AF325001

Financial Regulation in the EU

Raphaël Douady • Clément Goulet • Pierre-Charles Pradier
Editors

Financial Regulation in the EU

From Resilience to Growth

Editors
Raphaël Douady
Labex RéFi and Centre d'Economie de la
Sorbonne
Panthéon Sorbonne Université Paris 1 and
SUNY Stony Brook
Paris and New York, France and USA

Clément Goulet
Labex RéFi and Centre d'Economie de la
Sorbonne
Université Paris 1 Panthéon-Sorbonne
Paris, France

Pierre-Charles Pradier
Labex RéFi and Centre d'Economie de la
Sorbonne
Paris, France

ISBN 978-3-319-44286-0   ISBN 978-3-319-44287-7   (eBook)
DOI 10.1007/978-3-319-44287-7

Library of Congress Control Number: 2016957537

Cover illustration: David Lyons / Alamy Stock Photo

Printed on acid-free paper

This Palgrave Macmillan imprint is published by Springer Nature
The registered company is Springer International Publishing AG
The registered company address is: Gewerbestrasse 11, 6330 Cham, Switzerland

Contents

List of Figures

1

Introduction

Raphaël Douady, Clément Goulet,
and Pierre-Charles Pradier

It is almost ten years ago now that, in the wake of the financial crisis of 2007–2008, the European Parliement, European Commission and European Central Bank undertook a dramatic overhaul of European Union (EU) financial regulation. During these years, the EU experienced, along with the regulatory drive, a protracted recession and an apparent powerlessness of economic policies. Both the new legislature and the Commission asked for a pause so that the effects of the new rules could be understood rather better. As the new Commissioner in charge of Financial Stability, Financial Services and Capital Markets Union, Lord Hill declared to the *Financial Times* on 1 October 2015: "when you've done 40 major pieces of legislation in five years (…) common sense tells you that you are unlikely to have been able to work out all the consequences and interconnections. It is sensible to look at it." Two months later, the European Parliament responded with a resolution (2015/2106(INI)) brought by Burkhard Balz "stress[ing] that the impact of individual legislative measures differs from their cumulative impact; call[ing] on the Commission services (…) to conduct a comprehensive quantitative and qualitative assessment every five years of the cumulative impact of EU

R. Douady (✉)
SUNY Stony Brook, New York, NY, USA

C. Goulet (✉) • P.-C. Pradier (✉)
LabEx RéFi and CES, Université Paris 1 Panthéon-Sorbonne, Paris, France

R. Douady et al. (eds.), *Financial Regulation in the EU*,
DOI 10.1007/978-3-319-44287-7_1

financial services regulation (…); stress[ing] the importance of performing detailed impact assessments and cost-benefit analyses for any future legislation in order to demonstrate the added value of legislation, in particular as regards economic growth and job creation." The last sentence appears especially symptomatic of the shift from an all-out regulatory assault on the financial sector during a crisis to a recession-weary longing for growth.

The concept of this book coalesced a few weeks before these influential political authorities made their voices heard. In January 2015, LabEx REFI and the European Parliament organized a European Finance Forum in Strasbourg, bringing together more than 1,000 students from higher education institutions across Europe to discuss three topics: European financial regulation, European budgetary supervision and financing growth. The links between these themes now appear obvious: while financial institutions funded a growth cycle for most of the 2000s, this came to an end amid bank failures and market breakdowns, with governments sometimes too fragile to rescue their financial sector. Since then a protracted crisis has resulted in economic stagnation and the massive strengthening of financial regulation, with many diverse voices claiming that over-regulation is the *cause* of stagnation. So far, no book has illustrated the big picture: the relationship between microeconomic incentives and macroeconomic growth, between financial regulation, macroeconomic policies and the future of the EU… Until now the path toward a better future together has appeared blurred.

The present book builds on the three workshops that were organized at the European Parliament in Strasbourg. Part 1 covers the supervision of member states' budgets. Since the Maastricht Treaty in 1992, European institutions have strengthened common budgetary rules to break the "deadly embrace" (Farhi and Tirole, 2016) of sovereign and financial sector balance sheets, and to build a steady growth path. Jose Martin Flores recalls this history of *historic compromises*, from the 1997 Stability and Growth Pact, amended in 2005 to the 2011 reforms. Pierre Aldama then elaborates the theory of fiscal sustainability, showing that fiscal rules can achieve debt sustainability together with price stability and remain compatible with the countercyclical motives of fiscal policy. While fiscal consolidation in good times can allow running deficits when needed, recent history has confirmed a serious procyclical bias that has jeopardized both fiscal sustainability objectives and economic growth and stability. Unfortunately, according to macroeconomic research, the recent reforms (six-pack, two-pack and Fiscal Compact) do not seem likely to reduce the procyclical bias of fiscal policy. In order to push the analysis further, Jérôme Creel and Francesco Molteni break down governments' expenses since 2000. They show that countries in the euro area reduced public investment following the tightening of European fiscal rules and the effort to conduct fiscal consolidation. The decline in public investment matches the *public* part of Juncker's Investment Plan. The chapter gives also definite reasons to believe that an investment stimulus implemented at European level could be more effective than one at country level, while a larger issuance of *safe* assets would help improve banking stability and the passing of stress tests. Finally, Christian de Boissieu shows how the banking sector has been strengthened by improvements in situational factors (recapitalization of banks, rupture of the so-called deadly embrace) and more consistently by the progress of the banking union: single rulebook, single supervisory mechanism for systemically significant institutions, single resolution mechanism. This chapter also draws on the LabEx RéFi (Giraud and Kockerols 2015) study that shows how the banking union made the Eurozone more resilient.

In contrast with the macroeconomic perspective, Part 2 aims to understand how the new regulatory framework has impacted the economic models of financial institutions and entities. Discussion of systemic risk might impact on the macroeconomic dimension, though, as bank, insurance and asset management regulation has shown in the recent years. As a prelude, Mathilde Poulain assesses the risks and mitigation of regulatory capture in the contemporary EU. She concludes that *materialist* capture is starting to be overseen, while *non-materialist* capture remains ungoverned, as the difficulty in defining the latter may explain the poor arrangements to control it. Nasser Saber then addresses the topic of derivatives regulation with a transatlantic perspective. Rather than focusing on the last crisis and the product details, he embraces a wide historical panorama to show how derivatives have become necessary to the working of the financial system, and cannot be ruled out without severe consequences. Hence the debate on derivative regulation cannot oppose radical stances but provides informed and pragmatic views that have an incremental impact. The same level of subtle, informed and pragmatic comments are delivered for different regulatory areas: insurance by Arnaud Chneiweiss and Pierre-Charles Pradier, banking business models by Eric Lamarque, banks' market risk measurements by Jean-Paul Laurent and rating agencies by Philippe Raimbourg and Federica Salvadè. All these contributions share a common structure: an overview of the regulatory evolution, assessment and recommendations. The conclusion of this section is that regulation since the late 2000s has imposed not only costs on financial institutions and their customers but also a kind of regulatory uncertainty, which might cause *uncertainty aversion*.

The final section, Part 3, is forward-looking, as the European agenda is full of promising challenges: better securitization and new instruments (under

MIFID II), fine tuning of supervision under delegated acts and regulatory technical standards for AIFMD, CRR-CRD IV and Solvency II will supply long-term funding in lieu of non-conventional monetary policies. At a macroeconomic level, member state policies will be coordinated by the European Fund for Strategic Investments and the European Investment Bank. The funding channels that inflated a bubble having been closed down by the regulatory overhaul, it is time to describe the new architecture of a safer and more efficient European financial system. However, Pierre-Charles Pradier and Hamza el Khalloufi offer a critical view of the current state of implementation of banking regulation: the monetary bazooka surely destroyed the rise in borrowing costs that Basel III was expected to provoke, but even now, when the demand from businesses is picking up after years of slump, banks are not lending enough to fuel economic growth in the EU. The Basel III regulatory package came with so many strings attached that it might be difficult to find the binding constraint, but the authors argue that the regulatory avalanche triggered uncertainty aversion with the banks, which are now expecting strong positive incentives to get back in the game. Fortunately, Daphné Héant, Sophie Vermeille and Yann Coatanlem offer another transatlantic perspective on securitization, which matches the EU Parliament agenda, as a draft directive on this topic was put forward by the Commission in September 2015. The point of the authors is not to sell a miracle drug, but to insist on the benefit of an incremental and piecemeal development of financial markets: in this context, securitization might supply middle-market companies with additional funding (collateralized loan obligations amounted to more than $140bn in 2014 in the USA), while asset-backed vehicles might unload the banks' balance sheet to enable a more dynamical funding of small and medium-sized enterprises (SMEs), in conjunction with the EU SME support factor initiative. The authors show that securitization will not find a healthy business model without a dramatic reform of bankruptcy law in the EU, since investors today face the deterring uncertainty that surrounds bankruptcy procedures, which are common among firms on the technological frontier. Finally, Douady and Antoine Kornprobst recall that funding innovation is not a matter of sending helicopter money into the ether, since institutions are crucial to providing a life-supporting ecosystem. Together they analyse the French and European research and innovation system, which enjoys a convenient state of preparedness: the funnels are well designed; all we need are funds and consumer demand.

So far, no book has given the big picture, the relationship between microeconomic incentives and macroeconomic growth, between financial regulation, macroeconomic policies and the future of the EU. We hope you will enjoy reading about this big picture as much as we enjoyed writing about it. Unfortunately, writing the book was perhaps the easiest task, as recent developments have shown: the recent British referendum adds yet more uncertainty, with the prospect of competition between jurisdictions and regulatory arbitrage. This is just one more challenge to overcome, one more reason to roll up our sleeves and build a better future.

References

Farhi, E., & Tirole, J. (2016). *Deadly embrace: Sovereign and financial balance sheets doom loops*. NBER working paper No. w21843. Available at SSRN: http://ssrn.com/abstract=2713547

Giraud, G., & Kockerols, T. (2015). *Making the European banking union macro-economically resilient. Cost of non-Europe report*. European parliamentary research service. PE 558.771. Downloaded from: http://www.europarl.europa.eu/think-tank/fr/

Part I

Supervision of Member States' Budgets

2

Political Economy of the European Monetary Institutions and Reform Proposals

Jose-Maria Martin-Flores

2.1 Introduction

When the European Monetary Union (EMU) was created, member states agreed on a set of rules that were governed by the Stability and Growth Pact (SGP). The deviation of member states from the provisions of this Pact, which was aggravated by the last economic and financial crisis, led to a new set of fiscal rules that were agreed by member states in order to restore equilibrium and improve economic governance.

Euro area member states also agreed on a series of reforms aimed at setting fiscal backstops and financial facilities during the crisis. The banking crisis became a fiscal crisis with unforeseen consequences and devastating effects on the real economy. But the commitment of and compromise between member states with regard to the survival of the euro temporarily reduced the distress on some countries' public debt, avoiding the collapse of the system.

The European Central Bank (ECB) also played a relevant role during the peak of the Sovereign Debt Crisis, when the famous "whatever it takes" of its President, Mario Draghi,[1] contributed to the relaxation of the bond spreads

---

[1] Mario Draghi, President of the European Central Bank, at the Global Investment Conference in London on 26 July 2012. The full quotation was: "Within our mandate, the ECB is ready to do whatever it takes to preserve the euro. And believe me, it will be enough."

J.-M. Martin-Flores (✉)
LabEx RéFi, ESCP-Europe, Paris, France

R. Douady et al. (eds.), *Financial Regulation in the EU*,
DOI 10.1007/978-3-319-44287-7_2

of euro area peripheral countries. After this statement, the ECB initiated a programme of Outright Monetary Transactions in secondary sovereign bond markets that led to a reduction of the risk premium paid euro area distressed countries avoiding the need for further fiscal assistance, mainly for Italy and Spain.

However, the strong institutional commitment shown in the critical moments has not yet culminated with a full fiscal integration. The strong opposition to a "mutualization" of budgets and debts from some member states is still one of the main obstacles in the way of Europe's move towards a Fiscal Union. From a political economy perspective, when it comes to fiscal insurance and transfers between member states, the commons problem arises: the idea of having politicians who spend money without the burden of the cost of raising it is refused, which stops further commitments in fiscal matters. The fear of an increasing demand for transfers over time leads to a permanent deadlock.

Regarding banking union (another important pillar of the economic union), we also observe light and shade. On the positive side, two of the three pillars of the new European Union (EU) banking framework have already been built up as a result of a joint willingness to have a more integrated economic union. A Single Supervisory Mechanism within the ECB in charge of the supervision of the largest euro area banking institutions and a Single Resolution Mechanism (including a resolution fund fed by banks) has been set up. However, the third pillar which implies the creation of a common deposit guarantee scheme is the object of intense debates, and agreement seems unlikely. Without common deposit insurance, the banking union is flawed. When the subject is insurance and transfers between member states, the situation enters into an impasse that impedes further economic integration.

We intend to provide throughout this chapter an overview of the different fiscal reforms and monetary policies undertaken over the period since the creation of EMU. This overview of the economic reforms regarding fiscal policy is followed by a review of some of the proposals for fiscal and monetary reform made by different economists since the beginning of the financial and economic crisis. The objective of this chapter is to better understand which economic reforms have led to the current state of the Economic Union as well as the debates about fiscal and monetary policies.

2.2 EMU Institutional System and Fiscal Policy: Theory and Historical Overview of the Reforms

2.2.1 Fiscal Policy in the EMU: Theory

Among the objectives of the fiscal policy, we should differentiate between short-term and long-term objectives:

- In the short term, public spending and debt work as automatic stabilizers to smooth asymmetric shocks and serve as a support for monetary institutions in the conduct of monetary policy. Cyclical fluctuations in economic activity exert a significant influence on government budget balance. During recessions tax receipts weaken and social transfers increase. Such changes in the budget balance in turn have a stabilizing influence on economic activity. Positive balances accumulated in the past may help to smooth asymmetric shocks through higher spending during recessions, fulfilling the role of budgetary automatic stabilizers. The dampening effect of the automatic stabilizers on output fluctuations mainly depends on the degree of openness of the economy and on the structure of tax and public expenditure systems. The more open countries therefore need, *ceteris paribus*, comparatively larger budgetary fluctuations in order to achieve the same degree of output smoothing as obtained in more closed economies, which have automatic stabilizers of smaller size (Buti and Sapir 1998).
- In the medium and long term, the goal is to ensure sustainable public finances and a fair impact of spending and taxation between generations. Sustainable public finances mean that public spending and debt are kept at manageable levels. In the EMU, the Maastricht Treaty and the SGP provide the thresholds for debt and deficit manageability. They set the limits to avoid fiscal imbalances that may lead to negative spillovers to other member states, and intertemporal imbalances.[2]

The public sector solvency condition can be satisfied in two ways: budget discipline that ensures that future budget surpluses match public debt commitments, or weak fiscal discipline accompanied by an expansionary

---

[2] An inter-temporal imbalance occurs when the present value of an exogenously given path of government spending exceeds the present value of government revenue.

monetary policy that allows the public sector to meet its debt obligations (Von Hagen and Wyplosz 2010). However, the latter is the typical channel through which fiscal indiscipline can be a source of inflation (Canzoneri et al. 2001; Woodford 2001). In order to avoid inflation episodes triggered by fiscal imbalances, the EMU equipped itself with two tools: the SGP that establishes the thresholds for budget deficits and public debt; and the no-bail-out clause included in the treaty of the ECB that avoids this institution being forced to print more money to assist EMU member states to meet their obligations.

The economic reasoning behind these two mechanisms is rooted in moral hazard: governments' myopia and the commons problem.

The first argument is driven by the short-termism of governments regarding public spending and the temptation to increase public support when there are upcoming elections. They decide to increase public spending or delay fiscal consolidation to attract more votes and increase the chance of re-election, as voters will tend to reward governments that use public resources to their benefit. Therefore, under this view, the economy shows a deficit bias and a debt accumulation that would be higher than the level chosen in the absence of political incentives (Alesina and Tabellini 1990). A similar reasoning applies to the inflationary monetary policy. If a high degree of discretion is granted to policymakers in the conduct of monetary policy, they will tend to adopt time-inconsistent strategies. This means that they will announce an *ex ante* inflation target and will then adopt inflationary measures after economic agents have made their decisions based on the announcement (Kydland and Prescott 1977). The reason why policymakers may be tempted to follow such a strategy is the use of an expansionary (inflation bias) monetary policy to meet the obligations derived from a weak fiscal discipline.

Concerning the second argument to explain weak fiscal discipline, we make use of the theory of the common pool (or the commons problem). Public money is considered a common good, managed by policymakers with distributive policies. One important implication of those policies is the fact that those benefiting the most from public funds are only a small portion of the more dispersed taxpayers that finance them. As a result, politicians representing the interests of social groups would tend to overestimate the benefits of targeted policies and disregard the costs that are spread over the rest of the taxpayers. Therefore, there is a divergence between taxpayer preferences (as only the needs of a small group are met) and the composition of public spending, leading to a principal–agent problem. The greater is the problem with regard to the common pool (common budget), the greater is the potential for excessive spending, taxation and public debt (Von Hagen 2002).

Other consequences deriving from large budget imbalances (apart from the negative spillovers and increasing inflation) serve as an argument for fiscal discipline. High levels of public debt and spending drive interest rates on sovereign bonds upwards. A monetary union may even exacerbate the cost of a deficit bias for other countries, since contagion effects would drive other countries' interest rates up as well (snowball effect). In such situation the deficit country may not be paying such high interest rates while other countries may be paying much higher interest rates than they should. High public indebtedness may trigger undesired effects regarding the allocation of public and private consumption over time. As interest rates in higher indebted countries rise, lending from the productive sector may be shifted to state debt instead of financing the productive economy (the crowding-out effect).

Another negative consequence is the risk of bankruptcy of one of the states and the increasing pressure that it may create on the monetary authority. In such a situation of distress, the central bank may feel obliged to monetize government debt to avoid insolvency.

2.2.2 The "Original" Stability and Growth Pact

Solid budgetary discipline is considered to be an essential condition for the success of the EMU, as shown in section 2.2.1. The requirement of achieving a sound budgetary position and maintaining budgetary prudence is at the core of the Maastricht Treaty.

Fiscal policy has remained a national competence. However, Article 121 of the Treaty of Functioning of the European Union (TFEU) provides the basic framework for the coordination of economic policies between EU member states.[3] The rules, policies and procedures for effective coordination were spelled out in detail in another piece of legislation: the SGP. This document was signed in 1997 as a response to the demand of member states to lay down in a single document all the provisions regarding fiscal policy. The goal of this document was to strengthen the monitoring and coordination of fiscal and economic policies to enforce the deficit and debt limits established by the Maastricht Treaty. The numerical fiscal rules limited governments' deficit to 3 % of GDP (gross domestic product) and public debt level to 60 % of GDP.

The SGP consists of two Council Regulations: Regulation 1466/97 EC whose legal basis is the above-mentioned Article 121 of the TFEU and includes provisions to prevent member states to deviate from fiscal targets via

---

[3] "Member States shall regard their economic policies as a matter of common concern and shall coordinate them within the Council, in accordance with the provisions of Article 98" (European Union 2012).

information exchanges and peer pressure (preventive arm). The second arm, Regulation 1467/97 EC, has its legal basis in Article 126 of the TFEU and the protocol on excessive deficit procedure.[4] It contains provisions to increase the pressure on member states deviating from the targets so that they return to discipline (corrective arm). The imposition of sanctions is foreseen by this regulation as well as the steps for implementation of the Excessive Deficit Procedure (EDP).

The starting point of the SGP is that member states must set medium-term budgetary targets which are close to balance or in surplus, thus allowing them to respect the 3 % ceiling even during economic downturns. According to these provisions, when an excessive deficit occurs (deficit to GDP exceeds 3 %) an EDP is activated. This procedure aims at reducing the deficit initiated by increasing the pressure on the deviating member state to take effective measures to correct the situation. If there are no corrective measures, specific sanctions may be applied to the deviating member state. The member state should bring back its deficit below the reference value (3 %) two years after the occurrence of an excessive deficit and one year after its identification, unless special circumstances are given.

Nonetheless, the SGP foresees that in exceptional situations the 3 % threshold can be exceeded without causing excessive deficit. The three conditions to be met in such situation are: exceptionality, the origin of the excess has to be outside the normal range of situation (i.e. presence of a severe economic downturn);[5] temporariness, the deficit is allowed to remain above 3 % of GDP only for a limited period of time; and closeness, the deficit must remain close to the reference value.

2.2.3 The Fiscal Reforms Accomplished as a Consequence of the Crisis

As reported by Briotti (2004), EMU member states followed a process of consolidation and convergence in the run-up to the creation of the EMU in 1999. Budget deficits tend to converge towards the 3 % criterion established by the Maastricht Treaty. Therefore, the creation of the EMU created a dynamic effect on EMU government budgets. The incorporation to the EMU boosted fiscal consolidation in countries such as Belgium, Greece, Italy

---

[4] Article 126 includes "Member States shall avoid excessive government deficits" (European Union 2012).

[5] A severe economic downturn is defined as follows: annual fall of real GDP of at least 2 % or annual fall of GDP lower than 2 % accompanied by an abrupt downturn or accumulated loss of output relative to past trend.

and Portugal that were running large deficits prior to 1997. However, after the "club" was created, we observe divergent paths in the years after 1999. Annett (2006) states that countries adapted to the requirements of the EMU on the surface, but in the years after the implementation of the EMU some of the growth assumptions turned out to be overoptimistic and some accounts were misreported. During the years after 1999, some EMU member states showed diverging paths: France and Germany broke off the excessive deficit procedures, Greece accumulated excessive deficits that have been present for a long period and Portugal deviated from the target in 2004. These imbalances prompted the calls for a reform of the SGP in 2005 (Annett et al. 2005), which led to extensive research conducted by the European Commission evaluating national and fiscal frameworks and the level of enforcement of numerical fiscal rules. The two regulations making up the preventive and the corrective arms of the SGP were revised in 2005 after the conflict between the European Commission and the ECOFIN Council in 2003,[6] which resulted in a judgement of the European Court of Justice in 2004.[7] The result was a reform of the SGP,[8] and Regulations 1055/2005 (preventive arm) and 1056/2005 (corrective arm) introduced more flexibility and member states ownership into the SGP. However, the Pact continued to be breached as governments responded to the 2007–2009 financial crisis by incurring significant deficits to combat the recapitalization of the banking system.

The negative consequences of the economic downturn were poor growth and mismanagement of public finances in some euro area member states, which led to fiscally weakened economies in the aftermath of the crisis. Fiscal imbalances linked to a fiscal expansion and support of the banking sector led to a sovereign debt crisis that added more pressure to euro area member states' public finances management and pushed some euro area countries (i.e. Portugal, Ireland and Greece) to request financial assistance from European institutions and other international bodies (Fig. 2.1).

Until the economic crisis in 2008, the reformed version of the SGP governed the fiscal rules in the euro area. However, the crisis proved that this set of rules was not enough to prevent the economic crisis in the euro area. Its lax enforcement was rooted in the lack of sanctions imposed on diverg-

---

[6] On 25 November 2003, ECOFIN decided not to follow the recommendations of the European Commission on the EDP against Germany and France.

[7] European Commission against the Council (C-27/04).

[8] The comments on the reform can be found in the Communication from the Commission to the Council and the European Parliament, Strengthening economic governance and clarifying the implementation of the Stability and Growth Pact Brussels available at: http://www.europarl.europa.eu/meetdocs/2004_2009/documents/com/com_com(2004)0581_/com_com(2004)0581_en.pdf.

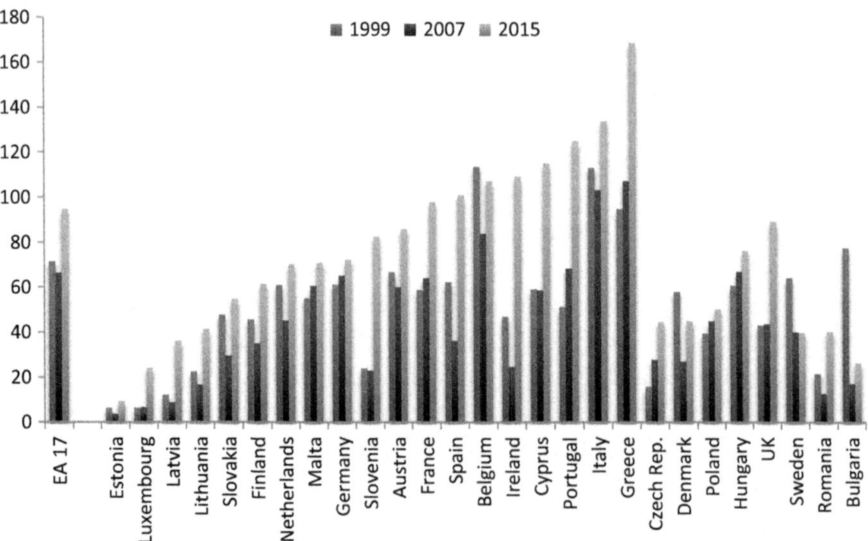

Fig. 2.1 Public debt over GDP (1999–2015) (*Source*: Eurostat)

ing countries and the inability of the EU institutional framework to enforce the provisions of the Pact (Ngai 2012). That is why, in 2010, the European Commission put forward a set of reforms to strengthen the existing fiscal tools and improve coordination between member states. In addition, further provisions regarding the "European Semester" were made, which led to its implementation in January 2011.

These proposals, which were aimed at strengthening the SGP, preventing and correcting fiscal imbalances accumulated before and during the crisis, establishing national fiscal frameworks and strengthening enforcement, gave rise to a set of agreements and directives that have been implemented in order to guarantee the sustainability of public finances in the future. They basically reshaped the architecture of the euro area.

We present below an overview of the newly established and ongoing reforms to describe their main features and the mechanisms used to tackle imbalances. The new mechanisms aim at addressing the problems raised by the crisis, enforcing compliance with the European goals and fostering economic policy coordination.

2.2.3.1 The Reform of the SGP

In 2011, Regulations 1055/2005 EC and 1056/2005 EC were amended to strengthen the surveillance and coordination of national budgets and clarify and make EDPs go faster.[9] These amendments included two main aspects: the so-called 1/20th rule that requires member states whose public debt is above the 60 % threshold limit to reduce it at a yearly rate of 1/20th of the difference between the actual ratio and the public debt threshold;[10] and a reform of how the medium-term budgetary objectives (MTOs) are set. Under the new amendments, member states were required to provide an MTO and the path to be followed in order to achieve it, including detailed policy measures to be taken and a detailed quantitative assessment. The MTOs are revised by the Council and subject to monitoring. Member states are required to meet its medium-term budgetary objective, with an annual improvement of 0.5 % of GDP as a benchmark, with more effort in good times and more limited effort in bad times.

Further to these amendments and as a result of the works performed by the Task Force chaired by the president of the European Council, Herman Van Rompuy, six new legislative proposals known as the "six pack" were released with effect from 2012.[11] These new proposals aimed at enhancing both budgetary and economic monitoring were organized under the European Semester. They were packaged in five regulations and one directive applicable to all EU member states.[12] At the moment the six pack was introduced, 23 out of 27 member states were immersed in Excessive Deficit Procedures that should now follow the new legislation.

The deficit threshold remained at 3 % of GDP. However, the new agreement included some specific sanctions for member states in an EDP that failed to comply with the recommendations of the Council. This sanction is activated unless a qualified majority of the member states vote against it in the Council. The new legislative package foresees a new surveillance and enforcement mechanism to identify and correct macroeconomic imbalances earlier than the former version of the SGP. This new mechanism is the so-called

---

[9] The amending regulations are the Council Regulations 1173/2011, 1175/2011 and 1177/2011.

[10] For instance, a country whose public debt represents 80 % of its GDP will have to reduce it annually at a rate of 1 % ((80-60)/20=1pp.).

[11] http://europa.eu/rapid/press-release_MEMO-11-898_en.htm.

[12] Regulation 1173/201 of 16 November 2011 on the effective enforcement of budgetary surveillance in the euro area;

Regulation 1175/2011 of 16 November 2011 amending Regulation 1466/97 on the strengthening of the surveillance of budgetary positions and the surveillance and coordination of economic policies; Regulation 1174/2011 on enforcement measures to correct excessive macroeconomic imbalances in the euro area;

Regulation 1176/2011 on the prevention and correction of macroeconomic imbalances;

Regulation 1177/2011 of 8 November 2011 amending Regulation 1467/97 on speeding up and clarifying the implementation of the excessive deficit procedure;

Directive 2011/85/EU of 8 Nov 2011 on requirements for budgetary framework of the Member State.

Excessive Imbalance Procedure (EIP). It incorporates a preventive arm that allows the European Commission and the Council to issue recommendations if a risk of deviation from the fiscal target is detected. Under the preventive arm, the European Commission and the Council guide member states towards their MTO to ensure fiscal sustainability. The new rules also define an expenditure benchmark that places a ceiling on public expenditure based on the MTO. Moreover, both institutions are provided with a corrective arm that allows them to open an EIP when they detect a serious deterioration of the fiscal position. Under this procedure member states will be requested to submit an action plan to correct the imbalances. In order to ensure the enforcement of the provisions of the SGP, a two-step approach is established. This consists of an interest bearing deposit that a deviating member state will have to create after one failure to comply with the corrective actions proposed. After a second failure to comply, the deposit becomes a fine of up to 0.1 % of GDP.

Regarding public debt, the benchmark remains at 60 % of GDP. However, the main novelty of this reform is that a member state that does not respect the 60 % threshold can be put into an EDP even if its deficit is below 3 % of GDP.

In May 2013 two new regulations were issued to introduce new monitoring tools and reinforce economic coordination. These new regulations are only applicable to the euro area member states and are known as the "Two-Pack." The first regulation improves and harmonizes the budgetary procedures, and imposes additional surveillance and reporting obligations in the case of an excessive deficit.[13] A common budgetary timetable is set with the following steps: (1) member states submit draft budgets before 15 October each year, (2) the European Commission examines them before the end of November, (3) the Commission's assessment is discussed in the Euro-Group and if required, it might be presented to the national parliament, and (4) budgets are approved by the end of December. Independent budget councils are created as a result of this regulation to verify compliance with the numerical fiscal rules. The second regulation focuses on special monitoring of troubled countries,[14] to ensure that they return to the financial markets,[15] and their public accounts are sound and sustainable. It aims at preventing spillovers in the EMU. This regulation mainly targets countries that required financial assistance or are experiencing financial stability difficulties that are subject to enhanced surveillance. For these countries the regulation foresees a

---

[13] Regulation (EU) No 473/2013.

[14] Regulation (EU) No 472/2013.

[15] In the situations in which countries are not able to finance themselves in the market and special financial assistance is needed.

macroeconomic adjusted programme that takes into account the specificities of the member state and suspends temporarily the application of other processes of budgetary surveillance, including the SGP.

2.2.3.2 The European Semester

The complex set of rules, agreements, a Treaty, plans and processes are coordinated via the European Semester, which was set up by the Van Rompuy Task Force. During the European Semester the European Commission and the Council analyse the fiscal policies and reforms of each member state before they are implemented, provide recommendations and monitor their execution. The European Semester integrates the surveillance of budgets and other macroeconomic and structural developments in a cycle of closer *ex ante* policy coordination. It brings together the following aspects: (1) the formulation and surveillance of the implementation of the Broad Economic Policy Guidelines (BEPG) of member states and the EU, (2) the member states' Stability and Convergence Programmes (SCPs),[16] and National Reform Programmes (NRPs),[17] and (3) the surveillance to prevent and correct macroeconomic imbalances.

The process of the European semester starts with an Annual Growth Survey (AGS) elaborated by the European Commission that identifies mutual economic challenges and determines the strategic policy stance around five priority axes: (1) sound and sustainable public finances, requiring fiscal adjustment based on a growth-friendly consolidation strategy, (2) stabilizing the financial system and restoring lending to the economy, especially to SMEs, (3) promoting economic growth and competitiveness, including competition-enhancing reforms in product markets, and the reduction of regulatory and administrative burden on companies, (4) addressing high and rising unemployment and promoting and inclusive labour market and adequate social protection and (5) promoting effective public administration.

Following the AGS, the European Council establishes the economic policy priorities based on the outcomes of the AGS. Member states then submit their medium-term economic and budgetary strategies on the basis of the European Council priorities. The European Commission assesses them and makes country-specific recommendations that are voted for in the Council. The final step of the process is the monitoring and assessment of the implementation of the policies agreed.

---

[16] SCPs are budget plans based on the MTO for each euro area member state.

[17] NRPs include similar provisions to SCPs but they are applied by non-euro area EU member states.

2.2.3.3 The Euro Plus Pact

In March 2011, euro area members adopted, under the Open Method of Coordination, a new reform known as the Euro Plus Pact. Although this reform was open to all EU member states, only 23 participated to it. This reform addresses the flaws detected in the fiscal enforcement mechanisms. The goals of the Euro Plus Pact are: (1) fostering competitiveness of the European economy with a strong focus on employment and (2) contributing to the sustainability of public finances and financial sector stability. This Pact further strengthens the economic pillar of the EMU and enhances the quality of economic policy coordination by securing more concrete commitments from the member states, since the measures announced in the national reform programs are often vague and non-committal. The Pact stipulates a set of quantitative targets in the fields of employment, public finances, taxation and financial stability that should foster the competitiveness of EU member states by preventing the accumulation of external imbalances (Gabrisch and Staehr 2014). Moreover, it stipulates a range of policy measures to achieve its goals. In the field of competitiveness, policy measures are geared to labour cost reduction and productivity increases. Regarding employment, the Pact foresees measures to increase flexibility, security and youth employment. Regarding public finances, the Euro Plus Pact is in line with the measures included in the SGP and the six pack and establishes sustainability indicators of debt and deficit, taking into consideration the specific characteristics of each member state in terms of ageing population, employment participation, health care system and so on. Taxation is a subordinated part of the Pact; however, while acknowledging that it is a national competence, the Pact pays attention to greater coordination in direct tax matters and cooperation in tax fraud and evasion.

In order to demonstrate the commitment towards these indicators, member states spell out a set of concrete actions to be implemented within a year that will remain the responsibility of each country.

2.2.3.4 The Fiscal Compact

On 2 March 2012, euro area countries agreed on a new treaty on stability, coordination and governance in the EMU. This new agreement is known as the Fiscal Compact or the Fiscal Stability Treaty. This treaty was signed by all EU member states but the UK and Czech Republic. It did not require the signature of every country to enter into force. However, non-signatory countries lose the right to receive funding if assistance is needed from the European Stability Mechanism (ESM).

This treaty requires member states to pass national legislation (preferably by modifying the Constitution) that forces them to run budget surpluses or balanced budgets.[18] The European Court of Justice fines a country up to 0.1 % of GDP if this is not done at least one year after the ratification of the treaty. The SGP was limited to the coordination of fiscal policies and the issuance of warnings and recommendations, while its execution remained a member state task. But this treaty puts all member states under the same practices and rules. It strengthens the budgetary targets set by the preventive arm through the MTOs. The purpose was to preserve debt and budget limits into their respective boundaries, including legally enforceable penalties for non-compliant member states.

The Fiscal Compact goes further than the SGP by requiring that the MTOs are above –0.5 % of GDP unless the ratio of government debt is below 60 % of GDP and the risks in terms of long-term sustainability of public finance are low. This MTO rule ensures the sustainability of public finance while allowing room for budgetary manoeuvre, in particular for automatic stabilizers or public investment. The Fiscal Compact also includes the 1/20th rule described above (Timbeau et al. 2015).[19]

2.2.3.5 Financial Facilities to Allow Member States to Benefit from Financial Assistance in Case of Distress

Sovereign bond yields increased to unsustainable levels in 2010 and they continued an increasing path until mid-2012. In order to reassure financial markets, European leaders wanted to show a strong determination to maintain sound public finances and a deep commitment towards the euro. As a result, all euro area countries agreed on the creation of the European Financial Stability Facility (EFSF),[20] and the European Commission created the European Financial Stability Mechanism (EFSM). These were two vehicles whose main aim was to provide financial assistance to euro area countries in distress. The

---

[18] The debt breaks were already introduced in Germany in its constitutional reform of 2009. The country introduced a debt to GDP ceiling of 60 % in its Constitution.

[19] The six-pack reform also includes some fiscal rules, though they neither differ from those in the SGP nor the Fiscal Compact. The most important reform with the six pack is certainly the macroeconomic imbalance procedure (MIP). MIP goes well beyond a discussion on fiscal rules, as it embeds a long list of nominal, real and social indicators which shall help monitor the macroeconomy of all EU member states.

[20] The financial assistance provided to Greece, Portugal and Ireland was channelled through this mechanism.

EFSF had €440 billion at its disposal for financial support to euro zone countries to be used if the funds of the EFSM were not enough. This entity has its debt guaranteed by euro area member states and was financed by member states' contributions. The EFSM raises its funds on the financial markets, having the EU budget funds as collateral. This emergency funding programme has participated in the Irish, Portuguese and Greek bailouts, making €60 billion available for financial support (Horváth and Huizinga 2015). This funding, together with the amount provided by the IMF, set aside €750 billion for support to troubled member states. Both the EFSF and the EFSM were replaced in October 2012 by the ESM, although they will continue its operations until the end of the assistance facility programme granted to Greece.

The creation of these institutions was a major step in the survival of the euro as a currency and implied an unprecedented change in fiscal policy coordination (Micossi et al. 2011). The no-bailout clause included in Article 125 of the TFEU forbade any European institution or member state from extending a credit line or a loan to pay back its debts, even in the case of serious risk of default. However, as the high likelihood of contagion from a default on any euro area member state's debt became a real threat, member states decided to bypass the EU law and agreed on granting a financial facility to Greece (Closa and Maatsch 2014). Instead of going through a change in EU treaties, a new regulation was passed, Regulation 407/2010, establishing an intergovernmental agreement that allowed the creation of the EFSF. The EFSF was created out of the EU legal framework as a private company located in Luxembourg and owned by member states.

In the same line, the creation of the ESM implied a revision of the EU treaties. The ESM was not based on Article 122 of the TFEU,[21] but on an amendment of Article 136 that was introduced to give legal legitimacy to this new mechanism (Christova 2011):

> "The Member States whose currency is the euro may establish a stability mechanism to be activated if indispensable to safeguard the stability of the euro area as a whole. The granting of any required financial assistance under the mechanism will be made subject to strict conditionality".

The ESM was granted with a fiscal capacity of €500 billion. The crucial aspect of its creation is that it must avoid fiscal transfers between member states. Its role shall rather be to intervene only if indispensable to preserve the stability of the euro area (Micossi et al. 2011).

---

[21] This article allows the Council, after a proposal of the Commission, to decide in the spirit of solidarity between member states measures appropriate to the economic situation.

2.3 The ECB and Monetary Policy Since the Creation of the EMU

2.3.1 Mandate and Structure

The Maastricht Treaty introduced the euro as a currency for the participating countries and gave power over monetary policy to an independent authority, the ECB, which together with the National Central Banks (NCBs) of each euro area member state constitutes the European System of Central Banks (ESCB).

This institutional architecture was based on two main principles: one was that the political independence of the ECB should be maintained and the second that the primary goal of the ECB was to pursue price stability within the euro area,[22] with other aspects such as the promotion of employment and growth or even the stability of the exchange rate being secondary objectives once the primary goal was secured. Price stability is defined as a year-on-year increase of the Harmonized Consumer Price Index below 2 %. However, the definition of the inflation target as well as the formulation of the monetary policy objectives and instruments belongs to the Government Council of the ECB (Micossi 2015). Comparatively, this is a more restricted mandate than the one attributed to other central banks such as the Federal Reserve in the USA and the Bank of England. The objectives attributed to the former are maximum employment, stable prices and moderate long-term interest rates, with no hierarchy or weights assigned, and the objective of the latter is to maintain price stability and, subject to that, support the economic policy of the country, including the objectives of growth and employment.

The independence of the ESCB is guaranteed by Article 130 of the TFEU and Article 7 of the statute of the ECB, which states that neither the ECB nor any of the national central banks shall take instructions from an European or national government body. Moreover, Article 125 of the TFEU and Article 21 of the ECB statute state that overdrafts or any other facility in favour of a European or national public body are prohibited. This constitutes a no-bailout clause, meaning that the ECB has no obligation to take over liabilities of another government body or institution. Independence and the no-bailout clause are two essential elements of the ESCB construction. Economic theory has pointed at the inflation bias (Kydland and Prescott 1977) as one of the main issues when monetary policy is left to political discretion. Governments

---

[22] Article 127.1 of the Treaty of Functioning of the European Union.

tend to increase inflation to benefit from temporary output increases by adopting time-inconsistent and inflationary policies. Delegation of this policy to an independent central bank neutralizes any possibility of inflationary policy.

Without jeopardizing its independence, the ECB must pursue a policy of transparency. Transparency requires some degree of disclosure of policy objectives, economic information and statistics, prompt announcement of its decisions and a description of how these decisions are implemented. Likewise, the ECB remains accountable to the European Parliament, to which it has to justify and accept responsibility for the decisions taken.

Regarding the implementation of the monetary policy, the ESCB follows a two-pillar strategy (Micossi 2015): The first pillar is related to the analysis of economic dynamics and shocks. This is aimed at assessing the short- to medium-term determinants of price developments, taking into account that price developments over this horizon are influenced by the interaction of supply and demand. On this pillar, the ECB determines the appropriate interest rate to achieve price stability over the established horizon. It also includes financial stability as one of the aspects to be taken into account, as financial sector imbalances can be the trigger of both output and price developments. The second pillar relates to the analysis of monetary trends. This focuses on a long-term horizon, exploiting the long-run relationship between output and prices.

2.3.2 Phases of the ECB Monetary Policy

Even if the mandate and objectives have remained the same since the creation of EMU, we can differentiate six different phases in the conduct of the monetary policy.

The first phase consisted in coping with the transition to monetary union and ran from mid-1998 until mid-1999. This period is characterized by low inflation in the euro area (below 1 %), a drop in oil prices, deregulation of the service sector and the aftermath of the Asian and Russian crises that began in 1997 and 1998 respectively. During this period the ECB set the reference interest rate at 3 %, then reduced it to 2.5 % until the end of 1999.

The second phase lasted from mid-1999 until the end of 2000 and was characterized by a period of rising interest rates to contain inflationary pressures. This rising inflation was driven by rapid economic growth, credit expansion and depreciation of the euro.

The third phase (early 2001 to mid-2003) consisted of a downward adjustment of key interest rates, mainly caused by the downward pressures on output and global economic uncertainty triggered by the dotcom crisis and the 9/11 terrorist attacks. This strategy sought growth fostering against the private sector declines and a shift in investments towards safer assets.

The fourth phase lasted from mid-2003 to the end of 2005 and was characterized by no change in the reference interest rate until 6 December 2005, when the interest rate rose 25 basis points to 2.25 %.

The fifth phase of the ECB monetary policy was marked by a withdrawal of monetary accommodation, and an expansion of money and credit to the private sector. There were also substantial increases in oil and commodities prices. The end of this phase was the start of the financial crisis in mid-2008. Interest rates were raised throughout this period by 200 basis points,[23] and remained high by the end of this phase. In order to counteract the first effects of the financial crisis in 2008, the ECB increased liquidity provisions through unlimited overnight liquidity, fine-tuning operations and swap lines.[24]

The last phase is mostly marked by the response of the ECB to the financial crisis. The main feature of this period has been a decreasing path of the key interest rate, reaching five basis points in September 2014. Over this period, the ECB took several measures to preserve market liquidity, avoid a financial collapse and contribute to stable inflation and output growth. The first measure that the ECB took was to target the banking sector in order to foster the flow of credit and ensure the transmission of monetary policy through the interest rate channel. These measures consisted in fixed-rate full allotment tender provisions of liquidity to banks, the expansion of the assets that were eligible as a collateral, longer-term liquidity provisions (LTROs), enhanced liquidity provisions in foreign currency, changes in the banks' reserve ratio, purchases of covered bonds, the Securities Purchase Market Programme (SMP) in May 2010 and the Emergency Lending Assistance (ELA). Despite the initial collapse, these measures managed to restore the interbank lending mechanism, foster confidence between financial institutions and allow the most distressed countries, Greece, Portugal and Ireland, to keep rolling over their debts until the arrival of the sovereign debt crisis in 2010, when they had to request financial assistance from international bodies.

Therefore, during this last phase the ECB assumed the role of lender of last resort. The ECB has continued to provide financial assistance to euro area governments indirectly (by buying distressed bonds in secondary markets rendering more liquid) and the banking system through rediscount facili-

---

[23] From 2.25 % in December 2005 to 4.25 % in July 2008.

[24] "The swap rate is the fixed rate that banks are willing to pay in exchange for receiving the average overnight rate for the duration of the swap agreement. It reflects the same negligible credit and liquidity risk premia as the overnight rate. The overnight index swap rate is therefore relatively immune to changes in liquidity or credit risk while the EURIBOR is not" (European Central Bank 2010).

ties, lower credit quality for eligible collateral and secondary market purchases of sovereign and corporate bonds through Outright Monetary Transactions (Acharya et al. 2016).[25] The last relevant measure of the ECB has been to set up a quantitative easing programme known as Public Sector Purchase Programme (PSPP), which started on 9 March 2015. The aim of this is to provide liquidity to the economy through a wide purchase of financial assets that are composed of sovereign bonds and securities from national and EU institutions. In order to foster further this liquidity injection, the deposit reserves at the ECB were reduced to negative levels.

2.3.3 Extension of the ECB's Tasks

One of the greatest changes in the structure of the ECB took place in 2013. Aiming at ensuring a common framework in banking supervision, the tasks of the ECB were further extended, incorporating a new branch to this construction, the Single Supervisory Mechanism (SSM). However, this new function remains separate from the monetary policy function.

To ensure a common framework, the European Council proposed to set up one single supervisor in charge of the supervision of euro area banks.[26] The objective is to make sure that all euro area members can have full confidence in the quality and impartiality of banking supervision.

Even if the responsibility and decision-making power for the overall functioning of the system are held by the ECB, the efficient day-to-day work of the SSM depends on the national supervisory agencies, whose expertise and proximity to the supervised entities are essential in ensuring that no aspect is overlooked (Verhelst 2013).

The supervision of the ECB is limited to credit institutions (CIs). As defined by Article 4 of the directive 48/2006,[27] credit institutions are "an undertaking whose business is to receive deposits or other repayable funds from the public and to grant credits for its own account." Banks that are active in other financial business (such as insurance or asset management) are only subject to ECB supervision with regard to their banking business, their other business being supervised by the competent national authorities.

---

[25] The ECB started this programme in the summer of 2012 as a response to the increasing spreads of the sovereign bonds of the most distressed euro area member states.

[26] The Council Regulation (EU) No. 1024/2013 foresees that non-euro members could voluntarily join the SSM as well.

[27] The reader should take into consideration that Directive 48/2006/EU has been replaced by Directive 36/2013/EU. However, for the purpose of our analysis the definition of credit institution remains valid.

According to Regulation 1024/2013, the SSM has the following tasks:

- SSM is responsible for authorization and micro and macro-prudential supervision of credit institutions, financial holding companies and mixed financial holding companies in participating Member States. Participating Member States are all euro area countries, and non-euro area countries that decide to opt-in.
- For subsidiaries and branches of non-euro area banks, the SSM assumes the role of host supervisor in relation to relevant prudential supervisory tasks. Verification of the licensing of new branches set up by a supervised or non-supervised bank is within the scope as well.
- Supervision of banks with regards to markets in financial instruments and anti-money laundering and terrorism financing.
- The European Banking Authority (EBA) remains responsible for the EU Single Rulebook and conducting EU-wide stress tests. National Competent Authorities (NCAs) remains in charge of conduct of business, financial crime and payment systems supervision, and transposition of EU Directives into national law.[28]
- ECB is able to use macro-prudential instruments, either at the request of national agencies or by adopting stricter measures than the ones at national level (some functions may overlap with the European Systemic Risk Board (ESRB)).
- The ECB directly supervises 'significant' CIs.[29] For 'less significant' CIs the ECB exercises oversight and issue regulations, guidelines or general instructions to NCAs, but delegates day-to-day responsibilities to NCAs.
- For a group headquartered outside the SSM, the ECB might seek to establish close cooperation agreements with the home supervisor.[30]
- The ECB receives supervisory data on all banks in the SSM.

When the ECB was created, its independence was one of the critical points. In the case of the SSM, this is also an essential aspect to be considered. In order to ensure its independence, the costs associated to this function are not borne by the member states but by the supervised institutions that are paying fees to the ECB. Without hampering independence, the SSM is also

---

[28] We also refer to National Competent Authorities as National Agencies.

[29] Representing roughly 80 % of the assets of the euro area banking sector. The list of institutions can be found in the decision of the ECB dated 4 February 2014 (http://www.ecb.europa.eu/pub/pdf/other/en_dec_2014_03_fen.pdf?21d953cb19106056a509a22888c646a8).

[30] An example would be the supervision of the subsidiary of the Swiss bank UBS in Luxembourg that falls under the scope of the SSM.

accountable to the European Parliament and the Council. Scheduled reporting is fixed in order to keep these two institutions updated on the tasks carried out by the SSM. National Parliaments can also submit observations to this reporting to which the SSM must reply.

The execution of the supervisory task implies some interactions with other institutions. The European Banking Authority (EBA) is part of this supervisory process and has as its main tasks ensuring that banks respect the existing legal framework, settling disagreements between national agencies and preparing and preventing crisis situations through stress tests and contingency plans. National supervisory agencies are subject to the ECB's broad oversight.

2.4   Review of the Different Proposals for a New Economic Governance in the EMU

The objective of this section is to discuss the main ideas and mechanisms for a new European economic governance in the aftermath of the crisis. Since its creation, the EMU has had a peculiar feature; monetary policy has been delegated to a common authority, the ECB, while fiscal policy remains under the responsibility of each member state. This implies that the EMU has a common currency, the euro, but it does not have a federal budget or a common fiscal mechanism to act as a stabilizer (Schiliro 2013). In this respect, there have been a series of proposals that aim at providing the EMU institutions with some fiscal power. Even if these proposals would not mean a fully fledged fiscal union, they foresee the creation of common fiscal backstops.

The first set of proposals analysed in this section deal with different mechanisms of tax revenue sharing and further labour market coordination, notably regarding unemployment subsidies and minimum wages.

Von Hagen and Wyplosz (2010) assess two different mechanisms of fiscal transfers among euro area member states as an alternative to external borrowing: tax revenue sharing and an euro area unemployment insurance.

Insurance through tax revenue sharing would imply the creation of a euro area tax fund that would be fed with transfers from each government. This fund would subsequently allocate these funds to other members based on a fixed per capita basis. The contribution of each country to the fund would vary depending on the evolution of the tax base over time. Under this mechanism, countries with lower tax bases would pay less than they receive. The reference tax base should ideally be the VAT base. There are two reasons for choosing VAT rather than direct taxes; VAT is more homogeneous across the EU and

VAT collection tracks better demand shocks as it is a tax on consumption. This system would allow member states to commit to countercyclical policies addressing asymmetric shocks, avoiding increasing deficits as the lack of tax collection would be compensated with higher transfers from the common fund. Nonetheless, this system has a moral hazard problem. Under such a system governments would not adjust their spending accordingly, as they can rely on additional transfers from the common fund. Moreover, they may tend to cheat and abuse as a way to circumvent the restrictions set by the EMU framework. Although this is not a problem for the euro area as a whole, it may lead to internal imbalances. However, the authors highlight that "it could be left up to the national electorates to make sure that their governments use the resources they have available properly."

An euro area unemployment insurance would imply direct payments to individuals rather than payments to each government. This system would be fed with contributions made by households in economies enjoying positive economic shocks. Funds would be distributed among individuals in countries suffering negative shocks. However, an additional contribution from governments would be added. As this mechanism would tend to replace the existing unemployment insurance schemes, no further burden would be added to the current taxes on labour. Again, moral hazard problems exist as such a system creates incentives for member states to raise unemployment figures in order to receive permanent transfers. Two alternatives would address this problem: First, a limitation on the duration of the subsidies coming from the common scheme and secondly, establishing a system of coinsurance in which each country would pay part of the subsidy while the rest would be provided by the common scheme.

Given the potential moral hazard implications of both systems, both at country and aggregate level, the authors proposed some mitigation measures. Regarding individual country level, in order to avoid that countries misstate their GDP figures to reduce their contributions to a common system, they propose to delegate the computation of the key figures to a politically independent agency or incorporate penalties that reduce the future transfers to be received. Concerning the aggregate level, countries may be tempted to abuse common schemes to circumvent the requirements of the EMU framework, or problems linked to the governance of the common insurance mechanism may arise. Regarding the former, governments running deficits above 3 % asking for payments from the common budget will be asked to run surpluses in future periods to pay back the amounts borrowed to finance these additional deficits. Concerning the latter, the problem could be mitigated by delegating the governance of the system to either the European Commission or the ECB as they are more independent bodies.

Another proposal for an euro area-wide unemployment insurance that has acquired some relevance in the policy debate is the one proposed by Dullien (2013). It consists of an EMU insurance scheme that would be financed by contributions paid by insured workers. Under such a scheme, eligible unemployed would receive benefits individually. These benefits would be adjusted relative to each country's wage level and could be topped up by national unemployment systems. The objective of this system would be to extend the benefits to all unemployed in all member states and not only to those countries suffering rising unemployment. Moreover, this system would have macroeconomic effects not only across member states but also across time. Revenue collected in one year would not need to be expended in that year as the insurance scheme could be running surpluses. Although the main fear is that this system causes permanent transfers, Dullien shows through a simulation exercise that such a scheme could be set up without causing large permanent transfers and would have a stabilization effect in all countries.

Aiming at increasing the coordination between member states in labour markets, Timbeau (2014) proposes a EU minimum wage policy. In a context in which labour costs dropped or grew moderately in the most fragile euro area countries as a way to increase external competitiveness, this proposal aims at setting a coordinated EU minimum wage to put an end to downward wage adjustments when a member state seeks to gain competitiveness through internal devaluations.[31] The idea is to set a minimum wage that takes into account the relative current account positions of each member state. This system would allow member states to equilibrate external imbalances while preventing member states facing imbalances from falling into the vicious circle of internal wages deflation. The EU-set minimum wage would not replace national minimum wages but would imply a minimum threshold under which nominal wages could not decrease.

On the subject of public accounts management and fiscal governance, there is a subset of proposals that aim at increasing fiscal coordination between euro area member states.

De Grauwe (2013) proposes a model of fiscal union that would help the euro area overcome the flaws of its design. He proposes a pooling of government debts as a way to protect the euro area from asymmetric shocks. Pooling debts should relax the panic in sovereign debt markets and make debt burdens more manageable for countries in distress. However, he acknowledges that

---

[31] This vicious circle gains special importance when unemployment levels remain at high levels.

such a system would imply moral hazard issues. As countries would become jointly liable, they might have a tendency to be more lax regarding public debt sustainability. Another obstacle is the fact that less indebted countries would pay higher interest than they would pay without pooling. De Grauwe proposes some measures to overcome both issues. Even if debts were to be pooled, a significant part should remain the responsibility of each member state. Moreover, an internal transfer mechanism should ensure that those countries with a lower creditworthiness would compensate those with higher ratings.

In line with the above proposal, Delpla and von Weizsacker (2010) and Delpla and Von Weizsäcker (2011) suggest that euro area members' debt could be "mutualized." They propose that a central treasury could issue European blue bonds that would pool up to 60 % of debt to GDP for each member state under joint and several liability senior debt. Under this system, blue bonds could obtain a higher credit rating and pay lower interest as a consequence of the joint liability. This mechanism would end moral hazard issues, as any debt above 60 % of GDP (red bonds) would be the sole responsibility of the issuing member state.

Steinberg (2015) proposes the creation of a new euro area central fiscal capacity that enables transfers between regions. He proposes the creation of a central fiscal authority (i.e. euro area treasury), headed by an euro area finance minister, that influences national budgets, monitors national accounts, issues debt and collects taxes. This institution would still delegate to national governments the decisions regarding tax and public spending but the central authority would determine the fiscal position of each member state. Likewise, member states would share the responsibility of debt issued by the common treasury.

There are three potential ways that Steinberg identifies for financing this central capacity: (1) the collection of euro area taxes (i.e. environmental taxes or financial transactions taxes), (2) direct contributions from member states with a system preventing countries always being net contributors or net receptors, and (3) the issuance of common bonds in a similar fashion as that proposed by De Grauwe (2013).

Other reform proposals target the institutional complexity of the EU and propose more simple frameworks.

Alcidi and Gros (2015) highlight that the current design of the EMU is an obstacle to a common and efficient response to asymmetric shocks. The only institution that has been equipped with tools to overcome a macroeconomic shock is the ECB, but this institution cannot act as a firewall in any situation because it is not in its mandate. They also point out that the institutional architecture designed to overcome the crisis may not be the best way to enhance policy coordination.[32] The need for policy coordination, if necessary imposing limitations to the degree of freedom that member states have regarding fiscal issues, would be a good response to avoid negative spillovers between euro area members. Therefore, their proposal is a new design of policy coordination that centralizes the fiscal and budgetary tasks, leaving less freedom at national level.

Andrle et al. (2015) presents some options for simplifying EU fiscal governance while enhancing its effectiveness. Their proposals are based on two axes: consolidating the preventive and corrective arms and shifting to a single fiscal anchor with a single operational rule.

Their approach consists of a consolidation of the preventive and corrective arms. Even though it would imply some ambitious legislative changes, it would notably simplify the procedure. Their reform proposal consists of replacing both arms with a two-step approach based on common rules.[33] Minor deviations from the reference debt figures would imply slight corrective actions and significant non-compliant cases would be subject to corrective actions and sanctions.

Regarding their proposal about shifting to a single fiscal anchor, they propose the elimination of deficit and debt targets, leaving a single debt to GDP objective. They suggest a two-pillar approach with a single anchor and a single operational rule. The rationale for setting a single anchor is that the ultimate objective of fiscal sustainability is debt sustainability. A stock variable such as debt to GDP is a more natural anchor than a flow variable such as deficit to GDP. The operational rule proposed should support a countercyclical fiscal policy that is transparent and easy to communicate to the public. They propose three possible operational rules. First, nominal budget balance rules with a focus on the variable that primarily influences the debt to GDP ratio (i.e. deficit). The drawback of such a rule is that it is specified in nominal terms and does not have stabilization features, potentially leading to procyclical effects. Secondly, structural balance rules (i.e. macroeconomic indicators not related to the budget) supplemented with a debt break incorporated in the national legislation. This type of rule would allow the automatic stabilizers to

---

[32] "Within the European Semester, the European Commission has to assess whether policies planned by national governments are 'appropriate' and issue recommendations accordingly. This is mostly based on the potential of such policies to meet certain targets. However, there are circumstances in which the assessment required is more complex and it is neither explicit nor clear whether the principle guiding the evaluation is the ad hoc optimisation of the overall good/welfare of the union or rather the idea that coordination always leads to a better outcome" (Alcidi and Gros 2015).

[33] As proposed by Eyraud and Wu (2015).

operate, so it can be more countercyclical. However, the disadvantage of this approach is that it is difficult to communicate and imply complex computations such as the estimation of the output gap. The third option is the use of expenditure rules. This implies the use of public spending in growth terms or in relative terms (i.e. the growth of the ratio of public expenditures to GDP). The advantages of this rule are that it allows the automatic stabilizers to operate and is easy to communicate.

Their simulations show that the expenditure rule should work better. They propose to combine it with an explicit debt correction mechanism. Moreover, they suggest that for this fiscal framework to work properly, it should be more automatic in enforcement, with credible sanctions and better coordination.

Carnot (2014) proposes a "rule of thumb" as an alternative to the existing framework for evaluating fiscal policies in the euro area member states. This new rule would balance the requirements of the fiscal policy with economic stabilization as a better way of achieving fiscal stabilization. The idea of this "rule" is to set long-term fiscal objectives while taking into account the possible tradeoffs with output stabilization in the short run. In practical terms, the proposal consists in setting a long-run objective (i.e. public debt equal to 60 % of GDP as required by the SGP) that serves as an anchor and then for each budgetary period; the rule suggests a fiscal impulse towards the debt objective while arbitraging symmetrically between this objective and a stable output. Under this system, debt stabilization would follow a smooth path without having a negative impact on growth. This rule would allow fiscal policy to be more countercyclical.

Regarding public debt sustainability, Blot et al. (2015) analyse the public debt targets and output dynamics imposed by compliance with those targets. They assess through a series of simulations the compliance path of 11 euro area member states towards the debt limits set by the SGP on the path established by the Fiscal Compact (1/20th of the adjustment yearly).[34] In their set of simulations they conclude that because of underoptimistic assumptions regarding deficit reduction and growth, some member states would not be able to reach the 60 % public debt threshold by 2032 (end of the 20-year horizon established by the Fiscal Compact). If debt consolidation was achieved by all member states it would be at the expense of a poor functioning of fiscal multipliers (thus, higher austerity). The consequence of this malfunctioning would be lower output growth, higher unemployment and higher volatility of euro area sovereign debt spreads, hampering the path towards the debt objective.

---

[34] These countries are Austria, Belgium, Finland, France, Germany, Greece, Ireland, Italy, the Netherlands, Portugal and Spain.

Therefore, they propose to eliminate front-loaded fiscal adjustment targets and instead delay fiscal austerity measures to avoid economic policy measures that are counterproductive in terms of return of public debt to its target.

The final set of proposals aims at changing the statute of the ECB to better serve the interests of the euro area.

A proposal that has been widely discussed is the possibility of giving a dual mandate to the ECB regarding monetary policy (Ragot 2013). This dual mandate would imply that ECB policy would have to pursue not only a price stability target but also an output target. However, economists such as Orphanides (2014) state that the primary objective of a central bank should be price stability without overburdening the institution with other objectives that dilute its efforts towards the primary objective. In his view, additional primary goals would reduce the contribution of the ECB to economic prosperity. Under New Keynesian theories, the existence of an output–inflation tradeoff relationship implies that in order to achieve higher levels of growth, policymakers have to allow for inflation to rise. Under such a framework, giving a double mandate to the ECB to pursue both maximum output growth and price stability can be seen as contradictory. Nonetheless, the theory states that in the long run this relationship ceases to exist, as employment and output return to their natural rate (Friedman 1968; Phelps 1968). Therefore, this would imply that in the long run either a double mandate or a mandate that only includes inflation would lead to the same results, which are the argument of those who support the double mandate view.

However, defendants of the current mandate argue that a dual target for monetary policy may lead to time inconsistent measures, meaning that the central bank has an incentive to communicate an inflation target and change it once the expectations of economic agents have been set. Moreover, they claim that a dual mandate would reduce the transparency of the ECB. Dual mandates imply that specific targets for both policy objectives are not fixed because accomplishing one but not the other would lead to criticism. Therefore, the ECB would have an incentive to avoid setting a quantitative definition for each objective (Smaghi 2007).

Alternatively, Blot et al. (2014) state that the incorporation of the Single Supervisory Mechanism (SSM) within the ECB (in charge of the microprudential supervision of banks) gives de facto a triple mandate to the institution. They distinguish then three mandates within the ECB: price stability given by the Treaty, output growth as the Treaty stipulates that without prejudice of price stability the European System of Central Banks shall support the general economic policies of the Union, and financial stability in the framework of the SSM. According to the authors, even if there is a hierarchy between each objective, in practical terms the ECB has been paying increasing attention to the evolutions of both inflation and growth. Therefore, the authors suggest an amendment of the ECB's mandate to include an output target like the one of the Federal Reserve.[35]

Another proposal that has been discussed is the one proposed by Burda (2013). He warns about the excessive "politicization" of the ECB's tasks and proposes an alternative system that would replace the current NCBs with a system more similar to the one in the USA, with decentralized Federal Reserve Banks. He proposes dividing the euro area territory into five different "monetary jurisdictions" that are not linked to the existing political division of states. Each jurisdiction would have a division of the ECB that represents large stretches of territory that reach beyond the borders. This main idea behind this system would be to secure a truly independent and neutral monetary policy.

2.5   Conclusions

Upon its creation, the euro area was equipped with a fiscal policy to ensure public finances' sustainability. However, the enforcement of these fiscal rules has been flawed and the situation was aggravated by the economic and financial crisis.

The euro area went through a reform of the fiscal rules before the 2008 crisis that did not put an end to excessive deficits and debt levels required by the SGP. Since then, there has been a set of important reforms to correct imbalances, but the enforcement leaves a high level of freedom to member states. Likewise, the last reforms may not be enough to end the procyclicality of national fiscal policies, which is one of the key matters to be addressed.

Policy proposals aim at simplifying the mechanism of control and enforcement of the fiscal rules as well as reducing discretion in the hands of member states.

The completion of an economic union requires more than temporary solutions and more integrating commitments in terms of fiscal policy. Last-minute solutions have been successful to solve critical problems and situations, not only in Greece but also in Portugal and Spain. However, the euro area lacks a clear project of economic union. In the light of the proposals analysed, a fiscal union shall incorporate transfers and a system of common debt issuance.

The ECB has been able to act to stop the meltdown at the decisive moment, but this just gives some additional time to the euro area member states to accomplish necessary reforms. Without further integration the euro area remains an imperfect (and potentially unsustainable) fixed exchange rate system, but not a common economic and political project.

---

[35] This new objective would add to the price stability objective and the financial stability objective of the SSM.

2.6   Annex

	Original 1997 SGP		SGP after the 2005 reform		SGP after the 2011 reform	
	Preventive arm	Corrective arm (Excessive Deficit Procedure)	Preventive arm	Corrective arm (Excessive Deficit Procedure)	Preventive arm	Corrective arm (Excessive Deficit Procedure)
	Regulation EC 1466/97	Regulation EC 1467/97	Regulation EC 1055/2005	Regulation EC 1056/2005	"Six-Pack": Regulations EU 1173/2011, EU 1174/2011, EU 1175/2011 amending R. 1466/97, EU 1176/2011, EU 1177/2011 amending R. 1467/97 ; Directive 2011/85/EU	
Objective	Close to balance or in surplus	Correct gross policy errors	Close to balance or in surplus	Correct gross policy errors	Close to balance or in surplus	Correct gross policy errors

Specification –					
	Limits: – Deficit < 3% of GDP – Debt < 60% of GDP or sufficiently diminishing	**Country specific Medium–Term Objective (structural terms)** – Safety margin against breaching the 3% of deficit limit – Rapid progress towards sustainability – Room for budgetary manoeuvre: limit for euro area and European Exchange Rate Mechanism II (ERMII) countries – => –1% of structural deficit/GDP	Limits: – Deficit < 3% of GDP – Debt < 60% of GDP or sufficiently diminishing	**Country specific Medium–Term Objective (structural terms)** – Safety margin against breaching the 3% of deficit limit – Rapid progress towards sustainability – Room for budgetary manoeuvre: limit for euro area and European Exchange Rate Mechanism II (ERMII) countries – => –1% of structural deficit/GDP **Expenditure benchmark** ensuring that expenditure net of discretionary revenue measures should grow in line with medium-term potential growth	Limits: – Deficit < 3% of GDP – Debt < 60% of GDP or sufficiently diminishing **Definition of sufficiently diminishing**: respect of debt reduction benchmark => reduction of 5% per year on average over 3 years of the gap to 60% taking the cycle into account or respect in the next two years

(continued)

Annex (continued)

	Original 1997 SGP		SGP after the 2005 reform		SGP after the 2011 reform	
	Preventive arm	Corrective arm (Excessive Deficit Procedure)	Preventive arm	Corrective arm (Excessive Deficit Procedure)	Preventive arm	Corrective arm (Excessive Deficit Procedure)
	Regulation EC 1466/97	Regulation EC 1467/97	Regulation EC 1055/2005	Regulation EC 1056/2005	"Six-Pack": Regulations EU 1173/2011, EU 1174/2011, EU 1175/2011 amending R. 1466/97, EU 1176/2011, EU 1177/2011 amending R. 1467/97 ; Directive 2011/85/EU	
Adjustment path	–	Defined within the Excessive Deficit Procedure (EDP)	**Annual adjustment:** benchmark of +0.5% of GDP (structural terms), more in good times, less in bad times **Possible temporary deviation** for major structural reforms with verifiable impact on long-term	**Annual adjustment:** at least +0.5% of GDP (structural terms) **Possible deadline extension if** (i) effective action has been taken and (ii) unexpected economic events beyond the control of the government with major unfavourable consequences for government finances (compared to forecasts underlying the recommendation)	**Annual adjustment:** – benchmark of +0.5% of GDP (structural terms), more in good times, less in bad times – adjustment > 0.5% in structural terms when debt >60% of GDP or pronounced risks of overall debt sustainability **Possible temporary deviation:** – for major structural reforms with verifiable impact on long-term	**Annual adjustment:** at least +0.5% of GDP (structural terms) **Possible deadline extension if** (i) effective action has been taken (ii) and unexpected economic events beyond the control of the government with major unfavourable consequences for government finances (compared to forecasts underlying the recommendation) or in case of severe economic downturn in the euro area or in the Union as a whole provided it does not endanger fiscal sustainability in the medium-term

				– in case of unusual events outside the control of the country with a major impact on the financial position of the general government – in case of severe economic downturn in the euro area or the union as a whole	
Enforcement mechanism	At the very end of the procedure	–	At the very end of the procedure	Procedure for correcting significant deviation Possible sanction (interest bearing deposit of 0.2% of GDP as a rule) in case of repeated non-compliance	Early and gradual sanction system to be activated at each stage of the EDP procedure

Note: This table reproduces tables 1.1, 1.2, 1.3 and 1.4 in European Commission, 2013, "Building a Strengthened Fiscal Framework in the European Union: A Guide to the Stability and Growth Pact", Publications Office

References

Acharya, V., Eisert, T., Eufinger, C., & Hirsch, C. (2016). *Whatever it takes: The real effects of unconventional monetary policy*, Working Paper.

Alcidi, C., & Gros, D. (2015). EMU governance and the limits of fiscal policy coordination. In *Redesigning European monetary union governance in light of the Eurozone crisis* (pp. 47–56). Barcelona: CIDOB.

Alesina, A., & Tabellini, G. (1990). A positive theory of fiscal deficits and government debt. *The Review of Economic Studies, 57*, 403. doi:10.2307/2298021.

Andrle, M., Bluedorn, M. J. C., Eyraud, L., Kinda, M. T., Brooks, P. K., Schwartz, M. G., & Weber, A. (2015). *Reforming fiscal governance in the European Union.* Washington, DC: International Monetary Fund.

Annett, A. (2006). *Enforcement and the stability and growth pact: How fiscal policy did and did not change under Europe's fiscal framework.* Washington, DC: International Monetary Fund.

Annett, M. A., Decressin, M. J., & Deppler, M. M. (2005). *Reforming the stability and growth pact.* Washington, DC: International Monetary Fund.

Blot, C., Creel, J., Hubert, P., & Labondance, F. (2014). Les enjeux du triple mandat de la BCE. *Revue de l'OFCE, 134*, 175–186.

Blot, C., Cochard, M., Creel, J., Ducoudré, B., Schweisguth, D., & Timbeau, X. (2015). Fiscal consolidation, public debt and output dynamics in the Euro area: Lessons from a simple model with time-varying fiscal multipliers. *Revue d'économie politique, 124*, 953–989.

Briotti, G.. (2004). *Fiscal adjustment between 1991 and 2002: Stylised facts and policy implications.* ECB occasional paper. Frankfurt am Main: European Central Bank.

Burda, M. (2013). *Redesigning the ECB with regional rather than national central banks.* London: Vox-EU.

Buti, M., & Sapir, A. (1998). *Economic policy in EMU: A study.* Oxford: Oxford University Press.

Canzoneri, M. B., Cumby, R. E., & Diba, B. T. (2001). Is the price level determined by the needs of fiscal solvency? *American Economic Review, 91*, 1221–1238.

Carnot, N. (2014). *Evaluating fiscal policy: A rule of thumb (No. 526), European economy economic papers.* Directorate General Economic and Financial Affairs (DG ECFIN), European Commission.

Christova, A. (2011). The European stability mechanism: Progress or missed opportunity? Baltic. *Journal of European Studies, 1*.

Closa, C., & Maatsch, A. (2014). In a spirit of solidarity? Justifying the European financial stability facility (EFSF) in national parliamentary debates. *JCMS: Journal of Common Market Studies, 52*, 826–842.

De Grauwe, P. (2013). *Design failures in the Eurozone: Can they be fixed?.* LEQS paper. Brussels: European Commission/Directorate-General for Economic and Financial Affairs.

Delpla, J., & Von Weizsacker, J.. (2010, May 2010). *The blue bond proposal*. Bruegel policy brief 2010/03. Brussels: Bruegel.

Delpla, J., & Von Weizsäcker, J. (2011). *Eurobonds: The blue bond concept and its implications*. Bruegel policy contribution. Brussels: Bruegel.

Dullien, S. (2013). *A euro area wide unemployment insurance as an automatic stabilizer: Who benefits and who pays?* European Commission (DG EMPL).

European Central Bank. (2010). *Monthly bulletin of October 2010*, Frankfurt am Main.Eyraud, L., & Wu, T. (2015).

Friedman, M. (1968). The role of monetary policy. *American Economic Review, 53*, 1–17.

Gabrisch, H., & Staehr, K. (2014). *The Euro plus pact: Cost competitiveness and external capital flows in the EU countries*. Working paper series 1650. Frankfurt am Main: European Central Bank.

Horváth, B. L., & Huizinga, H. (2015). Does the European financial stability facility bail out sovereigns or banks? An event study. *Journal of Money, Credit and Banking, 47*, 177–206.

Kydland, F. E., & Prescott, E. C. (1977). Rules rather than discretion: The inconsistency of optimal plans. *The Journal of Political Economy, 85*(3), 473–491.

Micossi, S. (2015). The monetary policy of the European central bank (2002–2015). *CEPS Special Report, 109*.

Micossi, S., Carmossi, J., & Peirce, F. (2011). *On the tasks of the European stability mechanism*. Centre for European policy studies. Brussels: CEPS.

Ngai, V. (2012). *Stability and growth pact and fiscal discipline in the Eurozone*. Wharton financial institutions center working paper 12–10. Pennsylvania: University of Pennsylvania.

Orphanides, A. (2014). *Changing the mandate of the ECB is not the solution to Europe's problems*, Speech addressed at the meeting of the "Cercle d' Economistes" of Aix-en-Provence. Aix-en-Provence, France.

Phelps, E. S. (1968). Money-wage dynamics and labor-market equilibrium. *The Journal of Political Economy, 76*, 678–711.

Ragot, X. (2013). *Should the ECB have a dual mandate?* Meeting papers 41st economics conference. Vienna: National Central Bank of Austria.

Schiliro, D. (2013). The crisis of euro's governance: Institutional aspects and policy issues. *Financial Aspects of Recent Trends in the Global Economy, 2*, 150–163.

Smaghi, L. B. (2007). The governance of the Euro area (Eight Years On). In: Forum Financier-Revue Bancaire et Financiaire Bank en Financiewezen-, Larcier, p. 162.

Steinberg, F. (2015). Building a sustainable Eurozone. In*Redesigning European monetary union governance in light of the Eurozone crisis* (pp. 35–46). Barcelona: CIDOB.

Timbeau, X. (2014). *From austerity to stagnation how to avoid the deflation trap: The independent annual growth survey 2014*, Sciences Po.

Timbeau, X., et al. (2015). *A diverging Europe on the edge: The independent annual growth survey 2015*.

Union, E. (2012). *Consolidated version of the treaty of functioning of the European Union.* Luxembourg: Office for Official publications of the European Communities.

Verhelst, S., (2013). *Assessing the single supervisory mechanism: Passing the point of no return for Europe's banking union.* Egmont paper No. 58, June 2013.

Von Hagen, J. (2002). Fiscal rules, fiscal institutions, and fiscal performance. *Economic and Social Review, 33,* 263–284.

Von Hagen, J., & Wyplosz, C. (2010). EMU's decentralized system of fiscal policy. In *The Euro, the first decade* (pp. 415–443). Cambridge: Cambridge University Press.

Woodford, M. (2001). Fiscal requirements for price stability. *Journal of Money, Credit and Banking, 33,* 669–728.

3

Fiscal Sustainability and Fiscal Rules in a Monetary Union: Theory and Practice in Europe

Pierre Aldama

3.1 Introduction

Over the last three decades, under what is usually called the "Great Moderation," both macroeconomists and policymakers involved in fiscal policy mainly focused on long-run issues. The consensus was that discretionary fiscal policy was mostly inefficient relative to monetary policy, to say the least. As a consequence, government should adopt rules ensuring the long-run sustainability of public finance, and let an independent central bank take charge of controlling inflation and stabilizing gross domestic product (GDP) growth and unemployment. This consensus was recently challenged following the experience of 2008's subprime crisis and the following "Great Recession." To some extent, fiscal policy has been restored as a powerful macroeconomic stabilization instrument during deep recessions, especially when monetary policy can no longer decrease the nominal short-run interest rate. But it also stressed the need of fiscal rules ensuring the long-run sustainability of public debt.

Nevertheless, the need for fiscal rules ensuring fiscal sustainability should not be seen as necessarily contradicting the short-run stabilization motives of fiscal policy. One of the lessons of European sovereign debt crisis may be that, in face of strong and negative demand shocks, a government must have

P. Aldama (✉)
CES, Paris School of Economics, Université Paris 1 Panthéon-Sorbonne, Paris, France

© The Author(s) 2017

R. Douady et al. (eds.), *Financial Regulation in the EU*,
DOI 10.1007/978-3-319-44287-7_3

enough "fiscal space" to use fiscal policy aggressively when needed (Blanchard et al. 2010).

What are the fiscal sustainability requirements? Despite being an (almost) infinitely lived-agent, government faces an intertemporal budget constraint like any other economic agent: it is expected to pay back its debts with future (present-value) primary surpluses; if not, it will at some point default—directly or indirectly—and lose access to financial markets as long as its borrower's credibility is not restored. Fiscal rules and monitoring of fiscal policy precisely aim at preventing government from engaging upon an unsustainable path; that is, violating its intertemporal budget constraint and eventually defaulting on its debt.

When this occurs, violations of the government intertemporal budget constraint may take different forms, depending on institutional framework: direct default on public debt repayments, monetization by the Central Bank and/or through an increase in present and (un)expected future inflation, which are actually indirect forms of default, through an inflation tax. At some point, from a theoretical point of view, violations of a government's sustainability constraint may result in some "unpleasant monetarist arithmetic," to use the words of Sargent and Wallace (1981). Thus monetary–fiscal interactions' effects on inflation, and more broadly speaking on macroeconomic stability, provide another set of theoretical arguments in favour of fiscal policy rules. Moreover, fiscal rules and fiscal surveillance are of great importance within a monetary union without federal budget. Uncoordinated national fiscal policies may have a significant impact on monetary policy's ability to control inflation; but it also makes room for countercyclical fiscal policy, since common monetary policy cannot react to country-specific or asymmetric shocks.

The issue of public debt sustainability and fiscal policy rules has been at the centre of European macroeconomic debate since the Maastricht Treaty (1992), the Stability and Growth Pact (SGP) (1997) and the creation of the European Monetary Union (EMU) (1999). The European fiscal framework has been intensively criticized since the beginning of the 1990s. Its detractors regularly denounce the economic growth and employment costs of alleged procyclical European fiscal rules, while its promoters argue that sound public finances and financial stability are the *sine qua non* for strong and sustainable economic growth and therefore full employment. Based on theoretical and empirical research on fiscal policy, fiscal sustainability and monetary–fiscal interactions, we propose a critical appraisal of the European fiscal framework.

This chapter is organized as following. In Sect. 3.2, we explain why and how fiscal policy needs to be constrained, in particular within a monetary union. Fiscal rules are usually designed and justified to ensure fiscal sustainability and to prevent sovereign default. We present different fiscal sustainability concepts—intertemporal budget constraint, convergence to stable debt-to-GDP ratios, maximum level of public debt and deficit and "fiscal limits"—in recent research on fiscal policy and their implications in terms of fiscal rules and surveillance. Second, monetary–fiscal interactions are essential to understand the need for fiscal policy rules, and even more within a monetary union. Fiscal policy may have a significant effect on the long-run nominal interest rate but also on present and future inflation, jeopardizing the central bank's ability to control inflation, and this would justify additional constraints on fiscal policy in order to prevent negative spillover effects between monetary union members and to prevent monetary policy from losing control of inflation. We also show that fiscal sustainability requirements and countercyclical fiscal policy should not be seen as necessarily antagonistic. In Sect. 3.3 we discuss the European Fiscal Framework based on empirical and theoretical research presented earlier. We argue that this framework might be both too tight and too loose: too tight because European fiscal rules are a priori much stricter than what would be required according to fiscal sustainability analysis; too loose because they induce a procyclical bias that, in addition to economic growth and employment costs, may be counterproductive in ensuring fiscal sustainability. We finally open the debate about the causes of the European sovereign debt crisis, which was at first interpreted as the result of irresponsible fiscal policies and therefore called for a tightening of fiscal rules. A new consensus narrative recently emerged which significantly changes the diagnosis as well as the economic policy responses it calls for. Section 3.4 draws some general conclusions about fiscal policy in a monetary union and more specific conclusions about the EMU and the European fiscal framework.

3.2 Why (and How) Does Fiscal Policy Need to Be Constrained?

Fiscal sustainability is usually defined for the government as the commitment to pay back its debt with future primary budget surpluses—budget surpluses excluding interest on public debt. Despite being quite intuitive, this assertion is actually very vague because government is (theoretically) infinitely lived. Consequently, it could roll over its debt forever and remain solvent as long as it runs enough future primary surpluses such that it pays back on average a small part of the interest charge: such a fiscal policy would *strictly* satisfy the government intertemporal budget constraint, despite government always being indebted. Considering this particular example, "fiscal sustainability" requirements—based on the government intertemporal budget constraint—seem very weak. Basically, research on fiscal policy tries to answer the following questions. What is "fiscal sustainability"? What are the minimum requirements the government intertemporal budget constraint (henceforth GIBC) imposes on fiscal policy—that is on taxes and non-interest spending, or primary budget surpluses? Is the GIBC sufficient to ensure fiscal sustainability or should we make additional assumptions—for instance on the maximum primary budget surplus a government can economically and politically run—to reach a robust fiscal sustainability criterion?

3.2.1 Public Debt Sustainability and Fiscal Policy Rules

Let us start from the GIBC (or present-value budget constraint). Consider a simplified representation of fiscal policy in which government non-interest spending is denoted by g_t and revenues by τ_t, both expressed in percentage of GDP. The stock of public debt at the end of year t is represented by b_t, in percentage of GDP. Define the primary budget surplus–GDP ratio as $s_t \equiv \tau_t - g_t$. Then public debt–GDP ratio evolves according the following public debt accumulation equation[1]:

$$b_{t+1} = \left(1 + i - g - \pi\right)b_t - s_{t+1} = \left(1 + r - g\right)b_t - s_{t+1}$$

where i is the average nominal interest rate on public debt, g is the average growth rate of real GDP and π is the inflation rate. For simplicity, we use Fisher's relation and define the real interest rate as $r = i - \pi$. It is worth noting that this accounting equation only describes the year-over-year accumulation of public debt; it does not per se yield any sustainability condition. Public debt–GDP ratio accumulation is mainly driven by primary surpluses (or deficits) and by public debt snowball effect $(r - g)b_t$: if $r > g$ public debt–GDP tends to increase by itself.

Studying sustainability of public debt and deficits requires examining the intertemporal budget constraint of government. From the public debt accumulation equation, one can deduce by successive iterations:

---

[1] For simplicity, this presentation neglects stock-flow adjustments (SFA), defined as the difference between total variation of public debt and overall public deficit. SFA are mostly a statistical and national accounting issue rather than a theoretical one. We also consider that interest rate, inflation rate and growth rate of real GDP are equal to their average values. This is a strong assumption to study public debt sustainability sometimes labeled as "ad hoc sustainability", see Bohn (2008); but we chose the most simple framework for clarity purposes.

$$b_t = \sum_{T=1}^{\infty} \frac{\mathbb{E}_t\left(s_{t+T}\right)}{\left(1+r-g\right)^T} \quad + \quad \lim_{T \to \infty} \frac{\mathbb{E}_t\left(b_{t+T}\right)}{\left(1+r-g\right)^T}$$

This intertemporal accounting equation states that initial stock of public debt (on the left-hand side) is equal to the sum of future expected present-value primary surpluses–GDP ratio and the expected long-run level of future present-value public debt–GDP ratio (on the right-hand side). From a purely accounting point of view, government can either repay initial public debt b_t with present-value primary surpluses or rolling over debt—but how much and how long can a government roll over debt? Thus, fiscal sustainability analysis usually imposes a solvency criterion, called the No-Ponzi Game (NPG) condition.[2] The NPG condition states that a solvent government cannot roll over debt *plus* interests forever but needs to cover *at least* a small amount of its debt-service with primary surpluses. This is equivalent to say that the average rate of growth of public debt must be strictly lower than the average interest rate (Hamilton and Flavin 1986; Bohn 2007). As a consequence, NPG condition implies long-run present-value public debt–GDP ratio must be equal to zero. Hence, a sustainable fiscal policy must satisfy the following "Transversality Condition" (henceforth TC):

$$\lim_{T \to \infty} \frac{\mathbb{E}_t\left(b_{t+T}\right)}{\left(1+r-g\right)^T} = 0$$

Then it is straightforward to derive GIBC:

$$b_t = \sum_{T=1}^{\infty} \frac{\mathbb{E}_t\left(s_{t+T}\right)}{\left(1+r-g\right)^T}$$

What are the implications in terms of fiscal rules—that is, constraints on fiscal instruments (primary surpluses, revenues or non-interest spending)—such that GIBC holds? Analogous to monetary feedback policy rules, such as the Taylor Rule that relates the short-term interest rate to the current (or past) inflation rate and output gap, Model-Based Sustainability analysis proposes to study fiscal sustainability using fiscal feedback policy rules. Following Bohn

---

[2] Named after Charles Ponzi's fraudulent investment operation.

(1998, 2008) and Mendoza and Ostry (2008) such empirical fiscal rules are generally specified as follows:

$$s_{t+1} = \alpha + \gamma b_t + \beta_x x_{t+1} + \beta_g g_{t+1} + \epsilon_{t+1}$$

These feedback rules basically assume that fiscal policy's instrument—in general, primary surplus–GDP ratio—reacts to:

- Initial level of public debt–GDP b_t, to account for fiscal sustainability motives;
- Contemporaneous output gap x_{t+1}, defined as the gap between actual and potential (or trend) real GDP,[3] to account for "automatic stabilizers" and countercyclical fiscal policy;
- Temporary fluctuations in public expenditures g_{t+1}, defined as the difference between actual and trend expenditures, to account for temporary primary surpluses or deficits;
- The constant term α would be different from zero and negative, accounting for the fact fiscal policy is not required to run primary surpluses all the time, if the fiscal policy rule is satisfying a debt-stabilizing criterion (see below).

Based on a dynamic stochastic general equilibrium model (DSGE), Bohn (1998) shows a necessary and sufficient condition on these fiscal policy rules to satisfy GIBC and TC on public debt is such that primary surplus–GDP must increase after an increase in public debt–GDP:

$$\gamma > 0$$

Thus, GIBC imposes very weak requirements per se (Bohn 2007). Theoretically, as long as government can roll over its debts on financial markets, it could accumulate an ever-increasing amount of public debt–GDP, provided that this ratio grows at a rate lower than the real interest rate adjusted for real GDP growth rate. As a consequence, GIBC does not imply per se any

---

[3] Potential real GDP is the level of real GDP that can be produced at a constant rate of inflation. It mainly depends on capital stock and utilization rate of capital, potential labour force, NAIRU (Non-Accelerating Inflation Rate of Unemployment) and factors' productivity.

Potential real GDP is generally estimated using structural models. As an alternative to structural methods, trend real GDP is an econometric approach consisting into the decomposition of real GDP between a trend component and a cyclical component, interpreted as the "output gap".

Although, each measure has advantages and shortcomings, structural methods are generally preferred to purely econometric methods because of the "end-point bias" (indeed econometric methods generally tend to underestimate the output gap at end of sample) but also because of "spurious business cycles."

upper bound on public debt–GDP ratio, raising questions whether GIBC and TC are really sufficient to ensure "fiscal sustainability." Yet additional considerations on fiscal policy would be required to justify bounded debt–GDP ratios, which would be a stronger definition of fiscal sustainability. A prudent answer could be that they are the *minimum requirements* for sustainability, but still they do not exclude sovereign default, if government was not able to roll over debt on financial markets.

There are two main arguments to justify an upper bound on public debt–GDP ratio. One approach is structural, using simulated or estimated DSGE models, and relies on the assumption of an upper limit on primary surplus–GDP ratio (Bi 2012; Bi and Traum 2012; Bi and Leeper 2013). The upper boundary for primary surplus–GDP ratio is justified by two main reasons:

1) The existence of a "Laffer curve" owing to distortionary taxation: there should be an optimal tax rate which maximizes tax revenue (Trabandt and Uhlig 2011);
2) The fact government may not be capable of decreasing public spending–GDP ratio beyond some level for political reasons.

Given that $s_t \leq s^{max}$ and using GIBC, one can define a maximum public debt–GDP ratio, called the "fiscal limit," at which government may default with a positive probability. The following equation combines the GIBC and the assumption made about s_t to yield an analytic expression for the "fiscal limit" b_t^{max}:

$$b_t^{max} = \sum_{T=1}^{\infty} \mathbb{E}_t \left(\Lambda_{t+T,t}^{max} \, s_{t+T}^{max} \right)$$

where $\Lambda_{t+T,t}^{max}$ represents the growth-adjusted stochastic discount factor, which also depends on the Laffer optimal tax rate, derived from general equilibrium models.

The fiscal limit is the maximum level of public debt–GDP ratio that could be backed by expected future present-value primary surpluses; beyond this level, fiscal policy would be *necessarily* playing a Ponzi Game against its creditors, implying a positive probability of default. A complete presentation of this concept accounts for uncertainty and effects of aggregate productivity shocks, or fiscal policy regime shifts on the future maximum primary surpluses (Bi 2012; Bi and Leeper 2013). Accounting for uncertainty implies the fiscal limit would not be deterministic but rather *stochastic*. Consequently, in a stochastic economy, sovereign default could occur at very various levels of public debt–GDP, even relatively low levels if the economy faces very adverse macroeconomic shocks and/or if a government is engaged on an unsustainable path, running persistent primary deficits.

Another approach accounts for the "fiscal fatigue" phenomenon (Ghosh et al. 2013). Using panel data on 23 advanced economies and covering the years 1970–2007, Ghosh et al. found a non-linear relationship between primary balance and public debt such that, at high debt levels, fiscal policy is no longer able to increase sufficiently its primary balance to stabilize public debt. Facing risk-neutral international investors, government hits the fiscal limit when primary surplus–GDP can no longer offset public debt's snowball effect $(r-g)b_t$ for high levels of public debt. The concept of fiscal limit leads to a definition of "fiscal space," which is the difference between the actual level of public debt and its estimated maximum sustainable level. Fiscal space offers an alternative and complementary measure for fiscal sustainability as the financial leeway of a government that allows it to face very adverse macroeconomic shocks.

Daniel and Shiamptanis (2013) show that, in the presence of "fiscal limits," a relevant fiscal sustainability criterion would be a debt-stabilizing rule around prudent public debt–GDP ratio—with sufficient fiscal space to face with adverse macroeconomic shocks. Such a debt-stabilizing rule requires that, on average, primary surpluses are greater than the growth-adjusted real interest rate; that is:

$$\gamma > r - g$$

Under a debt-stabilizing fiscal policy rule, it is straightforward to show that:

$$\alpha = \left((r-g) - \gamma \right) b^*$$

with b^* being the targeted level of debt–GDP (or steady-state) which also defines the debt-stabilizing primary surplus–GDP:

$$s^* = (r - g) b^*$$

As long the debt-stabilizing condition holds, α would be negative, as is usually found in the data. Thus, one can provide a comprehensive interpretation of linear–fiscal policy rules in terms of deviations from steady-state values:

$$s_{t+1} - s^* = \gamma\left(b_t - b^*\right) + \beta_x x_{t+1} + \beta_g g_{t+1} + \epsilon_{t+1}$$

Linear–fiscal policy rules do not imply that government must *always* run primary surpluses but only when its debt–GDP ratio is above its reference long-run value b^*.

Considering these long-run ratios, fiscal policy rules show themselves being useful theoretical and empirical tools both for fiscal sustainability analysis and the design of numerical reference values for fiscal variables—what we generally label "fiscal rules." Suppose policymakers take economic environment $r-g$ as given (which may be at some points a very restrictive assumption) and set reference values for b^*, then they can deduce how much fiscal policy must react to public debt (γ) and what must be the long-run average debt-stabilizing primary surplus s^*.

Fiscal sustainability analysis based on GIBC and fiscal policy rules yields important lessons on what constraints are needed for sustainability. First, a prudent fiscal policy should probably ensure convergence of public debt–GDP ratios towards prudent levels (Fall et al. 2015; Fournier and Fall 2015), with sufficient fiscal space in order to face adverse macroeconomic shocks, such as the 2008 financial crisis and the following Great Recession. Unfortunately, this does not definitively prevent government from hitting its fiscal limit when facing extremely adverse macroeconomic shocks, even if is committed to a strongly sustainable fiscal policy rule (i.e. the debt-stabilizing rule). Fiscal discipline cannot reduce fiscal risk to zero, and this fact may support the view that a central bank should act as a lender of last resort. Second, fiscal sustainability is a long-run requirement and fiscal numerical rules should account for the effects of automatic stabilizers or temporary public expenditures (or spending reversals); in practice, it supports fiscal numerical rules specified in terms of structural (or cyclically adjusted) balance.

3.2.2 Fiscal Discipline Within a Monetary Union

Since the very beginning of EMU, while the Maastricht Treaty was being negotiated, negative externalities coming from unsustainable fiscal policy at national level received a lot of attention (Wyplosz 1991; Buiter et al. 1993). Expansionary fiscal policy generally boosts demand and increases the real interest rate and the inflation rate. Outside a monetary union (MU), in a flexible exchange rate regime, these effects would be partially or totally offset through adjustment in the nominal exchange rate, as it often the case. On the contrary, within a monetary union adjustment occurs entirely through prices and real interest rate. Thus "excessive deficits" of one MU member may affect the real interest rate of all member countries and the inflation rate, in proportion to its relative size.

Concerns about undesirable effects of "excessive deficits" mostly focused on the monetary and financial instability that they could imply (Buiter et al. 1993). The motivation for preventing "excessive deficits" and unsustainable national fiscal policies, fiscal rules embedded in the Maastricht Treaty, was to ensure (nominal) convergence among members of EMU. What is the rationale behind fiscal rules as requirements for price-level stability?

There are two main approaches of monetary–fiscal interactions to the explanation of why fiscal policy should be constrained in order to control inflation stability: Sargent and Wallace's (1981) "unpleasant monetarist arithmetic" and the Fiscal Theory of Price Level (Leeper 1991; Sims 1994; Woodford 1995, 2001; Cochrane 2001, 2005). Both approaches focus on GIBC and link the need for fiscal rules that ensure the sustainability of public debt to achieve inflation stability.

In their seminal paper, Sargent and Wallace show that strategic interactions between fiscal and monetary authorities can jeopardize a central bank's ability to stabilize inflation, even in a purely monetarist economy. What matters is which authority moves first, the monetary or the fiscal authority. If fiscal policy decides to run excessive deficits, implying "fiscal dominance," then it will accumulate public debt until it reaches its maximum sustainable level, given the demand for public bonds. Thus, even when the central bank follows a strict monetarist rule, controlling money supply growth and inflation in the short run, it will be forced to monetize public debt and increase the money supply when public debt hits its maximum level. So here is the main result of Sargent and Wallace: "tighter money now can eventually mean higher inflation tomorrow" if fiscal policy is dominant and even if monetary policy is tight today. Even more, under fiscal dominance, tighter money today implies an even higher inflation rate tomorrow, compared to what it would have been if monetary policy had been easier today.

It is important that Sargent and Wallace's model does not depart from the quantity theory of money, since higher inflation arises from the fact that the monetary authority is forced to monetize public debt, which is to increase money supply. Sargent and Wallace show that the GIBC can affect the inflation rate significantly when fiscal policy dominates monetary policy. Consequently, achieving inflation stability requires *credible* and *binding* policy rules for each authority: the central bank must credibly commit to inflation stability and the government must commit to a sustainable fiscal policy. This supports the introduction of a no bailout clause between monetary and fiscal authorities; still, the credibility—and desirability—of such a clause remains questionable in the light of the recent sovereign debt crisis in Europe.

The Fiscal Theory of Price Level (FTPL) is somehow more radical than Sargent and Wallace's "unpleasant monetarist arithmetic." It basically states that "monetary policy alone does not provide the nominal anchor for an economy" and it is "a particular pairing of monetary policy and fiscal policy" (Canzoneri et al. 2010), which provides the nominal anchor and stabilizes inflation. According to the FTPL, even in the absence of seignorage revenue, binding rules on excessive deficits and public debt are necessary to achieve price stability. The FTPL starts from the assumption that government issues nominal debt rather than real debt and then rewrites the intertemporal budget constraint with nominal debt:

$$\frac{B_t}{P_t} = \sum_{T=1}^{\infty} \frac{\mathbb{E}_t S_{t+T}}{(1+r)^T}$$

where B_t is the nominal public debt (not scaled by GDP), P_t is the price level and S_t the real primary surplus of government. Fiscal theory considers the government's IBC as an *ex post* equilibrium condition rather than an *ex ante* budget constraint on fiscal policy. Then, if government does not adjust its fiscal policy to make this constraint hold *ex ante*, then price level will have to adjust *ex-post* to make it hold in equilibrium. Within FTPL's framework, two polar cases for fiscal policy arise. First, fiscal policy is Ricardian and future primary surplus adjusts such that GIBC holds *ex ante*; monetary authority can have full control over the price level through a standard interest rate rule. Second, fiscal policy is not Ricardian and does not satisfy its GIBC *ex ante*; GIBC is no longer a constraint for fiscal policy but a valuation equation for *real* public debt such that price-level P_t adjusts in order to equalize *ex post* the *real* value of public debt to the sum of future primary surpluses. In this case, monetary policy loses control of the price level.

Leeper's (1991) typology of monetary and fiscal interactions is a more restrictive definition of the FTPL. He studies different sets of monetary and fiscal policies achieving both *stable* inflation dynamics and *stable* nominal public debt dynamics, which requirements are stronger than the GIBC. He assumes monetary policy follows a Taylor Rule and fiscal policy follows a tax rule such that tax rate reacts to debt level. He characterizes monetary and fiscal policies as "active" and "passive":

- Monetary policy is labelled "active" if it satisfies Taylor's principle;[4] if not, it is "passive" and it reacts less aggressively to inflation.
- Fiscal policy is "passive" if the tax rate reacts to public debt more than the average interest rate, such it stabilizes debt; if not, it is "active" and does adjust taxes to debt (Fig. 3.1).

Consequently, Leeper describes four combinations possible for monetary and fiscal policies. Two combinations of monetary and fiscal policies—AM/PF or Regime M and PM/AF or Regime F—lead to a unique macroeconomic equilibrium, implying stable inflation and public debt dynamics along the balanced growth path. One combination—PM/PF—leads to indeterminacy and multiple equilibria: in this case, the economy is subject to self-fulfilling dynamics. The last case—AM/AF—leads to explosive dynamics of both inflation and public debt.

FTPL's detractors such as Buiter (2002) strongly criticized this interpretation of GIBC as an equilibrium condition. In his view, GIBC is a real constraint on government behaviour and GIBC must hold for any price level. As a result, macroeconomic equilibria described by the FTPL are "invalid" in Buiter's view. On the contrary, Woodford (2001) considers that government knows it can affect equilibrium price level and interest rates, which is not possible for other economic agents. Another question is the empirical validity of the FTPL: is there evidence of "fiscal inflation" episodes? Empirical literature has not reached any consensus yet. Canzoneri et al. (2001) show that fiscal sustainability imposes very weak restrictions, such that observed data on public debt and primary surplus would be consistent with GIBC and, as a result, making it difficult to distinguish between Ricardian and non-Ricardian fiscal policies. They show that US post-Second World War data

	Passive Monetary policy	Active Monetary policy
Passive Fiscal policy	Indeterminacy of inflation and debt dynamics *Multiple equilibria*	Regime M: inflation is determined by monetary policy *Unique equilibrium*
Active Fiscal policy	Regime F: inflation is determined by fiscal policy *Unique equilibrium*	Explosive dynamics of inflation and public debt *No equilibrium*

Fig. 3.1 Leeper's classification of monetary-fiscal interactions

---

[4]Taylor's principle implies that the central bank raises the short term interest rate by more than 1 percentage point in response to a 1 percentage point increase in the inflation rate.

may be well explained by the Ricardian regime. Creel and Le Bihan (2006) extend Canzoneri et al.'s method using cyclically adjusted balance data and find no evidence supporting the FTPL, using an international dataset that includes the USA, Germany, Italy, France and the UK.

Yet, using regime-switching techniques to estimate feedback policy rules for monetary and fiscal authorities, Favero and Monacelli (2005), Davig and Leeper (2007, 2011), Afonso and Toffano (2013) and Cevik et al. (2014) provide evidences of recurring changes in monetary and fiscal policy rules. Both monetary and fiscal policies periodically switch from active to passive (or passive to active), which would suggest that FTPL may be effectively at work (Davig and Leeper 2007, 2011).

One unexpected result of FTPL is that fiscal policy can eventually have large and significant effects on the economy. In a Regime F, debt-financed expansionary fiscal policy actually boosts aggregate demand through a positive wealth effect because Ricardian equivalence no longer holds and households expect that current deficits will not be financed through future taxes. As a result, government spending and tax multipliers are significantly higher when monetary policy is passive and fiscal policy active (Davig and Leeper 2011). When monetary policy becomes passive as it is constrained by the Zero Lower Bound (ZLB) on nominal interest rate, then fiscal multipliers would likely be much higher and inflation would be determined by fiscal policy. To sum up, the FTPL provides strong arguments to implement an active fiscal policy when monetary policy is constrained, as well as emphasizing the importance of public debt sustainability (or unsustainability) in the control of inflation.

Within a monetary union (a fortiori without coordinated fiscal policies), the FTPL as well as Sargent and Wallace's unpleasant monetarist arithmetic support the implementation of strong, binding, fiscal policy rules ensuring sustainability of public debt in the long run to avoid inflationary pressures. Yet both sustainability analysis and the FTPL show fiscal sustainability requirements do not fundamentally contradict the stabilization purpose of fiscal policy, and make room for business cycle stabilization motives (deficit spending in recessions) and temporary public spending measures (public spending reversals, one-off and exceptional measures).

In a large monetary union, all member countries do not necessarily face the same shocks: there are symmetric shocks affecting all countries in the same way and country-specific (or asymmetric) shocks affecting them differently. In an influential paper, Galí and Monacelli (2008) show that an optimal monetary–fiscal policy mix in a currency union would require that monetary policy stabilizes the economy by reacting to symmetric shocks, while national fiscal policies react to country-specific shocks at the national level. Thus research supports flexible fiscal policy rules both allowing for stabilization and ensuring the long-run sustainability of public debt at the national level.

3.3   European Fiscal Rules: Too Tight? Too Loose? Or Both?

The Maastricht Treaty on the European Union (1992) and the following SGP (1997) implemented numerical fiscal policy rules at European Union (EU) level, divided into a preventive arm and a corrective arm. The preventive arm specified a Medium-Term Objective (MTO) of close-to-balance or in surplus fiscal stance; the corrective arm, called the Excessive Deficit Procedure (EDP), specified procedures to correct deviations from the Treaty's reference values of 60 % of gross public debt-to-GDP and 3 % of deficit-to-GDP.[5] These rules were explicitly designed to ensure macroeconomic convergence and stability among EU member states, and in particular conditioning future participation to the EMU. Policymakers considered that sustainable fiscal policies were required to prevent both spillover effects among member states and inflationary effects of fiscal policy while monetary policy could successfully ensure price stability and promote economic growth.

Fiscal rules embedded in the Maastricht Treaty and the SGP have been intensively discussed over the last two decades. Are these rules sufficient to ensure fiscal sustainability and flexible enough to allow countercyclical fiscal policies? Some argued these rules, both the preventive and the corrective arm, were far too tight in regard to fiscal sustainability requirements. While at the beginning of the 2000s some argued there was no clear evidence that national fiscal policies had lost their ability to follow countercyclical stabilization objectives, recent research suggests the opposite: that national fiscal policies became more procyclical after the implementation of the SGP. More recently, the financial and economic crisis of 2008 and the following European sovereign debt crisis in 2010 raised concerns about the ability of European fiscal rules to prevent excessive deficits and debts within the EMU. Thus, we will present these debates on the European fiscal framework. Was the SGP too tight (with respect to the countercyclical objective of fiscal policy) or too loose (with respect to fiscal sustainability requirements)? Was the European sovereign debt crisis the result of excessive public deficits from euro area (EA) member states or rather the result of fundamental failures in the architecture

---

[5] These reference values are defined such that a 3 % deficit-to-GDP is compatible with a stable debt-to-GDP level of 60 %, assuming an average real GDP growth of 3 % and an average inflation rate of 2 %.

of the EMU? Did it call for a tightening of European fiscal policy rules and fiscal monitoring? Does Europe need stronger fiscal rules or more flexibility and country-specific requirements regarding fiscal sustainability?

3.3.1 Are European Fiscal Rules Ensuring the Sustainability of Public Finance?

During the 1990s and the move toward the creation of the EMU, most EU member states and future EA members focused on the Maastricht reference values more than on the medium-term objective of a close-to-balance or surplus budget position; see Collignon (2012). As a matter of fact, the corrective arm (the EDP) obviously dominated the preventive arm. What could be the rationale behind this?

Actually, the medium-term objective defined in the Maastricht Treaty (balanced budget or in surplus) does not find any economic justification from a standard sustainability analysis: a balanced-budget rule would imply an ever-decreasing debt-to-GDP ratio—which is a far too strong requirement for fiscal sustainability. From a more general point of view, balanced-budget rules would even increase aggregate economic instability (Schmitt-Grohe and Uribe 1997), being at odds with the Maastricht Treaty and the SGP!

Reference values of 3 % deficit-to-GDP and 60 % of debt-to-GDP are more sensible from a sustainability analysis' point of view since they are equivalent to a debt-stabilizing fiscal policy rule. Indeed, given a nominal growth rate of 5 % and a maximum value of 60 % gross debt–GDP ratio, we find that fiscal policy would stabilize debt by setting the deficit to 3 % of GDP. Yet the Maastricht Treaty's reference values rely heavily on assumptions made on real GDP growth rate and inflation rate, respectively 3 % and 2 %. As pointed out by Buiter et al. (1993), countries with higher real growth rate and inflation could support a higher deficit-to-GDP ratio. As a matter of fact, EA member states diverged in terms of real GDP growth and inflation rates, reinforcing the criticism of a nominal deficit reference value as a guideline for fiscal surveillance.

Regarding fiscal sustainability analysis, a nominal (with interest) deficit guideline would not seem the most appropriate way to monitor sound fiscal policy, in addition to Buiter, Corsetti and Roubini's criticisms. While a permanent deficit could still be consistent with (strong) fiscal sustainability, in other words stable debt-to-GDP ratio, fiscal policy should run primary surplus on average, over the business cycle—at least when $r > g$. What is more, the recent European sovereign debt crisis implied a strong divergence of real long-run interest rates among EA member states. This has asymmetric consequences on EA member states. It implies that stressed countries (higher real interest rates, lower real growth rate) are facing stronger sustainability requirements, implying a lower debt-stabilizing (with interest) deficit with respect to the 3 % deficit rule. Unstressed countries (lower real interest rates, higher real growth rates) are facing looser sustainability requirements, such that they could actually afford deficits close to 3 % of GDP (or maybe larger) without jeopardizing the long-run sustainability of public finances. As a result, the European deficit rule of 3 % appears to be sometimes too tight and sometimes too loose in a heterogeneous monetary and economic union. The bottom line is that one size *does not* fit all.

Are European fiscal policy rules sufficient to ensure fiscal sustainability? From a theoretical perspective, these rules are conceptually based upon a debt-stabilizing condition, which is most probably the relevant sustainability concept in an economy with fiscal limits. Still, if the real growth rate of GDP is to exceed the long real interest rate on a government's bonds (i.e. $r < g$) a stable debt–GDP ratio is not necessarily a proof of responsible fiscal behaviour. The relevant condition would rather be the NPG condition (i.e. a positive response of primary surplus to the initial level of public debt), which is not guaranteed to hold under a nominal deficit rule in this case. In addition, as explained earlier, a nominal deficit rule does not necessarily fit all member states, and it would be more efficient to impose a positive average (structural) primary surplus, which is the relevant fiscal indicator for sustainability analysis.

In the early 2000s, Afonso (2005) described what he called the "Unpleasant European Case." Despite their stabilizing of debt–GDP ratios by the end of the 2000s, he found many European countries were likely to be at risk regarding the sustainability of public finance. Yet Afonso's dataset stopped in 2003, which did not provide enough data to evaluate the European fiscal framework. In contrast with Afonso's results, more recent papers (Collignon 2012; Daniel and Shiamptanis 2013) found evidence that European fiscal policies became more responsible during the 2000s, after the implementation of the SGP. These empirical results suggest the European fiscal framework was sufficient to promote responsible fiscal policies in terms of primary surplus, and despite excessive deficit procedures engaged against EA member states during the first decade of EMU.

Following 2008, the European sovereign debt crisis has been immediately—maybe too rapidly—interpreted as the result of irresponsible (or at least imprudent) fiscal policies in the early 2000s; current account imbalances within the EA were also considered but with less emphasis in the public debate. The strengthening induced by the Six-Pack reform (2011), Two-Pack reform and the Fiscal Compact (2013) directly comes from this narrative of the crisis. We will develop these questions in Sect. 3.3.3.

During the 2000s, European policymakers tried to deal with the flaws of European fiscal framework by adding "exceptional measures" to the SGP, taking into account *structural* rather than *nominal* deficits and improving the preventive arm. Recent reforms (2005 and 2011 Six Pack Reform) of the SGP introduced several amendments. They reinforced the preventive arm of the SGP by defining MTOs in term of structural deficit rather than nominal. They also explicitly defined the required adjustment path toward them as a benchmark improvement of 0.5 % per year (or an average of 0.25 % per year during two consecutive years) of structural balance. 2011's reform toughened the structural adjustment (higher than 0.5 % per year) for member states with debt–GDP ratios above 60 %. Both reforms also specified when EA member states could deviate from their MTOs: "for major structural reforms with verifiable impact on long-run sustainability such as pension reforms" (2005's reform), "unusual events outside the control of the country with a major impact on the financial position of general government" and "in case of severe economic downturn in the euro area or the union as a whole" (European Commission 2013). Still, the corrective arm (the EDP) and especially the threshold of 3 % deficit–GDP ratio were not reconsidered. We think this results largely from ignoring the fact that EA member states diverge in terms of real growth, inflation and long-run interest rates. As long as European policymakers stick to the idea that EA member states will "naturally" converge in nominal and real terms, the deficit rule of 3 % might not be efficient at stabilizing both public debt and the economy.

Finally, one of the biggest flaws of the European fiscal framework was probably the exclusive focus on public debt and deficits while ignoring private debt and current deficits. As a result, ignoring private capital flows and private debt biases the analysis and narrative of the European sovereign debt crisis as being mainly the result of irresponsible fiscal policies; we will see further on that the European sovereign debt crisis might rather be analysed primarily as a classic sudden stop crisis. Still, the 2011 Six-Pack reform acknowledged the importance of external imbalances (Bénassy-Quéré and Ragot 2015), and the risk of a banking crisis and its consequences on public finances (Bénassy-Quéré and Roussellet 2014). Thus, it improved the European economic surveillance framework by introducing the Macroeconomic Imbalance Procedure (MIP), which follows the SGP pattern with a preventive and a corrective arm.

3.3.2 Procyclical Bias in European Fiscal Policy Rules

Beside fiscal sustainability issues, an important question was about the alleged "procyclical bias" of the European fiscal policy rules. From a theoretical point of view, both neoclassical (tax-smoothing models) and Keynesian economics (countercyclical fiscal policy) support deficit spending during recessions. This point was already made by Buiter et al. (1993): the SGP was really ambiguous about whether countercyclical deficits in excess of 3 % were acceptable. Actually, these excessive deficits were supposed to be *exceptional* and *temporary*, which support the view that the SGP induced de facto a procyclical bias in European fiscal policy.

In the early 2000s, Gali and Perotti (2003) produced empirical evidence against the conventional view that "the Maastricht Treaty and then Stability and Growth Pact have impaired the ability of EU governments to conduct a stabilizing fiscal policy and to provide an adequate level of public infrastructure." Using annual data from the Organization for Economic Cooperation and Development (OECD) Economic Outlook, ranging from 1980 to 2002, they estimated a linear fiscal policy rule linking the structural primary deficit–GDP ratio to output gap, initial debt–GDP ratio and past primary deficit–GDP. They found fiscal policy in EMU "has become more counter-cyclical over time, following what appears to be a trend that affects other industrialized countries." Regarding the decline in public investment, they found "industrialized regions not subject to the SGP have experienced an even greater decline." Still, they noted that deep, severe recessions have been rare in the post-Maastricht period, implying the SGP fiscal rules were not really binding. They concluded that the impact of the SGP could be different in the future.

Yet recent empirical research has challenged this result. Beetsma and Giuliodori (2010) distinguish two stages in fiscal policy: the planning stage and the implementation stage, using real-time data. They use panel data running from 1995 to 2006, for EU-14 plus the USA, Canada, Japan, Norway and Australia. Their results are twofold. First, they found planned fiscal policy was acyclical in EU countries but countercyclical in non-EU countries. Second, they provide evidence that EU countries react procyclically to unexpected changes in the output gap while non-EU countries react acyclically during the implementation stage. Collignon (2012) also provides empirical evidences that fiscal policy became more procyclical in the EU countries than in the non-EU countries.

These results are also confirmed by an International Monetary Fund (IMF) working paper (Eyraud and Wu 2015). Interestingly, this paper shows that, if European fiscal policy had been more countercyclical in the first decade of the EMU (1998–2008), it would have entered the crisis in a far stronger fiscal position (see figure 5, p. 13, op. cit.). It well illustrates the complementarity between the requirements of long-run sustainability of public debt and the need for a countercyclical fiscal policy. The lack of flexibility and the quasi-exclusive focus on fiscal sustainability within the European fiscal framework,[6] which likely induce the procyclical bias observed in the data, would eventually threaten the long-run sustainability of public debt.

What are the consequences of the procyclical bias of the European fiscal framework in terms of economic activity and employment? Creel et al. (2013) developed a medium-scale DSGE model with price rigidity and forward-looking agents to compare three different rules: the Maastricht Treaty (3 % of deficit–GDP), the Fiscal Compact framework and a public investment rule. Their simulations show that the Fiscal Compact is likely to be more deflationary and recessionary than both the status quo and the public investment rule. The public investment rule displays the lowest output cost. Creel et al. conclude by saying: "such a drastic consolidation strategy (i.e. the Fiscal Compact) embedded into EU constitutional laws threaten future macroeconomic performances of Eurozone countries."

One cannot oppose these two issues: fiscal sustainability requirements and countercyclical fiscal policy. Both theoretical research and empirical evidence rather suggest that fiscal sustainability is a long-run requirement and can support deficit-financed fiscal stimulus during recessions, on the condition that fiscal policy must tighten during expansions. Recent experience of non-EA countries with respect to EA countries shows that the first could both stabilize their debt–GDP ratio and reduce the output gap quicker than the latter while undergoing less austerity or, at least, not too soon following the Great Recession and with an accommodative (or passive) monetary policy.

The debate on "austerity" and procyclical fiscal consolidation focuses on the size of fiscal multipliers.[7] The consensus before the Great Recession was that fiscal multipliers were low, probably close to 0.5 or even lower. Yet both empirical and theoretical researches have challenged the common wisdom of low fiscal multipliers. Empirical research has shown the size of fiscal multipliers can vary a lot according to the state of the economy, and reach values well above 1 or even 2 in some cases. For instance, fiscal multipliers appear to be larger during recessions than expansions (Auerbach and Gorodnichenko

---

[6] Until the Six-Pack Reform and the implementation of the MIP, the European Semester was exclusively focused on public debt and deficits, neglecting current account deficits.

[7] Fiscal multipliers (public spending and tax multipliers) are generally defined as the extra euro(s) of real GDP generated by a 1 euro increase in public spending (or by a 1 euro decrease in taxes).

2012a, b). Riera-Crichton et al. (2015) show that fiscal policy has asymmetric effects depending on the state of the economy (expansion versus recession) and on the stance of fiscal policy (procyclical versus countercyclical) using a panel dataset of OECD countries. Two main results emerge from their analysis. First, estimated countercyclical fiscal multipliers are very large (the long-run multiplier is 2.3 in normal recessions and 3.1 in extreme recessions). Second, while the austerity motto "short-run pain, long-run gain" may be correct in normal recessions, it is no longer the case in extreme recessions, as they conclude: "applied to the current debate on austerity in the Eurozone, this would imply that debt to GDP ratios would increase in response to cuts in fiscal spending." Regarding the debate on austerity in Europe, Blanchard and Leigh (2013) produce empirical evidence that professional forecasters (including the IMF) have underestimated the size of fiscal multipliers in the years following the Great Recession and the sovereign debt crisis: while these multipliers were probably about 0.5 before the crisis, their results for European countries, in 2010–2011, indicate they were significantly above 1 in the early stage of the sovereign debt crisis.

Theoretical research also provides new explanations for larger fiscal multipliers. New Keynesian DSGE models with imperfect competition and staggered price-setting did not produce fiscal multipliers above 1 for one fundamental reason: in these models, the Ricardian equivalence holds,[8] and therefore fiscal spending shocks induce negative wealth effects for consumers, thus having a crowding-out effect on private consumption (being at odds with most empirical findings). This puzzle has been solved in many different ways. Relaxing some fundamental hypothesis of DSGE models dramatically changes the value of fiscal multipliers and produce a crowding-in effect in private consumption. For instance, taking into account Limited Asset Market Participation makes the Ricardian equivalence fall as a fraction of consumers are credit constrained and cannot smooth consumption over time (Bilbiie et al. 2008). Another way to solve the puzzle is to assume that consumers have non-separable preferences between consumption and labour such that hours worked and private consumption both increase after a positive government spending shock (Bilbiie 2011; Monacelli and Perotti 2008). Still one of the most important theoretical propositions is the analysis of fiscal policy when monetary policy is at the ZLB. Building on the old (Keynesian) wisdom that fiscal policy is more "effective" when monetary is accommodative,

---

[8] In the baseline DSGE model, fiscal policy is passive, that is, stabilizing public debt, and monetary policy is active, that is, strongly reacting to inflation, following Leeper's terminology. Therefore, what matters is the level of public spending, not the way public spending is financed, through tax or debt. To express it differently, the timing of taxation does not matter.

many theoretical papers have shown fiscal multipliers are far above 1 when the nominal interest rate is at the ZLB (Christiano et al. 2011; Corsetti et al. 2010; Denes et al. 2013; Eggertsson and Krugman 2012). And as already mentioned, an alternative monetary/fiscal policy mix can also make the Ricardian equivalence property fall and imply bigger fiscal multipliers (Davig and Leeper 2011). Yet the "sovereign risk channel" (i.e. the effect on private sector funding costs of sovereign default risk) can substantially reduce the size (and even invert the sign) of fiscal multipliers, suggesting that fiscal stimulus could eventually be self-defeating in countries in which sovereign financial distress tends to increase private sector funding costs (Corsetti et al. 2013).

3.3.3 Was the European Debt Crisis the Result of Irresponsible Fiscal Policies?

The European sovereign debt crisis revived the debate about fiscal policy rules in the EU and the EMU. It opposes two antagonist views of fiscal policy. The first is the orthodox view promoting balanced-budget rules and decreasing debt–GDP ratios, and is based on the Expansionary Fiscal Contraction (EFC) hypothesis, following the seminal paper by Giavazzi and Pagano (1990) and the work of Alberto Alesina and Silvia Ardagna (Alesina et al. 2015; Alesina and Ardagna 2010). This approach follows from the political economy of public debt and relies heavily on the so-called "confidence effect" of fiscal con-solidations. Taking the contrary view, the second one puts emphasis on new empirical evidences of state-dependent and time-varying fiscal multipliers as well as new theoretical results on fiscal multipliers in new Keynesian DSGE models (Auerbach and Gorodnichenko 2012b; Blanchard and Leigh 2013; Corsetti et al. 2010; Riera-Crichton et al. 2015). It also contradicts EFC supporters on empirical grounds, arguing for an upward bias in Alesina and Ardagna's estimates of expansionary effect of fiscal consolidation (Guajardo et al. 2014; Jorda and Taylor 2015).

Yet, despite serious criticisms of it, the EFC hypothesis obviously won the political battle in Europe at the very beginning of the European sovereign debt crisis. The early narrative of this crisis found the European irresponsible (or imprudent) fiscal policy was the main culprit, rather than excessive current account deficits and excessive private borrowing in the periphery countries. As mentioned earlier, it explains the strong tightening of the European fiscal rules after the six-pack, two-pack and Fiscal Compact reforms, and the relative disconnection between the SGP and the MIP; see (Bénassy-Quéré and Ragot 2015).

On the contrary, five years after the beginning of the European sovereign debt crisis, another consensus narrative emerged among macroeconomists. Lane (2012) had already suggested the so-called European sovereign debt crisis was not (primarily) caused by excessive deficits in the early 2000s,[9] but rather by original flaws in the EMU architecture (absence of banking union, federal buffer mechanisms), leading to large current account imbalances and excessive private borrowing within the EMU. More recently, a panel of economists from the CEPR (Centre for Economic Policy and Research) proposed a new consensus narrative of the European crisis (*The Eurozone Crisis* 2015), claiming it was a sudden-stop crisis, not a sovereign debt crisis as claimed by the EFC hypothesis supporters. According to this narrative, financial fragility, excessive private borrowing in non-productive sectors and current account imbalances were the source of the crisis, when the sudden stop occurred following 2008–2009's global crisis; and the sovereign debt crisis is rather a consequence than a cause of the financial crisis. This narrative also stresses the "causes of the causes" of the Eurozone crisis: "policy failures that allowed the imbalances to get so large," "lack of institutions to absorb shocks at the Eurozone level" and "crisis mismanagement" (Baldwin and Giavazzi 2015). To some extent, this narrative supports the view that the European fiscal framework (the Maastricht Treaty and in particular the "no bail-out" clause, the SGP) were probably not credible enough to prevent *both* excessive current account deficits *and* public deficits. In particular, they did not prepare the EU and the EMU to deal with a sudden-stop crisis, which was likely to cause a banking crisis and a sovereign debt crisis, for the simple reason that the European fiscal framework was implicitly built on the belief such a systemic crisis could not happen.

3.4 Conclusions

Fiscal rules are necessary to ensure public sustainability, around prudent debt–GDP ratios *and* to ensure monetary policy can reach its price-stability objective. According to macroeconomic theory on fiscal sustainability and monetary–fiscal interaction, these rules do not contradict countercyclical motives of fiscal policy. What is more, the recent economic and financial crisis has shown *how important* countercyclical fiscal policy is when the economy is hit by severe negative demand shocks. Future policymakers should keep

---

[9] Yet he acknowledges that "the failure of national governments to tighten fiscal policy substantially during the 2003-2007 was a missed opportunity, especially during a period in which the private sector was taking on more risk," in line with the claim that fiscal policy has been insufficiently countercyclical since the implementation of the SGP.

in mind that fiscal consolidation in good times can allow them to run large deficits when needed, with a sufficient safety margin against any "fiscal limit" on the public-debt-to-GDP ratio.

Yet the European fiscal framework has been shown to be sometimes too tight and sometimes too loose to ensure fiscal sustainability. In our opinion, the biggest flaw remains its serious procyclical bias, which jeopardizes both fiscal sustainability objectives and economic growth and stability; the recent reforms (Six-Pack, Two-Pack and Fiscal Compact) are not likely to reduce the procyclical bias of fiscal policy according to macroeconomic research.

A broader approach of economic surveillance now includes current account imbalances and private debt through the MIP, which is (in our view) the most important improvement in the European economic surveillance procedure. Further reforms should aim at simplifying European fiscal rules, reducing the procyclical bias (in particular in the implementation stage of fiscal policy) and giving a more important role to the analysis of current account imbalances.

References

Afonso, A. (2005). Fiscal sustainability: The unpleasant European case. *FinanzArchiv: Public Finance Analysis, 61*.

Afonso, A., & Toffano, P. (2013). Fiscal regimes in the EU. Working Paper Series No. 1529. European Central Bank.

Alesina, A., & Ardagna, S. (2010). *Large changes in fiscal policy: Taxes versus spending*. NBER Chapters. National Bureau of Economic Research, Inc.

Alesina, A., Barbiero, O., Favero, C., Giavazzi, F., & Paradisi, M. (2015). *Austerity in 2009–2013*. NBER Working Paper No. 20827. National Bureau of Economic Research, Inc.

Auerbach, A.J., & Gorodnichenko, Y. (2012a). *Fiscal multipliers in recession and expansion*. NBER Chapters. National Bureau of Economic Research, Inc.

Auerbach, A. J., & Gorodnichenko, Y. (2012b). Measuring the output responses to fiscal policy. *American Economic Journal: Economic Policy, 4*, 1–27.

Baldwin, R., & Giavazzi, F. (2015). *The Eurozone crisis: A consensus view of the causes and a few possible solutions*. VoxEU.org.

Beetsma, R., & Giuliodori, M. (2010). Fiscal adjustment to cyclical developments in the OECD: An empirical analysis based on real-time data. *Oxford Economic Papers, 62*, 419–441. doi:10.1093/oep/gpp039.

Bénassy-Quéré, A., & Ragot, X. (2015). *A policy mix for the Euro area (No. 21)*, CAE Reports. Conseil d'Analyse Economique.

Bénassy-Quéré, A., & Roussellet, G. (2014). Fiscal sustainability in the presence of systemic banks: The case of EU countries. *International Tax and Public Finance, 21*, 436–467.

Bi, H. (2012). Sovereign default risk premia, fiscal limits, and fiscal policy. *European Economic Review, 56*, 389–410.

Bi, H., & Leeper, E. (2013). *Analyzing fiscal sustainability.* Working paper. Bank of Canada.

Bi, H., & Traum, N. (2012). Estimating sovereign default risk. *American Economic Review, 102*, 161–166.

Bilbiie, F. O. (2011). Nonseparable preferences, Frisch Labor Supply, and the consumption multiplier of government spending: One solution to a fiscal policy puzzle. *Journal of Money, Credit and Banking, 43*, 221–251. doi:10.1111/j.1538-4616.2010.00372.x.

Bilbiie, F. O., Meier, A., & Müller, G. J. (2008). What accounts for the changes in U.S. fiscal policy transmission? *Journal of Money, Credit and Banking, 40*, 1439–1470. doi:10.1111/j.1538-4616.2008.00166.x.

Blanchard, O. J., & Leigh, D. (2013). Growth forecast errors and fiscal multipliers. *American Economic Review, 103*, 117–120.

Blanchard, O., Dell'ariccia, G., & Mauro, P. (2010). Rethinking macroeconomic policy. *Journal of Money, Credit and Banking, 42*, 199–215.

Bohn, H. (1998). The behavior Of U.S. public debt and deficits. *The Quarterly Journal of Economics, 113*, 949–963.

Bohn, H. (2007). Are stationarity and cointegration restrictions really necessary for the intertemporal budget constraint? *Journal of Monetary Economics, 54*, 1837–1847.

Bohn, H. (2008). The sustainability of fiscal policy in the United States. In R. Neck & J. Sturm (Eds.), *Sustainability of public debt* (pp. 15–49). Cambridge, MA: MIT Press.

Buiter, W. H. (2002). The fiscal theory of the price level: A critique. *The Economic Journal, 112*, 459–480. doi:10.1111/1468-0297.00726.

Buiter, W., Corsetti, G., & Roubini, N. (1993). Excessive deficits: Sense and nonsense in the treaty of Maastricht. *Economic Policy, 8*, 57–100. doi:10.2307/1344568.

Canzoneri, M. B., Cumby, R. E., & Diba, B. T. (2001). Is the price level determined by the needs of fiscal solvency? *American Economic Review, 91*, 1221–1238.

Canzoneri, M., Cumby, R., & Diba, B. (2010). The interaction between monetary and fiscal policy (Handbook of monetary economics). Elsevier.

Cevik, E. I., Dibooglu, S., & Kutan, A. M. (2014). Monetary and fiscal policy interactions: Evidence from emerging European economies. *Journal of Comparative Economics, 42*, 1079–1091.

Christiano, L., Eichenbaum, M., & Rebelo, S. (2011). When is the government spending multiplier large? *Journal of Political Economy, 119*, 78–121.

Cochrane, J. H. (2001). Long-term debt and optimal policy in the fiscal theory of the price level. *Econometrica, 69*, 69–116.

Cochrane, J. H. (2005). Money as stock. *Journal of Monetary Economics, 52*, 501–528.

Collignon, S. (2012). Fiscal policy rules and the sustainability of public debt in Europe. *International Economic Review, 53,* 539–567. doi:10.1111/j.1468-2354.2012.00691.x.

Corsetti, G., Kuester, K., Meier, A., & Muller, G. J. (2010). Debt consolidation and fiscal stabilization of deep recessions. *American Economic Review, 100,* 41–45.

Corsetti, G., Kuester, K., Meier, A., & Müller, G. J. (2013). Sovereign risk, fiscal policy, and macroeconomic stability. *Economic Journal, 123,* F99–F132. doi:10.1111/ecoj.12013.

Creel, J., & Le Bihan, H. (2006). Using structural balance data to test the fiscal theory of the price level: Some international evidence. *Journal of Macroeconomics, 28,* 338–360.

Creel, J., Hubert, P., & Saraceno, F. (2013). An assessment of the stability and growth pact reform in a small-scale macro-framework. *Journal of Economic Dynamics and Control, 37,* 1567–1580.

Daniel, B. C., & Shiamptanis, C. (2013). Pushing the limit? Fiscal policy in the European monetary union. *Journal of Economic Dynamics and Control, 37,* 2307–2321.

Davig, T., & Leeper, E.M. (2007). *Fluctuating macro policies and the fiscal theory.* NBER Chapters. National Bureau of Economic Research, Inc.

Davig, T., & Leeper, E. M. (2011). Monetary-fiscal policy interactions and fiscal stimulus. *European Economic Review, 55,* 211–227.

Denes, M., Eggertsson, G. B., & Gilbukh, S. (2013). Deficits, public debt dynamics and tax and spending multipliers. *Economic Journal, 123,* F133–F163. doi:10.1111/ecoj.12014.

Eggertsson, G. B., & Krugman, P. (2012). Debt, deleveraging, and the liquidity trap: A fisher-minsky-koo approach. *The Quarterly Journal of Economics, 127,* 1469–1513.

European Commission. (2013). *Building a strengthened fiscal framework in the European union: A guide to the stability and growth pact.* Publications Office.

Eyraud, L., & Wu, T. (2015). *Playing by the rules: Reforming fiscal governance in Europe.* IMF Working Paper No. 15/67. International Monetary Fund.

Fall, F., Bloch, D., Fournier, J.-M., & Hoeller, P. (2015). *Prudent debt targets and fiscal frameworks.* OECD Economic Policy Paper No. 15. OECD Publishing.

Favero, C.A., & Monacelli, T. (2005). *Fiscal policy rules and regime (In)stability: Evidence from the U.S.* SSRN Scholarly Paper No. ID 665506. Social Science Research Network, Rochester, NY.

Fournier, J.-M., & Fall, F. (2015). *Limits to government debt sustainability.* OECD Economics Department Working Paper No. 1229. OECD Publishing.

Galí, J., & Monacelli, T. (2008). Optimal monetary and fiscal policy in a currency union. *Journal of International Economics, 76,* 116–132. doi:10.1016/j.jinteco.2008.02.007.

Gali, J., & Perotti, R. (2003). Fiscal policy and monetary integration in Europe. *Economic Policy, 18,* 533–572.

Ghosh, A. R., Kim, J. I., Mendoza, E. G., Ostry, J. D., & Qureshi, M. S. (2013). Fiscal fatigue, fiscal space and debt sustainability in advanced economies. *Economic Journal, 123*, F4–F30. doi:10.1111/ecoj.12010.

Giavazzi, F., & Pagano, M. (1990). *Can severe fiscal contractions be expansionary? Tales of two small European countries*. NBER Chapters. National Bureau of Economic Research, Inc.

Guajardo, J., Leigh, D., & Pescatori, A. (2014). Expansionary austerity? International evidence. *Journal of the European Economic Association, 12*, 949–968. doi:10.1111/jeea.12083.

Hamilton, J. D., & Flavin, M. A. (1986). On the limitations of government borrowing: A framework for empirical testing. *American Economic Review, 76*, 808–819.

Jorda, O., & Taylor, A.M. (2015). The time for austerity: Estimating the average treatment effect of fiscal policy. *Economic Journal* n/a–n/a. doi:10.1111/ecoj.12332

Lane, P. R. (2012). The European sovereign debt crisis. *Journal of Economic Perspectives, 26*, 49–68.

Leeper, E. M. (1991). Equilibria under "active" and "passive" monetary and fiscal policies. *Journal of Monetary Economics, 27*, 129–147.

Mendoza, E. G., & Ostry, J. D. (2008). International evidence on fiscal solvency: Is fiscal policy "responsible"? *Journal of Monetary Economics, 55*, 1081–1093.

Monacelli, T., & Perotti, R. (2008). *Fiscal policy, wealth effects, and markups*. NBER Working Paper No. 14584. National Bureau of Economic Research, Inc.

Riera-Crichton, D., Vegh, C. A., & Vuletin, G. (2015). Procyclical and countercyclical fiscal multipliers: Evidence from OECD countries. *Journal of International Money and Finance, 52*, 15–31.

Sargent, T. J., & Wallace, N. (1981). Some unpleasant monetarist arithmetic. Federal reserve bank of Minneapolis. *Quarterly Review*, 1–17.

Schmitt-Grohe, S., & Uribe, M. (1997). Balanced-budget rules, distortionary taxes, and aggregate instability. *Journal of Political Economy, 105*, 976–1000.

Sims, C. A. (1994). A simple model for study of the determination of the price level and the interaction of monetary and fiscal policy. *Economic Theory, 4*, 381–399.

The Eurozone Crisis. (2015). *The Eurozone crisis: A consensus view of the causes and a few possible solutions*, ed. VoxEU eBooks. London: CEPR Press.

Trabandt, M., & Uhlig, H. (2011). The Laffer curve revisited. *Journal of Monetary Economics, 58*, 305–327. doi:10.1016/j.jmoneco.2011.07.003.

Woodford, M. (1995). Price-level determinacy without control of a monetary aggregate. *Carnegie-Rochester Conference Series on Public Policy, 43*, 1–46.

Woodford, M. (2001). Fiscal requirements for price stability. *Journal of Money, Credit and Banking, 33*, 669–728.

Wyplosz, C. (1991). *Monetary union and fiscal policy discipline*. CEPR Discussion Paper No. 488. CEPR Discussion Papers.

4

The Composition Effect of New Fiscal Rules in the Euro Area

Jérôme Creel and Francesco Molteni

An intense debate has been raging about the recent reforms in the euro area to enhance fiscal surveillance and to ensure the sustainability of budget deficits of its members, their consequences on governments' fiscal positions and the macroeconomic outcomes (in chronological order the six-pack, the Fiscal Compact and the two-pack). This chapter focuses on the spending side of governments' budgets and studies how expenditures evolved in the wake of the global financial crisis and in response to new regulations in the euro area. Following earlier reflections by Balassone and Franco (2000) and Mehrotra and Välilä (2006), we wonder whether abiding by the fiscal rules has changed the composition of public spending at the expense of public investment. Then we review the arguments on the possible impact of public investment (or capital) on economic growth (or gross domestic product, GDP), including a discussion about the so-called Juncker's Investment Plan, before making a few recommendations for increasing "safe assets."

J. Creel (✉)
LabEx RéFi, ESCP-Europe and Sciences Po, OFCE, Paris, France

F. Molteni (✉)
Labex ReFi and European University Institute, Fiesole, Firenze, Italy

© The Author(s) 2017
R. Douady et al. (eds.), *Financial Regulation in the EU*,
DOI 10.1007/978-3-319-44287-7_4

4.1 European Total Expenditures, by Country and Function

We conduct a granular analysis on disaggregated components of public spending in order to evaluate how members adjusted their policy to meet stricter fiscal criteria. Since the latter are always assessed in proportion to GDP, we adopt the same principle and show the evolution of different components of national public spending in GDP shares. It is noteworthy that these shares grow, all else being equal, with drops in GDP; hence, in an era of sluggish growth, stable or diminishing GDP shares of public spending are remarkable: they characterize rather sharp changes in public spending.

We rely on data published by the Organization for Economic Cooperation and Development (OECD) in its Economic Outlook (Number 97) annually on a consolidated basis. Total expenditure is decomposed in seven components according to their economic type:[1] government final non-wage consumption expenditure (CGNW), government final wage consumption expenditure (CWG), government fixed capital formation (IGAA), capital transfers paid and other capital payments (TKPG), subsidies to firms (TSUB), social security benefits (SSPG), gross government interest payments (GGINT). CWG is the amount of public wages and salaries and CGNW encompasses the intermediate goods purchased by the government. Their sum is the government consumption as defined by National Income and Product Accounts (NIPA) data largely employed in the empirical literature. Social security benefits include welfare spending (such as unemployment benefits) and pensions. Capital transfers paid and other capital payments register among other banking rescue plans. Although fiscal adjustments also take place through the revenue side of governments' budgets (Alesina and Perotti 1995; Alesina and Ardagna 2010, 2013; Alesina et al. 2015; Blot et al. 2015), OECD Economic Outlook Number 97 (2015) shows that between 2012 and 2014 following the introduction of new fiscal rules in the euro area the bulk of fiscal consolidation for European countries hinged upon the expenditure side. Understanding how public outlays were modified in response to new fiscal rules has important implications also for the assessment of the impact of fiscal consolidation on the weak economic recovery in the euro area, since different spending items have different multipliers (Pappa 2009; Valla et al. 2014). By looking at the evolution of disaggregated expenditures, this chapter does not try to disentangle discretionary interventions from changes due to the presence of

---

[1] The World Bank provides an alternative classification of public expenditure by function (e.g. military spending, health, education). Here we use the acronyms employed by the OECD.

automatic stabilizers. Coricelli and Fiorito (2013) and Coricelli et al. (2017) using the same OECD data propose a classification of discretionary and non-discretionary public spending on the basis of the statistical properties of disaggregated expenditures.

Figure 4.1 shows the evolution of the ratio of total public spending over GDP from 1990 to 2014. The left panel reports the series for France, Ireland, Italy and Spain. Even though their ratios differ in terms of size they are characterized by a similar pattern and their trend can be distinguished in four phases. (1) Between 1980 and 1992 the public expenditure in percent of GDP increased in all countries, especially in France and Italy where it was more than 50 %. (2) Following the introduction of the Maastricht Treaty in 1992, the ratio declined until the global financial crisis. (3) During the crisis fiscal stimuli and the contraction of economic activity led to a surge in the ratio of public expenditure to GDP. (4) The introduction and tightening of European fiscal rules curbed the evolution of public consumption with a progressive fiscal consolidation. The case of Ireland is peculiar because the bail out of the banking system boosted public outlays to 62.8 % of GDP in 2010 and the fiscal consolidation brought down this ratio to 36.7 % in 2014. The right panel shows the same ratio for Austria, Belgium, the Netherlands and Finland. For the first three countries public spending already declined during the 1980s and the Maastricht Treaty sharpened this trend. Similarly to Ireland, government spending spiked in Finland in 1993 in the aftermath of the financial crisis of Nordic countries, because of public intervention to rescue the banking sector and the contraction of GDP.

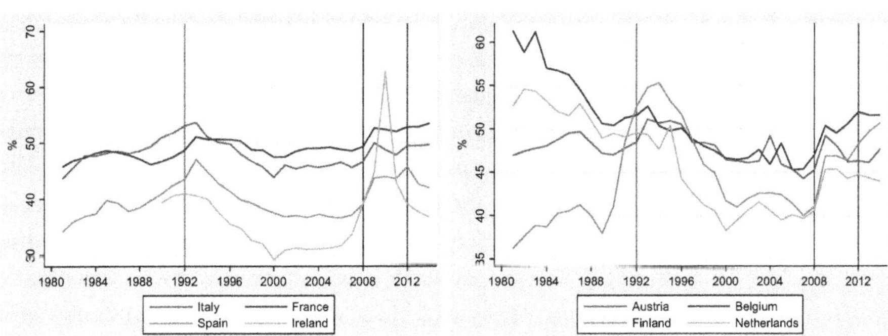

Fig. 4.1 Public spending (in percent of GDP) (*Note*: The green vertical line indicates the entry into force of the Maastricht Treaty, the black vertical line the global financial crisis and the red vertical line the new fiscal rules (six-pack and Fiscal Compact))

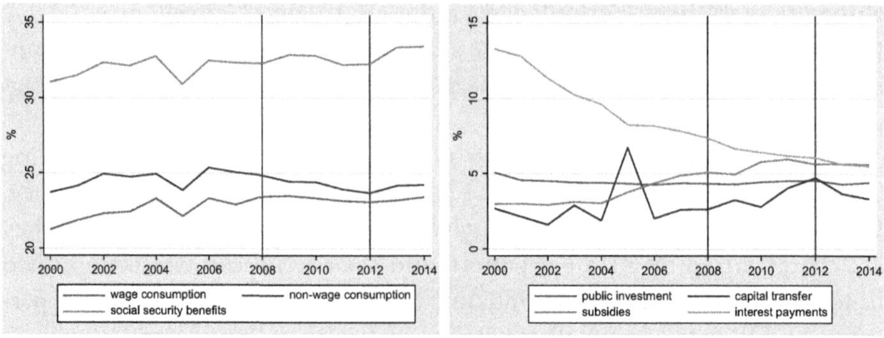

Fig. 4.2 Disaggregated public expenditures (in percent of total spending) in Belgium (*Note*: The black vertical line indicates the global financial crisis and the red vertical line the new fiscal rules (six-pack and Fiscal Compact))

For most of the countries considered here, the growth of public expenditure reduced in combination with the introduction of new fiscal rules: the six pack which entered into force on 13 December 2011 and the Fiscal Compact (Treaty on Stability, Coordination and Governance) signed on 2 March 2012 and entered into force on 1 January 2013. Finland and Austria are two exceptions, since total expenditure steeply increased over the period 2012–2014. However, they also register lower levels of public debt and deficits and have more room for manoeuvre than highly indebted countries for which new fiscal rules are more binding. For these countries (Belgium, France, Italy, Ireland, Spain) the analysis is deepened by focusing on disaggregated spending items. France, Ireland and Spain are also currently under the corrective arm of the Stability and Growth Pact (SGP), forcing members to correct excessive deficits by implementing the Excessive Deficit Procedure(EDP). Austria, Belgium, Finland, Italy and the Netherlands are instead currently under the overview of closed EDPs. Figures 4.2, 4.3, 4.4, 4.5, and 4.6 show the share of disaggregated outlays to total public expenditure.

Some interesting findings stand out. For all countries social security benefits are the main component of government spending, greater than CGNW and CWG, which are the second and third largest components respectively (left panel). Furthermore, its share increased in all countries following the introduction of new fiscal rules, except Ireland where it shows evidence of substantial swings and a decrease since 2012. The GGINT declined in those countries characterized by high precrisis levels of debt (Belgium, France and Italy) probably owing to a confidence channel and a reduction of government bond yields. By contrast, in Ireland and Spain where public debt rose sharply during the crisis, the share of interest payments kept growing after the

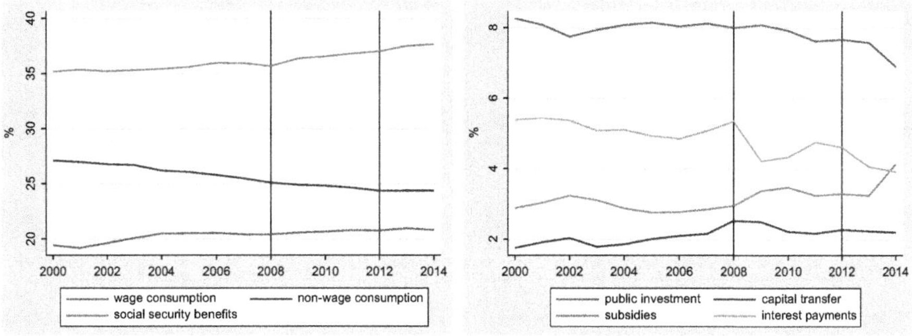

Fig. 4.3 Disaggregated public expenditures (in percent of total spending) in France (*Note*: The black vertical line indicates the global financial crisis and the red vertical line the new fiscal rules (six-pack and Fiscal Compact))

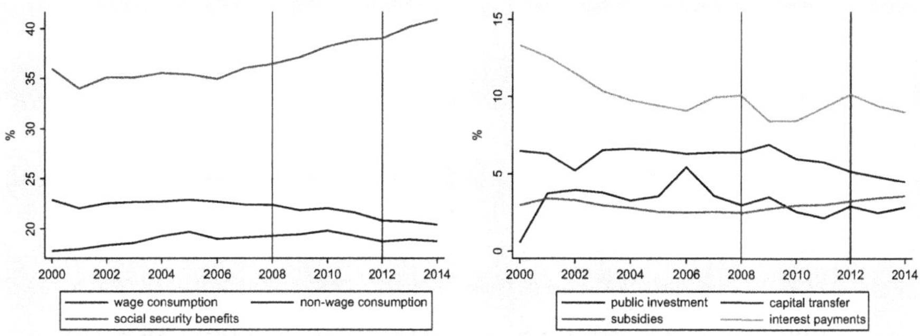

Fig. 4.4 Disaggregated public expenditures (in percent of total spending) in Italy (*Note*: The black vertical line indicates the global financial crisis and the red vertical line the new fiscal rules (six-pack and Fiscal Compact))

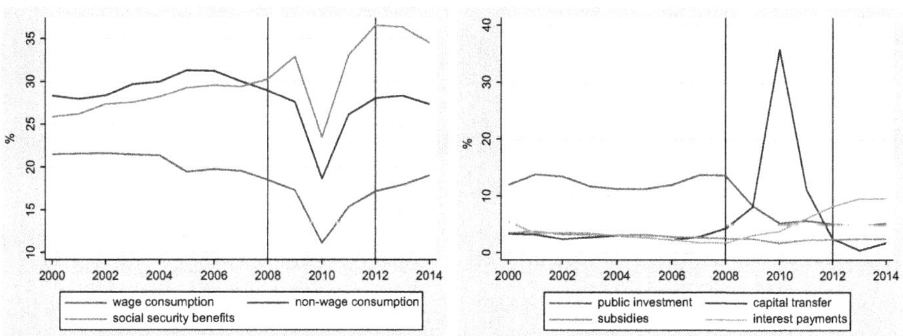

Fig. 4.5 Disaggregated public expenditures (in percent of total spending) in Ireland (*Note*: The black vertical line indicates the global financial crisis and the red vertical line the new fiscal rules (six-pack and Fiscal Compact))

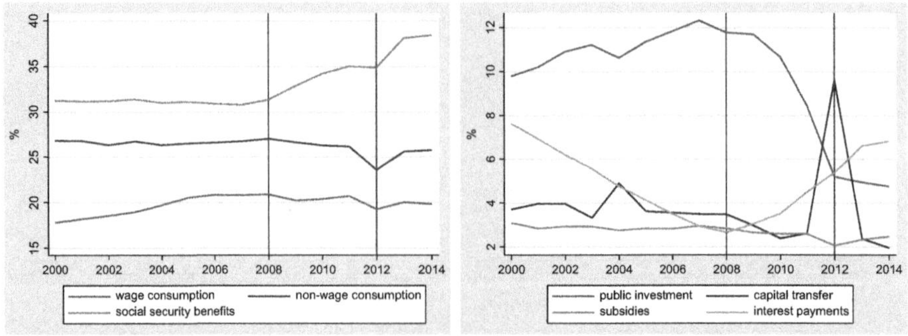

Fig. 4.6 Disaggregated public expenditures (in percent of total spending) in Spain (*Note*: The black vertical line indicates the global financial crisis and the red vertical line the new fiscal rules (six-pack and Fiscal Compact))

entry into force of new regulation. For these countries capital transfers paid and other capital payments spiked in the aftermath of the crisis. Finally an interesting result concerns public investment, which accounts for less than 10 % of total spending in all countries, its share steeply declining in the aftermath of the crisis and new fiscal rules (see also Berg et al. 2015).

Although the "investment clause" included in the SGP allows under certain conditions for deviating "temporarily from their medium-term budget objective or from the agreed fiscal adjustment path towards it, in order to accommodate investment"(European Commission 2015a), it seems that countries tend to adjust the public spending to meet fiscal criteria through a reduction in investment. Political economy arguments can provide an explanation for the observed contraction in public investment, since it is less costly for a government to cut it than other spending items such as public wages and pensions. In addition, public investment can be modified more easily since it does not involve the adoption of structural fiscal reforms that imply a long legislative process.

4.2   A Brief Literature Review of the Economic Impact of Public Investment

The decline in public investment may have contrasting effects on the economy: overall, it may decrease economic growth rate, whereas, more specifically, it may help restart private investment through the so-called "crowding-out" effect. In theory, public investment may have contradictory effects on private investment. On one side, it may compete with private funds for limited resources, thus crowding out private investment. This is an effect that we expect to be strong in "normal" times, when the economy is at (or close to) potential, but also in the short run when financing opportunities are scarce. On the other, it may crowd in investment. This may happen in the short run, because through Keynesian business cycle stabilization it improves the state of the economy and therefore expectations; but it can also happen in the long run, if public and private capitals are complementary in the production function, so that private investment productivity is enhanced by appropriate stocks of public capital.

The empirical literature devoted to the relationship between fiscal policy and economic growth certainly started with contributions by Ratner (1983) and Aschauer (1989a, b, c). The former concluded that US output elasticity with respect to public capital was positive but smaller than private capital (close to 6 %, whereas the output elasticity with respect to private capital was 22 %), whereas the latter pointed out a large elasticity of total factor productivity to public capital (around 0.4), and a crowding-out effect which was counterbalanced by the positive impact of public capital on the return to private capital. While his two former empirical contributions focused on US data, Aschauer (1989c) extended his analysis to G7 countries and highlights the positive impact of public investment on labour productivity.

A recent survey on the impact of public investment on the macroeconomy is provided by Pereira and Andraz (2013). Broadly speaking, the literature on public capital and growth can be divided into four main categories. First, papers based on the production function approach, which treat public capital as an input of the aggregate production function, and estimate its effects on output, as in Ratner and Aschauer. Second, papers based on the cost function approach, which are admittedly less demanding than the previous ones regarding the restrictions (for example on the degree of substitutability among factors) that they impose. Third, papers based on cross-section growth regressions à la Barro (1991), which include public capital among other explanatory variables. Fourth is the group of contributions that use Vector Auto Regressive (VAR) models or Vector Error Correction Models (VECM) including public capital; the advantage of this latter approach is that, by explicitly taking into account the dynamic links among variables, it allows to disentangle possible reverse causation (i.e. from output to capital/investment) and to differentiate the short run and long run relationships between public investment and GDP or public investment and private investment.

Romp and de Haan (2007) survey the literature on public capital and growth, explaining in detail each of the methodologies enumerated above, and reach a number of general conclusions. First, the majority of works surveyed, especially the most recent ones, conclude for a positive effect of public capital (or investment) on growth or on output. These effects are nevertheless considerably smaller than originally suggested by Aschauer. Such a positive but mild effect also emerges from the meta-analysis carried out by Bom and Lightart (2014) on a sample of 68 papers published between 1983 and 2008. Second, a number of papers (e.g. Batina 1998) suggest that reverse causation, from output to capital, is also significant and positive. Finally, and quite unsurprisingly, Romp and de Haan notice that the effects of public capital on growth differ across countries, regions and sectors.

Among the papers using a VAR approach, Pereira (2000) estimates an annual model in first differences for the USA. He identifies the model assuming Cholesky decomposition identification where innovations in public investment lead the other variables. He then finds permanent (long run) output level effects of a temporary increase in the growth rate of public investment or, which amounts to the same, a permanent increase in the level of investment. Afonso and St Aubyn (2009) estimate VARs for 17 developed countries and show that crowding-in effects go in both directions, from public to private investment and the other way round. The former effect varies across countries whereas the latter is more homogeneous across countries.

A regular feature of papers using the VAR approach is the use of yearly data. However, time series on a national basis and on a relatively short timespan may not show much variance. To overcome this issue, a few contributions have made use of quarterly data. Voss (2002) studies the impact of public investment on private investment in the USA and Canada, and (weakly) concludes for the crowding-out effect. Otto and Voss (1996) estimate a model in hours worked, GDP, public capital and private capital for the USA and Canada. They find weak evidence of a positive cointegration between private and public capital. They find a positive lagged effect on private capital (crowding in), but no significant effect on output. Mittnik and Neumann (2001) estimate a quarterly VAR model in levels with long-run cointegration restrictions (their results are not significantly different when they do not impose restrictions). Their model, estimated for six OECD countries, includes private investment and current government spending, and generally finds long-run, positive (but weak) effects of public investment on growth and on private investment (only for West Germany, does the long-run effect seem to be significant). The UK is the only country for which the effect is not significant even in the short run. Perotti (2004) estimates a structural VAR in levels for five countries (Australia, Canada, West Germany, the UK and the USA). His conclusions are not only that investment seems to have limited effects on GDP, but also that these effects are smaller than those of current spending.

A possible explanation that Perotti offers for these puzzling findings is that the level of public capital is so large in the countries considered that public investment is not productive enough. The crowding out of private investment hence more than compensates the direct effect on aggregate demand. Creel et al. (2009) offer a very different picture of the impact of public investment in the UK. In contrast with Perotti (2004), they also take into account the dynamics of public debt to GDP ratio in the empirical framework. They conclude that a positive and persistent effect of public investment on GDP robustly emerges. Further they find that this effect became more robust after the introduction of the golden rule of public finance in 1997, thus offering indirect empirical support to this institutional framework which allowed financing of public investment by debt issuance, in so far as current spending was financed by tax receipts over the business cycle.

Increasing the sample to a panel of countries may also increase variance and the power of the test, as argued in the literature (e.g. notably Temple 1999). According to Creel and Poilon (2008), the size of the different estimated production elasticities on a European panel are more realistic (with coefficients between 0.10 and 0.14) than those obtained with time-series regressions.

Recently, a few studies have concluded that the reduction in investment can drag the economic growth with a fiscal multiplier bigger than one. IMF World Economic Outlook (2014) finds empirical evidence that increased public infrastructure investment raises output in both the short and long term, especially during periods of economic slack and for advanced countries for which investment is more efficient. Valla et al. (2014) find that fiscal multipliers on public investment spending are significantly above one. Theoretical contributions also show the higher multiplier of public investment, especially with loose monetary policy (Coenen et al. 2012, 2013; Drautzburg and Uhlig 2013; Albertini et al. 2014). This can be particularly true in the current economic context of the euro area where private sector investment is reducing and is less than 20 % of euro area GDP, and the short-term crowding-out effect between private and public investment is smaller (Valla et al. 2014).

Regarding the crowding-in versus crowding-out effect, Creel et al. (2015) show with individual estimations on four countries (France, Germany, UK, USA) that causation, if any, runs from public to private investment. When trying to assess the sign of this causation, they conclude that for France there is reasonable evidence of textbook-like effects: increases of public investment generally trigger increases of private investment, unless the economy is overheating and/or public finances are in dire conditions. For the USA, the link is in general weaker, and tends to point to prevailing crowding-out effects, except for very low levels of public debt. The same can be said for Germany, where the relationship is even weaker than for the USA. The UK stands out as the country for which the results are more inconclusive. They interpret this latter outcome as the possible consequence of the adoption and implementation of the Code for Fiscal Stability (the golden rule of public finance), and then its abandonment.

4.3   Deficit of Public Investment and the Juncker's Investment Plan

In the first part of this chapter we have shown that countries in the euro area reduced public investment following the tightening of European fiscal rules and their effort to conduct fiscal consolidation. When we aggregate the data the picture becomes gloomier. For a set of 16 countries for which OECD data are available, investment dropped by €61.1 billion from 2009 to 2015,[2] hence a drop of €10 billion per year on average. At first sight, it might not prove substantial, but it disregards the fact that not only has public investment declined since the onset of the global financial crisis but also so has private investment. According to iAGS (2015), investment volumes in the European Union (EU) in 2014 were €370 billion below their historical pre-crisis level.

The decline in public investment matches 20 % of the recent Juncker's Investment Plan of overall (private *and* public) financing of €315 billion. In other words, one-fifth of the resources of the Plan, were it achieved, will only compensate the loss of capital formation owing to the reduction of investment activity by individual governments and will not therefore create a public investment stimulus; that is, a surge of public investment beyond what would have been achieved without the crisis. The "public investment retrenchment" is observed in many countries and is particularly strong in the periphery of the euro area. In Spain and Italy public investment contracted by €33.2 billion and €18.5 billion, respectively. It also declined in Greece (−€5.2 billion), France (−€3.8 billion), Netherlands (−€3.4 billion) and Ireland (−€2.5 billion), while it increased substantially in Germany (€5.5 billion).

The fall in public investment in euro area countries suggests that the Juncker's Investment Plan could be extended. There are many reasons for that. First and foremost, the amount of fresh public money invested in the European Fund for Strategic Investments (EFSI) has been limited to €21 billion. This is not much, as regards the reported drop in public investment

---

[2] Austria, Belgium, Estonia, Finland, France, Germany, Greece, Hungary, Ireland, Italy, Luxembourg, the Netherlands, Portugal, Slovak Republic, Slovenia, Spain.

between 2009 and 2015. Catching up the loss of public capital during the global financial crisis requires a bigger push to public investment. Second, the Investment Plan is not limited to infrastructure and innovation, but also encompasses financing of small and medium-sized enterprises (SMEs). There is a risk that funds associated with the Plan will be scattered. As of March 2016, 200 projects had been approved, for a total expected investment of €85 billion, 85 % of which was still expected to come from the private sector. On average, each project would receive €50 million from the EFSI. Third, the Plan is the third increase in capital or lending capacity of the Bank of European Investment since 2008: needless to say, the two former increases (of larger amounts than the latest one) neither produced a distinctive increase in public investment nor an improvement in public infrastructure. In June 2016, the European Council has agreed upon the extension of the Juncker Plan, both in length (until 2020 rather than 2017) and in volume (500 billion euros rather than 315 billion euros). The amount of fresh money (including an EU guarantee) will only grow by 12.5 billion euros though.

Although it may go against the principle of subsidiarity, there are also several reasons to believe that an investment stimulus implemented at European level could be more effective than one at country level. First, the Investment Plan can more easily finance cross-border projects in key sectors such as energy, transport and digital infrastructure, which can increase the productivity of the whole EU with long-term effects on economic growth, thus reinforcing the process of European integration.[3] Second, the adoption of stricter fiscal rules (e.g. the Fiscal Compact) to be incorporated in national laws limit the scope for budget deficits. An increase of 1 euro of investment must be compensated with a reduction of other expenditures or an increase in taxation by 1 euro during the same period. Drawing on a European stimulus would help circumvent domestic fiscal constraints. Otherwise economic agents in European economies will behave as "Ricardian" consumers, with the rise in public investment leading to a reduction in public or private consumption with small or no overall impact on economic activity. Finally, if the extension of investment plan is financed via the emission of bonds it could also enhance the functioning of the European financial system and the creation of the European capital market union, especially in the context of the zero lower bound and negative government bond yields.

The six-pack, Fiscal Compact and two-pack in the EU, together with the Debt Brake in Germany which imposes strict borrowing limits (Deutsche Bundesbank 2011), reduce the supply of government bonds that, per country,

---

[3] See the website of the European Investment Bank: http://www.eib.org/efsi/.

have been the *safest* and *most liquid* assets in Europe, hence failing to meet the increased demand for these assets. The capacity to issue debt against European investment projects can reduce this mismatch. Several authors point out the lack of a (relatively) safe asset in Europe, recommending alternative solutions. Brunnermeier et al. (2011) propose the creation of a synthetic safe asset formed by the senior tranches of a set of national bonds in fixed proportion (Euro-Safe-Bonds) that could lower the exposure of banks to their own sovereign and breaking the "diabolic loop." Garicano and Reichlin (2014) suggest that the Euro-Safe-Bonds could be an instrument used by the European Central Bank (ECB) for the outright quantitative easing (QE), preserving at the same time the market discipline. They argue that a government default would lead to fallout of the domestic banking sector. The ECB's unconventional policies, such as Outright Monetary Transactions (OMTs) and more indirectly the three-year Long Term Refinancing Operations (LTROs), relieved the strain on governments in the periphery of the euro area owing to the market pressure on the sovereign debt, but could foster their moral hazard. By loosening the link between sovereigns and banks, the Euro-Safe-Bonds would allow the market to monitor directly the governments instead of second guessing the bailout intentions of the ECB. Caballero and Fahri (2014) argue that reassessment of the European periphery sovereign debt contributed to the contraction of the supply of safe assets against an increasing demand for these assets owing to the rise in international reserves and global saving gluts, supporting the creation of a safe asset in Europe.

Since the financial crisis, the demand for *liquid* asset that can serve as collateral in the interbank market has increased, driven by market demand for more secured funding as well as new regulatory requirements, such as set out in the European Market Infrastructure Regulation (EMIR) (European Commission 2015b). Government bonds, and in particular German, French and Italian bonds, are the prime collateral in the European repo market (Molteni 2015). However, the ECB monthly purchase of €80 billion of mainly eurozone government bonds, based on self-imposed rules that limit how much it can acquire from individual governments, is reducing the net supply of these assets (Gerba and Macchiarelli 2015).[4] Analysts estimate that following those rules the supply of German bonds will be exhausted before the programme ends in March 2017, creating a policy dilemma for the ECB over which bonds

---

[4] The problem of scarcity of government bonds as collateral is more pronounced for Europe, where there is a smaller substitutability between public and private debt than in the USA (see Krishnamurthy and Vissing-Jorgensen 2012).

to buy.[5] Drawing on the decisions of the ECB, which were announced by Mario Draghi in mid-March 2016, the issuer and issuance limit on bonds from supranational institutions and national agencies has been raised from 33 to 50 % of their new issuances, up to a limit of 10 % of the ECB monthly purchases, i.e. €8 billion. It gives some new margins for manoeuvre to these institutions, among them the European Investment Bank, to raise capital and finance new investment projects.

Finally, a larger supply of *safe* and *liquid* assets would help achieve the construction of the European Capital Markets Union (CMU). The so-called "European sovereign-debt crisis" has fostered habit formation by savers: cross-border financial flows have diminished. The high mobility of capital between EU member states, which had been achieved since 1990, has been substantially weakened. The impetus for a CMU has come along this lower mobility in European capital. The objective is to push funding suppliers, especially institutional investors such as pensions and insurance sectors, to increase again the diversity of their European investments. For this to happen, they need some guarantees which usually take the form of substantial holdings in their asset portfolio of safe assets. A higher liquidity on sovereign bond markets would make a wider list of sovereign bonds safe again and would facilitate the high mobility of capital on which the EU has long developed upon. In addition, commercial banks, which remain key actors and participants in capital markets as issuers, investors and intermediaries, have to hold liquid assets in order to access the repo market and satisfy their funding needs. A larger issuance of safe assets would thus help improve banking stability and the passing of stress tests.

References

Afonso, A., & St Aubyn, M. (2009). Macroeconomic rates of return of public and private investment: Crowding-in and crowding-out effects. *Manchester School, 77,* 21–39.

Albertini, J., Poirier, A., & Roulleau-Pasdeloup, J. (2014). The composition of government spending and the multiplier at the zero lower bound. *Economics Letters, 122*(1), 31–35.

Alesina, A., & Ardagna, S. (2010). Large changes in fiscal policy: Taxes versus spending, NBER Chapters, In *Tax policy and the economy* (Vol. 24, pp. 35–68). National Bureau of Economic Research, Inc.

---

[5] This estimate was reported in the *Wall Street Journal*, "European Central Bank Faces Questions Over Which Bonds to Buy", 4 March 2016.

Alesina, A. & Ardagna, S. (2013). The design of fiscal adjustments, NBER Chapters, In *Tax policy and the economy* (Vol. 27, pp. 19–67). National Bureau of Economic Research, Inc.

Alesina, A., & Perotti, R. (1995). Fiscal expansions and adjustments in OECD economies. *Economic Policy, 21*, 207–247.

Alesina, A., Barbiero, O., Favero, C., Giavazzi, F., & Paradisi, M. (2015). *Austerity in 2009–2013*, CEPR discussion papers 10347, C.E.P.R. Discussion Papers.

Aschauer, D. A. (1989a). Is public expenditure productive? *Journal of Monetary Economics, 23*, 177–200.

Aschauer, D. A. (1989b). Does public capital crowd out private capital? *Journal of Monetary Economics, 24*, 171–188.

Aschauer, D. A. (1989c). Public investment and productivity growth in the group of seven. *Journal of Economic Perspectives, 13*, 17–25.

Balassone, F., & Franco, D. (2000). Public investment, the stability pact and the 'Golden Rule'. *Fiscal Studies, 21*(2).

Barro, R. J. (1991). Economic growth in a cross section of countries. *Quarterly Journal of Economics, 106*(2), 407–443.

Batina, R. G. (1998). On the long run effects of public capital and disaggregated public capital on aggregate output. *International Tax and Public Finance, 5*(3), 263–281.

Berg, J., Clerc, L., Garnier, O., Nielsen, E., & Valla, N. (2015). *From the investment plan to the capital markets union: European financial structure and cross border risk-sharing*, CEPII working paper No. 2015–34.

Blot, C., Creel, J., Ducoudre, B., & Timbeau, X. (2015). *Back to fiscal consolidation in Europe and its dual tradeoff: Now or later, through spending cuts or tax hikes?* Sciences Po publications info:hdl:2441/6018jmm8rk9, Sciences Po.

Bom, P., & Ligthart, J. (2014). What Have we learned from three decades of research on the productivity of public capital? *Journal of Economic Surveys, 28*(5), 889–916.

Brunnermeier, M. K., Garicano, L., Lane, P. R., Pagano, M., Reis, R., Santos, T., Thesmar, D., Van Nieuwerburgh S., & Vayanos, D. (2011). *European safe bonds (ESBies)*, The Euro-Nomics Group.

Coenen, G., Straub, R., & Trabandt, M. (2012). Fiscal policy and the great recession in the euro area. *American Economic Review, 102*(3), 71–76.

Coenen, G., Straub, R., & Trabandt, M. (2013). Gauging the effects of fiscal stimulus packages in the euro area. *Journal of Economic Dynamics and Control, 37*(2), 367–386.

Coricelli, F., & Fiorito, R. (2013). Myths and facts about fiscal discretion: A new measure of discretionary expenditure, Documents de travail du Centre d'Economie de la Sorbonne 13033, Université Panthéon-Sorbonne (Paris 1), Centre d'Economie de la Sorbonne.

Coricelli, F., Fiorito, R. & Molteni, F. (2017). Discretionary fiscal policy and recession. In *Rethinking fiscal policy after the crisis*. Cambridge University Press (forthcoming).

Creel J., & Poilon G. (2008), Is public capital productive in Europe?, *International Review of Applied Economics*, 22(6), November, 673–691.

Creel, J., Hubert, P., & Saraceno, F. (2015). Une analyse empirique du lien entre investissement public et privé. *Revue de l'OFCE, 144*, 331–356.

Creel, J., Monperrus-Veroni, P., & Saraceno, F. (2009, November). On the long term effects of fiscal policy in the United Kingdom: The case for a golden rule. *Scottish Journal of Political Economy, 56*(5), 580–607.

Deutsche Bundesbank. (2011). *The debt brake in Germany—key aspects and implementation*. Monthly Report October 2011.

Drautzburg, T., & Uhlig, H. (2013). *Fiscal stimulus and distortionary taxation*. Working Papers 13–46, Federal Reserve Bank of Philadelphia.

European Commission. (2015a). *Stability and growth pact: commission issues guidance to encourage structural reforms and investments*.

European Commission. (2015b). *Green paper: Building on a capital markets union*. COM (2015) 63 final, Brussels, 18th February.

Farhi, E., & Caballero, R. J. (2014). *On the role of safe asset shortages in secular stagnation. Secular stagnation: Facts, causes, and cures* (pp. 111–122). London: CEPR Press.

Garicano, L., & Reichlin, L. (2014). *A safe asset for Eurozone QE: A proposal*, VoxEu. org, 14 November.

Gerba, E., & Macchiarelli, C. (2015). *Sovereign bond purchases and risk sharing arrangements: Sharing: Myth and reality of the European QE*, SRC special paper, No. 9, October.

iAGS. (2015). *Give recovery a chance, OFCE-ECLM-IMK-AK-ENE report for the socialists and democrats' group at the European parliament*, November 25, http://www.iags-project.org/documents/iags_report2016.pdf.

Krishnamurthy, A., & Vissing-Jorgensen, A. (2012). The aggregate demand for treasury debt. *Journal of Political Economy, 120*, 233–267.

Mehrotra, A., & Välilä, T. (2006). Public investment in Europe: Evolution and determinants in perspective. *Fiscal Studies, 27*(4), 443–471.

Mittnik, S., & Neumann, T. (2001). Dynamic effects of public investment: Vector autoregressive evidence from six industrialized countries. *Empirical Economics, 26*(2), 429–446.

Molteni, F. (2015). *Liquidity, government bonds and sovereign debt crises, CEPII working paper, No. 2015–32. OECD, 2015*. The State of Public Finances 2015. Strategies for budgetary consolidation and reforms in OECD countries.

Otto, G. D., & Voss, G. M. (1996). Public capital and private production in Australia. *Southern Eastern Journal, 62*(3), 723–738.

Pappa, E. (2009). *The effects of fiscal expansions: An international comparison*. Working Papers 409, Barcelona Graduate School of Economics.

Pereira, A. M. (2000). Is all public capital created equal? *Review of Economics and Statistics, 82*(3), 513–518.

Pereira, A. M., & Andraz, J. M. (2013). On the economic effects of public infrastructure investment: A survey of the international evidence. *Journal of Economic Development, 38*(4).

Perotti R. (2004). *Public investment: Another (Different) look.* IGIER Working Paper No. 277, Bocconi University.

Ratner, J. B. (1983). Government capital and the production function for US private output. *Economics Letters, 13*, 213–217.

Romp, W., & de Haan, J. (2007). Public capital and economic growth: A critical survey. *Perspektiven der Wirtschaftspolitik, 8*, 6–52.

Temple, J. (1999). The new growth evidence. *Journal of Economic Literature, 37*(1), 112–156.

Valla, N., Brand, T., & Doisy, S. (2014). *A new architecture for public investment in Europe.* CEPII Policy Brief No. 4 July.

Voss, G. M. (2002). Public and private investment in the United States and Canada. *Economic Modelling, 19*(4), 641–664.

5

The Banking Union Revisited

Christian de Boissieu

The main purpose of this chapter is to give an account of the implementation of banking union in Europe. The benefits one may expect from a banking union are reviewed. Its components are analysed and discussed with a special focus on the supervision and resolution of banks. The challenges are both functional and institutional. They involve micro- and macroprudential considerations. As regards the European Central Bank (ECB), will there be possible conflicts of objectives when it cumulates its monetary policy function with its new supervisory role? For banking supervision, how is it possible to combine the division of labour between the ECB and the national competent authorities (NCAs) with the necessary coordination between them?

The same kind of challenge applies to resolution and deposit insurance. The chapter also relates the launching of banking union to other structural issues, such as the separation of bank activities and the financing of the real economy (investment and growth) in the new regulatory framework. At the end it touches upon the Capital Markets Union (CMU) project.

Christian de Boissieu is Professor at the University of Paris I (Panthéon-Sorbonne) and at the College of Europe (Bruges). He is also member of the board of the AMF (Autorité des Marchés Financiers). From 2003 to 2012 he was Chair of the Conseil d'Analyse Économique (CAE), which advises the French Prime Minister on economic and social issues.

C. de Boissieu (✉)
LabEx RéFi and CES, Université Paris 1 Panthéon-Sorbonne;
College of Europe, Bruges, Paris, France

© The Author(s) 2017
R. Douady et al. (eds.), *Financial Regulation in the EU*,
DOI 10.1007/978-3-319-44287-7_5

5.1   Background

Access to reliable, independent and comparable data is key to the banking union (hereafter BU), since transparency of bank data is a prerequisite for effective supervision and resolution by the competent authorities. Everyone acknowledges both the necessity and the difficulty of improving access to the relevant banking and financial data. It is worth noting that "market discipline" is at the core of Pillar 3 of Basel II and Basel III, and it implies more and better information disclosure by banks to all stakeholders. Some analysts even refer to a "battle of data," questioning the role of financial industry-led research which is not independent enough. This is a view which is strongly opposed by others, who stress the positive sum game between the regulators, the bankers, the stakeholders and the public at large regarding the collection and treatment of the relevant data. In their assessment of the first 18 months of BU, Dirk Schoenmaker and Nicolas Véron (2016) underline the persistent challenge of access to relevant and reliable data.

The obstacles to reliable and comparable data are manifold: excessive financial complexity (e.g. some exotic derivatives instruments), the difficult *ex ante* assessment of risks, persistent divergence across member states in the accounting and evaluation procedures despite their reliance on the same accounting rules (IFRS). As regards listed banks, IFRS are mandatory in the European Union (EU) but this harmonization does not apply to unlisted banks. There is still a high degree of heterogeneity in accounting and auditing rules and practices even within the euro area. Therefore it is not surprising that the ECB's comprehensive assessment of banks in the euro area implemented from November 2013 to November 2014 has emphasized more transparency for the purpose of "enhancing the quality of information available on the condition of banks" (JC 2014).

The Joint Research Centre of the European Commission, in cooperation with DG MARKT, has built the model SYMBOL (Systemic Model of Bank Originated Losses), which assesses the financial position of individual banks and the macro implications under exogenous shocks (Pagano et al. 2012). This model is still in progress since the collection of detailed and reliable data is indispensable. However, it is already a useful tool for assessing the probability of default of each bank. It takes into account contagion effects on the interbank market in order to analyse the micro/macro links, in particular the channels of transmission from individual bank risks (credit risks, market risks, operational risks, liquidity risks) to systemic risks and to simulate the impact of various shocks. In this respect such a modelization could be very useful in the implementation of future bank stress tests.

5.2 Benefits of Banking Union

R.Goyal et al. (2013) have presented a comprehensive survey of the economic foundations of BU. Without being exhaustive, it can be argued that BU in Europe is a means towards the following goals:

1) To deepen the single market for financial services and make it more effective. We are still far from an effective single market for banking and financial services and a true level playing field. One of the goals of BU is to make the single market a reality, in particular through the "single rulebook." However there is a debate on the financial reregulation process and the effectiveness of the single market. In many respects we are still far from a real single rulebook. Some analysts have regretted that even CRD IV and CRR leave too much room to the competent national authorities to incorporate idiosyncratic measures in the transposition of the directive and in particular in its interpretation, in such a way that we could be very far from a real level playing field. For instance, according to CRD IV the national authorities keep some discretionary power for the weights attached to real estate or for the implementation (or not) of the countercyclical buffer. This ongoing debate means that we will have to find the right balance between coordination and decentralization as regards the concrete implementation of Basel III. BU also implies such a search and clarification.

2) To overcome the current fragmentation of financial markets in Europe. This is another way to look at the single market puzzle. The Eurozone crisis has generated diverging interest rates and increasing spreads over the whole yield curve. Banks in countries under pressure still pay a premium on their debt compared to banks in core countries. The crisis has also fuelled an augmented "home bias" for investors which is well documented, a partial repatriation of financial assets, some form of "renationalization" of private savings and the necessity to compensate private capital flows from the south (Greece, Portugal, Spain) to the north of Europe by some public transfers from the north to the south.

3) To overcome the "impossible trinity." D. Schoenmaker (2011), referring to the concept of "financial trilemma," underlined the fact that we cannot have the three sides together: financial integration, financial stability and national policies for crisis prevention and management. If we want to maintain financial integration and to reach financial stability, we must pass to some supranational policies for the management of financial crises. This financial trilemma is as important for financial matters as the Mundell–

Padoa–Schioppa impossibility triangle is for monetary policy in an open economy with perfect capital mobility.

4) To get out of the vicious loop between banks and sovereigns. The Eurozone crisis has illustrated the manifold and bi-directional links between banks and sovereigns. In several cases the systemic banking crisis associated with private overindebtedness has led to state intervention as an investor of last resort in the banking sector and to an outburst in the public debt ratio (Ireland, Spain). Among other examples, the Cypriot crisis has illustrated the negative impact of non-performing sovereign debt on individual banks and on the banking system as a whole. In many cases spreads are the main channel of transmission from the sovereign to corporate debt (including bank debt). What to expect and what not to expect from the BU regarding the bank/sovereign loop? Banks will continue to buy sovereign debt, induced to do so by the scale of weights embedded in Basel III. But effective supervision at European level means that the supervisors are in a better position to contain on an *ex ante* basis the accumulation of bad debts on bank balance sheets. Moreover, a Spanish or an Irish scenario comparable to the one we had a few years ago would be much less likely in the future since the resolution of banks in BU relies on public funding as the last, not the first, solution. Compared to the pre-BU configuration, the probability for a bank crisis morphing into a sovereign debt crisis will significantly decrease, although it will not be zero.

5) To internalize externalities. The presence of externalities—either positive or negative—leads to under- or overutilization of some instruments. Here we come back to the classical argument à la Tinbergen (1954): the presence of externalities pushes towards coordination or even centralization (which represents the highest degree of coordination) of policy instruments. Cross-border banking and financial activities in the EU are still significant despite the recent fragmentation. The Cyprus crisis has shown that spillover effects fuelled by expectations and contagion could create a systemic problem from a configuration which was difficult to characterize as "systemic" on a purely *ex ante* basis. Potential negative externalities for the rest of Europe came from the initial and counterproductive decision of the Eurogroup to tax all deposits. The final decision to exonerate deposits up to €100,000 limited the externalities for depositors in the rest of the EU. The Cyprus case suggests that the transition from individual to systemic risks is much more complex than usually appreciated. It deserves more scientific and policy attention. The magnitude of externalities across member states explains the creation of the three European regulatory and supervisory bodies (ESMA, EBA, EIOPA) according to the recommenda-

tions of the de Larosière report made before the Eurozone crisis. This crisis means that we must go further regarding the internalization of financial externalities.

6) To reduce the risk of capture of regulators by the financial industry. The arguments are extensively discussed in the academic literature especially in light of the crisis and the growing focus on conflicts of interest. Supervision and resolution taken at national level would entail a risk of regulatory forbearance. This argument validates more integration and centralization. The idea that a supervisory mechanism centralized at European level would be less exposed to lobbies and pressures is based on the notion of "distance" from vested interests which are supposed to be more powerful at the national level than at EU or euro area level. Here the word distance could have several meanings: for sure geographical, but also functional, political, institutional and so on.

The emphasis on the benefits to be had from BU does not mean that there are no costs. The operational costs are difficult to estimate. The ECB had to recruit extensively (about 1,000 additional staff) in order to fulfil its new role as the main supervisor of banks. But a part of this recruitment came from a substitution effect: some experts left their NCA in order to work with the ECB on prudential issues. Likewise, how to measure the loss of national sovereignty through BU and the centralization of banking supervision and its costs for any member country? For the sake of transparency and accountability it would be useful to develop an *ex ante* assessment of the discounted costs/benefits of such a major economic and political change. The main challenge is to quantify so many qualitative changes and to value numerous externalities.

5.3 The Single Supervisory Mechanism

5.3.1 The Three Pillars and Their Sequencing

BU rests on three pillars: a Single Supervisory Mechanism (SSM), a Single Resolution Mechanism (SRM) and an integrated scheme of deposit insurance. The fact that Basel II and III also rest on three pillars does not imply that three has become the golden figure of financial regulation. This convergence is purely coincidental.

The three pillars of BU form a consistent system. They cannot be decoupled from each other. But, on the other hand, since BU relies not on shock therapy but rather on gradualism, proper sequencing is both required and fundamental.

It should take place in the following order: supervision, then resolution of banks and, at the end, deposit guarantee. Not in the steady state but during the transition period, which is expected to last at least a couple of years, the EU will face a dilemma: how to implement a credible and effective BU when it will be piecemeal during the transition phase, given the lags in effect between the respective integration of supervision, resolution and deposit insurance? The solution could be the following: to extend the monetary policy debate to financial regulation. In order to be time-consistent, each stage of the BU must be set in such a way that it is perfectly consistent with and conducive to the later stages. From the functional viewpoint the three stages (one for each pillar) are not separable even if they are implemented successively. This is what may be called the *non-separability principle* (de Boissieu 2013).

5.3.2 The Central Role of the ECB

The SSM benefits from the global reputation and credibility of the ECB. The independence and "distance" of the ECB from national authorities are valuable features of the SSM. Moreover, the ECB has a comparative advantage in collecting microeconomic information about bank condition and risks, and this advantage has been increasing with the implementation of unconventional monetary policy, which requires more transparency about bank balance sheets. The idea was to give the leadership to the ECB but to benefit from more coordination between the ECB, the European Banking Authority (EBA) and other existing institutions.

The ECB started its supervisory activity as of November 2014 by directly supervising the most "significant" banks of the Eurozone, 129 of them, which taken together represent a market share of 80–85 % of bank assets in the euro area (ECB 2016). Given the list of global systematically important banks (GSIBs) published each November by the FSB, which includes 30 banks at the world level (as of November 2015) of which eight have their seat in the euro area, it means that the ECB is supervising many non-GSIBs but "significant" banks. For a bank to be qualified "significant" the relevant criteria are: the size (namely assets over €30 billion, assets over 20 % of a member country's gross domestic product) and the magnitude of cross-border operations. These criteria differ from the ones put forward by the FSB to designate the list of systemic banks at world level (BCBS 2013) but they also concur with some of them.

5.3.3 The Necessity of Coordination

The coordination challenge is twofold: (1) cooperation between the ECB and the NCAs as regards the concrete functioning of the SSM, and (2) relationships between the ECB and other existing bodies in charge of prudential policy.

The first aspect raises a difficult but relevant issue. What will be for the SSM, both during the transition phase and in the steady-state regime, the balance between centralization forces giving a growing role to the ECB and decentralization forces maintaining a very significant role for NCAs because of their privileged access to local information, of the valuable argument of "proximity" (which is a multidimensional concept: geographic, cultural, political)? The answer, which is quite impossible to provide on an *ex ante* basis, will lie in the combination of two necessities: the fruitful division of labour between the ECB and the NCAs (in many cases the national central banks or institutions which are closely related to them), and the necessary cooperation between them. The basic split between large banks directly supervised by the ECB and the small and medium-sized banks ("less significant" banks which number slightly less than 3,200 as of 2016) directly supervised by the national authorities is useful and apparently clear cut. But even the size criterion will pave the way for some overlapping and competition between the "centre" and the "periphery." This wording is not intended to be pejorative, in view of the fact that the NCAs will continue to care for their "significant" banks whereas the ECB cannot neglect less significant banks in light of the Cyprus crisis and some other banking crises. Coordination does not mean the absence of hierarchy: the ECB is ultimately in charge and always able to look at some less significant banks. For the sake of consistency at Europe level, it exercises oversight of the NCAs. This fragile balance between cooperation and leadership is best illustrated by the concrete functioning of the Joint Supervisory Teams (JSTs), which gather both experts from the ECB and NCAs and undertake a review of significant banks. The chief of a JST is always from the ECB staff.

To be more concrete, let us consider two examples which raise the issue of the optimum degree of centralization (or decentralization) within the SSM.

With Basel II and Basel III, the supervisors have to assess the quality of internal models used by banks (in particular the A-IRB models for "advanced internal rating based") to compute their risk-weighted assets (RWA). This referee function is crucial for comparing and rating bank internal models and therefore creating a level playing field. In the SSM, the ECB and the NCAs will have to cooperate to fulfil this function. De facto, the ECB will be more involved in the rating of large banks' internal models while the NCAs will focus more on small and medium-sized banks (by the way, those banks mostly rely on the standard model or on the Foundation-IRB). But the two levels of decision have to be fully consistent since any significant discrepancy between them could generate competitive distortions.

A second example relates to the implementation of Pillar 2 of Basel II and III; that is, the competence of supervisors to tighten up solvency ratios required from a bank above the regulatory thresholds given the specific risk profile of that bank. The concrete exercise of such a discretionary power in the SSM will also imply a high degree of consistency and coordination between the "centre" and the "periphery."

The other aspect of the coordination puzzle concerns the relationships between the ECB and other existing institutions at the European level. A frequent debate concerns the role and the very existence of the ESRB (European Systemic Risk Board), which as a group is too large (about 60 people around the table), has no executive power and has no impact on the decision-making process. It has not issued any recommendation to any authority (Cyprus, Slovenia, etc). On the contrary, some economists pointed out the usefulness of the ESRB when it made some strong recommendations concerning money market funds at the end of 2012 and when it published scoreboards concerning systemic risks.

What will be the role of the EBA when a full BU is in place? No one really questioned the very existence of the EBA, but it will have to adjust to the new institutional framework. EBA could contribute to many aspects of the BU except that it cannot provide liquidity in case of a need for it. Some analysts point out to the fundamental limits of EBA because it is not a regulator. What can be considered to be fairly certain is that EBA will continue to be deeply involved in bank stress tests in cooperation with the ECB and the NCAs. The participation of EBA in the assessment of banks by the ECB is a positive token of the prevailing spirit of cooperation (rather than competition) between the various stakeholders of the BU. We are here also confronted with the question of what is the best incentive structure to fulfil the objectives defined by the European and national policymakers.

5.3.4 Micro- and Macroprudential Measures

Banking supervision is mostly microprudential. It is a continuous policy applied to all relevant financial institutions. Today everyone underlines the unavoidable "granularity" of macroprudential measures, namely the necessity to index them on the economic cycle in order to limit their procyclicality and if possible to make them contracyclical.

At present, this principle is widely accepted, whereas its concrete implementation is much more problematic. It suffices to refer to the status of the countercyclical buffer in Basel III, left to the discretionary appreciation of each national competent authority, or the ongoing debate since the London 2009 G20 summit about bank dynamic (or *ex ante*) provisioning. The concept of granularity is more complex, since it refers also to the optimal aggregation level for macroprudential policy. Here the optimum is not necessarily the most aggregated level, and I would support the suggestion that prudential policy must also be "meso" oriented by looking at intermediate-level patterns (e.g. prices on local or regional real estate markets). This is a form of geographic selectivity and fine tuning.

As Charles Goodhart has pointed out many times, it is much easier to tighten up banking and financial regulation in a boom than it is to relax it in a bust. Some empirical evidence of this asymmetry comes from convergent International Monetary Fund studies on macroprudential policy. Moreover micro- and macroprudential policies could work in opposite directions. Whereas during the boom both micro- and macropolicies converge to tightening (higher capital and liquidity requirements), they diverge during the bust with micropolicy pushing towards tougher measures and macropolicy trying to "lean against the wind" (i.e. to be contracyclical by lowering relevant ratios). Here there is a clear conflict of objectives within the overall prudential policy and the need for more instruments to reach the various objectives attached to financial stability. This is another application of the Tinbergen Rule, but we also have to consider the Mundell Rule; that is, how to assign the different prudential measures to the various goals of financial stability. We need here more research and academic analysis. Could we assess and implement the optimal degree of granularity and selectiveness as regards geographic and temporal criteria? The split between micro- and macromeasures is necessary but not sufficient, and in many respects we have to go beyond.

5.3.5 Potential Conflicts within the ECB

Possible trade-offs between monetary policy and prudential policy are well known and documented. It is known that such a trade-off could occur when monetary policy has to be tightened. The higher interest rate warranted from the monetary policy viewpoint could enhance the fragility of some banks whose financing costs are indexed on market rates. The impact could therefore challenge the supervisory function of the central bank.

There exists another potential conflict which is both functional and institutional. It relates to the links between the Governing Council and the Supervisory Board of the ECB. One option would have been the full separation between the two bodies, the Governing Council being no more than an observer at the Supervisory Board (and vice versa). There is some overlapping as regards the membership of the two Boards. A huge dose of pragmatism is required.

5.4   The Single Resolution Mechanism

From the viewpoint of the sequencing, the SRM is the second pillar of the BU. The problem of bank resolution was alluded to at the Washington DC, G20 Summit in November 2008, which called for a review of resolution regimes and bankruptcy laws "to ensure that they permit an orderly wind-down of large complex cross-border financial institutions." Owing to the impact of the Eurozone crisis on banks, the challenge of resolution has become still more topical. A sense of emergency has developed in particular after the Cyprus crisis. The 2014 BRRD (Bank Recovery and Resolution Directive, 2014/5/UE) has set the rule for banking resolution in the euro area.

5.4.1 The Legal Basis for Bank Resolution

In 2013–2014 the debate about the legal basis for bank resolution was still lively. For sure, there was and there is a consensus not to change the Treaties for this purpose. This is a sound position given the general mood in Europe and the economic and social circumstances. The SRM will facilitate the orderly resolution of cross-border banking groups and the belief that this is a single market issue.

Here the cross-border dimension of bank activity is underlined, but the SRM will be applicable to any credit institution "failing or likely to fail" whatever the respective weights of purely domestic and cross-border operations in its net income. The legal debate is over, at least for now (but we cannot discard completely the scenario of legal and judiciary disputes). A comprehensive analysis of the legal basis for resolution is proposed by Micossi et al. (2013).

5.4.2 The Basic Ingredients of Bank Resolution

The general idea was to set up a Single Resolution Board (SRB) which works in close cooperation with the NCAs. As for supervision, the debate concerning the balance between centralization versus decentralization forces does exist for resolution. However, the size criterion, which is relevant to assign responsibilities between the ECB and national supervisors, applies less to resolution. The SRM will cover all banks whatever their size and "significance." In this respect the ECB's view is at odds with that of the German authorities. Wolfgang Schäuble, the German Minister of Finance since 2009, has repeatedly said that the SRM must work as a network of the NCAs rather than as a centralized authority. This is not the view of the Commission, the ECB, the European Council or many member countries. There is even no place for a two-tier resolution system based on a size criterion as it could be for supervision. Nevertheless there could be no real decoupling between supervision and resolution. First, there exists a logical sequencing. The SSM (either the ECB or the NCAs) should be solely responsible for assessing whether a credit institution is failing or likely to fail. The supervisory assessment will therefore be a necessary precondition for putting an institution into resolution. Second, the relevant geographic areas for the SSM and the SRM have to coincide. A country cannot be part of one without participating in the other. As already mentioned, this is what the non-separability principle dictates.

5.4.3 Organizing Bail-in Procedures

The main objective of the new procedure is to count on private rather than on public money whenever a bank in the euro area is failing or likely to fail. Bail-in must be the rule, bail-out the exception. States and taxpayers will become payers of last resort, not of first resort as they were in 2008–2009 and more recently with the Irish, Spanish and Cypriot crises owing to the systemic nature of those crises and the prevalence of the "too big to fail" argument. Before coming to resolution, everything must be done to avoid such a situation through the adoption of preventive measures, early intervention with the power given to the authorities (European and national) to appoint a new management in case of a significant deterioration in the bank's financial situation or of serious violations of the law. Resolution itself is a multidimensional procedure since it could involve several steps, such as partial sale of bank business, defeasance operations (transfer of impaired assets to a special vehicle) and bail-in measures. Indeed a concise definition of bail-in has been put forward by the EU: "the imposition of losses, with an order of seniority, on shareholders and unsecured creditors" (Council 11228/13).

The directive on recovery and resolution introduces a strong hierarchy in the means to resolve a bank, a hierarchy which could be represented by a lexicographic order corresponding to the following order. First, shareholders solicited for a recapitalization. Second, creditors, in particular the ordinary, unsecured, non-preferred creditors. In any case creditors cannot suffer greater losses than they would have under the ordinary national insolvency procedure. Third, uninsured depositors (above €100,000). There is a long list of creditors and liabilities not eligible for bail-in procedures. For example, covered deposits (i.e. up to €100,000) are excluded from bail-in. Fourth, states (including the ESM at the European level) and taxpayers as last resort contributors. This ranking is reasonable. It has to be consistent with the company law of member states, which could still vary across countries despite the adoption of several EU directives in this field. In some cases national company law for bankruptcy will have to be adjusted to the new configuration created by the resolution directive. In practice, in light of past experiences, it is not evident that appeal to public money will become an exception and a last resort solution (see the Monte dei Paschi di Siena case in Italy). In order to avoid a gap between the desired objectives and reality, a strong political commitment from both national and European decision-makers is needed.

5.4.4 Governance, Funding and Fiscal Backstop

The SRB is based in Brussels and independent from the ECB in order to avoid conflicts of interest between supervision and resolution. The ECB has been very clear in its opinion on the SRM. "The ECB seeks representation in all plenary and executive meetings of the Single Resolution Board as an observer."

As far as funding is concerned there was also much convergence of views. The system has to be funded on an *ex ante* basis through premia paid by banks. This is very similar to most deposit insurance schemes which are also "funded," that is financed, on an *ex ante* basis. For most deposit insurance schemes, the premium paid by each bank has to be an increasing function of three factors: (1) a scale variable such as the level of bank liabilities eligible for a bail-in; (2) the global bank risk, computed in aggregating credit, market, liquidity and operational risks. A risk-based pricing is the way to deal with moral hazard; (3) the rate of global economic growth, taken as a proxy for the cycle. The positive relationship between premium and growth makes the system contracyclical since banks pay more during the boom, less during the bust.

We have exactly the same questions and answers for premia for resolution and deposit insurance. For instance, who is actually paying the quasi- taxes and premia? Under certain competition circumstances, banks could transfer part of or the entire bill to their customers, with higher lending rates and/ or lower deposit rates. The similarity between the funding of resolution and the financing of deposit guarantee means that it is not surprising that some experts and policymakers advocate their merger. However, it is preferable to start BU with a distinct and transparent Resolution Fund.

To finance the SRF, it has been decided to implement a gradual phasing in. The banks in the euro area are paying premia depending on the size and the risk profile of each bank. This regime comes from a compromise between the German (in Germany banking concentration is rather low compared to other European countries) and the French (in France banking concentration is much higher) and therefore from the necessity to combine the size and risk criteria. As of 2024, in the steady state, the SRF will get €55 billion, an amount which is sufficient to bail out a significant bank (e.g. a Landesbanken in Germany) but not enough to face a big systemic crisis. Therefore the creation of a common backstop to the SRF is crucial for the credibility of Pillar 2. The European Stability Mechanism (ESM) is a natural candidate for such a backstop. It manages around €500 billion, and such an amount could be enough to face a big systemic crisis in the Eurozone. Moreover the ESM has already some experience regarding the resolution of banks since it has been deeply involved in the resolution of several Spanish banks. The German authorities are still reluctant to give this new role to the ESM, seen by them as a way to inflate the European budget. The debate about the backstop illustrates the fact that the border between bail-in and bail-out, between private and public money, between prudential policy and fiscal policy, is tenuous and could be removed whenever the banking crisis reaches a certain threshold of intensity.

5.5 Deposit Insurance

So far deposit insurance, which is the third pillar of the BU, has drawn much less attention than the other pillars. There are at least two main reasons for the relative lack of attention. The timetable for Pillar 3 was not very clear until recently and in any case far delayed compared to the SSM and the SRM. Moreover, the topic could be more sensitive from the viewpoint of national sovereignty than supervision and resolution, which are already touchy issues.

Before 2007–2008 there was a significant heterogeneity across EU countries with respect to deposit insurance. The crisis has precipitated some convergence, in particular for the ceiling of insured deposits (€100,000).

It should be expected that coordination between the national deposit insurance authorities and any projected European fund will become necessary. Moreover, cooperation will be necessary but not sufficient. In the medium and long run, the EU will have to develop a more centralized system, such as a European Insurance Fund like that of the Federal Deposit Insurance Corporation (FDIC). The main reason is the non-separability principle mentioned earlier. In the steady-state regime, the three pillars of BU are not separable from each other. In the USA, which is more of an example than of a model, the FDIC is also deeply involved in the resolution of banks by addressing bank failures through mergers and acquisitions. In November 2015 the European Commission released a proposal in order to establish a European Deposit Insurance Scheme (EDIS, see IP/15/6051)[1] in three successive steps. (1) The reinsurance phase (2017–2018–2019): deposit insurance remains national and the European Deposit Insurance Fund (EDIF) will intervene as an insurer of last resort vis-à-vis the national Deposit Guarantee Schemes (DGSs). During this period EDIS may provide limited funding. (2) The coinsurance phase (2020 up to 2023 included) during which there will be a pragmatic division of labour between EDIF and the national DGSs. Coinsurance means that when necessary pay-outs would be shared between national DGSs and EDIF. (3) As of 2024 a fully integrated deposit insurance scheme, EDIF becoming therefore a FDIC-like European Insurance Fund with some important idiosyncracies when compared to the US case. Such an ambitious blueprint for Pillar 3 of BU still faces many uncertainties. In particular the Germans remain strongly opposed to the European Commission's proposal and timetable. Therefore we cannot take for granted that a compromise is going to be easily and quickly accepted for Pillar 3.

5.6   Other Structural Issues

5.6.1   The Ins and the Outs

It has been very clearly stated that the BU is also open to member states which are not in the eurozone. Some member states such as Poland seem to be interested to join whereas the UK, even before Brexit, and Sweden are very likely to stay

---

[1] http://ec.europa.eu/finance/general-policy/banking-union/european-deposit-insurance-scheme/index_en.htm.

outside. Jörg Asmussen (2013), then member of the Executive Board of the ECB, pointed out that the BU is "critical for the ins and desirable for the outs." If they join, the outs would participate on equal terms as euro countries to ensure a level playing field between the ins and the outs. They would also participate in the governance of the BU in a way which yet remains to be determined. Conversely, owing to the non-separability principle, the BU is a "package." It is not possible to be a member of one or two pillars without accepting the other(s). Hüttl and Schoenmaker (2016) have underlined that out countries could profit from joining BU, which is "a stable arrangement for managing financial stability." However, from a practical viewpoint, we must acknowledge that it would be uneasy and complex in terms of management and governance for a country to participate in BU without being a member of the euro area.

5.6.2 The Separation of Bank Activities

The crisis has opened a contentious debate on banking activities and whether it is necessary for the supervisory authorities to implement some "Chinese walls" between some of them. In the USA the Dodd–Frank Act and in particular the Volcker Rule (2010) took the option of a "soft" separation between banks and hedge funds. It is "soft" since this reregulation of banking activities in the USA is much less ambitious than the Glass–Steagall Act (1933). In Europe, the Vickers report in the UK and the Liikanen Group mandated by the Commission went further in their recommendations by advocating a strong separation between commercial banking and trading activities. This regulatory requirement is parallel to the transition to a BU, but they are not independent from each other and they will interact, since the structure of the banking industry conditions the way supervision, resolution and deposit insurance could be implemented.

The justification for bank separation is open for debate. At the start, the subprime crisis was very classical: the outburst of a real estate bubble. It had nothing to do with proprietary trading. Implementing the separation will be complex. On the one hand, separation between commercial banking and trading addresses two major challenges. (1) Time inconsistency: banking is long term while trading is short term. (2) The distribution of risks, which raises several problems such as transparency, traceability, risk shifting. On the other hand, however, banking and trading are so intimately connected that a full separation is not warranted. It is not always easy to separate market making from proprietary trading. Given the development of new forms of investment banking, regulators must be very pragmatic when implementing some separation of bank activities With one form or another of separation, where will the risks be allocated? What is the best place to manage them? To ask those questions is not a way to condemn separation but is an appeal for more academic research and more empirical (and historical) studies.

The debate about separation is still not over in Europe. Some member states (e.g. France) have taken regulatory initiatives even before the Liikanen Report was out. We have to avoid any significant discrepancies across countries in the implementation of the proposals in the Liikanen Report. Otherwise, there will be no level playing field, which is a core objective of the single market and one of the goals of BU.

5.6.3 CMU and the Financing of the Real Economy

In Europe as in many other areas, we are entering a new phase of disintermediation: less bank financing and more non-bank financing, which could be either market-based financing or fund-based financing. Beside markets and banks, it is useful to make more explicit the role of funds such as alternative investment funds (private equity, hedge funds, money markets funds, real estate funds, etc.) regulated in the EU under the AIFM directive. This new disintermediation will be induced by many factors including the impact of Basel III on the willingness of banks to lend to risky borrowers such as most small and medium-sized enterprises (SMEs). It will generate winners and losers, and it is very likely that many SMEs could belong to the losers group by facing bank credit rationing. Were it the case, a serious challenge for public policy would arise since in most EU and euro area countries SMEs and intermediate-sized firms are crucial for growth and job creation.

The prospect of changing financial structures has given the background for the launching of an action plan on building a CMU by the European Commission in the autumn of 2015 (COM(2015) 468).[2] Whereas BU primarily concerns the euro area, CMU applies to all EU countries, but not the UK after the Brexit takes place. There is still today a big gap between the very ambitious goals of CMU and the lack of a concrete and credible roadmap for such a project. The goals of CMU are clear and widely acceptable: (1) to boost investment, growth and employment; (2) to reduce financial fragmentation and deepen the single market for financial services; (3) to get more integrated, efficient and competitive financial markets. In this

---

[2] http://ec.europa.eu/finance/capital-markets-union/.

search for financial competitiveness, the action plan takes US capital markets as a reference to be replicated by European markets regarding their depth, liquidity and resilience.

The actions envisaged to reach such goals are numerous. The list deals with many items and persistent challenges: (1) to attract more SMEs on stock markets in order to facilitate their financing and growth; (2) to boost the rebound in private equity funding; (3) to speed up the development of securitization in light of the crisis that securitization had to face since 2007–2008, by promoting STS ("simple, transparent and standardized") vehicles possibly at the European level (see Daphné Héant et al., Chap. 16, this volume); (4) to promote the growth of crowdfunding in Europe; (5) to update some financial regulations such as the Prospectus directive. The list of actions given here is partial, but it is sufficient to understand that most actions are intended to boost non-bank financing (market or fund financing) tailored in particular to SMEs and intermediate-sized firms. CMU intends to make the new disintermediation phase which has just started sustainable and possibly positive for those firms. It has also to be analysed in connection with the implementation of the Juncker plan even if the time horizon of the two actions is different: three years initially for the Juncker plan (mid-2015/mid-2018) and an infinite horizon for CMU provided that it is actually implemented.

Will CMU be effective and succeed? It is clearly too early to have a definite answer. But we could already raise an incomplete list of issues. (1) The timetable of CMU is still too vague and not binding enough. (2) Concerning the canonical debate why SMEs are reluctant to go to stock markets, we know the long list of arguments put forward both by SMEs and by investors. But the action plan does not propose really new ways to overcome such structural difficulties. (3) Who is going to put the STS label on some securitization vehicles? ESMA or national financial regulators or independent rating agencies either already in place or to be created for such a business? If we want to get a true European market for securitization vehicles it would require a European STS label. (4) We have no European regulation for crowdfunding yet. Since Internet has no borders, if we want to reach a true level playing field for crowdfunding within the single market, we would need some specific EU regulation at some point in the future. (5) CMU means more intra-European harmonization regarding corporate law (e.g. bankruptcy rules) and corporate taxation. For reasons which are more political than technical we are very far from such a move. (6) Does CMU, like BU, entail more centralization of financial markets regulation at the European level? This topic is today somewhat taboo, but we can take it for granted that it will emerge as soon as CMU is made effective. Clearly ESMA could be a natural candidate for such a role.

5.7   Concluding Remarks

The main challenge of the ongoing reregulation process both at the world level and in Europe is the following: how to strengthen the banking and financial sector and to contain systemic risks without jeopardizing the financing of the real economy, growth and employment. An application of this general consideration is the transition from Basel II to Basel III and possibly to the controversial Basel IV and its implications for investment and growth. What is at stake is the good calibration of the new prudential rules. In the spring of 2016 and for the first time, the European Commission has recognized that the calibration challenge could be essential. It has already accepted some relaxation as regards Solvency II by reducing capital requirement for insurance companies when they finance infrastructure. This marginal evolution was necessary to make some prudential rules consistent with the concrete implementation of the Juncker plan's goals and means. For banks, the Basel Supervision Committee and thereafter the European Commission adjusted in early 2013 the definition of the LCR (liquidity coverage ratio) in a direction more favourable to bank financing. Possible adjustments in the long-term liquidity ratio (NSFR, or net stable funding ratio) could occur in the short term. The debate about the optimal calibration of the new prudential rules is going to stay there for long. Everyone including the European authorities has to be pragmatic in the search for a better balance between the main objectives of financial reregulation, financial stability on the one hand and the warranted financing of the real economy on the other.

In any case the business model of banks is likely to change with the capping of bank maturity mismatch generated by the conjunction of the two liquidity ratios. The impact of Basel III on the quantity and quality of bank financing is critical for European economies which are mostly "bank-based"(the UK being a "market-based" financial system, which is an exception in Europe). Since we cannot assume that market financing or private equity or more generally alternative investment funds will automatically substitute for bank financing if it becomes one way or another more selective and scarce, the capability of Europe to rebound in terms of investment, growth and job creation is at stake. We must not forget either that the implementation of the new prudential rules at the world level could generate a non-cooperative game (some countries staying apart from the new rules), which could lead us very far from the ideal configuration of a true level playing field.

At present, Europe is the "low pressure" zone in the world economy, posting low growth and high global and youth unemployment. By itself BU will not solve the challenges of the real economy; but it is an opportunity not only to improve the resilience of European finance but also to think and to act together for the long term, in a period of quasi-general myopia. BU is much more than a purely technical project, much more than the addition of integrated supervision, resolution and deposit insurance. It is one of the few political economy perspectives that we have in common today. It deserves a strong commitment, discipline and continuity from policymakers at European and national level, notwithstanding essential electoral cycles.

References

Asmussen, J. (2013, November 8). *The public and the private banking union*. Berlin: Humboldt Universität.

BCBS. (2013, July 3). *Global systemically important banks: Updated assessment methodology and the higher loss absorbency requirement*. Downloaded from http://www.bis.org/publ/bcbs255.htm.

de Boissieu, C. (2013, December). *Towards banking union: A report*. Joint Research Centre (European Commission) and college of Europe (Bruges).

ECB. (2016). *List of supervised entities as of 1 Jan 2016*. Downloaded from: https://www.bankingsupervision.europa.eu/banking/list/who/html/index.en.html.

Goyal, R., Brooks, P., Pradhan, M., Tressel, T., Dell'Ariccia, G., Leckow, R., Pazarbasioglu, C., & an IMF Staff Team. (2013). A banking union for the Euro area. *IMF staff discussion note*.

Hüttl, R., & Schoenmaker, D. (2016, February). Should the "outs" join the European banking union? *Bruegel Policy Contribution*.

JC. (2014, September 22). *Joint committee report on risks and vulnerabilities in the EU financial system*. JC 2014 063. Downloaded from http://www.eba.europa.eu.

Micossi, S., Bruzzone, G., & Carmassi, J. (2013, November 21). The new European framework for managing bank crises. *CEPS Policy Brief, 304*.

Pagano, A., Cariboni, J., & Giudici, P. (2012). SYMBOL model database and analyses for public finance sustainability. *JRC Technical Report*. JRC 77925. doi:10.2788/75033.

Schoenmaker, D. (2011). The financial trilemma. *Economic Letters, 111*, 57–59 (Duisenberg School of Finance – Tinbergen Institute discussion papers no. TI 11-019 / DSF 7). Available at SSRN: http://ssrn.com/abstract=1340395 or http://dx.doi.org/10.2139/ssrn.1340395.

Schoenmaker, D., & Véron, N. (Eds.). (2016). *European banking supervision: The first eighteen months*. Brussels: Bruegel Institute.

Tinbergen, J. (1954). *Centralization and decentralization in economic policy*. Amsterdam: North-Holland.

Véron, N. (2016, February 16). *European deposit insurance: A response to Ludger Schuknecht*. bruegel.org blog.

Part II

Supervision of Financial Entities

6

Regulatory Capture in Financial Supervision

Mathilde Poulain

On November 2014, the Banking Subcommittee on Financial Institutions and Consumer Protection of the Senate was asked to determine whether the US Federal Reserve was being "too cosy" with the industry it oversees. Suspicions were raised by one of its former examiners, Carmen Segarra. Indeed, a few weeks before Carmen Segarra had claimed she was "silenced" by her line managers during her supervision of Goldman Sachs.[1] She discovered in 2011 an important failure in Goldman Sachs conflict of interests policy and wanted to report her statement, but her Fed superiors pressured her to alter her report and her refusal cost her career.[2] The President of the Federal Reserve Bank of New York, William C. Dudley, who before taking office in the central bank was a Goldman Sachs economist, has been called to testify before the American Senate.

Three years before, the report of the Financial Crisis Inquiry Commission concluded that capture was one of the reasons leading to the financial crisis.[3] It created a favourable environment for the relaxation of the regulatory

---

[1] *The Guardian*, Carmen Segarra, the whistleblower of Wall Street, 5 October 2014 http://www.theguardian.com/commentisfree/2014/oct/05/carmen-segarra-whistleblower-wall-street-federal-reserve.

[2] NY Times Dealbook, Suit Revives Goldman Conflict Issue, 10 October 2013.

[3] The FCIC has been mandated to examine the causes of the financial crisis. A report was published in 2011.

M. Poulain (✉)
LabEx RéFi and CES, Université Paris 1 Panthéon-Sorbonne, Paris, France

© The Author(s) 2017
R. Douady et al. (eds.), *Financial Regulation in the EU*,
DOI 10.1007/978-3-319-44287-7_6

burden (Pagliari 2012) and hence allowed for excessive risk-taking by private institutions. Associated with lax supervision, all the necessary conditions were met to trigger a financial crisis. Hence, this hearing constitutes a beginning of awareness of the importance of capture in financial supervision.

Capture can touch on all the levels of public decision-making and action: government, parliament and even sometimes the scientific expertise that advises them. Hence, public decisions that "entails benefits or costs to groups that are likely to be involved in political lobbying" (Bénassy-Quéré et al. 2010) have been delegated to independent regulatory agencies (IRAs).[4] However, recent events tend to indicate that these independent agencies are not any less susceptible than the legislator to being influenced by special interests. Therefore, are financial supervisors protected from regulatory capture?

To answer this question, in Sect. 6.1 I first define the concept of capture as a departure of regulation and supervision from the general interest with respect to two subgroups: materialist and non-materialist capture. In Sect. 6.2 I then explain its normalization among supervisors with three processes derived from the literature on organizational behaviours: institutionalization, rationalization and socialization. In Sect. 6.3, I assess whether financial supervisors are from now on insulated from the influence of the financial industry. Finally, I attempt to explain the reason for financial supervisors' failure to prevent capture.

6.1   The Concept of Capture

At all times, industries have tried to protect and promote special interests. Their behaviour is completely rational: they apply pressures on the regulatory bodies in order to influence the decision-making process. Nevertheless, the industry should not have a disproportionate impact on this process.

Stigler (1971) observes that regulation is mostly designed for the benefit of the supervised sector. Hence, the industry has acquired a persistent and immoderate influence that disturbs the original balance of interests (Baxter 2011). Sometimes, the supervisor follows the prescription of the regulated industry and loses sight of the general interests. In this case, he is *captured* by the industry he regulates.

Since Stigler's definition, other types of capture have been highlighted by the literature. They can be gathered into two main groups: materialist capture and non materialist capture (Freeman Engstrom 2012). In both forms of

---

[4] It is, for instance, the case for the supervision of the pharmaceutical, nuclear or finance industries.

capture, the industry succeeds in influencing the regulatory and supervisory process at the expense of the general public.

The two concepts are based on polar assumptions regarding the supervisor's rationality. In materialist capture, the supervisor purposely favours the industry's interest over the general public's, while in non-materialist capture he ends up confusing or assimilating the industry's interest with the public's interest.

6.1.1 Materialist Capture

Materialist capture refers to the traditional form of capture that mostly figures in the seminal works. Stigler (1971) analyses the regulation of trucks in the USA, where in order to obtain lenient legislation the industry pays for the votes and resources a political party needs. Tirole (1986) and Laffont and Tirole (1991) introduce a model where the asymmetry of information creates an incentive to the industry in bribing the regulator to convince him not to tell the government the real situation regarding its costs (Dal Bó 2006). Martimort (1999) adds to the previous model Congress' response to the threat of capture. Less and less discretionary power is left at the agency but increased bureaucratization tends to decrease the agency's efficiency. Finally, Albino et al. (2013) formalize the interaction between firms and regulators and explicitly account for their mutual influence, thereby proving the incentive for collusion.

In materialist capture, the regulator is perfectly aware of the fact that he is harming general interests. He is confronted by a tradeoff between his own private interest or his regulator's duties. Thus, he takes into account selfish objectives such as personal enrichment (corruption and bribery), carrier concern (recruitment in higher paying jobs in the regulated industry, campaign contributions) or whether the IRA's funds depend on the supervised industry. Hence, materialist captures is also related to the literature on corruption and on revolving doors.

A structural problem, the asymmetric stakes among interest groups, allows "some interests to systematically win out over others" (Freeman Engstrom 2012). The financial industry has a stake in influencing regulation and supervision because it directly affects its profits. The industry is concentrated and well organized. Thus, it is tempted to influence its supervisors. The consumer group faces the well-known collective action problem (Olson 1965). Its diffuse nature and the resulting organizational problems prevent consumers from trying to influence regulation. In the light of the cost–benefit arbitrage, the profit from influencing the supervisor is not worth the costs incurred. There is an "asymmetry of stakes among interest groups" (Freeman Engstrom 2012).

To influence decisions, the financial industry offers personal benefits to the self-interested supervisor against a favourable regulation (Tai 2015). Such exchange of favours is only made possible because both sides are perfectly rational and have a positive incentive in shaping regulation toward special interests. As a result, the regulator favours industry interests over the general interest. Such a theory is therefore related to the rent-seeking and the government failure theories developed by public choice.

- Rent-seeking theory is defined as a situation where an individual, a company or an organization attempts to obtain economic gain from others without reciprocally creating wealth for society.
- Government failure theory analyses "the behaviour of governments under the assumption that all relevant agents pursue their self-interest" (Le Grand 1991). The main outcome is that government decision-making creates inefficiency and inequity.

6.1.2 Non-Materialist Capture

Non-materialist capture appeared more recently in the literature. It is a process of "colonization of ideas" (Freeman Engstrom 2012) that leads a supervisor to share the views of the regulated industry (Veltrop and de Haan 2014; Tai 2015). Unlike materialist capture, the regulator acts with the general interest in mind, and even the most well-intentioned supervisor would be captured. Non-materialist capture convinces him that making a pro-industry decision will be beneficial for everyone. It acts as a veil clouding the regulator's vision until he loses sight of the ultimate goal of the regulation (Benink and Schmidt 2004). Non-materialist capture does not derive from the government failure theory. On industry's part, the wish to influence a regulation stays unchanged.

* Information capture
  Any regulatory agency depends on the information provided by the regulated industry (Bagley 2010). This structural dependence creates de facto an asymmetry of information, where the regulated industry has an informational monopoly.
  This asymmetry of information is not particular to the regulation of finance. Any regulatory agency in charge of overseeing an industry is subjected to

this gap in information. According to Pagliari (2012), "'capture' is more likely when regulation is highly complex, and when information asymmetries between the regulated industry and the regulators are greater." Both are characteristics of financial regulation and supervision.

- Quantity of information
  Wagner (2010) explains how the industry captures the American Congress with an excessive use of information. As part of the rule-making process, legislators must proceed to public hearings and are "required by law to consider all the input received."[5] The regulated industry submerges the Congress with an extraordinary amount of information in order to overwhelm the legislators and attempt to brainwash the legislator as regards the industry's motives and intentions. Furthermore, "as the issues grow more numerous and technical, less well-financed interest groups find it hard to continue participating in the process" (Wagner 2010). Such a "machine-gun effect" associated with an asymmetrical participation between stakeholders leads to less pluralism and hence pro industry regulations.

  Such information capture, happening at legislator level, is likely to occur at the supervisory level of independent agencies. For matters such as enforcement and interpretation of the legislation, financial supervisors often proceed to hearings and other stakeholder consultations. As part of the supervisors' duty, these prescriptions ensure the agency is held accountable for its actions.

  It is particularly the case when the discussed matter highly technical or when it takes place within a period of legislative inflation. The financial industry has expertise and knowledge of the issues and thus benefits from the "effectiveness of comment" in the decision-making process (Baxter 2011). Pagliari (2012) argues that investors, deposit holders and other consumers of financial services "face greater challenges in coordinating and in mobilizing the organizational and informational resources required to compete with the financial industry groups in the marketplace for influencing regulation." As a result, the agency does not perceive the alternative views owing to the lack of representativeness and fundings of the stakeholders holding them. The interpretation of the "empowering legislation" is distorted (Baxter 2011).

---

[5] 5 U.S.C. § 553(c).

  – Quality of information

    Information capture may also occur through the use of highly sophisticated information. Hakenes and Schnabel (2015) argue that the financial industry captures the regulator through the use of highly complex information. The regulator is therefore unable to understand the argument of the industry owing to his lack of expertise. He does not have "the means or ability to review that information skeptically" (Bagley 2010). Instead of admitting his weakness, the regulator acts as if he understands the argument of the financial industry. He rubber-stamps banks even though regulation would be desirable from a social perspective.

    Two reasons prevent the unsophisticated regulator from admitting his shortcomings. First, he is concerned about his reputation and does not want to signal his lack of expertise. Second, he may be more easily convinced and shortchanged by the financial industry's *scientific* argument. Regarding the issue of capital requirements, Hellwig (2010) argues that "the regulatory community was so impressed with the sophistication of recently developed techniques of risk assessment and risk management of banks that they lost sight of the fact that the sophistication of risk modeling does not eliminate the governance problem which results from the discrepancy between the private interests of the bank's managers and the public interest in financial stability." Thus, by increasing the sophistication of the information, the industry raises the information gap and is more likely to convince a proud regulator.

• Intellectual capture
  Intellectual capture gathers several subdefinitions of non-materialist captures: cultural capture (Kwak 2013), social capture (Davidoff 2010), cognitive capture (Buiter 2008) and deep capture (Baxter 2011). Although named differently, their definitions are quite similar. They mostly refer to the regulator's education, background, experience, networks and other social interactions that tend to create an overall proindustry paradigm.

  Three mechanisms help to explain how intellectual capture occurs: identity, status and relationships (Kwak 2013).

  – *Identity*: "Regulators are more likely to adopt positions advanced by people whom they perceive as being in their in-group." This perception may be because the regulator used to work for the financial industry or because he works a lot with bankers and socially interacts with them.

- *Status*: "Regulators are more likely to adopt positions advanced by people whom they perceive to be of higher status in social, economic, intellectual, or other terms." The financial industry's representation in media and art may be at the root of this explanation. Although discredited after the last financial crisis, the financial industry used to be associated with success and popularity.
- *Relationships*: "Regulators are more likely to adopt positions advanced by people who are in their social networks." A regulators might know a lot of financial workers because of his education, past experience and so on.

The result of these three mechanisms is that the supervisor *identifies* with the industry. It is a process through which the arguments of the financial industry appear to the supervisor more legitimate and trustworthy. However, it is not because he does not understand the arguments. The supervisor is more familiar with the financial industry's concerns. He has internalized the objectives and interests of the financial industry. He understands the norms and values of the sector. He values the financial industry's work. Hence, the supervisor is more receptive when the argument comes from the financial industry.

In addition, identification also has an impact on the supervisors' perception of consumer advocates and other NGOs. They belong to a rival group that is not trusted. Their arguments appear less credible or even fallacious.

Despite this identification with the financial industry, working as a supervisor should also create another social identification. Identifying with the regulatory framework should contradict the identification with the financial industry and reduce its negative impacts on regulation and supervision (Dal Bó 2006). Nevertheless, regulatory agencies lack a strong institutional identity and a professional credibility. This prevents supervisors from developing a sense of belonging among the supervisors (Veltrop and de Haan 2014).

6.2   The Normalization of Capture

In the previous section, I define capture with a microlevel perspective. But capture is considered as one of the causes leading to the financial crisis. A microfounded phenomenon would not lead to such macrolevel consequences. Thus, capture spread like wildfire into the regulatory framework and created a totally uncontrollable chain reaction. How do we move from a captured regulator to generalized capture?

6.2.1 Institutionalization

Institutionalization is a process through which an isolated practice is banalized and becomes common practice in an agency (Ashforth and Anand 2003). Standardizing conduct leads to two outcomes. A normalization process rises a doubtful practice to the rank of a norm and an adaptation process impairs the regulator's awareness of the inappropriateness of his behaviour. Either way, bad practice becomes part of the day-to-day work.

The institutionalization process is reinforced by two factors. A "permissive ethical climate" leads to a *laissez-faire* approach where no one in the institution really cares about ethics and integrity. A weak leadership, which has internalized these poor practices, sends a negative signal to the institution as a whole. For instance in financial supervision, revolving doors have been totally institutionalized. The practice of hiring a banker for a regulatory position is nowadays as widespread in Europe as it is in Northern America. It may be both because of a weak ethical environment and because this is common practice among senior supervisors.

6.2.1.1 Rationalization

Rationalization is a process through which captured supervisors tend to legitimate their act. As corrupt persons do not view themselves as corrupt (Ashforth and Anand 2003), captured supervisors may not see themselves as captured. By rationalizing, supervisors deny the impact of capture on their decisions.

Ashforth and Anand (2003) highlight eight arguments used by decision-makers to rationalize corruption. Some of these arguments can be transposed to intellectual capture (Poulain 2016):

- the legality argument, "if it is not forbidden, it is not an issue," concerns all practices that are not yet legislated, such as the prior tenure of supervisor in the financial industry. The absence of legislation acts as a proof of the harmless nature of their behaviour. To justify their action, they can argue that one cannot criticize supervisors for the absence of a rule.
- the rationalization of ideologies tends to reconcile the general interest with the financial industry's interest by negating all the negative interpretation of a regulator's act. For instance, the argument of force used to justify revolving doors is often the need for expertise within the regulatory agencies. Another example is how a softer regulation is explained by the fact that tough supervision may hinder economic growth by weakening banks' profitability.

- The denial of injury consists, for the regulator, in denying that his act may have decreased the well-being or the utility of the general public. In the case of financial regulation, this argument appears quite useful as the impact of intellectual capture is pretty hard to assess (Kwak 2013).
- The denial of responsibility occurs when a supervisor argues that he had no other choice because of "circumstances beyond [his] control such as management orders, peer pressure, dire financial straits, being deceived, existing precedent, that everyone else does it" (Ashforth and Anand 2003).
- Refocusing attention is defined for intellectual capture quite differently from in the case of corruption. This argument consists in moving the object of discord to another issue. For instance, Villeroy de Galhau, the former banker recently named as the head of the Banque de France, attempted to prove his integrity and independence to the general public by getting rid of all his financial interests. Hence, by focusing the attention to financial interests, the original debate has shifted and intellectual capture has been totally forgotten.

6.2.2 Socialization

Socialization is the process that ends the cycle of normalization. It refers to the transmission of practices to newcomers. Hence, as institutionalization occurs at the macrolevel, socialization means internalizing practices at microlevel. In other words, it makes you learn how not to think outside the box.

The socialization process is effective when it combines two facts:

- The new recruit shall be sensitive to the practices. The institution (here the agency) chooses individuals that are familiar with these practices (through previous experience, organizations, networks). Hence, these new recruits are already *pre-socialized.*
- The newcomers shall be conventional rather than rebellious. Cressey (1986) argues that "White-collar criminals … should be viewed as conformists rather than as deviants."[6] Although used to explain the spread of corruption, conformism constitutes a good explanation for the normalization of the practices inducing non-materialist capture.

This socialization is even stronger and faster if top-level management teaches newcomers these new "rules." In addition to bond and affiliate with the senior

---

[6] Cressey quotes in Ashforth and Anand (2003).

members, they are also likely to identify with them, as they represent the hierarchy and with it success. Indeed, Zey-Ferrell et al. (1979) conclude that "perceptions of peers' behavior had a greater impact than the respondents' *own* beliefs about what constituted ethical behavior" (Ashforth and Anand 2003). This is also the conclusion of Kwak (2013):[7] "When senior New York Fed officials want their staff to go easy on Goldman Sachs they don't even need to lift a finger. The institutional culture takes care of it for them."

6.3   Are Financial Supervisors Insulated from Capture?

It is not possible to work on the psychological or sociological aspect of capture. Nor it is possible to expect the financial industry to "give up the fight." It is part of the supervisory game. Setting proper governance practices that ensure the institution's soundness and the supervisor's ethical behaviour is the remaining possibility. But how far are we from this goal?

6.3.1 Materialist Capture

Materialist captures occur when the industry offers personal benefits to acquire the supervisor's leniency. Such positive incentives are typically of two types: personal enrichment or carrier concerns.

- Personal enrichment
- Exchanging monetary favours for political support is illegal in most countries. Corruption and bribery are not allowed and are punished with all severity. In Europe, the anti-corruption package aims at implementing "a stronger monitoring and a proper implementation of existing legal instruments." In addition, the Commission "foresees a wide range of EU-level actions to adequately tackle corruption."[8] At international level, some policies such as the OECD Anti-Bribery Convention or the United Nations Convention against Corruption have been set up and are ratified by countries on a voluntary basis.

---

[7] Kwak, 30 September 2014, How not to regulate, *The Atlantic*. http://www.theatlantic.com/business/archive/2014/09/how-not-to-regulate/380919/.

[8] The European Commission, DG Migration and Home Affairs http://ec.europa.eu/dgs/home-affairs/what-we-do/policies/organized-crime-and-human-trafficking/corruption/index_en.htm.

- Regarding gifts and hospitality from interest groups, some restrictions (and even prohibition) are applied in most IRAs. For instance, the European Central Bank Guidelines lay down some ethical principles concerning this area. Notably, members of the Eurosystem central banks and their staff members are forbidden from "soliciting, receiving or accepting a promise related to receiving for themselves or any other person any advantage connected in any way with the performance of their official duties."[9]
- Campaign contributions or donations from industry to political campaigns are either forbidden or highly restricted. This is for instance the case in the USA with the Political Action Committee (PAC) system. When an interest group wants to get involved in the political process, it creates a PAC. This organization collects and receives money from the members of the interest groups and provides financial support to political campaigns. These PACs are submitted to several restrictions on the level of donation per candidate, political party and even election. Private firms and trustees cannot donate to PACs.
- Carrier concerns
- The prospect of higher paid employment may be considered as a supervisor's carrier concern. According to Pagliari (2012), "regulatory authorities often find in the firms they regulate and supervise the most common source of future employment." Worker flows from the public sector to the private sector constitute part of the revolving door issue. They may be governed either by a cooling-off period that forbids the former regulator to directly seek employment in the financial industry after termination of duties or a permanent ban. The severity of the rule depends on the seniority of the supervisor. These prescriptions are, for instance, set up at the US Security and Exchange Commission. However, these policies are still not sufficient. Between 2001 and 2013, the practice among financial institutions of hiring former employees of one of six US regulatory agencies increased by 18–55 % (Shive and Forster 2016).
- Although worthy of criticism, policies governing materialist capture are partially set-up. The existence of these prescriptions testifies that there is some beginning of recognition of the issue. However, there is still space for the improvement of regulation of regulators' post-employment.

---

[9] Guidelines (EU) 2015/[XX*] of the European Central Bank of 12 March 2015, Chapter IV Rules on the acceptance of gift and hospitality, Article 10 Prohibition on receiving advantages https://www.ecb.europa.eu/ecb/legal/pdf/en_ecb_2015_11__signed_r_f.pdf.

6.3.2 Non-Materialist Capture

The current legislation hardly controls the risk of non-materialist capture. Excessive social interactions may be conducted through three channels. First, the supervisory agency may want to hire a former banker. Second, the supervisory agency may organize hearings and a consultation process to benefit from financial institutions' expertise and information. Finally, the agency may be granted with advisory commissions that are composed of representatives of the financial sector.

Again, the worker flow from the private to the public sector remains unregulated (Poulain 2016). The only prescriptions set the basic requirements regarding the regulator's needed qualification. For instance in the USA, the Revolving Door Ban states that the regulator's recruitment shall be based on the "qualification, competence, and experience" of individuals.[10] Consequently, a growing number of supervisors come from the financial industry. In 2009, the OECD examined the revolving doors for a set of IRAs across eight countries. Apart from one supervisor (i.e. Iceland), all IRAs have recruited their senior employees from the financial industry.

Regarding public hearings and the consultation process, a control of the symmetrical participation of the stakeholders is never provided (Poulain 2016). The survey conducted by Pagliari and Young shows that "less than 10% of the stakeholders who respond to financial regulatory consultations belong to trade unions, consumer protection groups, non-governmental organizations, or research institutions." The financial industry lobby is well endowed. To lobby in the European Union, the financial sector employs around 1,700 lobbyists gathered into 700 organizations (Corporate Europe Observatory 2014). It is five times more than the NGOs, trade unions and consumer organizations.

Almost all the financial supervisors are granted advisory commissions and a scientific committee (Poulain 2016). However, their composition is never regulated. A recent report from Corporate Europe Observatory (2014) indicates similar results for the European Commission, where "70% of all advisors in [...] expert groups had direct ties with financial industry." Furthermore, the OECD (2015) concludes that "undue influence on the policy-making processes by vested interests is a persistent risk due to loopholes such as unbalanced representation of interests in government advisory groups."

Denial of this issue still exists, so it is not yet part of the public debate. In the absence of "the mere recognition of the possibility of self-interest on the

---

[10] An executive order signed by President Obama in January 2009.

part of regulators" (Boot and Thakor 1993), the likelihood of any change occurring is low. This capture is highly profitable for the industry: "No one has to be paid off, no one has to break the law, and no one asks too many questions" (Kwak 2013).[11]

6.4 The Limits of the Concept of Capture

Financial supervisors benefit from policies that insulate them from materialist capture. But the absence of prescriptions regarding non-materialist capture questions both the independence and the technocratic nature of supervisory agencies. Both constitute the pillars that supposedly motivated the creation of these institutions. Why did we let non-materialist capture reach the regulatory agencies?

While efforts have been made to prevent materialist capture in financial supervision, policies for insulating supervisors from non-materialist capture are struggling to emerge. Part of the issue lays in the difficulty in defining non-materialist capture.

When dealing with materialist capture, identifying the wrong practices and proving their existence is quite easy. It may be an exchange of favours, a monetary transfer, a recruitment. It is a tangible reality that no one can deny. Regarding the non-materialist version, either you prove the existence of an information/expertise gap between the supervisor and the industry or you demonstrate that a supervisor has identified with the industry. In both cases, the demonstration is obviously highly complex, time-consuming and even costly.

Measuring supervisory outcomes is extremely difficult. To assess the effectiveness of a regulation, one must know what the general interest is. Hence, if the regulation improves the general interest, then it is efficient and beneficial. And there is the rub. No one is actually able to define the notion of general interest. In addition, Freeman Engstrom (2012) argues that "virtually any policy position can be framed as furthering the public interest."

Finally, there exists no tangible proof of the link between poor regulatory outcomes and the presence of capture. The demonstration of this consists of enumerating a list of scandals and other regulatory failures that occur at individual level (such as the last Fed scandal with Carmen Segarra). Besides, a lot of external factors such as adverse economic conditions may be the

---

[11] Kwak, 30 September 2014, How not to regulate, *The Atlantic*. http://www.theatlantic.com/business/archive/2014/09/how-not-to-regulate/380919/.

source of regulatory or supervisory failures. Freeman Engstrom (2012) states that "arguments about capture necessarily turn on a difficult counterfactual inquiry about what public-interested regulation would look like in capture's absence."

6.5   Concluding Remarks

Financial regulators are still struggling with regulatory capture. Although materialist capture is starting to be overseen, non-materialist capture remains ungoverned. The regulatory dilemma and the difficulty in defining non-materialist capture may be part of the explanation for the poor arrangements that have been made to control this form of capture.

These past decades, we have surreptitiously given rise to the idea that the supervisor and the financial industry belong to the same side. An individual's belief in the institution can be much more powerful than written laws that reduce the risk of intellectual capture. If everyone has the conviction that the supervisor cannot be captured, then undue influence is less likely to occur. As stated by Freeman Engstrom (2012), "ideas can become self-fulfilling prophecies [...], it is common to hear that the administrative state is bad or that too much policy gets made by a runaway or captured bureaucracy. This rhetoric has a big effect. It degrades our faith in government. It undermines civic trust."

Hence, beyond the improvement of financial regulators' governance practices, there is a need for the creation of a strong institution that is never challenged by the general public or by the financial industry. It is about bringing about a culture of regulation.

References

Albino, D., Hu, A., & Bar-Yam, Y. (2013). *Corporations and regulators, the game of influence in regulatory capture*. Working Paper.

Ashforth, B., & Anand, V. (2003). The normalization of corruption in organizations. *Research in Organizational Behavior, 25*, 1–52.

Bagley, N. (2010). *Agency hygiene, Texas Law Review*. See also (Vol. 8, p. 1). University of Michigan Public Law Working Paper No. 224.

Baxter, L. (2011). Capture in financial regulation, can we channel it toward common good? *Cornell Journal of Law and Public Policy, 21*, 175–200.

Benassy-Quere, A., Coeure, B., Jacquet, P., & Pisani-Ferry, J. (2010). *Political economy: Theory and practice*. New York: Oxford University Press.

Benink, A., & Schimdt, H. (2004). Europe's single market for financial services: Views by the European shadow financial regulatory committee. *Journal of Financial Stability, 1*(2), 157–198.

Boot, & Thakor. (1993). Self-interested bank regulation. *The American Economic Review, 83*(2), 206–212.

Buiter, W. (2008). Lessons from the North Atlantic financial crisis. *The First Global Financial Crisis of the 21st Century*, 129.

Corporate Europe Observatory. (2014, April). *The fire power of the financial lobby*. Published by Corporate Europe Observatory (CEO), The Austrian Federal Chamber of Labour (Arbeiterkammer) and The Austrian Trade Union Federation (ÖGB).

Cressey, D. R. (1986). Why managers commit fraud. *Australian and New Zealand Journal of Criminology, 19*, 195–209.

Dal Bó, E. (2006). Regulatory capture: A review. *Oxford Review of Economic Policy, 22*(2).

Davidoff, S. M. (2010, June 11). *The government's elite and regulatory capture*. New York Times (2:00 PM).

Freeman Engrstrom, D. (2012). Corralling capture. *Harvard Journal of Law & Public Policy, 36*(1), 31–39.

Hakenes, H., & Schnabel, I. (2015). *Regulatory capture by sophistication*. Working Paper.

Hellwig, M. (2010). Capital regulation after the crisis: Business as usual? *CESifo DICE Report, 8*(2), 40–46.

Kwak, J. (2013). Cultural capture and the financial crisis. In D. Carpenter & D. Moss (Eds.), *Preventing capture: Special interest influence in legislation, and how to limit it*. Cambridge: Cambridge University Press, 71–98.

Laffont, J.-J., & Tirole, J. (1991). The politics of government decision making. *The Quarterly Journal of Economics, 56*, 1087–1127.

Le Grand, J. (1991). The theory of government failure. *British Journal of Political Science, 21*(04), 423–442.

Martimort, D. (1999). The life cycle of regulatory agencies: Dynamic capture and transaction costs. *Review of Economic Studies, 66*, 929–947.

OECD. (2015). *Government at a glance 2015*. Paris: OECD Publishing.

Olson, M. (1965). *The logic of collective action*. Cambridge, MA: Harvard University Press.

Pagliari, S. (2012). How can we mitigate capture in financial regulation? In Pagliari (Ed.), *Making good financial regulation. Towards a policy response to regulatory capture*. Guildford: Grosvenor House Publishing Ltd.

Poulain, M. (2016). *Are financial regulators insulated from regulatory capture*. Working paper.

Shive, S. A., & Forster, M. M. (2016). The revolving door for financial regulators. *Review of Finance*, rfw035.

Stigler, G. (1971). The theory of economic regulation. *The Bell Journal of Economics and Management Science, 2*(1), 3–21.

Tai, L. (2015). *Regulatory capture and quality*. Edmond J. Safra Research Lab Working Papers No. 66.

Tirole, J. (1986). Hierarchies and bureaucracies: On the role of collusion in organizations. *Journal of Law, Economics and Organization, 2*(2), 181–214.

Veltrop, & de Haan. (2014). *I just cannot get you out of my head, regulatory capture of financial sector supervisors*. DNB Working Paper No. 410.

Wagner, W. (2010). Administrative law, filter failure, and information capture. *Duke Law Journal, 59*(7), 1321–1432.

Zey-Ferrell, M., Weaver, K. M., & Ferrell, O. C. (1979). Predicting unethical behavior among marketing practitioners. *Human Relations, 32*, 557–569.

7

The Challenges of Regulation of Derivatives

Nasser Saber

7.1 Introduction

It is commonplace that to act is to act in the confines of the given conditions. That is another way of saying that to act one must *know* the conditions, or "what the shot is." The American colloquial expression captures the implied exigency and hints at the dangers of failing to do so.

The "shot" for the markets regulator is the role of derivatives in global financial markets. According to the Bank for International Settlements, the outstanding notional amount of derivatives in 2015 was \$550 trillion.[1] That sum does not include *synthetic* derivatives, so it grossly—by a factor of many multiples—undercounts the size of capital earmarked for derivatives-type trading.[2] I have shown elsewhere that such capital is the *anima mundi* of

---

[1] http://www.bis.org/publ/otc_hy1511.pdf.

[2] The notional amount in derivatives does not exchange hands (except in currency swaps.) It is, rather, the reference point for the calculation of the payments.

Nasser Saber is the author of *Interest Rate Swaps* (Business One Irwin, 1993) and the three volumes of *Speculative Capital* (Financial Times). The fourth and final volume is due to be released in 2017. He holds a master's degree in engineering from Case Western Reserve University and an MBA in quantitative analysis and finance from NYU.

N. Saber (✉)
New York, NY, USA

R. Douady et al. (eds.), *Financial Regulation in the EU*,
DOI 10.1007/978-3-319-44287-7_7

financial markets. What that means is the subject of the current chapter. We prescribe no policy here, only an adequate description of the conditions that exist in the markets with a focus on derivatives. Knowing those conditions is the prerequisite for regulation. An adequate explanation is an explanation in full. It accounts for the market dynamics in a precise manner, permits of no inconsistencies, and no future development will contradict it.

7.2   Structure of Derivatives

A derivative is a bet. That this bet is used in finance or that its outcome is determined with reference to the price of some security does not change the matter in the least.

A bet involves the realization of an event in the future. This definition applies to traditional commerce as well.[3] The maritime trade that gave rise to capitalism is entirely based on the forward delivery of goods, due when (and if) the ship arrived. The owners of the goods who needed money sold the bill of goods of as-yet-to-arrive merchandise in financial centres. Since there was always a risk of loss until the ship actually arrived, the buyers of the bills bought for less than full face value. Hence discount bills were born, one of the early securities.

A discount bill is a security because it represents a claim on *existing* merchandise. In agriculture, by contrast, a forward contract to deliver, say, wheat pertains to wheat that does not yet exist. That is why the contract to deliver it— unlike the *existing* goods travelling on a ship—is not a security but a derivative.

Independent farmers used derivatives to hedge their harvest.[4] A wheat farmer, for example, could enter into a forward contract to deliver wheat at, say, $1 a bushel. If by the time of harvest the price fell, he was guaranteed the $1 contract price.[5] On the other hand, by locking the price he would have to forego the benefit of any price appreciation above $1.20. That is how hedging works: it stabilizes the price in *either* direction.

But if there was no commodity to deliver, that is, *nothing to be owned yet*, speculators could also pretend to be farmers, i.e., mimic farmers' actions. They, too, could sell the commodities forward, hoping that by delivery time the prices would increase. Farmers had mixed feelings about the intrusion of speculators in "their" market. On one hand, speculators provided additional buying and

---

[3] I use "traditional" to distinguish it from the Internet-based "on-demand" commerce and near spontaneous trading. We will return to these topics later.

[4] Only independent farmers, that is, those without protection of landowners, were exposed to risk. Serfs and the European farmers working on the estate were "free" of such concerns. That is why the first organized attempts to regulate derivatives began in the USA.

[5] We will introduce counterparty default risk later in the chapter.

selling opportunities which meant more liquidity. But precisely for that reason, they could also create price volatility that damaged the farmers. We see this tension between the producers and speculators as early as the early twentieth-century USA in the rise of bucket shops and attempts to regulate them.

Bucket shops were the nascent form of present day exchanges and clearing houses. They connected buyers and sellers of forwards and earned a profit from the spreads.

The early capitalists who started the bucket shops did not grasp the impor-tance of capital—and if they did, they had no means to account for it.[6] Taking their chances, they lost not infrequently; if the market volatility was low so was the capital base of the bucket shops, so even small price changes led to their ruin. In the free-wheeling nineteenth-century USA such ruins in specu-lative markets carried little reputational risk.[7] When a bucket shop failed, its owner started a new one across the town. But farmers lost money. That is how "bucket shops" acquired their name and a pejorative connotation.[8] Bucket shops "bucketed", that is, *discarded*, the trade tickets because they had no intention of delivering the underlying commodity. But that was true of all exchanges and clearing houses, including the Chicago Board of Trade (CBT) and the Chicago Mercantile Exchange (CME), the two largest bucket shops, which thrived because they were well capitalized.

Under the pressure of farmers and populist politicians, the states passed bucket shop laws that forbade offering forward contracts without the abil-ity and intent to deliver. But the practical difficulties of the law—making a distinction between who had the intent to deliver and who did not—proved insurmountable. The two exchanges claimed that *their* trading reduced the price risk of commodities by offering hedging facilities to farmers. The bucket shops, by contrast, were interested in the price changes and speculation. Bucket shops disagreed. In 1912, the dispute reached the Supreme Court via *Board of Trade v. Christie.*[9]

The BOT sued Christie, a bucket shop, to prevent it from using the Board's price quotes. Christie claimed that the BOT was itself a bucket shop. The Court disagreed. Writing for the Court, Chief Justice Holmes said:

---

[6] We saw similar naiveté in the late twentieth and early twenty-first century in the USA, with regard to ecommerce. Taking e-retailing giant Amazon as the role model, thousands of individuals and families began selling books from their living rooms, only to shut down after much effort and expense.

[7] That is also true of the modern day USA. At the time of his successful presidential campaign in 2016, the Republican frontrunner, Donald Trump, has taken his companies to bankruptcy on at least four dif-ferent occasions.

[8] It is significant that unlike stock "boiler rooms" that were conceived as scams, the bucket shops were mostly genuine businesses, albeit with a deficient model.

[9] 198 US at 236.

Purchase made with the understanding that the contract will be settled by paying the difference between the contract and the market price … stands on a different ground from purchases made merely with the expectation that they will be satisfied with the offset.[10]

Note the Justices' struggle to distinguish between trading and speculation by talking of "different ground." The implication was that there was an opposition between "good and beneficial" trading and "bad" speculation. But such moralizations could not resolve the issue and the question of trade versus speculation, why one deserved support and the other censure, remained. As the uncertainty posed legal risk to the exchanges, they lobbied Congress, which passed the Futures Trading Act (FTA) in 1921. The Act mandated that all "contracts for future delivery" be traded in official, licensed exchanges. Over-the-counter forwards were banned.[11]

That is where things remained for half a century.

7.3   Collapse of Bretton Woods and the Rise of Hedging

The collapse of the Bretton Woods system of fixed exchange rates in 1971 threw currency relations into chaos and exposed multinational companies to new risks.

Take a corporation like IBM and assume it had a contract with a Japanese customer to deliver computers for ¥3 billion in three months. At the current exchange rate of $1 = ¥300, that translated to $10 million which included a $1 million built-in profit. If in the interim the yen weakened to $1 = ¥330, the contract price of ¥3 billion would be worth $9 million, wiping out the profit.[12] This was intolerable. The multinationals pressed their banks for a solution. The banks, taking a page from the old playbook of farmers, came up with hedging.

Take an international bank such as J.P. Morgan with long standing relations with leading industrial companies such as IBM and General Motors. Let us assume that GM, too, had negotiated to purchase land in Japan for a car assembly plant. The contract was expected to be signed in a few months for the agreed upon price of ¥3 billion. With the prevailing exchange rate that translated to $10 million. If in the interim the yen were to strengthen to

---

[10] Ibid.

[11] That is the historical background of the difference between a forward and a futures contract. A futures contract is a forward that is transacted in an exchange.

[12] ¥3 billion: 330 = $9 million.

say, $1 = ¥270, the land price would rise to $11 million. GM, too, wanted to protect itself against this eventuality. So it, too, went to J.P. Morgan for advice.

By placing itself in the middle, the bank could help both clients. From the diagram of the funds flow below, the solution is self-suggesting.

The bank entered into a contract to buy ¥3 billion from IBM for $10 million in three months. It also entered into a contract to sell ¥3 billion to GM for $10 million in three months. On the delivery date, IBM received ¥3 billion from its customer, which it paid to J.P. Morgan, which then passed it to GM. In return, the bank received $10 million from GM, which it paid IBM in exchange for the ¥3 billion it had received.

Superficially, that is, out of context, the arrangement resembles a bucket shop transaction: the Japanese yen is wheat, IBM is the farmer, GM the industrial food processor and the bank the bucket shop operator. But the same arrangement—a series of interlinked transactions—when adopted by speculative capital that was rising from the ashes of the Bretton Woods system, became the blueprint of the modern world, the key to its understanding.

7.4   Transformation of Hedging into Arbitrage

Speculative capital is capital engaged in arbitrage. It is the latest form in the evolution of capital that has come to dominate the financial markets in the twenty-first century.[13]

The genesis of speculative capital, like any other form of capital, is buying low and selling high; no one has yet invented another way of making money. Historically, the difference between the purchase and sales price was a function of space and/or time: to realize profit, commodities had to be either transported from one location to another or hoarded from one time to the next.[14]

But making a profit was never certain. Commodities could perish while being transported—or be stolen or confiscated. The borrowers could die, go broke or flee. And there was the ever-present risk that the price could drop for economic, natural or social reasons. As all these events took place in time, the early capitalists—they were merchants, traders and usurers before the rise of industrial capital—came to see time as the source of risk. The longer the

---

[13] The meaning of "dominate" will become clear in forthcoming pages. Briefly, it means that price changes in the financial markets are shaped by dynamics of speculative capital.

[14] This is not to say that space or time are the source of profit. We are distinguishing two modes of commerce without concerning ourselves with the source of profit. That the physical transportation of commodities also took time is a point that does not concern us here.

time between the purchase and sale, the greater the risk. Conversely, if by some magic one could buy a commodity and *simultaneously* sell it for a profit one could realize *riskless* profit. That was the Holy Grail of finance that had to remain in the realm of dreams until the collapse of the Bretton Woods system produced the conditions for its realization.

The Bretton Woods system was a regime of fixed exchange rates created by the governments; the exchange rate of $1 = ¥360 that held immediately in the post-war years between the US dollar and Japanese yen was a matter of agreement between the governments of the USA and Japan. Governments stabilize rates through decree.

The collapse of the system meant that governments washed their hands of exchange rates. Into the vacuum stepped private finance. Private finance stabilizes rates through arbitrage. Let us return to Fig. 7.1 and elaborate this point.

First, notice that what we have are private parties signed into private contracts. Yet the overall effect of the agreements is to isolate them from their economic "eco system." No matter how volatile the USD–JPY exchange rate, that is, no matter what happens in the "world," IBM and GM will exchange USD and JPY at the rate of $1 = 300¥. That is *hedging*, which insulates the companies' assets against market fluctuations. Setting aside counterparty default risk for now, IBM and GM have eliminated exchange rate risk.

As the middle man, J.P. Morgan faces no risk either, as it merely collects and forwards the payments to the main parties. In fact, strictly speaking, IBM and GM do not need the bank; they could have dealt with one another directly, *if they knew* of one another's need. That is exactly what "FinTech," the

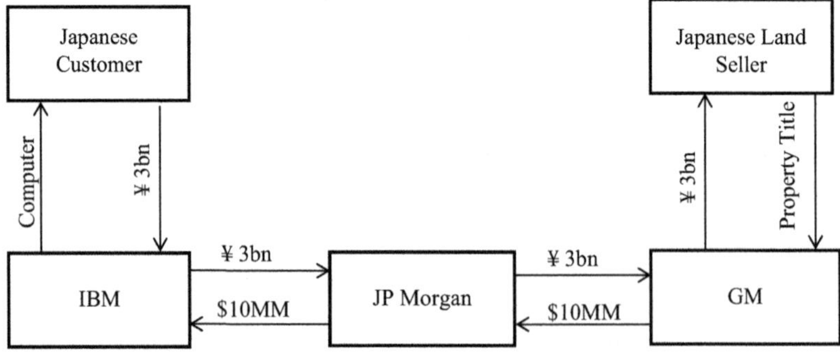

Fig. 7.1 Back-to-back transactions creating a currency hedge

technology driven financial app industry backed by venture capital, is aiming at: it wants to "disrupt" the business model of the bank intermediaries.[15]

But in the 1970s only the international banks with corporate contacts could arrange such multiparty deals. Naturally, they charged for their service either directly or, more commonly, by taking a "cut" from the deal by buying yens slightly cheaper from IBM and selling them slightly more expensively to GM.

The difference in buy–sell prices established the bid-offered "spreads." But recall that these were private deals. J.P. Morgan's USD–JPY spreads were different from those of Citibank or Credit Lyonnais. As these prices were posted in the shared interbank networks, traders took notice of arbitrage opportunities.

Now suppose a trader saw the following prices between the USD, JPY and Deutschmark (DEM)

$$1\,USD = 2.25\,DEM$$

$$1\,DEM = 150\,JPY$$

$$1\,USD = 330\,JPY$$

The trader could buy 2.25 MM DEM for $1MM USD and sell marks for 337.5MM JPY and pay that to buy $1,022,700 for a profit of about $22,700. The buying and selling was done through the phone so orders rapidly followed one another. This near simultaneous profitable buying and selling is arbitrage. Arbitrage means *simultaneously* buying low and selling high for a *riskless profit*. Capital earmarked for arbitrage is speculative capital.

Figure 7.2 shows the flows of funds in our example. Note the critical changes that have taken place compared to Fig. 7.1. The industrial corpora-

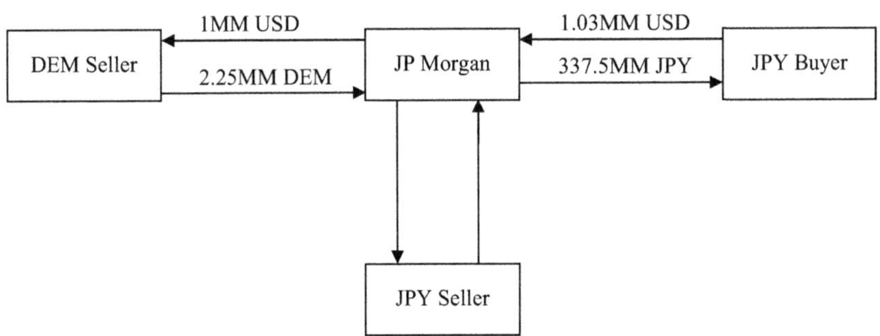

Fig. 7.2   USD–JPY arbitrage flow

---

[15] That is one of the focus areas of FinTech, albeit an important one.

tions are gone. What began as a service to bank clients is now currency transactions between generic buyers and sellers. Absent corporations, there can be no talk of their hedging needs. Indeed, there is nothing to hedge. Hedging is transformed into arbitrage.

The importance of this point is easy to miss, so let us develop it more methodically. The accounting equation is the place to start:

$$A = L + OE \tag{7.1}$$

In Eq. 7.1 A is assets, L is liabilities and OE is owners' equity. If an entity has $100 (A), either all of it is borrowed (L), or all of it belongs to the owner (OE), or, as is always the case for a corporation, a mix of the two, say L = $90 and OE = $10.

The objective of hedging is to insulate the capital against market fluctuations. That would be the owners' capital, OE. Rewriting Eq. 7.1 with respect to it, we get:

$$OE = A - L \tag{7.2}$$

In hedging, OE must remain constant "no matter what happens in the world." That is another way of saying that its value must not change. Denoting the change by Δ, we can express this condition mathematically as follows:

$$\Delta OE = 0 \tag{7.3}$$

If the left-hand side of Eq. 7.2 is to remain unchanged, its right-hand side must remain unchanged:

$$\Delta A - \Delta L = 0$$

Or:

$$\Delta A = \Delta L \tag{7.4}$$

Equation 7.4 is the condition of *hedge*. It states that for the equity of the entrepreneur to be preserved, the change in assets must equal the change in liabilities—or assets and liabilities must *match*.

That is also the condition of *arbitrage*. In the example above, J.P. Morgan successively converted

1) $1MM USD to 2.25MM DEM
2) 2.25MM DEM to 337.5MM JPY
3) 337.5 JPY to 1.022MM USD

In each stage, *equivalents* were exchanged so the bank had no risk. Yet, at the end, it earned a profit of $22,700. That is profit without exposure, or *riskless profit*, which is the driver as well as the condition of arbitrage.

To summarize, comparing hedging and arbitrage, hedging is matching assets and liabilities to insulate the *existing* capital. It is a defensive and conservative strategy.

Arbitrage is matching assets and liabilities to wangle a profit from "inefficiencies." An arbitrageur has neither an asset nor a liability. He looks for *any two positions* whose purchase and sale would create a profit for him. Arbitrage is an aggressive and predatory strategy.

After the fact, it is impossible to tell hedging from arbitrage; one only sees an asset matched by a liability, a long position matched by a short position. What conceptually separates the two is the *raison d'être* of the trades reflected in their order of execution. If the trades are sequential—an *existing* position is followed by another—the operation is hedging. If the trades are simultaneous, it is arbitrage.

In practice, the line between the two is easily crossed, hence the endless confusion about the "propriety" of the transactions after losses and wondering what went wrong in a conservative strategy.[16]

Since the difference between hedging and arbitrage is closely linked to their purpose and, from there, to the user, it would seem that one could draw a distinction between them by focusing on users. That is what the *Christie* Court tried to do but failed. The US Congress, as we saw, gave up trying and forbade non-regulated derivatives trading altogether.

More than a century later, the European Commission took the same track. Since there could be no talk of forbidding derivatives in the twenty-first century, the Commission went in a roundabout way, by increasing capital requirements for the use of derivatives. But unlike the US Congress which had earlier accommodated the farmers it made no exemption for the modern-day hedgers, the industrial user of derivatives. The result was an outcry from them:

---

[16] Such examples are legion. Here is J.P. Morgan's CEO, Jamie Dimon, talking about the $6 billion losses the bank suffered in the 'London Whale" incident (originally reported to be $2 billion): "I can't justify it. Unfortunately, these mistakes were self-inflicted." Mr Dimon added: "What this hedge morphed into violates our own principles." *DoJ probes JPMorgan's $2bn* loss, *Financial Times*, 16 May 2012, p. 1. Notice the words "self-inflicted" and "morph" the executive is using, without fully realizing their significance.

Ford, IBM, Airbus, BP and General Electric are among dozens of global businesses that have sharply criticised Europe's rules for the use of derivatives, claiming they unfairly push up costs for companies "that did not cause the financial crisis" … More than 40 institutions have written to policymakers at the European Commission urging them to rewrite the rules to be more like those in the US, which exempt non-financial corporations from some of the more onerous requirements.[17]

"Non-financial corporations" above is a byword for corporations that use derivatives for hedging. In light of their influence in Western capitals there is little doubt that the Commission will relax its rules. So it would seem that the regulation of derivatives could be bifurcated along the hedging-speculation divides. But the modern-day regulator of derivatives faces a far more complex challenge because the shell of derivatives is now claimed by the most potent force in the markets: speculative capital.

7.5   Speculative Capital

The subject of finance is not people. It is capital in circulation. The mind arrives at that conclusion through the compulsion of its reasoning as it moves from arbitrageur as a person to capital as a thing.

An arbitrageur's motive for trading is riskless profit. It goes without saying that to place the trade or write the algorithms, the arbitrageur acts as a person. But he cannot employ his capital in a development project in an emerging market or some long-term infrastructure project. If he does, he *ceases* to be an arbitrageur. An arbitrageur *must* employ capital in arbitrage trades. In consequence, he becomes an "agent" of capital, someone who must conform to capital's *modus operandi*. Capital then becomes the grammatical subject of the sentence as if it were alive: *capital* seeks arbitrage opportunities. Such capital is speculative capital. It is impossible to understand either the real life or theoretical developments in finance in the past 40 years without knowing speculative capital, its properties and the effects of its operations on markets. I have examined them in detail elsewhere. We briefly review them here as the prelude to the regulation of derivatives.

---

[17] *Global businesses urge Brussels to rewrite rules governing derivatives*, *Financial Times*, 28 January 2016, p. 13.

7.6   Characteristics of Speculative Capital

Arbitrage opportunities cannot exist in the open. Such situations would imply an infinite supply of fools on the receiving end of arbitrage who buy high and sell low. Arbitrage opportunities, rather, must be discovered. In Fig. 7.2, in addition to access to information, the bank trader must have some basic mathematical skills to unearth the hidden USD–JPY profit opportunity that passes through the USD–DEM intermediation. From there arises the need for mathematicians—later the "quants" and "rocket scientists"—who were recruited into finance in the rising era of speculative capital in the 1980s.

Precisely because arbitrage opportunities could appear at any time and anywhere, the manager of speculative capital must have the freedom to act quickly. He cannot operate with the traditional mutual funds bylaws which tie him to a particular strategy—say, value investing or growth. Hence the need for a legal structure that would give the investment officer *carte blanche* to invest in any form and fashion as he sees fit. These are hedge funds. They are the legal/organizational form that speculative capital assumes in the market.[18]

In terms of its main characteristics, speculative capital is, first and foremost, self-destructive: it eliminates the arbitrage opportunities that give rise to it. Buying low and selling high increases the price of what was low and decreases the price of what was high, creating a condition of "equilibrium" between the two.[19]

A system in equilibrium is a dead system.[20] Meanwhile, speculative capital is self-destructive by virtue of its *modus operandi* but it is not suicidal. Quite the contrary. It turns markets, societies and laws upside down to survive. So, after an arbitrage opportunity is grazed, it moves to the next.

---

[18] There was always bemusement as to why these aggressive investment vehicles were called *hedge* funds. Having studied the transformation of hedging to arbitrage, we know the answer. Nor were hedge funds the only legal/organizational structure under which speculative capital operated. "Propriety trading" under which large banks' in-house speculative capital operated was another. Its size eclipsed the size of hedge funds by many multiples.

[19] Before the arbitrage opportunity is eliminated, spreads begin to narrow. To compensate for the falling profit speculative capital increases its size, further accelerating the erosion of spreads.

[20] The idea of equilibrium appeals to a finance professor who concocts an "efficient market theory" or the "law of one price" around it. In efficient markets, one cannot make riskless profit. Hence the tautological buzzwords of modern finance—risk management, riskless profit, efficient markets, and equilibrium prices—all of which refer to speculative capital which remains unrecognized.

Arbitrage pricing is relative-value pricing *par excellence*. It prices A by comparing it against the price of B and in doing so, "links" A and B and synchronizes their price movement. That destroys portfolio diversification, which assumes that asset prices move asynchronously.

What is more, speculative capital does not have a command and control centre. It is dispersed amongst all the hedge funds and high-frequency trading desks and all arbitrage-seeking strategies in the world. The managers of these capitals use the same pricing sources and employ similar mathematical and algorithmic skills. So, when an arbitrage opportunity opens up, they all rush in. "Rushing in" is necessary because opportunities are short lived and the fastest arbitrageur will get the lion's share of profits.

Rushing in results in overshooting the target; what was overpriced becomes underpriced, and vice versa. The result is an increase in volatility that is transferred from one market to another. Market volatility, ironically, is the side effect of the attempts of speculative capital to restore equilibrium to the markets.

In search of virgin opportunities, speculative capital pushes for laws that facilitate globalization and transparency. Globalization expands the universe of arbitrage opportunities. Transparency enables it to uncover those opportunities.

Speculative capital, however, is not invincible. Temporarily setting its self-destructive nature aside, two potential threats to it always loom on the horizon. One is internal and hits the profit directly. The other is external and works in a roundabout way, but its impact is no less real or pernicious.

The internal threat is the counterparty default risk. It exists by virtue of the nature of private transactions from which speculative capital is born. If the party to the arbitrage defaults, the arbitrage fails and speculative capital incurs loss. The riskless profit which defined arbitrage is not truly riskless unless counterparty default risk is resolved.

Then there is the external threat that is regulation. Unlike the law which is enacted by the legislature, regulation is issued by regulatory agencies. Compared to the law, regulation is more focused and directly hits the areas it targets. The result is that the wiggle room is reduced, which is why regulation is the bane of speculative capital. It interferes with speculative capital's free movement and, by doing so, impairs and disrupts it.

Speculative resolves both problems through derivatives.

7.7   Forwards and Forward-like Derivatives

Derivatives are the functional form that speculative capital assumes in the market; one who speaks of derivatives speaks of speculative capital. To explain, let us examine the form. All derivatives are either forward-like or option-like.[21] We begin with the simple forward.

Forward contracts, as we saw, appeared in relation with agriculture. Let us take a commodity such as wheat and assume it is selling at $1 per bushel. If we have a contract to deliver a bushel of wheat in three months at the price of $1.15, we have a forward contract, as shown in Fig. 7.3.

S is spot price and F is the forward price.

How is F determined?

In the early twentieth-century USA, the forward price was "discovered" in the negotiation between farmers, silo owners, food companies and speculators.[22] Each day these actors came into a consensus after considering everything from national politics to foreign wars and, of course, the weather,[23] as to what price the various commodities should be in three, four, five months. Each price was an estimate and could change during the day in response to new information. But it was an estimate nonetheless, more art than science.

In "modern finance," the forward price F, of any asset whose spot price is S, is determined by the following equation:

$$F = S + CC$$

CC is the cost of carry. It includes all costs—actual as well as opportunity loss—associated with carrying the asset into the delivery. If the spot price of an asset is $100 and one-year interest .5%, the one-year forward price would be $100.5:

$$F = 100 + 100 \text{x} .005 = 100.5$$

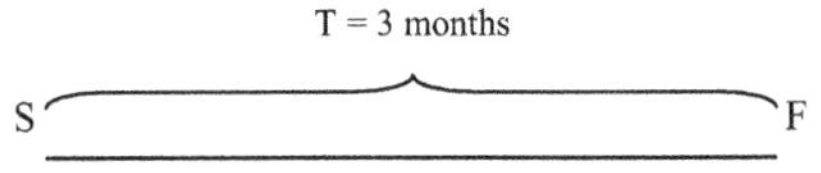

$$T = 3 \text{ months}$$

S ⌢⌢⌢⌢⌢⌢⌢⌢ F

Fig. 7.3 A forward time line

---

[21] Forward-like derivatives—forwards, futures, swaps—have no prepayment and theoretically unbound risk. Option-like derivatives have prepayments and limited risk. For ease of reference we will refer to them generically as forwards and options.

[22] FTA only banned the bucket shops. Speculation continued in the BOT and the CME.

[23] Hence the appearance of the famous "Farmers' Almanac" in the USA in the early nineteenth century.

The $.5 "cost of carry" in the above calculation arises from the opportunity cost of carrying the asset: if we had not purchased the asset we *could have* earned $.5 on our $100 with the prevailing rate. To make an investor "indifferent" between lending and purchasing the assets, the forward price of the asset must include that cost.

What happens if the forward price is *not* $100.5? In that case an arbitrageur could make a riskless profit.

- If the forward price is less, say $100, the arbitrageur could:

  (1) Buy forward at $100
  (2) Sell the asset short and place $100 at .5% with one year
  (3) At the end of the year, take the delivery of the asset (from 1) at $100, deliver it to satisfy the short position at (2) and keep the $.5 profit.

Buying forward and selling spot would increase the price of the forward and decrease the price of the spot, bringing them into the equilibrium, non-arbitrageable relation.

If the forward is more than $100.5, say, if it is $101, the arbitrageur could

(1) Sell forward at $101
(2) Borrow $100 and buy spot
(3) At delivery date, deliver the asset to satisfy forward, receive $101 (from 1), pay $100.5 towards the loan and its interest for a net profit of $.5

Selling forward and buying spot would restore the equilibrium.

The above reasoning, which is the basis of pricing of all derivatives, *presupposes* speculative capital: capital engaged in arbitrage.[24] Speculative capital is the mechanism that restores equilibrium to the markets.

A forward-like structure is too simple to be of practical use. Any discrepancy between the forward and spot prices would be detected and eliminated at once. That is why they are used almost exclusively for hedging. Vigilance of arbitrageurs ensures liquidity and tight bid/asked spreads.

---

[24] Arbitrage also "links" the debt and equity markets, producing the synchronizing we mentioned earlier.

Profitable arbitrage opportunities must be discovered as they lie hidden beneath the avalanche of data that is continually produced in financial markets. Speculative capital discovers them through option-like derivatives.

7.8   Options and Option-like Derivatives

All students of finance know of the Black–Scholes option valuation model. The problem of logically valuing options remained unsolved until in 1973 Robert Merton and, independently from him, Fischer Black and Myron Scholes produced a solution. In 1997 Merton and Scholes received the Nobel Memorial Prize in Economics for their discovery.[25]

The Black–Scholes formula has an imposing form. But that is because of the equation of stock price dynamics.[26] Otherwise the concept and the reasoning behind the valuation are simple. That a simple concept took more than a quarter of a century of work to be grasped—and was finally grasped in a misunderstood way, the way speculative capital operates—confirms what we stated earlier about the link between speculative capital and derivatives. Prior to the breakdown of the Bretton Woods system, speculative capital had not impressed itself sufficiently on the minds of traders and scholars for an option valuation formula to be possible.

We explain.

The Black–Scholes model begins with hedging, by creating a riskless portfolio of "Δ share of stock and one short call."

Assume the stock is trading at S = $100. We would like to price a one-year call option on this stock with the strike price of K = $100. At expiration, the asset price could be $105 or $95.[27]

A call option is a "right but not the obligation" to purchase the stock at the strike price. If the asset goes up to $105, the holder of the call who has the right to buy it at the strike price ($100) will make $5 profit. If the stock drops to $95, the holder would have no reason to pay $100 for an asset that is trading at $95. The option will expire worthless. Our problem is finding the value of this option.

---

[25] Fischer Black passed away in 1995.

[26] The Black–Scholes model is developed for options on stocks. It uses the equation of the stock price dynamics that was proposed in 1903 by Louis Bachelier. The success of the model was in no small part due to Bachelier's perceptive construct. See Nasser Saber, *Speculative Capital: Vol. 3 – The Enigma of Options*.

[27] This range constitutes the "volatility" of options. The calculation of volatility does not concern us here.

(1) We create a riskless portfolio with Δ shares of stock and 1 short call, C.[28] The value of this portfolio would be $100\Delta - C$. C is what we want to value.

(2) In 1 year, the stock price F, would be either \$105 or \$95.

  (i) F = \$105: The call option we have sold will be presented to us as demand for payment. The strike price of the call was \$100. With the stock price at \$105, the owner of the call will have the right to buy it for \$100, that is, \$5 cheaper than the market. Since we sold the call, we must bear the cost. The value of the portfolio would be $105\Delta - 5$.

  (ii) F = \$95: The call would expire worthless; the purchaser of the call option will not demand to buy the asset for \$100 if the asset is \$95. The value of the portfolio would be 95Δ.

These scenarios are shown in Fig. 7.4

(3) If the portfolio is riskless, its value must remain the same whether under condition (i) or (ii).[29] That is:

$$105\Delta - 5 = 95\Delta \Rightarrow \Delta = .5$$

(4) Substituting for Δ, the value of the original riskless portfolio would be $100 \times .5 - C$

(5) This value must remain unchanged at expiration:

$$100 \times .5 - C = 95 \times .5 = 105 \times .5 - 5 \Rightarrow C = \$2.5$$

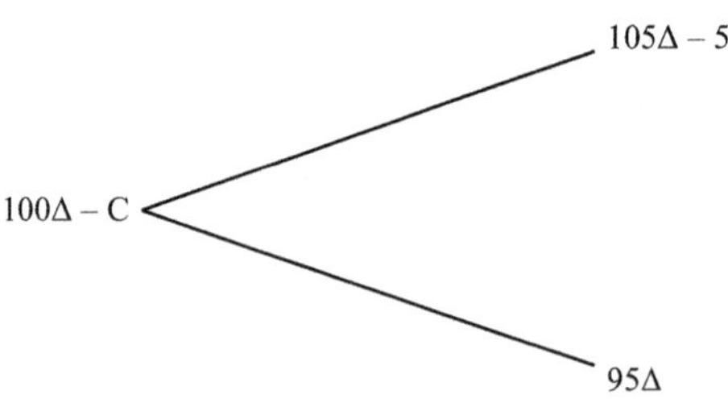

Fig. 7.4 Stock option pay-off

---

[28] Short call means that we have sold the call option (which we would like to value).

[29] The authors of the Black–Scholes equation reasoned that riskless portfolio must earn the riskless rate of return which they then associated with the yield of the US Treasuries.

Like the forward price we calculated, this call price is "rational" in the sense that it permits of no arbitrage. If the price is not $2.5 but, say, $3, an arbitrageur could sell the call at $3, and borrow $50 to buy .5 share of stock. The value of his portfolio is thus $100 \times .5 + 3 = \$53$. At expiration

(1) If F = $105
    He would deliver half a share of stock equal to $52.5 to the call and keep $.5 profit.
(2) If F = $95
    The call expires worthless. He sells half a share of the stock at $95 \times .5 = \$47.5$ and together with $3 from the sale of the call he returns the borrowed $50 for a profit of $.5

The driver of this way of option valuation is the *equivalent position*. The original portfolio of Δ shares of stock and one short call, $100\Delta - C$, is riskless because its value remains constant. That, recall from the condition of hedge in Eq. 7.4, can only happen if the change in the value of Δ share of stock and the change in the value of the call is the same. The call is valued from that equivalence.

An appropriately levered position in stock will replicate the future returns of a call. This is, if we buy shares and borrow against them in the right proportion, we can, in effect, duplicate a pure position in calls.[30]

In our example, .5 share of stock will earn $2.5 if the stock rises to $105; it will lose $2.5 if the stock falls to $95. That is exactly the call option's payoff. It will make $5 if the stock rises to $105, from which must be subtracted the call price of $2.5 for a total profit of $2.5. Otherwise, the option expires worthless and the initial $2.5 is lost.

That is how speculative capital operates, a process which the authors of Black–Scholes followed and uncomprehendingly copied.[31]

But beneath this procedural movement of speculative capital something deeper is going on. The clue to this is in the critical *leveraged* position. Why must the option valuation begin with a leveraged position? Why can we *not*

---

[30] John C. Cox, Mark Rubinstein, *Options Markets*, Prentice Hall, 1985, p. 167.

[31] The presence of interest rate further confused the authors of Black–Scholes. I have eliminated interest rate to: (1) conform to the current conditions; and (2) draw attention to the fact that that interest rate is an "exogenous" factor in option valuation, meaning that conceptually it has nothing whatsoever to do with it.

assume that the owner of the stock—someone who has already fully paid for it—is valuing the option?

Let us return to our forward contract and assume a mispricing that an arbitrageur wants to exploit. Recall that he has no position or equity. To buy the asset, he needs to borrow $100. So he goes to a lender. The following is an imaginary conversation between the arbitrageur (A) and the lender (L):

A: I would like to borrow $100 to buy a stock currently at $100. I will pledge the asset as the collateral for the loan.
L: Do you think that the stock will go up?
A: Yes. It will go up to $105.
L: Does the stock only go up? Can it drop to say, $95?
A: Yes, it can. But you and I would not care because I have shorted a forward on the stock with the strike price of $100. So no matter how low the asset drops, my counterparty *has* to buy it from me for $100.
L: Your forward counterpart is a *bucket shop*. Why would he buy the asset from you for $105 if the price has fallen to $95? And if you tell me the bucket shops no longer exist allow me to remind you of the carnage in the US housing market when the prices dropped below the outstanding mortgage: the borrowers just walked away.

At that point the conversation comes to a halt, the counterparty default risk being the central point of contention. That is what the US legislature in the early twentieth century tried to address by banning bucket shops and limiting derivatives to well-capitalized exchanges. And that is exactly what the European Union (EU) Commission attempted to do with its capital ruling on the use of derivatives.

After the crisis of 2008, the US legislators tightened the reins still further through the Volker Rule, which banned most propriety trading by banks, "proprietary trading" being a byword for (speculative capital driven) arbitrage trading. The reasoning was that banks should not expose "other people's money" to risky ventures.

Such banning is foreign to private finance. It is a diktat that is imposed from without, and like any "foreign" element it has the potential to disturb the environment sent to which it is introduced. Speculative capital solves the problem that arises out of finance using the tools of finance. Let us return to the conversation between the arbitrageur and the lender:

A: I have a way to address your concern. I will buy only half a share of the stock.

L: Some solution! In that case if the price goes down to $95 and your counterparty defaults, I will lose $2.5 instead of the previous $5. Your new solution reduces my loss but the fundamental problem of exposure remains, unless you have $2.5 to pay me in advance.

A: I do not. But I know how to get it. I will sell a call option for $2.5 to a gambler.

A: What is a call option and why would a gambler give you $2.5 for it?

A: Come and see.

Together they go to Gambler. Arbitrageur addresses him:

A: There is this stock trading at $100. I think it will go up in price. Would you like to share in its appreciation?

G: I would like to. But I don't have $100. And what happens if its price drops?

A: You don't need $100. All you need is $2.5. That sum will also take care of your concern re price drop. Here is how it works. The diagram below would help (Fig. 7.5):

Arbitrageur continues:

A: You bet on the price increase of the stock. It goes to $105, you make $5. Or more. The sky is the limit, really! Now you are concerned that the stock might drop to $95 in which case you would lose $5. But I will enter into a contract with you that if the stock drops, you could walk away without any obligation—no matter how far it drops, even to zero! All you need to pay for this all upside, no downside deal is $2.5.

G: How do I know that you could deliver on the "up" movement of the stock?

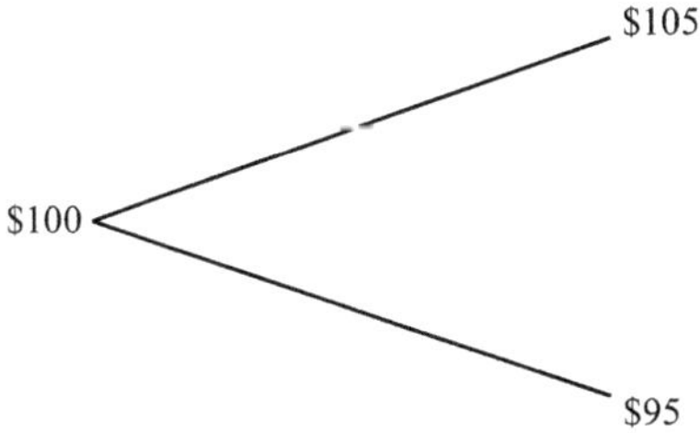

Fig. 7.5 Option outcome scenarios

A: Because I will have the stock. I am going to buy half a share of the stock. When the price increases from \$100 to \$105 it would result in a \$2.5 gain.

G: Where do you get the other \$2.5 to pay me \$5?

A: Why, that would be the \$2.5 that you are going to pay me in return for entering into this contract!

G: Does this contract have a name?

A: Yes. It is a call option.

The arbitrageur receives \$2.5 from the gambler for the call. He pledges it to the lender and receives \$50 from him with which he buys half a share of stock.

Note the position of the parties. The arbitrageur and lender are fully hedged. They have also eliminated the default risk, an ever-present risk in private contracts. For the lender, the loan is fully collateralized; for the borrower, the potential default is prepaid.

As for the option buyer, he is a bit player. He does not have enough money to invest in securities markets as capital demands a minimum size to be acquired. So he risks the meagre sum he has on a double or nothing bet that is the stock-in-trade of gamblers. More often than not, he loses.[32]

And yet he is a critical link in the circulation of speculative capital, which is why he is wooed, brought in and woven into the global network of capital markets.[33] Without the option buyer's money, the loan to purchase the stock would not be granted to the arbitrageur, meaning that arbitrage opportunities would go unexploited and the options could not be priced.[34]

7.9   Synthetic Derivatives

In creating the option structure, speculative capital scores two hits. We are forced to describe them sequentially but there is no "first" and "second," as they are intertwined and inseparable.

---

[32] "A former Blackstone Group managing director, Mr. Caspersen was well respected on Wall Street. [His] charmed life was thrown into turmoil [when] Federal prosecutors in Manhattan charged him in a criminal complaint with securities and wire fraud…[They] contend in a criminal complaint that Mr. Caspersen blew more than half of the \$25 million … on losing options in a personal brokerage account." "A Wall Street Family's Charmed Life Is Thrown Into Turmoil," *New York Times*, 6 April 2016, p. B1.

[33] In large-scale replication of options in financial markets that we about to discuss, speculative capital replaces the option player by putting down a small "equity" investment, the so-called skin in the game.

[34] The value of a call option increases with interest rates. Conversely, lowering rates makes call options cheap, which in turn fuels the expansion of speculative capital.

First, speculative capital makes itself impregnable through option structure. It can now confidently roam the global markets for arbitrage opportunities, having eliminated one scourge of private transactions, namely counterparty default risk. Little wonder that it creates this structure anywhere it can. Risk-parity, smart alpha, smart beta, exchange-traded funds, high-frequency trading:[35] these are the most recent names under which the synthetic structure is put to work. The extent to which speculative capital dominates the markets in that form is clear from the daily reporting of the financial press. A few examples should suffice:

Risk-parity
(1) The "systemic/technical investors" include risk parity funds and momentum investors known as CTAs. Initially commodity focused, they now invest across futures markets and are often computer driven. These investors, along with "smart beta" passive equity strategies that have become increasingly popular, adjust their exposures according to algorithms in response to market moves, meaning spikes in volatility can trigger a rash of automatic selling.[36]

(2) So-called risk parity is a next-generation passive strategy that seeks to give equity-like returns, while providing the relative stability of bonds in a crisis. Risk parity funds typically invest in a basket of stocks, bonds, and commodities, but "leverage" the traditionally safer fixed-income bets through derivatives to ensure each asset class contributes equally to a portfolio.[37]

(3) [Risk parity] is now a $400bn industry, and assuming an average 355 % leverage ratio—derived from the funds that issue public reports—it controls assets worth about $1.4 trillion. Even that figure is probably conservative, as it does not include in-house risk parity funds that have been established in some pension funds and insurers, which could easily bring the number up to $600 billion.[38]

---

[35] Speed in high-frequency trading is a technical aspect of the operation. The main point, the *way* to realize profit, is through establishing equivalent positions that are discovered through the algorithms: "Speed is proving to be little help to high-frequency traders as they battle stiff competition in a field now crowded by competitors … High frequency traders are instead turning their attention to developing strategies and computer algorithms that can carry out ultra-sophisticated arbitrage between asset classes, rather than darting in and out of market as fast as possible." "Super-fast traders feel heat from competition," *Financial Times*, 15 April 2011, p. 20.

[36] "'Systemic' trading comes under fire," *Financial Times*, 4 September 2015, p. 13.

[37] "'Risk parity' strategy blamed for fragile markets," *Financial Times*, 24 August 2015, p. 15.

[38] "Whatever the weather?," *Financial Times*, 24 August 2015, p. 8.

Exchange-Traded Funds (ETFs)

(1) ETFs were introduced only 25 years ago but now manage more than $3tn globally.[39]

(2) Many of the [exchange traded] funds are now "synthetic," relying on derivatives to deliver promised returns rather than holding the actual basket of goods as "physical" ETFs do. And despite the name, many exchange traded products change hands over the counter rather than on an exchange.[40]

(3) Synthetic ETFs, which use derivatives or structured products, have exploded; [they] account for 45 % of the market in Europe. And some ETFs are now using leverage; others are starting to purchase riskier assets such as risky loans.[41]

High Frequency Trading (HFT)

(1) Stock market: "[B]y any measure, HFT is a dominant component of the current market structure and likely to affect nearly all aspects of its performance."[42]

(2) Bond market: "More than $500bn in US Treasuries are traded daily and electronic trading accounts for 40 per cent of that, a number Nasdaq believes will increase. Nor is Nasdaq likely to stop at Treasuries. The group is planning geographical expansion, with new markets such as gilts, Japanese government bonds, repos and European sovereigns under consideration."[43]

(3) Currency market: "The gains are most visible in foreign exchange, where the global market share of high-frequency trading has soared to 40 per cent up from just a quarter in three years."[44]

(4) Commodities market: "The world's top sugar traders have attacked 'parasitic' computer traders, criticizing the New York-based exchange that hosts the main sugar futures contract for failing to clamp down on their activities."[45]

---

[39] "The index factor," *Financial Times*, 17 August 2015, p. 5.

[40] "Concern grows over 'synthetic' dangers," *Financial Times*, 5 October 2011, p. 23.

[41] "Why exchange-traded funds give uneasy sense of déjà vu," *Financial Times*, 6 May 2011, p. 20.

[42] https://www.sec.gov/marketstructure/research/hft_lit_review_march_2014.pdf.

[43] "Nasdaq sets stage for HFT in Treasuries," *Financial Times*, 5 April 2013, p. 22.

[44] "In search of fast buck," *Financial Times*, 20 February 2013, p. 7.

[45] "Sugar body blames 'parasitic' computer traders for volatility," *Financial Times*, 9 February 2011, p. 13.

Any farmer in 1910 would have understood the complaint of the sugar traders above, only that the "parasite" they complain about is no longer an tenuously solvent speculator but a force commanding trillions in euros, dollars, yens—what have you.[46]

Second, speculative capital uses derivatives to neutralize the external threat of regulation by performing a vanishing act. It shape-shifts from *product* to *strategy* and disappears in plain sight.

The derivative product form, you recall, was always tenuous; an option and a forward presuppose constantly arbitraging speculative capital to be priced. But this point was not adequately understood. Options, swaps, futures, captions—all were thought of, and presented as, products. The regulatory agencies claimed jurisdiction over them *as products.*

In its latest form, speculative capital goes a step further down the abstraction ladder. It decomposes the derivative structure to its constituent transactions—shorting Treasuries here, buying stock there—and executes them following a "strategy." To an outside observer these trades appear as innocuous, routine and unrelated.[47] There could be no talk of regulating them. Indeed, there is nothing to regulate. The booming business of index construction, for example, has little relation to derivatives. It revolves around creating the "best" index. That is, the most strongly correlated with a market segment and the cheapest to emulate index. The index is then used by the ETFs for arbitrage purpose.

Or take risk-parity, which is the age-old "60 percent stock, 40 percent bond" portfolio selection with only a change in the accent.[48]

It is only at the local command centre of speculative capital—a hedge fund, an asset management firm or a HFT shop—that the trades "come together" to form a de facto or *synthetic* derivative. This transformation of the product to strategy outmanoeuvres the regulator, a development which has not gone unnoticed:

The ban on proprietary trading ... has seemingly had a big impact since it was introduced in 2010. But are banks getting round this in part by dealing in

---

[46] Speed in HFT is a mere tool. The money is made not through speed per se but by exploiting the arbitrage opportunity: "High frequency traders are ... turning their attention to developing strategies and computer algorithms that can carry out ultra-sophisticated arbitrage between asset classes, rather than darting in and out of market as fast as possible." "Super-fast traders feel heat from competition," *Financial Times,* 15 April 2011, p. 20.

[47] The rivals can detect the strategy from the size of the trades. Hence, the rise of dark pools that protect the identity of the trader.

[48] Risk parity balances the portfolio with respect to the volatility of the asset classes as opposed to the traditional dollar value. Recall that volatility is one of the key attributes of options.

exchange-traded funds? … While the industry does not talk freely about its strategies, it is known that many revolve around index arbitrage, where traders exploit mispricing between ETFs and their underlying assets."[49]

The writer has the gist of the story right but it is not "banks"; it is speculative capital which resides increasingly in non-bank entities and, especially, these days, in asset managers that control trillions of dollars of individual investments including pensions.

Now it must be clear why we said speculative capital is the *anima mundi* of finance. It derives the innovation in finance and the technology serving it. It creates products, indexes and strategies and sees that they are implemented and used in serving its end. It links markets, products, securities and currencies through price relations that are transparent and fair; buyers and sellers would agree that they could not get any better prices. And it is efficiency-mad: it constantly drives down the bid/asked spreads to make trading in capital markets cheaper. These are the benefits of "modern financial markets" that finance professors teach without knowing their cause.[50]

This complex system is balanced on a razor's edge. The self-destructive tendency of speculative capital is ready to tip the balance any time and anywhere. The "mysterious" flash crashes that have plagued the US financial markets provide ample proof of that.

Treasury bond yield do not tumble 35 basis points in a few minutes every morning. There is no possible explanation for such a fall in the economic data that normally move the bond market, so yesterday's plunge in Treasury yield … suggests the market pathologies we grew to know during the crisis of 2008 are returning … Such a fall in such a liquid market implies someone, somewhere is under stress. Much like the "flash crash" of early 2010, which presaged a long period of volatility before the post-crisis rally resumed late the next year, it is a symptom of distress that cannot be ignored … The broader picture suggests the conventional wisdom is about to face a severe test. … There was no space in this world view for yield to fall, and certainly not to the 1.86 per cent level they briefly hit yesterday morning.[51]

---

[49] "Push-button perils: Why delta one is the new home of the exiled prop desk practitioners," *Financial Times*, 6 June 2011, p. 7.

[50] Market practitioners know more even if they cannot articulate. Here is the head of the Wall Street fixed income firm speaking about risk-parity: "It's a core structural change in the market place. Each investor is making a rational decision, but put them together and it has caused a dramatic change in markets. It has made the system more fragile." "'Risk parity' strategy blamed for fragile markets," *Financial Times*, 24 August 2015, p. 15.

[51] "Pathologies of crisis rise back to the surface," *Financial Times*, 16 October 2014, p. 1.

How speculative capital causes crashes is beyond our subject. The mechanics of the crash and whether it become a crisis is a function of many idiosyncratic factors.[52] The main point to note is that the much praised "efficiency" has two faces. On one hand, it ensures razor-thin spreads which is the good and the beneficial side that free-market supporters highlight.

But "in the most adequate and satisfactory tool, there is a hidden violence which is the reverse of its docility."[53] The efficiency also means that the margin of error is reduced, so that a small disturbance can trigger a crash—or a crisis. There, too, traders have noticed the vulnerability before the academics:

> The markets don't really need a Lehman or even Lehman-lite event for a credit dislocation," says [a hedge fund manager]. "You just need spreads to widen out or rates to go up for a significant impact on collateral movement for derivatives.[54]

Derivative products, *qua* products, are a small subset of this system. Nevertheless, because of the sensitivity of the system to outside stimulus, their regulation disturbs price relations. The protracted dispute between the USA and EU over derivatives regulated by the Commodities Futures Trading Commission that only recently led to an agreement is a case in point.[55] Each side claimed that an unfavourable collateral requirement made their derivatives more expensive, never mind that the dispute involved the relatively benign matter of minimizing default risk.

The effect is more pronounced when regulation targets the movement of speculative capital or bans it altogether, as in the Dodd–Frank Act and the Volker Rule. What results is a permanent dislocation of prices:

> Attention has focused on the sharp move in the spread between US Treasury yields and interest rate swaps … But it is not just US Treasury asset swap spreads that are behaving oddly. In foreign exchange markets, the so-called "cross-currency-basis" has rocketed. … Since the 2008 financial crisis, the difference between the theoretical and actual forward exchange rate, the "basis", has become more volatile. Recently, it has collapsed again. Credit and equity markets have

---

[52] See, for example, Nasser Saber, *The Upper Hand: Why Hedge Funds Lose Money*, Alpha, July/August 2007, pp. 40–46.

[53] Jean Paul Sartre, *Critique of Dialectical Reasoning*, p. 183.

[54] "Dangers to system from derivatives' new boom," *Financial Times*, 20 August 2014.

[55] "The two sides, which oversee about 90 per cent of the global derivatives market, had been unable to agree on common standards … The thrust of the agreement is that the EU will adjust some of its rules on the amount of margin customers must post at clearing houses, to bring its standards closer to those in the US. This will be doe through discussion among European regulators. In return the US will move towards the EU's more stringent standards on the amount of margin held by banks at clearing houses, most likely via changes to their rule book." "EU and US seal derivatives agreement," *Financial Times*, 11 February 2016, p. 22.

not been immune either. In both cases cash and derivatives markets have diverged, with the underlying cash assets cheapening significantly versus their related derivatives.[56]

Dislocated prices impact indices, and indices are the reference points for allocating trillions of investment capital. Their mispricing has serious implications for returns of investment portfolios and pensions alike. It is with consideration of all these matters that a derivatives regulator must act.

7.10 Conclusion

Highlighting the vulnerability of the financial system and its sensitivity to regulation is not a manifesto for laissez-faire or regulatory inaction. Quite the contrary. The vulnerability and sensitivity we discussed arise from the complexity of the markets: a dense web of interrelated segments kept in place by a self-destructive force whose incessant buying and selling is the condition of an equilibrium balanced on a razor's edge. Regulators approaching this complex web must do so with a firm theoretical grasp of the system. Only then will they be able to see what is happening, that is, what is changing and in what direction the changes are headed. That is the latest condition that arbitrage-driven speculative capital imposes on the markets: not only arbitrageurs but regulators, too, must recognize and adhere to the objective, mathematical relations that keeps markets in place. The days of regulation based on the "gut feelings" or moral considerations such as "prudence," "public good" or "common sense" are behind us.

References

Books

Cox, J. C., & Rubinstein, M. (1985). *Options markets* (p. 167). Englewood Cliffs: Prentice Hall.

Saber, N. (2006). *Speculative capital: Vol. 3 – The enigma of option.* SaberSystem.

Saber, N. (2007, July/August). *The upper hand: Why hedge funds lose money.* Alpha (pp. 40–46).

Sartre, J. P. (1976). *Critique of dialectical reasoning* (p. 183). London: NLB.

---

[56] "Real-world effects of mispriced derivatives too great to be ignored," *Financial Times*, 17 December 2015, p. 20.

Newspapers and Online

A Wall Street family's charmed life is thrown into turmoil. (2016, April 6). *New York Times*, p. B1.

Board of Trade v. Christie Grain & Stock Co. 198 U.S. 236. (1905). Justia US Supreme Court. https://supreme.justia.com/cases/federal/us/198/236/case.html

Concern grows over 'synthetic' dangers. (2011, October 5). *Financial Times*, p. 23.

Dangers to system from derivatives new boom. (2014, August 20). *Financial Times*.

DoJ probes JPMorgan's $2bn loss. (2012, May 16). *Financial Times*, p. 1.

Equity market structure literature review: Part II: High frequency trading. (2014, March 18). *US securities and exchange commission*, Staff of the divisions of trading and markets. https://www.sec.gov/marketstructure/research/hft_lit_review_march_2014.pdf

EU and US seal derivatives agreement. (2016, February 11). *Financial Times*, p. 22.

Global businesses urge Brussels to rewrite rules governing derivatives. (2016, January 28). *Financial Times*, p. 13.

In search of fast buck. (2013, February 20). *Financial Times*, p. 7

Nasdaq sets stage for HFT in treasuries. (2013, April 5). *Financial Times*, p. 22.

Pathologies of crisis rise back to the surface. (2014, October 16). *Financial Times*, p. 1

Push-button perils: Why delta one is the new home of the exiled prop desk practitioners. (2011, June 6). *Financial Times*, p. 7

Real-world effects of mispriced derivatives too great to be ignored. (December 17, 15). *Financial Times*, p. 20.

Risk parity' strategy blamed for fragile markets. (2015, August 24). *Financial Times*, p. 15.

Statistical Release: OTC Derivatives Statistics at end-June 2015. (2015, November). *Monetary and Economic Department, Bank for International Settlements*. http://www.bis.org/publ/otc_hy1511.pdf

Sugar body blames 'parasitic' computer traders for volatility. (2011, February 9). *Financial Times*, p. 13

Super-fast traders feel heat from competition. (2011, April 15). *Financial Times*, p. 20.

Systemic' trading comes under fire. (2015, September 4). *Financial Times*, p. 13.

The index factor. (2015, August 17). *Financial Times*, p. 5.

Whatever the weather. (2015, August 24). *Financial Times*, p. 8.

Why exchange-traded funds give uneasy sense of déjà vu. (2011, May 6). *Financial Times*, p. 20.

8

The challenges and implications of the Markets in Financial Instruments Directive (MiFID) and of its revision (MiFID II, MiFIR) on the efficiency of financial markets

Roland Gillet, Stéphanie Ligot, and Hassan Omidi Firouzi

8.1 Introduction

The Markets in Financial Instruments Directive (MiFID) is a European directive (Directive 2004/39/EC) published on 30 April 2004 in the *Official Journal of the European Union* and implemented since November 2007 across the 31 member states of the European Economic Area (the 28 EU member states plus Iceland, Norway and Liechtenstein). As of the effective date, 1 November 2007, it replaced the Investment Services Directive (ISD) through a framework directive (Directive 2004/39/EC), an implementing directive (Directive 2006/73/EC) and a regulation (Regulation 1287/2006).

This directive is one of the keystones concerning the Financial Services Action Plan (FSAP) set out by the European Commission in 1999. This plan has proposed a set of 42 measures to create an effective single market in the

R. Gillet (✉) • S. Ligot
Sorbonne Management School (PRISM and Labex RéFi), University Paris I
Panthéon – Sorbonne, Rue de la Sorbonne, 17, 75 231 Cedex 05 Paris, France

H.O. Firouzi
Labex RéFi, University Paris I Panthéon – Sorbonne,
Rue de la Sorbonne, 17, 75 231 Cedex 05 Paris, France

© The Author(s) 2017
R. Douady et al. (eds.), *Financial Regulation in the EU*,
DOI 10.1007/978-3-319-44287-7_8

financial services. The implemented measures harmonized the member states' rules on banking, securities trading, insurance, old-age pensions and other financial services. The FSAP is an integral part of the Lisbon Agenda, whose successor is the EU 2020 Strategy.[1]

MiFID is also the most significant piece of legislation introduced under the Lamfalussy procedure based on a four-level approach, where each level focuses on a specific stage of the legislation implementation:

1. At the first level, the piece of legislation is adopted by the European Parliament and Council of the European Union (EU)
2. At the second level, the sector-specific committees and regulators advise on technical details, then bring it to a vote in front of member-state representatives.
3. At the third level, the national regulators work on coordinating new regulations with other nations.
4. The fourth level involves compliance and enforcement of the new rules and laws.

This synthesis aims to highlight the challenges and the implications of the Markets in Financial Instruments Directive (MiFID) and of its revision (MiFID II, MiFIR) on the efficiency of financial markets.

In Section 8.2, we underline the context in which MiFID was implemented to understand more broadly its initial objectives. Section 8.3 briefly introduces the concept of financial markets efficiency as a key pillar of modern finance. At this level, the roles of market regulation within this concept will be brought forward. Section 8.4 presents the challenges and the key regulatory contributions of MiFID for the integration of the European financial markets in view of its objectives. Section 8.5 provides a first assessment of MiFID after 2011 to identify the remaining challenges for MiFID II and MiFIR in order to face the G20 requirements after the global crisis of 2008. Section 8.6 studies the implications of MiFID and its revisions (MiFID II and MiFIR) on the efficiency of financial markets through the selection of major academic work undertaken on this subject. Section 8.7 concludes with a discussion on the remaining challenges.

---

[1] The strategy 2020 is available at the following URL: http://eur-lex.europa.eu/LexUriServ/LexUriServ.do?uri=COM:2010:2020:FIN:EN:PDF.

8.2 Context in which MiFID was implemented and its first objectives

The London Stock Exchange's Big Bang on 27 October 1986, with the Financial Services Act established under Margaret Thatcher's government, was a rapid and complete deregulatory reform of the City market. The Big Bang was essentially a reprise of the deregulation of Wall Street in the 1970s. The main aims of the Act were to promote internationalization by allowing overseas firms to compete in London's market, making the City more competitive in equity transactions and confirming London's dominance in European markets.

Clemons and Weber (1990) underlines the main changes of this reform. It included an increase in the number of market participants, the opening to outsiders of ownership of stock exchange members, the breaking of the monopoly of brokers and the fixed brokerage commissions rule to make brokers more competitive. Moreover, an electronic dealing system was put in place allowing proprietary transactions, eliminating the separation between brokers and market makers and making trading off the order book possible.

Prior to these reforms, the City of London had difficulties competing with foreign banking. New York became a leading global centre of finance with a deregulation policy, which was at its pinnacle in 1975 with the end of fixed commissions on transferable securities, allowing liquidity on the equity and bond markets. This had to be replaced within the international monetary system context. For Thatcher's government, the two problems behind the decline of London banking were overregulation and the old structure of the financial markets. The solutions chosen were the free market doctrines of competition and meritocracy. The effects of the Big Bang led to significant changes in the structure of the financial markets and their regulatory environment, with the creation of the Financial Services Authority.

In 2007, the Market in Financial Instruments Directive (MiFID) was implemented. MiFID entered into force in November 2007 as a core pillar in European financial markets integration. This directive governs the provision of investment services in financial instruments by banks and investment firms, the operation of traditional stock exchanges and alternative trading venues. By reinforcing and harmonizing the financial regulatory framework at European level, MiFID aims to reinforce the integration of the European financial markets by increasing the competitiveness and the efficiency of European financial markets without neglecting investor protection to reduce the cost of capital and to generate growth.

After 2008, the global financial crisis and the European sovereign debt crisis of 2009 reminded us that the dynamics of financial markets are an ongoing process. Since the crisis, regulation has seemed to take over the vision of market structure itself, with a wide range of regulations impacting market structures all around the globe. The last global regulatory changes in the EU and in the USA are available in Table 8.1 in the Appendix.

The current trend is the reregulation of financial markets. This reregulation has to be placed in the institutional context of the G20 summits (Washington in 2008 and London and Pittsburgh in 2009). G20 was founded in 1999 with the aim of studying, reviewing and promoting high-level discussions on policy issues to promote international financial stability.

The following non-exhaustive list focus on the most significant items for G20 financial reform after 2008. According to Véron (2014), it could be divided into two main following objectives:

1. To tighten or strengthen the regulatory framework applying to entities or activities that had already been regulated before the crisis (a more demanding framework for the Basel III accord since its initial exposition in 2010, special regulatory treatment of systemically important financial institutions (SIFIs) and additional disclosure obligations for banks).
2. To tighten or strengthen the regulatory framework applying to entities or activities that until 2008 were mostly outside the scope of regulators such as the over-the-counter (OTC) derivatives, executive compensation, credit rating agencies, hedge funds, shadow banking and financial benchmarks (LIBOR and other similar reference rates).

In this context, the European Commission proposed to revise MiFID on 20 October 2011 with the aim of making European financial markets more efficient, resilient and transparent to strengthen the protection of investors and to be consistent with the evolution of financial markets after 2008. Consequently, a proposal for a new directive (MiFID II),[2] and a new regulation (MiFIR),[3] has been published to enter into force on 2 July 2014, with rules that should be applicable in 2018. The challenges and implications of MiFID relating to the efficiency of financial markets should be understood within this context.

---

[2] The directive 2014/65/EU of the European Parliament and of the Council of 15 May 2014 on markets in financial instruments and amending Directive 2002/92/EC and Directive 2011/61/EU is available at: http://eur-lex.europa.eu.

[3] The regulation (EU) No 600/2014 of the European Parliament and of the Council of 15 May 2014 on markets in financial instruments and amending Regulation (EU) No 648/2012 is available at: http://eur-lex.europa.eu.

8.3   The efficiency of financial markets

Based on the existing literature, Cobbaut, Gillet, and Hübner (2015) summarize the concept of market efficiency according to three points of view that underlie the role that the capital markets are expected to play in an economy:

1. **Allocation efficiency:** A market is considered as efficient when the price of assets evolves in a way that equates the marginal rates of risk-adjusted return between all savers and investors. The role of a capital market here is to optimally allocate scarce savings to productive investments in a way that benefits everyone, and that no profitable project is given up due to a lack of capital (Bauer 2004).
2. **Informational efficiency:** A market is informationally efficient if the asset prices incorporate, at each moment, all available information in order to reflect their underlying economic values.
3. **Operational efficiency:** A market is said to be operationally efficient if the transaction costs are fixed at a level where the intermediaries (dealers and market makers) provide services at competitive profits.

These three situations of efficiency represented on Fig. 8.1 are interdependent but should not be confused in order to avoid misinterpretations.

8.3.1 Informational efficiency and the Efficient Market Hypothesis (EMH)

Fama (1965, 1970, 1991) has significantly contributed to the definition and empirical testing of the Efficient Informational-Market Hypothesis (EMH),

Fig. 8.1   The efficiency of financial markets

which is a key assumption on which modern financial theory relies. This hypothesis is based on the random walk theory of asset prices introduced by Samuelson (1965), where the price changes are unpredictable in an informationally efficient market.

This idea was formerly proposed by Bachelier (1900) in his doctoral thesis. It illustrates that in an efficient market, at any point in time, the actual price of a security will be a good estimate of its intrinsic value and an accurate reflection of all available information. Fama (1991) proposed testing the informational efficiency of a market according to these three types of information:

1. Weak-form tests of return predictability, where it is impossible to systematically beat the market by using historical data.
2. Semi-strong form tests of event studies, where it is impossible to systematically beat the market by using publicly available information.
3. Strong-form tests of confidential information, where it is impossible to systematically beat the market using any information, public or private. This concept is hard to test because it requires access to the private information of all insiders.

Numerous tests of the EMH have suggested that information is reflected quickly and fully in prices confirming the semi-strong form of efficiency. Validation of this hypothesis does not need to confirm an efficient orders process but implies that the stock price movements are unpredictable. An informationally efficient market can have economically inefficient runs and crashes, so long as those crashes are not predictable.

The current paradigm of securities market regulation rests on the EMH, even if this hypothesis has been discredited by behavioural finance. Walter (2012) underlines that the EMH is still a stochastic convention for representing the markets as a martingale through the European prudential norms and in the directive MiFID.

8.3.2 Operational efficiency or the microstructure research area

From the operational efficiency point of view, the microstructure of financial markets has given rise to an abundant literature. O'Hara (1995) defines market microstructure as the study of processes and outcomes of exchanging assets under a specific set of rules. Microstructure theory focus on how the specific trading mechanisms affect the price formation process. According to Schreiber and Schwartz (1986), if the EMH refers to information efficiency given the design of the market, the price discovery process refers to design efficiency given the frequency with which information arrives. Moreover, the authors underline that the serial dependences in stock price changes do not violate the EMH, if after taking into account the transaction costs, the pattern is not concentrated enough for its exploitation to be economically viable. The autocorrelation of returns could be a manifestation of imperfections in our trading systems. In addition to the information changes and the liquidity trading, the following factors could account for the price changes that we observe: the bid–ask spread, the thin limit orderbook, the market maker interventions and the workings of price discovery process.

When transactions are costly to make and necessitate effort from intermediaries, a market maker or a dealer should be compensated through a bid–ask spread around the underlying value of the asset. The market is still informationally efficient if the underlying value fluctuates randomly, as being the centre of the spread. When information arrives, both the bid and the ask prices should move to different levels, such that their average is the new equilibrium value.

When the conditioning information is "all public information", the conditional expectation is sometimes called the fundamental value or the efficient price of a security, approximated in the long run by random walks. According to Cochrane (2009), the martingale behaviour of asset prices is a classic result, arising in many economic models with individual optimization, absence of arbitrage or security market equilibrium. This result is contingent on assumptions of frictionless trading opportunities.

However, as mentioned by Hasbrouck (2006), this result is not appropriate in most microstructure applications. At this level, the improvement of market structures, described as the state of a market with respect to its competition, is necessary to ensure the viability and stability of markets. The technology innovations, market fragmentation or consolidation, costs, volatility, transparency, policy interventions and regulations shape the market structure to ensure the competitiveness and efficiency of financial markets. At this level, the MiFID directive and its revision have key roles to play in the integration of European financial markets around its key objectives: competitiveness and efficiency.

8.3.3 Allocative efficiency

In order to be allocatively efficient, a market must meet the prerequisites of being both informationally efficient and operationally efficient. If all conditions are met, capital flows should direct themselves to the places where they will be the most effective, providing an optimal risk–return scenario for the investors.

An allocation is Pareto efficient if there does not exist a possible redistribution which would make at least one person better off without harming another person. In finance, this idea can be translated by the concept of optimal risk-sharing. The concept of allocative efficiency is related to the investment choices of firms and to the consumption/saving decisions of consumers. The roles of informational and operational efficiencies on allocative efficiency through the study of private information and liquidity on price equilibrium have been studied.

However, it remains difficult to assess the part that is due to the informational component and the part that is due to the liquidity component in the price determination of financial assets. According to Shiller (2003), we should look at the stance we take up in relation to the presumption that financial markets always work well and that price changes always reflect genuine information. Behavioural finance should be integrated in order to understand how human behaviours and arbitrary feedback relations could fuel stock market booms and crashes, which could generate a real and substantial misallocation of resources.

While some economists deny that bubbles occur, it remains difficult to identify them with certainty and this concept could lead to arbitrary judgements. Moreover, the causes of bubbles could be multiple and they often remain disputed. Among them, we could mention liquidity causes, inflation causes and the diverse social psychological factors that affect the behaviour of market participants. In the current non-conventional context, there is a considerable amount of research interest in understanding the interactions between asset prices, monetary policy changes and regulations.

1. From the regulation point of view, financial regulation changes could play a critical role in the severity and consequences of bubbles. Bubbles could lead to the failure of financial regulation by outlining five dynamics (Gerding 2014): the regulatory stimulus cycle, compliance rot, regulatory arbitrage frenzy, procyclical regulation and promotion of investment herding, which could affect the financial institution leverage and the supply of credit-fuelling bubbles, and making the markets vulnerable to a crash.

2. From monetary policy changes, Rigobon and Sack (2004) estimated the response of asset prices to changes in monetary policy through a new estimator that is based on the heteroscedasticity existing in high-frequency data. The results indicate that an increase in short-term interest rates results in a decline in stock prices and in an upward shift in the yield curve that becomes smaller at longer maturities. On the opposite side, a too cheap interest rate could reinforce instabilities with bubbles on the financial markets and real estate markets. The prices of assets could no more reflect their fundamental realities. This situation could become perverse if the central banks have to lead the dance, as

the thoughts of investors themselves should make the market. To make the financial markets efficient, investors need to assess properly their risks instead of believing that the central bank will be their saviour of last resort. To the extent this happens, the markets could fail to provide risk-sharing for individuals and access to risk capital for firms and entrepreneurs in the long run.

However, beyond monetary policy, there are also budgetary and fiscal policies. At European level, most member states of the EU participate in economic and monetary union (EMU) based on the euro, but most fiscal and budgetary decisions remain at national level. Therefore, although the EU has a monetary union, it does not have a fiscal union. At this level, the EU Treaty adopted the Stability and Growth Pact among members of the Eurozone to coordinate the fiscal policies of Member States.

This one defines an excessive budget deficit as one that is greater than 3 % of gross domestic product (GDP) and public debt is considered excessive under the Treaty if it exceeds 60 % of GDP without diminishing at an adequate rate (defined as a decrease of the excess debt by 5 % per year on average over three years). Its extension is the Treaty on Stability, Coordination and Governance (TSCG) signed in March 2012, which introduces a new fiscal discipline through three pillars: the fiscal compact, economic policy coordination and their convergence with the governance of the Eurozone.

8.4   The challenges and the key regulatory contributions of MiFID

MiFID reinforces the competitiveness and the efficiency of European financial markets, as it is a continuation of the Single European Act signed at Luxembourg on 17 February 1986.

This act was the first major revision of the 1957 Treaty of Rome, opening the path to the Treaty on the European Union in 1992, which established a single market through the creation of an area without internal frontiers, thereby ensuring the free movement of persons, goods, services and capital in accordance with the provisions of this Treaty. It came into effect on 1 July 1987 under the Delors Commission.[4]

The launch of the euro at the end of the 1990s, the Council Directive 93/22/EEC on investment services in the securities field and the Financial

---

[4] For a review of the European challenges post-1992, see Jacquemin, Wright and Silberston (1994)

Services Action Plan of 2005 were major milestones for European economic and financial integration in that they tackled currency and regulatory segmentation. With the euro, the Eurozone is at least an economic and monetary union with an independent monetary policy, which makes fixed exchange rates impossible according to Mundell (1961), but capital can move freely. Mundell developed a theory around optimum currency areas that underlay the key necessary features of a monetary union in order for it to endure. It is necessary to put in place specific mechanisms for adjustments to absorb the asymmetrical shocks that affect only some of its countries. Without a monetary devaluation being possible, the solution proposed by the author is a perfect mobility of production factors. If this solution is not totally possible, the monetary union should make possible budgetary transfers within the union to reduce disequilibria in order to allow the convergence of economic policies and to continue economic and monetary union. What remains needed at this level is the will to accomplish the convergence of economic policies and agreements on those convergences.

In the meantime, financial integration is particularly important within the economic and monetary union. The Eurosystem, according to Praet (2012), defines financial integration as a situation whereby there are no frictions that discriminate between economic agents in their access to the investment of capital, particularly on the basis of their location.

At this level, MiFID plays an important role because it improves the remaining challenges of the Investment Services Directive (ISD) with those of the passport system. We have decided to present the main contributions of MiFID and the main challenges facing it around four pillars: the competitiveness and efficiency of financial markets, the investor protection, the transparency and quality of the markets, and the supervision and enforcement of financial regulations.

8.4.1 Challenges around the competitiveness and the efficiency of financial markets

To face the challenges around the need for more competitiveness and efficiency in the European financial markets, it was necessary to abolish the monopoly of traditional stock exchanges, to remove obstacles to the free circulation of capital among European countries and to encourage the emergence of an integrated and competitive trading infrastructure. At this level, MiFID abolished the possibility for Member States to require all trading in financial instruments to take place on national traditional exchange places by suppressing the rule of national concentration of orders.

Moreover, it introduced new market players with the introduction of alternative venues, such as Multilateral Trading Platforms (MTFs) and Systematic Internalizers (SIs) alongside the traditional exchange places to execute securities transactions. SIs are financial institutions which decide to internalize the matching of client orders without putting out the orders on the regulated market. This change aims to enable European-wide competition between traditional exchange places and alternative venues to eliminate barriers to cross-border trading and to inject competition into the European investment services industry.

8.4.2 Challenges around the investor protection

The challenge was also to grant banks and investment firms a strengthened European passport for providing investment services across the EU in compliance with both organizational and reporting requirements as well as comprehensive rules designed to ensure better investor protection. This change was aimed at improving due diligence through the development of business conduct rules in the internal organization of financial institutions. At this level, some rules concern the definition of a "best execution policy" for the orders of clients and a classification of clients according to their level of financial knowledge in order to provide appropriate financial advice. Investor protection was needed to attract new investors to the EU capital markets and to encourage sustainable growth.

This directive affects the internal organization of financial institutions from the front office to the back office with impact at pre-trade, execution and post-trade levels of the transaction. The organizational requirements concern also the skills of the managerial teams and information on the shareholders and members who exercise a qualifying holding on an investment firm or a significant influence on the management of a regulated market.

The investment firms and the regulated markets must undertake their responsibilities in order to prove their compliance with the directive in their work processes. At this level, the identification of possible conflicts of interest and the procedure to manage them has to be clearly established. A risk management approach must be developed among actors concerned by MiFID in order to identify the significant risks which could impede their appropriate functioning. Investment firms have to organize internal control processes with an independent internal audit department. Regulated markets have to facilitate the finalization of transactions in an efficient way and with sufficient financial resources. Moreover, MiFID requires firms to categorize clients according to clear procedures to assess their suitability for each type of investment product. The appropriateness of any investment advice or suggested financial transaction must be verified before being given. The different categories are the following:

1. Eligible counterparts are supposed to have expertise in the field of investments as they operate on the financial markets. They do not benefit from specific protection.
2. Professional clients have competences to evaluate the risks and to make their investment decisions. They have to communicate less information and there is less protection than for retail clients.
3. Retail clients benefit from an increasing level of protection.

The investment firm has to assess risk profile through the collection of information on each client in order to propose appropriate products and services. Specific information also has to be communicated to the clients depending on their category.

8.4.3 Challenges around transparency and the quality of markets

The directive requires transparent and non-discretionary rules to ensure a fair and ordered negotiation process through the definition of a best execution policy with objective criteria to obtain the best possible result in the execution of an order for a client, unless there is a specific request from the client. The best possible outcome includes the execution price, cost, speed, likelihood of execution, likelihood of settlement and any other relevant factor. This policy is applicable for orders coming from professional and retail clients.

From the pre-trade transparency point of view, MiFID requires that operators of continuous order matching systems aggregate order information on liquid shares available at the five best price levels on the buy and sell side and that on quote-driven markets, the best bids and offers of market makers are available. From the post-trade transparency point of view, MiFID requires firms to publish the price, volume and time of all trades in listed shares, even if executed outside a regulated market, unless certain requirements are met to allow for deferred publication.

8.4.4 Challenges around the supervision and the enforcement of the financial regulation

Firms willing to benefit from the European passport have to be authorized and regulated by their "home state" competent authority. The firm is then able to use the MiFID passport to provide services to customers in the other European Member States.

The European passport means that the investment firm can exercise its activities within the EU under the permanent control of the home country regulatory authority if the investment firm has an approval from that national authority. The home country is the country where the investment firm, the credit firm or the regulated market has its headquarters or head office. The transparency of transactions will be toward the home country regulatory authority, which will organize information exchanges with other regulatory authorities concerned by the transactions. In order to facilitate and accelerate cooperation and information exchange, the Member States have to choose an authority that will be a contact point for this directive.

8.5   A first assessment of MiFID with the remaining challenges for MiFID II and MiFIR

In 2011, a first assessment of the directive MiFID was achieved. Increasing competition between venues in the trading of financial instruments has occurred, with more choices for investors in terms of service providers and available financial instruments. Moreover, several technological advances with high frequency trading (HFT) and algorithmic trading (AT) have been developed. Finally, transaction costs have decreased and integration has increased. However, this more competitive landscape has given rise to new challenges:

1. The benefits from this increased competition have not flowed equally to all market participants and have not always been passed on to the end investors, retail or wholesale. The market fragmentation implied by competition has also made the trading environment more complex, especially in terms of collection of trade data. The absence of a consolidated tape since MiFID's initial introduction in 2007 has impacted the buy-side traders. They are suffering from a decline in the quality of market data that drives their investment decisions, which could reinforce uncertainty on the

markets. Moreover, the issuers have difficulties in rebuilding their liquidity on the markets.

2. The market and technological developments have outpaced various provisions in MiFID. The common interest in a transparent level playing field between trading venues and investment firms was undermined.
3. The financial crisis of 2008 has exposed weaknesses in the regulation of instruments other than stocks, such as bonds and derivatives, traded mostly between professional investors through Over-The-Counter (OTC) markets. This crisis has also underlined that the challenges concerning the organization of financial markets are beyond the EU and should be studied with a more international approach.
4. The rapid innovations and growing complexity in financial instruments underline the importance of an up-to-date high level of investor protection. As AT and HFT have grown rapidly, they have increased the complexity of the market dynamics. A current controversy concerns the extent to which they improve or degrade the functioning of financial markets and also influence market volatility and the risk of instability.
5. Finally, the sovereign debt crisis of 2009 in the EU has exposed weaknesses in EU governance that affect the viability and the solidarity of the EU. The situation of Cyprus in 2013 and the situation of Greece in 2015 have made us question what has been accomplished around the integration of European financial markets.

In October 2011, owing to the crisis context and to improve the drawbacks of MiFID, the European Commission put forward proposals for revising MiFID, with the aim of establishing a safer, sounder, more transparent and more responsible financial system and more integrated, efficient and competitive European financial markets.[5] A proposal for a new directive (MiFID II) and a new regulation (MiFIR) were published on 20 October 2011. The directive evolved from a set of rules to protect retail investors (MiFID) to a set of proposals to increase transparency among the fragmented European trading venues (MiFID II/MiFIR). The objectives of MiFID II are mainly to:

1. Reinforce supervisory powers.
2. Make financial markets more robust and efficient.
3. Increase transparency of both equity and non-equity markets.
4. Introduce a stricter framework for commodity derivatives markets.
5. Strengthen investor protection.

---

[5] See the following regulation COM(2010)301 Final. For further details see: http://ec.europa.eu.

The revision of MiFID through MiFID II and MiFIR has been a way of delivering G20 commitments after the crisis of 2008 and tackling the less regulated and more opaque parts of financial systems, improving the organization, transparency and oversight of various market segments, especially in those instruments traded mostly OTC,[6] complementing the legislative proposal on OTC derivatives, central counterparts and trade repositories.[7] Improvements are also required to enhance transparency on commodity derivatives markets in order to ensure their hedging and price discovery functions.[8]

The main modifications covered by MiFID II/ MiFIR are underlined in the factsheet from Linklaters (2014) available in Table 8.2 in the Appendix. Briefly, on one side, MiFID II amends specific requirements regarding the provision of investment services, the scope of exemptions from the current Directive, the organizational requirements for investment firms and trading venues, the authorization and ongoing obligations applicable to the providers of data services, the powers available to competent authorities, and the sanctions and rules applicable to third-country firms operating via a branch. Important parts are dedicated to HFT, to OTC market obligations through Organised Trading Facilities (OTFs) and to supervision mechanisms.

On the other side, MiFIR sets out requirements in relation to the disclosure of trade transparency data to the public and of transaction data to competent authorities and it removes the barriers to non-discriminatory access to clearing facilities. It also sets out requirements in relation to the mandatory trading of derivatives on organized venues, the specific supervisory actions regarding financial instruments, the positions in derivatives and the provision of services by third-country firms without a branch.

In line with recommendations from the de Larosière Group and the conclusions drawn by the ECOFIN Council, the EU has committed to minimize, where appropriate, discretions available to Member States across European financial services directives, in order to establish a single rulebook for European financial markets across all areas covered by the review of MiFID.[9]

---

[6] See the following regulation COM (2009) 563 Final. For further details see: http://ec.europa.eu.

[7] See the following regulation COM (2010) 484. For further details see: http://ec.europa.eu.

[8] See the following regulation COM (2011) 656. For further details see: http://ec.europa.eu.

[9] See the following regulation COM (2011) 656 Final. For further details see: http://ec.europa.eu.

8.6   The implications of MiFID and MiFID II/MiFIR on the efficiency of financial markets

The implications of MiFID have been studied mainly on the operational efficiency side through the microstructure research area, but this regulation has brought spillovers on the informational and allocative sides of financial market efficiency. The following list of academic research is not exhaustive but helps us to highlight some of the main MiFID efficiency implications. For MiFID II and MiFIR, it is a bit too early to assess their implications, because the rules will be implemented in 2018. Nevertheless, some implications may be anticipated. We have structured these implications around four pillars of market microstructure research: the developments of market structures, the design rules, information and its disclosure, and the interface of microstructure with other areas of finance.

8.6.1   Developments in market structures: The implications of the suppression of the national order flow concentration rule and of the introduction of alternative venues (MTFs, SIs and OTFs) on the liquidity

This directive is related to the introduction of the Regulation of National Market Securities (Reg NMS) in the USA with the objective of enhancing competition on the financial markets. Petrella (2010) presented a comparison of both regulations around microstructure principles to show that the EU and the USA adopt different provisions with respect to the best execution duty, the consolidation of market data and the disclosure of execution quality information. It appears to be more effective for the USA in strengthening competition for order flow among trading venues.

A consolidated tape of transactions has been available in the USA since 1976, whereas the situation is quite different in the EU. This could be because of the structure of the European financial markets, which are diverse in terms of securities exchanges, central securities depositories and central counterparty clearing statistics, as we can observe from the statistics of the European Central Bank (2014) on Fig. 8.2. This diversity represents the different European economies. However, a certain level of consolidation seems apparent through the additional statistics on Securities Exchanges, Central Securities Depositories and Central Counterparty Clearing, available in Fig. 8.5 up to Fig. 8.10 in the Appendix.

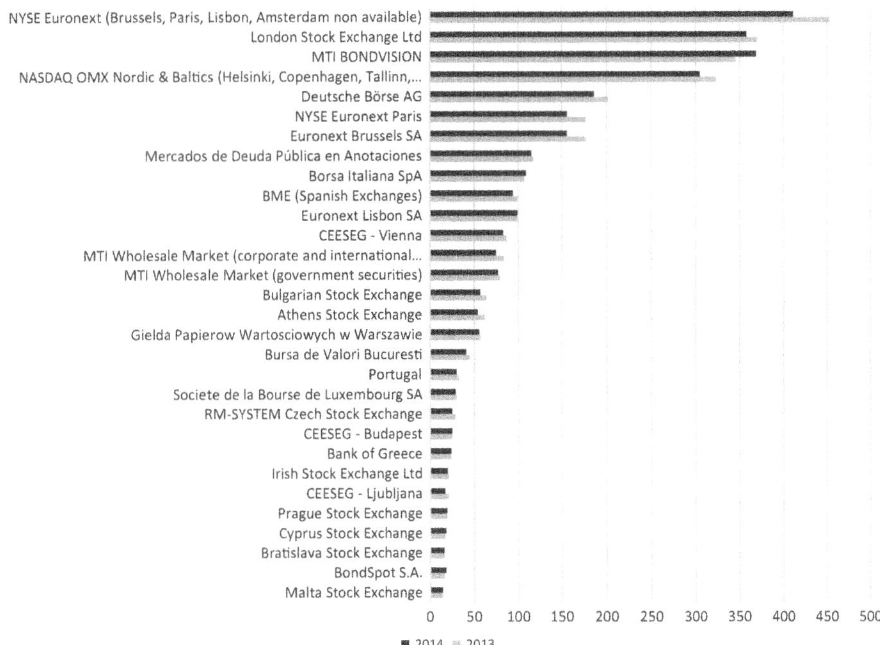

Fig. 8.2   Securities Exchange Statistics: Number of participants (*Source*: ECB - June 2015)

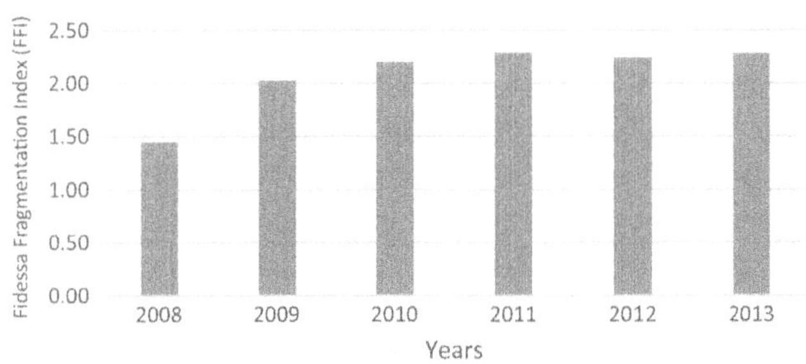

Fig. 8.3   Evolution of the Fidessa Fragmentation Index (FFI) for the CAC40 Index (*Source*: Fidessa)

Market structures and design rules are critical to understanding the price formation process in financial markets. The major objectives of a stock exchange are to provide liquidity and price discovery functions. In this section, we will focus on the implications of market structures changes brought about by MiFID with regard to liquidity. Price discovery implications will be discussed in the following section, through an analysis of developments in design rules.

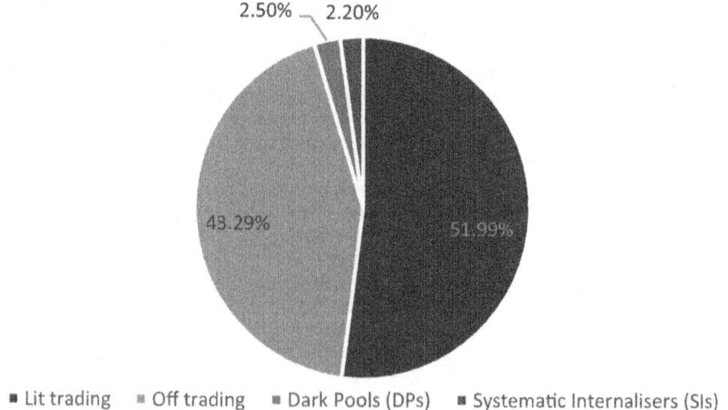

Fig. 8.4 Transaction execution mode for the CAC 40 Index in 2013 (*Source*: Fidessa)

There are several dimensions of liquidity. An asset is considered to be liquid if it can be converted to cash with ease. According to Krishnamurti (2009), liquidity can be measured by the cost of trading an asset for cash immediately, broken down into explicit costs (brokerage commissions and taxes) and implicit costs (rounding of prices, bid–ask spreads, market impact effects and imperfections in the price determination process). A liquid market is characterized by its breadth (existence of orders in substantial volume), its depth (existence of orders on both sides of the market near the current equilibrium price) and its resiliency (responsiveness of new orders to price changes caused by temporary order imbalances). A market is not resilient when the order flow does not quickly adjust to errors in price discovery.

At this level, we can observe that with the introduction of MiFID in 2007, there is a significant evolution of the Fidessa Fragmentation Index (FFI) for the CAC 40 index since 2008 on Fig. 8.3. The FFI is defined as the inverse of the sum of squares of the market shares of each individual trading venue, and it is often used to measure the level of competition in an industry. An index of 1 means that the stock is traded at one venue. Once the FFI of a stock exceeds 2, it means that its liquidity has fragmented to the extent that it no longer belongs to its originating venue. The causes of the fragmentation induced by MiFID are related to the abolition of the national order concentration rule and the introduction of the possibility of executing transactions on alternative venues through the MTFs and the SIs. On Fig. 8.4 and Table 8.1, we can observe the transaction execution mode for the CAC40 Index in 2013.

Several studies had been undertaken to study the implications of the abolition of the national order concentration rule and the introduction of alternative trading venues on the operational efficiency of financial markets, and

Table 8.1 Transaction execution mode for the CAC40 Index in 2013 (*Source*: Fidessa)

Lit trading	2013 (%)
Euronext Paris	32,29
BATS Chi-X CXE	10,75
BATS Chi-X BXE	1,69
Turquoise	4,63
Euronext Amsterdam	0,93
Off trading	**2013 (%)**
Boat Xoff	28,24
Swiss Exchange	7,41
Euronext OTC	3,78
LSE Xoff	2,97
LSE	0,45
Dark pools	**2013 (%)**
Instinet BlockMatch	0,25
Posit	0,36
BATS Chi-X BXE	0,41
BATS Chi-X CXE	0,44
UBS MTF	0,63
Systematic internalisers	**2013 (%)**
OMX OTC SI	0,02
Boat SI	2,15
SI	0,07

more specifically on the improvements in market liquidity. According to Doumayrou (2008), the effects of MiFID on liquidity could be difficult to anticipate. On one hand, the increased competition could decrease transactions costs but on the other hand, the order flow fragmentation could decrease liquidity. Fleuriot (2010) underlines that the impacts on liquidity should be mitigated owing to the global financial crisis of 2008 and the fact that a multitude of factors could impact the liquidity of markets.

According to Cherbonnier and Vandelanoite (2008), the number of SIs on liquid securities listed on Euronext Paris could be between five and ten in the medium term, and represented 5 % of turnover on CAC 40 securities per annum. Moreover, the institutional investors could carry out around 6 % of their annual turnover on MTFs organized as crossing systems. However, this analysis underestimates the volume likely to be lost by Euronext owing to the block trades executed in the orderbook and those executed outside the orderbook by non-residents (not subject to reporting requirements) or by residents on another regulated market (such as SEAQI) not being included.

Gresse (2010a) looked at four monthly periods to compare market liquidity before and after the entry into effect of MiFID, based on two samples of non-financial large caps from the FTSE 100 and the CAC 40 and a third sample of non-financial mid-caps from the SBF 120. The order-flow fragmentation reached substantial levels but it was less pronounced among the mid-caps of the SBF 120. The results of this paper underline that the primary markets continue to dominate the European securities trading landscape with a significant decline in price spreads among trading venues, which is relatively proportionate to the strength of competition at the cost of a reduced depth at best limits. According to Gresse (2010a), competition and the rise in AT have resulted in orders being more broken up, reducing the average transaction size and the frequency of trading, whereas the quote changes have increased greatly.

Gresse (2014b) underlines that in Europe three trading platforms have become significant players. Their joint market share exceeds 30 % of lit trading volumes. Regulated dark pools do not execute more than some 5 % of total trading volumes and OTC trading makes a large share of total volumes. According to Gresse (2014b), price quality does not appear to be significantly affected by market fragmentation in the European stock markets, which improves liquidity for global traders who connect to several platforms and provides greater liquidity gains on large capitalization stocks.

Foucault and Menkveld (2008) study the rivalry between Euronext and the London Stock Exchange (LSE) in the Dutch stock market. Their main findings are that the consolidated limit order book is deeper after entry of the LSE and a higher trade-through rate in the entrant market coincides with less liquidity supply in this market cross-sectionally. The fragmentation of order flow can enhance liquidity supply, and protecting limit orders against trade-throughs is important.

Schacht, Cronin, Allen, and Preece (2009) also find that fragmentation has not had a detrimental effect on markets overall, based on a sample of 44 stocks issued by Europe-based companies in the Dow Jones Stoxx 50 index. The average bid–ask spreads have slightly fallen at the aggregate level, in particular amongst the UK stocks. However, according to Fleuriot (2010), we should be prudent when assessing changes in spreads because they could be contradictory. The Federation of European Securities Exchanges (FESE) observed a widening of spreads in 2008 and 2009. In fact, according to Fleuriot (2010), the spreads both grew and narrowed over the period. Spreads narrowed slightly over the period as a whole since November 2007. The key question is whether the widening of spreads between September 2008 and January 2009 was an exceptional event or the result of an increase in volatility, which doubled over the period from November 2007 to June 2009, compared to the period from the beginning of 2006 to November 2007.

8.6.2 Developments in the design rules: The implications of the Best Execution policy and financial innnovations on price formation and the price discovery process

8.6.2.1 *Developments in the design rules and the Best execution policy*

As set out in Schreiber and Schwartz (1986), the major regulatory objectives for a securities market are:

1. To assure a fair and honest market.
2. To increase competitive efficiency in the provision and pricing of broker/dealer services.
3. To enhance market efficiency with regard to the price discovery function.

A major securities market regulatory problem is that, in large part, the three regulatory objectives are not mutually consistent. This conflict of objectives is closely related to the regulatory dilemma noted by Bloch and Schwartz (1978), where enhancing the efficiency of competition in the market for broker/dealer services can impair the efficiency of competition in the market for the stocks that are traded and vice versa. As underlined by Schwartz (2013), achieving a price discovery of high quality has remained a woefully neglected regulatory goal, while considerations such as providing transparency on transactions and competition in the marketplace have received the lion's share of regulators' attention.

For any financial marketplace, a key economic function is to find the price of a security; this function is reinforced with the mark-to-market accounting requirements. Markets are known for providing liquidity and price discovery, as mentioned by O'Hara (2003). If liquidity refers to the matching of buyers and sellers and the emergence of a spread to compensate the middleman, it is largely accepted that the price discovery process involves the incorporation of new information into the asset prices as defined by Schreiber and Schwartz (1986).

This definition of the price discovery process is completed by the market search for a new equilibrium price. The price that should be discovered is defined as a value that best reflects a broad array of buy and sell desires, namely an equilibrium value. This function of price discovery for a market has attributes of "public good." The question of how the fragmentation in its temporal and spatial aspects impacts the accuracy of the price discovery process is an interesting one, and remains a big challenge for the integration of European financial markets.

From the spatial fragmentation point of view, some studies have studied the contribution of trading venues to price discovery for cross-listed stocks in the EU after the implementation of MiFID. Harris and Di Marco (2012) underline that the price discovery efficiency in London and Paris has declined with the fragmentation of order flow post-MiFID. However, according to Aitken, Sensenbrenner, and Harris (2010), there is no price discovery migration away from the central exchange with the fragmentation of financial markets in London. After a stark clearing and settlement fee schedule change by Chi-X, a surprisingly large information impounding was attributable to the migration of high-frequency traders to Chi-X. At this level, it should be interesting to study the parameters that influence these changes.

The CFA underlines, through a survey, the difficulty in obtaining a complete and clear picture of market prices in the EU. Of the survey respondents, 70 % concluded that dark pools are problematic for price discovery, while 68 % agreed that market fragmentation has created difficulties in trade reporting obligations. According to the CFA, these results support the necessity of a consolidated tape for quote and trade data for the European equity markets.

The impact of temporal fragmentation, known as order fracturing, on the price discovery process has been less studied in the post-MiFID context. However, this fragmentation could increase the informational non-fulfilment and runaways, particularly with the arrival of HFT and AT.

In absence of a consolidated tape for the European financial markets, it is particularly difficult to assess the best execution policy duty required by MiFID. Moreover, its multicriterion approach makes its evaluation more complex. However, this approach is important to permit the channelling of orders to the most efficient market.

8.6.2.2   *Developments in design rules and financial innovations*

Under MiFID II, the rules designed to address the financial stability risks posed by the HFT and AT will also require investment firms and the operators of trading venues to enhance their systems, processes and controls. One of the key areas that MiFID II will address at this level is the so-called flash crashes for which the regulators are asked to investigate market abuses related to HFT. A flash crash is a very rapid, deep and volatile fall in security prices occurring within an extremely short time period as defined by Bozdog, Florescu, Khashanah, and Wang (2011).

Two notable flash crashes in the current decade took place on 6 May 2010 and 23 April 2013. HFT is an algorithmic form of trading which entails using extraordinarily high-speed order systems and algorithms for automated decision-making. All processes in HFT should be operated in a short period of time. HFT could be considered as one reason for flash crashes, but there are some studies which show that other factors can be regarded as the main reasons. Cohen and Schwartz (2001) underlined the importance of call auctions as a mechanism to equalize informational sources and time reactions in order to determine a unique price. This point is particularly important with the HFT phenomenon, where speed is an advantage in the trading.

There are two different views towards HFT. One group, supporters of HFT, argues that it provides liquidity to markets, reduces volatility in most circumstances and enhances the price discovery process. The other group, more sceptical, argues that the liquidity provided by HFT is false and that it can vanish during periods of market stress. Zhang (2010) finds that HFT is negatively associated with the market's ability to incorporate news about a firm's fundamentals into asset prices by exaggerating otherwise sound price reaction and by increasing the stock price volatility. While the HFT may reduce volatility most of the time, it is also responsible for periodic flash crashes, brief periods of extremely high volatility (Brogaard, Hendershott, and Riordan 2014). One of the risks in the HFT environment that market makers have to face is the risk of adverse selection.

Adverse selection refers to a market process in which undesired results occur when buyers and sellers have asymmetric information. In Easley, Lopez de Prado, and O'Hara (2012a), the authors introduce the concept of order flow toxicity, which helps to study the risk of adverse selection within the HFT context. In this paper, it is stated that the order flow is toxic when it adversely selects market makers, who may be unaware that they are providing liquidity at a loss. To measure the order flow toxicity, Easley, Lopez de Prado, and O'Hara (2012a) and Easley, Lopez de Prado, and O'Hara (2012b) present the Volume Synchronized Probability of Informed Trading (VPIN) metric.

This metric is a new procedure to estimate the probability of informed trading based on volume imbalance and trade intensity. VPIN is an update of the well-known PIN model of Easley, Kiefer, O'Hara, and Paperman (1996) with four main characteristics: the broader definition of information, sampling in volume-time, bulk classification of buys and sells and the incorporation of trade size according to Abad and Yague (2012). Some interesting results obtained in Easley, Lopez de Prado, and O'Hara(2012a) are the following:

1. When the VPIN is low, the subsequent absolute returns are also low (when absolute returns are large the immediately preceding VPIN was rarely small).
2. When VPIN is high, the conditional distribution of subsequent returns is much more dispersed. It takes persistently high levels of VPIN to reliably generate large absolute returns.
3. VPIN anticipates a large proportion of extreme volatility events, and toxicity-induced volatility seems to be a significant source of overall volatility.
4. High levels of VPIN signify a high risk of subsequent large price movements, deriving from the effects of toxicity on liquidity provision.

This liquidity-based risk is important for market makers who directly bear the effects of potential toxicity, but it is also significant for traders who face the prospect of toxicity-induced large price movements. One important consequence of using the VPIN metric is the possibility of reducing volatility clustering. Since large price moves are associated with large volumes, sampling by volume, which is an important characteristic of VPIN metric, can therefore be viewed as a proxy for sampling by volatility.

Easley, Lopez de Prado, and O'Hara (2012a) have shown that with volume sampling we get a collection of observations whose distribution is closer to the normal and is less heteroskedastic than it would be if we sampled uniformly in clock-time. Therefore, this approach can be seen as an alternative to GARCH models in capturing volatility clustering. The VPIN metric could be a useful tool to help to reduce and capture market risk for market makers and traders in a context of HFT and AT. The authors also believe that the VPIN could alert market regulators to an impending flash crash. However, not everyone agrees (Andersen and Bondarenko 2014).

Nevertheless, the debate around VPIN or no VPIN should be useful as MiFID II introduces closer regulation and monitoring of algorithmic trading, imposing new and detailed requirements on algorithmic traders and the trading venues on which they trade.

8.6.3 Information and disclosure: The implications for the transparency and the quality of markets

Madhavan (2000) defines market transparency as the ability of market participants to observe information about the trading process. Differences in trade disclosure across markets may induce order flow migration, affecting the liquidity and price discovery functions of the markets. Transparency is a major factor for electronic dealing systems in ensuring the quality of financial markets. However, as transparency rules change, it could impact the behaviour of market participants and affect the degree of market informational efficiency. As mentioned by Harris (2003): "the traders are often ambivalent about transparency because they favour transparency when it allows them to see more of what other traders are doing, but they oppose it when it requires that they reveal more of what they are doing. Generally, those who know the least about market conditions most favour transparency. Those who know the most oppose transparency because they do not want to give up their informational advantages."

From the regulation point of view, the art is finding the degree of transparency on the markets that is compatible with the consolidation of transactions and the fragmentation of markets and players, and thereby encourages competition. To address the impacts of fragmentation on market quality issues in the USA, O'Hara and Ye (2011) use the SEC Rule 605 data, which is a set of execution metrics that must be reported monthly on a per stock basis by all execution venues in the USA. It allows comparison of execution quality (effective spreads, realized spreads and execution speeds) and price efficiency quality (short-term return volatility, variance ratio tests and return autocorrelations).

In Europe, Gresse (2014a) presents an empirical analysis of the effects of market fragmentation on price quality, which is measured by price inefficiency coefficients (PICs) based on the variance ratios for a sample of European large and medium capitalization stocks. Gresse (2014a) underlines that there is no clearly significant impact of market fragmentation observed on the price quality, except for the PICs based on 1-s to 5-s return variance ratios.

Boneva, Linton, and Vogt (2015) investigate the effects of fragmentation of equity trading on the quality of trading with a focus on volatility, liquidity and volume for the FTSE 350 stocks over the period 2008–2011, following the implementation of MiFID. They find that volatility is lower in a fragmented market when compared to a monopoly, and that trading volume at the LSE is lower but global trading volume is higher if order flow is fragmented across multiple venues. According to these authors, the decline in LSE volume can be attributed to the visible fragmentation, while the increase in global volume is down to dark trading.

With MiFID II, no more than 8 % of an individual stock in the EU should be traded in dark pools. The issue is that it could potentially impede trading of large institutional orders in Europe. Pricing behaviour of SIs introduced in the post-MiFID context have been little studied from the market quality improvement point of view. Hautcoeur, Lagneau-Ymonet, and Riva (2010) underline that regulated markets should be entrusted at European level with a general interest mission of centralization, consolidation and publication of the post- and pre-trade information considered as a public good, without the possibility that economic development will be harmed.

From the transparency and the quality of markets points of view, MiFID II and MiFIR have a specific mission in order to tackle the G20 commitments. The biggest change will be on the derivatives markets and on the bonds markets, with the introduction of OTFs in order to move more OTC derivatives and bonds trading on to these trading venues. Consequently, the OTC trading or off-trading without any supervision of the exchange should be significantly reduced. Moreover, MiFID II will increase transparency for derivatives commodities in order to reduce speculation on these markets, with new disclosures, position reporting rules and quantitative limits on positions for both investment firms and the operators of trading venues.

Lastly, MiFID II should establish a regime for a European consolidated tape. One of the aims of MiFID II and MiFIR is to ensure that Regulated Markets (RMs), MTFs and OTFs have the same transparent rules and procedures, in order to build a fair and orderly trading environment with the setting of objective criteria for an efficient execution of orders and an obligation of a transparent, fair and non-discriminatory fee structure for these trading venues.

At this level, the European Securities and Markets Authority (ESMA), created in 2010 in Paris, aims to safeguard the stability of European financial markets and to address shortcomings in European financial supervision. This European supervisory authority comprises the market regulators of the Member States of the European Economic Area, a European Commission representative, a representative of the European Banking Authority (EBA) and a representative of the European Insurance and Occupational Pensions Authority (EIOPA).

This new European authority has key roles to play in the regulation and supervision of financial markets and is involved in setting common standards and practices in regulation and supervision, in issuing opinions for regulation and in building shared interpretations of European legislation through its recommendations and guidelines for national regulators. The aim is to harmonize regulation on the financial markets with specific missions around investor protection and to monitor the development of innovative financial solutions. At this level, it is important to maintain independent supervision.

8.6.4 Market microstructure interfaces with the other areas of finance

As underlined by Madhavan (2000), the market microstructure affects asset values and price efficiency, and it also has important implications for the other areas of finance: asset pricing (through liquidity as a factor in expected returns and other behavioural explanations), corporate finance (through pricing of initial public offerings (IPOs) and stock splits) and international finance (through American depositary receipts (ADRs) and multiple share classes, cross-border flows and the microstructure of foreign exchanges markets with the hot potato models and the exchange rates movements).

8.7   Conclusion : United in diversity after the Big Bang and the crisis of 2008 ?

This widening of the European markets could be quite risky from the investor protection and efficiency points of view in the current context facing the Member States of the EU. The fragmentation of liquidity within the European markets may be a reality and causes some damage. At this level, Modigliani and Perotti (2000) underline that when the minority investors rights are poorly protected, the ability of firms to raise equity capital is impaired, leading to less finance for new ventures, and the provision of funding shifts from risk capital to debt and to a predominance of intermediated over market finance.

According to Hamon, Jacquillat and Saint Étienne (2007), stock exchange consolidation is an inevitable process in a globalized world where capital flows are at the forefront of globalization through the increase in liquidity and the decrease in transaction costs. They mention that the development of communication and information technology is important at this level because it makes possible the electronic interconnection of order books to organize a system of competing markets that most effectively replicates the impact of consolidation of supply within a single market. Therefore, compatibility is possible between the consolidation of transactions and the fragmentation of markets and players, which encourages competition. However, Hamon, Jacquillat and Saint Étienne (2007) stress the importance of having appropriate supervision; otherwise the concentration of orders is detrimental to competition and leads to an increase in the margins of stock exchange operators, which in turn restricts the growth in volume of transactions.

As for the efficiency of financial markets, the key question is whether the best execution policy introduced under MiFID allows the channelling of orders to the most efficient market. At this level, few studies have been undertaken. This is perhaps because it is extremely difficult to test it in the current pre- and post-trading environment with no consolidated tape and an increasing level of HFT and AT. At this level, the organization of the post-trading environment will have important implications.

With the crisis of 2008 and the European sovereign debt crisis of 2009, we have seen that the EU has some problems of governance to overcome in order to ensure the viability and the stability of the EU, composed as it is of 28 Member States. Consolidating financial integration and enhancing the future financial stability of European financial markets remain big challenges for the future.

"United in Diversity" is the official motto of the EU, adopted in 2000, and this is a perfect representation of a game where cooperation is possible despite the existence of diverging preferences. It means unity without uniformity and diversity without fragmentation. Let us hope that Europe will find its path to more integrated and efficient European financial markets in order to reduce the cost of capital, to generate growth and to reinforce international competitiveness within the EU without neglecting the rights and duties of its citizens and investors.

8.8   Appendix

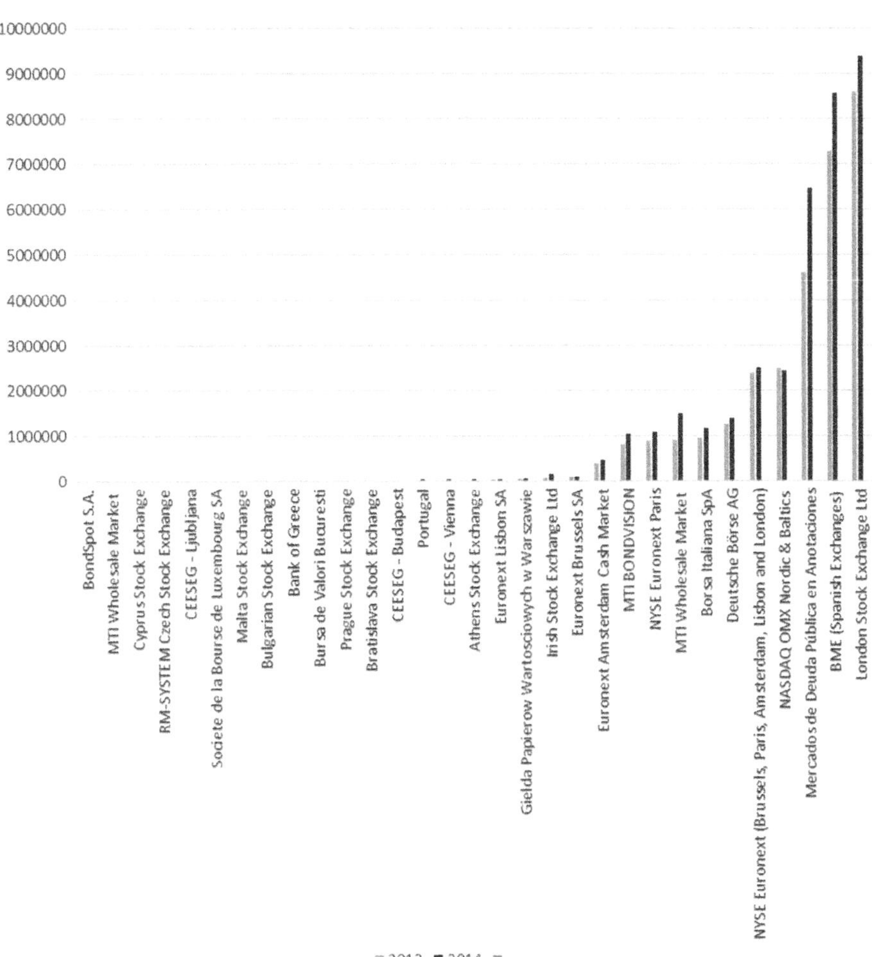

Fig. 8.5   Securities Exchange Statistics: Value of executed trades in millions of Euros (*Source*: ECB - June 2015)

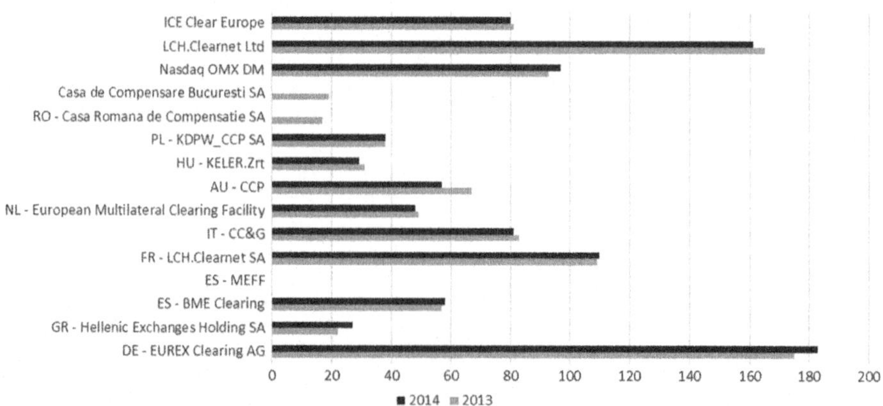

Fig. 8.6 Central Counterparty Clearing: Number of participants (*Source*: ECB - 2015)

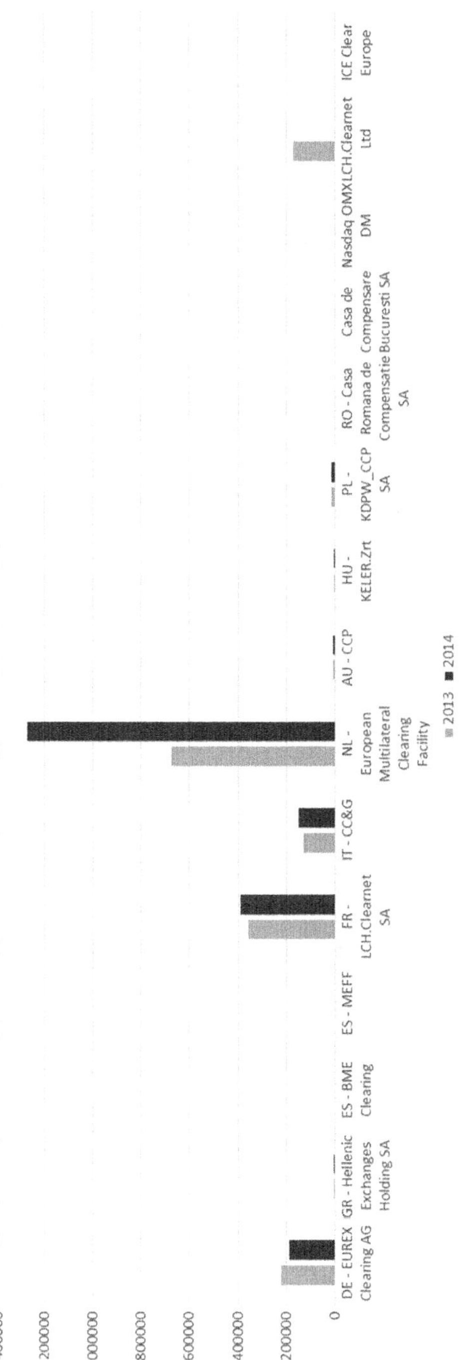

Fig. 8.7 Central Counterparty Clearing: Number of cash (outright) securities transactions in thousands (*Source*: ECB - 2015)

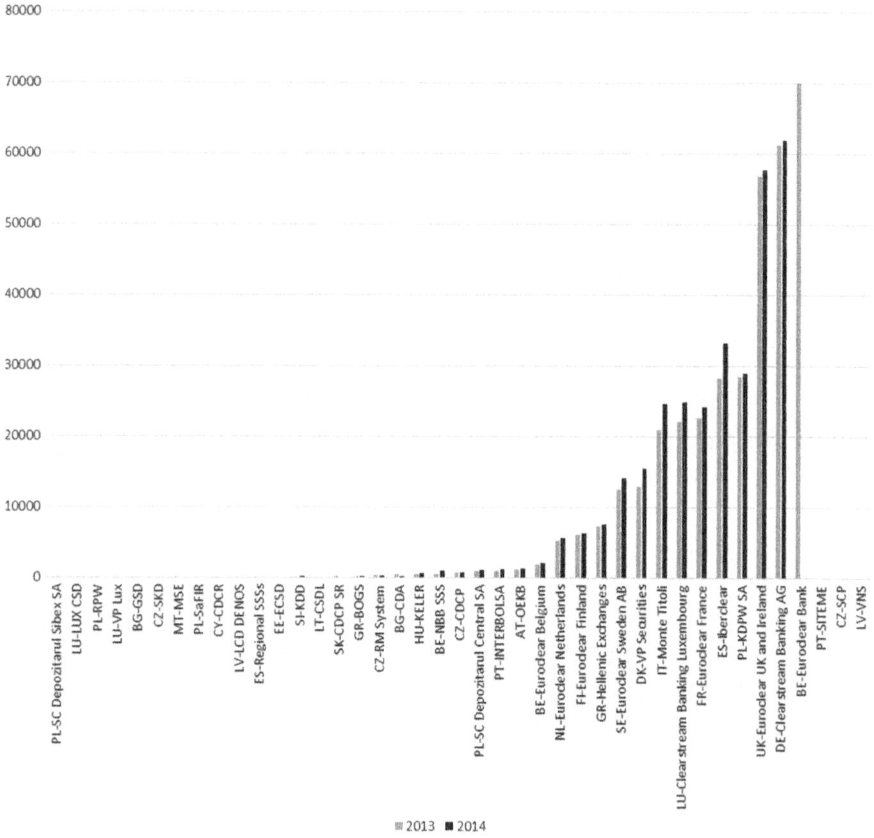

Fig. 8.8 Central Securities Depositories: Number of transactions in thousands (*Source*: ECB - 2015)

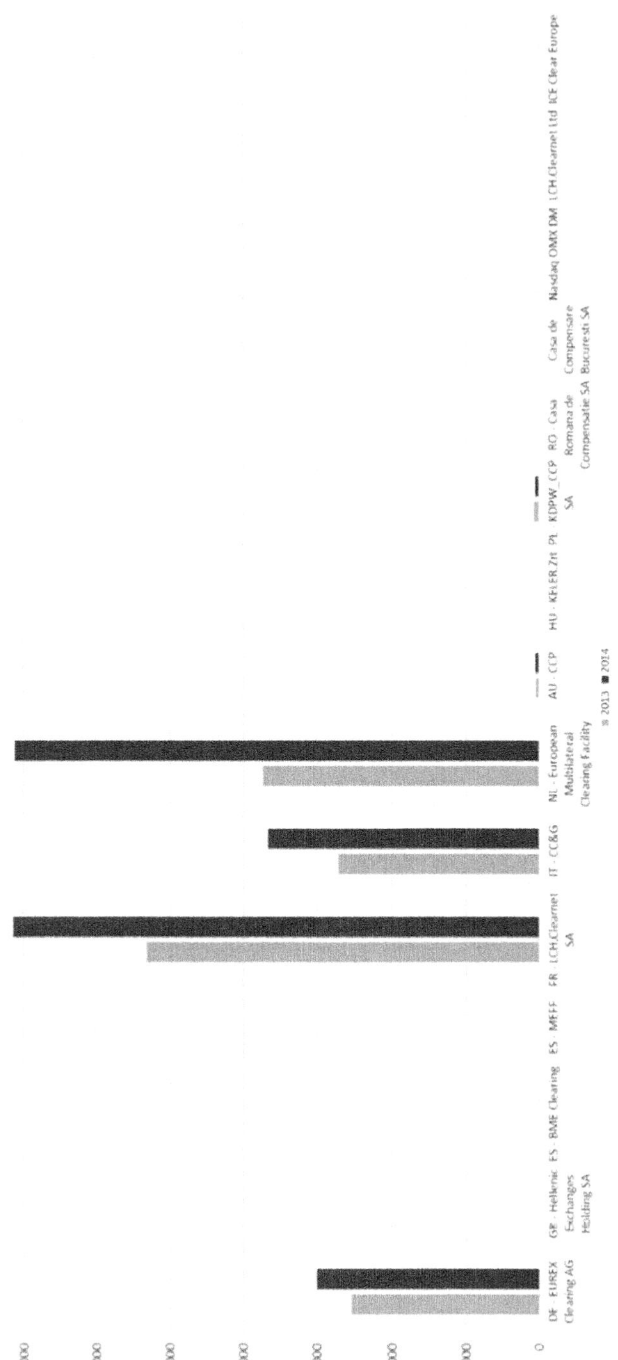

Fig. 8.9 Central Counterpart Clearing: Value of cash (outright) securities transactions in billions of Euros (*Source*: ECB - 2015)

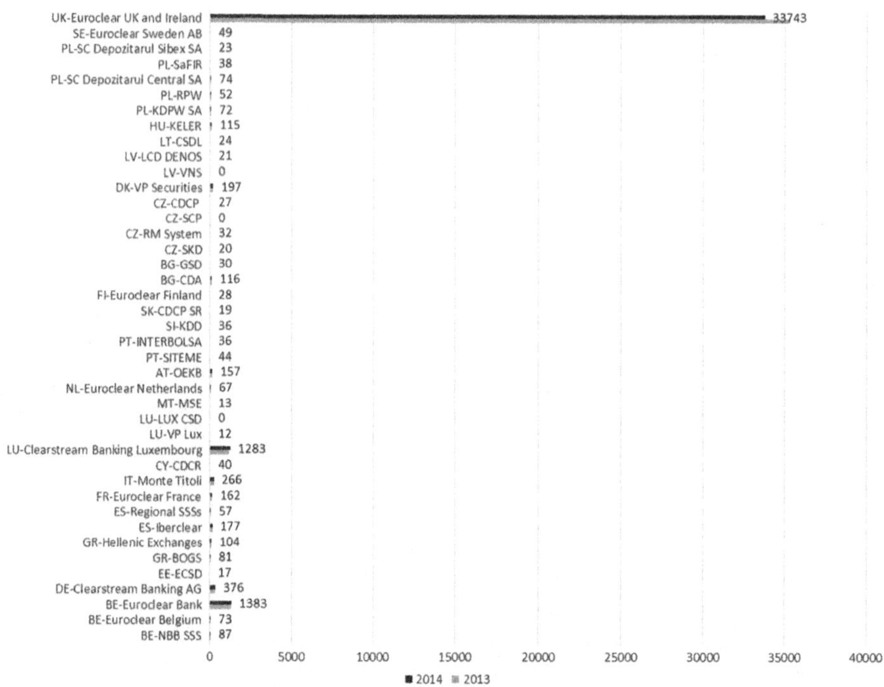

Fig. 8.10 Central Securities Depositories: Participation (End of period) (*Source*: ECB - 2015)

Table 8.2 Global regulatory changes

Date	Status of (de) regulatory change	Regulatory change description
1986	London Big Bang	Deregulation of the UK financial markets
1988	First Basel Accord signed	Publication of a set of minimum capital requirements for banks
1994	Riegel-Niel Interstate banking and branching efficiency Act	Restore the laws' competitiveness with the recently relaxed laws governing state chartered banks.
1996	FED reinterprets Glass-Steagall Act	Allowing bank holding companies to own investment bank affiliates with up to 25 % of their business in securities underwriting.
1999	European Financial services action plan (FSAP)	The Financial Services Action Plan (FSAP) is a key component of the European Union's attempt to create a single market for financial services.

(continued)

Table 8.2 (continued)

Date	Status of (de) regulatory change	Regulatory change description
1999	Gramm-Leach-Bliley Act	An Act to enhance competition in the financial services industry by providing a prudential framework for the affiliation of banks securities firms and other financial service providers and for other purposes
2000	Commodities futures modernization Act	Modernization regulation of financial products known as over-the-counter derivatives.
2004	Basel II published	Amend international standards that controlled how much capital banks need to hold to guard against the financial and operational risks banks face.
2004	Regulatory National Market System – Reg NMS	Set of rules proposed by the SEC to modernize and strengthen the regulatory structure of the U.S. equity markets adopted under Section 11A of the Securities Exchange Act of 1934.
2007	Markets in Financial Instruments Directive published	This directive governs the provision of investment services in financial instruments by banks and investment firms and the operation of traditional stock exchanges and alternative trading venues.
2008	On set of global recession	Reregulation move of the financial markets
2009	G20 meeting in Pittsburgh	It commits governments to improve transparency of the OTC Derivatives Markets
2010	Dodd – Frank Wall Street Reform and Consumer Protection Act signed	An Act to promote the financial stability of the United States by improving accountability and transparency in the financial system to end too big to fail to protect the American taxpayer by ending bailouts to protect consumers from abusive financial services practices and for other purposes.
2012	Volcker rule published	The rule is often referred to as a ban on proprietary trading by commercial banks whereby deposits are used to trade on the bank's own account, although a number of exceptions to this ban were included in the Dodd-Frank law
2012	European Market Infrastructure regulation (EMIR) passed into law	A European Union regulation designed to increase the stability of the over-the-counter (OTC) derivative markets throughout the EU states

(*continued*)

Table 8.2 (continued)

Date	Status of (de) regulatory change	Regulatory change description
2013	Dood – Frank swap dealer registration and swap data repository deadlines	Swap data repositories (SDRs) are new entities created by the Dodd – Frank Wall Street Reform and Consumer Protection Act (Dodd-Frank Act) in order to provide a central facility for swap data reporting and recordkeeping where all swaps whether cleared or uncleared are required to be reported to registered SDRs
2013	Phased implementation of rules for Basel III begins	Basel III is a global voluntary regulatory framework on bank capital adequacy stress testing and market liquidity risk.
2014	FATCA withholding begins	The Foreign Account Tax Compliance Act (FATCA) is a United States federal law requiring United States persons (including those living outside the U.S.) to have yearly reported themselves and their non-U.S. financial accounts to the Financial Crimes Enforcement Network (FINCEN) and requires all non-US (Foreign) Financial Institutions (FFI's) to search their records for suspected US persons for reporting their assets and identities to the US Treasury.
2017/2018	MiFID II/MiFIR implementation expected	The legislation in the form of a Directive that recasts MiFID (MiFID II) and a new Regulation (MiFIR) is one of the most important pieces of the post crisis regulatory reform puzzle.
2019	Vickers reforms deadline	With the Liikanen report, one of three proposed models for changing the structure of banks: Volcker in the US, Vickers in the UK and Liikanen in the European Union. Liikanen proposes that banks' trading business should be placed in separate subsidiaries.
2019	Basel III	Capital, leverage and liquidity requirements effective

Table 8.3 Broad overview of the key changes set out in MiFID II/MiFIR (*Source*: Linklaters – Factsheet 03 July 2014)

MiFID II/MiFIR	Key change	Description
MiFID II, Recitals 9–11, 39, 40, 87–89, Annex I, Sections A,B,C	Scope of MiFID	The entities, activities, and instruments to which MiFID will apply have been amended. The operation of an OTF, emission allowances and commodity derivatives have been added. Moreover, some provisions of MiFID have been extended to credit institutions and investment firms when selling or advising clients is in relation to structured deposits.
MiFID II, Recitals 53–55, Articles 9,45,63	Corporate governance	MiFID II includes new requirements for management bodies of investment firms, RMs, and data reporting services providers. RMs are subject to governance requirements similar to those for investment firms, including with regard to numerical limits on directorships, diversity, and nomination committees. Data reporting services providers are subject to more limited governance requirements, with no numerical limits on directorships or requirements for diversity or nomination committees.
MiFID II, Recitals 141–150, Articles 69–75	Supervisory Power and Sanctions	More defined measures have been introduced giving Member States less flexibility with regard to powers, remedies and sanctions. The main changes to the current regime include the following: *Competent authorities will be given the power to suspend the marketing or sale of investment products in certain circumstances, and require the removal of a person from the management board of an investment firm or market operator. *In the case of a breach, sanctions and other measures can be applied to members of the management body and other responsible persons, subject to national law. *Sanctions or measures imposed by competent authorities must be published and reported to ESMA, though this does not apply to sanctions of an investigatory nature. *When determining the type and level of sanctions, competent authorities must take specified factors (including turnover or income and net assets of the responsible person) into account. *Competent authorities may exercise their sanctioning powers directly, in collaboration with other authorities, by delegation to other entities and by application to judicial authorities. *With regard to agricultural commodity derivatives, competent authorities should cooperate with and report to public bodies responsible for regulating physical agricultural markets. *Competent authorities must implement effective mechanisms to encourage reporting of potential or actual breaches, including protections for whistle blowers. *Member States may decide not to impose administrative sanctions on infringements which are already subject to national criminal law as long as Member States communicate to the Commission the relevant criminal law provisions and measures are in place to cooperate and exchange information with other Member States and with ESMA.

(continued)

Table 8.3 (continued)

MiFID II/MiFIR	Key change	Description
MiFID II, Recitals 52,57,71, Article 16	Organisational requirements	*Organisational requirements have been expanded to include an approval process for new financial instruments and adaptations of existing financial instruments before they are marketed or distributed to clients, specifying the target market and ensuring that risks to the target market have been identified and that the distribution strategy is consistent with the target market. *Information security, recording of telephone conversations and electronic communications and the safeguarding of client assets are concerned by organisational requirements.
MiFIR, Article 23	Trading Rules for Equity instruments	*Transactions in shares admitted to trading on an RM or traded on a trading venue must take place on an RM, MTF or SI, or an equivalent third country trading venue, unless they are non-systematic, ad-hoc, irregular and infrequent, or carried out between eligible and/or professional counterparts and do not contribute to the price discovery process. *Investment firms that operate an internal matching system which executes client orders in shares and other equity instruments on a multilateral basis must be authorised as an MTF. These provisions were not included in the Commission's proposal.
MiFID II, Recitals 70–106, Articles 24–30	Investor protection	*A number of amendments and additions have been made to the investor protectionprovisions of MiFID. *The design, marketing, and distribution of products by investment firms must be tailored to the target market. Remuneration and sales targets should not incentivise staff to recommend inappropriate financial instruments to retail clients. *Member States may impose additional requirements in exceptional circumstances. *Best execution for retail clients will be determined based on total consideration, including the price of the financial instrument and all costs and expenses related to execution. *When assessing different execution venues, firms must take into account their owncommissions and costs for executing the order on different venues. *Firms may not receive any remuneration, discount or non-monetary benefit for routing orders to a particular venue that would be in breach of requirements on conflicts of interest or inducements. *Trading venues, SIs and execution venues must publish at least annually data relating to the quality of execution of transactions on that venue. *Investment firms must inform clients where orders have been executed. *Firms that execute client orders must also publish annually, for each class of financial instrument, the top five execution venues in terms of client orders, as well as information on quality of execution.

MiFID II, Recitals13,14, 112, Articles 4(1) (22), 4(1) (23),18–20; MiFIR, Recitals 7–9, Article 23	Trading venues: OTFs and MTFs	*An organised trading facility is a multilateral system in which mul tiple third-party buying and selling interests are able to interact in the system in a way that results in a contract under MiFID (limited OTFs to bonds, structured finance products, emission allowances and derivatives). *OTFs will have discretion as to how to execute orders, subject to pre-transparency and best execution obligations. OTFs are prohibited from executing client orders against their proprietary capital, which distinguishes them from SIs. *The requirements for MTFs have been aligned with those of RMs so that investment firms and market operators operating an MTF will be required to have (a) systems and measures in place to manage, identify and mitigate risks, (b) effective arrangements for the efficient and timely finalisation of transactions executed under its systems and (c) sufficient financial resources for its orderly functioning. *OTFs and MTFs must set arrangements in place to identify and manage conflicts of interest.
MiFIR, Recital 29, Articles 39–43	Product Intervention	*Nationalregulators, ESMA, and the European Banking Authority (EBA) will have new product intervention powers. ESMA and national regulators will monitor the market for financial instruments and, where appropriate, ban or restrict financial instruments, activities or practices. A competent authority must notify ESMA and other Member State regulators before it takes action, though it may take urgent action with less notice in exceptional circumstances. ESMA will play a coordinating role. *ESMA or the EBA may take action to address a significant investor protection concern or a threat to markets or to the stability of the financial system in the EU if applicable regulatory requirements do not address the threat and competent authorities have not taken adequate action. *In the case of agricultural commodities derivatives, ESMA will be required to consult with the regulators of physical agricultural markets before taking action.

(continued)

Table 8.3 (continued)

MiFID II/MiFIR	Key change	Description
MiFID II, Recitals 59–68, Articles 18(5), 48, 49, 50	Trading venues: Systems resilience, circuit breakers and electronic-trading	*RMs, MTFs, and OTFs will be required to implement systems, procedures andarrangements to ensure that their trading systems are resilient, have sufficient capacity, are able to ensure orderly trading under conditions of severe market stress, are fully tested, and are subject to business continuity arrangements and to reject orders that exceed pre-determined volume and price thresholds or are clearly erroneous. *Trading venues must have systems, procedures and arrangements in place to prevent and manage disorderly trading conditions arising from algorithmic trading systems, including by limiting the ratio of unexecuted orders, slowing order flow, enforcing minimum tick sizes, and requiring members or participants to test algorithms. *Trading venues must be able to halt or constrain transactions if there is a significant price movement in a short period and, in exceptional cases, to cancel, vary or correct transactions. *Parameters for halting trading must be reported to competent authorities. *Trading venues must have systems, procedures and arrangements in place to ensure that only authorised investment firms and credit institutions are able to provide direct electronic access, that they retain responsibility for trades executed using that service, and that they assess the suitability of persons to whom access is provided. *Trading venues must enter into agreements with market makers and have schemes in place to ensure a sufficient level of liquidity. The content of such agreements must be notified to competent authorities, and trading venues must monitor and enforce compliance by investment firms. Rules on co-location services must be transparent, fair, and non-discriminatory. *Fee structures must be transparent, fair, and non-discriminatory and must not create incentives for disorderly trading or market abuse. Venues must impose market making obligations in individual shares or a suitable basket of shares in exchange for any rebates and may impose higher fees on cancelled orders and high frequency traders. It has also been agreed that trading venues and their participants must synchronise the business clocks they use to record the date and time of reportable event.

MiFIR, Recitals 1,5,10, 12–18, 22,23, 26, Articles 3–22; MiFIDII, Recitals 117–119, Articles 64,65	Pre- and Post-trading: Transparency requirements	*The current requirements under MiFID, which are limited to shares, will be extended to cover other equity-like instruments such as depositary receipts and exchange-traded funds, as well as non-equity instruments including bonds, structured finance products, emission allowances, and derivatives, in each case including actionable indications of interest. *Pre-trade transparency may be waived, and post-trade disclosures deferred, in certain circumstances. Pre- and post-trade transparency for non-equity instruments may also be temporarily suspended if liquidity falls below a given threshold. While identical transparency requirements will apply to all trading venues, SIs will be subject to a different, tailored pre-trade transparency regime. *The agreed version of MiFID II also includes an amended version of the Commission's proposals for a consolidated tape provider (CTP), which will consolidate post-trade information into a continuous electronic data stream and made it publicly available as close to real time as technologically possible on a reasonable commercial basis and free of charge after 15 minutes. Both APAs and CTPs are new concepts under MiFID II and MiFIR. As of yet, no CTP has been identified.
MiFID II, Recitals 125–131, Articles 57, 58,69(2)(j), (o), (p); MiFIR, Recitals 30, 31,Articles 44, 45	Commodity derivative position, limits and reporting	*Member State regulators will set limits on the size of a net position that a person can hold at all times in commodity derivatives traded on trading venues as well as economically equivalent OTC contracts. *Limits will not apply to positions held by or on behalf of non-financial entities for hedging purposes. The limits will be established in accordance with a methodology for calculation determined by ESMA, on the basis of all positions held by a person individually and on its behalf at aggregate group level, in order to prevent market abuse and support orderly pricing and settlement conditions. *The methodology will take a number of factors into account, including maturity of the contracts, the deliverable supply of the underlying commodities, the overall open interest in the contract and other financial instruments having the same underlying, market volatility, the number and size of market participants, the characteristics of the underlying commodity market, and the development of new contracts. *Member States can apply stricter limits on a temporary basis in exceptional cases. The limits will be intended to ensure, in particular, the convergence between prices of derivatives in the delivery month and spot prices for the underlying commodity. * Trading venues will be required to publish aggregate positions in commodity derivatives or emission allowances or derivatives thereof by category of person on a weekly basis, but only when the number of persons and their open positions exceed minimum thresholds.

(continued)

Table 8.3 (continued)

MiFID II/MiFIR	Key change	Description
MiFIR, Recitals 25–27, Articles 28–34	Derivatives Trading	*In order to meet G20 commitments, derivative contracts declared subject to the trading obligation by ESMA will be required to be traded on an RM, MTF, or OTF. *The trading obligation will only apply where both counterparts are subject to clearing obligations under EMIR, and excludes intra-group transactions and portfolio compression exercises. *ESMA will determine which classes of derivatives are subject to the trading obligation. In order for the trading obligation to take effect, the class of derivatives must be sufficiently liquid. *MiFIR also includes a new requirement that transactions in cleared derivatives must be submitted and accepted for clearing as quickly as technologically practicable using automated systems, including derivatives not subject to the clearing obligation under EMIR.
MiFID II, Recitals 109–111, Articles 39–43; MiFIR, Recitals 41–44, Articles 46–49, 54	Third Country Firms	The Commission had proposed a passporting regime for third country firms providing services to retail clients from a branch in a Member State as well as those providing services to eligible counterparties (ECPs) and professional clients (PCs) without a branch. In each case, the Commission would have required a determination that the firm was subject to equivalent supervision in its home jurisdiction.
MiFID II, Recitals 132–135, Article 33	SME growth markets	*In order to help small and medium-sized entities access capital, MiFID II introduces a new category of MTFs known as SME growth markets. At least 50 % of the issuers whose financial inst ruments are traded on an SME growth market should be SMEs. *For these purposes, an SME is defined as a company that had an average market capitalisation of less than EUR 200,000,000 on the basis of end-year quotes for the previous three calendar years.

MiFIR, Recitals 32–36, Articles 24–27; MiFID II, Article 66	Transaction Reporting and recordkeeping	*While investment firms will still have to report details of their transactions in instruments admitted to trading or traded on an RM or MTF (and now also an OTF) to their national competent authorities, they will now also have to report transactions in financial instruments (a) where admission to trading has been requested, and (b) where the underlying is a financial instrument (or an index or basket of financial instruments) traded on a trading venue. The reporting obligation applies regardless of whether the transaction is carried out on the trading venue. *The reported information must include the identity of the client (using legal entityidentifiers where appropriate) and the person or algorithm responsible for the investment decision and execution. Short sales and any applicable waivers must also be identified. In the case of commodity derivatives, the report must indicate whether the transaction reduces risk in an objectively measurable way in accordance with MiFID II. *Recordkeeping requirements for investment firms will be extended to trading venues, and ESMA will be able to access investment firm records. Investment firms must keep data relating to all orders (as well as transactions). Records maintained by trading venues must include data that constitute the characteristics of an order, including data that link orders to executed transactions.
MiFID II, Recitals 59–68, Article 17	Investment Firms: Algorithmic Trading and Direct Electronic Access	*Investment firms that engage in algorithmic trading must have in place suitable systems and controls to ensure their trading systems are resilient and have sufficient capacity, are subject to appropriate trading thresholds and limits, and prevent erroneous orders or the system otherwise functioning in a way that could create or contribute to a disorderly market.

(continued)

Table 8.3 (continued)

MiFID II/MiFIR	Key change	Description
		*Firms must have business continuity arrangements in place and ensure that their systems are tested and monitored. They must also have systems and risk controls to ensure that their trading systems cannot be used in any way that is contrary to the Market Abuse Regulation or the rules of a trading venue to which they are connected. *A firm which provides direct electronic access to a trading venue must have systems and controls in place to review the suitability of clients using the service, to prevent clients from exceeding pre-set trading and credit thresholds, to monitor trading, and to implement appropriate risk controls. Direct electronic access without these controls is prohibited. *The investment firm will be responsible for ensuring that its clients comply with the requirements of MiFID II and the rules of the trading venue. Rights and obligations must be set out in a binding written agreement between the firm and the client, under which the firm retains responsibility under MiFID. *Firms that act as a general clearing member for their clients must have systems and controls in place to ensure that clearing services are only provided to suitable persons who meet clear criteria and that requirements are imposed on these persons to reduce risks to the firm and the market. Rights and obligations must be set out in a binding written agreement.
MiFID II, Recitals 29,42, Article 3	Optional Exemptions	The scope of optional exemptions by Member States has been extended to include persons who provide investment services exclusively in (a) commodities, emission allowances and/or derivatives thereof for the sole purpose of hedging the commercial risks of local electricity undertakings and/or natural gas undertakings or (b) emission allowances and/or derivatives thereof for the sole purpose of hedging the commercial risks of operators of installations subject to the EU directive on emissions trading (2003/87/EC), provided in each case that these clients jointly hold 100 % of the capital or of the voting rights of such persons, exercise joint control and would be exempt under the ancillary business exemption if they carried out the investment services themselves.
MiFID II, recitals 18–25, 35, 41, Article 2(1)	MiFID Exemptions	A number of changes have been made to the list of MiFID exemptions. *Dealing on own account exemption: Currently, persons who do not provide investment services other than dealing on own account are exempt, unless they are (a) market makers or (b) deal on own account outside an RM or MTF on an organised, frequent and systematic basis by providing a system accessible to third parties. This exemption has been amended so that it will not apply to dealing on own account in commodity derivatives, emission allowances or derivatives thereof. Members of and participants in an RM or MTF, persons who have direct market access to a trading venue, and persons engaged in high frequency trading will also be excluded from the exemption.

*Emission allowances trading by installation operators: MiFID II will not apply tooperators with compliance obligations under the EU directive on emissions trading(2003/87/EC) who, when dealing in emission allowances, do not execute client orders or provide any investment services or perform any investment activities other than dealing on own account, provided they do not apply a high frequency trading technique.

*Ancillary business exemption: The dealing on own account limb of this exemption will be restricted to commodity derivatives, emission allowances or derivatives thereof, and will include market makers (provided that market making in commodity derivatives is not their main business). As proposed by the Commission, it will exclude persons who deal on own account by executing client orders. The exemption also applies to persons who provide investment services (other than dealing on own account) in commodity derivatives, emissionallowances or derivatives thereof to the customers or suppliers of their main business. The activity must be ancillary on an individual and group basis, and high frequency traders will not be able to use the exemption. Firms will be required to notify regulators annually that they are using the exemption and, upon request, report the basis on which they consider an activity to be ancillary.

*Commodities dealer exemption: As proposed by the Commission, the exemption for persons who deal on own account in commodities and commodities derivatives has been deleted.

*Locals exemption: The exemption for locals (i.e. those who exclusively deal on own account on derivatives and cash markets for hedging purposes or who deal for accounts of other market members or make prices for them, where performance is guaranteed by clearing members) has been deleted. Commodity related systems The Commission's proposed new exemption for transmission system operators has been amended to include persons acting as service providers on behalf of transmission system operators, as well as certain other persons, and limited to relevant activities in commodity derivatives. The exemption will not apply to the operation of a secondary market.

*Central Securities Depositaries: Central Securities Depositaries (CSDs) will be authorised under the CSD Regulation, which was agreed in trilogue in December 2013. They will be subject to MiFID rules where they carry out MiFID services or activities that are not expressly mentioned in the Annex to the CSD Regulation.

Source: Linklaters – Factsheet 03 July 2014

Bibliography

Abad, D., & Yague, J. (2012). From PIN to VPIN: An introduction to order flow toxicity. *The Spanish Review of Financial Economics, 10*(2), 74–83.

Aitken, M., Sensenbrenner, F., & Harris, F. (2010). Price discovery in liquid UK shares Pre and Post MiFID, *Available at SSRN 2250459.*

Andersen, T., & Bondarenko, O. (2014). VPIN and the flash crash. *Journal of Financial Markets, 17,* 1–46.

Bachelier, L. (1900). Théorie de la spéculation, Gauthier-Villars.

Bauer, G. (2004). Typologie de l'efficience des marchés, *Revue du système financier,* 39–42.

Bloch, E., & Schwartz, R. (1978). The great debate over NYSE rule 390. *The Journal of Portfolio Management, 5*(1), 5–8.

Boneva, L., Linton, O., & Vogt, M. (2015). The effect of fragmentation in trading on market quality in the UK equity market. *Journal of Applied Econometrics, 31, 192-213.*

Bozdog, D., Florescu, I., Khashanah, K., & Wang, J. (2011). Rare events analysis for high-frequency equity data. *Wilmott, 2011*(54), 74–81.

Brogaard, J., Hendershott, T., & Riordan, R. (2014). High frequency trading and price discovery. *Review of Financial Studies, 27*(8), 2267–2306.

Cherbonnier, F., & Vandelanoite, S. (2008). The impact on financial market liquidity of the markets in financial instruments directive (MiFID). *Banque de France – Financial Stability Review, 2, 75.*

Clemons, E., & Weber, B. (1990). London's Big Bang: a case study of information technology, competitive impact, and organizational change. *Journal of Management Information Systems, 6*(4), 41–60.

Cobbaut, R., Gillet, R., & Hübner, G. (2015). La gestion de portefeuille: Instruments, stratégie et performance, De Boeck Supérieur.

Cochrane, J. (2009). *Asset pricing.* Princeton: Princeton University Press.

Cohen, K., & Schwartz, R.. (2001). An electronic call market: Its design and desirability, In *The electronic call auction: Market mechanism and trading,* volume 7 of The New York University Salomon Center Series on Financial Markets and Institutions, pp. 55–85, Springer.

Doumayrou, B. (2008). Entre concurrence et efficience: l'impact de la directive MIF sur la liquidité des marchés actions reste difficile à anticiper, *Bulletin de la Banque de France,* (169), 49.

Easley, D., Kiefer, N., O'Hara, M., & Paperman, J. (1996). Liquidity, information, and infrequently traded stocks. *The Journal of Finance, 51*(4), 1405–1436.

Easley, D., de Prado, M. L., & O'Hara, M. (2012a). Flow toxicity and liquidity in a High-Frequency world. *Review of Financial Studies, 25*(5), 1457–1493.

Easley, D., de Prado, M. L., & O'Hara, M. (2012b). Bulk classification of trading activity. *Johnson School Research Paper Series, 8.*

ECB, Statistical Data Warehouse. (2014). http://sdw.ecb.europa.eu. Online; accessed 16-July-2015.

Fama, E. (1965). The behaviour of stock-market prices. *Journal of Business, 38*(1), 34–105.

Fama, E. (1970). Efficient capital markets: A review of theory and empirical work. *The Journal of Finance, 25*(2), 383–417.

Fama, E. (1991). Efficient capital markets II. *The Journal of Finance, 46*(5), 1575–1617.

Fleuriot, P. (2010). The review of the markets in financial instruments directive (MiFID), *Working Group Report to the French Minister for the Economy, Industry and Employment.*

Foucault, T., & Menkveld, A. (2008). Competition for order flow and smart order routing systems. *The Journal of Finance, 63*(1), 119–158.

Gerding, E. (2014). Law, bubbles, and financial regulation, http://corpgov.law.harvard.edu. Online; accessed 16-July-2015.

Gresse, C. (2010a). Multi market trading and market liquidity, *Technical report, Université Paris-Dauphine.*

Gresse, C. (2014a). Market fragmentation and market quality: The European experience. In *Market microstructure and nonlinear dynamics* (pp. 1–24). Cham: Springer.

Gresse, C. (2014b). Market fragmentation: Assessments and prospects? *Revue du Conseil scientifique de l'Autorité des marchés financiers, 1*, 23–37.

Hamon, J., Jacquillat, B., & Saint Étienne, C. (2007). Consolidation mondiale des bourses, *La Documentation francaise.*

Harris, L. (2003). *Trading and exchanges: Market microstructure for practitioners.* Oxford/New York: Oxford University Press.

Harris, F., & Di Marco, E. (2012). European market quality pre- and post-MiFID: A panel discussion of metrics for market integrity and efficiency. *The Journal of Trading, 7*(4), 7–26.

Hasbrouck, J. (2006). *Empirical market microstructure: The institutions, economics, and econometrics of securities trading.* Oxford/New York: Oxford University Press.

Hautcoeur, P.-C., Lagneau-Ymonet, P., & Riva, A. (2010). L'information boursière comme bien public: Enjeux et perspectives de la révision de la directive Européenne des marchés d'instruments financiers. *Revue d'économie financière, 98*(98–99), 297–315.

Jacquemin, A., Wright, D., & Silberston, A. (1994). The European Challenges Post-1992: Shaping factors, shaping actors. *Economic Journal, 104*, 678–679. Wiley on behalf of the Royal Economic Society.

Krishnamurti, C. (2009). Introduction to market microstructure. In *Investment management* (pp. 13–29). Springer.

Linklaters. (2014). Revision of the markets in financial instruments directive (MiFID II), http://www.linklaters.com. Online; accessed 16-July-2015.

Madhavan, A. (2000). Market microstructure: A survey. *Journal of Financial markets, 3*(3), 205–258.

Modigliani, F., & Perotti, E. (2000). Security markets versus bank finance: Legal enforcement and investors' protection. *International Review of Finance, 1*(2), 81–96.

Mundell, R. (1961). A theory of optimum currency areas. *The American Economic Review, 51*(4), 657–665.

O'Hara, M. (1995). *Market microstructure theory*. Cambridge: Blackwell.

O'Hara, M. (2003). Presidential address: Liquidity and price discovery. *The Journal of Finance, 58*(4), 1335–1354.

O'Hara, M., & Ye, M. (2011). Is market fragmentation harming market quality? *Journal of Financial Economics, 100*(3), 459–474.

Petrella, G. (2010). MiFID, Reg NMS and competition across trading venues in Europe and the USA. *Journal of Financial Regulation and Compliance, 18*(3), 257–271.

Praet, P. (2012). European financial integration in times of crisis, https://www.ecb.europa.eu. Online accessed 24-July-2015.

Rigobon, R., & Sack, B. (2004). The impact of monetary policy on asset prices. *Journal of Monetary Economics, 51*(8), 1553–1575.

Samuelson, P. (1965). Proof that properly anticipated prices fluctuate randomly. *Industrial Management Review, 6*(2), 41–49.

Schacht, K., Cronin, C., Allen, J., & Preece, R. (2009). Market microstructure: The impact of fragmentation under the markets in financial instruments directive. *CFA Institute Centre for Financial Market Integrity, 2009*(13), 60.

Schreiber, P., & Schwartz, R. (1986). Price discovery in securities markets. *The Journal of Portfolio Management, 12*(4), 43–48.

Schwartz, R. (2013). Opening remarks: Good price discovery, the neglected regulatory objective. In *Rethinking Regulatory Structure* (Vol. 10, pp. 1–5). New York: Springer, 2013.

Shiller, R. J. (2003). From efficient markets theory to behavioural finance. *The Journal of Economic Perspectives, 17*(1), 83–104.

Véron, N (2014). The G20 financial reform agenda after five years, *Technical Report 11, Bruegel Policy Contribution*.

Walter, C (2012). La martingalisation des marchés financiers: l'efficacité informationnelle comme convention stochastique.

Zhang, F. (2010). High-frequency trading, stock volatility, and price discovery. *Available at SSRN 1691679*.

9

The Evolution of Insurance Regulation in the EU Since 2005

Pierre-Charles Pradier and Arnaud Chneiweiss

9.1 Introduction

While the consequences of the 2008 financial crisis seem to roll away, with many countries either back to growth or facing different problems, there is still a common tendency to blame the financial sector for the grim economic situation of the Eurozone, as if every financial institution bore a portion of liability for high unemployment, low investment and poor economic outlook. Some seem even more liable than others: in a report to the G20 members, the International Monetary Fund (IMF) (2009) chose to study the cases of Northern Rock, Lehman Brothers and American International Group (AIG). Is this to say that the insurance sector is responsible for *one-third* of the misfortunes of the time? This would be highly questionable. Nevertheless, there is a widespread idea that strong regulation of the insurance sector is needed to improve overall welfare. In the European Union (EU), the legal framework has shifted from the "Solvency I" set of third generation EU directives (2002/13/EC for non-life insurers and 2002/83/EC for life insurers) implemented in

P.-C. Pradier (✉)
LabEx RéFi and CES, Université Paris 1 Panthéon-Sorbonne, Paris, France

A. Chneiweiss
Fédération Française de l'Assurance, Paris, France

199

R. Douady et al. (eds.), *Financial Regulation in the EU*,
DOI 10.1007/978-3-319-44287-7_9

2004 to Solvency 2 (S2), passed in November 2009 as directive 2009/138/EC, eventually implemented from 1 January 2016 after many delays. Meanwhile a European Insurance and Occupational Pension Authority (EIOPA) was created in 2010 together with banking (EBA) and market (ESMA) counterparts to enforce the law and supervise the corresponding actors. To what aim?

The International Association of Insurance Supervisors (IAIS) issued in 2011 "insurance core principles" (later ICP) defining the objectives of supervision: "maintaining a fair, safe and stable insurance sector for the benefit and protection of the interests of policyholders" (IAIS 2013c p. 4). Decoding is needed to understand that "fair" is related to market or conduct regulation, "safe" to solvency regulation and "stable" to the system-wide consequences of firm-level problems, hence systemic risk.[1] The EU Commission, on the other hand, takes into account a broader picture, where regulation aims at economic growth and employment through adequate microeconomic incentives (DG ECOFIN 2007). European regulation, though, must also develop the European single market, while the insurance sector still appears fragmented at country level. A true European insurance market is needed to enable students and workforce to move freely inside the EU; it would make local innovation available at EU level; it would thus benefit employment and growth.

In order to analyse in due detail the aforementioned themes, the remainder of the chapter is organized as follows: Sect. 9.2 deals with market regulation; Sect. 9.3 is concerned with solvency; Sect. 9.4 with systemic risk; Sect. 9.5 summarizes the costs of regulation and their consequence; while Sect. 9.6 looks at the consistency of the whole and offers some further developments and alternatives.

* * *

9.2 Market Regulation

Market regulation is related to business conduct, comprising both business-to-business and business-to-consumer relationships. We will review price regulation (Sect. 9.2.1) and explicit consumer protection (Sect. 9.2.2) before

---

[1] The recent reference paper on insurance regulation in the *Handbook of insurance* (Klein 2014) uses different words to address the same issues: "(1) catastrophe risk, (2) competition and (3) systemic risk," with catastrophe being connected to solvency, competition to market and conduct and systemic risk being obvious. See also recital (16) of S2: "The main objective of insurance and reinsurance regulation and supervision is the adequate protection of policy holders (...) Financial stability and fair and stable markets are other objectives of insurance regulation."

turning to solvency, which can be understood as a particular form of consumer protection.

9.2.1 Price Regulations

Back in the 1980s or early 1990s, insurance firms were in many continental European countries under close supervisory tutelage since EU member states could introduce "laws, regulations or administrative provisions concerning, in particular, approval of general and special policy conditions, of forms (…) of premiums…" (Dir. 1988/357/EC on non-life insurance art. 18, Dir. 1990/619/EC on life insurance art. 12). The 1992 Directives terminated this "interventionist era" and abolished prior approval of prices and forms (see especially art. 39 of Dir. 1992/49/EC on non-life and art. 29 of Dir. 1992/96/EC on life insurance). By that time, 31 US states also had prior rate approval for automobile insurance (Harrington 2002 p. 292). The rationale for the EU's liberal move was the inefficiency of prior approval; as Harrington later brilliantly summed up: "There is little or no evidence that prior approval on average has a material effect on average rates for any given level of claim costs. This finding is consistent with an inability of rate regulation to reduce average rates materially and persistently in competitively structured markets without significantly reducing product quality or ultimately causing widespread exit by insurers" (Harrington 2002 pp. 310–311).

In fact, some marginal price regulation remained, such as the compulsory "bonus" system in France (*code des assurances* A. 121); the basic idea behind it was to allow comparison of prices over time, a feature now rendered useless by Internet price comparison sites and on-demand contract termination (enabled by the recent 2014-344 law on consumption in France). The strongest point on pricing policy, though, was made by the European Court of Justice ruling of 1 March 2011 in the Test-Achats case (C-236/09), which gave insurers until 21 December 2012 to change their pricing policies in order to treat individual male and female customers *equally* in terms of insurance premiums and benefits. The scope of the ruling has since then been thought (Rego 2015) as encompassing all topics covered by Article 21 of the Charter of Fundamental Rights of the European Union (2000/C 364/01): "Any discrimination based on any ground such as sex, race, colour, ethnic or social origin, genetic features, language, religion or belief, political or any other opinion, membership of a national minority, property, birth, disability, age or sexual orientation shall be prohibited." It is now uncertain whether place of residence will remain a valid basis for price discrimination after the EU commission decided in July 2015 to probe Eurodisney for charging Northern European customers more (Barker 2015). But the general idea is this: the supervisor is no longer supposed to decide on insurance prices; only the principles of pricing policy are amenable to regulation according to general non-discrimination principles.

The overall effect of the liberalization of insurance marketing since the 1990s seems quite satisfactory. Table 9.1 shows that the price of insurance grew overall at almost the same pace as general inflation, with property-casualty insurance (as exemplified by dwelling and transport insurances) even slower than Consumer Price Indices, and health insurance growing faster since health expenses outpaced other consumption items in the EU. Appendix 9.1 shows that prices in the EU grew not as fast as in the European Economic Association, for instance, indicating that EU regulation could be better than its neighbour countries'. Now if we look at price convergence in the EU, the Eurostat Harmonised Index of Consumer Prices (see Appendix 9.1) is not precise enough, since it provides only variations, not absolute levels; hence all we can learn is that Eastern Europe (apart from Romania and Bulgaria) experienced a relative fall in prices, which can be interpreted as convergence toward Western European prices. It seems difficult to go farther than this conjecture, since average price for insurance contracts computed by most member states' insurance associations do not feature the same guarantees from one country to another. Overall, the general moderation of prices tends to show that competition is working better than under the previous overdone supervision. Until recently, academic evidence interpreted the Internet as a disciplining device: Brown and Goolsbee (2002) had shown that the use of the Internet significantly reduced the price of insurance products which were offered through online channels, and hence were amenable to easy comparison. This evidence has been recently challenged by theoretical papers (Edelman-Wright 2015; Ronayne 2015), which proved that price comparison websites do not warrant the desirable properties of perfect competition (e.g. a unique price for a given service); furthermore these sites add their margin to the price paid by the consumer, which has a significant negative welfare impact. The combined effect has to be taken into account, not before business models in distribution are stabilized after further innovation likely to happen in the coming years.

Table 9.1 Evolution of insurance prices 1996–2014 as percentage of CPI

Average	Dwelling	Health	Transport	Other
104.26	91.07	164.43	99.58	186.86

Source: Eurostat, HICP COICOP CP125

Our inquiry so far proves that consumer protection issues have changed dramatically since the 1980s: with increased competition, overpricing is no longer a concern for the supervisor. Concern remains on misinformation and misselling on the one hand dealt with by "conduct authorities," while on the other hand "prudential authorities" focus on solvency (Sect. 9.3, below), which might become an issue when contracts are underpriced (see also Plantin and Rochet 2007).

9.2.2 Consumer Protection

Most new rules pertaining to consumer protection are related to information: S2 articles 183 to 186 list precisely what information should be included in the contracts. Moreover, the Packaged Retail and Insurance-based Investment Products (PRIIPs, Regulation EU1286/2014) defines the set of key facts (assembled in a Key Information Document or KID), which should be provided to retail customers by investment product manufacturers; the number of pre-sale obligations also rise (from 29 to 102 according to Insurance Europe). The Insurance Distribution Directive (Directive EU 2016/97 due for implementation in national law in 2018) will force brokers to disclose the incentives and remuneration given to them by insurance companies. This normative approach is in fact different from prior form approval, as it existed before 1992, since consumer information is now in a process of being harmonized among member states, not the contractual clauses themselves.

It should be emphasized that a common legal framework does not imply uniform supervision, as recent history has shown: the appointment of Martin Wheatley as head of the Financial Conduct Authority of the United Kingdom in 2011 was seen as a symbol of an especially tough stance, which now seems to have reached its limits in the UK (FT 2015). Martin Wheatley had a personal record of solving a difficult case at Hong Kong's Securities and Futures Commission, where thousands of savers lost money in complex structured products linked to Lehman Brothers. George Osborne, the UK Chancellor of the Exchequer, chose him to broker a solution in the Personal Protection Insurance (PPI) misselling crisis, as more than 1 million complaints have already been filed against intermediaries for various misselling of these products (which were usually sold to people who already enjoyed an income insurance in case of illness or unemployment, or were sold on wrong promises). The boss of the Financial Conduct Authority (FCA) set up a simplified process, which enabled the plaintiffs to get their money back (FCA 2014). As of May 2016, more than 15 million complaints have been filed, leading to more than £23.8

billion in redress being paid since 2011.[2] Never had such a large sum been paid as the result of a financial regulator's decision. The need for funding led to price increases in the UK (see Appendix 9.1), which appeared to be detrimental to the consumer in the long run; this ultimately led Wheatley to resign.

The punitive approach is still fashionable on the Continent, especially in France, where every foreign example is followed rigorously:

1. the French Conseil d'Etat decision n° 353885 (23 July 2012) about loan insurance mimics the FCA approach to PPI,
2. the French and Belgian action in favour of dormant life insurance contracts is inspired by the reparation of Nazi Germany crimes against the Jews.

In France, complaints against loan insurance are very common, and the PPI is a regular reference among commentators. There is an undeniable problem as competition between banks crushed their profit margins, so most of the money they make when lending is on loan insurance: a typically perverse situation which has led to many complaints. In 2012, the Conseil d'Etat eventually settled the pending cases by deciding that (1) a section of the *code des assurances* (article A. 331–3) was illegal before an ordinance of 23 April 2007 was issued to correct the problem; and (2) no redress was to be awarded, since decision 307089 of 5 May 2010 by the same Conseil d'Etat had already established that only a clause in the contracts (which was banned by the aforementioned article A. 331–3) could have justified such redress. In the end, the Conseil did not go far enough to make the State liable for its past error, but the symbolic aspect of the decision was widely commented upon.

The French and Belgian action about dormant life insurance contracts has its origin in the action taken in reparation for Aryanization by Nazi Germany. An International Commission on Holocaust Era Insurance Claims was set up in 1998 (ICHEIC 2007b), which eventually permitted the award of more than $300 million to 48,000 claimants (ICHEIC 2007a). In Europe, the Directive 2002/83/CE included some provisions to enable the claims to be processed; they were translated in France by law 2005-1564 15 December 2005 and in Belgium by the 24 July 2008 law, after an independent commission reported on the extent of looting of Jewish property during the war (Buysse 2008). Hence a one-off reparation of past injustices led to a permanent jurisprudence with non-negligible consequences: in France alone, two more laws were passed to settle the case of dormant insurance contracts (law 2007-1775,

---

[2] https://www.fca.org.uk/consumers/financial-services-products/insurance/payment-protection-insurance/ppi-compensation-refunds.

17 December 2007 and 2014-617, 13 June 2014). Media coverage boasted billions retained by the insurers while the vice-president of the supervisor (ACPR, the *Autorité de contrôle prudentiel et de résolution*) claimed the insurers to have behaved "scandalously" (Le Monde 2013), but no formal impact assessment was performed; in the end, the French legal provisions organize the custody of dormant contracts via the state-owned *Caisse des Dépôts* before they are taken over after 20 years: the State is so much concerned by customer protection that it has appointed itself as perpetual trustee. Apart from these good intentions, the main result for the time being has been administrative penalties imposed upon some insurance companies by ACPR, the largest so far in French history.[3]

* * *

Since the liberal reform of 2002, Europe has been relying on effective competition to achieve price discipline in the insurance sector, with apparent success. Consumer protection is now seen by European authorities as provision to the prospect or consumer of exhaustive product information. Recently, some national insurance supervisors or regulators have taken a tougher stance, which contrasts with a legal approach aimed at European harmonization. Let us look now more precisely at the solvency regulation, which is designed to enforce the policyholder's right to indemnification.

9.3   The Solvency II Process

The S2 regulatory package contains provisions for consumer protection, but as the name implies, its main focus is on solvency. We introduce the objectives and features of the regulatory package (Sect. 9.3.1) before we review the positive aspects (Sect. 9.3.2) and the more controversial, still unsolved issues (Sect. 9.3.3).

9.3.1   Objective and Features of the Solvency II Package

The proposed directive was introduced with an accompanying document (EC 2007) that looks like an extended set of recitals, stating four weaknesses of the then current regulatory regime and four objectives for the planned one:

---

[3] €10 million for Cardif on 7 April 2014, €40 million for CNP on 31 October 2014, €50 million for Allianz on 19 December 2014.

1) Weaknesses of existing regime

   a) (**w1**) Lack of risk sensitivity (the capital requirement of Solvency I was a function of premia or claims, not of the effective risk faced by insurance institutions);
   b) (**w2**) Restriction of the single market (Solvency I "sets out minimum standards that can be supplemented by additional rules at national level") ;
   c) (**w3**) Insufficient supervision of conglomerates and groups;
   d) (**w4**) Lack of convergence with both the banking regulation (i.e. Basel) and the international standards (as promoted by the International Association of Insurance Supervisors) leading to the possibility of regulatory arbitrage.

2) Objectives of planned reform

   a) (**o1**) Deepen the integration of the EU insurance market;
   b) (**o2**) Enhance the protection of policyholders and beneficiaries;
   c) (**o3**) Improve the international competitiveness of EU insurers and reinsurers;
   d) (**o4**) Promote better regulation;

3) One should now add

   (a) (**o5-r**), financial stability, which was not a major issue in 2007, but became the main concern of policymakers when the crisis broke out and took momentum.

While **o4** seems an obvious objective for any concerned lawmaker and **o1** seems to respond to **w2** by extending the scope of the EU regulation (thus leaving less to do at the national level to prevent regulatory arbitrage between countries), **o3** and **o2** might appear conflicting as the protection of policyholders raises the cost function of the insurers, while greater international competitiveness could only be achieved by extracting a higher profit from the domestic consumers. Alternatively, the idea behind the reform package is simply that insurance buyers are paying to be sure that they will get relief in case of an unfortunate event; in other words they are buying the insurance company's solvency. Better regulation (**o4**) can then warrant solvency (hence the name) and thus raise consumer satisfaction in order to improve insurer competitiveness.

The constraints **w4** and **w3** determine S2 to converge with the banking sector regulation to guarantee conglomerates are correctly monitored and to prevent regulatory arbitrage between sectors. Hence the architecture of the new reform looks very much like the then-in-force Basel II standards, with three "pillars"[4]:

- Pillar 1—quantitative (capital) requirements—includes market-consistent valuation of the balance sheet leading to a risk-sensitive (**w1**) assessment of capital requirements.
- Pillar 2—is relative to corporate and risk governance.
- Pillar 3—is concerned with disclosure and transparency requirements.

More precisely, Pillar 1 introduces deep changes with former practices:

1. All assets and liabilities obey a market consistent valuation (art. 75).[5] Insurance liabilities that cannot be valued using market prices are split into a best estimate (current estimate of expected cash flows, discounted using the risk-free yield curve) and a risk margin (costs of ensuring that the capital needed to support the insurance obligations, based on a cost-of-capital rate given by the supervisor).
2. Then a Solvency Capital Requirement or SCR is calculated as the sum of partial risks plus correlation factors. For every risk class, an assessment is made of the loss that may arise with a 0.5 % probability over the next 12 months[6]: this is the (100%–0.5 %=) "99.5% 1-year Value-at-Risk."

---

[4] Although neither the pillars themselves nor their designation appear in the Directive, every analytical introduction to Solvency II describes these pillars by analogy with Basel II.

[5] Prudential accounting standards are specific, albeit close to IFRS 4 "phase I," which are compulsory for listed companies and will be replaced by "phase II," likely to be implemented in 2019 after two exposure drafts in 2010 and 2013. For a comparison of the two standards, see Visser and McEneaney (2015).

[6] The solvency capital requirement is such that it must provide the insurance firm with enough of its own funds to absorb the operating loss that could occur 199 years out of 200 (if the financial future is consistent with the observed history since 1971). Conversely, there is only a one in 200 chance that the solvency capital requirement is not enough to overcome the operating loss.

This operating loss can be computed with an *internal model* authorized by the relevant supervisor or with the *standard formula* as the sum of partial risks (EIOPA 2014) broken down into three categories (basic SCR, operational risk and adjustment); BSCR features six modules and 35 sub-modules, every one being the Value-at-Risk at 99.5 % of the corresponding risk. The standard formula takes correlation into account, through the definition equation:

$$BSCR = \sum_{i=1}^{35} SCR_i + \sum_{i=1}^{35}\sum_{\substack{j=1\\j\neq i}}^{35} \sqrt{\rho_{i,j} SCR_i SCR_j}$$

or more generally

3. If the own funds (classified in three tiers according to their quality) are below SCR, then the supervisor should take appropriate action.
4. Minimum Capital Requirement (MCR) is a lower threshold[7]: if the own funds are insufficient to cover MCR, immediate and ultimate supervisory action is triggered.

Pillar 2 (art. 40–50) defines the central Own Risk Self Assessment (art. 45) and imposes strong requirements on the key functions (art 41–49: actuarial function, internal audit, internal control, risk management plus governance), which should be performed by fit and proper persons. **Pillar 3** defines specific prudential accounting standards as well as disclosure modes to the supervisor (art. 27–39, revised in Omnibus) and to the public (art. 51–56).
This important regulation had a mixed reception.

9.3.2 Positive Interpretation

By comparison with other regulatory frameworks, S2 was generally welcomed by academics. In particular, Doff (2008), Holzmüller (2009), Lorent (2010) among others, compared the planned reform to other frameworks by applying a set of criteria: EU solvency appears to clearly dominate the US regulations, and does marginally better than the Swiss in some respects, as their summary table shows.

These criteria, while being somewhat shared among insurance academic specialists, are not aligned with the Insurance Core Principles as defined by the IAIS, for instance (IAIS 2013c). There is some overlapping among the sets of criteria, though: for instance item 1 "getting appropriate incentives," in Holzmüller is connected to ICP7 (corporate governance) and ICP17 (capital requirements); item 2 is reminiscent of ICP16 (ERM for solvency purposes)[8]

$$BSCR = \sum_{i=1}^{35}\sum_{j=1}^{35}\sqrt{\rho_{i,j} SCR_i SCR_j}$$

where $\rho_{i,j}$ denotes the linear correlation coefficient between SCR_i (for sub-module i) and SCR_j provided by the supervisor.

[7] Article 129 of the Directive introduced calculation principles for the MCR, which were rather vague, and article 130 enabled the Commission to adopt implementing measures. The final rules (Delegated Regulation EU 2015/35 art 248–253) are far more complex than the usually alleged "1-year 85% VaR" of the original Directive. The most striking feature of the complete rule set is that MCR is not fully risk-sensitive. To be more precise, MCR is the maximum of a linear formula (involving mostly technical provisions of the company) and of 25 % of the SCR, capped at 45 % of the SCR.

[8] Cf. 16.16.13 "risk sensitive regulatory financial requirements should provide the incentive for optimal alignment of the insurer's risk and capital management and regulatory requirements."

and ICP17; item 3 is relative to preliminary impact assessment which should meet, among others, ICP17 at a micro level and ICP24 at a macro level; item 4 is also connected to ICP24; item 5 is related to ICP14 (valuation); and so on.

Preliminary impact assessment generally concluded that sound principles were correctly implemented by the projected reform, and that they would enable more effective competition and supervision, leading to healthier insurance firms and better pricing of products, hence a higher demand and consumption of insurance products, leading to enhanced consumer satisfaction with a positive impact on growth, as academic research such as Outreville (1990) and Webb et al. (1992) had shown. While "the direct *macroeconomic effect of Solvency II would be rather marginal*," the study ordered by the European Commission in 2007 concluded that the process would lead to better efficiency and better European integration of both the insurance industry and the financial markets (DG ECOFIN 2007). The ECB was more prudent in identifying possible short- to medium-term issues (see below Sect. 9.5.3). In the long term, though, the effect was to be positive for the aforementioned reasons. It should be emphasized that, in comparison with the Basel regulation for banks (see Pradier and El Khalloufi in Chap. 15, this volume), the impact studies were mostly qualitative, with no precise forecasting of impact on the EU economy.

The a priori impact assessments were then supplemented by a series of Quantitative Impact Studies (QIS) : five rounds have been carried out by the former insurance supervisor committee (CEIOPS) and voluntary insurers, from 2005 to 2010. The summary information shown in Table 9.2 deserves interpretation:

1) QIS and QIS2 were *reviews* intended to set up the methodology and new accounting rules. Hence not all participating firms were able to compute even the best estimate of insurance liabilities, let alone the probabilistic distribution thereof (needed to provide percentiles). Increased participation between QIS and QIS2 resulted in a falling response rate.
2) QIS3 and later were true calibration experiences, testing the practicability of the standard formula among various social forms, such as insurance groups and mutual insurers.[9]
3) In QIS4 and QIS5, a significant share of the participants used internal models, so that their output should be compared to the result of using the standard formula.

---

[9] QIS3 noted about the mutual insurers that a "severe fall was detected in their financial position and this might be an insolvable issue because of the limited possibilities these firms have in raising own funds" (p. 23). Additional reflection was thus devoted about the mutuals' specific capitals through supplementary member calls to be tested in QIS4.

Table 9.2 Summary of Quantitative Impact Studies

Exercise name	QIS	QIS2	QIS3	QIS4	QIS5	LTGA (S0)	LTGA (S12)	LTGA (S10)	LTGA (S1)	2014 ST (base)	2014 ST stressed
Year	2005	2006	2007	2008	2010	2012	2004	2009	2012	2014	2014
# of participating firms	272	514	1027	1412	2520	427	427	427	427	167/225	167/225
Market share (premium)	44 %	60 %	>65 %	>75 %	>85 %	70 % (TP)	70 % (TP)	70 % (TP)	70 % (TP)	55–60 %	55–60 %
% of participants reporting *best estimate*	90	80	91	100	100	100	100	100	100	100	100
% of participants reporting 90th percentile	66	68	most	100	100	100	100	100	100	100	100
% of participants with partial internal models	nil	some	13	50	42	n/a	n/a	n/a	n/a	n/a	n/a
% of participants with total internal models	nil	some	some	n/a	10	n/a	n/a	n/a	n/a	n/a	n/a
% of participants that do not meet MCR	n/a	n/a	2	1.20	4.60	28	4	3	10	6–8	?
% of participants that do not meet SCR	n/a	n/a	16	11	15	46	13	12	29	14–16	20–44
Additional regulatory capital (S2 RC – S1 RC)	n/a	n/a	n/a	(€46 bn)	€56 bn	n/a	n/a	n/a	€88 bn	n/a	n/a
Cost of capital (EY Euro Upper Bound + 6% as of QIS5)	–	–	–	10.5 %	10 %	–	–	–	11.5 %	–	–

Source: CEIOPS (2006), (2007a), (2007b), (2008), (2009); EIOPA (2011), (2013), (2014); authors' calculations

4) QIS5 involved 50 % of all EU insurers totalling 85 % of underwritten premiums and 95 % of insurance provisions. 4.6 % of the participants did not meet the MCR, which triggers "immediate and ultimate supervisory action."

This latter figure was both very high, as it meant 116 companies should be resolved or have their portfolio transferred, and rising quickly in comparison with QIS4, where the MCR failure rate was 75 % lower. QIS5 was therefore a turning point in the preliminary assessment, with a significant deterioration of the companies' solvability. While this can be partly attributed to the consequences of the financial crisis, it could be feared that smaller, more fragile insurance undertakings surfaced with the extension of the sample, hence even more should follow among the 2,500 remaining firms who did not take part in QIS5.

As a result, an additional impact study was performed under the title Long-Term Guarantees Assessment (LTGA), testing a few scenarios to fine-tune S2. While **S0** provides the baseline scenario (S2 as of the 2009 Directive), **S1** introduced some accounting changes so that the failure rate was kept at a more reasonable level. 10 % is still a very high failure rate, in comparison with the historical values recompiled for 2004 and 2009, even if one keeps in mind that the assessment did not make use of (generally less demanding) internal models. The latest simulation to date, a set of stress tests conducted in late 2014 (EIOPA 2014), also showed a high level of SCR/MCR violation (respectively 14–16 % and 6%–8 %) in unstressed scenario, climbing up to 44 % in the case of stress. Meanwhile, critics became increasingly vocal.

9.3.3 Criticism

The advent of a protracted financial crisis interfered with the consultation and deployment process and displayed disappointing consequences of the planned framework. Critical features included procyclicality and the feedback loop between accounting rules and capital requirements (Sect. 9.3.3.1), impact on investments (Sect. 9.3.3.2) and (Sect. 9.3.3.3) low predictive power of the *capital requirements*. While the appropriateness of a bank-based prudential model is still controversial, we save this criticism for later discussion (see Sect. 9.4).

9.3.3.1   Accounting-Capital Requirements Feedback Loop

In stark contrast with the lenient preliminary impact assessment (DG ECOFIN 2007), some economists issued a critical appraisal of the interaction between market value accounting and capital requirements: the Glachant et al. (2010) volume by the French economic council (the prime minister's counselling team) issued an early warning shot. First, Valla (2010) recalled that an investor with liquidity constraint might be forced to sell his assets in order to get cash; if forced to do so in time of trouble, he would be caught in a feedback loop: I need some cash therefore I sell assets, but by doing so I increase the excess supply of assets, which leads to falling prices and the need to sell more assets in order to obtain the same amount of cash, and so on. As Rodarie (2010) shows, the business model of insurance (with inverted production cycle) normally leads to positive cash flows; hence no liquidity constraint should be experienced unless the firm is poorly managed, in which case the supervisor should intervene *before* the liquidity problem arises. Eventually, thinking in terms of liquidity constraints is just like thinking all insurers are doing badly, which does not seem a sound basis for supervision.

Lombard and Mucherie (2010) advance a step further, showing that the combination of market valuation of asset *and* one-year value-at-risk (VaR) actually transforms the risk of feedback loop into certain procyclicality: when the balance sheet of the insurance company is assessed according to market value, the value of the asset side will follow the economic cycle, while the liabilities (being mostly insurance provisions) will stay steady; hence the own funds fluctuate according to the cycle (while the target SCR is approximately constant). Insurance firms will then need to build up capital requirements in the downturns. If they cannot raise any more own funds, they will need to sell part of their asset to diminish their SCR. In the first case, they will crowd out other borrowers, hence negatively contributing to the long-term financing of the economy. In the second case, they will start fire sales that could cause market crash according to Valla's feedback loop model. In both cases, the capital requirements are procyclical and only add problems in time of crisis.

In the same volume, La Martinière (2010) shows that Value-at-Risk (VaR) is not intrinsically perverted: if one-year VaR means that we consider stress on the economic environment while the assets set to be held to maturity (of the corresponding liabilities, as stocks, for instance, do not have an intrinsic maturity) are valued at their "long-term" price, then the procyclicality would disappear. The problem is that most supervisors interpreted one-year VaR to be computed on the liquidation value of assets, which leads to procyclicality. Once again, this would mean that all insurance firms are supervised in a way which contradicts their business model. Overall, the Glachant volume calls for changes in accounting rules, in order to limit the prudential undervaluation of assets needed for long-term financing (mostly stocks and securitized assets) as well as the volatility of the whole balance sheet.

The facts proved the authors of the 2010 volume to be correct. As we have seen, from QIS5 on (2010), worsening market conditions led to rising SCR for life insurance companies so that many of them were no longer able to cover their SCR (Planchet Leroy 2012), as the 2014 stress tests ultimately showed (Table 9.2). The same authors diagnosed that the standard formula incentivized sovereign bonds against other instruments: this is another line of criticism.

9.3.3.2   Long-Term Financing and Asset Concentration

The distribution of investments of the insurance firms dramatically changed in the last ten years as Table 9.3 shows. Between 2005 and 2013,[10] the relative weight of shares fell by almost 50 % (or 18 percentage points) while bonds, particularly sovereign securities, rose by a comparable amount: the private sector has been losing billions of potential funding to EU states. Given the primary importance of the insurance sector in the funding channels of the EU economies, this could lead to severe consequences regarding the financing of long-term growth. Laas and Siegel (2015) have shown this tendency to be a direct result of the standard formula, which imposes far higher capital requirements on stocks than on sovereign debt, thus negating the benefits of the formers' excess return.

Table 9.3 Distribution of investments of EU insurance firms

	2000	2005	2010	2011	2012	2013
Land and buildings	5.24 %	4.2 %	3.1 %	3.1 %	3.1 %	3.4 %
Participating interests	3.80 %	4.4 %	6.3 %	6.2 %	7.9 %	7.8 %
Shares and variable yield	36.72 %	37.5 %	31.0 %	30.9 %	21.0 %	19.5 %
Debt securities and fixed-income	30.98 %	35.7 %	41.6 %	41.8 %	50.4 %	52.4 %
Loans, including mortgages	16.36 %	10.6 %	10.7 %	10.3 %	13.2 %	13.6 %
Deposits	1.07 %	2.4 %	2.5 %	2.4 %	1.3 %	1.4 %
Other investments	5.84 %	5.3 %	4.8 %	5.5 %	3.0 %	1.8 %

Source: Insurance Europe

---

[10] No satisfactory consolidated regional data exist beyond 2012 since the ECB and OECD statistics rely on different typology (for instance, OECD statistics usually consider a significant share of "other" investments which have to be broken down). The state-level data confirm that the 2012 level is still valid in 2015 for many countries.

It seems difficult to disentangle the combined effects of a major financial crisis from the anticipation of S2 by the companies in order to form a definite opinion of the impact of the Directive on the financing of long-term growth; however, Pradier and El Khalloufi in Chap. 15, this volume argue that regulatory uncertainty surrounding Basel III is detrimental to the funding of the EU economy by the banks; the same point could be made about S2 and the insurance companies. A more detailed look at some countries will show that the current structure of investment differs greatly from one EU country to another (Table 9.4): Eastern and Latin Europe countries exhibit a very low relative weight for shares and conversely a large share of bonds; Scandinavian countries are just the reverse; German insurers grant a large amount of loans. One would hardly see a common pattern; hence the change might not be entirely attributable to S2, as S2 is supposed to imply convergence.

Diversity across countries of the EU would avoid asset concentration, which has been shown in the banking sector (Blundell-Wignall and Atkinson 2012) to be responsible for the build-up of systemic risk. The level of asset concentration is notwithstanding high enough for the EIOPA to recently announce it will "monitor consistency and convergence of supervisory practices" relative to "the modelling of Sovereign Exposures" (EIOPA 2015). As the internal models are supposed to be approved by national supervisors, it shall be asked whether the difference in Table 9.4 proceeds from national idiosyncrasies or from incentives provided by the National Competent Authorities (national supervisors; hereafter NCAs). One possible explanation is that NCAs in over-indebted countries are especially lenient toward the holding of domestic sovereign debt by insurers. This raises questions about a possible conflict of interest of national supervisors (an issue which will be discussed in Sect. 9.4), for instance in assessing the need for regulatory action, now supposedly prompted by capital requirement thresholds.

Table 9.4 Distribution of investment of insurance firms in selected countries (2013)

	Real estate	Mortgage loans	Shares	Bonds	Loans, non-mortgage	Other investments
Denmark	0.8 %	0.0 %	50.7 %	40.2 %	1.1 %	7.2 %
Germany	1.8 %	5.2 %	5.8 %	38.6 %	18.9 %	29.7 %
Hungary	2.0 %	0.0 %	1.9 %	88.5 %	0.1 %	7.5 %
Portugal	2.3 %	0.0 %	2.6 %	75.0 %	0.0 %	20.1 %
Sweden	3.0 %	0.1 %	35.6 %	52.9 %	1.1 %	7.4 %
United Kingdom	3.9 %	2.9 %	16.6 %	51.1 %	1.6 %	23.9 %

Source: OECD insurance database, authors' calculations

9.3.3.3   Very Low Predictive Power

In a risk-sensitive framework, the capital requirements of any firm are proportional to the level of risk it is facing, and the probability of a failure should rise with the capital gap. So far, many tests of the US prudential framework have been performed to assess its predictive power.[11] Cummins et al. (1999), for instance, tested on a large sample of insurance companies whether the US Risk Based Capital (RBC) formula correctly predicted corporate failures and their results were disappointing: type I error (i.e. wrongly assessing a failing firm as solvent) as high as 89 % (p. 442), which means that almost 9 out of 10 insolvency cases are not predicted. This figure can be diminished at the price of rising type II error (i.e. wrongly assessing a healthy firm as insolvent): for a 5 % type II error, type I error ranges from 48 % to 84 % according to the year and the test in consideration, while for a 20 % type II error, type I comprises between 18 % and 52 %. The lack of predictive power is a serious problem, since type I error means failures are not predicted and type II error means measures would be taken against healthy firms: in both case, the legitimacy of the supervisor is likely to be eroded.

Further advances have shown that prediction is in fact difficult for purely statistical reasons: Kartasheva and Traskin (2011) have shown that very low insolvency rates lead to low predictive accuracy. As the EU experienced far lower failure rates than the USA, as can be seen in Table 9.3, the predictive accuracy of the SCR/MCR, whatever their sophistication, is likely to be even lower than the often-criticized US RBC model. As a comparison, failure rate was equal to zero for the whole 2008–2012 period in many EU countries, while 4.6 % (2010) to 28 % (2012) of companies were reported as amenable to "immediate and ultimate supervisory action" (DR 2015/35 art. 378–380). Type II error is then at 100 % for countries without failures (and above 95 % on average): this seems intolerably high after five years of calibration; moreover type I error is still undocumented in countries with failed firms (Tables 9.5 and 9.6).

While statistical literature has emphasized the importance of using twin threshold (see for instance Lalkhen and McCluskey 2008), the only acceptable way to deal with the MCR/SCR should be to calibrate them more finely in order to guarantee that SCR (which triggers supervisory inquiry) will minimize type I error, which is obtained at the cost of very high type II error.

---

[11] It should be recalled here that the laws governing US insurance activity and supervision are enabled at the state level. The National Association of Insurance Commissioners has nevertheless developed and sponsored a prudential framework known as "risk-based capital," which has been passed into law in most states.

Table 9.5 Fraction of total insurance sector's liabilities in default, p. 15

Percentage of world assets (2012)	Country	2008	2009	2010	2011	2012	2008–2012
27 %	United States	0.042 %	0.006 %	0.012 %	0.013 %	0.004 %	0.0151 %
24 %	Japan	0.078 %	0.000 %	0.000 %	0.000 %	0.000 %	0.0147 %
12 %	United Kingdom	0.000 %	0.001 %	0.000 %	0.000 %	0.001 %	0.0002 %
9 %	Germany	0.000 %	0.000 %	0.000 %	0.000 %	0.333 %	0.0075 %
5 %	France	0.000 %	0.000 %	0.000 %	0.000 %	0.000 %	0.000 %
3 %	Netherlands	0.000 %	0.000 %	0.000 %	0.000 %	0.000 %	0.000 %
3 %	Switzerland	0.000 %	0.000 %	0.000 %	0.000 %	0.000 %	0.000 %
3 %	Sweden	0.355 %	0.002 %	0.034 %	0.056 %	0.004 %	0.0820 %
2 %	Denmark	0.000 %	0.000 %	0.000 %	0.000 %	0.000 %	0.000 %
1 %	Ireland	0.000 %	0.000 %	0.867 %	0.000 %	0.000 %	0.1613 %
1 %	Italy	0.058 %	0.012 %	0.078 %	0.017 %	0.000 %	0.0326 %
1 %	Spain	0.000 %	0.005 %	0.056 %	0.000 %	0.009 %	0.0155 %
0 %	Belgium	0.000 %	0.000 %	0.000 %	0.052 %	0.000 %	0.0102 %
94 %	Global default rate	0.038 %	0.002 %	0.020 %	0.006 %	0.005 %	0.0139 %

Data from Baranoff (2015), The Geneva Association

Standard, low-cost procedures should be designed for further inquiry. On the contrary, MCR, which prompts immediate action, should be calibrated to minimize type I error under type II error constraint of, say 1 or 5 %. These figures should be made public so that the supervisory procedures become easier to understand for the stakeholders.

* * *

The S2 package is a comprehensive legal reform package, which goes far beyond solvency, since it also features provision for consumer protection and aims above all at European integration. While the initial assessments of the microprudential incentives and the macroeconomic effects were enthusiastic, a protracted tuning process has shown, from 2010 on, a significant number of the insurance firms not able to meet the capital requirements and, more generally, time has paved the way for criticism. The procyclicality issue has been reduced by the Long-Term Guarantees Assessment (LTGA) package, but S2 (as Basel II–III) still leads to asset concentration on sovereign debt, and the usefulness of crucial capital requirements to predict insurance firm failures seems unsatisfactory. One can argue that these are necessary costs to prevent regulatory arbitrage with the banking sector. Before we can judge on this matter, we should add the cost of systemic risk regulation to the equation.

Table 9.6 Number and rate of property-casualty insurance insolvencies per year

Year	1990	1991	1992	1993	1994	1995	1996	1997	1998	1999	2000
Number of companies	1897	1968	2012	2061	2065	2084	2100	2096	2096	2042	1952
Number of failures	23	33	21	22	7	8	25	6	10	18	16
% failed	1.21	1.68	1.04	1.07	0.34	0.38	1.19	0.29	0.48	0.88	0.82

Source: Kartasheva and Traskin (2011)

9.4   Systemic Risk Regulation

Whether the insurance sector is subject or source of systemic risk is still debatable. While the Financial Stability Board (FSB) has concluded that it is (Sect. 9.4.1), a large body of evidence suggests it is not (Sect. 9.4.2). We shall then distinguish more precisely the type of insurance activity or products exhibiting systemic risk.

9.4.1 From Academic Evidence to Enhanced Supervision of GSII

In the wake of their landmark paper on financial contagion, Allen and Gale circulated in the early 2000s a paper about "systemic risk and regulation." They showed that "there is evidence that risk has been transferred from the banking sector to the insurance sector. One argument is that this is desirable and simply reflects diversification opportunities. Another is that it represents regulatory arbitrage and the concentration of risk that may result from this could increase systemic risk" (Allen Gale 2007 p. 342). Only months later, the US government had to rescue AIG in order to prevent a failure with possible systemic implications. The subsequent IMF (2009) report clearly proved that the problems with AIG were entirely due to the sale of credit default swap together with securities lending, carried on by a London branch called AIG-Financial Products, which was clearly not active in the insurance business. Nevertheless, the report by the FSB at the November 2010 G20 Summit in Seoul insisted on the role of Systemically Important Financial Institutions (SIFIs) in financial crises and proposed to mitigate systemic risk by identifying such firms and taking appropriate measures. A list of Global Systemically Important Banks (G-SIBs) was published in November 2011 and has been updated every year, while for insurance the IAIS proposed a list of nine Global Systemically Important Insurers (GSIIs) in July 2013,[12] which was confirmed by the FSB in November 2014 (IAIS 2015) and updated in 2015.[13]

Together with the listing of G-SIIs, a framework of policy measures was published (IAIS 2013a, 2013b). These measures include:

1) Enhanced Supervision comprises both supplementary prudential requirements decided by national authorities and proper international coordination of supervisors.

---

[12] These are: AIG, Allianz (Assicurazioni) Generali, Aviva, Axa, MetLife, Ping An insurance, Prudential, Prudential financial.

[13] On 15 November 2015, the list became: Aegon NV, AIG, Allianz, Aviva, Axa, MetLife, Ping An insurance, Prudential, Prudential financial.

2) Effective resolution of SIFIs in an orderly manner without destabilizing the financial system and exposing the taxpayer to the risk of loss should be made possible for the supervisors.
3) Higher Loss Absorbency capacity for GSIIs to reflect the greater risks that these institutions pose to the global financial system.

As of 2016, IAIS is still consulting the stakeholders to agree on what will be done precisely from 2019 on.

It should be emphasized that there has been a fierce opposition to the classification of insurance institutions as systemic.

9.4.2 The Insurance Business Is Not Systemic

Since 2009, numerous authors have shown that the insurance business model is not systemic by design: the inverted production cycle allows the building up of capital reserves before payments are due. Only non-traditional and non-insurance activities, as in the case of AIG, lead to systemic risk. Thimann (2015) reviewed the theoretical literature on this topic and offers a nice classification of insurance activities, as well as product and balance sheet management tools according to their systemic riskiness. For example, pure life annuities are typical insurance business (they rest on a mortality table and the law of large numbers) while variable annuities with living benefits rely on the uncertain performance of financial instruments, hence they could be systemic: as Baranoff 2015 has shown, most failures of large insurance companies are linked with interest rate risk (especially in Japan during the 2000s). The aforementioned GSIIs are financial conglomerates (amenable to the Financial Conglomerates Directive (Dir 2002/87/EC) (FiCoD), and their systemic riskiness does not come from their insurance business. Overall, it appears that the key issue is to distinguish which activities and products could really build up systemic risk, being clear that pure insurance business is not concerned: Thimann (2015) shows that current typologies are not entirely consistent in 2015. Further research seems necessary in this area.

Very recently, empirical papers made a contribution to the question. In particular, Bierth et al. (2015) has shown that "the insurance sector predominantly suffers from being exposed to systemic risk, rather than adding to the financial system's fragility." Very significantly, they added that "our study reveals that both the systemic risk exposure and the contribution of international insurers were limited prior to the financial crisis with all measures of systemic risk increasing significantly during the crisis. In contrast to the banking sector, however, systemic risk in the insurance sector does not appear to lead but rather follow macroeconomic downturns as evidenced by our analysis." While these results have to be confirmed, they add empirical evidence to the theoretical assertion that the bank metaphor could be misleading.

9.4.3 Is the Bank Metaphor Fully Justified?

The rationale for capital requirements for banks shall be recalled: banks create money by giving credit. They are thus subject to liquidity risk, which can be prevented by holding cash balances and having enough own funds to absorb losses. Moreover, the banks enjoy a high level of public concern, with both a deposit guarantee scheme (which prevents bank runs) and a lender of last resort (which provides the banks with liquidity). As beneficiaries of public spending, it seems obvious that they *should* be regulated. Not only do the banks benefit from public spending, they also have invisible costs for the society: an implicit subsidy, which is more or less the difference between what they should pay to borrow at the cost incurred by their standalone credit rating and what they do with an implicit state support that will not let them fail (Hoenig 2014). The reason why the state will not let the large bank fail is simply their systemic relevance. Overall, too-big-to-fail or systemic banks rely on hypothetic or probable public support: they should accept some regulation in exchange. Basically, capital requirement lessen the probability of their failure and can so be used to diminish the moral hazard, which grows with their systemic significance.

For the insurance firms, the picture is quite different: at any rate, the expected cost of bailout for an insurance company is small as the probability appears minimal; the liabilities side of the balance sheet is only marginally borrowed, hence a minimal implicit subsidy; insurance companies do not have access to the lender of last resort (such access qualifies a bank in most jurisdictions) and the insurance liabilities are not guaranteed by a public insurance scheme in the EU (and nothing like this is planned, albeit there has been a white paper: see EC 2010). Overall, the dependence of insurance on possible public spending is far less than for banking institutions. And, very significantly, it does not seem necessary to pile up own funds to start an insurance business, as payment is made by the customer up front, while a borrower must repay the bank for months or years before the bank gets its money back. Hence, correctly priced insurance contracts should not consume own funds, and the prime motive for supervision is simply to check whether the pricing of contracts covers the expenses.

It seems then legitimate to ask whether the whole project of convergence with banking regulation is healthy. While it makes some sense to impose on insurers the same kind of constraints the banks experience in order to guarantee that the insurers will not host clandestine banking operations, it does not necessarily make sense to impose the same set of constraints on *true* insurance business. The aforementioned supervisor tendency to assume every company will act in contradiction to the business model of insurance (Sect. 9.3.3.1) adds up to the idea that insurance regulation the way it is brought by the S2 framework is, unless appropriately proved, not optimal and must thus have social costs, which were not appropriately accounted for in the preliminary impact assessment. What can be said about this?

9.5   From Private to Social Costs

It appears now that all the costs of the S2 reform have not been taken into account. We try to list (Sect. 9.5.1) and assess (Sect. 9.5.2) these costs before thinking of the consequences (Sect. 9.5.3).

9.5.1 How Many Costs?

So far, we have mentioned many cost sources which are amenable to categorization. Impact studies usually distinguish between the direct cost of regulation (i.e. funding of regulatory authorities through taxes) from indirect costs, featuring a one-off cost of implementation of the reform (a project team should be set up in order to meet the new supervisory expectation, IT systems are often in need of a revamp, etc.) and the recurring cost of compliance (additional capital and reporting requirements). In the case of S2, the literature has taken into account administrative costs, but costs of additional regulatory capital (as S2 commands more costly capital than the current framework) for instance, or cost of asset concentration (since sovereign bonds have a lower return than stocks, especially in conjunction with OECD-wide Quantitative Easing) should have been reviewed.

It should even be noticed that, while impact studies usually consider the cost of optimally working regulation, the process of fine-tuning S2 through the QIS is still far from this ideal state. Chneiweiss and Schnunt (2015) recently argued that the distribution of power among authorities has not yet reached an equilibrium point; on the contrary they give many examples for what they call "competition between authorities [...] to take an ever larger share of the market regulation." Taking a more theoretical approach, Plantin and Rochet (2007) concluded their remarkable book with a warning that "public regulators might aim to expand the scope of their mission in order to increase their resources." A few examples will show how the legal innovation of the past years opened many avenues for coordination problems, both inside member states of the EU and between local and regional authorities.

Inside member states, interesting cases of competition between authorities involve, for instance, the following:

1) *Double jeopardy*—The European Court of Human Rights (ECHR 2014) recently settled the Grande Stevens v. Italy case condemning Italy for various procedural offences as well as a double punishment in the same case. The plaintiff has been imposed an administrative sanction by CONSOB (Italy's financial market regulator) together with a sentence by a criminal court; this contradicts a legal principle that has held since the Roman Republic: *non bis in idem.*

2) *Insufficient legal provision*—The French Conseil Constitutionnel (2015) ruled against the national supervisor (ACPR), which transferred for solvency reasons an insurance company's portfolio to another company: the French *Code monétaire et financier* was ruled unconstitutional, violating property right, as the plaintiff was not given the opportunity to find a buyer for his portfolio.

As to the relationship between national and regional authorities, there has been a clear distribution of powers in the banking sector with first the Eurosystem and then the banking union. In the insurance sector, EIOPA is producing standards and recommendations according to the Lamfalussy process, but also *opinions*, which might contradict the ACPR *instructions* (eight such texts about insurance have been produced between 2010 and 2015 without a clear legal status; see Thourot 2015). Another example is the interpretation of the insurance Directives: we already mentioned in Sect. 9.3.3.1 how the one-year VaR was interpreted in the most counterproductive way; today there are some worries on the implementation of the "fit and proper" condition as part of Pillar 2. As the IMF assessment of observance of the ICP has shown the French regulator was too lenient on the suitability of persons, there seems to be room for "setting an example," especially with the administrators of (small) mutual insurance societies. ACPR first held that the chairman of the board could not be counted as executive director, but since 2015 it has held to a "one-size-fits-all" approach to "properness," in contradiction to ICP2.5: "the supervisor applies [requirements and procedures] consistently and equitably, taking into account the nature, scale and complexity of insurers." It seems fairly obvious now that some member states' regulators (e.g. Ireland and Luxembourg) adopted a more relaxed and business-friendly stance than some others; different interpretation from country to country would mean different costs to the companies, this therefore being a case of regulatory arbitrage among jurisdictions.

Regulatory arbitrage incurs social costs, as it leads to capital misallocation and above all increased risks, hence a larger probability of a more serious financial crisis. Among other social costs, one can imagine that larger capital requirements will raise the demand for capital, which could cause a crowding out effect (although probably not in the same amount as Basel III: Oliveira Santos-Elliott 2012). While crowding out has been prevented by years of relaxed monetary policy, regulatory arbitrage is precisely what S2 was aiming to destroy: albeit there can still be competition among authorities as illustrated by Chneiweiss and Schnunt (2015), risk transfer from banking to insurance seems under control, as Laas and Siegel (2015) have shown that it is usually more costly (in terms of regulatory capital) to hold assets under S2 than under B3. One could be tempted to think, then, that the current European regulatory framework is successful at controlling social costs at the expense of the insurance sector. The next section elaborates on this idea to compute the cost to the sector.

9.5.2 The Cost to the Insurance Sector (See Also Appendix 9.2)

While some preliminary impact studies made some significant contributions to the computation of regulatory costs, it should be made clear that the costs and their effects were considerably underestimated, both at sector and individual firm level.

9.5.2.1 Sector-Wide Costs

From QIS4 on, the preliminary impact studies have computed the overall surplus, that is to say, the difference between the excess regulatory capital in the whole insurance sector under solvency 2 minus the same under solvency 1. While this overall surplus provides an indicator of the sector's health, it has no practical meaning for cost computation since it gives no information about the distribution of shortage (which implies effective costs) among companies. Under the vague assumption of conserving the same level of overall surplus with a mean cost of capital (see Table 9.2), QIS5 would imply €10 billion additional cost of capital per year, but this figure is extremely variable from one QIS to another and sensitive to the distribution of surplus/shortfalls.

While it could be computed straightforwardly (national supervisors publish detailed reports), the direct cost of regulation is rarely mentioned since supervisors usually argue their mandate is country-specific. Eling and Kilgus (2014) produced a notable breakthrough by computing the cost of supervision per employee in the financial sector in Austria, Germany and Switzerland. In order to expand the comparison, we performed additional computation for France and the UK. The results appear in Table 9.7.

France and Germany seem to enjoy the same cost per employee, while the financial centres of the UK and Switzerland are higher, with Austria somewhere in between. Nevertheless, it should be emphasized that the data for the UK were taken before the split of the Financial Services Authority (FSA) into the Prudential Regulation Authority (PRA) and the Financial Conduct Authority (FCA). The budget of the PRA alone, which is closer to the current definition of ACPR and BaFin, is of the same order of magnitude (**), while the FCA has a larger budget. Evolutions should be taken into account: for instance FSA/FCA+PRA had the strongest growth since 2008 with the budget doubling; in France the tax on insurance was raised sharply in 2013; hence the cost of regulation per employee in the insurance sector is 50 % above the average cost per employee in the overall financial sector (*). While a comparative appraisal of the value for money of regulation remains to be done, there is much room for European harmonization, and regulatory arbitrage.

9.5.2.2 Individual Level Costs

Preliminary impact studies focused on administrative costs (linked to reporting and governance requirements of Pillars 2 and 3 in S2): CEIOPS (2007 p. 16) counted €2.7 billion overall for the whole EU27, or €40,000 for each insurance company, on the basis of two months' equivalent full-time job for each of the four "key functions." A report by the Centre d'Etude des Assurances on the very same year (CEA 2007 p. 22) counted twice as much overall, while in 2011 Ernst and Young estimated with the FSA that the figure was close to £1.8 billion (€2.3 billion) for the UK alone, accounting for one-

Table 9.7 Cost of supervision in € per employee in the financial sector in 2012

AT	CH	DE	FR	UK
467.07	593.62	231.45	222.30	645.07
		2014:	334.2*	244.71**

fifth of the European insurance market. The implementation costs have then been multiplied at least by five between 2007 and 2011, and they continue to grow with every new QIS, with the recurring cost of compliance still difficult to assess. The only certainty about these recurring costs is that the 4 x 2 months-persons are insufficient to staff the key functions and fulfil the reporting obligations: Chneiweiss and Schnunt (2015) lists the 21 reports to be prepared annually for the stakeholders (including the supervisors) and reviewed by board members. Administrative costs thus appear as non-negligible fixed costs, which must be added to the legal uncertainties reviewed in Sect. 9.5.1, and, rather unexpectedly, to regulatory capital-linked fixed costs.

Regulatory capital as it appears in Pillar 1 of the S2 reform is supposedly risk-based; it should then be treated as a variable cost. Nevertheless, the QIS5 and later quantitative assessments have shown that the internal models were able to save a considerable amount of capital.[14] More precisely, they benefited large insurance companies more than medium and small ones, as Table 9.8 demonstrates:

While the standard formula leads the large companies to halving their overall surplus, internal models allow them to boost their surplus by 137 % and look even better under S2 than under S1. The boost is less than 20 % for both medium and small companies, which cannot reclaim under S2 the surplus level they have under S1. Internal models thus appear as an investment: they are costly to develop but can save regulatory capital and lower the mean cost of capital, since firms with better solvency experience better financial rating and lower funding costs. A very productive investment, since they save the large companies more than €70 billion (hence at 10 % WACC (weighted average cost of capital), which was the working assumption of QIS5, close to

Table 9.8 Solvency global surplus and internal models

Insurance company type	S1 surplus	S2 surplus/Standard formula	S2 surplus/Internal model
Large	109.4	54.6	129.5
Medium	26.7	15.5	18.3
Small	64.3	43.6	49.5

Source: CEIOPS (2010) p. 136

---

[14] More recently, Picagne and Tam (2016) have shown that the definition of capital was broadened during the S2 maturing process, with additional categories (such as Deferred Tax Assets) being added under the pressure of companies to achieve more easily the requirement threshold. This analysis marginally lowers the overall cost of S2 without changing the argument in this section (on the contrary, these authors show that new capital categories were included as a consequence of efficient lobbying by larger insurance companies).

€7 billion a year). While it seems obvious that the largest companies need a more complex model, there is still a minimum cost to these internal models, which make them look like fixed costs.

The discussion of implementation and compliance cost might seem trifling in comparison with what has been lost on investments in crisis-stricken countries or with potential losses in life insurance when interest rates will revert to their normal level. Although trifling at industry level, they are more or less in the nature of fixed costs (larger insurers had larger project teams but some of them prepared internal models to save regulatory capital); hence they weigh far more on small businesses and must lead to concentration.

9.5.3 From Costs to Concentration and Uniformization

The preceding section has argued that most recent reforms, whether prudential (such as S2) or consumer oriented have been basically adding to fixed costs, thus promoting concentration in the sector. Do we really observe concentration in the insurance industry? While the summer of 2015 saw many merger announcements, Table 9.9 shows the broader perspective. It features the rate of reduction in the number of insurance firms, hence a positive rate means the number of firms is falling and conversely a negative rate means a rising number of firms. Perimeter is crucial to the understanding of concentration in Europe. In EU28, the number of firms is most often rising, with an exception between 1998 and 2003; EU12 seems to be less dynamic with 0.5–1 % more concentration per year, probably because the market is more mature. But only the UK has a rising number of firms: with the UK excluded, the EU12 market is experiencing accelerating concentration: more than 3 % of insurance firms disappear every year between 2008 and 2013. A line EU28 minus UK is added for symmetry: it should be pointed out that without the UK, the entire EU insurance sector has been experiencing consolidation since the beginning of the century (Table 9.9).

Is the acceleration of concentration the effect of regulatory proliferation or the proof that additional regulation is necessary? Given the institutional variety of the insurance sector, takeover is not the only possibility for firms to merge: one can also go on runoff and choose its legatee, in the case of mutuals friendly fusions are also possible directly (in France, the legal regime thereof has been modernized by decree 2014–12, 8 January 2014 on fusion of mutual insurance societies), or through specific forms such as SGAM (*société*

Table 9.9 Concentration rate in the EU insurance industry

	1993	1998	2003	2008	2013
EU28	5083	5173	4756	4914	4968
Yearly concentration rate		−0.3504 %	1.6951 %	−0.6515 %	−0.2183 %
EU28 – UK	4255	4341	3984	3942	3739
Yearly concentration rate		−0.3994 %	1.7312 %	0.2122 %	1.0630 %
EU12	*4284*	*4212*	*3804*	*3741*	*3611*
Yearly concentration rate		0.3396 %	2.0586 %	0.3346 %	0.7099 %
EU12 – UK	*3456*	*3380*	*3032*	*2769*	*2382*
Yearly concentration rate		0.4457 %	2.1968 %	1.8313 %	3.0567 %

Source: Insurance Europe

de groupe d'assurance mutuelle) or even complex business agreements where a large group backs a small insurer by providing it with solutions to complete its product range, and comply with S2. These kind of packages make the smaller insurer look more like a front for the larger group without economic capital links (although the group can provide regulatory capital through reinsurance treaties, for instance). Hence it is likely that the concentration process is underestimated by counting the number of companies: the driver of this trend does not seem to be multiple failures calling for additional supervision, but the financial crisis, changes in consumer tastes and distribution channels (especially investments required to follow the evolution of digital technologies) leading to increased competition might have their impact, as well as the increase in the cost of regulation. Therefore, the acceleration of concentration deserves attention.

Concentration will lead to larger firms: while the US experience shows that very small insurance firms are more prone to bankruptcy (see e.g. Baranoff 2015), further concentration has serious drawbacks, illustrated by the banking industry. A paper by Demirgüç-Kunt and Huizinga (2011) has shown that relative (to their home economy) size is "a liability, as it lowers return without an offsetting reduction in risk," and that systemic size protects banks from market discipline and supervisory action through moral hazard resulting from being too big to fail. Recent empirical studies confirm the increasing risk of concentration. Mühlnickel and Weiß (2015), for instance, conclude that "insurance mergers thus (expectedly) on average do not lead to immediate crashes of the financial system, *they nevertheless coincide with a significant increase in the potential of a system-wide crash* [emphasis added]. Thus, our key result is that mergers in the insurance industry can have a destabilizing effect on both the insurance as well as the banking sector." A more general statement was made in a previous paper by the same authors, since Weiß and Mühlnickel (2014), after studying a sample of US insurance companies, concluded that "contrary to current conjectures of insurance regulators, we find that the contribution of insurers to systemic risk is only driven by insurer size."

There are hence some converging signs that the cost of regulation is leading to concentration and through concentration, to systemic risk. A concurrent process of uniformization deserves attention of its own. The S2 process is a strong factor of uniformization. ECB (2007) has already interpreted convergence in terms of "herding behaviour," possibly leading to systemic risk:

> As S2 aims at consistency with the banking regulatory framework and at reducing regulatory arbitrage opportunities, a certain degree of convergence will be achieved regarding risk and capital management across the two sectors. As a result, more homogeneous risk assessment and management within the European financial landscape may be expected from the implementation of S2. This could result in herding behaviour if a growing number of financial institutions were to adopt a common risk modelling framework, possibly posing risks of adverse dynamics at times of market stress.

Herding behaviour may result in cycles and systemic risk, two notions the authors of the ECB report purposively refrained from using because they are infamous keywords. The idea is nevertheless simple: if all decision-makers decide on the same grounds, they might find no counterparty in time of uncertainty. This is what happens during panic when all owners of an asset try to sell while nobody wants to buy. So far, the insurance business has been safe as most decisions have been driven by "industrial" reasons with rigid asset management rules (the life insurance business is an exception since the huge balance sheet is financial in nature). S2 leads give insurance decision-makers much more freedom to optimize but at the cost of thinking in financial terms: this might induce decisions to be strongly correlated, especially for those who do not have the means to behave as sophisticated investors. Recently, Danielsson, Shin and Zigrand (2013) provided a theoretical framework for this unpalatable phenomenon labelled "endogenous risk."

Since John Maynard Keynes, there has been some literature about the unexpected composition effect of individual decisions. A paper by De Long et al. (1990) is especially interesting since it showed how overconfident speculators can benefit from self-fulfilling returns, at the cost of augmented risk. The model by De Long could describe the behaviour of insurers under S2, not because the insurers overestimate the return on risky assets, but because the insurers' metric is different from the other players on the market: the insurers subtract from the return experienced by other players the cost of regulatory capital. The result is concentration on sovereign debt (Frunza 2014 p. 22), which no longer appears risk-free and paradoxically exposes the companies to capital shortfall when the interest rates rise to their long-term average. It should be emphasized that, without the current QE, the interest rate risk would be a major risk for insurance companies.

A recent paper by Lévy-Vehel (2015) gives an even more precise example of how new management rules could polarize financial decisions. If one thinks of S2 as a global valuation of risk, as opposed to rigid rules (such as concentration thresholds) in S1, then S2 leads to match regulatory capital with both asset management and underwriting policy. The latter being given, the optimization problem is focused on the 99.5 % VaR of Pillar 1. This is the precise point of Lévy-Vehel, who shows that under the (false) assumption of continuous prices, while prices actually make jumps, trying to minimize VaR under a constraint of activity leads to *maximizing* the value-at-risk of the decision portfolio. Hence, improper implementation of a rational management rule turns out to produce adverse effects. The Lévy-Vehel model could well be interpreted to account for asset concentration on sovereign debt: insurance companies' balance sheets appear almost riskless until it is too late to react.

It might seem ironic that the solvency framework, which focuses on individual firm solvency, and was amended (LTGA) with much care in order to avoid procyclicality as seen in Basel II, might nevertheless lead to systemic risk through the polarization of decisions. Scholes had already argued in 2000 that this unexpected result was the consequence of an outdated conception of systemic risk, inherited from 1929, when initial failures triggered a chain reaction of bankruptcies. This model still dictates our response to systemic risk with the prevention of individual failures. The FSB approach to systemic risk directly inherits from this tradition, as it calls for more regulatory capital in individual firms. While the contagion and build-up kind of systemic risks are consciously addressed by the current regulatory evolution,[15] the polarization of financial decisions problem, noticed by ECB (2007) and documented by our examples, did not deserve much attention. It should be emphasized that not just decision-making processes are subject to uniformization: the Directive also does not seem neutral about ownership structures.

It has been stated already that a first draft of S2 did not incorporate specific provisions for "the limited possibilities [the mutuals] have in raising own

---

[15] Geneva Association (2010) has shown that some "non-core activities [when] they are conducted on a huge scale and using poor risk control frameworks" could have the potential for systemic risk. S2 has targeted sources for systemic risk as excessive concentrations on a given class of asset that could build up structural fragility set to detonate when asset price dynamics changes (see e.g. the connection between mortgage backed securities and the bursting of the real estate bubble in the USA). Recent research has tried to assess the potential for systemic risk in the equity sub-module (Martin 2013, Eling-Pankoke 2014): generally speaking, firms with a systemic potential are likely to develop an internal model; hence the control of systemic risk is at the discretion of the supervisor.

funds" (CEIOPS 2007b, p. 47). Though this had been corrected by incorporating supplementary member calls in Tier 2 capital by the 2009 Directive, this demonstrates how difficult it is to find a common measure between stock and mutual insurers. Another instance of the same problem might appear with the Pillar 1/Pillar 3 articulation: while MCR prompts for immediate and ultimate supervisory action, SCR is more likely to be a signal for stakeholders, together with the yearly Solvency and Financial Condition Report. It is very unlikely that the policyholders will read these reports: Plantin and Rochet (2007) rightly pointed out that their personal stake in the firm is too low to invest much time in reading all the reports of all operating companies before choosing one. As members of a mutual association have basically the same amount at stake than policyholders, the agency problem is the same for them. Only large investors with a significant interest in the firm will take their time to read the supervisory report. It seems, then, that the whole architecture of the Directive can be interpreted as promoting an ownership structure open to large investors, that is, large joint-stock companies.

While the European Community never agreed to this idea, the nature of information disclosed to parties, as well as the tendency toward concentration with the rising cost of regulation, are undeniable evidence of a bias in favour of joint-stock insurers. While joint-stock companies have without doubt been a powerful vector of economic progress since the eighteenth century, there is some misplaced irony in trying to shape insurance after them when mutual insurance societies have been the basis of insurance since antiquity. The sharing economy is experiencing a very peculiar moment, with the information economy allowing for direct contact between people and direct support to projects (such as crowdfunding). Start-up companies recently introduced some fresh new ideas into the insurance business through shared deductible (e.g. Friendsurance in Germany, Guevara in the UK, Inspeer in France): none of these platforms offer real insurance activity, only legal counsel for drafting the sharing contract between the coinsured. It should then be asked whether the current regulation does not act as a barrier to entry for new schemes. While EC (2015) boasts the numerous measures designed to lower the cost of small insurance businesses, the planned framework might be too complex for new, innovative ventures as well as small mutuals and other grassroots projects. This could both hinder innovation and lessen resilience of the insurance sector.

* * *

The legal package under elaboration in the EU has so far raised the administrative costs of insurance businesses. It is likely also to raise the costs of capital requirements, especially for insurers without internal models. While the social costs seems to be efficiently blocked—in the long run S2 will rule out regulatory arbitrage, and in the short run crowding out is unlikely under QE—the insurance sector seems to bear the brunt of the regulatory overhaul after a crisis to which it did not significantly contribute. Other unpalatable aspects of the planned reform include a protracted tuning process, with competition among authorities and rising administrative cost, all being very likely to add fixed costs to insurance businesses, leading to increased concentration in the sector. Adding uniformization of decision processes to the picture leads to the conclusion that the current package is probably building up moderate but significant systemic risk. The common FSB–IAIS effort to supplement GSII supervision draws a path for further regulation; one could nevertheless ask whether this is the only avenue for the insurance sector.

9.6 Rationale for Regulation and Future Agenda

So far, the evolution of the EU regulation appears as a drive to rule out insolvency of individual financial institutions; this concern constrained a no arbitrage between sectors approach, which appears costly for the insurance business while it leads to significant increase in complexity. This whole process seems in contradiction to the intuitive appeal of a European market, which should bring in simplified procedures, lower prices and increasing opportunities for stakeholders. Before we suggest further moves, one should understand how the stakeholders behave. To this end, Table 9.10 gives some insight into the rationality they pursue.

From this table, it is clear that most European insurance supervisors were largely sleeping partners until recently: insurers under the direct monitoring of the State, who offered to be lenient in exchange for arbitrary levies and employment protection (Plantin-Rochet 2007 pp. 13–14). When supervisors became independent, the mandate remained the same: no fuss, employment must be protected, hence no strong action should be taken against firms because that would push consumer toward foreign firms with better credibility. At best, this could be interpreted as a delegation of public authority to a supervisory body in charge of brokering deals that would serve "general interest" in the way they would interpret it. Since the mid-2000s the political authorities chose a stiffer stance on finance and the supervisory authority chose to "set examples" in order to attract attention and further resources. Generally speaking, the current approach to supervision is confused: the politicians are struggling to convince the voters they are tough on finance so they should vote for them, the supervisory authority is struggling to convince

Table 9.10 Rationale of stakeholders and likely consequences

Agent	Shareholders	Managers	Policyholders	Supervisor	Political authorities	EC administration
Rationale	Maximize expected utility of asset according to their own risk-loving utility function	Depends on the incentive scheme. Joint-stock companies: usually aligned with shareholders. Mutual societies: likely to favour employment	Look for simpler package, then maximize expected utility of net technical provisions according to their own risk-averse utility function.	Maximize its resources. Try to convince the other stakeholders that he must be awarded more powers.	Far-sighted: maximize the expected present value of future taxes. Myopic (election-cycle driven): maximize next period employment.	Maximize its resources. Try to convince the other stakeholders that he must be awarded more powers.
Likely Consequences	Favour risky decisions, "gamble for growth".	JS: as shareholders. MS: no general answer.	Likely to "play safe". Would recommend definite action in case of problems.	Depends on incentives.	FS: protect policyholders interest. M: protects (local) employment.	Introduces new, more complex regulations

the politicians that they should invest with them to show how tough they are, while the European Commission and European Parliament are playing their own part. This looks very much like competition between authorities at all possible levels with rising costs and efficiency missing in action. We believe, therefore, that the problems should be fixed as further integration of the EU market takes place. In the next sections we offer three main lines for the agenda.

9.6.1   Addressing Transition Costs and "Regulatory Avalanche"[16]

The European Commission is conscious of the general problem of overlapping or competing authorities and has addressed it by describing as much as possible the future practices of the insurance sector: put together, the 2009 and 2014 Directives plus the 2015 Delegated Regulation amount to 1,013 pages in the *Official Journal of the European Union* (at 5,000 typographical signs per page). This is far less than the literature surrounding the US Dodd–Frank Act, but the aim is more modest, with directives of pending implementation such as the Packaged Retail and Insurance-based Investment Products (PRIIPs, Regulation EU1286/2014 due for implementation in national laws in late 2016) and Insurance Distribution Directive (EU 2016/97, due in early 2018) about to further impact the insurance sector. The "simplification" effort looks somewhat contradictory, though, as adds to the regulatory burden (see for instance art. 56–61 of Delegated Regulation 2015/35). Eventually, the law, as any contract, can never describe completely every possible event: this should be taken into account in organizing the delegated supervision of the financial institutions.

It is of course the responsibility of national authorities to adapt *smartly* to the European regulation, reducing double costs and double jeopardy by avoiding competing authorities. The UK has taken a dramatic step in this direction with the better regulation initiative, which seeks simplification of regulation and questions the utility of government involvement in private affairs (NAO 2006). Nevertheless, in the banking sector, this drive is not left to member states, and a banking union has superseded the principle of subsidiarity: Regulations 1022/2013 and 1024/2013 established the ECB as supervisor for the largest European banks, with national supervisors being left with the non-significantly systemic institutions; Regulation 806/2014 established a single resolution mechanism intended to cover the banking sector as well

---

[16] The expression "regulatory avalanche" appears in Chneiweiss and Schnunt (2015).

as conglomerates operating under the FiCoD (which can include insurance groups and notably GSII) and subsidiaries thereof. In the insurance sector, we surveyed two reasons to proceed in much the same way:

1) EIOPA is concerned with possible conflict of interest between states as borrowers and states as supervisors in assessing the internal models related to sovereign exposures (see above Sect. 9.3.3.2),
2) Competition between authorities has led to misinterpretation of EU rules (see above Sects. 9.2.2, 9.3.3.1, 9.5.1) and redundant costs.

We believe that a direct European supervision should be relevant in the insurance sector too. A true European supervision agency would solve at the same time the competing authorities and complexity issues as well as the agency problem of delegated supervision. Hence it might be convenient to think of an insurance union that would produce harmonization by teaming together member states' supervisors: the banking union has taken this course, at a high cost since 1,000+ positions have been created. In order to reduce costs, a ten or 15 year schedule for extinction of member state authorities can be set up, with progressive transfer of volunteers to the new entity.

Complexity, cost and barrier-to-entry issues could be more broadly targeted by easing up the present complex rule-based approach by enabling principles-based simplification, especially for smaller and innovative businesses. Unfortunately there is no reason for the supervisors nor the EU Commission to follow this simplifying trend on its own (Table 9.9). Hence, simplification has to be incentivized: this is a complex matter of political science (OECD 2010), and of political priority. The "best idea for red tape reduction award" could be restarted, for instance, and given a sectorial declination to promote cooperation between firms and supervisors. While the trend of regulation since 2009 has been in the opposite direction, it seems necessary to recall the academic evidence for focused supervision.

9.6.2 Toward Focused Supervision

While S2 and the Insurance Core Principles of the IAIS offer an all-encompassing supervisory program that derives from the banking metaphor, Plantin and Rochet (2007) in their landmark contribution advocated for a more focused approach to supervision. Their book started from case studies of insurance failure to introduce the peculiar feature of the so-called inverted production cycle. As the true production cost of insurance is only known years after the premium has been paid, since long-tailed events can span on decades, risk-loving insurance stockholders and managers may have a tendency to underwrite too much contracts at too low a price to gather premiums, underestimate future liabilities and pocket "profits," which are overvalued at the expense of policyholders. Plantin and Rochet show with some insolvency cases that even well-established companies may be guilty of this misconduct by trying to "gamble for resurrection" when their economic model has lost momentum. They argue that the policyholders hold insufficient incentive to take action against the stockholders and managers, hence the conflict of interest is aggravated by asymmetric information: public intervention is then needed to prevent the collapse of the insurance business that simply could not exist with too much information asymmetry. The precise role of supervision is then to act as an informed policyholder and make sure that the money collected from customers is not "gambled" for further growth.

The case made by Plantin and Rochet is especially important under strictly competitive pressure, when insurers cannot charge the customer too much. As we have seen in Sect. 9.2, this seems to be the case in Europe now. As the customer decision is mainly concerned with the price/service arbitrage, only the supervisor is able to deduce from periodical reporting the true probability of failure of the insurance company. In case this probability becomes significant (so as, for instance, the customer would not have bought insurance from the company), the supervisor takes all necessary action to ensure that the policyholders will be paid accordingly to the contract they signed. This might involve radical measures such as the transfer of the portfolio to another firm or resolution of the failed firm. But this is not the only way in which the supervisor could act. Table 9.9 summarizes the likely objective of the stakeholders: while it has its own agenda, the supervisor could be incentivized to act on behalf of others. There must be a clear political choice of which point of view the supervisor is supporting.

We think the mandate for supervisory authority should be to protect policyholders against conflicting interests of other parties. Period. The other consumer protection issues related to business conduct should be dealt with by a separate entity in order to curb the tendency of the supervisor to seek new resources. Moreover, the insurance supervisor should focus on its insurance expertise and leave complex asset schemes for the single supervisor already set up for banks and financial conglomerates. This will lead to a reduction in the cost of supervision, a useful reversal of the recent trend. Meanwhile, the steering of risk aggregates should be left to higher-level authorities.

9.6.3　From (Infinite) Layer Cake to Fitness Menu

With the Insurance Capital Standard and other GSII requirements under elaboration by the IAIS, European insurers might by 2019 experience three levels of regulatory compliance: national, European and global. The overall result will probably look like a layer cake where different layer are produced by competing authorities with no overall regulation. This will add more fixed costs, and, as we have shown in Sect. 9.5, this approach to systemic risk is basically flawed since it is likely to produce endogenous risk. The idea of a more holistic approach (or macroprudential policy) has been put forward by many authors. In the insurance context, this could take the form of EU level reserves for specific risks, which would be broken down among companies according to individual prudential indices (see for instance Macron 2016 or Rodarie 2015 p. 357–9). This approach seems necessary to address systemic risk, and to decide at what price (in terms of regulatory capital) insurance companies should continue non-insurance business. This seem to be a matter for the European Systemic Risk Board, but there is no reason to think its action should not be supervised by the European Parliament, in order to add a slice of transparency and accountability in this menu, which should target a more appropriate balance between regulatory capital and EU-wide perceived risk.

* * *

9.7　Conclusion

Since the Directives of 2002, Europe has abandoned direct price supervision and is relying on effective competition to achieve price discipline in the insurance sector. This move has had positive results in terms of prices, without degrading the soundness of the insurance businesses, which proved far more resilient than banks during the overstretched financial crisis. Nevertheless, governments and supervisors adopted a tough stance toward the insurance sector, which somewhat hijacked the Solvency 2 reform: competition among authorities produced a rigid interpretation of European texts, leading to infamous cases such as the condemnation of the French supervisor by the Conseil d'Etat, or the resignation of the head of the UK conduct authority. On the strictly prudential side of the reform, while the initial assessments of the microprudential incentives and the macroeconomic effects were enthusiastic, a protracted tuning process has shown a significant part of the insurance firms not to meet the capital requirements and, more generally, time has paved the way for criticism. The procyclicality issue has been reduced by the LTGA package, but S2 (as Basel II–III) still leads to asset concentration on sovereign debt, and the usefulness of crucial regulatory indices (the capital requirements) to predict insurance firm failures seem unsatisfactory. While the social costs seems to be efficiently blocked—in the long run S2 will rule out regulatory arbitrage, and in the short run crowding out is unlikely under QE—the firms experience costs, which have been vastly underestimated. The insurance sector seems to bear the brunt of the regulatory overhaul after a crisis to which it did not significantly contribute.

Focusing on the cost of regulation brings some unexpected results: regulatory capital charges are not just variable costs increasing with the insurers' risks. Thank to internal models, the larger insurers can save significant amounts of capital. Internal models are but fixed costs, adding to the already burdensome reporting and governance requirements, and to the protracted implementation and legal uncertainty. All these costs are more or less fixed costs: overall, the reform package weighs more on small businesses, and is likely to strengthen a trend of concentration in the sector. Adding uniformization of decision processes to the picture leads to the conclusion that the current package is probably building up moderate but significant systemic risk. The common FSB–IAIS effort to supplement Insurance Capital Standard and GSII supervision draws a path for further regulation; one could nevertheless ask whether this is only an avenue for the insurance sector. The agenda is thus consistently addressing the foreseen issues, but at rising costs which penalize future activity and innovation.

To prevent rising costs, it seems necessary to focus on the rationale of stakeholders and design incentive schemes to improve efficiency of the supervising process. We advocate a clear mandate for a single European supervisor, with strong incentives to simplify an overly complex regulation and a steering of regulatory capital from a higher-level authority, preferably with European Parliament approval. Moreover, we would like to plea for the advent of a more European insurance market. At the moment, it is difficult to insure a German-registered car with a Spanish insurer, or a home in Italy with the Belgian branch of a Danish insurer; it is almost impossible to transfer motor insurance personal records as a French driver to the Irish market, even at branches of French companies. Moreover, the Spanish leader is unknown to Italian customers, as is Germany's number two insurer, and so on. While these facts do not seem a problem for most EU consumers, they are likely to limit workers' mobility inside the EU, and they would be solved by further integration: now that insurance companies obey the same supervisory framework, it should be easier; let us hope for the benefit of all stakeholders that further unification will result from simplification.

Appendix 9.1: Relative Insurance Prices in EU28

The following table shows the average level of insurance prices relative to CPI in 2014, where base 100 was in 1996, 2000 or 2005 according to data availability.

Country	Insurance price in 2014 / CPI	Base 100 in
AT – Austria	98.29	1996
BE – Belgium	104.27	1996
BG – Bulgaria	206.95	2000
CH – Switzerland	96.33	2005
CY – Cyprus	103.06	1996
CZ – Czech Republic	129.46	2000
DE – Germany	104.94	1996
DK – Denmark	130.97	1996
EE – Estonia	75.16	2000
EEA[a]	113.92	1996
EL – Greece	89.09	1996
ES – Spain	123.73	1996
EU28	104.26	1996
FI – Finland	144.23	1996
FR – France	100.74	1996
HR – Croatia	81.26	2005
HU – Hungary	72.34	2005
IE – Ireland	225.93	1996
IS – Iceland	125.46	1996
IT – Italy	180.66	1996
LT – Lithuania	83.95	1996
LU – Luxembourg	85.23	1996
LV – Latvia	63.70	1996
MT – Malta	97.37	1996
NL – Netherlands	123.22	1996
NO – Norway	132.27	1996
PL – Poland	78.90	2000
PT – Portugal	101.39	1996
RO – Romania	361.48	2005
SE – Sweden	156.24	1996
SI – Slovenia	124.67	2000
SK – Slovakia	127.70	1996
TR – Turkey	100.36	2005
UK – United Kingdom	187.63	1996

Reading the table: "Between 2005 and 2014, the average price of insurance contracts grew 81.26% of the consumer price index in Croatia"

[a]EEA = European Economic Area = EU28 + Iceland, Lichtenstein, Norway

Appendix 9.2: Cost of Insurance Regulation in EU28

Short name	Description	Reference	Fixed or variable cost	Current solutions	Alternative solutions
Direct cost of regulation	Paid to fund prudential supervision/consumer protection	Eling and Kilgus (2014) This study	Mainly variable		Simplification (needs incentives)
Indirect costs of regulation					
Administrative cost	Cost of staffing to meet the regulatory/ supervisory requirements	CEIOPS 2007 CEA Europe 2007 EY 2011	Mainly fixed		Simplification (needs incentives)
Cost of regulatory capital	Cost of additional regulatory capital under S2 in comparison with current regulation (S1)	QIS4, QIS 5, LTGA This study	Variable but internal models add a fixed component		
Cost of asset concentration	Opportunity cost of total asset returns under S2 in comparison with current regulation (S1)	?[a]	?	(securitization)	Single European Supervision
Cost of competing authorities			Likely fixed		Single European Supervision
Social costs					
Business failure/ systemic risk			n. a.	S2	European market development
Crowding out		Oliveira Santos- Elliott 2012	n. a.	QE Securitization	
Regulatory arbitrage			n. a.	S2	Simplification (needs incentives)

(continued)

Appendix 9.2 (continued)

Short name	Description	Reference	Fixed or variable cost	Current solutions	Alternative solutions
Concentration, Uniformity, see below			n. a.	See § 6	

[a]There is no literature on this subject. A rough estimate could be computed with some assumptions. For instance, considering the MSCI world as an equity index and the euro area ten-year Government Benchmark bond yield (ECB) as the proxy for return of fixed yield instruments, the return on the 2010-composition portfolio (that is 31.0 shares and 41.6 bonds) would have been 38 % for the period between 2010 and 2015. Now adjusting the composition of the portfolio yearly with respective shares evolving linearly between 2010 and 2015, the return for the same 2010–2015 period would have been 29 %. Considering the total investment value of insurance companies in 2010 (€7,547,690 million), the opportunity cost of asset concentration on debt instrument is in the order of magnitude of €350 billion for the 2010–2015 period. This rough measure obviously neglects the dividend received in the case of shares and the risk premium on corporate debt

Appendix 9.3: Insurance Core Principles

While the banks have enjoyed since 1974 an international Committee on Banking Supervision (BCBS 2014), which produced the three Basel Agreements plus an enormous literature on good supervision practices, the insurance relative (International Association of Insurance Supervisors or IAIS, also hosted by the Bank of International Settlements since 1994) did not provide for a similarly globally accepted framework. Nevertheless, the role of IAIS has dramatically increased since the US financial crisis, with the G20 establishing the Financial Stability Board (FSB) at the London Summit in 2009. Since then, the IAIS has been producing recommendations in three areas to international convergence: (1) Insurance Core Principles (ICP); (2) a Common Framework (ComFrame) for the Internationally Active Insurance Groups (IAIG) and a global Insurance Capital Standard (ICS); and lastly (3) additional supervision requirements for Global Systemically Important Insurers (G-SIIs).

Insurance Core Principles (ICP)

The aim of the ICP is to provide a globally accepted framework for the supervision of the insurance sector. These principles are supposed to apply in every jurisdiction, whatever the level of development of the insurance market and the type of activity being supervised. They define the objectives of supervision—"maintaining a fair, safe and stable insurance sector for the benefit and protection of the interests of policyholders" (IAIS 2013c p. 4)—as well as the limits of the insurance sector. In this respect, the framework states that entities providing reinsurance and intermediation services are not directly under the scope of supervision, but their indirect impact on insurance activity command supervisory attention. For reinsurance, the supervisor should ensure that the guarantee provided by the reinsurance treaties effectively meets the expectations of the cedants (as reported in the assets side of their balance sheet). For insurance intermediaries, the ICP prescriptions are far more stringent, since they cover consumer relationship management at large in ICP18 (intermediaries), ICP19 (conduct of business), ICP21 (countering fraud) and ICP22 (AML-CFT regulations enforcement). Eventually, IAIS recommends a careful monitoring of intermediaries and reinsurers, but this is not necessarily to be done by the supervising body of insurance companies.

Table A.9.1 Overview of insurance core principles implementation

	Singapore	Switzerland	Australia	Italy	France	Japan	Belgium	Ireland	Malaysia	USA	Denmark	Spain	South Africa	Brazil	Nigeria
ICP1 Objectives, Powers and Responsibilities of the Supervisor	3	3	2	3	3	3	2	3	2	1	2	3	2	2	3
ICP2 Supervisor	2	3	1	1	2	1	1	1	2	1	1	1	1	1	2
ICP3 Information Exchange and Confidentiality Requirements	3	3	3	3	2	3	3	3	2	2	3	3	3	2	2
ICP4 Licensing	3	2	3	3	2	3	3	3	2	2	3	3	3	2	2
ICP5 Suitability of persons	3	2	2	2	1	2	2	2	2	2	2	2	3	2	1
ICP6 Changes in Control and portfolio transfers	3	3	2	3	2	3	3	3	2	3	3	3	2	3	1
ICP7 Corporate Governance	3	3	3	3	1	2	2	2	2	1	2	1	1	1	2
ICP8 Risk Management and Internal Controls	3	2	3	3	2	3	3	3	2	2	1	1	1	3	2
ICP 9 Supervisory Review and Reporting	3	2	2	1	2	2	2	1	3	2	2	2	2	2	1
ICP 10 Preventive and Corrective Measures	3	3	3	3	3	2	3	2	3	3	3	3	3	3	2
ICP11 Enforcement	3	3	3	2	3	3	3	3	2	3	3	3	3	3	2
ICP12 Winding-up and Exit from the Market	3	3	2	3	3	3	3	3	3	3	2	3	1	2	3
ICP13 Reinsurance and Other Forms of Risk transfer	3	2	3	3	3	2	2	2	2	3	3	2	2	2	1

ICP14 Valuation	3	3	3	1	2	1	2	2	3	1	3	1	2	2	1
ICP15 Investment	3	3	3	3	3	3	2	2	2	3	2	3	2	3	2
ICP16 Enterprise Risk Management for Solvency purposes	2	3	2	3	1	2	2	2	1	2	2	1	1	0	1
ICP17 Capital Adequacy	2	3	2	1	2	2	1	1	2	2	2	1	2	2	1
ICP18 Intermediaries	3	1	3	1	3	2	2	3	1	2	2	1	3	1	1
ICP19 Conduct of Business	3	1	1	3	3	3	2	2	2	2	1	2	2	2	1
ICP20 Public Disclosure	2	1	1	2	1	2	1	1	2	3	2	2	1	3	1
ICP21 Countering Fraud in Insurance	3	2	3	2	3	3	3	3	2	3	1	0	1	3	1
ICP22 Anti-Money Laundering and Combating the Financing of Terrorism	3	3	3	2	3	3	3	2	3	2	1	3	1	2	2
ICP23 Group-wide Supervision	3	3	2	3	3	3	2	1	1	1	2	3	1	0	0
ICP24 Macroprudential Surveillance and Insurance Supervision	3	2	3	2	2	1	3	3	3	2	1	1	2	1	1
ICP25 Supervisory Cooperation and Coordination	3	3	3	3	3	2	3	3	3	2	3	3	3	1	1
ICP26 Cross-border Cooperation and Coordination on Crisis Management	2	3	2	2	3	1	2	2	1	2	2	1	2	0	0
Total	73	65	63	61	61	60	60	58	55	55	54	52	49	48	37

These principles are not just theoretical. In April 2009, the London G20 summit decided to have the IMF producing detailed assessments of the observance of the ICP as part of the Financial Sector Assessment Program. Since 2011, 15 countries have been surveyed and the results are shown in Table A.9.1. While KPMG 2014 insists that "the reviews demonstrate major themes that permeate the ten reviews,"[17] the whole picture shows large differences in practices among countries, even inside the EU: for 11 of the 26 insurance core principles,[18] the difference between the most and the least compliant EU member state is two notches or above on a four notch scale (from 0 – principle not observed to 3 – observed). Large differences in insurance supervision across countries pave the way for supervisory arbitrage; this is particularly the case in the EU, as passporting enables companies to operate across jurisdictions. While the EU has a specific approach to this issue (see above Sect. 9.2.1), the objective of tightening supervisory gaps seems of general relevance: IAIS is then working on a common framework for insurance groups operating across borders.

Common Framework for International Groups and Capital Standard

The IAIS issued its first exposure draft of the Concept Paper on ComFrame in July 2011 (IAIS 2011). The idea behind this project, which is due for implementation in 2019, is to impose convergent prudential rules to Internationally Active Insurance Groups (IAIGs) in order to prevent supervisory arbitrage. Around 25 IAIGs have volunteered to work on the project, since they too would be more comfortable with a harmonized regulation rather than multiple group supervision framework in the jurisdictions they are operating in.

ComFrame is to include a risk-based insurance capital standard (ICS), which will set minimal rules that can be supplemented by additional rules at local level ("goldplating"), in contrast to the European S2 regime (see below Sect. 9.3), which is based on maximum harmonization. While IAIS is still consulting to determine these capital standards, the definition of internationally active insurance groups (IAIGs) is now accepted as

- writing premiums in at least three jurisdictions,
- total assets must be at least US$50 billion
  or gross written premiums at least US$10 billion.

---

[17] Five more have been published since the KPMG survey.

[18] These are ICP7, ICP8, ICP14, ICP16, ICP18, ICP19, ICP21, ICP22, ICP23, ICP24, ICP25. For ICP2, ICP17 and ICP20, EU member states appear to perform poorly overall: Solvency II is addressing these issues in priority.

According to this definition, the IAIS expects there to be about 50 IAIGs worldwide (IAIS 2014). The process of refining this Insurance Capital Standard is complex, involving IAIS consultations of insurance companies and detailed responses with no synthesis to date (see http://www.iaisweb.org/page/news/consultations/closed-consultations/insurance-capital-standard-ics//file/58015/ics-cd-resolution-of-comments-october-stakeholder-meeting).

It should be noted that these capital standards will also apply to Global Systemically Important Insurers (G-SIIs), although the definitions of IAIGs and G-SIIs are not exactly aligned. First, there are no clear-cut criteria for defining a G-SII: G-SIIs are designated by the FSB following consultation with the IAIS and national authorities. Then, proceeding from the definition of IAIGs, it appears that a solo national insurer of global systematic significance could be a G-SII without being active in three jurisdictions, hence without being an IAIG. Ping An for instance, while being a global systematically important financial institution with geographically diversified interests in banking, is underwriting mainly in China, hence it would not necessarily qualify as an IAIG if it were not designated by the FSB as a G-SII.

While the G-SIIs will be submitted to the same requirement as the IAIGs, they will deserve additional supervisory attention since national supervisors might not correctly address the systematic risk.

Additional Supervision Requirements for G-SIIs

See above Sect. 9.4. Systemic risk regulation.

Bibliography

ACPR. (2012–2014). Questionnaires sur l'application des règles destinées à assurer la protection de la clientèle.

ACPR. (2015). *Analyse de l'exercice 2014 de préparation à Solvabilité II*. Analyses et synthèses. N° 41. Février. Retrieved from: https://acpr.banque-france.fr/solvabilite2/actualites/actualite/article/analyses-et-syntheses-n41-analyse-de-lexercice-2014-de-preparation-a-solvabilite-ii.html

Allen, F., & Gale, D. (2007). Systemic risk and regulation. In M. Carey & R. M. Stultz (Eds.), *The risks of financial institutions*. Chicago: University of Chicago Press. ISBN: 0-226-09285-2.

Baranoff, E. (2015). *U.S. and Japan Life insurers insolvencies case studies: Lessons learned from resolutions*. The Geneva Association. Downloaded from: https://www.genevaassociation.org/media/913756/ga2015-insurance-resolution.pdf

Barker, A. (2015, July 28). High Ho! Disneyland Paris faces Brussels pricing probe. *Financial Times*. 6:17 pm. Retrieved from FT.com

BCBS. (2014). *A brief history of the Basel Committee*. BIS. Retrieved from: http://www.bis.org/bcbs/history.pdf

Bierth, C., Irresberger, F., & Weiß, G. N. F. (2015). Systemic risk of insurers around the globe. *Journal of Banking & Finance, 55*, 232–245.

Blundell-Wignall, A., & Atkinson, P. E. (2012). *Basel regulation needs to be rethought in the age of derivatives, Part I*. VoxEU.org column. Retrieved from: http://www.voxeu.org/article/rethinking-basel-part-i

Brown, J. R., & Goolsbee, A. (2002). Does the internet make markets more competitive? Evidence from the life insurance industry. *Journal of Political Economy, 110*(3), 481–507.

Buysse, L. (2008). *Commission pour le dédommagement des membres de la Communauté juive de Belgique pour les biens dont ils ont été spoliés ou qu'ils ont délaissés pendant la guerre 1940–1945*. Rapport final 4 février 2008. Retrieved from: http://www.combuysse.fgov.be/

CEA Europe. (2007, March). *Consequences of Solvency II for insurers' administrative costs*. Downloaded from: http://ec.europa.eu/finance/insurance/docs/solvency/impactassess/annex-c08b_en.pdf

CEIOPS. (2006, March 17). *QIS1 – Summary report – Sanitized version*. CEIOPS-FS-01/06. Retrieved from: https://eiopa.europa.eu/Publications/QIS/CEIOPS-FS-0106Rev32006-03-17PA.pdf

CEIOPS. (2007a). *QIS2 – Summary report – Public report*. CEIOPS-SEC-71/06S. Retrieved from: https://eiopa.europa.eu/Publications/QIS/QIS2-SummaryReport.pdf

CEIOPS. (2007b, November). *CEIOPS' report on its third Quantitative Impact Study (QIS3) for Solvency II – Public report*. CEIOPS-DOC-19/07. Retrieved from: https://eiopa.europa.eu/Publications/QIS/CEIOPS-DOC-19-07%20QIS3%20Report.pdf

CEIOPS. (2008, November). *CEIOPS' report on its fourth Quantitative Impact Study (QIS4) for Solvency II*. CEIOPS-SEC-82/08. Retrieved from: https://eiopa.europa.eu/Publications/QIS/CEIOPS-SEC-82-08%20QIS4%20Report.pdf

Chneiweiss, A., & Schnunt, M. (2015). Compliance: une illusion dangereuse. *Risques, 102*, 82–87.

CNIL. (2014). *Pack de conformité assurance*. Edition juillet 2014. Retrieved from: http://www.cnil.fr/fileadmin/documents/Vos_responsabilites/Packs/Assurance/PACK_ASSURANCE_complet.pdf

Conseil Constitutionnel. (2015). Décision n° 2014-449 QPC du 06 février 2015.

Cummins, D., Harrington, S., & Niehaus, G. (1994). An economic overview of risk-based capital requirements for the property-liability industry. *Journal of Insurance Regulation, 11*, 427–447.

Cummins, J. D., Grace, M. F., & Phillips, R. D. (1999). Regulatory solvency prediction in property-liability insurance: Risk-based capital, audit ratios, and cash flow simulation. *The Journal of Risk and Insurance, 66*(3), 417–458.

DG ECOFIN. (2007, March). *Impact assessment: Possible macroeconomic and financial effects of Solvency II.* DG ECFIN/C-4(2007)REP 53199. Retrieved from: http://ec.europa.eu/internal_market/insurance/docs/solvency/impactassess/annex-c06_en.pdf

Danielsson, J., Shin, H. S., & Zigrand, J. P. (2013). Endogenous and systemic risk. In J. G. Haubrich & A. W. Lo (Eds.), *Quantifying systemic risk.* Chicago: University of Chicago Press.

Demirgüç-Kunt, A., & Huizinga, H. (2011). *Do we need big banks? Evidence on performance, strategy and market discipline* (CEPR discussion papers 8276). CEPR Discussion Papers. Retrieved from: http://cepr.org/active/publications/discussion_papers/dp.php?dpno=8276#

De Long, J. B., Shleifer, A., Summers, L. H., & Waldmann, R. J. (1990, August). Noise trader risk in financial markets. *Journal of Political Economy, 98*(4), 703–738.

DG ECOFIN. (2007). *Impact assessment: Possible macroeconomic and financial effects of solvency II,* March 2007 (DG ECFIN/C-4(2007)REP 53199). Retrieved from: http://ec.europa.eu/internal_market/insurance/docs/solvency/impactassess/annex-c06_en.pdf

Doff, R. (2008). A critical analysis of the Solvency II proposals. *The Geneva Papers on Risk and Insurance: Issues and Practice, 33,* 193–206.

Dupuydauby, M. *Solvabilité 2 est une chimère dangereuse.* Banque et Stratégie — ENAss Papers. 293.

EC. (2007). Accompanying document to the proposal for a directive of the European Parliament and of the Council concerning life assurance on the taking-up and pursuit of the business of Insurance and Reinsurance—Solvency II—Commission staff working document, 2007-07-10, Brussels.

EC. (2010). *White paper: On insurance guarantee schemes.* Retrieved from: http://ec.europa.eu/internal_market/consultations/docs/2010/whitepaper-on-igs/whitepaper_en.pdf

EC. (2015, January 12). MEMO/15/3120. *Solvency II overview—Frequently asked questions.* Brussels. Retrieved from: http://europa.eu/rapid/press-release_MEMO-15-3120_en.htm

ECB. (2007, July). *Potential impact of solvency II on financial stability.*

ECB. (2014). Decision of the European Central Bank of the 2 July 2014 on the provision to the European Central Bank of supervisory data reported to the national competent authorities by the supervised entities pursuant to Commission Implementing Regulation (EU) No 680/2014 (ECB/2014/29).

ECHR. (2014, March 4). *European Court of Human Rights. 2014. Grande Stevens and others v. Italy.* Applications #18640/10, 18647/10, 18663/10, 18668/10 et 18698/10. Retrieved from: http://hudoc.echr.coe.int/sites/eng/pages/search.aspx?i=001-141370

Edelman, B., & Wright, J. (2015). *Price coherence and excessive intermediation*. Retrieved from: http://www.benedelman.org/publications/pricecoherence-2015-03-12.pdf

EIOPA. (2011, March 14). *EIOPA report on the fifth Quantitative Impact Study (QIS5) for Solvency II*. EIOPA-TFQIS5-11/001. Retrieved from: https://eiopa.europa.eu/Publications/Reports/QIS5_Report_Final.pdf

EIOPA. (2012–2014). *Consumer trends reports*.

EIOPA. (2013, June 14). *Technical findings on the long-term guarantees assessment*. EIOPA/13/296. Retrieved from: https://eiopa.europa.eu/Publications/QIS/EIOPA_LTGA_Report_14_June_2013_01.pdf

EIOPA. (2014, November 28). *EIOPA insurance stress test 2014*. EIOPA-BOS-14-203. Retrieved from: https://eiopa.europa.eu/Publications/Surveys/Stress%20Test%20Report%202014.pdf

EIOPA. (2015, April 14). *EIOPA opinion on the preparation for internal model applications*. Retrieved from: https://eiopa.europa.eu/Publications/Opinions/EIOPA-BoS-15-083%20Opinion%20on%20IMs%20(April%202015).pdf

Eling, M. (2015). The complexity risk of regulation: An article on the complexity of Solvency II. *Newsletter Risk Management: The Geneva Association, 55*, 18–19.

Eling, M., & Kilgus, S. (2014). *Wirksamkeit und Effizienz der Regulierung in der deutschsprachigen Assekuranz—Eine juristische und ökonomische Analyse*, technical report.

Eling, M., & Pankoke, D. (2014). Basis risk, procyclicality, and systemic risk in the Solvency II equity risk module. *Journal of Insurance Regulation, XXXIII*, 1.

Ernst and Young. (2011). *Solvency II cost benefit analysis*. Retrieved from: http://www.fsa.gov.uk/pubs/other/ey-solvencyii-cba.pdf

European Commission. (2003). Design of a future prudential supervisory system in the EU—Recommendations by the Commission Services, Markt/2509/03, Working Paper, 2003-03-03, Brussels.

European Court of Human Rights. (2014, March 4). *Grande Stevens and others v. Italy*. Applications #18640/10, 18647/10, 18663/10, 18668/10 et 18698/10. Retrieved from: http://hudoc.echr.coe.int/sites/eng/pages/search.aspx?i=001-141370

FCA. (2014, August). *Redress for payment protection insurance (PPI) mis-sales update on progress and looking ahead*. Thematic Review TR14/14. Retrieved from: https://www.fca.org.uk/news/tr14-14-redress-for-ppi-mis-sales

Frunza, M. C. (2014). La réglementation prudentielle appliquée aux banques et aux assurances. In Ch. de Boissieu, F. G. Le Theule, & P. Bailo (Eds.), *Comment la régulation financière peut-elle sortir l'Europe de la crise?* Strasbourg: ENA. ISBN 2133273V.

FSB. (2009, October). *Report to G20 Finance Ministers and Governors—Guidance to assess the systemic importance of financial institutions, markets and instruments: Initial considerations*.

FT. (2015, July 17). *A stubborn crusader gets his marching orders*. 6:41 pm. Retrieved from: FT.com

Geneva Association. (2010, March). *Systemic risk in insurance—An analysis of insurance and financial stability.*

Glachant, J., Lorenzi, J. H., Quinet, A., & Trainar, Ph. 2010. *Investissements et investisseurs de long terme* (Conseil d'analyse économique report n° 91). Retrieved from: http://www.cae-eco.fr/IMG/pdf/091.pdf.

Harrington S. (2002). Effects of prior approval rate regulation of auto insurance. In J. D. Cummins (Ed.), *Deregulating property-liability insurance –Restoring competition and increasing market efficiency.* Washington, DC: Brookings. ISBN: 0-8157-0243-4.

Hoenig, T. (2014). *Too big to fail subsidy for large banks—Literature review.* Federal Deposit Insurance Corporation. Retrieved from: https://www.fdic.gov/news/news/speeches/literature-review.pdf

Holzmüller, I. (2009). The United States RBC standards, Solvency II and the Swiss Solvency test: A comparative assessment. *The Geneva Papers on Risk and Insurance: Issues and Practice, 34,* 56–77.

IAIS. (2011, July). *Common framework for the supervision of internationally active insurance group—Concept paper—Invitation for comments.* Retrieved from: http://www.actuaries.org/LIBRARY/Submissions/Temporary_Draft_Comments/ComFrame_Concept_Paper_Final.pdf

IAIS. (2013a). Global systemically important insurers: Initial assessment methodology (July).

IAIS. (2013b, July 18). *Global systemically important insurers: Policy measures.* Retrieved from: http://iaisweb.org/index.cfm?event=openFile&nodeId=34256

IAIS. (2013c). *Insurance core principles, standards, guidance and accepted methodology.* Amended 19 October 2013. Retrieved from: http://iaisweb.org/index.cfm?event=getPage&nodeId=25224

IAIS. (2014). *ComFrame FAQs.* Updated 17 December 2014. Retrieved from: http://iaisweb.org/index.cfm?event=openFile&nodeId=41664

IAIS. (2015, June 25). *Frequently asked questions for IAIS financial stability and Macroprudential Policy and Surveillance (MPS) activities.*

ICHEIC. (2007a, March 19). *ICHEIC claims process.* Retrieved from: http://www.icheic.org/

ICHEIC. (2007b, June 18). *Finding claimants and paying them: The creation and workings of the International Commission on Holocaust Era Insurance Claims.* Retrieved from: http://www.icheic.org/

IMF. (2009, October 28). *Guidance to assess the systemic importance of financial institutions, markets and instruments: Initial considerations.* Background Paper. Retrieved from: https://www.imf.org/external/np/g20/pdf/100109a.pdf

Jenkins, P. (2016, January 26). Analysis: FCA must now look at its governance. *Financial Times.*

Kartasheva, A., & Traskin, M. (2011). Insurers' insolvency prediction using random forest classification. *Wharton School Working Paper.*

Klein, R. W. (2014). Insurance market regulation. In G. Dionne (Ed.), *Handbook of insurance* (2nd ed., pp. 909–939). New York: Springer.

KPMG. (2014, March). *Evolving insurance regulation. The kaleidoscope of change.* Retrieved from: http://www.kpmg.com/au/en/issuesandinsights/articlespublications/evolving-financial-services-regulation/pages/evolving-insurance-regulation-march-2014.aspx

La Martinière, G. de. (2010). Les assureurs comme investisseurs de long terme. In Glachant, et al. (Eds.), (pp. 177–186).

Laas, D., & Siegel, C. F. (2015, February 27). *Basel III versus Solvency II: An analysis of regulatory consistency under the new capital standards.* Available at SSRN: http://ssrn.com/abstract=2248049 or http://dx.doi.org/10.2139/ssrn.2248049

Lalkhen, A. G., & McCluskey, A. (2008). Clinical tests: Sensitivity and specificity. *Continuing Education in Anaesthesia, Critical Care and Pain, 8*(6), 221–223.

Le Monde. (2013, November 1). *Assurance-vie: le scandale des contrats en déshérence.* Retrieved from http://www.lemonde.fr/argent/article/2013/11/01/assurance-vie-le-scandale-des-contrats-en-desherence_3507035_1657007.html#7oCfoVkjCClsFuLl.99

Lévy-Véhel, J. (2015). A simple isochore model evidencing regulation risk. Colloque « volatilité », SMA-BTP, 26 novembre.

Lombard, E., & Mucherie, M. (2010). Veut-on faire de l'épargne longue une espèce en voie de disparition ? In Glachant, et al. (Eds.), (pp. 171–176).

Lorent, B. (2010). *Insurance solvency regulation: Regulatory approaches compared* (Working papers CEB 10-041). ULB – Universite Libre de Bruxelles.

Macron, E. (2016). Interview. *Risques*, 105, 11.

Martin, M. (2013, November 10). *Equity risk under Solvency II: Internal models and procyclical effects.* Available at SSRN: http://ssrn.com/abstract=2340430 or http://dx.doi.org/10.2139/ssrn.2340430

Mühlnickel, J., & Weiß, G. N. F. (2015). Consolidation and systemic risk in the international insurance industry. *Journal of Financial Stability, 18*, 187–202.

NAO. (2006, June 28). *National Audit Office. Evaluation of regulatory impact assessments 2005–06.* Retrieved from: http://www.nao.org.uk/wp-content/uploads/2006/06/05061305.pdf

OECD. (2010). *Why is administrative simplification so complicated? Looking beyond 2010.*

Oliveira Santos, A., & Elliott, D. (2012). *Estimating the costs of financial regulation* (IMF staff discussion note). SDN 12/11. Retrieved from: https://www.imf.org/external/pubs/ft/sdn/2012/sdn1211.pdf

Outreville, J.-F. (1990). The economic significance of insurance markets in developing countries. *The Journal of Risk and Insurance, 57*(3), 487–498.

Philipponnat, T. (2013). Contribution to "Scission bancaire: débat". *Revue Projet.* Available on: http://www.dailymotion.com/video/xx2y5z_scission-bancaire-debat-thierry-philipponnat_news

Picagne, P., & Tam, R. (2016). *Solvency II will lead tohigher ROE forEuropean re/ insurers—At what cost?* (ENAss Papers 11, Banque et Stratégie 347, pp. 21–29).

Planchet, F., & Leroy, G. (2012). « Comment adapter Solvabilité 2 à la crise ? », *la Tribune de l'Assurance* (rubrique «le mot de l'actuaire »), n°172 du 01/09/2012.

Plantin, G., & Rochet, J. C. (2007). *When insurers go bust.* Princeton: Princeton University Press.

Rego, M. L. (2015). Statistics as a basis for discrimination in the insurance business. *Law, Probability and Risk, 14,* 119–134.

Rodarie, H. (2010). Investisseurs de long terme : une disparition révélatrice. In Glachant, et al. (pp. 201–212).

Rodarie, H. (2015). *La pente despotique de l'économie mondiale.* Salvator.

Ronayne, D. (2015). *Price comparison websites* (Warwick economics research paper series). Retrieved from: http://www2.warwick.ac.uk/fac/soc/economics/research/workingpapers/2015/twerp_1056b_ronayne.pdf

Scholes, M. (2000). Crisis and risk management. *American Economic Review, 90,* 17–21.

Thimann, C. (2015, February 26). The economics of insurance, its borders with finance and implications for systemic regulation (CESifo Working Paper Series No. 5207). Available at SSRN: http://ssrn.com/abstract=2573633

Thourot, P. (2015). L'EIOPA: du rôle de consultant au contrôle des groupes européens d'assurance. *ENAss papers, 9 (Banque et Stratégie, 336),* 4–9.

Valla, N. (2010). Investisseurs de long terme: fournisseurs de liquidité. In Glachant, et al. (Eds.) 2010, (pp. 157–164).

Webb, I., Grace, M., & Skipper, K. (2002). *The effect of banking and insurance on the growth of capital and output.* Department of Risk Management and Insurance, WP 02-1, Georgia State University.

Weiß, G. N. F., & Mühlnickel, J. (2014). Why do some insurers become systemically relevant? *Journal of Financial Stability, 13,* 95–117.

10

The Impact of Basel III on the Operations of Retail Banks

Eric Lamarque

For many bankers, Basel III has led to a change of world, a change of model and for some even a change of profession. These views initially reflect the content of the Basel principles relating to two major indicators of bank stability, namely: (1) solvency via the level of equity capital required and (2) liquidity in terms of assets held. The mainstream financial press and bankers have largely discussed the impact of these measures on the banking sector and the wider economy. There is no doubt that they have significant consequences on banks' activities and financing capacity. But Basel III also deals with other issues relating to the organisation and governance of financial institutions. These have been less publicized, but affect banks and the way actors operate on a daily basis as much, if not more.

Basel III is a system based on three pillars. Pillar 1 is detailed in EU Directive CRD4. It concerns the definition of equity required to cover exposure to credit, market and operational risks. Such exposure is gauged by risk-weighted assets (RWAs), and regulatory equity capital is defined differently compared to usual accounting definitions. Pillar 2 leads to the implementation of control measures of equity capital, of exposure to risks. It also includes measures to be pursued to meet these requirements. Lastly, Pillar 3 relates to

E. Lamarque (✉)
LabEx RéFi and GREGOR, Sorbonne Graduate Business School, Université Paris 1 Panthéon-Sorbonne, Paris, France

© The Author(s) 2017

R. Douady et al. (eds.), *Financial Regulation in the EU*,
DOI 10.1007/978-3-319-44287-7_10

market discipline, with emphasis on the information financial institutions must communicate in terms of risks.

The motives of regulators in adopting Basel III clearly follow the banking crisis in September 2008: they seek to ensure that governments will no longer be obliged to protect banks from filing bankruptcy. The decisions to take capital holdings in banks in October 2008 were not understood by the public, even if the public monies committed were recovered with a profit. The political cost of such interventions has been so high that it is no longer possible for governments to find themselves in a similar situation. Public regulators have had the mission of reinforcing the safety and financial stability of banks, as well as ensuring and reinforcing the quality of internal bank controls and those carried out by national and European supervisory agencies.

The European Capital Requirements Directive (CRD 4) runs to nearly 340 pages. It covers the three pillars and aims to provide precise recommendations on how banks can protect themselves against insolvency risks with sufficient levels of equity capital, and how to protect themselves against liquidity risks to prevent sudden bankruptcies. These two risks lie at the heart of regulatory concerns. But the Directive also addresses the conditions under which banks are supervised, the bodies involved in such supervision and the resolution mechanisms they put into place. Basel III therefore addresses criteria for risk and financial management as much as it stresses organizational and strategic criteria.

The aim of this chapter is to review and assess the two dimensions of the consequences induced by these new texts. It seeks to see what is truly new and how financial institutions will adapt—more or less easily—to the new conditions for exercising their trade.

The chapter will therefore focus on two questions. It will look first at how Basel III hopes improving banks' solvency, mainly in their retail activities. The aim is to assess the improvement in institutions' financial stability. Subsequently, the chapter will review the principles put forward to improve banks' control by focusing on the organization of internal control, the resolution mechanisms and the role played by governance bodies, which have a special place in Basel III.

In these two areas, particular attention will be paid to how the new regulations affect cooperative banks, which are a particular type of actor in the retail banking. This sector is indeed characterized by a diversity of governance models. Financial cooperatives have a special position, especially in France, where they are even dominant actors. The regulations set out in Basel III make no distinction concerning such banks, assuming that operating conditions should be the same for everyone. Furthermore, the cooperative sector as a whole has to deal with special legislation that sometimes interferes with measures put forward by regulators. This chapter also sets out to address these specific issues.

10.1 Improving the Reliability and Safety of Financial Institutions

The question of improving banks' safety is the very basis of the Basel Committee's existence, which has looked at the matter for nearly 30 years. The risk of solvency may be defined as the risk of a bank not being able to meet losses linked to its activities (credit, markets and operations). In this case, equity capital must be able to cover losses. As with any company, liquidity risks involve not being able to meet short-term payments. The two are linked, but the Basel Committee has only been interested in the latter since the 2008 banking crisis. This chapter starts by examining issues linked to equity capital and the consequences for banks, as well as their clients. It then examines problems of liquidity, in order to identify changes to the financial management of banks.

10.1.1 The Progressive Increase in Capital Equity Required by Regulators

Basel I introduced the requirement for banks to cover their credit risks with sufficient equity at the end of the 1980s. Equity capital had to be equivalent to 8 % of risk exposure. The Basel II agreement, which was initiated in 2004, came into force in January 2007. This extended the range of risks covered, by including market risks and operational risks, while maintaining the 8 % threshold. However, the impact of this agreement was not really felt, owing to the rapid increase in bank failures that year. Basel III was signed in 2010, and will be fully implemented by 2019. It has not changed the risks requiring cover, but it has raised equity capital requirements further, bringing these up to a minimum of 10.5 % and even 15 or 16 % in certain cases. Basel III has also brought in new demands in terms of liquidity: Table 10.1 below sets out the accord's obligations.

The general principle is that prudential equity capital is equal to a minimum of banks' exposure to risks, according to the principles of banking regulation. In the case of the Basel III framework, all actors expect that equity requirements will rise, even if thresholds are not increased, given present portfolio

Table 10.1 From Basel II to Basel III

	From Basel II to Basel III
Pillar 1 Equity capital requirements	The minimum requirements in equity capital in view of the assessment of exposure to credit, market and operational risks $$\frac{\text{Prudential equity capital}}{\text{Credit risks} + \text{market risks} + \text{operational risks}} > 10,5 \text{ to } 18\%$$ Regulators are increasingly restrictive in terms of the elements that can be included in prudential equity capital and also demand models for evaluating exposure to different risks that are increasingly "stressful": that is, corresponding to extreme situations. The methods used for evaluating risks are put forward or validated by regulators. Thresholds have been set in a range from 10.5 % to 15 %, depending on the banks and the countries in question, as part of the Basel III process. This method requires calculating two variables: – The exposure to RWAs: it depends on the content of balance sheets, but also on how they operate on a daily basis. For banks, this exposure stems mainly from credit risks (at least 85 % of total risks). On top of this, there are market risks (about 5 %) and operational risks (about 10 %). It is therefore necessary to assess exposure, which provides the basis for estimating required equity, under the auspices of the European Central Bank or the resolution authority (*Autorité de Contrôle Prudentiel et de Résolution*, or ACPR) in France. – Prudential equity capital: financial services are one of the few sectors in which the perimeter defining equity capital has a regulatory dimension. As a result, the value of such capital may diverge from accounting equity values and a series of processing measures need to be taken into account in these calculations. In particular, intangible assets, often arising from goodwill associated with external growth, need to be eliminated. Institutions which engage in such acquisitions in order to expand may be penalized. – One novelty of Basel III is the proposition of a new ratio linked to solvency risks: the leverage ratio is set at the 3 % threshold at least. $$\text{leverage ratio} = \frac{\text{Tier one capital}}{\text{Exposure}}$$ Exposure = balance sheet excluding derivatives and pensions + off-balance sheet {derivatives + pensions} withdrawn prudentially Furthermore, liquidity ratios need also to be included: the Liquidity Coverage Ratio (LCR) is the available liquidity over one month, and the Net Stable Funding Ratio (NSFR) is the liquidity for one year $$LCR = \frac{\text{High Quality Liquid Assets}}{\text{Total net cash out flows over the next 30 calendar days}} \geq 100\%$$ $$NSFR = \frac{\text{Available amount of stable funding to 1year}}{\text{Required amount of stable funding to 1year}} \geq 100\%$$ The numerator and denominator of each ratio are defined by BCBS specific document. All these thresholds have to be reached by 2019.

Table 10.1 (continued)

	From Basel II to Basel III
Pillar 2 Supervision of the adequacy and management of equity capital	Banks are required to implement a prudential supervision system, in coordination with the regulatory authorities. This system is called SREP—the Supervisory Review and Evaluation Process—and aims to analyse all risks on a permanent basis, including solvency risks and liquidity for Pillar 1, as well as to calculate equity capital needs. It has four components: An analysis of banks' business models, by market and by entity in order to assess the sustainability of the model, at a given date in the future. The assessment of the adequacy of equity capital relative to risks, using quantitative and qualitative measures. This component clearly envisages overloading equity capital depending on the assessment, in order to ensure the sustainability of the business model. The assessment of liquidity and funding by quantitative and qualitative measures, according to the risks that may affect it. The ability to search for resources is a key aspect of this assessment. The assessment of governance, as well as management and control processes. This component complements the implementation of the internal control system which has existed for several years in France, in particular. The supervisor can demand higher equity capital or the implementation of any action capable of improving the safety of the institution.
Pillar 3 Market discipline	This pillar aims at improving banks' financial transparency, obliging them to communicate information needed to allow third parties to appreciate the adequacy of their equity capital. It is hoped that this will lead to better market discipline.

Source: Adapted from the BIS—Basel Committee 2013a, European Commission and ECB

activities and assets held on balance sheets. If on top of this requirements continue to rise, as is the case for banks, then considerable changes have been envisaged by banks, in terms of strategic and commercial positioning, including withdrawing or reducing finance to certain types of clients. Three trends can be identified today, as follows.

10.1.2   The Reduction in the Risk Exposure

Banks track permanently the use of equity capital associated with each of their activities and especially their credit policy. As shown in Table 10.2 below, the latter influence the amount of required equity capital, first and foremost.

Table 10.2 The exposure to risks measured by RWAs

RWAs (in millions of euros)	Retail banking and services		Corporate and institutional banking		Securities services	Other activities	Total
	Domestic markets	International financial services	Corporate banking	Global markets			
Credit risk	**179,089**	**141,022**	**92,042**	**8,988**	**1,44**	**26,7**	**449,282**
IRB approach	116,985	14,377	86,769	6,396	1,069	3,145	228,74
Standardized approach	62,105	126,645	5,273	2,592	372	23,556	220,542
Banking book securitization	**909**	**646**	**221**	**9,676**	**1**	**1,173**	**12,625**
IRB approach	757	79	221	9,675	1	1,173	11,905
Standardized approach	151	567	0	2	0	0	720
Counterparty credit risk	**2,636**	**909**	**23**	**24,021**	**1,548**	**91**	**29,228**
CCP	0	0	0	1,385	1,048	0	2,432
CVA Charge	138	334	22	2,919	12	81	3,507
Counterparty Credit Risk excL CCP and CVA charges	2,498	575	1	19,718	488	10	23,289
Equity risk	**5,329**	**33,595**	**2,869**	**1,962**	**358**	**13,966**	**58,079**
Market risk	**170**	**424**	**1,488**	**19,573**	**57**	**2,052**	**23,764**
Internal model	0	28	280	18,693	0	2,038	21,039
Standardized approach	170	395	1,208	142	57	14	1,986
Trading book securitization positions	0	0	0	739	0	0	739
Operational RISK	**16,367**	**15,706**	**9,122**	**15,456**	**2,675**	**1,222**	**60,548**
Total	**204,501**	**192,301**	**105,765**	**79,677**	**6,079**	**45,203**	**633,527**

Source: Document de Référence, BNPP, 2015

The table indicates that two factors affect total exposure in particular: credit risk accounts for more than 71 % of total exposure. This does not include counterparty risks, the importance of exposure to risks associated with international activities, in respect to the scale of such activities in banks' balance sheets.

10.1.2.1   The Consequences in Terms of Credit Risk Policies

The mechanics of calculating required equity capital under Basel II was relatively simple. The more a bank finances a risky client, the more equity it has to accumulate to deal with bankruptcy. The more a bank is exposed to a sector which is sensitive to economic conditions, the more it has to cover itself. A bank's policy in terms of taking risks determines its capital requirements directly. This situation is especially sensitive in the corporate market (especially for small and medium-sized enterprises, SMEs). This market has traditionally been more risky than the household sector.

Some sectors are impacted by economic conditions and the business cycle. They risk facing credit rationing, because default risks are too high. The principle of individualized credit rating for each "corporate" client is now a key instrument in decision-making.

Looking at the above example in detail, it is clear how trends in the exposure to risks are combined with an increase in thresholds under Basel III.

It is clear here that the reduction in exposure to credit risk between 2011 and 2012 allowed the bank to "save" €2.7 billion in equity capital. Conversely between 2013 and 2014, the rise in exposure meant that another €2 billion had to be found. Lastly, between 2014 and 2015, the volume of credit distributed expanded by 4 %, but total exposure only increased by 1.6 %. This implies that such credit was mainly granted to safe counterparties.

In addition, companies represent more than half of this total exposure, and hence the variations of exposure on this market affect regulatory capital first and foremost.

For all retail banks, three factors explain the changes in exposure:

1) The quality of borrowers: the more banks lend to highly ranked borrowers (1–2 on a scale running to 9) the more RWAs will be minimal or even zero. Thus the best clients will have no problems in satisfying their demand for credit, whereas the most risky borrowers will have problems in obtaining finance. This is especially so for SMEs.

2) The economic situation: in times of slow or even negative growth, the number of troubled borrowers will increase. When specific sectors are facing problems, risks to actors increase. At that point, exposure and equity capital increase for a given level of debt. As a result, certain sectors experiencing worsening economic problems risk having less access to bank finance.

3) The volumes of credit granted: the volume of credit granted impacts the level of RWAs upwards or downwards, in a fairly mechanical way. In economic slowdowns, retail clients borrow less and vice versa.

It is hard to say which of these three effects has been the most important in recent years. All have undoubtedly been significant. Some banks publish a statement analyzing the different effects impacting exposure between the two last years. But economic actors with average rating clearly face real difficulties, or at least are at the limit of what banks accept today. Institutions quite evidently set themselves boundaries which are not overstepped. Credit policy thus includes a new dimension which is more or less explicit, namely clients' ratings.

In the retail banking sector, this conflicts with the positioning sought by cooperative banks in terms of risk policy, and raises questions of the ability of actors to pursue more accommodative policies in this area. Indeed, within the framework of their local (territorial) commitment to local firms, some cooperative players are more inclined to accept and finance clients with more risky ratings. Such a policy is consistent with their cooperative engagements. But it generates problems because this policy automatically leads to greater equity requirements. Cooperative banks cannot therefore increase their shares of such clients without having large surpluses of equity capital and accepting the costs of higher risks.

This illustrates a phenomenon which we will find throughout this chapter, namely the fact that regulatory principles largely oppose the natural positioning of cooperative banks. As a result, they too behave more and more like traditional banks, favouring less risky clients too. In fact, they often argue that their specificity lies in the fact that they carry lower risks, which is quite paradoxical.

10.1.2.2   When Retail Banks Develop Internationally

External growth strategies are largely favoured by retail banks to obtain positions in new countries. These strategies may not always be successful. However, the search for new sources of growth and the acquisition of banks with many clients is always tempting. But such growth also generates extra credit risks and extra operational risks.

Credit risks arise because most of these acquisitions take place in emerging countries, where policies for granting loans are probably less supervised than in France. Risks in the company sector are more important and the quality of information they provide to assess default risks is not the same as in developed countries. Moreover, systems of evaluation are not exactly identical and so there are problems with reporting and consolidation of exposure to such risks. This can put a brake on such initiatives, given that the quality of data on risks is an important issue at present, owing to reforms concerning the principles for registering accounts.

Lastly, the acquisition of retail banks in a foreign country often leads to an increase in operational risks that come under Basel III. These risks are linked to the inadequacy of the systems, procedures and practices, as well as to external events that may lead to direct losses, legal risks or more often to reputational risks. Credit activity is subjected to these kinds of risks when procedures are not respected and clients are granted loans they should not have been able to obtain. These risks also arise in the collection of deposits, when measures appropriate to controlling the origin of funds collected are not implemented.

The distance between the subsidiary and the parent company makes it more difficult to implement required controls. This leads to higher risks automatically, and hence a greater demand for equity capital. International development thus requires more investment in equity.

Credit policies and international development are two fundamental components of investment banking. Since the beginning of 2015, Pillar 2 has come into force, and actors have to think in terms of risk appetite. As a result, there is an explicit link between strategic positioning in terms of products, clients and geographical zones, as well as the exposure to risks. A way for managing such exposure clearly resides in the redefinition of a bank's business model, unless it has no problems in finding the equity capital required to cover risks. Here again, the diversity of models within the banking sector means that many actors have to be taken into account, especially financial cooperatives. Actors may not always be able to deal with positions they may take, concerning clients facing the greatest difficulties.

For universal banks, changes to their business model involve dropping certain activities in some countries. Several actors have sold some activities deemed to be non-strategic in recent years, though on the basis of criteria that are not very clear. Apart from the two cases referred to in the previous table, the sale by BBVA of its life insurance subsidiary in Spain may be mentioned, as can the management of assets by Santander. In France, Société Générale has pulled out of the asset manager Amundi, while BNPP has given up insuring certain types of financing (planes and ships), and has reduced its investment banking activities in several geographic regions. Consumer credit and credit leasing have also been much affected by the rundown of operations.

Finding a new balance between strategic positioning and the capacity for satisfying equity capital requirements has become the decision-making model of the sector today

10.1.3 Raising Equity Capital and the Capacity to Absorb Losses

The preceding examples all point to the conclusion that equity capital needs to be increased. Table 10.3 shows the strong rise in capital for shareholder capital banks. Generally speaking, the equity capital of European banks rose by nearly 50 % between 2009 and 2014, and is expected to rise by a further 25 % by 2018 (Table 10.4).

Apart from what has been already highlighted out in the preceding point concerning the need to change banks' business model to raise the level of equity capital, regulatory changes also impose new management of equity in retail banks. There are three components to this:

Table 10.3 Trends in RWA credit and equity capital requirements

€ billions	2015 Basel III	2014 Basel III	2013 Basel III	2013 Basel II ½	2012 Basel II ½	2011 Basel II
Total credit granted	685	657	612	617	630	666
Total RWA credit	449	442	418	411	411	446
Equity capital required to cover credit risk	35.9	35.3	33.4	32.8	33	35.7
RWA "company" credit	257	246	232	234	236	254
Equity capital required to cover "company" credit risks	20.6	19.6	18.5	18.7	18.8	20.3

Source: Documents de Référence, BNPP

Table 10.4 Change in equity capital with respect to balance sheets (in € billions)

Banks	Book equity 2007	Total balance sheet 2007	Book equity 2015	Total balance sheet 2015
Société Générale	31	1071	62.6	1334
BNPP	59	1694	100	1994
BPCE	47.8 (2009)	1029 (2009)	57.6	1166
CA SA	46	1414	59.4	1529

Sources: Reference documents
Note: Consolidated accounts for BPCE have only been available since 2009

1) Further improvement of financial results: the most virtuous way to achieve this increase is above all to raise operational performance and to have the capacity to improve net earnings. Looking at the situation of retail banks today, however, shows that achieving this goal is difficult, and banks are increasing layoffs across the world. The first reason for this lies in the fall in interest rate spreads (the difference between the rates paid by clients and the rates at which banks can refinance themselves). The fall in rates has led to a wave of loan renegotiations by clients. As banks favour less risky clients, interest rate margins have fallen all the more. This fall in interest rate spreads has not been compensated by higher commissions on the sale of products and services (as most clients do not easily accept such payments), nor by higher returns on market products. The latter have in fact been affected by new regulations concerning market risks, which push banks and other institutional investors to turn towards safer financial products (such as government bonds), that are less profitable.

   Net bank earnings have therefore been stagnating in France for two years and forecasts are not optimistic. As a result, the only way to obtain margins is by limiting operational costs (more than 60 % of which are made up of wage bills), and limiting the costs of risks (see Lamarque 2014). This leads to credit policies that are as riskless as possible, which in turn weighs on GDP.

2) Paying fewer dividends to shareholders: a seductive solution for many is to limit payments to shareholders and hence retain more earnings for equity capital. Publicly listed banks and more generally banks with shareholder capital face a dilemma, however. Limiting dividends over the long term runs the risk of encouraging potential investors and existing shareholders to turn to other shareholdings. The most spectacular example in recent years has been the way General Electric (GE) has pulled out of financial services, which accounted for half the group's earnings in 2000. Not only have immediate returns on dividends been reduced, but falls in stock prices following the crisis in 2008 have yet to be recovered, despite a general rise in market values.

   The main explanation for this is a structural decline in Return on Equity (ROE or financial profitability), which is a benchmark for many shareholders. Not only are earnings no longer rising, in fact they are stagnating and falls are to be expected. At the same time, equity capital requirements are rising endlessly. For retail banking, ROE has fallen from between 12 % and 15 % in 2007, to between 6 % and 8 % today.

3) Having the capacity to raise equity capital quickly: the last solution to raising equity capital is to have quick access to investors who can provide

further capital. A publicly listed bank has an advantage from this point of view, because it is easy to issue new shares, even though this may lead to a low share price. To overcome uncertainties faced by shareholders, the regulator is now clearly envisaging the possibility of transforming bond debt into capital in an authoritarian way, which broadens the notion of equity capital.[1]

This raises a new problem faced by cooperative banks, as the retention as equity capital of all net earnings lies at the very heart of the cooperative system, which is not constrained by the fact of having to reward shareholders. Cooperative banks should have an advantage from this point of view. However, the regulator and supervisor are wary about the stability of equity capital and the ability to raise further equity quickly. On the first point, it is true that members of a cooperative who provide funds, which can be deemed to be equity capital, can ask to be paid back by the cooperative every year. The cooperative has to make such paybacks. If a large number of members make similar demands, then the institution is threatened. This cannot occur with shares, whose transfer between shareholders does not affect the level of equity capital available. As a result, the regulator is quite tempted to view share certificates in a cooperative more as a form of debt. This is all the more the case as they are often sold as a financial investment to clients of the cooperative bank.

Another difficulty in the event of financial distress concerns the speed with which cooperative banks can issue new share certificates. Following the implementation of the Basel regulations, all financial cooperatives have embarked on ambitious plans to issue share certificates. Without going into too much technical detail, different types of share certificates exist, some of which enhance cooperatives' stability. Efforts to collect and reinforce capital have met with some success, but for long timespans. However, this is not enough in the face of short-term liquidity shortages. In this case, the essential thing is to have the capacity to react quickly when incidents threaten bank liquidity. What matters most is the possibility of accessing sources of liquidity as quickly as possible. Rightly or wrongly, it often seems that of all possibilities for obtaining liquidity, the reactivity of shareholders is greater than that of members of cooperatives.

The Total Loss Absorbance Capacity (TLAC) and the Minimum Requirement for Eligible Liabilities (MREL), as a percentage of TLAC, are new ratios that have been established to deal with liquidity issues. Leaving

---

[1] Supervisors introduced Total Loss Absorbance Capacity (TLAC) as a new indicator of resources that can be mobilized in a balance sheet to meet exceptional losses.

aside technical questions, the basis of these ratios is the "bail-in" mechanism, in other words the capacity of banks to mobilize resources to meet liabilities, aside equity capital, in order to absorb losses that threaten the survival of the institution. These mechanisms are now much under discussion, and the ability of transforming certain types of bearers of bank-issued bonds into shareholders in an authoritarian manner raises legal issues. Here again, cooperatives and their system of share certificates, which can be paid out to members on demand, are especially affected. So the question of their current remuneration needs to be looked at.

10.1.4   Strengthening Liquidity

Equity capital was very much an issue at the forefront in the years 2010–2015. Many banks strove to comply with the new Basel III thresholds, under pressure from the rating agencies in particular. Today's main issue concerns liquidity, and all thresholds have to met by 2019. We have already briefly looked at the ratios to be used (LCR for 30 days and NSFR for one year). A detailed analysis of these elements takes into account the numerator and denominator of each of these ratios,[2] and makes it possible to anticipate the consequences for financial institutions.

Liquidity risks lay at the heart of several bank restructuring operations in France, such as with Dexia or Crédit Immobilier de France. They were operating using a non-viable refinancing model, despite having equity capital. Northern Rock in 2007 in the UK, Washington Mutual and the Royal Bank of Scotland in 2008 were similarly affected. At some point, these banks were no longer able to access liquidity in the financial markets owing to investor wariness. The drop off in liquidity put them in great difficulty in meeting their commitments and they were unable to access other sources of funding. It also became apparent that most of France's major banks were operating with insufficient liquidity, in other words, loans granted exceeded the sum of available deposits accounts. The dependency on refinancing through borrowing in capital markets is always held to be risky, and weighs on banks' ratings. Similarly, demands by clients to extend loans were not balanced by the lengthening or greater stability of deposits. Most bank deposits are sight deposits and are therefore subject to significant variations.

---

[2] BIS, Basel Committee, *Basel III: The Liquidity Coverage Ratio and liquidity risk monitoring tools*, January 2013.
BIS, Basel Committee, *Basel III: The Net Stable Funding Ratio, Consultative Document*, 11 April 2014.

The awareness of the fragile financial structure of certain bank balance sheets has led to several changes, notably with the aim of consolidating and diversifying access to liquidity:

1) Business policy: this is surely the most visible consequence for consumers. France is one of the few countries to have allowed a situation of insufficient liquidity to arise, in other words to have a stock of bank deposits which are less than loans granted. This is even true for the cooperative banks, which historically were in the opposite situation, with far more deposits than loans. The indicator measuring this phenomenon is the Loan to Deposit Ratio (Total Loan / Total Deposits)[3] The ratings agencies have penalized and continue to penalize institutions with a Loan / Deposit > 1, because they are dependent on financial markets for refinancing. The retail banks have taken this situation into account and have adopted, or attempted to adopt, changes in their business policy to reduce the gap between the two components of this ratio, in order to return to a more balanced position. This has led the banks to review their relations with their customers. From about 2012 onwards, account managers have been clearly instructed to achieve more balanced relationships in terms of liquidity. For years, the main priority was to sell loans, accompanied possibly with the hope of recovering flows and savings from their clients. But this latter objective was not followed up much. This requirement has now been strengthened, although legislation does not demand this. As a result, two situations may be observed: banks do not provide all financing demanded buy the borrower or they put pressure on customer to manage more savings and current accounts from them. This reduces liquidity needs. This change in business policy has taken place quite quickly, and has been strongly felt by customers, who have not fully understood the reasons for it, and have viewed it as a worsening of their bank relationships.

   In the same logic, it can be pointed out that some banks linked to car producers, such as PSA Finance or RCI Banque (Renault Group), have begun collecting deposits by offering savings accounts. This acceleration in the collection of deposits risks keeping relatively high interest rates on such accounts. Special offers by some market players of interest rates at between 3 % and 4 % for several months bear this out. Another indicator is the interest rate on France's traditional savings account for small savers—the Livret A—which is surely overvalued at present, given prevailing economic circumstances. Changes in this business strategy have stretched interest

---

[3]Total credits granted to clients/total deposits by clients.

rate margins—the main source of income—a little. This, however, complicates banks' capacity for increasing equity capital out of profits.

2) The acquisition of retail banks in developing countries: many institutions in these countries have an excess of liquidity coming from an amount of deposits higher than credits. In these countries, the number of depositors is growing with the trend to opening accounts leading the granting of financing. Even if there is no transfer of liquidity between merged entities, consolidated accounting methods mean that all deposits and loans can be consolidated in the same balance sheet. Liquidity ratios are assessed mainly using consolidated accounts, so that the ratios may improve mechanically.

3) Access to liquidity in the markets: In situations where there is a lack of liquidity, access to financial markets is unavoidable. Banks generally have two options. Either they can turn to the interbank market, or they can access classical market debt directly. The interbank market was relatively unreliable in providing liquidity after the collapse of Lehman Brothers and at the height of the euro crisis. Banks lost confidence in the market and the ECB had to intervene to reestablish some visibility. However, quantitative easing will not continue indefinitely. Banks have turned more and more to debt markets to refinance themselves recently. But this supposes that:

   a. Markets are given visibility through the proposal of creating a multi-annual programme to provide access to liquidity, indicating when a bank issues paper and for how long.
   b. Better long-term and short-term management of ratings in order to provide visibility of interest rates offered to investors. Tracking such ratings is particularly sensitive as the least worries linked to a downward change in ratings may provoke a liquidity crisis. In the autumn of 2012, for example, the cut in the rating of the PSA Group led to an automatic fall in the rating of PSA finance. The French government was obliged to intervene to guarantee access of the French car-maker's bank to markets as investors adapted to this new situation.

4) Managing the banks' balance sheet: this last change follows modifications in regulations in terms of liquidity. It concerns the necessary adaptation of investment policies and investments. Indeed, the very definition of the LCR and even more the NSFR ratios assumes the availability of balance sheet assets with low risks when being transformed into liquidity. Accordingly, banks are tempted to hold high-quality assets, above all government bonds. There is thus a danger that banks buy more of such assets, at the expense of providing credit to companies or buying up corporate bonds.

5) Another evolution linked to these new ratios lies in the comeback of securitization. This technique was emblematic of the subprime crisis, the main channel through which the banking crisis was transmitted to the whole economy. Securitization is now being used more and more by the banks. Indeed, given that the ECB recognizes the quality of such security issues, banks are once again tempted to use securitization to make their best loans more liquid (mortgage loans on housing): in other words credit with the highest ratings. This constitutes a return to the historical balance sheet management practices that were misused by American banks in the 2000s.

The question of liquidity securitization is not therefore merely a simple technical matter. Instead, it affects the whole of an institution's strategy, as do the new equity capital requirements. These two ratios have thus become the essential determinants of top managements' strategic choices (BRI 2013a and BRI 2014).

10.2 Improving the Control of Financial Institutions

The prudential regulations issued by the Basel Committee not only concern quantitative ratios. They also have a qualitative dimension stemming from the implementation of supervisory measures. These are based on the Supervisory Review and Evaluation Process (SREP) which translates the philosophy of Pillar 2 of the Basel regulations. SREP deals both with the control of levels of equity capital and liquidity, the definition of an institution's "risk appetite" and the governance mechanisms set up to ensure supervision of these issues. Changes are surely likely to be most sensitive for actors concerning the question of governance, notably governance of financial cooperatives (10.2.1.). It should also be noted that as part of the continuity of these supervisory measures, major financial groups will have to present their organizational structures in which responsibilities for controls are clearly identified (10.2.2.).

10.2.1 The Strengthening of Financial Institutions' Governance

The roles of governance, top management and company boards are central to the systems of internal control set up by financial institutions (Lamarque and Karfoul 2009). The concern for the quality of governance, however, does not only affect questions of control, but also reinforces the weight and contribution of control in strategic decisions and in the fixing of risk taking. This shift is the logical consequence of criticisms made by the authorities of the passivity of governance bodies (company boards and supervisory boards) about controls over risk-taking by institutions which these bodies should have been supervising in theory. In July 2015, the BCBS published its latest recommendations on the principles of company governance for the banking sector.

10.2.1.1 Regulatory Requirements in Terms of Governance Quality

Since 2012, these requirements have mainly been fixed by the European Banking Authority (EBA), which was given its official mandate as part of CRD 4 (Art 91-12) to put forward Guidelines. The latter relate to the competence, experience and honorability of top executive managers: the Management Body. These guidelines are generally translated today as requiring managers and directors to be "fit and proper," and are grounded in the following principles:

a. The allocation of enough time by top managers to their commitments;
b. Adequate knowledge, competence and collective experience;
c. Concepts of honesty, integrity and independence of judgement;
d. Concepts of human and financial resources that are adequate for the training of members of the executive and the supervisory functions of the bank;
e. Concepts of diversity.

Box 10.1 European Banking Authority Guidelines for "Fit and Proper" Board Directors

1. **Appropriate knowledge and experience**

   a. Relevant training: diploma, on-the-job learning, in-house training programmes
   b. Relevance of the content of training: banking, finance, insurance, economics, law, management
   c. Specific knowledge of strategic planning, risk management, rules of governance and analysis of financial statements
   d. Work experience: level of responsibilities held, duration (five years), number of subordinates, size of organization, date of leaving position (three years at most)

2. **Professional behaviour**: search for indices aiming to verify such behaviour:

   a. Potential conflicts of interest with other functions, relations between interested parties and shareholders or companies in the group, relations with senior executives
   b. Excessive number of mandates/directorships (positions held)
   c. Verification of directors' independence in the positions given to them

3. **Skills:** decision-making abilities, a faculty for judgement, communication capacities, abilities to detect risks, leadership, loyalty, independence, power of persuasion, resistance to stress, capacities to work with others, courage and so on.
4. **The weighting of the above criteria according to:**

   a. The characteristics of the financial institution: the nature of activities, size (employees, balance sheet, number of clients)
   b. The functions the person will need to conduct: chair of the company board—the ability to act as chair, leadership, strategic direction
   c. Collective expertise by the board: checking whether the expertise of the board is guaranteed by the candidate. In case the director is replaced, checking the expertise he/she applied, in order to replace it and reinforce the training of present administrators in the area

Adapted from the European Banking Authority 2012

These principles affect not just members of a bank's top management but also persons responsible for supervision, in other words a bank's company boards. Specific criteria are not assessed here. However, it is to be noted that as of 2012, the EBA set out factors to help evaluate a certain number of characteristics of the individuals concerned (see Box 10.1).

The principles of bank governance put forward by the Basel Committee on Banking Supervision in July 2015 support the same approach. They include points on the composition and qualifications of company boards. There is thus a general convergence for raising the level of expertise of governance bodies so that they can increase their supervisory powers over management decisions in good conditions, and so that boards can challenge such decisions. But moreover, boards should undoubtedly be able to meet their responsibilities concerning strategic choices and policy risks.

These changes led to stricter control by supervisors of the quality of governance and challenges to certain appointments of bank directors and top managers. The result is a form of certification of members of leading governance bodies, to check whether they can really carry out their missions. The desired profile of directors and the way they are selected have been directly affected by this new regulatory context.

10.2.1.2 Consequences for the Recruitment of Directors

The very use of the word recruitment for directors may seem incongruous, given that they are elected by general assemblies of shareholders (for banks with publicly listed shares) or by certificate shareholders (or their representatives for cooperative banks). There are no plans to change the way board members are appointed. Independent directors must also be elected by general assembly. However, it is clear that candidates for election will have to meet the "fit and proper" criteria.

The task is not easy, whatever model the bank adopts. Large, publicly listed banks, with a majority of independent directors, will need to put up candidates for election who have both the necessary financial skills and also the time to carry out their missions. This is not always easy, and suggests that the number of mandates held by any one director should be limited, if banks want to see renowned directors elected to their boards. As for the small number of family banks which still exist, electing board directors with no experience to represent shareholders may raise problems when the expertise of boards is assessed. Other consequences for governance also include the obligation of separating the role of chairman of the board and CEO (chief executive director), and no longer having one person doing both jobs.

Electing directors with experience in finance is even more difficult for cooperative banks. As cooperatives of customers, these banks have governance systems that lead customers to be elected to governance bodies. In these systems, financial expertise used to be secondary in view of members' interests. The application of the principles means that certain chairpersons elected by the boards of cooperative banks have already lost their status as executive directors. Crédit Agricole even filed a suit with France's top administrative court (Conseil d'Etat) on this matter in October 2014. But it is likely to be more difficult to find candidates for directorships that have the necessary skills to meet the new principles. These banks must therefore examine new ways of retaining both the specificities of their business model and the ability of constituting boards which bring together the right skills so that they can be effective collectively.

Furthermore, all banks are set to train their board members in order to raise their expertise. However, in view of the complexity of managing banks and its associated regulations, it is not certain that training programmes currently being designed will be enough to bridge the skills gap. Apart from this compliance which worries many actors, it is widely recognised today that the effectiveness of governance bodies and the quality of their decision-making contribute to banks' competitive advantage. Many companies have started work to increase boards' effectiveness and the quality of their contributions.

10.2.2 Clearer Organization and Responsibilities

Following these changes, regulation of the functioning of financial groups as a whole reflects the principles put forward by the Basel Committee. CRD 4 clearly reflects the will to see the missions and responsibilities of central bodies being defined unmistakably, especially concerning risk management. Accordingly the Directive stipulates:

1) In terms of supervising credit risks, it is necessary to have an overall measure for consolidated groups, a common rating and the definition of the body responsible for rating;
2) The solvency and liquidity of the central body as well as all its affiliated institutions must be followed up using consolidated accounts for these institutions;
3) The management of the central body is empowered to give instructions to the management of affiliated institutions.

For the first point in particular, the implementation of instruction memorandum BCBS 239 of January 2013 illustrates well the necessary changes in organizations and their governance (BRI 2013b). This instruction memorandum relates to the aggregation of risks in group finances as well as the reporting of risks. The memo stresses in particular the importance of reinforcing and improving "infrastructures" (in terms of information organization and systems). The aim is to provide the best possible information in reporting to governance bodies and top management, so that they can identify, assess and manage risks.[4]

---

[4] BCBS 239, Principles for effective risk data aggregation and risk reporting, January 2013. http://www.bis.org/publ/bcbs239.pdf.

More generally, the reinforcement of risk management skills is expected to take place quickly, in view of improving decision-making and ensuring effective supervision of groups' entities. The aim is to have truly a better vision of exposure to risk on a consolidated basis.

From this perspective, the operation of financial groups has been questioned and institutions are in the process of changing their organisation and governance, more or less rapidly. The cooperative banks surely have to meet the greatest challenges. On the whole, they are strongly decentralized in France, and these regulatory changes oblige them to adapt the way they operate, and it has been possible to observe changes in these groups' structures.

For a while, Crédit Agricole considered a Reorganization of its Central Body (*Réorganisation de son Organe Central*, or Projet ROC). The project involved transferring the functions of the central body set out above from the company listed on the stock exchange (Crédit Agricole SA or CASA) to a National Federation of the Crédit Agricole (Fédération Nationale du Crédit Agricole). The latter today is an organization that owns a majority of CASA shares through a holding company. The project did not go ahead, but it highlights the complexity of governance structures for cooperatives and mutual in general, as well as the difficulties for the bank regulators and supervisors to decipher them. Crédit Agricole nevertheless went ahead in making adjustments to governance, by bringing political authorities onto the board of CASA. The bank has also clarified the financial structure of the group by selling the cooperative investment certificates it held in regional banks to regional banks themselves.

With the same idea, in 2013 the BPCE Group simplified its capital structure when its regional banks bought back their cooperative investment certificates from Natixis, which had been supporting a certain number of subsidiaries on behalf of the group. The distribution of roles between BPCE, the central body and the listed structure of Natixis is clear and has been consolidated by the strict separation of capital ties between the regional parts of the group (Caisses d'épargne and Banques Populaires) and BPCE on the one hand, and between BCPE and Natixis on the other hand.

These two examples of major French financial cooperative groups illustrate well the importance of clarifying their organization and governance, in order to increase their efficiency but also their external transparency. The examples have followed directly changes in the Basel texts, since 2010. These texts have addressed such structural questions as much as the issues of equity capital levels and liquidity. However, it remains difficult here to describe the consequences of the relations between the regional entities and the central body. Indeed, several studies have shown that the regulatory measures are encouraging the increasing centralization of decision-making, which in turn is undermining a key component of the differentiation across banks (Ory et al. 2006; Ory et al. 2012; Deville & Lamarque 2015). In fact, it is increasingly said that the cooperative model is becoming hybrid as it draws on the conventional model of banking.

The traditional banks are also being affected by these regulations. At the national level their structures are being integrated (see principles of corporate governance for banks, july 2015). But with a far greater international presence and subsidiaries that have been bought up, these banks must present high-quality information to supervisors. This raises numerous questions in terms of consolidation and steering, and several banks have had problems with this.

10.3 Conclusion

This chapter has sought to provide a general assessment of the impact of Basel regulations on solvency and liquidity ratios of retail banks, as well of associated changes in internal control and governance measures. The consequences have been numerous, and have considerably affected the functioning of institutions. They have led to changes which, viewed from outside, may appear to be merely technical.

However, the conditions of a profound change in banks' business models have been implemented. To begin with, conditions for financing the economy, the requirements for equity capital and liquidity are providing a new framework for the ability to lend. Moreover, the French and European authorities clearly expect bank intermediation to diminish, to the advantage of financial markets. The retail banks have therefore started analysing how to adapt to these new conditions, by having fewer branches, by becoming financial advisors rather than just being lenders, by helping companies combine various sources of financing and so on. Apart from adapting marketing practices, banks are dealing with the upheavals of a new organizational and governance model. This is especially so for cooperative banks. They are being destabilized by requirements about organizational structure, the quality of data, as well as the clear identification of individual and collective responsibilities. Banks must therefore carry out a twofold business and organizational transformation, as other major changes to their operating environment are taking place (most notably the digital revolution).

The accumulation of regulations in a very short timespan may be regretted, along with instability and a clear and notorious underevaluation of their internal human consequences for banks' employees. The tensions generated by this context moreover risk mitigating the scope of financial and technical developments that have been promoted by the Basel Committee. These tensions could lead to operational risks and the emergence of alternative actors that are free from all constraints.

References

BRI, Comité de Bâle, Bâle III: Ratio de liquidité à court terme et outils de suivi du risque de liquidité, Corporate governance principles for banks Janvier 2013a.

BRI, Comité de Bâle, BCBS 239, Principles for effective risk data aggregation and risk reporting, Janvier 2013b. http://www.bis.org/publ/bcbs239.pdf.

BRI, Comité de Bâle, Bâle III: Ratio structurel de liquidité à long terme, Document consultatif, 11 Avril 2014.

BRI, Comité de Bâle, Corporate governance principles for banks Juillet 2015.

Deville, A., & Lamarque, E. (2015). *Diversity of cooperative bank governance models questioning by regulation: An international qualitative research*. Working paper, Chaire Management et Gouvernance des cooperatives financière, IAE de Paris, Mai 2015.

European Banking Authorities. (2012). Guidelines on the assesment of the suitability of members of the management body and key function holder.

Karfoul, H., & Lamarque, E. (2009). Gouvernance des banques et maîtrise des risques. *Revue Française de Gouvernance d'Entreprise*, n°5, Septembre.

Lamarque, E. (2015). *Stratégie des banques et des assurances*. Paris: Dunod.

Ory, J.-N., Gurtner, E., & Jaeger, M. (2006). The challenges of the recent changes in the French Cooperative Banking Groups. *Revue Internationale de l'Economie Sociale, RECMA* (référencée ESSEC et ECONLIT), October—version française dans le numéro de juin 2006.

Ory, J. N., De Serres, A., & Jaeger, M. (2012). Comment résister à l'effet de normalisation: le défi des banques coopératives, *Revue des Sciences de Gestion*, n°258, novembre.

11

The Knowns and the Known Unknowns of Capital Requirements for Market Risks

Jean-Paul Laurent

11.1 Introduction

A new era is beginning for bank intermediation in financial markets. Under the leadership of the Trading Book Group of the Basel Committee, the calculation of risk-weighted assets (RWAs) associated with market and trading book risks is being upended. The Fundamental Review of the Trading Book (FRTB) led to the publication of a set of rules in January 2016.[1] It should be recalled that RWAs are the denominator of the solvency ratio.

In the first part of this text, the FRTB is situated in the vast movement that has reinforced regulatory and prudential requirements.

The present reforms are a subtle compromise. On the one hand, they perpetuate the autonomous function for monitoring risks within banks, under

I thank Hassan Omidi Firouzi and Michael Sestier for their assistance in preparing this document and Pierre-Charles Pradier for useful comments on a draft version. Any errors of fact or interpretation are of course my sole responsibility.

J.-P. Laurent (✉)
LabEx RéFi and PRISM, Université Paris 1 Panthéon-Sorbonne, Paris, France

---

[1] See in particular *Minimum capital requirements for market risk*, http://www.bis.org/bcbs/publ/d352.pdf. For a brief introduction see also the Basel Committee document, again published in January 2016, entitled *Explanatory note on the revised minimum capital requirements for market risk*, http://www.bis.org/bcbs/publ/d352_note.pdf.

R. Douady et al. (eds.), *Financial Regulation in the EU*,
DOI 10.1007/978-3-319-44287-7_11

the control of bank supervisors. On the other hand, they set up a safety net to avoid any drift linked to self-regulation.

The emphasis here is therefore placed on the uncertainties linked to the final calibration of the new framework and the implications for economic banking models and market intermediation, namely:

1) The reduction in financial market banking intermediation will benefit managers of bond funds and insurance companies, which are less regulated than banks.
2) The fall in over-the-counter (OTC) derivative trading will confirm the rising strength of standardized markets in futures and swaps.[2] The development of new market infrastructures is associated with new issues of financial stability, including the creation of systemic nodes and clearing houses that have to be regulated and supervised. This will not occur without consequences for final users, who will continue to want to use customized products. They will have to take on "basis risks" or face extra costs charged by banks.[3]

Lastly, the chapter will stress operational issues linked to piloting this transformation process for regulated banks, which are facing a lot of uncertainty.

11.2 Market Regulation

The future rules for weighted averages of trading books are part of the new regulatory framework. Nearly ten years after the 2008 financial crisis, the broad outlines put forward at the G20 summits in 2009 and by the Financial Stability Board (FSB),[4,5] the work on bank regulation (by the Basel Committee on Banking Supervision (BCBS) or simply the Basel Committee), the markets and financial infrastructures (Committee on Payments and Market Infrastructures or CPMI) are taking shape.

---

[2] See Litan (2010), Duffie (2013), Rosenberg and Massari (2013).

[3] The new regulations relating to OTC derivative products will have major consequences for end users, especially companies. The latter may be led to changing the risk profile of rates on their debts, via profiled asset swaps according to the bonds issued. These non-standard products are not cleared centrally. The cost of managing financial risks to companies is thus increased, either directly through a rise in intermediation margins on asset swaps, or indirectly through an increase in "basis risks," if companies decide to take out insurance cover using standardized products. Culp and Miller (1995) illustrate the importance of basis risks in the case of Metallgesellschaft.

[4] See for example, *The financial crisis and information gaps*, published October 2009 https://www.imf.org/external/np/g20/pdf/102909.pdf.

[5] *A Coordination Framework for Monitoring the Implementation of Agreed G20/FSB Financial Reforms*, October 2011, http://www.financialstabilityboard.org/wp-content/uploads/r_111017.pdf.

The main aim is to improve financial stability and to eliminate incentives to create risks, which are costly to taxpayers. However, reforms must not penalize economic growth, the granting of loans or the management risk functions carried out by markets and financial intermediates.

The range of new regulations for banks and markets is vast, and the regulation process is particularly ambitious and complex. This chapter focuses on measuring market risks and credit risks of trading books. However, other issues include:

1) The reinforcement of the quantity and quality of equity capital required for risk.
2) The role played by "risk-based" solvency ratios relative to leverage ratios and the use of stress tests by supervisors, especially in the USA.
3) An examination of liquidity transformation.
4) An examination of OTC bank intermediation for derivative products.[6]

In banking, Basel III has profoundly modified regulations concerning bank solvency.[7] Changes include: the increase in solvency ratios; more restrictive definitions of equity capital relative to risks, a stronger framework relating to internal models for banking book risks (in terms of loans and securities); stricter regulation of counterparty risks and higher leverage ratios. The redesigning of ways for calculating average weighted assets for their trading book risks is only one aspect of this whole set of measures.

11.2.1   Higher Solvency Ratios (CET1/RWA)

The minimum Core Equity Tier One (CET1) solvency ratio has increased from 2 % to 7 % (4.5 % + 2.5 % for a "conservation buffer"). There is a supplementary buffer that can run to 3.5% for globally systemically important banks (G-SIBs): in practice, this means 1 % to 2.5 % for the banks in

---

[6] This includes:

1) The obligation for transactions in the simplest derivative products to be booked through clearing houses, with the aim of reducing the counterparty risks on these products. The clearing houses have been placed at the heart of the new market architecture for derivative products. For more detail on this matter. <AU Last sentence of Footnote 6 point 1 is incomplete: please correct>
2) The introduction of bilateral initial margins (guarantee deposits) for derivative products that are not centrally cleared, again in view of reducing counterparty risks and contagion via derivative products.
3) The improvement of pre- and post-trade transparency.
4) The use of trading platforms (Swaps Execution Facilities, SEFs).

[7] See *"A brief history of the Basel Committee"*, October 2014, http://www.bis.org/bcbs/history.pdf and Blundell-Wignall and Atkinson (2010) for a first assessment of Basel III.

question.[8] Apart from increases already adopted, there are further plans to implement counter-cyclical buffer reserves of up to 2.5 % of RWAs, as well as a buffer of possibly up to 5% for systemic risk: the latter is specific to the European regulatory framework. This is mentioned in CRD IV, as well as in the Basel rules. The aim is to prevent the emergence of speculative bubbles. In this case, the solvency ratio could rise from 2% under Basel II to a maximum of 18% under Basel III.

11.2.2   A More Restrictive Notion of Prudential Equity Capital (CET1) as the Numerator of Solvency Ratios

Prudential capital equity is obtained by subtracting from booked equity capital a certain number of elements which do not have the required "loss absorption capacity".[9] These include non-eligible minority interests,[10] dividends to be paid, intangible assets, goodwill, and deferred tax assets on losses carried forward. Similarly, adjustments for risks to equity capital, especially elements of Debit Valuation Adjustment (DVA) that affect the evaluation of the fair value of derivative products, are deduced from equity capital. Lastly, a certain number of filters are applied to obtain fair value. These are Additional Valuation Adjustments (AVAs) that have been introduced within the European framework.[11] Such valuation adjustments take into account especially market price uncertainty (MPU), the costs of liquidation or closeout costs, model risks and concentrated provisions. Apart from reserves that are already accounted

---

[8] See https://www.bis.org/bcbs/gsib/ for the criteria classifying systemically important banks.

[9] Apart from the capacity to absorb losses, the Basel Committee has set out precise criteria for defining Core Equity Tier 1 capital, as a function of its capacity to absorb losses, its permanency and flexibility for payments. These latter two points have led to the exclusion of certain hybrid securities from CET1.

[10] In December 2009, the Basel Committee (http://www.bis.org/publ/bcbs164.pdf) proposed deducting minority shareholdings in subsidiaries from equity capital because they cannot cover losses at consolidated group level. The handling of minority interests has subsequently evolved. The reader may refer to the following documents by the Basel Committee concerning the definition of equity capital:

1) Basel III: A global regulatory framework for more resilient banks and banking systems, June 2011, http://www.bis.org/publ/bcbs189.pdf (the first version was published in December 2010, the June 2011 version introduced an equity capital charge for variations in Credit Valuation Adjustment (CVA);
2) The press release in January 2011, http://www.bis.org/press/p110113.pdf.

The FAQ available on the Basel Committee website (last update October 2011): http://www.bis.org/publ/bcbs211.htm.

[11] Capital Requirements Regulation (CRR) and the technical document of the EBA on prudent valuation https://www.eba.europa.eu/documents/10180/642449/EBA-RTS-2014-06+RTS+on+Prudent+Valuation.pdf.

for by banks concerning the preceding factors, the AVAs lead to further deductions in equity capital. In presenting its results for Q1 2014, Deutsche Bank valued the impact of these adjustments to its equity capital at €2 billion.[12]

11.2.3 Improved Monitoring of Counterparty Risks

In addition, Basel III has increased charges on capital linked to counterparty risks on derivative products, including the introduction of a charge on capital linked to the variability of CVA and capital requirements for bank exposures to central counterparties (CCP).[13] Lastly, specific measures have been taken to discourage interbank exposure: for example, increases in RWAs to cover exposure to large financial sector entities or to unregulated financial entities.[14]

11.2.4 Leverage Ratio Acting in Principle as a Backstop

For the Basel Committee, the solvency ratio, with risk-sensitive-based capital ratios as the denominator, is the dominant indicator. The leverage ratio should only serve as a safeguard (Estrella, Park and Peristiani 2000; Blum 2008). The Americans, however, do not see things like this, and have a different approach to regulation. In the USA, there has for a long time been a leverage ratio based on US accounting standards (US GAAP). In order to ensure consistency with the Basel framework,[15] a Supplementary Leverage Ratio (SLR) was introduced in September 2014: the enhanced SLR (eSLR).[16] This indicator concerns the eight major US banks identified as G-SIBs, and essentially makes the new US leverage ratio comparable to that applied by European banks. Both, overall,

---

[12] https://www.db.com/ir/de/images/Deutsche_Bank_1Q2014_results.pdf page 6.

[13] See the Basel Committee documents *Review of the Credit Valuation Adjustment Risk Framework* issued in July 2015, http://www.bis.org/bcbs/publ/d325.pdf, *Reducing variation in credit risk-weighted assets – constraints on the use of internal model approaches*, issued in March 2016, http://www.bis.org/bcbs/publ/d362.pdf, *Capital requirements for bank exposures to central counterparties - final standard*, April 2014, http://www.bis.org/publ/bcbs282.pdf.

[14] See for example http://www.allenovery.com/SiteCollectionDocuments/Capital%20Requirements%20Directive%20IV%20Framework/IRB%20approach%20to%20credit%20risk%20in%20the%20Banking%20Book.pdf.

[15] US accounting standards are different from IFRS standards in terms of netting repo activities and security financing transactions (SFTs). Deutsche Bank showed that the size of its balance sheet according to US GAAP was twice as weak when compared to calculation based on international accounting standards, this being essentially because of the way repos are processed. The Basel ratio is the result of a compromise between international and US practices. It should be noted that the denominator of the leverage ratio (the exposure measure) includes off-balance sheet items, especially credit derivatives, as well as the exposure to risk on derivative products.

[16] See for example http://www.usbasel3.com/docs/Final%20SLR%20Visual%20Memo.pdf.

broadly comply with Basel III. The new minimal leverage ratio is 5 % for major systemically important banks, and 6 % for their subsidiaries managing deposits (Insured Depository Institutions). This compares to only 3 % set out in Basel III. The work on setting out the methods for calculating leverage ratios should be completed in 2017, for effective implementation in 2018. Until then, the banks must publish their leverage ratio every quarter. As of the beginning of 2015, the major US banks were already implementing ratios above those required (by US regulations of course). Market discipline has led European banks to follow US norms, which have therefore become de facto extraterritorial. This doubles the constraints induced by the Basel leverage ratio. If at the end of the day, the constraint associated with the leverage ratio becomes binding, then there will no longer be much point in banks investing in tools to monitor market risks.

The preceding rules complete the measures relating to the ordered liquidation of systemically important financial institutions, with the aim of protecting depositors and avoiding the commitment of public monies in saving banks that are too big to fail.

The revision of the principles and method of calculating RWAs is thus only one part of a whole set of measures.

11.3 The Reasons for Overhauling the Calculation of Risk Weighted Assets on Trading Books

The FRTB is part of the implementation of the new prudential standards under Basel III, initiated at the G20 summits in London and Pittsburgh in 2009 and by the FSB.

The project builds on previous Basel rules.[17] The document updating the processing of market risks under Basel II was released in July 2009.[18] It addresses certain shortfalls in the previous regulations, highlighted by the crisis in 2008, including:

1) The inclusion of Stressed VaR (Value at Risk) in calculating RWAs. This is a calibrated measure of market risk throughout a period of instability.

---

[17] The Market Risk Amendment of 1996 (http://www.bis.org/publ/bcbs24.pdf), see also the Basel Committee's document entitled *International Convergence of Capital Measurement and Capital Standards* (http://www.bis.org/publ/bcbs128.pdf), published in June 2006 as a consolidated version.

[18] http://www.bis.org/publ/bcbs158.pdf, see also *Analysis of the trading book quantitative impact study* (http://www.bis.org/publ/bcbs163.pdf), published in October 2009.

Previous measures of risk did not include such events in their calculation (Dowd et al. 2011). This could lead to an underestimation of risk, when current volatility is weak.

2) Taking into account risks of bankruptcy and migration (i.e. a change in ratings) within a trading portfolio, via an Incremental Risk Charge (IRC). Under Basel II, credit risks in such trading portfolios only showed up in the risks of credit margin variations. As its name indicates, IRC aims to complete previous regulation which neglects such risks.

3) The specific processing of portfolio correlation, including especially corporate CDOs (Comprehensive Risk Measure or CRM). If internal models can be used, a regulatory floor calculated using the standard approach (CRM floor) has de facto become an active constraint.

Regulators have nevertheless found it useful to go further and to carry out profound reforms for calculating RWAs. The so-called Basel 2.5 rules, whatever their usefulness, were designed under emergency conditions, and did not benefit from the same preparation and formulation that went into the various ingredients of Basel III. The relevance of this revision in ways of calculating RWAs for trading book risks is discussed below. Several underlying principles of the new regulatory framework are also set out, namely the supervision of internal models and the development of a standard approach whose own principles converge on internal models.

It should be first recalled that the Basel Committee has put forward three criteria for assessing risk models: the capacity to measure risks effectively (risk sensitivity), simplicity and comparability.[19]

The regulation of trading book risks seeks to structure better the methods used by banks in calculating risks, and hence their RWAs. This will favour the comparability of results across banks and should prevent drift in practices. It is useful to start with a historical overview in understanding the proposed changes.

Basel II was not applied uniformly internationally. Since this agreement, solvency ratios—the levels of equity capital required to carry out banking activities—have been determined according to risks, and less in the flat-rate way that existed previously. This especially concerns the Advanced Internal

---

[19] *The regulatory framework: balancing risk sensitivity, simplicity and comparability*, http://www.bis.org/publ/bcbs258.pdf. Other references include the speech by the Secretary General of the Basel Committee in February 2013 (http://www.bis.org/speeches/sp130226.pdf) and a document by the Fed and the OCC relating to risk models, which has become the reference text for US supervisors: *Supervisory Guidance on Model Risk Management* (https://www.federalreserve.gov/bankinforeg/srletters/sr1107a1.pdf). We also refer to Aikman et al. (2014).

Ratings Based Approach (IRBA) used by large banks to take into account credit risks in their banking books. Some important aspects in calculating exposure, such as the dependency between default events, are controlled by the Basel Committee. Yet banks have certain latitude in determining default probabilities and recovery rates.

The 1996 amendment for taking into account market risks was a supplementary step. Regulated institutions were henceforth able to calculate their market risks (risk-weighted assets) using internal models for assessing extreme losses (risk distribution quantiles or VaR).

This led to a paradigm shift based on:

1) the emergence of quantitative models for measuring risks, such as VaR; and
2) the possibility for banks to develop internal models to measure risks, with regulators only setting out general principles and supervisors ensuring their correct implementation.

The characteristics retained for measuring risks (VaR) in the present regulatory framework have often been criticized (for example by Danielsson et al. 2015):

1) In certain cases, though seldom, the capital required for a diversified portfolio may be greater than the sum of capital required for the components of the portfolio (there being no benefits from diversification).
2) Other criticisms concern the liquidation horizon (ten days), which is insufficient, especially for concentrated positions owing to the proportionality between portfolio size and risk measures.
3) This concerns microprudential regulation, which does not take into account the systemic effects linked to the accumulated exposure of large, regulated institutions (De Long et al. 1990; Lowenstein 2000). The regulation is held to be procyclical (Danielsson, Shin and Zigrand 2004); Gordy and Howells 2006; Rochet 2008), as regulated capital requirements increase with the price volatility of assets, which may lead to forced sales in times of market tensions (see for example Adrian and Shin (2013) on banks' deleveraging).

The underlying theoretical concepts of credit risk assessment (VaR) and Expected Shortfall are simple (see Acerbi and Tasche 2002; Tasche 2002; Yamai and Yoshiba 2002): VaR is a quantile associated with the distribution of losses over a given horizon; Expected Shortfall is the average loss beyond VaR. Their implementation is not, however, easy or transparent (see Jackson and Perraudin 2000; Pérignon and Smith 2010a; Alexander and Sarabia 2012), as:

1) internal bank models for valuing risks are complex, and hence difficult for supervisors to audit;
2) their specific nature to each bank makes comparisons difficult;
3) excessive detail in identifying risks is associated with instability in determining correlations and so poor assessment of the benefits of diversification;
4) by contrast, a lack of detail means that some risks are underestimated; and
5) lastly, adjustments to take into account the persistent character of high volatility or extreme risks imply delicate modelling choices which may be more or less arbitrary.

The Basel Committee has set up procedures of "backtesting" risk models, in order to ensure that effective market losses are not abnormally frequent. This involves a "traffic light" approach in which internal models are distributed across three categories (green, yellow and red), according to whether the number of days or trading losses were greater to the measure of risks during the preceding 12 months.[20] This approach entails incentives: above a certain threshold, which corresponds to entry into the yellow zone, abnormally high losses lead to increased requirements in terms of equity capital. The procedures retained by the Basel Committee can be improved at the margins. It is, however, difficult to invalidate a poorly specified VaR model, owing to the relative scarcity of the abnormalities considered (see for example Kupiec 1995).

From a positive point of view, a set of techniques and good practices has been progressively put into place over 20 years, both for the entities being regulated as well as for the supervisors (see Ediz, Michael and Perraudin 1998; Jorion 2002; Liu, Ryan and Tan 2004; Barakova and Palvia 2014).

By contrast, it has been argued that the complexity of models for measuring risks favours large banking institutions, given the scale of their resources available when compared to supervisory bodies. This asymmetry provides banks with margins of manoeuvre (see, for example, Groeneveld et al. 1999; Jones 2000; Blum 2008; Pérignon, Deng and Wang 2008; Pérignon and Smith 2010a; Behn et al. 2014; Colliard 2015; Mariathasan and Merrouche 2014;

---

[20] This approach and terminology were initially described in a Basel Committee document entitled *Supervisory framework for the use of 'backtesting'*, published in January 1996 http://www.bis.org/publ/bcbs22.pdf.

or Begley, Purnanandam and Zheng 2016). In the so-called "London Whale" scandal involving J.P. Morgan, the internal models for measuring credit risks were being revised at the same time as the bank was taking out important positions in the market for credit default swaps, as part of its main balance sheet management. The revision contributed largely to hiding the scale of excessive risks being taken on by the bank.

Comparability studies of hypothetical portfolios, carried out under the auspices of the Bank for International Settlements (BIS),[21] and the European Banking Association (EBA),[22] have revealed significant variations in RWAs. For different types of portfolios, especially portfolios actually held by banks, it is difficult to identify if banks are underestimating their RWAs. The studies nevertheless demonstrate that the use of internal models is far from providing a uniform vision of bank risks. The International Monetary Fund (IMF) has published a study showing the large variation in RWA density (Le Leslé and Avramova (2012)). Such variations may be explained by different banking cultures, as well as the varying relative importance of financial markets in Europe and the USA. The latter never applied Basel II, and the US approach to regulation has traditionally favoured leverage ratios rather than capital requirements relative to risk.

The analysis of market losses by banks relative to their risk profile (VaR) indicates that internal models smooth out volatility estimates. As a result, VaR was a poor indicator of banking difficulties during the crisis in 2008 (see for example Haldane and Madouros 2012). It also discriminated little between banks. This is clearly problematic from a prudential point of view.

Banking supervisors need to be vigilant, be they the OCC, the Fed LISCC (Large Institution Supervision Coordinating Committee), the New York Fed in the USA, the Single Supervisory Mechanism (SSM) and national regulators in the Eurozone, or the Prudential Regulatory Authority (PRA) in the United Kingdom. The credibility of instruments for calculating risk-weighted assets does not depend on banking regulation, but on the capacity of supervisors to audit internal models developed by banks. This is a challenge. In the case of the USA, the culture of banking supervision and the inappropriate nature of its formalism were recently called into question relating to J.P. Morgan's Chief Investment Officer following the London Whale scandal (mentioned

---

[21] Documents in 2013: http://www.bis.org/publ/bcbs240.pdf and http://www.bis.org/publ/bcbs267.pdf, document submitted to the G20 in 2014: http://www.bis.org/bcbs/publ/d298.pdf.

[22] December 2013, https://www.eba.europa.eu/documents/10180/15947/20131217+Report+on+variability+of+Market+RWA.pdf, May 2014 https://www.eba.europa.eu/documents/10180/711669/EBA-CP-2014-07+%28CP+on+RTS+and+ITS+on+benchmarking+portfolios%29.pdf.

above).[23] The fact that the significant intellectual resources available to central banks have actually been focused on the methods for quantifying risks can only been strongly applauded, as can the fact that supervisory teams have been reinforced by experts from the financial services industry. It is also desirable that regulated banks provide extra information (disclosure, the third Basel pillar, http://www.bis.org/bcbs/publ/d309.pdf) concerning internal models of risk calculation.

11.4 The Present State of Reforms in the Calculation of Risk Weighted Assets on Trading Books

The first consultative document by the Basel Committee concerns the fundamental review of the trading book, published in May 2012.[24] Two further documents were distributed in October 2013 and December 2014 respectively.[25] These consultative documents have led to many responses, mainly from the financial services industry, notably through ISDA, IIF and GFMA channels.[26] Furthermore, Quantitative Impact Studies (QISs) in February 2015 and July 2015 include updates of the preceding documents.[27] Lastly, the official rules were published in January 2016, based on the July 2015 impact study.[28]

It should be noted that recommendations by the Basel Committee are not legally binding and need to be transposed into national legislation, as for example in the European Union (EU) with the CRD IV, the CRR regulation,

---

[23] See for example the summary of the report by Fed's Office of Inspector General (http://oig.federalreserve.gov/reports/board-supervisory-processes-jpmorgan-chase-oct2014.pdf), the Senate report (http://www.hsgac.senate.gov/download/report-jpmorgan-chase-whale-trades-a-case-history-of-derivatives-risks-and-abuses-march-15-2013) and numerous other commentaries in the press.

[24] *Fundamental review of the trading book: A revised market risk framework*, Basel Committee on Banking Supervision http://www.bis.org/publ/bcbs265.pdf.

[25] *Fundamental review of the trading book - second consultative document*, Basel Committee on Banking Supervision http://www.bis.org/publ/bcbs265.htm, "*Fundamental review of the trading book: outstanding issues*", Basel Committee on Banking Supervision

http://www.bis.org/bcbs/publ/d305.pdf.

[26] The Basel Committee has published its responses: see for example, http://www.bis.org/bcbs/publ/comments/d305/overview.htm for the third consultative document.

[27] https://www.bis.org/bcbs/qis/biiiimplmoninstr_feb15.pdf, https://www.bis.org/bcbs/qis/instr_impact_study_jul15.pdf.

[28] "*Minimum capital requirements for market risk*", http://www.bis.org/bcbs/publ/d352.pdf. See also *Explanatory note on the revised minimum capital requirements for market risk* (http://www.bis.org/bcbs/publ/d352_note.pdf) published in January 2016 by the Basel Committee, which provides some information on the origin of rules published the same month, and on the impact of new measures.

the Regulation Technical Standards (RTS) and the Implementation Technical Standards (ITS) of the EBA or of the European Supervisory Authorities (ESAs). Divergences in interpretation and the actual effective implementation within different jurisdictions of the Basel Committee rules are not without negative consequences. The USA never wanted to implement Basel II fully, and implemented its own rules with the Dodd–Frank Act, prior to recommendations of the Basel Committee. As for the EU, it has applied favourable treatment to sovereign exposures, even though these have created real problems for the Union. The Basel Committee checks the compliance of national regulations. However, nothing guarantees geographical convergence, given a lack of political will. The negative consequences of regulatory fragmentation are not insignificant: compliance costs with multiple standards that are sometimes contradictory, the absence of a "level playing field" which allows competition to function normally (see Acharya 2003). The result is competition to weaken regulation, in order to favour national champions, as well as geographical fragmentation. This fragmentation is detrimental to global management of excess savings, financing needs and services provided to global companies.

11.4.1   The Rise of Standardized Approaches

The new regulatory project does not challenge the internal models approach (IMA) for quantifying market risks. It nevertheless confirms the increasing strength of standardized approaches in which risk models are stipulated by regulators.

1) The eligibility criteria of trading desks with respect to internal models (backtests and above all explanations of profits and losses by models monitoring risks (P&L attribution tests) have been strengthened considerably. Much uncertainty remains concerning the share of trading activities, which are eligible for inclusion in internal models. Otherwise, desks that do not qualify for inclusion are subject to standard requirements, which potentially use up much more equity capital.
2) The publication of risk measures using the standard approach is compulsory in order to facilitate the comparison of results published by banks.
3) The use of regulatory floors for the outputs of internal models. The calculation of regulatory equity capital requirements cannot be less than the percentage of the result provided by the standard formula. The higher this percentage is, the smaller the scope for applying internal models. In many

cases, the formula applicable will simply be a percentage of RWAs, calculated using the standard approach.

4) The application of a "residual risk add-on" capital charge that is proportional to the notional value of exotic instruments.
5) The risks associated with credit valuation adjustments (CVAs) for which the standard approach is prescribed.
6) Correlation Trading Portfolio (CTP) instruments including CDOs are also excluded from the perimeter of internal models.

These moves towards standardized approaches result from scepticism of numerous regulators and economists concerning the pertinence of self-evaluation models of market risks used by banks.

The standard approach has changed a lot since the first consultative document published by the Basel Committee in May 2012, following feedback and interaction with the financial services industry after its QISs. The standard approach has been designed as a credible alternative to internal models. As an approximate order of magnitude, it involves around 5,000 risk factors.[29] Processing the concavity associated with option positions is included in the Basel Committee document. Nevertheless, essentially the standard approach to market risks is linked to preservation shocks on risk factors and to correlations prescribed by the Basel Committee. At first sight, this involves a parametric VaR (or Expected Shortfall).

The sensitivities to risk factors defined by the Basel Committee continue to be calculated based on each bank's internal pricing models.[30] It is therefore important that the audits of the model, such as the Asset Quality Review in the Eurozone, are followed up and extended to other jurisdictions, in order to ensure good comparability for outputs using the standard model. This assumes that supervisors have adequate resources and that priorities are clearly defined, though it should be noted that stress tests such as the CCAR in the USA are very time-consuming. The preceding remark applies to tools for "mapping" sensitivities to risk factors used in front office "pricers" with sensitivities to risk factors defined by the regulator. The role of supervision (see Agarwal et al. 2014; Eisenbach et al. 2015) will therefore remain crucial and benchmarking exercises may be carried out on hypothetical portfolios to establish zones of

---

[29] The level of granularity of internal models by banks is more detailed (typically including several tens of thousands of risk factors).

[30] More specifically, the risk factors are the finite differences from which it is possible to quantify the scale of directional positions (the "deltas") and negative convexity (negative Gamma or "curvature risk" in Basel terminology).

divergence concerning the calculation of sensitivity and whether it should be remedied.[31]

Given the high fixed costs involved in the compliance of internal models, certain so-called tier two banks could opt for the standard approach.[32]

A bank's choice (which is indeed optional) for calculating market risks using the standard approach eliminates uncertainty associated with trading desks no longer deemed qualified for inclusion in the internal model. The capital charges linked to the standard approach seem to be clearly higher than those associated with internal models, given the present state of projected regulations and their implementation by banks. The failure of a desk to meet eligibility criteria for using the internal model could imply a leap in the overall capital charge.

Risks to a bank's reputation can also be mentioned, if its internal model is invalidated for some of its major trading activities. Lastly, this will affect decisions in allocating the bank's assets, with marginal costs being different according to standard approaches and internal models. Moreover, despite its numerous merits, the standard approach is not entirely adapted to measuring risks associated with certain positions on options. For example, the purchase of out-of-the-money options does not represent a major risk, as the losses are limited to the option premium. In this case, the standard approach could overvalue real risk. If the internal model is well specified, the ratio of charges between the internal model and the standard approach will be abnormally high. This will set off false alarms with supervisors and audits of models or inappropriate use of regulatory floors.

It is important to remember the truly Herculean task that the Basel Committee has had to deal with over the 2012–2016 period. Proposing a standardized approach for measuring market risk to big banks has been a substantial challenge, which has been met to a large extent. However, the generalization of the use of standardized approaches has not gone ahead without raising serious questions:

1) Apart from the overall capital equity requirements (see below), the relative costs of different risks changed a lot from the project distributed to banks for the monitoring exercise at the end of 2015 and the final rules set out in January 2016. Yet these costs determine banks' optimal portfolio allocations.

---

[31] The valuation models used for interest rate options differ from one bank to another, particularly as regards the sensitivity to interest rates. This raises the question of whether to harmonize models, albeit at the expense of innovation. It is also possible that the reconciliation exercises, which should be conducted with the establishment of bilateral initial margins for derivatives that are not centrally cleared, lead spontaneously to such convergence.

[32] It has also been suggested that higher fixed costs owing to compliance could constitute an entry barrier.

This leads to two questions: (a) have these relative costs been determined correctly by the regulator (the calibration methodologies were not made public, and so far there are no available academic studies concerning the pertinence of the standard approach); and (b) do they lead to good incentives? This is all the more important given that the uniformity resulting from a wider scope of application for the standard approaches will show up in banks' allocation of resources. This greater parallelism is not without consequences for financial stability (exposure to common factors and heightened procyclicality).

2) The detail of the risk analysis with the standard approach is less than in internal models. Risk buckets, especially for equity and credit, draw together very heterogeneous risks. For example, credits risk on sovereign debt only fall into two categories: Investment Grade and other risks. As a result, there is a possibility of risk drift within the categories set out by the Basel Committee. Moreover, exiting the Investment Grade category is extremely costly in terms of capital. Therefore, while the standard approach is calibrated in an acyclical way, there is in fact the risk of a sharp rise in equity capital requirements in times of crisis, given threshold effects. This could lead to a contraction of balance sheets and the amplification of exogenous shocks via the credit channel.

3) Two mechanisms have been implemented as far as option contracts are concerned: (a) treatment of negative curvature risks limited to parallel shocks on all risk factors taken together (idiosyncratic gamma); and (b) a residual risk add-on for exotic options. Exotic options here are options for which the underlying assets have particularly low liquidity, and options which do not correspond to combinations of calls and puts (i.e. which are not so-called "plain vanilla" options). For second order risks, crossed risks are not taken into account. Risks associated with hybrid products and spreads options are not therefore correctly taken into account. In defence of the Basel Committee, it must be said that an exhaustive approach would have been largely impractical. Concerning "residual risk add-on," difficult questions are likely to arise over the definition of notional values and the perimeter of products covered. The Basel framework sets general rules, whose transposition into different jurisdictions could de facto lead to quite different treatments.

The main problem with the standard approach is that it is a compromise. It satisfies neither the proponents of leverage ratio, who are deeply resistant to the very notion of risk weighted assets and risk-sensitive capital ratios,[33]

---

[33] See for example the presentation by Anat Admati, https://www.gsb.stanford.edu/sites/default/files/research/documents/Slides.pdf.

nor those actors who believe in the necessity for banks to carry out sufficient investments needed to measure their risks effectively:

1) The standard approach meets the goals of comparability of risk-weighted assets and a better sensitivity to risks. But this comes at the price of a certain complexity, which is contrary to the initial aims of the regulators, including the simplicity of models.
2) Excessive recourse to the standard approach, for example in terms of constraining floors, could have negative implications, such as the renunciation of the development and use of internal risk models.

11.4.2   The Reformulation and Supervision of Internal Models

The transition from the Basel 2.5 framework to Basel III (or 3.5 or even IV—no trademark seems to have been deposited for this!) shows itself in changing risk metrics. Recall that under Basel 2.5, risks calculated using internal models are the sum of VaR and stressed VaR, calculated over a ten-day horizon with a 99 % confidence level (the issue of multipliers applied to quantities, as well as temporal smoothing effects are set aside). The new framework considers Expected Shortfall, calculated during the stressed period at a confidence level of 97.5 %. The horizon is variable according to the liquidity of the risk factors in question. Moreover, for validation purposes, banks are asked to calculate, among other things, VaRs with a one-day horizon and at the 97.5 % and 99 % confidence levels.

11.4.3   Differentiated Liquidity Horizons and the Limits to Benefits from Diversification

There is a large literature about the relative merits of VaR and Expected Shortfall, the favoured tool henceforth for regulators when it comes to measuring market risks. Expected Shortfall makes it possible to take into account the scale of losses beyond VaR.[34] While this debate may stimulate theorists of risk measures and statisticians, it is not sure that it is very important from

---

[34] Expected Shortfall is a subadditive measure in contrast to VaR. This makes it possible to remedy the fact that the benefits of diversification are not taken into account. This new risk indicator, however, is not unanimously supported. It is criticized for being overly dependent on a few extreme events (a lack of statistical robustness), the theoretical problems of carrying out backtesting. Eventually, the measured risks are proportional to positions, without taking into account the negative impact of concentrated positions.

the point of view of financial stability. That said, the Basel Committee has introduced a new concept of "partial" Expected Shortfall, which is calculated on subsets of risk factors (and not on portfolios). Furthermore, the Basel Committee has implemented limits on the "benefits of diversification," though situations can be found in which the mechanism put forward operates in a way opposite to the laudable aims of its designers, for example with hybrid products. Similarly, the introduction of differentiated liquidation horizons by risk factor and not by financial product is based on pertinent economic and financial intuitions. But its mathematical formulation is not beyond criticism. The rules have in fact been amended to limit perverse effects. The calculation of the regulatory metric stems from rationale in which profitability has a Gaussian distribution and is independent. For the informed reader, this will limit the impact of the preceding debate on the choice of risk metric. Overall, Expected Shortfall is really the name given by regulators to a new concept, but it should not be confused with the term that has the same, academic meaning. Again, no trademark has been declared in financial mathematics!

11.4.4   Default Risks in the Trading Book

Turning to default risks in the trading book, the possibility of using internal models to calculate RWAs have been confirmed by the Basel Committee: securitizations are excluded, for which the standard approach is prescribed. The treatment of default risks for securitizations in the trading book is explicitly linked to the banking book (according to the new reference text on the subject: "Revisions to the securitisation framework," http://www.bis.org/bcbs/publ/d303.pdf, released in December 2014 by the BC). This excludes correlation portfolio trading which was already covered specifically by Basel 2.5, via the CRM. Hopefully, the new regulations will facilitate the marketization of credit risks, though avoiding the excesses which occurred during the previous crisis.[35] As for other risks, the quality of supervision is of primary importance, even given an appropriate regulatory framework.

Regarding the risk of default outside securitizations, the changes are not to be underestimated either, though the principles of Basel 2.5 have been preserved. The IRC has been replaced by a Default Risk Charge (DRC). The new charge does not explicitly take into account the risk of migration (which was not a major factor in the IRC, but which is now included in the charges

---

[35] On the issue of securitization, see Daphné Héant et al., Chap. 16, this volume.

on changes in credit margins, via lengthened liquidity horizons). A number of changes should be noted:

1) The introduction floors on default probabilities (at three basis points), which will not be without problems in the EU, where there is not yet a capital charge for sovereign risk.
2) The use of default probabilities and recovery rates based on internal models, which is again associated with the challenges in terms of data quality and consistency with the data used for the banking book.
3) The inclusion of equity risk in the perimeter: in case of default, the share price is expected to fall to zero, with a horizon of three months, compared to one year for other classes of products, shares or credit derivatives.

For a more technical presentation of the new DRC and the theoretical and implementation issues, the reader may refer to Wilkens and Predrescu (2015) or Laurent Sestier and Thomas (2015).

In addition to market and credit risks, a new class of risk has appeared on the regulators' monitor. CVA is related to value adjustments for the counterparty risk of derivative products that are not cleared centrally. The rise in counterparty risks during the financial crisis was the source of significant losses in the trading portfolios of some banks, mainly through the increase in CVA. A capital charge for the risks in variations of CVA was introduced in the Basel framework in 2011 (http://www.bis.org/publ/bcbs189.pdf). This was also reflected in European law (see for example Section 381 of the CRR for a definition of the CVA), or in the rules adopted by US regulators in July 2013. In spring 2016, the Basel Committee decided that from 2019 onwards the capital charges for the variability of the CVA would be calculated using the standardized approach. The text of January 2016 gives guidelines for the methodology based on other categories of risk.

Capital charges for counterparty risks are not covered here. These charges will largely diminish owing to the establishment of bilateral initial margins and the rise of the central clearing for derivative trades.[36]

It should be noted that banks' preparation for the new rules applicable from 2019 has mobilized significant resources for several years, even though the previous work programme—for Basel 2.5—is still being finalized: the expensive developments being undertaken to ensure compliance with capital charges for CVA variability will expire while barely finalized.

---

[36] This is not, however, the case for sovereign risks, given the exemption margins from which they benefit.

11.5 Future Trends

The implementation of the new recommendations by the Basel Committee and their transposition into national law are planned for 2019. For Europe, this should result in an amendment of the Capital Requirements Regulation (CRR). This ensures direct and uniform implementation across the EU. In addition, the European Banking Authority (EBA) has been delegated to edit technical standards. It is possible that Community law will deviate on some important points from the Basel Committee's recommendations, such as the treatment of sovereign risks.

Improving the qualitative content of RWAs in the trading book is the cornerstone of the new prudential framework, and the best response to the sensitivity deficit concerning risks of leverage ratios.[37] The QISs and "monitoring exercises" are designed to quantify the impact of the new rules for calculating RWAs in the portfolios of participating banks. These impact studies and "monitoring exercises" also allow banks to prepare for the operational implementation of the new regulations. They are an opportunity for exchanging views between the Basel Committee and the national regulatory authorities (NRAs) on the one hand, and the financial industry and banks on the other hand. The Basel Committee has decided, as part of the redesigning of RWA calculations for trading books, to get involved in concrete, pragmatic and precise engineering of banks' risk management: in short, the Basel Committee is getting its hands dirty. However, the complexity of measuring risk in trading books and the many exchanges between regulators and the financial industry will undoubtedly fuel prejudices.

The credibility of the new methods of calculating RWAs will also depend on the quality of supervision. Recall that even under the standard approach, model inputs include sensitivities to risk factors, calculated using banks' internal pricing models. The supervision of market risks therefore implies audits of such pricing models. These audits should not be limited to an analysis of compliance, but should also focus on the relevance of the models used. This requires that supervisors have top level capacities in quantitative risk engineering, the qualitative understanding of the business models of banks' trading activities and finally that they interact effectively with regulated entities, by maintaining a high level of expertise and intellectual independence. In addition to these high demands, the main risk lies in the excessive standardization

---

[37] See for example Kim and Santomero (1988) for an illustration of the distortions in the allocations of assets and the destabilizing incentives induced by the leverage ratio effect. See also Lautenschläger (2013) for a critical presentation of this ratio.

of internal models (which will become de facto standards); the destabilizing effects (any model error is multiplied and behaviours also tend to standardize); and limited incentives for vigilance. There are also dangers in risk measurement methods being frozen and little adapted to emerging risks, such as counterparty risks to clearing houses. Compliance with norms could become the one and only guarantee against prosecution for bank losses. Some commentators have jokingly welcomed the return of "boring banking." It is to be hoped that the overseers of bank risk do not take them at their word...

At present, some quantitative information is available about the impact of the new rules on equity capital requirements. The impact study published in November 2015 deserves attention. It relates to trading positions at 31 December 2014.[38] Another study was published in January 2016,[39] while benchmarking exercises were conducted by ISDA in October 2015 and April 2016.[40] The results are derived from using rules published in January 2016, applied to trading positions at 31 December 2015. They allow the issues at stake to be better identified, and further studies will be conducted on positions at 30 June and 31 December 2016.

The mandate of the Trading Book Group of the Basel Committee was not to increase the overall amount of RWAs, but to improve their quality and information content, as well as the comparability of RWAs. However, there is no evidence that recalibration of the rules in January 2016, or of the introduction of regulatory floors will not lead to an increase in RWAs for trading portfolios. Furthermore, to know what rules will ultimately be applicable, it will be necessary to await the final arbitrations made by the regulators within the Basel Committee, in conjunction with other bodies (the Group of Governors and Heads of Supervision (GHOS) and the FSB) sometime in 2017. Moreover, these will be followed by various transpositions of the Basel framework into national jurisdictions.

The QISs are based on existing portfolios, constituted according to previous regulatory requirements. The new rules for calculating RWAs will induce changes in the compositions of trading portfolios, and hence in the amount and composition of RWAs. Banks will monitor more inventory costs of

---

[38] *Fundamental Review of the Trading Book – interim impact analysis* http://www.bis.org/bcbs/publ/d346.pdf.

[39] http://www.bis.org/bcbs/publ/d352_note.pdf on the database, June 2015.

[40] *Industry FRTB QIS Analysis*, 22 October 2015, https://www2.isda.org/functional-areas/risk-management/

ISDA/GFMA/IIF published the industry FRTB QIS analysis, 18 April 2016, https://www2.isda.org/attachment/ODM0OA==/QIS4%202015%20%20FRTB%20Refresh%20Report_Spotlight__FINAL.pdf.

market-making activities (Cheshire, 2015), for example for bond trading. The reduction in volumes of activity and numbers of participants in the market for corporate Credit Default Swaps (CDSs) is a concrete sign of the changes underway. It is unclear whether institutional investors will return as counterparties in sufficient scale to offset the reduction in market bank intermediation.[41] Erratic movements in bond prices and credit spreads are to be feared during times of turbulence (stress) in the markets.[42]

11.6 Rethinking Banks' Capital Markets Activities

It is hard to comment on the implications of the new rules for calculating RWAs, but one can examine the evolution of bank profitability in capital market activities. This issue must be looked at comprehensively. Indeed, the new solvency ratio has seen the rules for calculating its denominator—RWAs—change. Yet, it is mostly expected for this ratio to increase, and therefore for capital requirements to rise. At the same time, the perimeter of regulatory equity capital required to cover bank losses (Common Equity Tier 1 and the numerator of the ratio) has been greatly restricted, in order to enhance its quality and "loss absorbing" character. These new equity capital requirements induced by Basel III have in fact been applied by banks in anticipation of regulation. As a result, banks should amend the products they offer, their pricing and their strategic positioning for market activities.

---

[41] A study entitled *Has corporate bond market liquidity fallen?*

https://bankunderground.co.uk/2015/08/27/has-corporate-bond-market-liquidity-fallen/ published on the blog of the Bank of England by Yuliya Baranova, Lousia Chen & Nicholas Vause concludes that, "These findings support the claim that the market-making capacity of dealers has fallen in recent years, reducing secondary market liquidity." It may be hoped that funds develop contrarian strategies and/or develop market-making activities to provide the market with liquidity. De Long et al. (1990) instead emphasize the dangers of procyclical and destabilizing investment strategies. To get an idea of inventory costs under the new framework, in a letter sent in October 2015 to Mario Draghi (in his capacity as Chairman, GHOS), and to Stefan Ingves (as Chairman, BCBS), the financial services industry indicates that about €1 of capital is needed (using the standard approach) for every €1 invested in 30-year German government bonds (the letter is available on the ISDA site). The total lack of any leverage effectively means that banks in practice have become investment funds. This situation far exceeds the 20 % to 30 % equity capital ratios put forward by Anat Admati https://www.gsb.stanford.edu/sites/default/files/research/documents/Slides.pdf. Alex Brazier, Executive Director for Financial Stability Strategy at the Bank of England indicated in March 2016 that "after a point, another unit of capital buys a much smaller fall in the probability of bank failure. There may be seriously diminishing returns. And at the same time, it's possible that ever more bank capital may not best serve the real economy" (speech entitled "A macroprudential approach to bank capital: Serving the real economy in good times and bad." http://www.bankofengland.co.uk/publications/Documents/speeches/2016/speech887.pdf.

[42] On this subject, see the study published by PWC in August 2015, *Global financial markets liquidity study*, https://www.pwc.se/sv/financial-services/assets/global-financial-markets-liquidity-study.pdf.

The new regulations will primarily penalize the least profitable banks and those whose market share is insufficient to absorb the fixed costs associated with the new constraints. Banks' structures will also be shaped by their internal rules for determining the cost of capital, as well as the new expectations of financial analysts in these areas.

The implementation and compliance costs of internal models will increase. This may be limited by some cost sharing, be it for databases for model calibration, or methods and structures allowing banks to harmonize their tools for risk calculation. Nevertheless, the effectiveness of such instruments and measures can doubted, as:

1) the largest banks have no interest in such mutualization;
2) governance tools such pooling structures are difficult to implement; and
3) the most complex risks are very specific to each bank.

These implementation costs relate on the one hand to data, and on the other hand to the alignment between pricing models and representations of front office risk, as well as to the costs of teams modelling risks internally.

Regarding the quality of data, the risk factors included in the internal models may be considered as Modellable Risk Factors (MRFs). Otherwise, the corresponding risks are subjected to detrimental processing under stress scenarios. The latest QIS or "monitoring exercises" have shown up considerable capital charges associated with Non-Modellable Risk Factors (NMRF). The idea of the regulator is that risks eligible for inclusion in internal models should be associated with "real" markets for which transaction prices or "committed quotes" are available. Since the price manipulation scandals in the money and foreign exchange markets, there have indeed been legitimate suspicions about data formed by market consensus, based on the opinions of banks. This is a major operational project. It is important to rethink the organization, collection and governance of data, and the notion of risk factors (the so-called "representations of risks"), even at the level of front office tools.

A second major constraint lies hidden in the jargon of "P&L attribution tests." It involves ensuring the consistency between the models actually used by the front office and internal models of risk calculations. This concerns both the alignment of the definition of the perimeter of risk factors and the methods for revaluing portfolios following shocks to these risk factors. The third element of the new regulatory arsenal lies in tracking models used at trading desks (in the order of several dozen per bank). At first glance, the thresholds of acceptable anomalies (the number of days when the losses exceed VaR) are not very constraining. Yet in practice they will highlight the operational weaknesses of risk models. Overall, the Basel Committee is asking banks wishing to continue using internal models to do work that is far from being trivial.

Banks must rethink their overall architecture for managing their internal data and their internal models. There is a move towards a greater integration of data and pricing tools. This involves heavy operational projects and structural choices for banks that want their trading desks to remain eligible for internal models.

Banks are thus faced with significant operational issues. More conceptual questions are nestled within these practical considerations, and include: the choice of calculation methods (historical or Monte Carlo), methods for revaluing portfolios, pricing models, representations of risks, costs of capital and portfolio allocation.

The new regulation of market risk is leading to strategic choices, with banks facing choices of whether to abandon some activities that have become insufficiently profitable and/or move to "bank 2.0" operations. This would not involve banks outsourcing their vital functions. They must reconcile agility, quality and cost control by transforming and thinking intelligently about existing internal tools. Otherwise, banks will be engulfed by the current regulatory wave and will no longer be able to control their business processes. Only some market players will have the force to imagine themselves operating in this new world, even as intermediation in OTC derivative markets is likely to decrease.

As regards financial stability, the better integration of front office tools and risks needs to be managed appropriately, if this trend persists. It is indeed necessary to maintain the principles of (1) risk management which is independent from the front office (though independence does not mean isolation); and (2) of governance, based on practices such as the independent audit of models.

Finally, to assess the impact of the new regulations of market activities, it is also necessary to be able to quantify changes in expected profitability (ROE, or return on tangible equity) and to risk premiums (and therefore betas). Many banks have already announced a reduction in their ROE target, which makes sense when leverage has decreased. However, more precise responses are difficult to establish. In terms of financial theory, increasing capital ratios lowers the costs of financial distress and the value of implied guarantees made by governments to depositors. This is difficult to quantify and differs between regimes of business recovery and liquidation, the credibility of governments and central banks in terms of bail-out exclusions and the intrinsic profitability of banks.

11.7 Conclusion

FRTB began in May 2012 and led to the "Minimum capital requirements for market risk" document, which was published by the Basel Committee in January 2016. The new rules will have considerable but unquantifiable consequences for the capital requirements for trading activities. The calculation of the denominator of the solvency ratio (RWAs) for the trading book will be changed greatly. As of 2019, the new rules will replace the 1996 amendment to market risks, as well as the "add-ons" introduced after the financial crisis, which are commonly known as Basel 2.5.

The draft regulation on the calculation of risk weighted assets for market risks comes on top of a set of measures which have themselves not been finalized. These include: the composition of equity capital in the numerator of the ratio (especially prudential value adjustments in the balance sheets, the so-called Additional Valuation Adjustments, or AVAs); the leverage ratio for derivatives and securities financing activities; regulatory floors; constraints on the modelling choices concerning the banking book; the calculations of capital surcharges for systemic institutions, and so on.

The intellectual and practical consistency of this comprehensive package of measures is far from assured. Nearly a decade after the great financial crisis, the coming years will be marked by regulatory uncertainty and major operational difficulties, as the effective implementation of the new rules is complex. The banks themselves have underestimated implementation costs: instead of focusing on the development of new services to the economy as well improving existing counterparty services and providing liquidity, a large share of banks' intellectual and financial resources will be devoted to the implementation and management of new prudential regulations. The issues related to international harmonization and the transposition of Basel rules into national law, along with the real ability of supervising risks are also underestimated.

Global governance of the transformation process of the prudential framework is clearly a problem. This is the result of fundamental differences of analysis among the architects of the new international financial system (the FSB, the GHOS, the Basel Committee and its various working groups, regulatory and supervisory agencies, major central banks, as well as the European Commission). As the French theologian and moralist Jacques-Joseph Duguet observed long ago with reference to governance and public goods, "the worst of all parties is to take none."[43] Outstanding questions thus remain:

---

[43] Jacques-Joseph Duguet (1649–1733), *Institution d'un prince, ou traité des qualitez, des vertus et des devoirs d'un souverain,* published posthumously in 1739.

1) What role should be given to the leverage ratio relative to "risk-based" solvency ratios? For some, mainly European regulators, the leverage ratio should not be the binding constraint, but a "backstop." For US systemic banks, the SLR, which is quite close to the Basel ratio in the principles of its calculation, is set at 5 %, compared to 3 % for the Basel rules. Yet this 5 % level seems to have become the standard for financial analysts.

2) To what extent can the internal models developed by banks to measure their risks and the ability of supervisors to "monitor" these models be trusted? Is it even desirable or reasonable to delegate to banks the responsibility for assessing their own market risks? Opinions differ radically on these issues.

3) Should the level and the proportion of equity capital set aside to deal with market risks be increased or not? Without going into a long analysis of statements by regulators, objectives fluctuate between targeting a stable level of equity capital, its resizing based on the total RWA (10 % set aside to cover market risks), or the absence of any objective, with capital targets based just on the application of established rules.

4) What is the accepted social function assigned to "customised" risk management products (OTC derivatives)? The direction given to the regulation and calibration rules varies fundamentally according to a priori views.

5) What should be the main tool for supervising large banks? Solvency ratios, which are the main subject of this article, or stress tests (CCAR), as is now the case in the USA.

As of mid-2016, it is not possible to quantify realistically the impact of these new measures, despite numerous consultative documents issued since 2012, impact studies and "monitoring exercises," as well as the interactions between regulators and the financial services industry. This is true for overall capital requirements for market risks, and more so when breaking down assessments by categories of risk (interest rates, foreign exchange rates, shares, credit, raw materials/commodities). The operational nature of impact studies already conducted is illusory, and it is impossible for financial institutions to perform any strategic management of their market activities:

1) these impact studies are conducted on the basis of existing portfolios, even though the new rules will result in significant reallocations of exposure, or indeed significant cutbacks in market activities;

2) the quality of banks' contributions to impact studies is highly variable; and

3) most of all, the rules are not determined. In particular, the calibration of regulatory floors constraining the use of internal models, or the interpretation of the Basel texts concerning the criteria for implementing and validating internal models could change the very philosophy of the new rules.

The economic models of Corporate and Institutional/Investment Banking (CIB) need rethinking and depend crucially on the regulatory framework which is developing, sometimes in an opaque and unpredictable way. The new prudential rules will determine the comparative costs and benefits of bank intermediation in financial markets, compared to non-regulated actors (pension funds and hedge funds). The markets for OTC derivatives will be affected depending on the amount of equity capital required, the transformations related to the automation of transactions, and the specific rules relating to the organization of these markets (bilateral initial margins and geographical fragmentation). There is great uncertainty about changes in overall business volumes, the perpetuation of market intermediation in several asset categories, the level of sophistication of the products sold by banks, the degree of concentration of financial industry, the value of banking franchises and the creation of shareholder value. It is probably only with time and experience that it will be possible to determine the extent of the reconfiguration of banking intermediation in financial markets.

The new prudential regulations have a worthy goal: making banks safer. However, the effectiveness of the new system is not guaranteed from the point of view of financial stability (see Veron 2014 for similar remarks), due to complexity, geographic fragmentation and the lack oft risk sensitivity in the standardized approaches.

With respect to services rendered to the economy, increased use of standardized derivatives could push "basis risks" and liquidity risks onto final players: for example, the use of "plain vanilla" swaps or futures contracts instead of asset swaps in managing the risks of rates on corporate bond liabilities.

It may be asked whether the new equity capital requirements will reduce the ability of the banking system to ensure market-making functions. This cannot be ruled out. The rise of players which are less regulated than banks testifies to this: insurance funds and companies have developed their consultancy activities in the field of capital markets and now offer price quotes for the purchase and sale of derivatives.[44]

Is this outsourcing desirable? Yes, if one is willing to consider that only sight deposits and not long-term savings should be protected, that insurance companies or big fund managers do not pose any systemic risk,[45] and that problems of moral hazard cease at the frontiers of the banking world. Furthermore, it is important that systemic risks associated with new nodes

---

[44] For example, BlackRock Solutions https://www.blackrock.com/aladdin/blackrock-solutions or the Multi Asset Client Solutions services provide by Axa IM Corporate.

[45] As mentioned by Hansen (2012), systemic risk is uneasy to define. We refer to the review paper of Benoit et al. (2016) for comments about the systemic point of view on banking regulations.

(clearing houses) are well quantified and monitored. The new regulatory environment for banks is leading to this kind of outsourcing. Regulators have developed sophisticated banking supervision tools. The regulated banks have embarked on expensive developments in terms of compliance and monitoring market risks. Yet the risks will have moved to less supervised areas.[46]

So has something been gained in terms of asset price stability? It is possible, for example, to have doubts about the evolution of the depth of bond markets. The fleeting nature of liquidity was well illustrated by the sharp rise in long-term rates observed in the European markets for public debt markets in 2015, or the "taper tantrum" in the USA in 2013 (Neely 2014; Fisher 2015). These are warning signals.[47] So, too, have been the repeated warnings about the development of bond bubbles (de Larosière 2016).

The prudential regulation of market risks must meet diverse goals that are hardly compatible.[48] This regulation involves firstly ensuring financial stability and bank solvency, which in turn implies an adequate level of equity capital. Yet such capital serves only as short-term guarantees. Longer term, it is the profitability of banking activities that guarantees the viability of the banking system. Changes in Price to Book ratios, which give an idea of the value creation associated with new business, are probably worth considering. Krugman (2010) illustrated the importance of banking franchises for financial stability with a maxim: "do not kill the cash cow that kept laying golden eggs."[49] It is desirable that increased equity capital requirements and higher compliance costs do not penalize excessively the profitability of market activities (a reduction of market intermediation could reduce the ability of banks to absorb risks), nor the financing of the economy. The degree of substitutability

---

[46] See the FSB reports, *Shadow Banking: Strengthening Oversight and Regulation* (2011), http://www.fsb.org/wp-content/uploads/r_111027a.pdf and *Strengthening Oversight and Regulation of Shadow Banking* (2013), http://www.fsb.org/wp-content/uploads/r_130829a.pdf.

[47] As mentioned in the study reported on the blog of the Bank of England (cited above), this reduction in market depth, which is specific to OTC markets, is hardly measured by the usual liquidity metrics. In a document published by Blackrock, *The liquidity challenge,* in June 2014, (http://www.blackrock.com/corporate/en-mx/literature/whitepaper/bii-the-liquidity-challenge-us-version.pdf), Peter Fisher (Senior Director of the BlackRock Investment Institute) states that, "The whole system relies on liquidity illusion". The International Monetary Fund in its *Global Financial Stability Report* of April 2015 (http://www.imf.org/external/pubs/ft/gfsr/2015/01/pdf/text.pdf) provides the same analysis. The reader may refer to Elliott 2014 or Fender and Lewrick 2015, or more generally to the lively debate on the evolution of liquidity in the bond markets.

[48] See for example the summary presentation by Krugman (2010), http://krugman.blogs.nytimes.com/2010/04/18/six-doctrines-in-search-of-a-policy-regime/.

[49] See the revealing article by Calomiris and Nissim (2014), the analyses by Keeley (1990), Allen and Gale (2000), Hellmann, Murdock and Stiglitz (2000), Repullo (2004) about bank franchises and that by Gorton (2012) on "quiet banking." Unfortunately, the regulators only look at tangible equity, and not the market value of shares, for the reason that intangible assets cannot be ceded easily in case of liquidation. However, such arguments cannot be applied to incentives or moral hazard.

between banks and other unregulated market participants also needs to be controlled. In short, we are conducting a full-scale experiment, and time will tell which of the very different views on this subject are closest to the truth.

Bibliography

Acerbi, C., & Tasche, D. (2002). Expected shortfall: A natural coherent alternative to value at risk. *Economic Notes, 31*(2), 379–388.

Acharya, V. V. (2003). Is the international convergence of capital adequacy regulation desirable? *The Journal of Finance, 58*(6), 2745–2782.

Adrian, T., & Shin, H. S. (2013). Procyclical leverage and value-at-risk. *Review of Financial Studies*, hht068.

Agarwal, S., Lucca, D., Seru, A., & Trebbi, F. (2014). Inconsistent regulators: Evidence from banking. *Quarterly Journal of Economics, 129*(2), 889–938.

Aikman, D., Galesic, M., Gigerenzer, G., Kapadia, S., Katsikopoulos, K. V., Kothiyal, A., & Neumann, T. (2014). *Taking uncertainty seriously: Simplicity versus complexity in financial regulation* (Bank of England Financial Stability Paper 28). London: Bank of England.

Alexander, C., & Sarabia, J. M. (2012). Quantile uncertainty and value-at-risk model risk. *Risk Analysis, 32*(8), 1293–1308.

Allen, F., & Gale, D. (2000). *Comparing financial systems*. Cambridge, MA: MIT press.

Barakova, I., & Palvia, A. (2014). Do banks' internal Basel risk estimates reflect risk? *Journal of Financial Stability, 13*, 167–179.

Begley, T. A., Purnanandam, A. K., & Zheng, K. K. (2016). *The strategic underreporting of bank risk* (Ross School of Business Paper 1260). Ann Arbor: Ross School of Business.

Behn, M., Haselmann, R. F., & Vig, V. (2014). The limits of model-based regulation.

Benoit, S., Colliard, J. E., Hurlin, C., & Pérignon, C. (2016). Where the risks lie: A survey on systemic risk. *Review of Finance*, rfw026.

Blum, J. M. (2008). Why 'Basel II'may need a leverage ratio restriction. *Journal of Banking & Finance, 32*(8), 1699–1707.

Blundell-Wignall, A., & Atkinson, P. (2010). Thinking beyond Basel III. *OECD Journal: Financial Market Trends, 2010*(1), 9–33.

Calomiris, C. W., & Nissim, D. (2014). Crisis-related shifts in the market valuation of banking activities. *Journal of Financial Intermediation, 23*(3), 400–435.

Cheshire, J. (2015, March). Market making in bond markets. *RBA Bulletin*, 63–73.

Colliard, J. E. (2015). Strategic selection of risk models and bank capital regulation. Available at SSRN 2170459.

Culp, C. L., & Miller, M. H. (1995). Metallgesellschaft and the economics of synthetic storage. *Journal of Applied Corporate Finance, 7*(4), 62–76.

Danielsson, J., Embrechts, P., Goodhart, C., Keating, C., Muennich, F., Renault, O., & Shin, H. S. (2001). An academic response to Basel II.

Danielsson, J., Shin, H. S., & Zigrand, J. P. (2004). The impact of risk regulation on price dynamics. *Journal of Banking & Finance, 28*(5), 1069–1087.

DeAngelo, H., & Stulz, R. M. (2013). *Why high leverage is optimal for banks* (No. w19139). National Bureau of Economic Research.

de Larosière, J. (2016). *Cinquante ans de crises financières.* Paris: Odile Jacob.

De Long, J. B., Shleifer, A., Summers, L. H., & Waldmann, R. J. (1990). Positive feedback investment strategies and destabilizing rational speculation. *The Journal of Finance, 45*(2), 379–395.

Dowd, K., Cotter, J., Humphrey, C., & Woods, M. (2011). How unlucky is 25-sigma? arXiv preprint arXiv:1103.5672.

Duffie, D. (2013). Futurization of swaps.

Duguet, J. J. (1743). Institution d'un prince, ou Traité des qualitez, des vertus et des devoirs d'un souverain [par M. l'abbé Duguet]. chez J. Nourse.

Ediz, T., Michael, I., & Perraudin, W. (1998). The impact of capital requirements on UK bank behaviour. *Economic Policy Review, 4*(3), 15–22.

Edwards, F. R. (1999). Hedge funds and the collapse of long-term capital management. *Journal of Economic Perspectives, 13,* 189–210.

Eisenbach, T. M., Haughwout, A., Hirtle, B., Kovner, A., Lucca, D. O., & Plosser, M. C. (2015). Supervising large, complex financial institutions: What do supervisors do? *FRB of New York Staff Report,* (729).

Elliott, D. J. (2014). *Bank liquidity requirements: An introduction and overview.* The Brookings Institution.

Estrella, A., Park, S., & Peristiani, S. (2000). Capital ratios as predictors of bank failure. *Economic Policy Review, 6*(2).

Fender, I., & Lewrick, U. (2015, March). Shifting tides-market liquidity and market-making in fixed income instruments. *BIS Quarterly Review.*

Fischer, S. (2015). The federal reserve and the global economy. *IMF Economic Review, 63*(1), 8–21.

Gordy, M. B., & Howells, B. (2006). Procyclicality in Basel II: Can we treat the disease without killing the patient? *Journal of Financial Intermediation, 15*(3), 395–417.

Gorton, G. (2012). *Misunderstanding financial crises: Why we don't see them coming.* New York: Oxford University Press.

Groeneveld, H., Hancock, D., Jones, D., Perraudin, W., Radecki, L., & Yoneyama, M. (1999). *Capital requirements and bank behaviour: The impact of the Basle Accord* (No. 1). Bank for International Settlements.

Haldane, A. G., & Madouros, V. (2012). The dog and the frisbee. *Revista de Economía Institucional, 14*(27), 13–56.

Hansen, L. P. (2012). *Challenges in identifying and measuring systemic risk* (No. w18505). National Bureau of Economic Research.

Hellmann, T. F., Murdock, K. C., & Stiglitz, J. E. (2000). Liberalization, moral hazard in banking, and prudential regulation: Are capital requirements enough? *American Economic Review, 90,* 147–165.

Jackson, P., & Perraudin, W. (2000). Regulatory implications of credit risk modelling. *Journal of Banking & Finance, 24*(1), 1–14.

Jones, D. (2000). Emerging problems with the Basel capital accord: Regulatory capital arbitrage and related issues. *Journal of Banking & Finance, 24*(1), 35–58.

Jorion, P. (2002). How informative are value-at-risk disclosures? *The Accounting Review, 77*(4), 911–931.

Keeley, M. C. (1990). Deposit insurance, risk, and market power in banking. *The American Economic Review,* 1183–1200.

Kim, D., & Santomero, A. M. (1988). Risk in banking and capital regulation. *The Journal of Finance, 43*(5), 1219–1233.

Krugman, P. (2010, April). Six doctrines in search of a policy regime. In *Speech at the 19th annual Hyman Minsky conference, April 2010.*

Kupiec, P. H. (1995). Techniques for verifying the accuracy of risk measurement models. *The Journal of Derivatives, 3*(2), 73–84.

Laurent, J. P., Sestier, M., & Thomas-Simonpoli, S. (2015). *Trading book and credit risk: How fundamental is the Basel review?* Available at SSRN 2678834.

Lautenschläger, S. (2013, October). The leverage ratio-a simple and comparable measure. In *Speech at the evening reception of the Deutsche Bundesbank/SAFE conference "Supervising banks in complex financial systems", Frankfurt am Main, October 21, 2013.*

Le Leslé, V., & Avramova, S. Y. (2012). Revisiting risk-weighted assets.

Litan, R. E. (2010). *The derivatives dealers' club and derivatives markets reform: A guide for policy makers, citizens and other interested parties.* Washington, D.C.: Initiative on Business and Public Policy at Brookings.

Liu, C. C., Ryan, S. G., & Tan, H. (2004). How banks' value-at-risk disclosures predict their total and priced risk: Effects of bank technical sophistication and learning over time. *Review of Accounting Studies, 9*(2–3), 265–294.

Lowenstein, R. (2000). *When genius failed: The rise and fall of Long-Term Capital Management.* New York: Random House Trade Paperbacks.

Mariathasan, M., & Merrouche, O. (2014). The manipulation of basel risk-weights. *Journal of Financial Intermediation, 23*(3), 300–321.

Miles, D., Yang, J., & Marcheggiano, G. (2013). Optimal bank capital. *The Economic Journal, 123*(567), 1–37.

Neely, C. J. (2014). Lessons from the taper tantrum. *Economic Synopses,* (2).

Pérignon, C., & Smith, D. R. (2010a). The level and quality of value-at-risk disclosure by commercial banks. *Journal of Banking & Finance, 34*(2), 362–377.

Pérignon, C., & Smith, D. R. (2010b). Diversification and value-at-risk. *Journal of Banking & Finance, 34*(1), 55–66.

Pérignon, C., Deng, Z. Y., & Wang, Z. J. (2008). Do banks overstate their Value-at-Risk? *Journal of Banking & Finance, 32*(5), 783–794.

Repullo, R. (2004). Capital requirements, market power, and risk-taking in banking. *Journal of Financial Intermediation, 13*(2), 156–182.

Rochet, J. C. (2008). Procyclicality of financial systems: Is there a need to modify current accounting and regulatory rules? *Financial Stability Review, 12*, 95–99.

Rosenberg, G. D., & Massari, J. R. (2013). Regulation through substitution as policy tool: Swap futurization under Dodd-Frank. *Columbia Business Law Review, 667*.

Tasche, D. (2002). Expected shortfall and beyond. *Journal of Banking & Finance, 26*(7), 1519–1533.

Véron, N. (2014). The G20 financial reform agenda. *Bruegel Policy Contribution Issue 2014/11*, September 2014.

Wilkens, S., & Predescu, M. (2015). *Incremental Default Risk (IDR): Modeling framework for the 'Basel 4' risk measure.* Available at SSRN 2638415.

Yamai, Y., & Yoshiba, T. (2002). On the validity of value-at-risk: Comparative analyses with expected shortfall. *Monetary and Economic Studies, 20*(1), 57–85.

12

Reforming Rating Agencies

Philippe Raimbourg and Federica Salvadè

12.1 Rating Activity's Characteristics

12.1.1 Rating Agencies Give Information to Investors About the Credit Risk of Issuers

This is the rationale of the agencies: they inform investors who would not be able to assess the credit risk of issuers without their help.

Is that true?

Partially. First, we may reasonably think it is true on the primary market, that is at the issuance of new bonds. In that case, investors do not have a precise knowledge of the issuer and the help of such agencies may be required. It is commonplace to assert that rating agencies help new issuers decrease the cost of the money they borrow.

It is also true for products that seem difficult to value by some specific investors. Imagine a German city wanting to issue bonds to be sold to some Japan institutional investors. It appears to be very difficult for these investors to assess the credit risk of the German city. They need the help of an advisor in credit risk such as a credit rating agency. It is the same for sophisticated financial products that cannot be easily analysed by investors. For instance, it

P. Raimbourg (✉) • F. Salvadè (✉)
LabEx RéFi and PRISM, Université Paris 1 Panthéon-Sorbonne, Paris, France

R. Douady et al. (eds.), *Financial Regulation in the EU*,
DOI 10.1007/978-3-319-44287-7_12

would be very complicated to invest in a CDO (collateralized debt obligation) without any rating from a credit rating agency.

Regarding other issues, we are led to distinguish informed investors from uninformed ones. The former, for the most part, do not need the agencies to assess the credit risk of an issuer. The latter, which we may call "trustful investors," do not have superior information; they need the help of rating agencies and follow their ratings.

12.1.2   Issuer Paying System

The rating agencies activity consists in selling information about the credit risk of bonds and other quoted debt contracts. Since the 1970s, the investors benefiting from the credit risk information are not the ones who pay for it: the issuers (the ones who are rated) buy the ratings from the agencies. It is an important characteristic of the agencies that immediately raises the question of collusion between the rater and the issuer paying for being rated.

The answer of the agencies is: reputation. They argue that they spend a lot of money and efforts when they start the company to achieve a good reputation with investors; and this reputation is indeed the main asset they own. It would be a really bad strategy to dilapidate this asset by colluding with the issuer.

Roughly, this may be true. But there are always some situations in which it does not work. For simple products such as domestic bonds, investors can make up their own idea about the credit risk of an issuer. For more complex issues (foreign issues, issues relevant to an unknown bankruptcy law or sophisticated financial products such as a CDO), basic investors may have some difficulties assessing the level of risk of the issue and they may need some kind of an expert to rate the default probability of such products. These investors will easily trust rating agencies. And these "trustful" investors will give the agencies the opportunity to do, let us say, a quick job. As we have seen during the subprime crisis, sophisticated products may not be rare and a wrong appreciation of their risk may give birth to a financial crisis. A new regulation for CDO rating has been enacted, but there are still many other products about which some investors are not well informed and have to be trustful.

Is it possible to come back to an investor paying system, such as the one used before the 1970s?

It may be a good solution, but we think it might not work with the present organization of the rating sector. The problem comes from the ability of investors to duplicate the analyses and ratings of the agencies. In the 1950s and at the beginning of the 1960s paper copies were not so easy to get. Nowadays, the creation of an electronic copy requires only a simple click. How can the free scattering of the work of the rating agencies be avoided?

As a niche sector, one can imagine a rating service dedicated only to investors paying an annual fee, with rating and analyses being consulted on a website without any possibility of copying the files. In such a case, the rating company would work as if it were a subsidiary of the investors. Such an organization presumes a long-term and trustful relationship between the rating agency and the investors. It would be very difficult to organize for a global and international rating agency without a reliable investor base. Many investors would choose not to pay the annual fee.

Another difficulty implementing an investor paying system comes from the very cause of the success of rating agencies; that is the very simple and synthesized way they express their analyses. A letter scale is an easy way to express the opinion of the rating agencies about credit risk since everyone can easily understand it. But of course it can easily be copied. Another way is to establish a report about each issuer or at least to multiply the criteria of appreciation of an issuer's credit risk so that a synthesis through a single mark (the rating) would be difficult. During the 1960s and the 1970s, an English rating agency specialized in the rating of banks (IBCA) drew well-known reports about the credit risk of banks. To synthesize the whole report in a single mark would have meant to strongly reduce the high-quality content of this report. Copying such a report would have had no meaning.

These two conditions seem necessary if one wants to set up an investor paying system: credit rating agencies working in a niche sector with a reliable investor base and strongly enriching their rating with a report that would mitigate this rating.

12.1.3   Rating Through the Cycle

If some investors are not perfectly aware of the risk level of financial products, others are. Some institutional investors indeed choose to dedicate a team of analysts to a specific sector they estimate fundamental for their investment strategy. For the issues of that sector, the institutional investor's analyses generally appear to be timelier than the ones of the rating agencies while being as accurate. As a result, the institutional investor can anticipate the rating agencies' decisions and buy or sell the bonds before the rating announcement. In perfect financial markets, the movement in price resulting from the action of buying or selling bonds is enough to inform other investors of the change in the issuer's credit risk, and there is no need for a rating agency. That is the point of view of many investors. To go against that idea, the rating agencies claimed that they were rating "through the cycle." One has to understand that they are not influenced by the business cycle and that the rating does not move each time the activity goes up or down. It is a kind of long-term or medium-term rating. If this concept appears quite clear from a theoretical point of view, it is not so clear from an operational point of view. An important power of decision seems to be left to the analyst who decides if an event will trigger or not a rating action. As a result:

1) Rating actions are deliberately late compared to market reactions (changes in prices).
2) Market reactions are supposed to be much more frequent than rating actions, some of them being thought of as not fundamental by the agency.
3) Even if two agencies agree about the credit risk level of an issuer, split ratings should be the rule as these agencies may not agree about the time to disclose the new rating.

12.1.4   The International Credit Rating Sector Is an Oligopoly

At the national level, rating agencies are not an oligopoly. In the USA, ten rating agencies are registered (Nationally Recognized Statistical Rating Organizations, NRSRO) by the Securities and Exchange Commission and can operate all over the country. Three of them work at the international level, and seven of them at the national level. Within Europe, 16 rating agencies are registered, the same three international ones and 13 agencies (mainly German ones) working at a national level. In Japan, China and Canada, we also observe rating agencies working at the national level. All over the world, there are about 130 credit rating agencies.

At the international level, there are only three agencies: Moody's, Standard and Poor's and, with a lower market share, Fitch. Some competitors are trying to challenge these agencies (the US agency Rating and Investment Information (R&I), the Japanese Japan Credit Rating and the Canadian Dominion Bond Rating Services), but the sector is still an oligopoly.

Why is it so? First, for economic reasons. The main asset of rating agencies is their reputation. And it takes a long time to build it up. Investors appreciate the quality of an agency work based on its results and the agency has to work for a long time before being trusted by investors. Moody's and Standard and

Poor's (which comes from the merging of Henry Poor's Publishing Company and the Standard Statistics Company) are the oldest agencies; the present company Fitch comes from the merging of several agencies (IBCA, Duff and Phelps, Thomson Bankwatch and the former Fitch) that were well known for bank rating (IBCA) and securitized bond rating (Fitch).

Second, for regulatory reasons. The action of authorities had two effects: setting up a new market for rating agencies by filtering out the companies which are authorized to rate the issuers, and making this new market an oligopoly by confining to a small figure the number of authorized rating agencies. As early as 1936 in the USA, the accounting rules regarding high yield bonds became different from those for investment grade bonds; it made financial companies hold mainly investment grade bonds and, at the same time, it put the rating agencies in a central position. In France, bonds from securitizing vehicles have to be rated. More recently, Basel II agreements gave an important role to the external ratings of rating agencies. These rules and agreements contributed strongly to the growth of the rating sector. At the same time, the authorities decided which agencies which were authorized to rate. In 1975 in the USA, the Securities and Exchange Commission created the NRSRO which counted at first only three agencies. In Europe, the European authorities did the same by recognizing 16 agencies that could operate across Europe. So an oligopoly of rating agencies with a protected market was created.

What are the consequences of such a market structure?

First, and classically, rating agencies' fees tend to be high. The revenues of rating agencies come from new ratings and from the reexamination of former ones, as it is very difficult for a company, once it has been rated, to withdraw its rating from the market. It means the operational risk of rating agencies is quite low, just as the volatility of their revenues. We don't know much about the prices of ratings and the profits of agencies. Nevertheless, in 2011, the operational profit of Standard and Poor's and Moody's was about 40 %; and Fitch's was 31 %. For the first nine months of 2011, the revenue of Standard and Poor's reached US$ 1.3 trillion for about 1,400 analysts. The figures for Moody's were US$ 1.2 trillion for 1,300 analysts. These figures make for an annual revenue per analyst higher than US$ 1 million, which is quite high.

The other consequence is about reputation. It is obviously true that at the beginning of its life a rating agency needs to care a lot about its reputation, which is seen by economists as a price to pay to get in the rating sector (and then as a barrier to the entry of competitors). But, as we have seen, there is another barrier to entry that is the status of NRSRO, which rules the incumbents out of the sector. And, at least in the short run, this regulatory barrier can appear as a sufficient protection for the international agencies and be the origin of a relaxing of their reputational constraint. This can explain the greed of rating agencies concerning collateralized issues before 2008, and today the possibility for an issuer to do his "shopping" among the agencies before being rated. Reputational effects can be a guarantee of quality (to some extent) only if reputation is the only (or at least the most important) barrier of entry into the sector, which is not the case for credit rating agencies. The protection given by the regulator may give birth to a downward competition between the agencies, which is obviously the opposite of the aim of such a protection.

12.2 Criticisms Towards the Activity of Rating Agencies

Three kinds of criticisms have been formulated against the rating agencies during these last 20 years.

12.2.1 Conflict of Interest

Rating agencies were at the very heart of the financial crisis that subverted the whole financial world in 2007–2008.

The main point is the handling of the securitization operations by rating agencies. Such operations mean packaging classical debt contracts in new bundles, assessing the credit risk of each bundle and then issuing new debt contracts backed on each bundle. The rating agency steps in at several levels of the process. First, it helps the issuer fix the size of each bundle, that is to set up the financial structure of the special purpose vehicle used to issue the debt contracts. Then it assesses the credit risk level of each bundle of new debt. This credit risk depends of course on the financial structure of the special purpose vehicle, a financial structure that has been chosen and assessed by the rating agency itself. The agency has a conflict of interest: it sets up the special purpose vehicle and appreciates the default risk of this vehicle. It gave birth to an underestimation of the credit risk and, owing to a large dissemination of junk debts in the balance sheets of banks, to a tremendous financial crisis.

Rating agencies were asked to build a "Chinese wall" between their advisory and rating activities, and the problem nowadays seems much less acute.

12.2.2   Sluggishness

Apart from a systematic undervaluation of the credit risk of securitized issues, credit rating agencies were blamed for informing investors late. This sluggish attitude has three consequences.

First, investors were not warned in due time of the bankruptcy of the issuer. In 2002, four days before Enron went bankrupt, the rating of this issuer was still good. It was the same for the Lehman Brothers' bank during the last financial crisis.

Then, even if the downgrading of the issuer does not lead to a bankruptcy, it induces a partition of investors between the ones who can appreciate the risk level of the issuer by themselves, without the help of the agencies (the informed investors) and other investors. The former benefit from the fact that the latter are informed late by selling them at a high price the bonds that will be downgraded. The sluggishness of the agencies induces a wealth transfer between informed investors and other investors.

And at last, if rating agencies do not inform investors in due time, the whole bond market appears not to be not regulated and the usefulness of rating agencies to be very limited.

12.2.3   Toughness

In some cases, when the agency proved not to have foreseen the fall in credit risk of the issuer, it tried to compensate for this blindness by tough downgrading which did not seem to be justified. For instance, during the Asian crisis at the end the twentieth century, rating agencies were blamed for making the crisis worse with harsh ratings. It was the same with securitized issues, which were deeply downgraded after the beginning of the crisis.

12.3   The Utility of Rating Agencies

12.3.1   Credit Rating Agencies Have a Certification Function

As credit rating agencies are late in disclosing their new ratings, we may wonder what their usefulness on the financial markets is. An observation of the market reactions, for instance in the credit default swap (CDS) market, will certainly give more complete and timely information to the investors. What is the function of the agencies?

Their role is indeed to specify, among all the market reactions, the ones that will last over time and can be qualified as fundamental changes, and the ones that will quickly disappear. Only the first ones will correspond to a change in rating. The function of the agencies is to confirm that the change in prices corresponds to a change in the level of credit risk. This is a certification function.

Is this certification function important for the market? We don't think it is for institutional investors who specifically analyse some issuers: they know before the agencies what the changes in credit risk of the issuers are and they do not need the agencies to select their investments. But the agencies may be useful for other investors from two points of view:

1) The agencies inform these investors that the change in prices is due to a change in credit risk and is definitive; of course, this affects their investment strategy.
2) They also inform these investors about the importance of the change in credit risk. Even if these investors guess that the market price reaction is due to a modification of the credit risk, they may not be sure of the importance of that change, the price reaction being possibly followed by another one. The rating disclosure gives a clear indication of the new credit risk of the issuer.

So the financial market, or at least some investors, needs the credit rating agencies' appreciations of credit risk. This information transmission to these investors also means a coordination of all the investors' expectations.

12.3.2 Credit Rating Agencies Have a Stabilizing Effect on the Bond Market and Give a Profit Opportunity to Informed Investors

With the coordination of investors' expectations comes the stabilization of bond prices and spreads.

Let us assume there is a downgrading. Uninformed investors first experience a fall in price resulting from the selling decision of informed investors. This decrease in price can be a nice opportunity to invest for the uniformed investors if it does not last long. On the opposite, it means a loss of money if this decrease corresponds to a change in the credit quality of the issuer. So uninformed investors wonder how to interpret the decrease in bond price and they don't know what should be the fair price of the bond. It means bond price volatility increases after the observation of the change in the bond price.

When the rating agency announces a downgrading, the expected fair price of the uninformed investors meets the price of the informed investors, and bond price volatility decreases. A change in the credit risk of an issuer has a destabilizing effect on the bond price, and the rating agency's announcement has a stabilizing effect. Of course, it works exactly in the same way in the case of an upgrading, but with a less acute intensity because an upgrading is good news for every investor, and uninformed ones are less keen to trade their bonds.

In which cases do rating agencies' announcements have a destabilizing effect? First, when it is a surprise event. Sometimes, the rating agency has information about the issuer the informed investors do not have. The agency reacts first causing a change in bond price and an increase in volatility.

A destabilizing effect also occurs when the rating agency disagrees with the informed investors. Informed investors are now assumed to react first, and then the rating agency discloses its new rating. But this announcement can be inconsistent with the informed investors' reaction. For instance, in case of a fall in price, the downgrading announced by the agency can be tougher than expected. This disagreement between the agency and the informed investors makes the bond price volatility increase.

We must also notice that this behaviour of the rating agencies gives a profit opportunity to informed investors. As the agencies are late to give information about an issuer's credit risk to uninformed investors, informed ones have time to sell their bonds at a high price in case of a downgrading, or to buy them at a low price in case of an upgrading. Why do uninformed investors agree to buy or to sell bonds? Because they are not aware of the change in the issuer's credit risk. As soon as uninformed investors become doubtful and wonder if there is any change in the issuer credit risk, the bond price volatility increases, and the announcement by the rating agency should stop this increase in volatility. So the sluggish behaviour of the rating agency, which gives birth to a stabilizing effect, is also at the origin of a profit opportunity for informed investors. If rating agencies were to react in a timely manner, their announcements would increase volatility (in the short run) and there wouldn't be any wealth transfer between investors.

12.4 Improving Bond Market Regulation

As they reduce asymmetry between informed investors and less informed ones, and by doing so stabilize bond prices, rating agencies seem to be necessary to a good regulation of the bond market.

Apart from treachery, which should be fought (a Chinese wall between rating activities and advisory ones is absolutely necessary), the main complaints against rating agencies seem to be sluggishness (which gives birth to wealth transfers between investors) and high fees. Rating shopping does exist as issuers often use the rating advisory services of banks, but it is not a huge problem when multiple ratings are quite compulsory and the point of view of agencies is more or less the same (split ratings diverge only by one notch). We may think the best incentive to make rating agencies work harder and decrease their fees is *competition*. Other ways to regulate agencies do not seem very appropriate:

1) Controlling *ex ante* the rating agencies' methods: necessary, but insufficient.
2) Allocating blindly an agency to an issuer, in order to avoid the rating shopping: a very theoretical solution which would destroy the commercial relationship between the agency and the issuer.
3) Making the agencies liable for the consequences of their errors: this would make the rating business disappear because of the difficulty of predicting a default and the importance of the consequences.

If we want to go a little further and look at the way the whole rating industry may be organized at the European level, we should first mention that a rating agency is a private company that fulfils a general interest mission. Other companies or individuals do exactly the same; for instance, chartered accountants and accounting auditors who have to certify the accounting books of other companies. This could be a good example to use to organize the rating industry.

Raters, and not only rating agencies, should be regulated. The organism in charge of regulation should approve the new raters who want to get into the business only if they fulfil some specific conditions in terms of training (as for registered accountants, an academic path, with examinations and internships, should be followed by applicants who want to become raters). Rating agencies could only be created by approved raters. We can expect an increase of the number of rating agencies, and at last of competition among the rating industry, as everyone fulfilling the training conditions could be a rater.

We think such an organization would create a good balance between a compulsory monitoring of the rating agencies and a free right to get into the market in order to increase competition.

Bibliography

Alsakka, R., & Ap Gwilym, O. (2010). Leads and lags in sovereign credit ratings. *Journal of Banking and Finance, 34,* 2614–2626.

Altman, E. I., & Rijken, H. A. (2004). How rating agencies achieve rating stability. *Journal of Banking and Finance, 28,* 2679–2714.

Boot, A. W., Milbourn, T. T., & Schmeits, A. (2006). Credit ratings as coordination mechanisms. *Review of Financial Studies, 19*, 81–118.

Cheng, M., & Neamtiu, M. (2009). An empirical analysis of changes in credit rating properties: Timeliness, accuracy and volatility. *Journal of Accounting and Economics, 47*, 108–130.

Dallocchio, M., Hubler, J., Raimbourg, P., & Salvi, A. (2006). Do upgradings and downgradings convey information? An event study of the French bond market. *Economic Notes, 35*(3), 293–317.

Grier, P., & Katz, S. (1976). The differential effects of bond rating changes among industrial and public utility bonds by maturity. *Journal of Business, 49*, 226–239.

Hand, J. R., Holthausen, R. W., & Leftwich, R. W. (1992). The rating agency announcements on bond and stock prices. *The Journal of Finance, 47*, 733–752.

Heinke, V. G., & Steiner, M. (2001). Event study concerning international bond price effects of credit rating actions. *International Journal of Finance and Economics, 6*, 139–157.

Hettenhouse, G., & Sartoris, W. (1976). An analysis of the informational value of bond rating changes. *Quarterly Review of Economics and Business, 16*, 65–78.

Hite, G., & Warga, A. (1997). The effect of bond-rating changes on bond price performance. *Financial Analysts Journal, 53*, 35–51.

Hubler, J., Louargant, C., Ory, J. N., & Raimbourg, P. (2014). Do rating agencies' decisions impact stock risks? Evidence from European markets. *The European Journal of Finance, 20*(11), 1008–1036.

Jeon, D. H., & Lovo, S. (2013). Credit rating industry: An helicopter tour of stylized facts and recent theories. *Toulouse School of Economics*, WP n° 376.

Jorion, P., Liu, Z., & Shi, C. (2005). Informational effects of regulation FD: Evidence from rating agencies. *Journal of Financial Economics, 76*, 309–330.

May, A. D. (2010). The impact of bond rating changes on corporate bond prices: New evidence from the over-the-counter market. *Journal of Banking and Finance, 34*, 2822–2836.

Ory, J. N., & Raimbourg, P. (2015). European rating actions, investor reaction and bond spread volatility. *Economic Notes, 44*(2), 333–360.

Ory, J. N., Raimbourg, P., & Salvi, A. (2011). Does it really hurt? An empirical investigation of the effects of downgradings and negative watches on European bond spreads. *The Journal of Fixed Income, 20*, 86–96.

Raimbourg, P. (2013). Rating agencies and financial regulations: Thirty years of academic research. *Bankers, Markets & Investors*, (123), 54–61.

Sénat. (2012). *Rapport d'Information*, N° 598.

Weinstein, M. I. (1977). The effect of a rating change announcement on bond price. *Journal of Financial Economics, 5*, 329–350.

13

The Regulation of Alternative Investment Funds in Europe: The Alternative Investment Fund Managers Directive

Marco Dell'Erba

13.1 Introduction

The new European Union (EU) framework that concerns financial regulation, supervision and oversight has been strongly influenced by the financial and economic crisis of 2007–8. The role of systemic risk, in particular, even if its definition is not clear, has determined the design of the new institutional and regulatory framework.

The 2007 financial crisis has demonstrated that a model exclusively oriented towards microprudential supervision can fail. Therefore, the European regulators have adopted a different approach, emphasizing the macroprudential dimension of economic supervision.

At the same time, important institutional changes have determined the creation of a new entity, the European Systemic Risk Board (a homologue of the US Financial Stability Oversight Committee, FSOC), and the substitution of the Lamfalussy Committees with new European Authorities (ESMA, EBA, EIOPA).

This institutional transformation has been completed with a regulatory approach that has tended to provide more effective regulation for all those

---

We wish to thank John P. Drohan III, Esq. for helpful comments and encouragement.

M. Dell'Erba (✉)
Post-Doctoral Fellow LabEx ReFi, IRJS - Université Paris I Panthéon Sorbonne,
Paris, France

© The Author(s) 2017
R. Douady et al. (eds.), *Financial Regulation in the EU*,
DOI 10.1007/978-3-319-44287-7_13

entities that are considered responsible for the financial crisis. In this context, the regulation of alternative funds (especially hedge funds and private equity funds) has played a crucial role. The adoption of the Alternative Investment Fund Manager Directive (AIFMD) in Europe has been significant, as was the Dodd-Frank Act in the USA. With respect to alternative investment funds (AIFs), a category that has been identified by adopting broad terms (the notions of AIF in the EU and "private investment fund" in the USA), both the American and European regulators decided to adopt, together with other complementary regulatory tools, a direct regulatory approach, providing, inter alia, requirements in terms of registration, governance and leverage.

The AIFMD, adopted by the European Parliament on 11 November 2010, and published in the *Official Journal of the European Union* on 1 July 2011, is a crucial text in the European post-crisis regulation. In the Commission's approach, it is part of a more comprehensive and ambitious project: the creation of a single rulebook in relation to hedge funds, private equity funds and more generally all those non-harmonized funds.

Two elements have to be taken into account in relation to AIFs, explicitly mentioned within the AIFMD.

Firstly, the adoption of the AIFMD is an acknowledgement of the prominent role of hedge and private equity fund managers within financial markets, since they are responsible for the management of a significant number of assets invested in the EU, account for significant amounts of trading in markets for financial instruments, and can exercise an important influence on markets and companies in which they invest (Recital 1).

Secondly, with the AIFMD, the European regulators emphasized the positive consequences of the presence of alternative investments within the market: the AIFMD confirms that hedge funds did not cause the financial crisis, as already argued in the de Larosière Report[1]; in addition, even if the financial crisis has demonstrated that the activities of AIFs may spread or amplify risks throughout the system, they also have a beneficial impact on the markets in which they operate (Recital 2).

From a broader perspective, the AIFMD should be considered as part of a general rethinking and evolution of the European legal system with reference

---

[1] This position is consistent with paragraph 86 of the de Larosière Report, excluding any responsibilities of hedge funds in causing the financial crisis: "Concerning hedge funds, the Group considers they did not play a major role in the emergence of the crisis. Their role has largely been limited to a transmission function, notably through massive selling of shares and short-selling transactions. We should also recognize that in the EU, unlike the US, the great bulk of hedge fund managers are registered and subject to information requirements. This is the case in particular in the UK, where all hedge funds managers are subject to registration and regulation, as all fund managers are, and where the largest 30 are subject to direct information requirements often obtained on a global basis as well as to indirect monitoring via the banks and prime brokers."

to financial intermediation, or a real reregulation of the relevant discipline,[2] and in particular of funds. Many regulations have been issued that affect fund management companies and that concern the distribution of financial products: the UCITS Directives,[3] the Directive on distance-selling of financial products,[4] the Directive on pension funds,[5] the E-commerce Directive,[6] MiFID I,[7] and II,[8] Prospectus,[9] and Transparency Directives,[10] which also display some consequences for the activities of AIFs.

In particular, the Directive 85/611/EEC of 20 December 1985 (UCITS I) has been an important stage in the construction of financial Europe: "harmonisation de l'essentiel / agrément unique / contrôle par les autorités de l'Etat d'origine."[11] Such a legal regime is not so different in its essence from the one adopted nearly 30 years later to regulate AIFs; its central idea has been the harmonization of the essential elements, emphasizing the importance of authorizing funds by supervisory authorities from the state of origin of the fund manager.

The UCITS I Directive established basic principles for authorization, supervision and investment policies, providing prudential limits, risk

---

[2] IOCCA M.G. (2009), Gli investitori istituzionali, in VELLA F. (ed) Banche e mercati finanziari (Giappichelli), Torino, 483.

[3] UCITS means "Undertakings for Collective Investment in Transferable Securities Directives"; the acronym is thus used to call both the directive and the objects regulated by it (i.e. funds). Directive 85/611/EEC (UCITS I), (UCITS II was never passed), 2001/107/EC and 2001/108/EC (together form UCITS III), 2009/65/EC (UCITS IV), 2014/91/EU (UCITS 5).

[4] Directive 2002/65/EC of the European Parliament and of the Council of 23 September 2002 concerning the distance marketing of consumer financial services and amending Council Directives 90/619/EEC, 97/7/EC and 98/27/EC.

[5] Directive 2003/41/EC of the European Parliament and of the Council of 3 June 2003 on the activities and supervision of institutions for occupational retirement provision.

[6] Directive 2000/31/EC of 8 June 2000 on certain legal aspects of information society services, in particular electronic commerce, in the Internal Market ("Directive on electronic commerce").

[7] Directive 2004/39/EC of 21 April 2004 on markets in financial instruments amending Council Directives 85/611/EEC and 93/6/EEC and Directive 2000/12/EC of the European Parliament and of the Council and repealing Council Directive 93/22/EEC.

[8] Directive 2014/65/EU of 15 May 2014 on markets in financial instruments and amending Directive 2002/92/EC and Directive 2011/61/EU Text with EEA relevance.

[9] Directive 2003/71/EC of 4 November 2003 on the prospectus to be published when securities are offered to the public or admitted to trading and amending Directive 2001/34/EC (Text with EEA relevance).

[10] Directive 2013/50/EU of 22 October 2013 amending Directive 2004/109/EC on the harmonization of transparency requirements in relation to information about issuers whose securities are admitted to trading on a regulated market, Directive 2003/71/EC on the prospectus to be published when securities are offered to the public or admitted to trading and Commission Directive 2007/14/EC laying down detailed rules for the implementation of certain provisions of Directive 2004/109/EC. Text with EEA relevance.

[11] SYNVET H. (2011), La gestion collective: à l'aube d'une ère nouvelle?, RD banc. Fin. n. 1, étude 5, in lexisnexis.com.

diversification, transparency requirements and investor information for UCITS funds. Moreover, in accordance with the provisions of Article 67 of the Treaty establishing the European Economic Community (known as the Treaty of Rome, which provides, among other principles, for the abolition of restrictions on the free movement of units of UCITS), the main purpose of this coordination was the harmonization of competition between UCITS within the EU and at the same time effective and uniform protection for investors. It also introduced the principle of mutual recognition, a novelty at the time for the financial sector: a UCITS that has been authorized in the member state of origin may, after notification to the competent supervisory authorities of the other EU countries concerned with the distribution of its units, market such units without further permission of the host state.[12]

The main purpose of subsequent Directives has been to harmonize legislation in the field of mutual funds, encouraging pan-European marketing and aligning it with the latest trends in the European asset management industry.

The UCITS Directives are useful in emphasizing and understanding the role of harmonization in Europe with reference to financial intermediation.

It is precisely the role of harmonization that AIFMD intendsto implement for all those managers that do not fall within the UCITS Directive. The AIFMD has been a further step in the construction of a regulatory framework that over the years has become more and more structured, through the adoption of measures that have also partially affected the activities of hedge funds (EMIR Directive, Prospectus and Transparency Directives).

This chapter is structured as follows: it first provides a historical background to the AIFMD, then explains the notion of AIFM, as regulated by the AIFMD and the further interventions of ESMA, before analysing the main tools of direct regulation contained in the AIFMD; finally, the chapter provides some critical remarks and conclusions.

13.2 The Difficulties in Approving the AIFMD

The AIFMD was approved by the European Parliament on 11 November 2010 (published on 1 July 2011 in the *Official Journal of the European Union*) after a negotiation that proved long and difficult, and the date for its implementation was set for 2013. Luxembourg was the fastest in transposing the AIFMD, whereas other member states have had more difficulties. Among these is France, which completed the transposition after a long consultation

---

[12] Iocca M.G., quoted, 486.

process, and Italy, one of the "first movers" in the regulation of hedge funds in 1999, which launched the consultation procedures only in mid-2013 and completed the transposition of the Directive in July 2014.

The difficulties around the negotiation of the AIFMD emphasize its political dimension[13]: underlying conflicting interests in recent years have driven the debate about the need for regulation of alternative investments, especially hedge funds, in connection to the different positions of member states and their different approaches to financial economy in the context of each economic model. Consistently with these considerations, the focus of the Directive on the objective of regulation has been interpreted as a reflection of the desire of some member states, in particular France and Germany, to find "a suitable scapegoat for the excess of Anglo-Saxon capitalism" that these countries, along with others, believed responsible for the acceleration and amplification of the global financial crisis.[14]

At the European level there was no organic and appropriate regulation of AIF activities,[15] despite a few provisions applicable to hedge funds and private equity funds.[16] European regulation was rather fragmentary because of its systematic delegation to the laws of member states. Such a circumstance might have posed a serious regulatory gap, in consideration of the transnationality and internationality of the activity of alternative management.[17]

Unlike other regulatory initiatives, the debate around the regulation of hedge funds was not intrinsically linked to the last financial crisis of 2008[18]: the regulatory issues posed by alternative investments had been identified long before.[19] The issue had first arisen after the collapse of LTCM in 1998.

---

[13] Awrey D. (2011), The limits of EU hedge fund regulation, Law and Financial Markets Law Review, March 2011, 124.

[14] Awrey D. (2011), *The limits of EU hedge funds regulation, Law and Financial Markets Review*, March 2011, 124.

[15] Ferran E. (2011), The Regulation of Hedge Funds and Private Equity: A Case Study in the Development of the EU's Regulatory Response to the Financial Crisis, Law Working Paper N°.176/2011 February 2011, available at http://ssrn.com/abstract=1762119, 5.

[16] Clerc C. (2009), *Faut-il une réglementation européenne de la gestione alternative?*, in *Revue Trimestrielle de Droit Financier*, n. 3, 2009, 4.

[17] See Engert a., (2010), Transnational Hedge Fund Regulation, EBOR, 11, n. 03, 375, quoted. The European Commission in the AIFM Proposal states that "Currently, the activities of AIFM are regulated by a combination of national financial and company law regulations and general provisions of Community law. They are supplemented in some areas by Industry-developed standards. However, recent events have indicated that some of the risks associated with AIFM have been underestimated and are not sufficiently addressed by current rules. This is partly a reflection of the predominantly national perspective of existing rules: **the regulatory environment does not adequately reflect the crossborder nature of the risks** [emphasis added]. This is particularly striking in relation to the effective oversight and control of macro-prudential risks."

[18] Synvet H., quoted.

[19] Ferran E., quoted, 3.

The Motion for a European Parliament Resolution (the Motion),[20] in Recital F, explains this non-correlation with the last financial crisis, since "EU and national institutions have long before the current financial crisis, analysed potential concerns in relation to hedge funds and private equity as regards financial stability, risk management standards, excessive debt (leverage) and the valuation of illiquid and complex financial instruments."

In 2005, the European Commission initiated a public consultation regarding possible ways in which to improve the European regulatory framework for investment funds: "While the debate focuses primarily on retail investment funds that fall within the existing legislative framework (UCITS), the Commission also notes the strong growth of the alternative investment market, consisting of inter alia, private equity funds and hedge funds."[21] There followed an intense debate; in particular, in 2006 the *Report of the Alternative Investment Expert Group to the European Commission Managing, Servicing And Marketing Hedge Funds In Europe* was published.[22] After this report, many other contributions from different sectors broadened the debate. Such contributions can be considered to constitute the preparatory documents of the AIFMD.

However, the financial crisis gave a strong impetus to the development of a new regulatory framework. The Motion,[23] with recommendations to the Commission on Hedge Funds and Private Equity of 11 September 2008, emphasized the importance of rethinking the activities of AIFs and the planning of further steps in subsequent years. In the context of the Motion, the European Parliament officially "requests the Commission to submit to Parliament by the end of 2008, on the basis of art. 44, art. 47(2), or art. 95 of the EC Treaty, a legislative proposal or proposals covering all relevant actors and financial market participants, including hedge funds and private equity." Such an initiative had to respond to seven principles corresponding to seven different areas.[24]

---

[20] Motion for a European Parliament Resolution with recommendations to the Commission on Hedge Funds and Private Equity of 11 September 2008, available at http://www.europarl.europa.eu/sides/getDoc.do?pubRef=-//EP//NONSGML+REPORT+A6-2008-0338+0+DOC+PDF+V0//IT.

[21] Report of the alternative investment expert group to the European commission managing, servicing and marketing hedge funds in Europe, 2007, 3, available at http://ec.europa.eu/internal_market/investment/docs/other_docs/reports/hedgefunds_en.pdf.

[22] Supra.

[23] Motion, quoted.

[24] Such seven principles have been provided in Recital AE in relation to seven areas:

– regulatory coverage: existing Community legislation should be reviewed to identify any regulatory gaps; national variations should be reviewed and harmonization should be promoted, for example through colleges of supervisors or otherwise; international equivalence and cooperation should be pursued;

Recitals A and B of the Motion point out a practical need for regulation of hedge funds (and in general to alternative investments), in a perspective of harmonization of national legislation, because it considers that "there is at present national and EU regulation concerning financial markets that directly or indirectly, though not exclusively, applies to hedge funds and private equity," and that "Member States and the Commission should ensure the consistent implementation and application of that regulation; all further adjustments to existing legislation should be the subject of a proper cost/benefit analysis and should be non-discriminatory."

Together with the issue of regulating alternative investments, there is also the need to pursue financial stability. In this sense, enhanced regulation seeks to rethink the model of supervision: Recital L refers to a "better supervisory cooperation, including at the global level, which logically requires, continuing improvements of current EU supervisory arrangements including regular exchanges of information and enhanced transparency of institutional investors."

Furthermore, as can be understood from the expression "regular exchanges of information and enhanced transparency of institutional investors," the importance of transparency and the relevance of information emerge in this context. Transparency is crucial for different reasons: the possibility of regulating off-shore market players globally (Recital M); the consideration that appropriate levels of transparency towards investors and supervisory authorities are crucial to ensure well-functioning and stable financial markets and promote competition between market actors and products (Recital N); the importance of monitoring and analysing the effects of the operations of hedge funds and private equity and to consider putting forward a directive on mini-

---

- capital: capital requirements should be mandatory for all financial institutions and should reflect risk from the type of business, exposures and risk control; longer liquidity horizons should also be considered;
- originate and distribute: to achieve a better alignment of the interests of investors and originators, originators should generally retain exposure to their securitized products by holding a representative stake in the product; disclosure should be made of the level of the stakes originators keep in loan products; as an alternative to retention, other measures to align interests of investors and originators should be investigated;
- accounting: a smoothing technique to counter the procyclical effects of fair value accounting should be considered;
- rating: to increase transparency and understanding in the ratings market, Credit Rating Agencies should adopt codes of conduct regarding visibility of assumptions, product complexity and business practices; conflict of interest should be managed; unsolicited rating should be independently categorized and not used as a means of pressure to obtain business;
- derivative trading: open and visible trading of derivatives should be promoted whether on-exchange or otherwise;
- the long term: reward packages should be aligned with longer term outcomes, reflecting losses as well as profits.

mum transparency rules on how investments are financed in the future, risk management, methods of assessment, managers' qualifications, possible conflicts of interest as well as the disclosure of ownership structures and the registration of hedge funds (Recital O); in the adoption of binding measures in terms of corporate governance with a view to achieving greater transparency, which must also be made public, and calls for an improvement of controlling mechanisms (Recital Q).

Together with transparency, two other important elements emerge: "external" conflicts of interest (depending on the operational model of private equity and hedge funds and so emerging from the relationship between those vehicles and other entities within the financial markets) (Recital Z), and "internal" conflicts of interest, which comprise remuneration of the managers, characterized by inappropriate incentives that lead to excessive risks (Recital AA).

The European Parliament has emphasized the importance of adopting principle-based regulation as an appropriate approach to regulating financial markets, as it is better able to keep up with market developments (Recital AD), as the Financial Services Authority (FSA, now Financial Conduct Authority, FCA) already did. Consistent with this approach, the European Parliament has identified seven central issues that must be taken into consideration (Recital AE).

The European Parliament adopted the proposed motion on 23 September 2008 with a very large majority: 562 votes in favour, 86 against and 25 abstentions.[25] With this, the long preparatory work of the Commission Ecofin was officially closed and the European Commission was given the mandate to provide for the regulation of hedge funds and private equity funds. The European Parliament Resolution emphasized in Recital AF a crucial element for the type of activity that characterizes hedge funds and private equity funds[26]: regulatory action "whereas such action would provide a legal basis, universal and comprehensive, encompassing all financial institutions above a certain size, mutually taking into account international supervisory and regulatory practices."

Even at international level, the financial crisis of 2008 played a significant role in reviving the debate and the need to propose uniform regulation of

---

[25] The statistics about the vote of the Resolution are available at http://www.europarl.europa.eu/oeil/popups/sda.do?id=16041&l=en.

[26] EP (2008) European Parliament resolution of 23 September 2008 with recommendations to the Commission on hedge funds and private equity, P6_TA(2008)0425, available at http://eur-lex.europa.eu/legal-content/EN/TXT/?uri=CELEX:52008IP0425.

alternative management. This has resulted in a dual track, at both European and international level.[27]

The G20, almost simultaneously with the Resolution of the European Parliament, in sessions in November 2008 in Washington and April 2009 in London, took a position on this topic, laying out two basic principles: the regulatory principle of universal coverage, according to which any actor, instrument or systemically important financial market must be subject to oversight, adapted to the type of activity, and abiding by a principle of international coordination, according to which appropriate mechanisms of supervision should be put in place to enable a fruitful exchange of information between national supervisors, together with international coordination of these supervisors, to prevent systemic risks.

With the aim of implementing the G20 recommendations, the International Organization of Securities Commissions (IOSCO), as already mentioned, had launched a public consultation concerning the regulatory standards related to hedge funds.[28] The G20 was supported by a special task force, the Task Force on Unregulated Entities, which had been created within IOSCO and was chaired by Commissione Nazionale per le società e la borsa (CONSOB) and the FSA (now FCA). The action of the IOSCO Task Force culminated in the publication, immediately after the G20 summit in London in June 2009, of a final document (Hedge Funds Oversight: Final Report),[29] in which a series of guiding principles for regulation of hedge funds, written from the perspective of harmonization, were proposed. Moreover, IOSCO provided in the Objectives and Principles of Financial Regulation a new principle specifically dedicated to hedge funds: "(r)egulation should ensure that hedge funds and/or hedge funds managers/advisers are subject to appropriate oversight."[30]

On 30 April 2009, the European Commission filed a first proposal for a directive, adopting a new regulatory approach for alternative management. In the past, the European Institutions persistently refused to consider the possibility of regulating the hedge funds (and private equity) industry in the previous years,[31] and above all was supposed to represent, in the words of

---

[27] C. CLERC, *Faut-il une réglementation européenne de la gestion alternative?*, in *Revue Trimestrielle de Droit Financier*, 2009, 4, emphasizes the "*double origine*" of the AIFMD: European and international.

[28] See *Consults on Regulatory Standards for Funds of Hedge Funds* published on 6 October 2008. See also *Technical Committee Task Forces to Support G-20 Aims*, which was announced on 25 November 2008, coordinated with the G-20.

[29] The Report is available at http://www.iosco.org/library/pubdocs/pdf/IOSCOPD293.pdf.

[30] IOSCO, Objectives and Principles of Securities Regulation, June 2010.

[31] CLERC C. (2011), *La Directive AIFM, des avancées significatives au prix de compromis complexes*, in *Revue Trimestrielle de Droit Financier*, n. 3, 2011, 22.

the Commission, the European answer to financial crises. The Commission's main objective was to extend appropriate regulation and supervision to all entities and all activities involving significant risks,[32] recalling the positions expressed in this regard by the European Parliament,[33] and the de Larosière Group,[34] as well as the G20, IOSCO and the Financial Stability Forum, with reference to all funds not governed by the UCITS Directive.[35]

In the course of the negotiations for the AIFMD, three distinct positions emerged: the European Parliament was convinced of the need for comprehensive regulation; the Council maintained a rather minimalist approach, based on a variety of technical topics; and the Commission held an intermediate position. The consequence has been that, in the face of strong political will expressed by European political parties, prime ministers and governments of the major economic powers, as well as by the Commission, the Council, in consideration of its technical approach, played a role in mediation that actually resulted in a complication of the text.[36] The Directive proposal has been substantially redrafted, and numerous parties have lobbied the EU Commission and Parliament to accept their changes.[37] The process that led to the approval of the AIFMD was not only a policy process but also a political process.[38]

The first proposal of the European Commission in April 2009 has been substantially amended and redrafted. A strong position on the proposed text was expressed by one of the committees of the British House of Lords, which stated that the British government should not have given its approval to the proposal, underlining its incompatibility with the international regulatory regime, and even claiming that "the Directive will seriously damage the EU and UK economy unless it is fully compatible with the global approach to

---

[32] Commission calls on EU leaders to stay united against the crisis, move fast on financial market reform and show global leadership at G20, march 2009, available at http://europa.eu/rapid/pressReleasesAction.do?reference=IP/09/351&format=HTML&aged=0&language=EN&guiLanguage=en.

[33] Report of the European Parliament with recommendations to the Commission of hedge funds and private equity (A6-0338/2008) [Rasmussen Report] and the transparency of institutional investors (A6-0296-2008) [Lehne Report].

[34] High level group on financial supervision, Report, 25 February 2009, 25.

[35] Directive 2009/65/EC of the European parliament and of the council of 13 July 2009 on the coordination of laws, regulations and administrative provisions relating to undertakings for collective investment in transferable securities (UCITS).

[36] CLERC C., quoted, 22.

[37] KAAL W. A. (2011), Hedge Fund Regulation Via Basel III. *Vanderbilt Journal of Transnational Law*, Vol. 44, p. 389, available at http://ssrn.com/abstract=1806252. See also WATTS J. (2010), United Kingdom: AIFM Update, *MONDAQ Bus.*, 24 Mar. 2010, available http://www.mondaq.com/article.asp?articleid=96668.

[38] AWREY D., quoted, 124.

the regulation of AIFM and it permits the marketing of non-EU funds in the EU. Restrictions on non-EU managers should also be removed."[39]

Strong pressures arising mainly from lobbyists representing industry associations even led to the production of two different versions of the AIFMD: one in November 2010 issued by the Council of the European Union (known as the Revised Compromise Proposal, also known as the Swedish Proposal, because of the Swedish presidency of the European Council), and a second one issued by Jean-Paul Gauzès, a member of the Committee on Economic and Monetary Affairs, known as the Gauzès Report (Gauzès 2010),[40] for the European Parliament. The two versions had important differences in their approach to significant issues, including the applicability of the Directive to certain or all the funds, regardless of their dimensions and exposures, the valuation of assets and the AIFMs belonging to countries outside the EU doing business in the EU.[41]

After this tumultuous process, on 11 November 2010 political agreement was reached by the European Parliament and the Council of Ministers on the text for the Directive, which was promulgated and took effect in July 2013.

13.3 The Creation of a Residual Category

13.3.1 The Notion of "Alternative Investment Funds" in the AIFMD

The AIFMD regulates alternative fund managers and not AIFs. The reason depends on the difficulties of harmonizing AIFs in relation to their heterogeneity. Recital 10 of the AIFMD implicitly points out the difficulties of defining AIFs: it would be disproportionate to regulate the structure or composition of the portfolios of AIFs managed by AIFMs at EU level, and it

---

[39] House of Lords—*Directive on Alternative Investment Fund Managers—European Union Committee*, available at http://www.publications.parliament.uk/pa/ld200910/ldselect/ldeucom/48/4802.htm: "Key concerns raised by the letter included: The provisions related to marketing of non-EU funds and possible restrictions on non-EU managers marketing in the EU could prevent investment in and out of the EU; The lack of differentiation between different sorts of alternative investment—the one size fits all approach—would lead to inappropriate unintended consequences; Some elements of the proposals for supervision of managers were unnecessary and disproportionate; and The proposal provided an unnecessary level of protection to well-informed institutional investors and banks".

[40] Gauzes J. –P. (2010 A7-0171/2010 Report on the proposal for a directive of the European Parliament and of the Council on Alternative Investment Fund Managers and amending Directives 2004/39/EC and 2009/.../EC (COM(2009)0207—C7-0040/2009—2009/0064(COD))·

[41] See Kaal W. (2011), quoted.

would be difficult to provide for such extensive harmonization owing to the very diverse types of AIFs managed by AIFMs.[42] The consequence of such a choice made by the European regulator might be a fragmentation of provisions applicable to funds: the AIFMD does not prevent member states from adopting or continuing to apply national requirements with respect to AIFs established in their territory.[43]

Moreover, in response to the question of why the AIFMD regulates fund managers instead of funds, the Commission replied (EC 2009) that the AIFMD is focused on regulating the activities of AIFM,[44] since the AIFM is responsible for all key decisions regarding the management of the fund. Financial stability and investor risk stem primarily from the conduct and organization of the manager and the providers of key services, notably the depositary and valuation agents. The most effective response is therefore to focus on these entities.

Therefore, the choice to regulate the funds' managers and not the funds has an impact on the scope of the Directive: in terms of applicability, subject to the exceptions and restrictions provided for, the AIFMD should be applicable to all EU AIFMs managing EU AIFs or non-EU AIFs, irrespective of whether or not they are marketed in the EU, to non-EU AIFMs managing EU AIFs, irrespective of whether or not they are marketed in the EU, and to non-EU AIFMs marketing EU AIFs or non-EU AIFs in the EU.[45]

Some entities do not fall within the scope of the AIFMD: holding companies, institutions for occupational retirement provision which are covered by Directive 2003/41/EC, supranational institutions, such as the European Central Bank, the European Investment Bank, the European Investment Fund, the European Development Finance Institutions and bilateral development banks, the World Bank, the International Monetary Fund, and other supranational institutions and similar international organizations, in the event that such institutions or organizations manage AIFs, and in so far as those AIFs act in the public interest; national, regional and local governments

---

[42] AIFMD, Recital 10.

[43] AIFMD, see art. 2, paragraph 1, and Recital 10.

[44] EC (2009) European Commission—MEMO/09/211. Directive on Alternative Investment Fund Managers (AIFMs): Frequently Asked Questions, 29/04/2009, available at http://europa.eu/.

[45] AIFMD, Recital 13. In this regard, in relation to the scope of the AIFMD only in relation to managers, see Puel S. and Goffin G. (2013), *La notion de fonds d'investissement alternatifs dans la Directive AIFM*, *Revue Trimestrielle de Droit Financier*, n.2—2013, 108: «*L'idée selon laquelle la Directive AIFM a pour seule ambition de régir les gestionnaires de FIA est à nuancer dans une très large mesure. En effet, à travers les obligations mises à la charge des gestionnaires, la Directive AIFM vient encadrer la structure des FIA (obligation de recourir à un dépositaire), les stratégies de gestion mises en oeuvre (encadrement du recours à l'effet de levier, aux prime brokers, à l'investissement dans des positions de titrisation) ainsi que la commercialisation des parts et actions émises par les FIA (régime du passeport)*».

and bodies or other institutions which manage funds supporting social security and pension systems; employee participation schemes or employee savings schemes; securitization special purpose entities.

Investment firms do not fall within the scope of the AIFMD.[46] They are mentioned in the Recital of the Directive, which states that investment undertakings, such as family office vehicles which invest the private wealth of investors without raising external capital, should not be considered to be AIFs.[47]

Moreover, investment firms authorized under MIFID (2004/39/EC), as well as credit institutions authorized under the Capital Requirement Directive (2006/48/EC), should not be required to obtain an authorization under the AIFMD in order to provide investment services such as individual portfolio management. However, investment firms should be able to provide, directly or indirectly, shares or units of an AIF to investors in the EU or sell those shares to investors in the EU only to the extent that the shares may be sold in accordance with the AIFMD.[48]

Notwithstanding the choice to regulate fund managers, the AIFMD proposes a definition of "alternative investment fund," but it does not propose a definition of hedge funds nor of private equity funds and real estate funds, all subcategories that the AIF notion encompasses. The AIFMD provides a definition of AIF managers: AIFMs means legal persons whose regular business is managing one or more AIF.[49]

The definition of AIF has been amended between the proposal and the final version of the AIFMD. In the Proposal, AIFs were defined as "any collective investment undertaking including investment compartments thereof whose object is the collective investment in assets and which does not require authorisation pursuant to art. 5 of Directive 2009/.../EC [the UCITS IV Directive]."

In the final version of the AIFMD, Article 4 defines AIFs simply as:

"collective investment undertakings, including investment compartments thereof, which: (i) raise capital from a number of investors, with a view to investing it in accordance with a defined investment policy for the benefit of those investors; and (ii) do not require authorisation pursuant to art. 5 of Directive 2009/65/EC."

---

[46] Investment firms are defined in art. 4 of the MIFID as "undertakings the regular occupation or business of which is to provide investment services and/or perform investment activities on a professional basis. Its scope should not therefore cover any person with a different professional activity." Before MIFID, investment firms were regulated by Directive 93/22/CEE.

[47] AIFMD, Recital n. 7.

[48] AIFMD, Recital n. 9.

[49] AIFMD, art. 4, paragraph 1, lett. b).

Two fundamental elements of these funds emerge from this definition: first, a positive content, consisting of the activity of raising capital from a number of investors whose investment objective is a return for themselves through an investment strategy (generally speaking, an activity in their interest); secondly, a negative content, in terms of the clear distinction with UCITS funds, in the sense that the funds covered by the AIFMD do not require authorization pursuant to Article 5 of UCITS IV Directive (2009/65/EC).[50] With reference to the negative content of the definition,[51] some concerns with respect to this formulation have been expressed.[52]

An important element to be considered is the possibility that AIF managers may sell AIFs to retail investors[53]: "Without prejudice to other instruments of Union law, Member States may allow AIFMs to market to retail investors in their territory units or shares of AIFs they manage in accordance with this Directive, irrespective of whether such AIFs are marketed on a domestic or cross-border basis or whether they are EU or non-EU AIFs."[54] In such circumstances, member states may impose stricter requirements on the AIFM or the AIF than the requirements applicable to the AIFs marketed to professional

---

[50] TORCK S. (2013), La notion de fond d'investissement alternatif (FIA), *RTDF*, –special issue, 41. See also PUEL S. GOFFIN G., quoted, 108.

[51] The negative content of the definition is well radicated in the context of the EU: in this sense, it has to be considered even the *CESR's Guidelines on a common definition of European money market funds*, 19 May 2010, available at http://www.esma.europa.eu/system/files/10_049.pdf.

[52] See TORCK S., quoted, 40: "*Une définition négative des FIA eut toutefois été proprement insuffisante pour délimiter le périmètre de la directive AIFM car, au-delà de la nécessité de tracer une frontière nette entre OPCVM coordonnés et OPC non coordonnés, il était d'évidence nécessaire, ratione materiae cette fois, de dégager les principaux critères de nature à déclencher la mise en œuvre des règles chargées d'encadrer l'activité des sociétés gérant des fonds d'investissement dits alternatifs.*"

[53] According to art. 4, let. (aj) of the AIFMD, "retail investor" means an investor who is not a professional investor.

[54] AIFMD, art. 43. Recital 72 of the AIFMD specifies that "Member States should be able to allow the marketing of all or certain types of AIFs managed by AIFMs to retail investors in their territory. If a Member State allows the marketing of certain types of AIF, the Member State should make an assessment on a case-by-case basis to determine whether a specific AIF should be considered as a type of AIF which may be marketed to retail investors in its territory. Without prejudice to the application of other instruments of Union law, Member States should in such cases be able to impose stricter requirements on AIFs and AIFMs as a precondition for marketing to retail investors than is the case for AIFs marketed to professional investors in their territory, irrespective of whether such AIFs are marketed on a domestic or cross-border basis. Where a Member State allows the marketing of AIFs to retail investors in its territory, this possibility should be available regardless of the Member State where the AIFM managing the AIFs is established, and Member States should not impose stricter or additional requirements on EU AIFs established in another Member State and marketed on a cross-border basis than on AIFs marketed domestically. In addition, AIFMs, investment firms authorised under Directive 2004/39/EC and credit institutions authorised under Directive 2006/48/EC which provide investment services to retail clients should take into account any additional requirements when assessing whether a certain AIF is suitable or appropriate for an individual retail client or whether it is a complex or non-complex financial instrument."

investors in their territory in accordance with the Directive.[55] Member states that permit the marketing of AIFs to retail investors in their territory were to, by 22 July 2014, inform the Commission and ESMA of the types of AIF which AIFMs may market to retail investors in their territory, and any additional requirements that the member state imposed for the marketing of AIFs to retail investors.[56]

The choice of European regulators to provide the possibility for member states to allow the marketing of AIFs to retail investors confirms the erosion of one of the "common" characteristics of hedge funds; that is, their exclusive availability for qualified (professional) investors.

13.4 Further Specifications by ESMA

The definition contained in the AIFMD of AIF appears rather vague and not well determined, like many other definitions developed with reference to AIFs in general and hedge funds in particular. Considering the need to better specify the content of that definition in some of its key parts, ESMA launched a consultation process,[57] which ended with the enactment of the *Final Report Guidelines on key concepts of the AIFMD*.[58] This indicated more precisely the meaning and the scope of some essential elements traceable in the definition of AIF provided by the AIFMD: the notion of "collective investment undertakings", the activity of "raising capital", the "number of investors" and the notion of "defined investment policy."

Regarding the notion of "collective investment undertakings," ESMA has specified their content as follows:

(a) the undertaking does not have a general commercial or industrial purpose;
(b) the undertaking pools together capital raised from its investors for the purpose of investment with a view to generating a pooled return for those investors; and

---

[55] AIFMD, art. 43, subpara. 1.

[56] AIFMD, art. 43, para. 2.

[57] ESMA, *Consultation paper: Guidelines on key concepts of the AIFMD, ESMA/2012/845*, 19 December 2012, available at http://www.esma.europa.eu/system/files/2012-845.pdf.

[58] ESMA, *Final report Guidelines on key concepts of the AIFMD*, 24 May 2013, available at, http://www. esma.europa.eu/system/files/2013-600_final_report_on_guidelines_on_key_concepts_of_the_aifmd_0. pdf.

(c) the unit holders or shareholders of the undertaking—as a collective group—have no day-to-day discretion or control. The fact that one or more but not all of the aforementioned unit holders or shareholders are granted day-to-day discretion or control should not be taken to show that the undertaking is not a collective investment undertaking.[59]

With reference to the commercial activity, ESMA defines it as the commercial activity of taking direct or indirect steps by an undertaking or a person or entity acting on its behalf (typically, the AIFM) to procure the transfer or commitment of capital by one or more investors to the undertaking for the purpose of investing it in accordance with a defined investment policy should amount to the activity of raising capital mentioned in Article 4(1)(a)(i) of the AIFMD.[60]

The problem concerning the number of investors, which is undefined in the definition provided by the AIFMD ("raise capital from a number of investors"), has been clarified in the sense that an undertaking which is not prevented by its national law, the rules or instruments of incorporation, or any other provision or arrangement of binding legal effect, from raising capital from more than one investor should be regarded as an undertaking which raises capital from a number of investors in accordance with Article 4(1)(a)(i) of the AIFMD; and this should be the case even if it has in fact only one investor.[61] Moreover, it specifies the possibility that an undertaking involves only one investor: an undertaking which is prevented by its national law, the rules or instruments of incorporation or any other provision or arrangement of binding legal effect from raising capital from more than one investor should be regarded as an undertaking which raises capital from a number of investors in accordance with Article 4(1)(a)(i) of the AIFMD if the sole investor: (a) invests capital which it has raised from more than one legal or natural person with a view to investing it for the benefit of those persons; and (b) consists of an arrangement or structure which in total has more than one investor for the purposes of the AIFMD.[62]

---

[59] ESMA, *Guidelines on AIFMD key concepts*, 31. With reference to the proposed notion of collective investment, in the consultation process two respondents (asset managers' associations) recommended a clear identification of the boundary between an AIF(M) and a holding company. Moreover, another respondent asked for clarification to the expression "an entity whose purpose is to manage the underlying assets as part of a commercial or entrepreneurial activity"; in particular, this respondent asked ESMA to clarify the difference between this concept and an ordinary company with general commercial purpose.

[60] ESMA, *Guidelines*, quoted, 32.

[61] Ibid., 31.

[62] Ibid., 31.

Another crucial element is that of investment policies: an undertaking which has a policy about how the pooled capital in the undertaking is to be managed to generate a pooled return for the investors from whom it has been raised should be considered to have a defined investment policy in accordance with Article 4(1)(a)(i) of the AIFMD.[63] Moreover, ESMA identifies some elements that, singly or together, tend to indicate the existence of such a policy: (a) the investment policy is determined and fixed, at the latest by the time that investors' commitments to the undertaking become binding on them; (b) the investment policy is set out in a document which becomes part of or is referenced in the rules or instruments of incorporation of the undertaking; (c) the undertaking or the legal person managing the undertaking has an obligation (however this is defined) to investors, which is legally enforceable by them, to follow the investment policy, including all changes to it; (d) the investment policy specifies investment guidelines, with reference to criteria including any or all of the following: (i) to invest in certain categories of assets or conform to restrictions on asset allocation; (ii) to pursue certain strategies; (iii) to invest in particular geographical regions; (iv) to conform to restrictions on leverage; (v) to conform to minimum holding periods; or (vi) to conform to other restrictions designed to provide risk diversification.[64]

From the point of view of the structure of an AIF, it is important to consider Article 2, paragraph 1 of the AIFMD: via the definition of the scope of AIFMD, the European regulator has confirmed the non-significance of the structure of the fund in relation to the definition, since an AIF can be both open-ended or closed-ended (letter a) and can be created under contract law, under trust law, under statute or with any other legal form (letter b). Also in this regard, the Commission Delegated Regulation,[65] stating that an AIFM may manage both open-end funds and closed-end funds, implicitly confirms that an AIF can be both an open-end and a closed-end fund. In this context, following a consolidated approach, closed-end funds are defined in opposition to open-end funds. Therefore, for the latter it is possible to identify certain characteristics which are not detectable for closed-end funds.

The reason why it is important to distinguish open-end funds from closed-end funds even in the context of alternative investments depends on the

---

[63] Ibid., 32.

[64] Ibid., 32.

[65] Commission Delegated Regulation (Eu) 231/2013 of 19 December 2013 supplementing Directive 2011/61/EU of the European Parliament and of the Council with regard to regulatory technical standards determining types of AIF managers, available at http://ec.europa.eu/internal_market/investment/docs/alternative_investments/131217_delegated-regulation_en.pdf.

possibility to apply correctly the rules on liquidity management and the valuation procedures of Directive 2011/61/EU to AIFMs.[66]

The identification of the distinguishing criteria of the Commission Delegated Regulation proposed by ESMA in the Final Report Draft regulatory technical standards on types of AIFMs partially differs with respect to the final version (see note) adopted by the Commission.[67]

In the ESMA proposal, in fact, it can be read that:

"An AIFM of open-ended AIF(s) shall be considered to be an AIFM which manages at least one AIF, some or all of its unit holders or shareholders have the right to redeem their units or shares out of the assets of the AIF where all the following conditions are present:
(a) the right to redeem may be exercised at least once a year;
(b) in accordance with the rules or instrument of incorporation of the AIF or any prospectus the redemption is to be carried out at a price that, before any redemption fee is applied, does not vary significantly from the net asset value per unit/share of the AIF available at the time when the price is determined in accordance with the rules or instrument of incorporation of the AIF."[68]

Substantially, in the final version of the Commission Delegated Regulation, the conditions referred to in points (a) and (b) have been repealed.

Moreover, in order to define the type of fund, it has no significance for this purpose: first, a decrease in the capital of the AIF ("in connection with distributions according to the rules or instruments of incorporation of the AIF, its prospectus or offering documents, including one that has been authorised by a resolution of the shareholders or unitholders passed in accordance with those rules or instruments of incorporation, prospectus or offering documents"); and, secondly, based on the model of UCITS Directive,[69] the possibility that shares or units can be negotiated on the secondary market and repurchased or redeemed by the AIF.[70]

Taking into consideration the texts just mentioned, it is clear that there is no reference to hedge funds as an autonomous entity, nor is there a specific reference either to private equity funds, both of which are particularly relevant to AIFs. Moreover, Article 4, after specifying what is meant by AIFs (using a

---

[66] Commission Delegated Regulation, quoted, recital 2.

[67] ESMA (2013), *Final report, Draft regulatory technical standards on types of AIFMs*, 2 April 2013, available at http://www.esma.europa.eu/system/files/2013-413_0.pdf.

[68] ESMA, *Final report*, quoted, art. 1 para. 2.

[69] UCITS Directive, art. 1 (2) b.

[70] Commission Delegated Regulation, quoted, art. 1, para. 2.

rather general formula), highlights the absence of the same authorization for the activities of AIFs otherwise provided for harmonized investment funds that fall under the scope of the UCITS Directive.

Not only is there no specific reference to hedge funds as a separate entity, but the definition of Article 4, excepted for the authorization under the UCITS Directive, does not contain even a defining element that can distinguish AIFs from traditional funds.

This approach is justified by the European Commission: "while the focus is currently on hedge funds and private equity, the European Commission believes that it would be ineffective and short-sighted to limit any legislative initiative to these two categories of AIFM: ineffective because any arbitrary definition of these funds might not adequately capture all the relevant actors and could be easily circumvented; and short-sighted because many of the underlying risks are also present in other types of AIFM activity. The regulatory solution which is likely to prove the most enduring and productive is therefore to capture all AIFM whose activities give rise to those risks."[71]

This choice is consistent with the choice of the European regulator, in theory oriented to regulate the activities of AIFs, instead of identifying a precise definition.[72]

13.5   The AIFMD as a Model of Direct Regulation

The aim of European regulators was to provide a reference model of direct regulation for hedge funds and alternative investment vehicles not only at the European level.

Regulatory approaches—direct and indirect—correspond to two very different choices: while the first approach adopts regulatory tools such as registration, capital, leverage, margin and reporting requirements to directly regulate hedge funds and their activities, the latter focuses on entities related to hedge funds that act on them indirectly. However, despite obvious differences in the regulatory philosophy of the two approaches, many regulators favour a development in this direction.

A substantial convergence of regulatory solutions has been proposed in the text of the AIFMD and the Dodd-Frank Act, its Title IV discussing

---

[71] AIFMD, 5.

[72] In this sense the following sentence in the AIFMD can be read: "This proposal focuses on those activities that are specific or inherent to the AIFM sector and hence need to be addressed by targeted requirements," 5.

the Investment Adviser regulation: in both texts, a middle way was chosen between direct and indirect regulation.[73]

The debate about the usefulness and efficiency of one or the other approach originated in the USA in the aftermath of the crash of LTCM in 1998 (for the rescue of which the Federal Reserve organized and coordinated the activities of a pool of 16 banks). A President's Working Group, consisting of representatives of the Department of the Treasury, the Federal Reserve, the SEC (Securities and Exchange Commission) and the Commodity Futures Trading Commission, was set up. This had the merit of making the debate on hedge funds more systematic.

The President's Working Group referred to "indirect regulation," emphasizing the role played by hedge funds' counterparties and the importance of "market discipline" and "self-regulation" as capable of ensuring a reasonable level of leverage.[74]

One important aspect of the assessment of a direct or indirect regulatory approach is that hedge funds depend almost entirely on regulated companies for a variety of essential services, such as investment banking, prime brokerage, insurance and loans. Investment banks and broker–dealer firms often offer prime-brokerage services to hedge funds.[75]

---

[73] Kaal W. A., quoted.

[74] See President's Working Group (1999), Hedge Funds, Leverage, and the Lessons of Long-Term Capital Management, April 1999, available at http://www.cftc.gov/tm/tmhedgefundreport.htm: "in our market-based economy, market discipline of risk taking is the rule and government regulation is the exception. Generally, government regulation becomes necessary because of market failure or the failure of the pricing mechanism to account for all social costs. Government regulation of markets is largely achieved by regulating financial intermediaries that have access to the federal safety net, that play a central dealer role, or that raise funds from the general public. Any resort to government regulation should have a clear purpose and should be carefully evaluated in order to avoid unintended outcomes." See Cole R.T., Feldberg G. and Lynch D. (2007), Hedge funds, credit risk transfer and financial stability, in *Banque de France • Financial Stability Review—Special issue on hedge funds*—No. 10, 11. They underline that "Policy makers have subscribed to an indirect approach in dealing with many of the issues surrounding hedge funds. A key element of the indirect approach is the reliance upon market discipline—that is, relying on hedge fund investors, creditors, and counterparties to reward well-managed hedge funds and to reduce their exposure to risky, poorly managed hedge funds. To provide proper discipline, of course, market participants need to understand the activities of the hedge funds with which they do business, in order to assess their creditworthiness and risk-adjusted returns. While hedge funds are very reticent about sharing that kind of information, and are not usually required to do so by law or regulation, it is the responsibility of investors and counterparties to pressure funds to improve their disclosures. Well-managed funds should find that it is to their advantage to be more open about their activities. Lack of transparency should come at a great price, measured by fewer investors and less favorable treatment by banks. Although basic information about hedge fund activities has begun to flow, investors and counterparties still too often obtain very limited disclosure from hedge funds.".

[75] Pierre Louis L. N. C. (2009), *Hedge Fund Fraud and the Public Good*, Fordham Journal of Corporate and Financial Law, Vol. 15, No. 21, 21-95. 2009, 51.

In the following paragraphs the basic mechanisms of the AIFMD's implementation of a direct regulatory approach to alternative management will be analysed.

13.6 Authorization

The AIFMD has established the requirement of authorization in order to allow management of an AIF. The decision to establish an authorization system is the starting point in terms of model and mechanism behind the regulation of hedge funds. The consequence in terms of the regulatory model is the creation of a model that could be defined as "integrated" in the sense of a combination between a model of indirect regulation, aimed primarily at individuals and entities that interact with hedge funds, and one of direct regulation. The first instrument for the establishment of a direct regulation is authorization (equivalent to American registration), which is generally based on the provision of some limitations in relation to heterogeneous elements (leverage, capital requirements, organizational requirements). This regulatory framework is integrated with other provisions which directly affect the activities of hedge funds.

Through the implementation of a system of authorization, the AIFMD first puts in place the recommendations of IOSCO, in the sense of a combination of direct and indirect regulation.[76]

Through the provision of this authorization, AIF managers have to disclose some information to national authorities. Together with the preliminary information provided to the national authorities of the member states, they must provide additional information both to the authorities and investors over time.

Article 6, paragraph 1 is quite trenchant in establishing that member states shall ensure that no AIFMs manage AIFs unless they are authorized in accordance with the AIFMD. The authorization may be withdrawn by the competent authorities of the member state of the AIFM (Article 11) or amended in relation to its scope.[77]

Member states have to provide a mechanism according to which the AIFM must submit an application to the competent authorities of its home member

---

[76] IOSCO, Hedge Funds Oversight, quoted, 23. The IOSCO criteria on a mixture of direct and indirect regulation has been accepted by the majority of the respondents: "a balanced mixture of indirect and direct regulation of the hedge funds and/or their managers/advisers, consistent with the principle of proportionality and a risk-based approach."

[77] AIFMD, art. 11.

state (which is the only one that can release it) to obtain the authorization,[78] while ESMA shall keep a central public register identifying each AIFM authorized under this Directive, a list of the AIFs managed and/or marketed in the Union by such AIFMs and the competent authority for each such AIFM.[79] Moreover, in order to ensure consistent harmonization in this sense, ESMA has been granted the power eventually to develop draft regulatory technical standards to specify the information to be provided to the competent authorities in applying for authorization of the AIFM, including the programme of activity.[80]

The purpose of the creation of such an authorization system is to ensure a model of supervision and oversight that is effectively extended to all AIFMs operating in the EU without taking into consideration the domicile of the managed funds,[81] whose central element, or at least the initial stage around which to build this model, is the information to be provided by fund managers, together with the provision of their initial own capital and eventual additional capital.

13.7 Information To Be Provided

Authorization by the member states is realized only after the presentation of certain information. This information directly impacts on one of the main features of hedge funds, or more generally AIFs, which, as mentioned at the beginning of this chapter, share the characteristic of being secretive.

Managers of AIFs must provide the competent authorities of their home member state with much different information.

The first set of information relates specifically to AIF managers. In this it is possible to identify two subcategories: the first refers to the identification and participation of the managers, the fund and their partners of different kinds (letters a) and b)); the second refers more precisely to the activity of the fund (letters c), d), e)).

With reference to the first subcategory, information is required about the persons effectively conducting the business of the AIFM,[82] and, secondly,

---

[78] AIFMD, art. 7, paragraph 1.

[79] AIFMD, art. 7, paragraph 5.

[80] AIFMD, art. 7, paragraph 6.

[81] Baffi E., Lattuca D., Santella P. (2011), Extending the EU Financial Regulatory Framework to AIFM, Credit Derivatives, and Short Selling, p. 5, available at http://ssrn.com/abstract=1792993 or http://dx.doi.org/10.2139/ssrn.1792993.

[82] AIFMD, art. 7, paragraph 2, lett. a).

information about the identities of the AIFM's shareholders or members, whether direct or indirect, natural or legal persons, that have qualifying holdings, and the amounts of those holdings.[83]

With reference to the second subcategory (activities), the AIFMD requires information in relation to the programme of activity, setting out the organizational structure of the AIFM, including information on how the AIFM intends to comply with its obligations provided by the AIFMD.[84] The AIFMD also requires information on remuneration policies and practices, as well as information on arrangements made for the delegation and subdelegation to third parties of functions as referred to in Article 20.[85]

A second set of information that the manager of the AIF shall provide to the competent authorities of its home member state concerns information about the funds that the manager intends to manage.[86] Fund managers should first of all provide information about the investment strategies, including the types of underlying funds if the AIF is a fund of funds.[87] Moreover, information is required about the AIFM's policy with regard to the use of leverage, and the risk profiles and other characteristics of the AIFs it manages or intends to manage, including information about member states or third countries in which such AIFs are established or are expected to be established.[88]

Other information concerning the place where the master AIF is established, if the AIF is a feeder AIF, is required,[89] together with information on the rules or instruments of incorporation of each AIF the AIFM intends to manage,[90] as well as information on the arrangements made for the appointment of the depositary for each AIF that the AIFM intends to manage (in accordance with the provisions in this regard by the Directive),[91] and any additional information (information about investors referred to in Article 23 of the Directive).[92]

The information about the investment strategies adopted is particularly important. The request for this type of information is also linked to the pursuit of so-called "risk-transparency." The problem is that the pursuit of risk

---

[83] AIFMD, art. 7, paragraph 2, lett. b).

[84] AIFMD, art. 7, paragraph 2, lett c).

[85] AIFMD, art. 7, paragraph 2, lett. d) ed e).

[86] AIFMD, art. 7, paragraph 3.

[87] AIFMD, art. 7, paragraph 3, lett. a).

[88] AIFMD, art. 7, paragraph 3, lett. a).

[89] AIFMD, art. 7, paragraph 3, lett. b).

[90] AIFMD, art. 7, paragraph 3, lett. c).

[91] AIFMD, art. 7, paragraph 3, lett. d).

[92] AIFMD, art. 7, paragraph 3, lett. e).

transparency can lead to a contraction of a fundamental aspect of hedge funds, or the "proprietary nature of hedge fund investment strategies."[93]

The request for detailed information about the investment strategies for the purpose of authorization from the member states is, according to the perspective of the European regulators, a necessary condition for the pursuit of transparency. For it to be effective, a series of standards related to risk management (contained in Article 15 of the AIFMD), liquidity management (Article 16) and organizational requirements must be met. Chapter IV of the AIFMD, entitled "Transparency obligations," refers to a different period, since these reporting requirements concern the real course of business. They correspond to two obligations with respect to investors and national authorities. In relation to the former, the AIFM has to provide an annual report which contains the disclosures set out in the AIFMD Directive (Article 22) and implemented with the 2013 Commission Delegated AIFMD Regulation, together with the initial disclosures for the AIFs and the period disclosures (Article 23).[94] In relation to the latter, "an AIFM shall regularly report to the competent authorities of its home Member State on the principal markets and instruments in which it trades on behalf of the AIFs it manages. It shall provide information on the main instruments in which it is trading, on markets of which it is a member or where it actively trades, and on the principal exposures and most important concentrations of each of the AIFs it manages."[95]

13.8 Initial Capital and Own Funds

Among the conditions provided by the AIFMD for the purposes of authorization, member states shall require that an AIFM which is an internally managed AIF has an initial capital of at least €300,000.[96] Where an AIFM is appointed as external manager of AIFs, the AIFM shall have an initial capital of at least €125,000.[97]

Where the value of the portfolios of AIFs managed by the AIFM exceeds €250 million, the AIFM shall provide an additional amount of own funds.

---

[93] Lo W. (2001), *Risk Management for Hedge Funds: Introduction and Overview* (June 7, 2001), available at SSRN: http://ssrn.com/abstract=283308.

[94] See Moloney N. (2014), *EU Securities and Financial Markets Regulation* (Oxford University Press, 3rd edition), 303.

[95] AIFMD, art. 24. The frequency of the reports depends on the size and the complexity of the funds managed.

[96] AIFMD, art. 9, paragraph 1.

[97] AIFMD, art. 9, paragraph 2.

That additional amount shall be equal to 0.02 % of the amount by which the value of the portfolios of the AIFM exceeds €250 million; however, the required total of the initial capital and the additional amount shall not exceed €10 million.[98] But member states may authorise AIFMs not to provide up to 50 % of the additional amount of own funds referred to in paragraph 3 if they benefit from a guarantee of the same amount given by a credit institution or an insurance undertaking which has its registered office in a member state, or in a third country where it is subject to prudential rules considered by the competent authorities as equivalent to those laid down in EU law.[99]

Together with additional funds, the AIFMD requires other funds to be provided to cover potential professional liability risks resulting from activities that AIFMs may carry out, for both internally managed AIFs and external AIFMs, that shall either have additional own funds which are appropriate to cover potential liability risks arising from professional negligence,[100] or hold a professional indemnity insurance against liability arising from professional negligence which is appropriate to the risks covered.[101]

All the own funds shall be invested in liquid assets or assets readily convertible to cash in the short term and shall not include speculative positions.[102] This confirms their nature as "guarantee funds," and therefore they must be able to be easily sold.

13.9 Operational Requirements

One of the parts of the Directive which can lead to some considerations primarily focused on fund governance relates to operating conditions for AIFM, and this is divided into several sections. The first section outlines the general requirements, the second is devoted to organizational requirements, the third is dedicated to the delegation of AIFM functions, and the last is dedicated to the custodians, a key role from many points of view.

Reading the headings of the various sections contained in this part of the Directive, it can be assumed that the aim of the European regulators was to model a sort of mandatory structure for AIFs. In some respects such a structure could be defined as a fund governance model. With reference to the

---

[98] AIFMD, art. 9, paragraph 3.

[99] AIFMD, art. 9, paragraph 6.

[100] AIFMD, art. 9, paragraph 7, lett. a).

[101] AIFMD, art. 9, paragraph 7, lett. b).

[102] AIFMD, art. 9, paragraph 8.

practice, hedge funds are generally characterized by a thin structure, in which three entities can be identified (investors, the fund or funds managed, and the investment adviser/management company). For this reason AIFs (especially hedge funds) can be characterized by an *non-corporate governance*.[103]

In this first section of Chapter III of the AIFMD, elements related to the organizational perspective are approached: the issue of managers' remuneration together with general conflicts of interest within the fund, as well as more specific functions within the funds, such as risk management (Article 15) and liquidity management (Article 16).

These issues are typical for an analysis focused on corporate governance. In the specific context of the governance of hedge funds, it should take into account the specific problems between the various entities within the fund (investors, the fund and the investment/adviser/management company) and out of the fund, considering the other market players and stakeholders involved, since topical issues such as market integrity (see Article 12 paragraph 1, letter b)), systemic risk and liquidity risk not only involve internal entities in the fund. Such components may influence (and de facto influence) the governance of AIFs, especially hedge funds.

In general, hedge funds have tried to adopt forms or types of companies which have guaranteed a sort of *non-corporate governance*.[104] However, it is possible to identify a concept of fund governance of hedge funds,[105] with different issues and characteristics from those of mutual funds, as well as from those of classic companies and corporations, especially for reasons related to the different relationship between investors and fund managers and the different role of managers.

The corporate governance of hedge funds has steadily aroused interest over time. This is a consequence of the exponential increase of investments

---

[103] SHADAB H.B. (2009), The Law an Economics of Hedge Funds, *in Ber. Bus. Law J.*, Vol. 6.2, 247.

[104] See Part I of this work.

[105] On hedge fund governance see PLENDER J., A call to fix hedge fund governance, in *Financial Times*, 6 May 2012, available at http://www.ft.com/cms/s/0/f97ee96e-9467-11e1-8e90-00144feab49a. html#axzz2Iv09vpOy. See also DICKINSON C., *Feature Investor and regulatory pressures continue to force change in hedge fund corporate governance*, *Hedge Funds Review*, 6 July 2012, available at http://www. hedgefundsreview.com/hedge-funds-review/feature/2186894/investor-regulatory-pressures-continue-force-change-hedge-fund-corporate-governance. See also the PwC Survey on fund governance in Luxembourg, and UCITS and non-UCITS are compared, available at http://www.ila.lu/docs/ Presentation/2010/ILA%20PwC_151823_Mutual%20Fund%20Governance%20Survey_BAT%20 -%202010.03.10.pdf. For a survey on hedge fund governance, see CARNE, Global Financial Services, Corporate governance in hedge funds: Investor Survey 2011, available at https://www.castlehallalter-natives.com/upload/resources/CarneHedgeFundGovernanceSurveySept2011.pdf. See also, ASPINALL R., SMITH S. (2011), Corporate governance in investment funds Duties and responsibilities of directors revisited, available at http://www.deloitte.com/assets/Dcom-CaymanIslands/Local%20Assets/ Documents/R%20Aspinall%20article.pdf.

in hedge funds by institutional investors.[106] Whether the issue is considered from the point of view of hedge funds or investors, the development of fund governance has positive implications: from the point of view of hedge funds, it results in a greater interest from institutional investors and therefore the risk of losing these customers decreases; from the point of view of institutional investors, the development of corporate governance of hedge funds might lead to a mitigation of adverse selection.

A number of crucial elements related to the management, in a broad sense, of hedge funds emerge. After a series of general principles that open Chapter III of the AIFMD, some important areas are identified: the remuneration of managers (refer to the first part of this work for considerations of the peculiar structure of the remuneration of managers), conflicts of interest, risk management (with different characteristics from those existing in a different context) and the management of liquidity.

The remuneration policy requirements, detailed and controversial, reflect the crisis-era focus on the link between remuneration and risk management.[107] They are strongly influenced by those contained in the Capital Requirements Directive (as indeed evidenced by the regulator). Of course, the key principle is the same, and consists of the idea that "remuneration policies which encourage excessive risk-taking behavior can undermine sound and effective risk management of credit institutions and investment firms."[108]

Conflicts of interest are crucial from the perspective of the European regulators. Article 14 of the Directive, entitled Conflicts of Interest, reaffirms the obligation to take all reasonable steps designed to identify, prevent, manage and monitor conflicts of interest in order to prevent them from adversely affecting the interests of the AIFs and their investors. Moreover, the AIFMD expressly refers to typical conflicts of interest, in particular the one between the AIFM (including its managers, employees or any person directly or indirectly linked to the AIFM by control) and the AIF managed by the AIFM, or the investors in that AIF; two AIF or their investors; an AIF and another client of the AIFM, or, alternatively, a UCITS (or its investors) managed by the AIFM; finally, two clients of the AIFM.

---

[106] See MOODY'S INVESTOR SERVICE, *Hedge Fund Governance and Oversight*, July 2011. "Corporate governance practices for hedge fund firms are more closely examined today than at any other time in the history of the industry [...] hedge funds firms have experienced a shift in their investor composition from high net worth individual investors to institutional investors [...]. Institutional investors have shown that they view the evaluation of governance and oversight as it relates to risk management, valuations, operational controls, transparency and the investment process as important as analysing a hedge fund manager's investment performance."

[107] See N. Moloney, quoted, 295.

[108] See, for example, Recital 62 of the Capital Requirements Directive.

The AIFMD goes in the direction of ensuring the independence of the risk management function, both functionally and hierarchically, from all other operational functions, including even portfolio management.[109] The risk management function must not only be functionally and hierarchically independent, but must also be permanent.[110]

In Sect. 13.2, the AIFMD approaches some issues more specifically related to the organizational structure, since topical issues such as the valuation of the assets as well as the delegation of functions to third parties and the role of depositaries are addressed here. The valuation of the fund's assets, particularly in the sense of a more or less marked independence from the AIFM in carrying out the assessment, was one of the most debated issues in the course of the negotiation of the AIFMD, because hedge fund managers consider this element central in maintaining the confidentiality of their investment strategies.

13.10 Leverage

Under the AIFMD, leverage is defined as "any method by which the AIFM increases the exposure of an AIF it manages whether through borrowing of cash or securities, or leverage embedded in derivative positions or by any other means."[111] Leverage is a concept typically associated with banking regulation,[112] but the necessity to obtain more detailed information about the use of leverage in alternative management (especially for hedge funds) induced the European regulators to introduce some provisions in this regard.

The AIFMD provides for a lighter regime for AIFM when the cumulative AIFs under management are lower than the threshold of €100 million, or €500 million for those AIFM the managed funds of which are not leveraged and do not grant investors redemption rights for a period of five years.[113] But

---

[109] AIFMD, art. 15, paragraph 1.

[110] Commission Delegated Regulation, art. 39: "AIFM shall establish and maintain a permanent risk management function."

[111] AIFMD, Art. 4, para. 1, v.

[112] Moloney. N., quoted, 301.

[113] Such a choice of the European Commission depended on the circumstance that extending these regulatory requirements to small managers would impose costs and administrative burden, which would not be justified by the benefits. Moreover, on this basis, supervisory attention will be focused on the areas where risks are concentrated. A threshold of €100 million implies that roughly 30 % of hedge fund managers, managing almost 90 % of assets of EU domiciled hedge funds, would be covered by the Directive. It would capture almost half of managers of other non-UCITS funds and provide an almost full coverage of the assets invested in their funds. See in this sense European Commission, Proposal, quoted, 7.

it is clear that such a quantitative distinction has no implications in terms of the definition of different subcategories of AIFs.

The methods of calculation of the leverage, provided in the Commission Delegated AIFMD Regulation, are the same provided for the UCITS Directive (so-called "gross" and "commitment").

The use of leverage shall be disclosed to investors (in the initial document and periodically) as well as to supervisory authorities (since the authorization process and periodically). The purpose of disclosure to supervisory authorities consists of identifying systemic risk in the financial system, risks of disorderly markets or risks to the long-term growth of the economy.[114] The AIFM shall set a maximum level of leverage which it may employ for each AIF it manages, taking into account inter alia the type of AIF, the investment strategy and the source of leverage.[115] The AIFM shall also demonstrate that the leverage limits set by it for each AIF it manages are reasonable and that it complies with those limits at all times. The competent authorities shall assess the risks that the use of leverage by an AIFM with respect to the AIFs it manages could entail, and, where deemed necessary in order to ensure the stability and integrity of the financial system, the competent authorities of the home member state of the AIFM, after having notified ESMA, the ESRB (European Systemic Risk Board) and the competent authorities of the relevant AIF, shall impose limits to the level of leverage that an AIFM is entitled to employ or other restrictions on the management of the AIF with respect to all the AIFs under its management, to limit the extent to which the use of leverage contributes to the build up of systemic risk in the financial system or risks of disorderly markets.[116]

13.11   Critical Remarks

Following the recommendations issued by IOSCO, the EU combined a direct and an indirect regulatory approach to regulate AIFs. At the same time the European regulators have opted for highly detailed regulation, which may have the effect of limiting the role of self-regulation.

Considering the direct regulatory approach, the benefits of this choice will consist especially in providing information and data about the alternative investments that otherwise could never have been collected.

---

[114] AIFMD, art. 25, para. 1.
[115] AIFMD, art. 15, para. 4.
[116] AIFMD, art. 23, para. 3.

A few comments about the American context will be very helpful in evaluating the concrete role and the benefits arising from the direct regulation of AIFs (defined in the Dodd-Frank Act as "private funds").[117] As is well known, the USA has successfully adopted a strategy that is similar to the European one, both in terms of definition of a broad category of AIFs and in terms of direct regulation combined with indirect regulation. The American regulators implemented the obligations of the registration for the majority of the investment vehicles through the Dodd-Frank Act, which considerably amended the previous regulatory framework (in particular amending the Advisers Act), characterized by numerous exemptions granted to hedge funds and private equity funds.

For the first time since the enactment of the new regulatory framework, the SEC has published a report on private funds,[118] taking into account the information collected under the new registration regime (with the ADV and PF forms that have to be filed by the majority of the asset managers).[119] As the chairman of the SEC Marie Jo White has emphasized, "Registration and reporting have given us significant insight into the nearly 30,000 private funds managed by 4,500 registered advisers, which helps us to understand potential risks for both individual firms and the broader financial system. We have learned, for example, a great deal about the size, geographic distribution, and investment concentrations in the industry. We have also begun to analyse data reflecting private fund strategies, including the use of leverage and counterparty exposures. Excessive leverage, lack of liquidity, and asset concentrations have in the past been at the root of financial crises, and we now have the regulatory tools to help better identify and appropriately mitigate potential problems."[120] Similar data will soon be available even in the European market.

The next steps will consist in understanding how these data may be useful in providing some structural modifications to the recent regulatory framework

---

[117] The Dodd-Frank Act (§ 402) defines a "private fund" as an issuer that would be an investment company, as defined in Section 3 of the Investment Company Act of 1940, but for Section 3(c)(1) or 3(c)(7) of that Act. This complexity in the formulation depends on the system of exemptions from registration for funds with fewer than 100 investors or funds whose investors are all "qualified purchasers," usually natural persons who have assets equal to at least $5 million or even advisers who possess or discretionally invest at least $25 million. The most common definition provided in the USA states that they are "any pooled investment vehicle that is privately organized, administered by professional investment managers, and not widely available to the public."

[118] SEC, Division of Investment Management, Private Funds Statistics, Fourth Calendar Quarter 2014, 16 October 2015, available at https://www.sec.gov/divisions/investment/private-funds-statistics/private-funds-statistics-2014-q4.pdf.

[119] See for example Form PF, available at https://www.sec.gov/about/forms/formpf.pdf.

[120] WHITE M. J. (2015), Five Years On: Regulation of Private Fund Advisers after Dodd-Frank, 16 October 2015, available at http://www.sec.gov/news/speech/white-regulation-of-private-fund-advisers-after-dodd-frank.html.

adopted by the different jurisdictions, in particular the European and the American ones.

These data will also give the opportunity to conduct a more consistent cost–benefit analysis (ex-post) that may have an impact on the decisions of regulators, not only in relation to alternative investment management, but also in relation to the shadow banking system as well as the banking sector and its transformations in general. It will be important to evaluate the adoption of a model more clearly oriented towards a risk-based approach, which will emphasize the importance of monitoring the activities existing in the market, independently of the formal categories of the entities that generate it.

In addition, it will be important to clarify, from a risk-based perspective, whether many regulatory solutions in relation to the corporate governance of AIFs, disclosure and reporting requirements implemented by the AIFMD are driven by the need to protect investors or to ensure financial stability: regulators seem to have overestimated the importance of protection from risks related to systemic risk and financial stability. A clear example in this sense is related to the risk management function in hedge funds: this function proved to be robust even before the enactment of the AIFMD. The reason for the robustness of the risk management processes within hedge funds is the relationship between these processes and "alpha" yields: in fact, the more efficient the risk management, the higher the yields,[121] and managers are the first to be interested in high "alpha" yields. The manager has an economic interest in efficient risk management.[122] With regard to this particular issue, rather than making substantial changes, the AIFMD seems to have simply taken note of the soundness of the results derived from a model of self-regulation that already contained the minimum requirements of risk management.

From a structural perspective, a direct regulatory approach may have some consequences: each national market authority as well as ESMA shall consider creating working groups that are more and more focused on alternative management and analysis of the data arising from the new direct approach, as the American SEC did. The American agency has successfully implemented its structure, with the creation within the Division of Investment Management (Risk and Examinations Office) of a group focused on the analysis of hedge funds and private equity funds.

Taking into account the second issue (highly detailed regulation), one of the consequences of the AIFMD relates to the role of self-regulation, enhancing the importance of public regulation in the context of AIFs. The choice

---

[121] Lo A. W. (2001), quoted.

[122] Awrey D., quoted, 122. See also Shadab H.B., *The Law and Economics of Hedge Funds*, quoted, 11.

to reduce the role of self-regulation is politically driven and is based on the assumption that self-regulatory organizations mainly operate in the interest of their members. This raises concerns in relation to inadequate incentives for the enforcement of a set of rules, the purpose of which may be the effective protection of communities' interests.

A strong limitation of self-regulation as well as a weak dialogue between self-regulatory organizations and public institutions may be highly inefficient and counterproductive, considered the high specialization required in this field. Self-regulation can have advantages for both regulators and the industry. For this reason IOSCO recommended the importance of a well-integrated public regulation with self-regulation.[123] A clear example of the advantages of an intense dialogue between private and public authorities has been the regulation of hedge funds in the UK: the FSA (now FCA) developed an efficient mechanism of consultation that involved different categories of professionals, with the consequence that a flexible and effective regulatory framework for alternative management was provided.[124]

In the future, a revitalization of the role of self-regulatory organizations will be crucial in order to improve the regulations implemented in the different jurisdictions.[125]

13.12 Conclusions

The decision to regulate hedge funds has had a strong political dimension: the AIFMD is therefore a political product. This explains the difficulties surrounding its approval and implementation.

Notwithstanding this political approach to the regulation of AIFs, the AIFMD is undoubtedly a further step towards a complete and effective regulation of the alternative entities existing and operating in the financial markets.

The AIFMD, through its rules on authorization, initial capital and funds, operational requirements and leverage, clearly establishes direct regulation for

---

[123] IOSCO (2009), Technical Committee, Hedge Funds Oversight, June 2009, paragraph 5.

[124] TIFFITH L. (2007), *Hedge Fund Regulation: What the FSA Is Doing Right and Why the SEC Should Follow the FSA's Lead. Northwestern J. of Int Law & Bus* 27 (2007 2006), 497.

[125] See CAFAGGI F. (2006), Rethinking Private Regulation in the European Regulatory Space, Reframing Self-Regulation, *in European Private Law*, Kluwer Law Publ. Paper, 2006. Available at http://cadmus.eui.eu/bitstream/handle/1814/4369/LAW2006.13.PDF;jsessionid=C75C897F5D17F4052CCC2500F282B83D?sequence=1, 4. The author notes that "the expansion of private regulation is perceived—somewhat ideologically—either as an expression of privatization or as a tool intended to reregulate liberalized or deregulated fields in a more regulated-friendly environment." Indeed, "the more relevant role of private actors does not (necessarily) coincide either with deregulation or with a lower degree of regulation."

AIFs (technically for AIF managers), which are defined through the adoption of a broad categorization. The benefits arising from this choice will emerge in the next few years, when the data and general information collected by regulators will be helpful in strategically addressing further development of the regulation.

At the same time, European regulators will have to consider a revitalization of the role of self-regulation, enhancing the critical interaction of public regulation with self-regulatory organizations.

14

The Regulation of CCPs in Europe: The European Market Infrastructure Regulation (EMIR)

Marco Dell'Erba

14.1 Introduction

Market infrastructures and clearing houses are established entities in the context of financial markets. With the establishment of the Dojima Rice Exchange in Osaka in 1697, commodity futures were regularly exchanged.[1] The London Clearing House Clearnet (LCH) was created in 1888 as a central counterparty (CCP) for commodities.[2] Starting from that time, clearing houses became powerful institutions, capable of sustaining trading activities in financial markets.[3]

---

[1] Treadwell T. (2013), OTC Clearing in Japan: Solid Start for Interest Rate Swaps, Future Industry, January 2013, 41.

[2] Papathanassiou C. (2015), Central counterparties and derivatives, Kern A. and Dhumale R. (ed.), Research handbook on international financial regulation (Routledge I ed. 2015), 217.

[3] Yadav Y. & Turing D. (2015), The Extra-Territorial Regulation of Clearing Houses, 8.

We wish to thank John P. Drohan III, Esq. for helpful comments and encouragement.

M. Dell'Erba (✉)
Post-Doctoral Fellow LabEx ReFi, IRJS - Université Paris I Panthéon Sorbonne, Paris, France

© The Author(s) 2017
R. Douady et al. (eds.), *Financial Regulation in the EU*,
DOI 10.1007/978-3-319-44287-7_14

"

In the last two decades, the debate about designing resilient market infrastructures (particularly CCPs) has become more and more relevant.

Since 1998, the G10 report on settlement of over-the-counter (OTC) derivatives has provided a strong impetus for the expansion of CCP services from exchange-traded to OTC derivatives,[4] with the purpose of mitigating counterparty risk.[5]

From 2001 onwards, the activity of the Committee of Payment and Settlement Systems (CPSS) and the Technical Committee of the International Organization of Securities Commissions (IOSCO) has been more and more focused on market infrastructures.[6] In November 2004, the CPSS and Technical Committee of IOSCO issued 15 Recommendations for CCPs, which addressed the major types of risk faced by CPSS and a methodology for assessing a CCP's observance of each recommendation. In January 2009, a working group was created to provide guidance on the application of these recommendations to CCPs that clear OTC derivative products.

The financial crisis of 2007–8 significantly contributed to the enhancement of cooperation at international level in order to establish and regulate CCPs, in particular the positive experience related to the resolution of futures portfolios in the Lehman default.[7] The G20 (Pittsburgh, September 2009) confirmed the importance of strengthening the International Financial Reporting Standards (IFRS), expanding the scope of regulation and oversight, with tougher regulation of OTC derivatives, stating that "All standardized OTC derivative contracts should be traded on exchanges or electronic trading platforms, where appropriate, and cleared through central counterparties by end-2012 at the latest. OTC derivative contracts should be reported to trade repositories. Non-centrally cleared contracts should be subject to higher capital requirements. We ask the FSB and its relevant members to assess regularly implementation and whether it is sufficient to improve transparency in the derivatives markets, mitigate systemic risk, and

---

[4] CPSS-IOSCO, 'OTC derivatives: settlement procedures and counterparty risk management', 1998, available at http://www.bis.org/cpmi/publ/d27.pdf.

[5] Papathanassiou C., quoted, 217.

[6] See CPSS-IOSCO (2001), Core principles for systemically important payment systems, January 2001, and CPSS-IOSCO, Recommendations for securities settlement systems (RSSS), November 2001.

[7] See Chander A. & Costa R. (2010), Clearing Credit Default Swaps: A Case Study in Global Legal Convergence, *Chicago Journal of International Law*, Winter 2010, 10, 2, 647.

protect against market abuse."[8] In 2012, the CPSS and the IOSCO issued the principles for financial market infrastructure. Since then there has been a constant monitoring of the level of implementation of the Regulation in each jurisdiction.[9]

In the aftermath of the financial crisis, the majority of jurisdictions have implemented or are in the process of implementing regulations to accommodate the clearing obligation for derivatives and the establishment of CCPs. According to the Financial Stability Board, which on an annual basis conducts an assessment of the major jurisdictions with respect to, inter alia, the implementation of the central clearing regulation, the majority of jurisdictions has central clearing requirements in effect and in the process of further implementations.[10]

This chapter provides some preliminary information in order to understand CCPs: it approaches the definition of clearing houses and their functions, highlights the advantages and disadvantages of CCPs, and provides an overview of the European Market Infrastructure Regulation (EMIR).

14.2   Definition of Market Infrastructure and CCPs

Various institutions have provided a definition of market infrastructures and clearing houses.

IOSCO (Principles for Financial market infrastructures, April 2012) has defined a market infrastructure as a multilateral system among participating institutions, including the operator of the system, used for the purposes of clearing, settling or recording payments, securities, derivatives or other financial transactions. Market infrastructures typically establish a

---

[8] G20 Leaders Statement (2009), The Pittsburgh Summit, 24 September 2009, point 14.

[9] See CPSS-IOSCO Implementation monitoring of PFMIs – Level 1 assessment report, August 2013, available at http://www.bis.org/cpmi/publ/d111.pdf. See also FSB, OTC Derivatives Market Reforms Eighth Progress Report on Implementation, 7 November 2014, available at http://www.financialstabilityboard.org/wp-content/uploads/r_141107.pdf?page_moved=1.

[10] See Financial Stability Board (2016), 20 August 2016, OTC Derivatives Market Reforms Eleventh Progress Report on Implementation, available at http://www.fsb.org/wp-content/uploads/OTC-Derivatives-Market-Reforms-Eleventh-Progress-Report.pdf.

set of common rules and procedures for all participants, a technical infrastructure and a specialized risk management framework appropriate to the risks they incur. Their main activities concern centralized clearing, settlement and recording of financial transactions among themselves or between each of them, and a central party to allow for greater efficiency and reduced costs and risks. IOSCO emphasizes that through the centralization of specific activities, market infrastructures also allow participants to manage their risk more efficiently and effectively, and in some instances to eliminate certain risks. Financial market infrastructures can also promote increased transparency in particular markets. Some market infrastructures are critical to helping central banks conduct monetary policy and maintain financial stability.

Another characteristic associated with market infrastructures is their heterogeneity, since they can differ in organization, function and design.[11]

Consistent with the definition provided by IOSCO,[12] American regulators in the Dodd-Frank Act Wall Street Reform and Consumer Protection Act of 2010 provided a definition of financial market utilities (FMUs): they are defined as multilateral systems that provide the infrastructure for transferring, clearing and settling payments, securities and other financial transactions among financial institutions or between financial institutions and the system.[13]

The Oxford Finance Group noted that a possible definition of an infrastructure encompasses these characteristics: "1) is, or provides, the basic framework that supports or underlies a system, defined quite broadly; 2) is essential to support commerce, economic activity and development, or whatever other activities are facilitated by the system it operates; 3) is, or operates, a network, which in the economic sphere facilitates the delivery of goods and services; 4) exhibits economies of scale; 5) requires large, long-term, and sunk investments; 6) is, or operates, a natural monopoly; 7) provides beneficial public goods or services, in addition to the specific goods and services it delivers directly; 8) has some form of government or public sector involvement, defined very broadly."[14]

---

[11] CPSS-IOSCO, Principles for Financial Market Infrastructures, quoted.

[12] Lubben S. (2014), Nationalize clearing houses!, June 2014, available at Seton Hall Public Law Research Paper No. 2458506. Available at SSRN: http://ssrn.com/abstract=2458506 or http://dx.doi.org/10.2139/ssrn.2458506.

[13] Board of Governors of the Federal Reserve (2015), Designated Financial Market Utilities, available at http://www.federalreserve.gov/paymentsystems/designated_fmu_about.htm.

[14] Lee R. (2010), The Governance of Financial market Infrastructure, Oxford Finance Group, 2010, viii.

More difficulties are posed by the notion of CCP. "A wide range of factors have led to disagreement and uncertainty in such a topic, and also to some confusion about which organizations should be classified as an exchange, a CCP, or a CSD (Central Securities Depository)."[15]

In this respect, IOSCO defines CCPs as "persons that interpose themselves between counterparties to contracts traded in one or more financial markets, becoming the buyer to every seller and the seller to every buyer, through a mechanism of novation."[16] EMIR adopts this definition.

Moreover, despite the generally accepted understanding of how clearing, settlement and other post-trade activities are organized, there are particular difficulties in classifying the processes of clearing and settlement.[17]

EMIR defines "clearing" as the process of establishing positions, including the calculation of net obligations, and ensuring that financial instruments, cash or both are available to secure the exposure arising from those positions.[18]

In responding to the Commission Communication *Clearing and Settlement in the European Union* (COM(2004)312), the European Association of Counterparty Clearing Houses (EACCH) has proposed a functional approach (i.e. focusing on the functions carried out by clearing houses in order to provide a definition) for clearing houses, as well as for each single activity of "clearing," "settlement" and "custody."[19]

The document emphasizes that "clearing" is performed on different levels; "firstly by trading parties for their clients, secondly at central counterparty clearing houses (CCP Clearing) and thirdly at central securities depositories (CSD/ICSD Clearing) or banking institutions (for internal executions) for public market participants."[20] It further specifies that "CCP clearing concentrates on trade management, position management, collateral and risk management, and delivery management" and that "it exists in two forms, either as a CCP, in which case the CCP becomes the counterparty of the original buyer and seller, or as a facilitator, in which case the original buyer and seller remain legal counterparties to each other."[21] With regard to the latter, "clearing focuses on validating and matching the delivery instructions; the result

---

[15] Ibid.

[16] CPSS-IOSCO, quoted, para. 1.13, 9.

[17] Lee R., quoted, ix.

[18] EMIR, art. 2, n.2).

[19] European Association of Counterparty Clearing Houses (2004), Functional Definition of a Central Counterparty Clearing House (CCP), available at http://ec.europa.eu/internal_market/financial-markets/docs/clearing/2004-consultation/each-annex3_en.pdf.

[20] Ibid.

[21] Ibid.

of which is forwarded to settlement."[22] "Due to these specifications, CCP clearing takes place prior to the clearing performed by CSDs. CSD clearing concentrates on validating and matching the delivery instructions; the result of which is forwarded to settlement."[23]

A CCP may also be involved not only in the activity of clearing but also in the settlement. It can be effected using netting within a CCP process, as a facilitation service provided by central security depositories in conjunction with their custodian services and central banks or correspondent banks. In the case of internal trade, however, this process is also performed by banking institutions.[24]

In addition, EACCP underlined that "netting, risk management and collateral management are often associated with CCP," whereas "delivery versus payment" and "free of payment" are often associated with settlement, and corporate actions are generally referred to custodians.[25]

14.2.1   The Functions of CCPs

CCPs should serve as a source of financial stability, even in extreme market conditions, by virtue of their risk-reduction benefits.[26] From this perspective, credit and liquidity risk management, together with the adequacy of financial resources, is crucial.

CCPs, and more generally financial market infrastructures, are designed to enhance safety and efficiency in the different post-trade phases, as well as to limit systemic risk and foster transparency and financial stability.[27] As already mentioned, CCPs interpose themselves between counterparties to contracts traded in one or more financial markets, becoming the buyer to every seller and the seller to every buyer, through a mechanism of novation.[28] More precisely, multilateral netting is at the basis of this mechanism. Netting consists in "offsetting an amount due from a member on one transaction against an amount owed to that member or another, to reach a single, smaller net

---

[22] Ibid.

[23] Ibid.

[24] Ibid.

[25] Ibid.

[26] See CPSS-IOSCO, Principles for financial market infrastructures, April 2012, 9 and 36, available at http://www.bis.org/cpmi/publ/d101a.pdf. The IOSCO principles provide a set of principles on credit risk management, collateral, margin and liquidity risk management, and they are clearly interconnected.

[27] Ibid., quoted, 10.

[28] Ibid., quoted, para. 1.13, 9.

exposure: when trades are centrally cleared, the original counter-parties' contracts with one another are replaced or 'novated' – with a pair of equal and opposite contracts with a CCP, so the CCP becomes the buyer to the original seller, and the seller to the original buyer."[29]

The potential to significantly reduce risks is based on the multilateral netting of trades as well as on more effective risk controls, assuming that reducing risks to participants implies reducing systemic risk.[30]

Financial market infrastructures may "face systemic risk because the inability of one or more participants to perform as expected could cause other participants to be unable to meet their obligations when due."[31] In the context of derivatives, together with the underlying trading risk, a major source of risk is the counterparty credit risk that can be dangerous in the context of credit default swaps.[32] Counterparty credit risk is "the basic way in which OTC derivatives may cause systemic risk and it is precisely one of the causes that central clearing houses address: it is extremely different to hedge and is inherent in every derivatives transaction."[33]

Liquidity risk may be connected to systemic risk. It is defined as "financial market infrastructures and their participants may face liquidity risk, which is "the risk that a counterparty, whether a participant or other entity, will have insufficient funds to meet its financial obligations as and when expected, although it may be able to do so in the future."[34] Financial market infrastructure as well as their participants may be exposed to liquidity risk and increase systemic risk: "liquidity problems have the potential to create systemic problems, particularly if they occur when markets are closed or illiquid or when asset prices are changing rapidly, or if they create concerns about solvency."[35]

---

[29] Rehlon A. & Nixon D. (2013), Central counterparties: what are they, why do they matter and how does the Bank supervise them?, Bank of England Quarterly Bulletin 2013 Q2, available at http://www.bankofengland.co.uk/publications/Documents/quarterlybulletin/2013/qb1302ccpsbs.pdf.

[30] CPSS-IOSCO, quoted, 9.

[31] CPSS-IOSCO, quoted, para. 2.2.

[32] Griffith S.J. (2012), Governing Systemic Risk: Towards a Governance Structure for Derivatives Clearinghouses, *Emory Law Journal*, Vol. 61, No. 5, 2012; Fordham Law Legal Studies Research Paper No. 2157693. Available at SSRN: http://ssrn.com/abstract=2157693.

[33] Griffith S.J., quoted, 1163. On the causes of systemic risk through derivatives see also Whitehead C.K. (2010), Destructive Coordination, *Cornell Law Review*, Vol. 96, No. 2, p. 323, 2011; Cornell Legal Studies Research Paper No. 010-012. Available at SSRN: http://ssrn.com/abstract=1656075 and the Volcker Rule and Evolving Financial Markets (June 1, 2011). *Harvard Business Law Review*, Vol. 1, 2011; Cornell Legal Studies Research Paper No. 11-19. Available at SSRN: http://ssrn.com/abstract=1856633. See also Duffie D. & Lubke T. (2010) Policy Perspectives on OTC Derivatives Market Infrastructure Li, Policy Perspectives on OTC Derivatives Market Infrastructure (March 2010). FRB of New York Staff Report No. 424. Available at SSRN: http://ssrn.com/abstract=1534729.

[34] CPSS-IOSCO, quoted, para. 2.6.

[35] Ibid.

Together with netting, risk management and collateral management are typical operations and functions of CCPs.[36]

The so-called default-waterfall mechanism is determinant in this sense. Its purpose consists in managing credit risk, more specifically replacement cost risk.[37] A default-waterfall mechanism consists of a series of rules, arrangements and resources to ensure that CCPs can respond in an orderly and efficient way to a member defaulting.[38] This is sometimes achieved through an "auction" of the defaulter's positions among surviving members. In terms of resources to cover its obligations, CCPs typically have access to financial resources provided by the defaulting party, the CCP itself and the other, non-defaulting members of the CCP.[39] The order in which these are drawn down helps to create appropriate incentives for all parties (members and CCPs) to manage the risks they take on.[40]

Collateral plays a primary role in the context of the risk-waterfall mechanism: together with regulatory capital, they are "a primary method of reserving against losses arising in the event of a counterparty default."[41] Collateral is crucial from the perspective of credit and liquidity risk management operations. IOSCO recommends that a financial market infrastructure "should accept collateral with low credit, liquidity, and market risk,"[42] because of the importance of its confidence in "the collateral's value in the event of liquidation and of its capacity to use that collateral quickly, especially in stressed market conditions."[43]

Collateral plays a dual role in relation to credit risk and liquidity risk. With respect to the former, in the context of risk waterfall,[44] collateral provided by the defaulting member is the first line of defence.[45] At the same

---

[36] EACCP, Functional Definition of a Central Counterparty Clearing House (CCP).

[37] Wendt F. (2015), Central Counterparties: Addressing their Too Important to Fail Nature, 2015, 8, available at https://www.imf.org/external/pubs/ft/wp/2015/wp1521.pdf. The author notes that other tools exist to manage liquidity risk, such as accepting only high quality liquid collateral, monitoring payment flows, stress testing liquidity needs and maintaining committed credit lines with commercial banks and/or a routine intraday credit line with the central bank if available. A CCP can in no way count on emergency liquidity assistance of a central bank to manage its liquidity risk.

[38] Ibid.

[39] Ibid.

[40] Ibid.

[41] Chander A. & Costa R., quoted. About regulatory capital the authors underline that it is unimpaired equity that must be held on the balance sheet of regulated entities, such as banks and broker dealers.

[42] CPSS-IOSCO, quoted, Principle 5: Collateral.

[43] Ibid., quoted, para. 3.5.2.

[44] A risk waterfall is a tiered loss absorption mechanism consisting of layers of protection that a CCP accesses to satisfy the losses following the default of a clearing member: see Wendt F., quoted, 8, available at https://www.imf.org/external/pubs/ft/wp/2015/wp1521.pdf.

[45] Rehlon A. & Nixon D., quoted.

time, collateral plays a crucial role with respect to liquidity risk.[46] CCPs require an initial and a variation margin. The initial margin serves to "cover potential future exposures in the interval between the last margin collection and the close out of positions following a participant default."[47] Variation margin (or "mark-to-market margin") "reflects the rapid changes in prices, positions, or both, that may have the effect to rapidly increase the exposures to clearing members."[48]

Together with collateral, in a risk waterfall-mechanism there are different layers: the default fund of the defaulting clearing member, the CCP's capital or "skin in the game" (pre-defined contribution to the loss allocation waterfall, a part of its own capital), the default fund contributions of surviving clearing members, the assessment calls to be made by the CCP (requesting replenishment of funds by surviving clearing members and/or other loss-sharing calls) and finally the remaining capital of the CCP, which will cease its operations when the capital is exhausted.[49]

14.3 Pros and Cons of CCPs

14.3.1 Benefits of Clearing Houses

Many advantages of CCPs are connected to stronger risk-management practices as well as enhanced transparency, which has many consequences.

From a general risk-management perspective, "the reduction (through netting and collateralisation), the mutualisation and the orderly distribution of losses are the key differences comparing trades that are centrally cleared with non-cleared transactions."[50]

CCPs may provide a multilateral netting of exposure: this means in concrete terms that, differently from a bilateral netting, "a given level of risk protection can be achieved with a smaller amount of collateral, or vice versa, and a given amount of collateral can achieve a higher level of risk

---

[46] Other instruments are represented by monitoring payment flows, stress testing liquidity needs and maintaining committed credit lines with commercial banks and/or a routine intraday credit line with the central bank if available. See F. Wendt, quoted, 8.

[47] CPSS-IOSCO, quoted, para. 3.6.6.

[48] Ibid., quoted, para. 3.6.11. See also Chander A. & Costa R., quoted, 647.

[49] See Wendt F., quoted, 8–9.

[50] Rehlon A. & Dan Nixon D., quoted.

protection."[51] Moreover, compared to CCPs margin and risk management methods, bilateral schemes either rely "on standardised margining methods that are not very risk-sensitive or on bank-internal margining models whose standards may not be as high as the ones that CCPs are required to meet."[52]

From a transparency perspective, CCPs may have an impact in reducing information asymmetries, in the context of a market characterized by heterogeneous participants. This depends on two reasons that are interconnected. First, trading with a single counterparty facilitates the due diligence process and risk management practices that counterparties have to face.[53] Second, CCPs can make pricing and volume data public[54]: this is connected to the standardization of products, because by using standardized financial products CCPs are in a position to report trades regularly.[55] Standardization has the further advantage of facilitating price comparison even for occasional traders, "inducing regulars to sharpen their pricing, narrowing the spread between what they pay and what they charge for the same deal. Because a clearinghouse with public pricing gives outsiders the same information as the regular traders, spreads narrow. Trading becomes less expensive."[56]

Finally, transparency is connected to the regulatory advantages of centralization: "when trading is dispersed, regulators cannot readily see the system's aggregate risk-taking", whereas "with centralized clearing they can examine the clearinghouse's books," and this may support the action of policymakers.[57]

---

[51] Cœuré B. (2014), Risks in CCPs, Speech at the policy panel during the conference "Mapping and Monitoring the Financial System: Liquidity, Funding, and Plumbing" organized by Office of Financial Research and Financial Stability Oversight Council, Washington DC, 23 January 2014, available at https://www.ecb.europa.eu/press/key/date/2014/html/sp140123_1.en.html. In the bilateral context, netting reduces the aggregate amount owing between two counterparties under a master agreement to the sum of amounts owing under the individual transactions entered into under that master agreement; in the cleared context, netting reduces the aggregate amounts owed by the customer to the clearing member and reduces the aggregate amount owed by a clearing member on behalf of its customers (and separately, in its proprietary capacity) to the clearing house. See Beylin I. (2015), A Reassessment of the Clearing Mandate: How the Clearing Mandate Affects Swap Trading Behavior and the Consequences for Systemic Risk (May 18, 2015). Available at SSRN: http://ssrn.com/abstract=2612755 or http://dx.doi.org/10.2139/ssrn.2612755. On multilateral vs bilateral netting, see also Cont R. & Kokholm T., (2012) Central Clearing of OTC Derivatives: bilateral vs multilateral netting, available at: http://ssrn.com/abstract=2233665.

[52] Ibid.

[53] Cœuré B., quoted.

[54] Roe M. (2013), Clearing House Overconfidence, California Law Review, 2013, 13 and Cœuré B., quoted.

[55] Ibid.

[56] Ibid.

[57] Ibid.

14.3.2 Negative Effects

CCPs may have some negative effects given different perspectives.

First, risk concentration is a major issue. "Risk concentration within CCPs will grow, both nationally and internationally. CCPs are increasingly turning into institutions of unprecedented systemic importance."[58] Therefore, it is important that CCPs view themselves and are viewed as systemic risk managers[59]: "as a higher proportion of trading is cleared across CCPs, more and more credit, liquidity and operational risks will be concentrated in these institutions, which will themselves become potential sources of systemic risk."[60] This risk concentration is also favoured by the fact that "CCPs have strong natural monopoly characteristics,"[61] and "this tendency towards the dominance of clearing by a small number of large CCPs will contribute to make these entities highly systemically important."[62] At global level, "a growing number of banks will participate in key CCPs" and therefore "it is essential that financial institutions participating in and relying on CCPs should be in the condition to conduct effective due diligence to understand the risks they face as members and take appropriate steps to mitigate those risks."[63]

This concentration of risks should lead to the consideration that the failure of CCPs may be seriously disruptive (potentially catastrophic).[64] For this reason, it is important to put in place sound risk management, supported by an effective recovery and resolution regime for CCPs.[65] Considering mutualization from the perspective of an event of defaults, "losses and liquidity shortfalls in the event of a member default may spread to other participants and crisis propagation may be further driven by interdependencies of changing complexity, favoured for example by interoperability arrangements."[66] Mark

---

[58] ICMA, quoted.

[59] Hermans L., McGoldrick P. and Schmiedel H. (2013), Central Counterparties and systemic risk, European Systemic Risk Board, Macro – Prudential Commentaries, Issue N. 9, November 2013, 8.

[60] ICMA, quoted.

[61] Pirrong C. (2011), The Economics of Central Clearing, Theory and Practice, ISDA Discussion Papers Series, Number One – May 2011., 15.

[62] Ibid.

[63] Cœuré B., quoted.

[64] Ibid.

[65] Ibid., quoted. The author emphasizes the role of the globalization process that has triggered a trend towards global clearing that in itself may lead to further unintended consequences and may create new risks. The trend towards increasingly large global CCPs is similar in nature to that of horizontal integration which the CPSS looked at in greater detail in a report of 2010, concluding that larger global CCPs may have certain advantages, but may also lead to systemic risks, reduced benefits of central clearing, and regulatory frictions.

[66] Ibid.

Roe emphasizes the fact that "clearing houses transfer but do not eliminate risks, especially in critical financial crisis," since they rather push that risk elsewhere.[67]

Concentration also has some negative consequences with respect to client clearing services, which seem to be dominated by a few large global intermediaries. Two factors may have an impact on the concentration among a few banks as clearing service providers. First, "higher compliance burdens may play a role, where only the very largest of firms are capable of taking on cross-border activity."[68] Second, considered that clearing service providers are credit institutions, capital requirements, in particular leverage ratio, introduced with Basel III, have direct implications on their activities. Major financial institutions access clearing houses directly, whereas other categories of investors (including asset managers and hedge funds) tend to go through a bank-owned clearing member. An increasing number of financial institutions abandoned this business because it has become less profitable since an increasing level of capital, operating and investment costs for banks have reduced potential profit margins. [69]

There are also concerns about client access to this limited number of firms offering client clearing services, since CCPs may not be suitable for all types of market users, in particular for smaller firms in connection with the costs of netting.[70]

Adopting a general perspective in terms of risk reduction, for netting to be efficient it requires "standardisation of financial instruments. Less customisation means that residual risks have to be managed in the uncleared market or left with the end-user."[71] Moreover, the real benefits of netting may be lim-

---

[67] Roe M., quoted.

[68] Cœuré B., quoted.

[69] Rennison J. (2015), CFTC head calls for leverage ratio fix, *Financial Times*, 29 September 2015, available at http://www.ft.com/intl/cms/s/0/f62c38ec-66c9-11e5-a57f-21b88f7d973f.html#axzz3rHlwpaCu. At the moment, according to a report of the CFTC, the five largest banks in the US account for more than 70 % of the market by the amount of customer collateral required. For this reason, the CFTC has reiterated calls for a softening of bank capital requirements (in particular the leverage ratio, introduced with Basel III) blamed for a decline in the number of clearing firms.

[70] ICMA, quoted: "Netting is only cost-effective for institutions with two-way flows of business, i.e. intermediaries rather than end-investors. Many end-users are unused to margining and may be deterred from trading by the cost and effort of margining." In addition Cœuré B., quoted, also notes that "there is some evidence of clearing firms 'cherry picking' clients, while other end-users are commercially unattractive customers and hence unable to access centrally cleared markets."

[71] Ibid., since "uncleared business will be subject to higher regulatory capital requirements (with the purpose to encourage migration, where possible, to CCPs), the latter outcome may be common. To this extent, financial markets will be constrained from their essential task of managing financial risks and allowing non-bank financial and non-financial institutions to focus on their core business."

ited for two other reasons: first, "most financial assets (including most credit instruments) are not eligible for clearing across CCPs;"[72] second, "CCPs tend to be specialise in particular products or asset classes. Use of CCPs therefore reduces the scope for netting across products, a practice that institutions currently put in place on a bilateral basis."[73]

From a risk management perspective, "greater use of CCPs means greater collective reliance on a limited range of risk management methodologies, whose effect may consist in synchronised reactions to any news and generate," consistently with the risks of connected to financial coordination,[74] "procyclical shocks to the financial system."[75] Moreover, "although CCPs apply more rigorous risk management practices than many market users, their methodologies may not be transparent, because they are often proprietary and for this reason opaque,"[76] and even clearing members, who clearly have a critical dependence on such methodologies, may struggle to obtain information in this regard.[77]

Considering margins more specifically, they may have an impact in terms of extra costs for clearing members and consequently will raise the cost of funding to all market-users.[78]

With respect to market liquidity, "banks will have to apply credit limits to CCPs, taking account of the fact that, if they are clearing members, they will also have contingent obligations to help bail out the CCP should a default by another member or several other members exhaust the CCP's margins and default fund. These limits may constrain market liquidity."[79]

From the same perspective of market liquidity, another issue may be related to collateral transformation, the technique of "transforming" assets which are not accepted as collateral by CCPs into assets which are. A very simple form of this transaction may involve the counterparty to the derivatives trade borrowing eligible, liquid assets from an intermediary and posting its ineligible, illiquid assets as collateral to that intermediary. This means that the intermediary lends a liquid asset and holds an illiquid asset as collateral, resulting in the

---

[72] Ibid.

[73] Ibid.

[74] See generally Whitehead C., quoted.

[75] ICMA, quoted.

[76] Ibid.

[77] Ibid.

[78] Ibid.: "the initial margins or haircuts imposed by CCPs are very high compared to current market practice, and the remuneration of cash margin paid to members is low."

[79] Ibid.

intermediary holding the liquidity risk of the transaction. This poses potential problems for the regulatory objectives of CCPs. The CCPs' effectiveness in managing liquidity risk, and thereby reducing systemic risk, is reduced, as the liquidity risk is shifted to the intermediary rather than managed. Further, the intermediaries are often key players in global finance. Collateral transformation potentially increases the overall risk exposure by these intermediaries, raising counterparty default risk, the very risk CCPs were supposed to reduce.

Competition (from the perspective of collaterals) among CCPs may be another source of risk: liquid and high-quality collateral is crucial for CCPs, but an easy way to compete may consist in accepting more illiquid and low-quality assets as collateral.[80]

Another major risk is related to distorted incentives in the presence of information imperfections: "risk sharing mechanisms are frequently subject to moral hazard and CCPs, like virtually all mutual protection arrangements, are vulnerable to moral hazard and adverse selection problems that impose real costs."[81]

14.4 An Overview of EMIR

14.4.1 General Elements

In line with the recommendations provided by the international mandate of the G20 in 2009, the High-Level Group chaired by Jacques de Larosière concluded that the supervisory framework of the financial sector of the European Union (EU) needed to be strengthened to reduce the risk and severity of future financial crises and recommended far reaching reforms to the structure of supervision of that sector.[82]

---

[80] Thomas Murray Data Services (2014), The risks in CCPs and central clearing, 19 September 2014, available at http://ds.thomasmurray.com/opinion/risks-ccps-and-central-clearing. "It is one of those very strange questions […] Some people would say that there are too many CCPs and that, even though it sounds counterintuitive, you would be better off with one CCP where you can net everything. For the dealers, there is a netting piece and there is a governance piece. As there are a lot of CCPs, these challenges add up. Theoretically, the ideal would be to have one or two CCPs globally and that would be it. That, of course, is never going to be the case. Some people view that as a failing of the CCP model."

[81] Pirrong C., quoted: "this vulnerability depends on who participates in the protection (clearing) arrangement, and the kinds of products protected (cleared). Thus CCP membership requirements, the products that should be cleared, and the power of decision over membership and the clearing slate, should depend on moral hazard and adverse selection considerations. If this is not done, CCPs are more vulnerable to systemically damaging failure."

[82] EMIR, Recital 1.

In Europe and in the United States the financial industry was opposed to the adoption of a regulation providing detailed rules for clearing. Therefore the European regulators have clearly affirmed the disutility of incentives to promote the use of CCPs, because they have not proven to be sufficient to ensure that standardized OTC derivative contracts are in fact cleared centrally.[83] This is a strong argument against the possibility to adopt effective self-regulatory practices in this context. For this reason, the European regulators have considered CCP clearing requirements for those OTC derivative contracts that can be cleared centrally as necessary,[84] exactly as the IOSCO had concluded.[85] Moreover, from the European perspective, the fact that Member States could adopt *"divergent national measures was perceived as an actual risk, therefore an obstacle to the smooth functioning of the internal market and detrimental for market participants and financial stability"*.[86] A uniform application of the clearing obligation in the Union has been considered as necessary in order *"to ensure a high level of investor protection and to create a level playing field between market participants"*.[87]

As EMIR emphasizes, in the context of the EU, the role of the European Commission consists in a monitoring function, *"to ensure that those commitments are implemented in a similar way by the Union's international partners: the adoption of decisions on equivalence of the legal, supervisory and enforcement framework in thirds countries is explicitly mentioned"*.[88] The first equivalence decisions for CCP regulatory regimes have been signed with Australia, Hong Kong, Japan and Singapore on October 2014. The European Securities and Markets Authority (ESMA) played a key role in this regard, after that the European Commission requested its technical advice. The technical advice provided by ESMA is conducted by adopting a holistic perspective and by conducting *"a line-by-line analysis that takes into account the differences and similarities between the different regulatory frameworks"*.[89]

EMIR came into force on 16 August 2012 and introduced requirements aimed at improving the transparency of OTC derivatives markets and to reduce the risks associated with those markets. In order to achieve this, EMIR

---

[83] EMIR, Recital, 13.

[84] Emir, Recital 13.

[85] CPSS-IOSCO, Principles For Financial Market Infrastructures, quoted.

[86] EMIR, Recital 13.

[87] EMIR, Recital 14.

[88] EMIR, Recital 6.

[89] See Artamonov A. (2015), Cross-border application of OTC derivatives rules: revisiting the substituted compliance Approach, *Journal of Financial Regulation*, 2015, 13.

requires first that OTC derivatives which fulfil certain requirements are subject to the clearing obligation and second that risk mitigation techniques apply for all OTC derivatives that are not centrally cleared. In addition, all derivative transactions need to be reported to trade repositories (TRs). Finally, EMIR establishes organizational conduct of business and prudential standards for both TRs and CCPs.

The next paragraphs of this section will specifically focus on the regulation of CCPs provided by EMIR.

14.5 The Provisions of EMIR for CCPs

EMIR introduces uniform authorization regime and requirements for CCPs and, given the relevance of the risks, connected to a potential CCP's failure, the process of authorization as well as the supervisory phase are national prerogatives.[90] At the same time the Regulation empowers ESMA to develop technical standards in the view of ensuring *an uniform and objective application of these standards across the E.U.*[91] *From this perspective the provision of specific requirements (organizational, conduct of business and prudential requirements)*[92] *is crucial.*

The authorization regime is based on the 2012 CPSS-IOSCO Principles for Financial Market Infrastructure, but is significantly more detailed than the Principles, and engages with EU-specific risks, including issues related to cross-border supervision.[93] A legal person established in the EU that intends to provide clearing services as a CCP shall apply for authorization to the competent authority of the member state where it is established (the CCP's competent authority), in accordance with the procedure set out by the Regulation.[94] A CCP shall fulfil the capital requirements: in particular it shall have a permanent and available initial capital of at least €7.5 million to be authorized.[95] In general, a CCP's capital shall be proportionate to the risk stemming from the activities of the CCP. It shall at all times be sufficient to ensure an orderly wind-down or restructuring of the activities over an appropriate time span

---

[90] Moloney N. (2014), EU Securities and Financial Markets Regulation (Oxford University Press 2014, III Edition), 604.

[91] Awrey D., quoted.

[92] Ibid.

[93] Moloney N., quoted, 604.

[94] EMIR, article 14, para. 1.

[95] EMIR, article 16, para. 1.

and an adequate protection of the CCP against credit, counterparty, market, operation, legal and business risks which are not already covered by specific financial resources.[96]

According to the Regulation, each member state shall designate the competent authority responsible for carrying out the duties descending from the Regulation for the authorization and supervision of CCPs established in its territory.[97]

A key element in the authorization process designed by EMIR is the College, which can exercise material and unusually intrusive powers with respect to CCP authorization.[98] Each clearing house shall have a college. It consists of different members, chosen from the different authorities that supervise the clearing houses. In detail, members of the college are: ESMA; the CCP's competent authority; the competent authorities responsible for the supervision of the clearing members of the CCP that are established in the three member states with the largest contributions to the default fund of the CCP on an aggregate basis over a one-year period; the competent authorities responsible for the supervision of trading venues served by the CCP; the competent authorities responsible for the supervision of trading venues served by the CCP; the competent authorities supervising CCPs with which interoperability arrangements have been established; the competent authorities supervising CSDs to which the CCP is linked; the relevant members of the ESCB responsible for the oversight of the CCP, and the relevant members of the ESCB responsible for the oversight of the CCPs with which interoperability arrangements have been established; the central banks of issue of the most relevant EU currencies of the financial instruments cleared.[99]

The college has specific duties. These include the preparation of an opinion, exchange of information, agreement on the voluntary entrustment of tasks among its members, coordination of supervisory examination programmes based on a risk assessment of the CCP, and the determination of procedures and contingency plans to address emergencies.[100] The national authorities may grant authorization only when they are fully satisfied that the CCP complies with all the requirements laid down under EMIR and where the CCP college has not exercised its veto. In making its decision the national

---

[96] EMIR, article 16, para. 2.

[97] EMIR, article 22, para 1.

[98] Moloney N., quoted, 606.

[99] EMIR, article 18.

[100] EMIR, article 18, para. 4.

competent authorities must consider the risk assessment required of the college in relation to the CCP. A CCP may not be authorized where all the members of the college reach an unanimous joint opinion that the CCP shall not be authorized.[101]

A CCP established in a third country may provide clearing services to clearing members or trading venues established in the EU only where that CCP is recognized by ESMA.[102]

14.5.1 Corporate Governance of CCPs

Adopting the same regulatory approach that has been chosen for other contexts (e.g. the AIFM Directive), EMIR provides requirements for the corporate governance of CCPs. In such a context the corporate governance has a systemic relevance: CCPs should be organized so as to align the control of risks with those who bear the consequences of risk management decisions. Failure to align rights with risk-bearing will tend to decrease the effectiveness of CCPs in reducing systemic risk.[103]

In general terms a CCP shall have robust governance arrangements, which concretely means a clear organizational structure with well-defined, transparent and consistent lines of responsibility, effective processes to identify, manage, monitor and report the risks to which it is or might be exposed, and adequate internal control mechanisms, including sound administrative and accounting procedures.[104] Moreover, the organizational structure has to ensure continuity, an orderly functioning in the performance of its services and activities,[105] a clear separation between the reporting lines for risk management and those for other operations of the CCP,[106] a remuneration policy which promotes sound effective risks

---

[101] See Moloney N., quoted, 606.

[102] EMIR, article 25, para. 1. In relation to this topic, it is necessary to refer to the Eurosystem Oversight Policy Framework of the ECB and the recent challenge by the General Court of Justice. The Eurosystem Oversight Policy Framework required central counterparties to be located in the Eurozone. This requirement has been recently challenged by the General Court of the European Union, with the decision of 4 March 2015, Judgment in Case T-496/11 United Kingdom v European Central Bank. It has been affirmed that the ECB does not have the competence necessary to impose such a requirement on central counterparties involved in the clearing of securities. See, General Court of the European Union, Press Release No 29/15, Luxembourg, 4 March 2015.

[103] Pirrong C., quoted, 3.

[104] EMIR, article 26, para. 1.

[105] EMIR, article 26, para. 3.

[106] EMIR, article 26, para. 4.

management,[107] adequate information technology systems,[108] information about governance arrangements, rules governing the CCP and admission criteria for clearing membership publicly and freely available,[109] and independent audits.[110]

The senior management of a CCP shall have a sufficiently good reputation and sufficient experience so as to ensure the sound and prudent management of the CCP.[111]

The existence of a board is compulsory, and at least one-third of the members of the board shall be independent.[112]

The risk committee shall be composed of representatives of its clearing members, independent members of the board and representatives of its clients.[113] It must be independent and the CCP shall clearly determine the mandate and the governance arrangements to ensure its independence.[114] Its role consists in advising the board of any arrangements that may impact the risk management of the CCP (e.g. significant change in its risk model, default procedures).[115] A CCP may decide not to follow the advice of the risk committee but shall promptly inform the competent authority of any decisions of this kind.[116]

A key element for a CCP, in order to obtain authorization by the competent authority, is the identity of the shareholders or members (direct or indirect, natural or legal persons) that have qualifying holdings, and the amounts of those holdings.[117] EMIR provides a consistent flow of information to be provided to the competent authorities.[118]

---

[107] EMIR, article 26, para. 5. This reflects the crisis-era concern across EU securities and markets regulation to break the link between remuneration and incentives for excessive risk-taking. See Moloney N., quoted, 607: "many CCPs strongly criticized ESMA's approach (which did not, however, change) as being disproportionate, more restrictive than requirements applying in other regulated sectors, and potentially compromising CCPs' ability to recruit high-calibre employees, ESMA responded that CCPs were systemically important institutions and merited special treatment, which could be more prescriptive than for other regulated entities and that remuneration could generate severe conflicts of interest."

[108] EMIR, article 26, para. 6.

[109] EMIR, article 26, para. 7.

[110] EMIR, article 26, para. 8.

[111] EMIR, article 27, para. 1.

[112] EMIR, article 27, para. 2.

[113] EMIR, article 28, para. 1.

[114] EMIR, article 28, para. 2.

[115] EMIR, article 28, para. 3.

[116] EMIR, article 28, para. 4.

[117] EMIR, article 30, para 1.

[118] See EMIR, articles 31 and 32.

Conflicts of interest are strongly emphasized by EMIR (as has been the case in the context of the AIFM Directive). A CCP shall maintain and operate effective written organizational and administrative arrangements to identify and manage any potential conflicts of interest between itself, including its managers, employees or any person with direct or indirect control or close links, and its clearing members or their clients known to the CCP.[119] In the same way, a CCP shall establish, implement and maintain adequate business continuity policy and disaster recovery plan aiming at ensuring the preservation of its functions, the timely recovery of operations and the fulfilment of the CCP's obligations.[120]

With reference to the conduct of business, together with the duty to act fairly and professionally in accordance with the best interests of such clearing members and clients (Article 36 para. 1), a CCP shall establish participation requirements,[121] and publicly disclose the prices and fees associated with the services provided.[122]

In relation to the participation requirements, a CCP shall establish, where relevant per type of product cleared, the categories of admissible clearing members and the admission criteria, upon the advice of the risk committee.[123] These criteria shall have some key characteristics, in view of preserving and protecting the totality of the clearing members: they shall be non-discriminatory, transparent and objective so as to ensure fair and open access to the CCP and shall ensure that clearing members have sufficient financial resources and operational capacity to meet the obligations arising from participation in a CCP.[124] It is important to note that restricted access shall be permitted only to the extent that the objective is to control the risk for the CCP.[125] Moreover, a CCP may only deny access to clearing members who meet the criteria provided by the CCP where duly justified in writing and based on a comprehensive risk analysis.[126]

Clearing members who clear transactions on behalf of their clients shall have the necessary additional financial resources and operational capacity to perform this activity.

---

[119] EMIR, article 33, para. 1.

[120] EMIR, article 34, para 1.

[121] EMIR, article 37.

[122] EMIR, article 38.

[123] EMIR, article 37, para. 1.

[124] Ibid.

[125] Ibid.

[126] EMIR, article 37, para. 5.

A CCP may impose specific additional obligations on clearing members, such as the participation in auctions of a defaulting clearing member's position. Such additional obligations shall be proportional to the risk brought by the clearing member and shall not restrict partition to certain categories of clearing members.[127]

An important element is transparency: the CCP and its clearing members shall publicly disclose the prices and fees associated with the services provided.[128] These shall be provided separately (also disclosing discounts and rebates and the conditions to benefit from those reductions). A CCP shall allow its clearing members, and where relevant, its clients separate access to the specific services provided.[129]

EMIR provides different regimes of disclosure, in relation to the specific type of information to be provided. The CCP shall disclose:

- to clearing members and clients the risks associated with the services provided;[130]
- to its clearing members and to its competent authority the price information used to calculate its end of day exposure to its clearing members[131];
- publicly, the operational volumes of the cleared transactions for each class of instruments cleared by the CCP on an aggregated basis,[132] together with the operational and technical requirements relating to the communication protocols covering the content and message formats it uses to interact with third parties, including the operational and technical requirements,[133] and any breaches by clearing members of the criteria to be admitted as clearing members.[134]

Concerning segregation, EMIR requires, first of all, that a CCP keeps separate records and accounts that shall enable it, at any time and without delay, to distinguish in accounts with the CCP the assets and positions held for the account of one clearing member from the assets and positions held for the account of any other clearing member and from its own assets.[135]

---

[127] EMIR, article 37, para. 6.

[128] EMIR, article 38, para. 1.

[129] Ibid.

[130] EMIR, article 38, para. 2.

[131] EMIR, article 38, para. 3.

[132] Ibid.

[133] EMIR, article 38, para. 4.

[134] Such disclosure will not take place where the competent authority, after consulting ESMA, considers that such disclosure would constitute a threat to financial stability or to market confidence or would seriously jeopardize the financial markets or cause disproportionate damage to the parties involved.

[135] EMIR, article 39, para. 1

A CCP shall offer an omnibus client segregation and individual client segregation: in the first case the CCP will keep separate records and accounts enabling each clearing member to distinguish in accounts with the CCP the assets and positions of that clearing member from those held for the accounts of its clients[136]; in the second case the CCP will keep separate records and accounts enabling each clearing member to distinguish in accounts with the CCP the assets and positions held for the account of a client from those held for the account of other clients.[137] At the same time all clearing members have to keep separate records and accounts that enable them to distinguish both in accounts held with the CCP and in their own accounts their assets and positions from the assets and positions held for the account of their clients at the CCP.[138] Moreover they have to offer their clients, at least, the choice between omnibus and individual client segregation and inform them of the costs and level of protection.[139]

CCPs and clearing members shall publicly disclose the levels of protection and the costs associated with the different levels of segregation that they provide, and shall offer those services on reasonable commercial terms.[140]

14.6 Prudential Requirements for CCPs

EMIR provides prudential requirements for CCPs. They are constituted by specific provisions on margin requirements, the creation of a default fund and the management of other financial resources, as well as liquidity risk controls, collateral requirements, specific rules on the investment policy and default procedures.

EMIR reflects the typical waterfall mechanism. First of all it provides a general duty for CCPs, since they shall measure and assess its liquidity and credit exposures to each clearing member and, where relevant, to another CCP with which it has concluded an interoperability arrangement, on a near to real-time basis. For this reason a CCP shall have access in a timely manner and on a non-discriminatory basis to the relevant pricing sources to effectively measure its exposures.[141]

---

[136] EMIR, article 39, para. 2.
[137] EMIR, article 39, para. 3.
[138] EMIR, article 39, para. 4.
[139] EMIR, article 39, para. 5.
[140] EMIR, article 39, para. 6.
[141] EMIR, article 40, para. 1.

Moreover a CCP shall impose, call and collect margins to limit its credit exposures form its clearing members and, where relevant, from CCPs with which it has interoperability arrangements.[142]

Such margins shall have some characteristics. They shall:

- be sufficient to cover potential exposures that the CCP estimates will occur until the liquidation of the relevant positions;
- be sufficient to cover losses that result from at least 99 % of the exposures movements over an appropriate time horizon;
- ensure that a CCP fully collateralizes its exposures with all its clearing members and, where relevant, with CCPs with which it has interoperability arrangements, at least on a daily basis.[143]

In this regard a CCP has some specific obligations. It shall:

- regularly monitor and, if necessary, revise the level of its margins to reflect current market conditions taking into account any potentially procyclical effects of such revisions[144];
- adopt models and parameters in setting its margin requirements that capture the risk characteristics of the products cleared and take into account the interval between margin collections, market liquidity and the possibility of changes over the duration of the transaction[145];
- call and collect margins on an intraday basis at least when predefined thresholds are exceeded[146];
- call and collect margins that are adequate to cover the risk stemming from the positions registered in each account.[147]

In order to limit its credit exposures to its clearing members further, a CCP shall maintain a pre-funded default fund to cover losses that exceed the losses to be covered by margin requirements, arising from the default, including the opening of an insolvency procedure, of one or more clearing members.[148]

The CCP shall establish a minimum amount below which the size of the default fund is not to fall under any circumstances.[149]

---

[142] EMIR, article 40, para. 2.

[143] EMIR, article 41, para 1.

[144] Ibid.

[145] EMIR, article 41, para. 2.

[146] EMIR, article 41, para. 3.

[147] EMIR, article 41, para. 4.

[148] EMIR, article 42, para. 1.

[149] Ibid.

A CCP shall establish the minimum size of contributions to the default fund and the criteria to calculate the contributions of the single clearing members. The contributions shall be proportional to the exposures of each clearing member.[150]

The default fund shall at least enable the CCP to withstand, under extreme but plausible market conditions, the default of the clearing member to which it has the largest exposures or of the second and third largest clearing members if the sum of their exposures is larger.[151]

A CCP shall maintain sufficient pre-funded available financial resources to cover potential losses that exceed the losses to be covered by margin requirements and the default fund.[152]

At the same time a CCP shall at all times have access to adequate liquidity to perform its services and activities. To that end, it shall obtain the necessary credit lines or similar arrangements to cover its liquidity needs in case the financial resources at its disposal are not immediately available. A clearing member, parent undertaking or subsidiary of that clearing member together shall not provide more than 25 % of the credit lines needed by the CCP.[153] The potential liquidity needs shall be measured by the CCP on a daily basis.[154]

A CCP shall use the margins posted by a defaulting clearing member before other financial resources in covering losses.[155] Where the margins posted by the defaulting clearing member are not sufficient to cover the losses incurred by the CCP, the CCP shall use the default fund contribution of the defaulting member to cover those losses.[156]

A CCP shall use contributions to the default fund of the non-defaulting clearing member and any other financial resources only after having exhausted the contributions of the defaulting clearing member.[157]

A CCP shall use its dedicated own resources before using the default fund contributions of non-defaulting clearing members. A CCP shall not use the margins posted by non-defaulting clearing members to cover the losses resulting from the default of another clearing member.

A CCP shall accept highly liquid collateral with minimal credit and market risk to cover its initial and ongoing exposure to its clearing members.

---

[150] EMIR, article 42, para. 2.

[151] EMIR, article 42, para. 3.

[152] EMIR, article 43, para. 1.

[153] EMIR, article 44, para. 1.

[154] Ibid.

[155] EMIR, article 45, para. 1.

[156] EMIR, article 45, para. 2.

[157] EMIR, article 45, para. 3.

For non-financial counterparties, a CCP may accept bank guarantees, taking such guarantees into account when calculating its exposure to a bank that is a clearing member. It shall apply adequate haircuts to asset values that reflect the potential for their value to decline over the interval between their last revaluation and the time by which they can reasonably be assumed to be liquidated. It shall take into account the liquidity risk following the default of a market participant and the concentration risk on certain assets that may result in establishing the acceptable collateral and the relevant haircuts.[158]

EMIR provides specific provision in relation to the investment policies of a CCP. It shall invest its financial resources only in cash or in highly liquid financial instruments with minimal market credit risk. A CCP's investments shall be capable of being liquidated rapidly with minimal adverse price effect.

A critical element is one of the default procedures, to be put in place where a clearing member does not comply with the participation requirements of the CCP within the time limit established by CCP procedures.[159]

In this case a CCP shall take prompt action to contain losses and liquidity pressures resulting from defaults and shall ensure that the closing out of any clearing member's positions does not disrupt its operations or expose the non-defaulting clearing members to losses that they cannot anticipate or control.[160]

Where a CCP considers that the clearing member will not be able to meet its future obligations, it shall promptly inform the competent authority before the default procedure is declared or triggered.[161]

A CCP shall verify that its default procedures are enforceable. It shall take all reasonable steps to ensure that it has the legal powers to liquidate the proprietary positions of the defaulting clearing member and to transfer or liquidate the clients' positions of the defaulting clearing member.[162]

A CCP shall regularly:

- review the models and parameters adopted to calculate its margin requirements, default fund contributions, collateral requirements and other risk control mechanisms. It shall subject the models to rigorous and frequent stress tests to assess their resilience in extreme but plausible market conditions and shall perform back tests to assess the reliability of the methodology adopted. The CCP shall obtain independent

---

[158] EMIR, article 46, para. 1.
[159] EMIR, article 48, para. 1.
[160] EMIR, article 48, para. 2.
[161] EMIR, article 48, para. 3.
[162] EMIR, article 48, para. 4.

validation, shall inform its competent authority and ESMA of the results of the tests performed and shall obtain their validation before adopting any significant change to the models and parameters[163];

– test the key aspect of its default procedures and take all reasonable steps to ensure that all clearing members understand them and have appropriate arrangements in place to respond to a default event.[164]

As is well known, CCPs may enter into an interoperability arrangement with another CCP. In this regard EMIR provides some requirements in terms of risk management, provision of margins and approval of interoperability arrangements.

14.7 Critical Considerations

From the specific perspective of the regulation of CCPs, EMIR clearly appears as a document strongly consistent with the European regulation provided in the post-crisis era: it is highly detailed, emphasizing the relevance of conflicts of interests, the importance of risk-management practices, the relationship between policy remunerations and excessive risk-takings.[165]

The European regulation of clearing houses has to be considered by contextualizing and comparing it with other regulations developed by other jurisdictions. In this context it is not possible to provide an accurate analysis from a comparative perspective. To briefly consider the different approaches to regulation in different jurisdictions it may be interesting and useful to refer to the comparative analysis provided by ESMA in relation to EMIR and its homologues in Hong Kong,[166] Singapore,[167] Japan,[168] and the USA.[169] As already mentioned, the European Commission mandated ESMA to provide

---

[163] EMIR, article 49, para. 1.

[164] Ibid.

[165] See Moloney N., quoted.

[166] ESMA, Technical advice on third country regulatory equivalence under EMIR – Hong Kong, September 2013, available at http://www.esma.europa.eu/system/files/2013-1160_technical_advice_on_third_country_regulatory_equivalence_under_emir_hong_kong.pdf

[167] ESMA, Technical advice on third country regulatory equivalence under EMIR – Singapore, September 2013, available at http://www.esma.europa.eu/system/files/2013-1161technical_advice_on_third_country_regulatory_equivalence_under_emir_singapore.pdf.

[168] ESMA, Technical advice on third country regulatory equivalence under EMIR – Japan, September 2013, available at http://www.esma.europa.eu/system/files/2013-1158_technical_advice_on_third_country_regulatory_equivalence_under_emir_japan.pdf.

[169] ESMA, Technical advice on third country regulatory equivalence under EMIR – US, September 2013, available at http://www.esma.europa.eu/system/files/2013-1157_technical_advice_on_third_country_regulatory_equivalence_under_emir_us.pdf.

it with technical advice on the equivalence between those different regulatory regimes and different aspects of the EU regulatory regime under EMIR. The equivalence assessment conducted by ESMA followed an objective-based approach, where the capability of the regime in the third country to meet the objectives of the EU Regulation was assessed from a holistic perspective.[170]

This document highlights a strong inhomogeneity in the regulatory approach to clearing houses. There are many discrepancies with respect to key areas. Considering the USA, there are relevant differences with respect to margins, default-risk management, financial backstopping and governance.[171] Moreover, comparing both the regulations of Hong Kong and Singapore with EMIR, for example, a lack of details in the Hong Kong and Singaporean regimes emerge. In this respect ESMA emphasized that this does not imply that the same rules are not adopted by the clearing houses themselves, independently of the public regulation approved. ESMA, in its assessment, constantly recalls the internal policies, procedures, rules, models and methodologies of individual CCPs. Specifically, this demonstrates a different approach in terms of regulatory strategy, more oriented towards a self-regulatory approach.

This clearly shows that a uniform approach to the regulation (both in terms of specific provisions and regulatory approach) of market infrastructures, particularly in the context of CCPs as the G20 explicitly requested, has not been adopted by the principal jurisdictions.

It is still unclear whether these differences will concretely affect the practical operations of CCPs and their regulations. Regulators may face problems of regulatory arbitrage, in the sense that parties can select the clearing house and jurisdiction that will deliver settlement at lower possible cost.[172] Furthermore, differences in regulation between jurisdictions may be a major issue when considering eventual failures of systemically important clearing houses. In this sense the eventual adoption of a transnational resolution regime may be even more complicated if compared to the debate around the resolution of systemically important banks.

At the same time, it is not clear whether the existing differences considering each specific provision as well as the general regulatory framework and strategies adopted by each jurisdiction will lead to a fragmentation of the derivatives markets instead of enhancing a stronger and efficient cross-border cooperation in this field, as the G20 and IOSCO required.[173] A letter from

---

[170] See one of the documents on the Technical advice on third country regulatory equivalence.

[171] See Yadav Y. (2015), Clearinghouses and Extra-Territorial Regulation, Vanderbilt Law & Economics Research Paper No. 15-24, available at SSRN: http://ssrn.com/absract=2659336.

[172] Ibid., 37.

[173] See Artamonov A., quoted.

the Ministers of Finance of different jurisdictions from Europe, Asia and America to Secretary Lew explicitly refers to the risk of fragmentation in the OTC market: "We are already starting to see evidence of fragmentation in this vitally important financial market, as a result of lack of regulatory coordination. We are concerned that, without clear direction from global policymakers and regulators, derivatives markets will recede into localised and less efficient structures, impairing the ability of business across the globe to manage risk. This will in turn dampen liquidity, investment and growth." A phenomenon of fragmentation has been particularly clear in the context of the IRS swaps,[174] with the introduction of the US swap execution facility (SEF) regime in October 2013.[175] The trend in fragmentation has been confirmed by International Swap Dealer Association (ISDA).[176]

In light of these considerations, the European regulators, as well as their homologues in the most relevant jurisdictions, should be more concerned with the issue of an effective coordination and cooperation on the regulation of clearing houses.

14.8 Conclusions

The role of CCPs in the context of financial markets will become increasingly relevant. The activity of CCPs may strengthen financial stability, but at the same time has major risks, including their possible default. Considered their systemic importance, the implementation of a coordinated response at the international level is necessary in the short term.

Through the adoption of EMIR, the EU provided an important contribution to the regulation of CCPs, consistently responding to the mandate of the G20. A preliminary comparison of the European regulatory response with the principal jurisdictions shows significant discrepancies that may pose a threat to the concrete capacity of CCPs to absolve their functions in an international context. For this reason, all the regulators should make an effort to aim for stronger coordination in the next years, avoiding a race to the bottom with the purpose of attracting more financial players.

---

[174] See Ministers of Finance from Brazil, European Commission, France, Germany, Italy, Japan, Russia, Switzerland, South Africa, United Kingdom to Secretary Lew, Cross-Border OTC Derivatives Regulation, 18 April 2013.

[175] See Artamonov A., quoted, 1–20.

[176] ISDA (2014), Cross-Border Fragmentation of Global OTC Derivatives: An Empirical Analysis, January 2014, and Cross-Border Fragmentation of Global Derivatives: End-Year 2014 Update, April 2015.

Part III

Funding Innovation, Financing Growth

15

The Impact of Regulatory Capital Regulation on Balance Sheet Structure, Intermediation Cost and Growth

Hamza El Khalloufi and Pierre-Charles Pradier

While support for strengthening financial regulation was unanimous after the financial crisis (with the customary exception of both radical groups and financial lobbies),[1] there have been recently some notable breaches in the consensus. Prominent European politicians have publicly expressed the idea that a break was needed to complete an overall assessment of past work (EP 2016), "remove unnecessary burden" and cut red tape (Brunsden 2015), while some took a more aggressive stance in front of their domestic audience: Emmanuel Macron (2016) and Gianfelice Rocca (Sanderson 2016) have been vocal against excessive financial regulation, which would have become a burden for corporations, and might be responsible for the enduring recession in the European Union (EU). The same argue that the USA and emerging countries quickly recovered after the 2007 financial crisis and resumed growth in two years at most, so they enjoyed a full business cycle before experiencing the current slowdown. On the contrary, Europe has experienced a protracted finan-

---

[1] Such as the Institute of International Finance, see IIF (2010, 2011).

We wish to thank Jean-Paul Laurent and Nuno Coimbra for their advice and comments. All errors remain ours.

H. El Khalloufi (✉)
LabEx RéFi and PRISM, Université Paris 1 Panthéon-Sorbonne, Paris, France

P.-C. Pradier (✉)
LabEx RéFi and CES, Université Paris 1 Panthéon-Sorbonne, Paris, France

R. Douady et al. (eds.), *Financial Regulation in the EU*,
DOI 10.1007/978-3-319-44287-7_15

385

cial crisis, with commercial banks' failures and fragilities not yet resolved, as recent developments in Portugal (Wise 2016) and Italy (Hale 2016) have proven. At the same time, the economy has been growing slowly or negatively in the during the last years, especially in the Eurozone: fiscal consolidation and banking sector balance sheet unwinding had an obvious negative macroeconomic impact. With the economic policy offering some relief, as an EU-centred scheme (the Juncker Plan) opened opportunities for removing targeted government expenses from deficit constraints, and the European Central Bank (ECB) flooded the markets with cheap money and promises to continue, one should have expected the beginning of business cycle to rely on credit. Loans to corporations notwithstanding failed to improve as Fig. 15.1 shows, and gross domestic product (GDP) growth stayed weaker than before the crisis.

The situation is especially worrying for small and medium-sized enterprises (SMEs), which account for 67 % of EU employment (in non-financial corporations, NFCs) since "SME bank lending has suffered a significant backdrop in volumes, from a peak of EUR 95 billion in mid-2008 to approximately EUR 54 billion in 2013/2014" (EBA 2016b, p. 8). SMEs are especially reliant on bank credit (through overdraft or loans) since they enjoy limited access to other financing options available to larger corporations (Figure 2 from EBA 2016b, p. 19), especially from securitization, which is low in Europe in

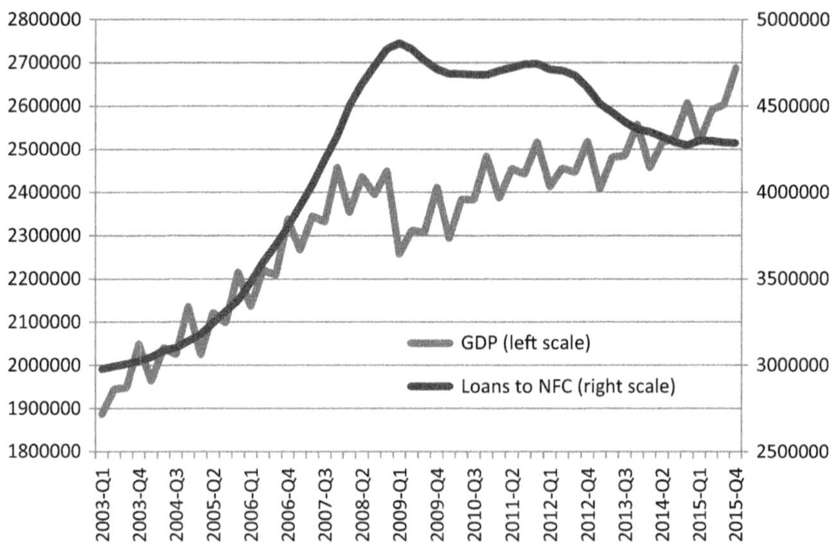

Fig. 15.1 GDP and amount outstanding of loans to NFCs in the Eurozone, € million (*Source*: ECB statistical datawarehouse)

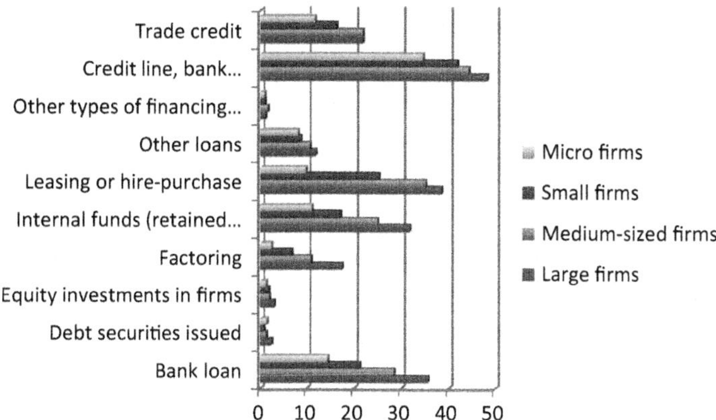

Fig. 15.2   Use of various sources of finance in the EU 28 by entreprise size (2015 H_2) (*Source*: ECB statistical datawarehouse)

comparison with the USA (see Daphné Héant et al., Chap. 16, this volume) (Fig. 15.2).

As conventional and unconventional economic policy tools seem to have exhausted their virtue, one can then ask whether the overall tightening of bank regulation is not responsible for the current state of low growth and missing foregone business cycle through declining credit to corporations, especially to the smaller ones.

In order to answer this question, one must maybe look at the *currently* implemented or announced measures, which imposed new costs to financial institutions, these costs being eventually paid by the customer. But the expected developments might also matter: banks might be reacting to the expected future regulation, and the credit tightening might be the result of uncertainty aversion in a context of uncertain public policies. It would thus be difficult to assess the steady state impact of any regulatory measure. Moreover, non-conventional monetary policies are distorting the usual economic signals: first, negative interest rates on deposits with the European central bank plus repeated quantitative easing (QE) operations have driven short-term returns so low that investors and banks together have lost their usual points of reference in the risk/return space. In the case of banks, many observers believe their economic model is being deeply challenged by both the flatness of yield curve (return on maturity transformation) and the low level of interest rates (return on deposits). Conversely, current regulation might be interpreted as a mild constraint: the single resolution mechanism, for instance, is designed to organize bail-in and rescue troubled banks without the influx of taxpayer money, but the whole scheme is just a tentative "credible threat" since nobody really expects, in the current European economic environment, that governments will let any large bank get bankrupt, endangering the whole economy. Hence implicit government support still biases the risk/return arbitrage in a way, which is difficult to determine. Given these three problems (convergence is not steady state, QE displaces and distorts the yield curve, a change in implicit government support), it seems especially difficult to understand how the new Basel III metrics change the Basel II-adjusted risk/return filtering, transforming the asset-side structure of banks' balance sheets.

While it seems difficult to answer such a complex problem, we will try to disentangle the effect of every set of causes, taking into account expected future rules. The rest of this chapter is organized as follows: we will first recall the main novelties of the Basel III package as implemented in the EU (Sect. 15.1) before we turn to impact assessments (Sect. 15.2), trying to discover what definite constraint is binding at the moment (Sect. 15.3) and offer some remediation (Sect. 15.4) before concluding (Sect. 15.5).

15.1 Novelties of Basel III (CRD IV/CRR) and Their Anticipated Effects on Lending

The European implementation of the Basel III package (through CRD IV and CRR) aims at "[strengthening] the resilience of the EU banking sector so it would be better placed to absorb economic shocks while ensuring that banks continue to finance economic activity and growth" (EC 2013), especially in Europe where banks are the main financing actors (Schackmann-Falli and Weiss 2014). Among the novelties of the Basel III regulatory package, the most significant in terms of impact on corporate lending practices are likely to be capital requirements (Sect. 15.1.1), overall leverage (Sect. 15.1.2) and liquidity ratios (Sect. 15.1.3). Let us review them in this order.

15.1.1 Capital Requirements

Basel III increased the capital requirements in order to strengthen the banks at a microprudential level: Table 15.1 describes the increase in overall quantity, but the capital quality is also enhanced and the risk weighted assets (RWA) computation rules are stiffened so that overall the amount of required capital for a given balance sheet has been raised (see Jean-Paul Laurent, Chap. 11, this volume). The table also features the systemic risk surcharge imposed by the Financial Stability Board, which has still to be passed in European law.

Table 15.1 Regulatory capital requirements: Basel II versus Basel III

Capital category	Basel II reqd cap % RWA	Basel III reqd cap % RWAs of 2016	Authority in charge
Common Equity Tier 1 capital	$\cong$4	4.5	ECB or National Supervisor[a]
Additional Tier 1 capital	0	1.5	ECB or National Supervisor
Tier 2 capital	T2: max 100 % of T1 T3: max 250 % of market risk T1	2	ECB or National Supervisor
Capital conservation buffer	0	2.5	ECB or National Supervisor
Partial sum (basic capital)	8 %	10.5	Multiplier: 1.31
Countercyclical buffer	0	0–2.5	National Competent Authority
G-SIB Buffer	0	0–5	Financial Stability Board
D-SIB Buffer	0	0–5	National Competent Authority
(Pillar 2 buffers)	0	0–2	ECB
TLAC	8 %	10.5–20%	Multiplier: 1.31–2.5

[a]ECB for ECB directly supervised banks (Since 4 November 2014, "significant" banks are directly supervised by the European Central Bank. According to Council Regulation (EU) No 1024/2013 art. 6, a bank is deemed significant if it fulfils at least one of the following conditions (1) The value of its assets exceeds €30 billion; (2) The value of its assets exceeds both €5 billion and 20 % of the Gross Domestic Product of the member state in which it is located; further regulation added; (3) The bank is among the three most significant banks of the country in which it is located; (4) The bank has large cross-border activities and (5) The bank receives, or has applied for, assistance from Eurozone bailout funds (the European Stability Mechanism or European Financial Stability Facility)), National Supervisory Authorities for other financial institutions

The table shows that the basic capital amount is only lightly impacted (10.5 % instead of 8 %) but the Total Loss Absorption Capacity might be as high as 20 % for banks with maximum systemic surcharge: this would commend a 150 % increase over the Basel II framework. Recent reports have measured the *actual* increase in regulatory capital: from 5.5 % to 12.5 % between 2009 Q1 and 2014 Q4 in the US (Tier 1 alone, Fed 2015, p. 2), from 4.9 % to 12 % in Eurozone between the December 2010 Quantitative Impact Study and the EBA Monitoring Exercise of September 2015 (Group 1 banks only,[2] Quignon 2016, p. 25). These are overall figures, though, and the *specific* provision of

---

[2] Group 1 banks are banks with Tier 1 capital in excess of €3 billion and internationally active. All other banks are categorized as Group 2 banks.

regulatory capital for business loans is not distinguished. It seems reasonable to conjecture that these provisions have increased in a slightly higher proportion, since corporate debt is in the higher bracket of capital requirement, especially in comparison with mortgage loans or EU sovereign bonds.[3]

At this point, we establish a concomitance between increased capital requirements and decreasing loans to financial corporations. This is not a satisfying causal explanation, though, but a partial description of the Basel III framework implementation. Let us proceed to the other features of the same package.

15.1.2   Overall Leverage

The Basel III framework requires the banks to have their capital equal to 3 % at least of their balance sheet; this limit implies a maximum 33:1 leverage. While this is not directly binding for corporate lending, as the basic capital charge of 10.5 % implies a 9.5:1 leverage (which is often less as corporate loans can be charged above 100 % of the basic requirements according to the borrower's creditworthiness), it might be indirectly binding. Banks listed in the USA are required to apply a Supplementary Leverage Ratio of 5 %, or 6 % for IDR (Insured Depository Institutions). But US banks are far above this floor: the last published figure was 8.8 % on average (Fed 2015, p. 3), with the only two banks in the sample missing the stress tests being US branches of European banks. For Group 1 European banks competing at a global level, it seems almost impossible to steadily display lower figures than their American counterparts, hence capital build-up might not be over. If we take in consideration the average US bank's leverage as the "desired leverage," it might become a binding constraint as most assets carry a capital charge lower than corporate loans: the former might thus contribute to the saturation of the leverage constraint, effectively crowding out the latter.

15.1.3   Liquidity Ratios

Basel III features two liquidity ratios: a short term Liquidity Coverage Ratio (LCR) under progressive implementation in the EU and a longer term Net Stable Funding Ratio (NSFR), whose possible implementation remains to be decided.

---

[3] In the standardized risk approach, corporate debt must be backed by 20 % (for AAA-rated borrowers) to 150 % of the standard regulatory capital provision, while claims secured by residential property only need 35 % of the standard provision and EU sovereign debt 0 %.

15.1.3.1   Short-Term Liquidity

The LCR is defined as the ratio of the value of the stock of high quality liquid assets (in stressed conditions) divided by net cash outflows over the next 30 calendar days. It is supposed to be above 70 % in 2016, with this constraint being stiffened in the coming years (80 % from 1 January 2017 and 100 % from 1 January 2018). It is thus expected that LCR implementation will have a growing, effect on lending since loans are not liquid, hence they do not count in the numerator of the LCR. On the other hand, this effect is only indirect: only banks with an insufficient volume of liquid assets might be restricted from lending. For this reason, the European Banking Authority (EBA) is minimizing the effect of LCR on bank lending behaviour (EBA 2014, p. 23). Is it any different for the long-term ratio?

15.1.3.2   Long-Term Liquidity

The NSFR is such that Available Stable Funding (ASF) divided by Required Stable Funding (RSF) on a one-year horizon should be above 100 %. These quantities may be computed using haircuts detailed in BCBS (2014): ASF weighs liabilities (for instance Tier 1 regulatory capital is weighted at 100 % while deposits are weighted between 50 % and 95 % according to their stability) and RSF weighs assets (from 0 % for coins and banknotes to 100 % for assets encumbered for a period of one year or more). This being said, most performing corporate loans are weighted at 85 % (non-performing loans receiving a 100 % weight). This means that banks must hold not only regulatory capital but also 85 % of the amount lent as stable funding, for instance 85 % of regulatory capital or 85:0.9 = 94.44 % on stable deposit accounts of the amount lent. This constraint would likely be binding for many banks, if only NSFR were due for implementation in the EU. At the moment there is no deadline for such plan, but the EBA is pushing for NSFR implementation (EBA 2015).

The obvious conclusion of this first section is that lending to business is likely to be penalized by almost every aspect of the new regulatory package. This is leading us to the question of the overall effect of this package on economic growth via the firm-financing channel.

15.2   Regulatory Impact on Financing Businesses

In this section, we will distinguish between impact studies reliant on the interest-rate methodology (Sect. 15.2.1) from newer ones, which were inspired by new theoretical developments (Sect. 15.2.2). The latter seem to better fit the current state of the EU economy but the former are still usually produced and cited, see for example Quignon (2016).

15.2.1   Interest-Rate Reliant Impact Studies

The earliest assessments of the Basel III package addressed an important causal chain: rising regulatory capital will raise the cost of borrowing, leading to reduction in lending and ultimately to less output. Oliveira Santos and Elliott (2012), for instance, surveyed the early impact studies carried on by the regulators (BCBS) and the industry (IIF) (Table 15.2)

All these impact studies concluded that the additional capital requirements were likely to substantially raise the borrowing costs, leading to falling equilibrium lending with a definite impact on . More recently, Quignon argued that the rise in regulatory capital (+7 % of RWA) was far higher than considered by BCBS (2010) assessments (+1.3 %), hence the consequences should be reassessed and the impact on growth would appear more significant.

The problem with all these studies is obvious since they rely on a transmission mechanism, which has been deactivated by the ECB monetary policy since the massive quantitative easing carried on under Mario Draghi's presidency. Figure 15.3 shows how the banks cost of lending sharply decreased after the €489 billion package of December 2011, the Long Term Refinancing Operation (LTRO) of February 2012 and the beginning of the QE in September 2012. Although the Joint Committee recently stated that the banks margins were "low (…) in the context of a low interest rate environment" (JC 2016, p. 4), the borrowing costs could hardly be lower. Hence the negative effects pointed out by the aforementioned array of impact studies are likely to have disappeared with the current monetary policy.

Table 15.2 Basel III impact studies

Study	Impact on credit spread (bps)		Impact on GDP growth (%)	
	Europe	World	Europe	World
IIF (2011) for 2012–2019	328	281	−0.4	−0.2
IIF (2011) for 2011–2015	291	364	−0.6	−0.7
Slovik and Cournède (2011)/ OECD	54	53	−0.23	−0.16
BCBS (2010) model 1	52	52	−0.07	−0.07
BCBS (2010) model 2	25	25	−0.03	−0.03
BCBS (2010) model 3	66	66	−0.08	−0.08

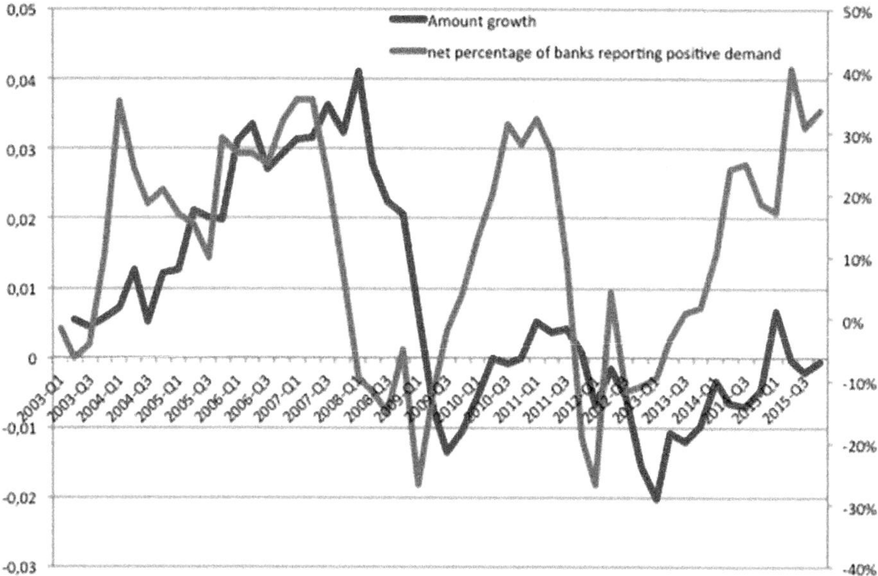

Fig. 15.3   Changes in demand and amount growth for loans or credit lines to enterprises in the EU (net percentages of banks reporting positive demand) (*Source*: ECB statistical datawarehouse)

One could still ask whether the impact studies were not pointing to substantial issues for the years 2009–2013, as the borrowing costs were still high and likely to be raised by the imminence of Basel III implementation. According to the ECB *Credit Monitor* data, it is likely that loan demand was depressed when the crisis broke out in 2008–2009 then around 2012 (ECB 2015, p. 38). On the contrary, the net percentage of banks reporting positive loan demand from Non-financial counterparty (NFC) was high during 2010 and 2011, and it began to rise again since 2012 Q4, the growth of loans still being negative. It seems then that, while *demand* for loans from NFC has been low in the wake of the crisis, it is rising now since the beginning of QE, but the amount lent failed to pick up yet. It is then necessary to ask whether this failure is not the side effect of the Basel III package, as we have seen some reason to think it might be. New theoretical grounds have been given to assess the performance of the newly implemented reform.

15.2.2   New Theoretical Developments

In 2008, Borio and Zhu issued a seminal contribution, first as BIS working paper republished as a journal article in 2012. The title explicitly mentioned risk-taking as a transmission mechanism of monetary policy.

It thus rationalized the idea that the impact of the Basel III package not only depended on interest rate. In particular, the paper discusses the difference between *threshold effect* in capital requirements (which raises the borrowing cost, as already seen) and *framework effect*, which might twist asset allocation as some classes of assets might be favoured or incentivized by the overall framework while others would not. EU sovereign bonds, for instance, benefit from positive framework effect, and it shall be asked whether corporate loans were not negatively affected by the framework effect.

The question was given a more general scope with the development of the risk-taking channel concept, which inaugurated a huge literature, involving both theoretical and empirical research. Basically, the risk-taking channel is a possible new channel of monetary policy, which leads investors to invest more, when interest rates fall, than investment function of interest rate would have predicted. Three convergent effects are at work with the risk-taking channel:

1) "One set of effects operates through the impact of interest rates on valuations, incomes and cash flows." This is the idea behind the real balance effect of Pigou (1943) or financial accelerator (Bernanke et al. 1999), allowing for "time-varying risk aversion," which makes it even more procyclical than the former. In this respect, lowering interest rate through monetary policy not only make investors richer, hence more willing to spend and invest all things being equal; they might also experience a drop in their risk aversion leading to even higher spending and investment.

2) "A second set of effects operates through the relationship between market rates and target rates of return." This is to say that institutions linked by a sticky rate (life insurance companies with a contractual rate of return, for instance) might experience a margin squeeze with relaxed monetary policy: these institutions then engage in search for yield, which lead to select riskier assets.

3) "A third set of effects operates through the communication policies and reaction function of the central bank. (…) By increasing the degree of transparency or commitment accompanying specific moves, and hence removing uncertainty about the future, the central bank can compress risk premia—a 'transparency effect', adding an extra kick to the effect of those moves." This is more or less the theoretical rationalization of new communication policies such as *forward guidance*.

The paper triggered a tidal wave of empirical research. For instance Antipa and Matheron (2014) established with a dynamic stochastic general equilibrium model calibrated to euro area data that forward guidance is very effective at the "zero lower bound" (= zero nominal discount rate), by providing a substantial boost to demand and reducing the costs of private deleveraging at the same time. The underlying mechanism relies on inflation announcement that create negative *real* interest rate expectations. In the Eurozone, though, the main financing operations rate has been below inflation since 2011, but the ECB failed both to raise inflation enough to produce definitely negative real interest rates expectation, and to have the amount lent to NFC picking up with pre-crisis level. Overall, while QE is hopefully negating the impact of Basel III on interest rates, the risk-taking channel is not working as intended. We shall then ask, given the previously gathered evidence, which element of the reform package appears to act as binding constraint in lending to corporations.

15.3 What Is the Binding Constraint?

Taking together unpalatable empirical facts (Sect. 15.3.1) with theoretical explanations for the mixed results of the Basel III implementation (Sect. 15.3.2.) we try to offer a convincing narrative (Sect. 15.3.3).

15.3.1 Unpalatable Empirical Facts

We would like to introduce three categories of such facts.

Measurement Error

A recent paper in ECB (2015) has shown that the previously issued statistics on amount lent were reporting optimistic figures in comparison with the new methodology implemented in September 2015. While the difference appears (ECB 2015, p. 26) small for NFC (one half of a growth point in 2015 and even less for the previous years) in comparison with households for instance (more than one point), the new methodology confirms that the amount outstanding of loans to NFC diminished for the 2012 Q3–2015 Q4 period, while banks were reporting increasing funding demand from the NFC.

Loan Rejection Figures

We have just established that, from 2012 Q3 to 2015 Q4 the amount outstanding of loans to NFC has been falling, although business demand was significantly increasing. During that time, loan rejections figures consistently

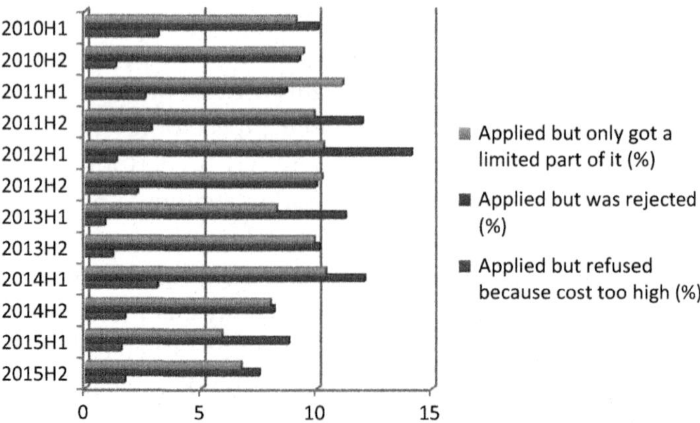

Fig. 15.4 Loans rejection evolution (*Source*: ECB statistical datawarehouse)

dropped (see Fig. 15.4). The only way to account for these statistics and to make them consistent would be that the banks are granting more loans, but constraining more tightly the amount lent per application, so that the global outstanding volume would be stalling. Such rationing behaviour would not allow the businesses to carry on their projects, barring a significant recovery of investment, output and employment.

Bank Asset-Side Unwinding
It shall be emphasized that, in the Eurozone, the fulfilling of regulatory constraints has not been obtained only by raising the amount of regulatory capital but also by a reduction of the RWA, as Fig. 15.5 shows. It is quite likely, then, that in order to save capital, the most impacted assets were those with the higher RWA per euro: corporate loans might hence have been impacted for this reason. While one may think this gives reason to hope this is over now that the banks have enough regulatory capital, one might not forget that US leverage rules and EU rules under overhaul (such as credit risk measurement) are likely to induce prudence from the banks. Unless it has been proved, this argument remains theoretical, though.

15.3.2 Theoretical Explanations

In Chap. 11, this volume, Jean-Paul Laurent insisted the quantitative impact studies so far proved to be wrong for three reasons at least: they were done on the basis of prereform portfolios likely to be changed once the reform was enacted, then the contribution of banks to impact studies were probably

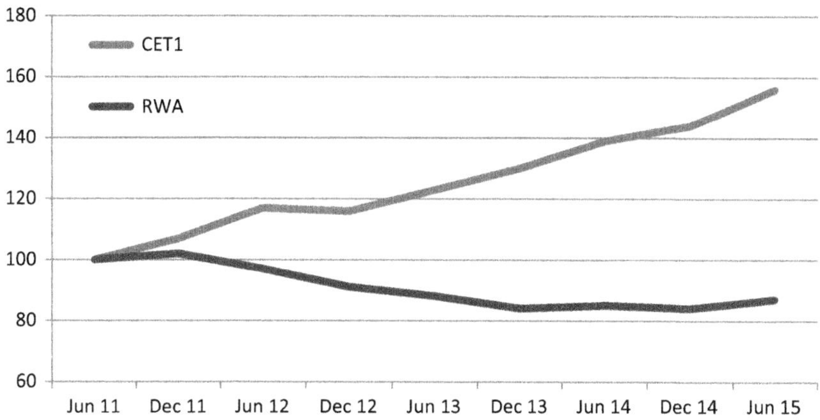

Fig. 15.5 Evolution of CET1 capital versus RWA over time (for Group 1 banks) under full implementation of CRD IV—CRR (*Source*: EBA)

(selection-) biased, eventually the exact rules were not determined, hence the banks' response could not be considered reliable. We would like to stress the later phenomenon.

The mechanism discovered by the risk-taking channel, especially the "forward guidance channel," is likely to work if it builds up significant inflationary expectations, but all empirical evidence shows that it does not work as of spring 2016. On the contrary, as the amount lent is not picking up, negative expectations are at work on the banks' side. The most likely reason of these negative expectations might be the future evolution of regulation: the Basel Committee on Banking Supervision (BCBS) is asking for a revision of the credit risk standard approach measurement (BCBS 2015), while the EBA has launched a regulatory review of the internal rating based approach (EBA 2016a), which is likely to lead to a stiffened risk valuation model, hence increased regulatory capital for credit risk, that is, for corporate loans. There is nothing certain in this process, except that the banks are reacting prudently. Eventually it might happen that the binding constraint be the banks' expectations about future regulation.

Contrary to a widely shared opinion, according to which the banks have lobbyists in Brussels, which allow them to influence the regulator, there are good reasons for banks to be overly risk averse in appraising the future state of regulation since they currently have no power to shape its evolution. We already mentioned that US leverage regulation has an impact on US-listed European banks: here they have no command of a regulatory impact, which is quite subtle as the problem is not about the leverage itself, but about how investors would perceive a higher leverage of EU banks. Another very delicate issue at the moment is the competition among authorities: this is the situation where authorities do not coordinate themselves in order to produce aligned incentives. If we take for instance the regulatory capital, then it is clear that the EU rules organized a playing field which is neither level nor coordinated. Looking back at our Table 15.1, one may notice that Group 2 banks which are not supervised by the Single Supervisory Mechanism (SSM) have their capital requirements checked (and Pillar 2 buffers decided) by their national supervisor and their countercyclical buffer tuned by their nationally competent authority (which is usually not the same as the supervisor). For Group 2 banks supervised by the SSM and Group 1 non-globally systemic banks, this SSM (ECB) plays the role of the national supervisor. Eventually, for Group 1 globally systemic banks (G-SIB), that G-SIB is decided by the Financial Stability Board (FSB). That is to say, these banks depend on national correspondent central bank (CCB), European (Pillar 2 + supervision) and global (FSB) regulators, with no one being able to commit to a comprehensive capital level. It seems clear thus that the bank interpret the future decisions of these competing authorities as potentially more damaging if they were used to a rather familiar relationship with their formerly unique supervisor, and acquire risky assets such as corporate loans.

The "risk-taking channel" of monetary policy is just not effective enough as of spring 2016, while the risk-taking channel of anticipated regulation is probably strengthening the banks' overall risk aversion. This is the end of the narrative we sketched so far, so let us describe it more completely.

15.3.3   A Narrative Since the Crisis

Table 15.3 summarizes the information of this section. The pre-crisis and immediate post-crisis profile led to a falling amount of NFC financing as a consequence of the slowdown: while demand has been slowly growing in 2009–2010, the banks have been strongly turning down NFC demand for additional credit as a result of growing risk aversion against crisis (2008), then against possible, plausible and imminent reform: as soon as January 2009, the BCBS offered a consultative document about "proposed enhancement to the Basel II framework"; the Basel III package was eventually disclosed in December 2010, with CRD IV proposed by the European Commission in July 2011, voted two years later for implementation on 1 July 2014. Hence the likelihood of reforms has been increasing since 2009 in a harsh environment, where banks were made responsible for the financial crisis and the

Table 15.3 Information summary

Year	Banks RWA	Demand for loans	NFC loans outstanding amount growth	Constraint by new regulation	Constraint by anticipated future regulation
2008		Falling	Slowing	No	No
2009		Low	Negative	No	Possibly
2010		Rising	Negative	No	Possibly
2011	Rising	Falling	Constant	No	Likely
2012	Falling	Falling	Negative	No	Likely
2013	Falling	Rising	Negative	Likely	Almost certain
2014	Constant	Rising	Negative	Likely	Almost certain
2015	Rising	Rising	Constant	Likely	Almost certain

subsequent economic misfortunes, and were submitted to a regulatory avalanche that was not built as a consistent project but as a pile of recriminations.

While demand for loans was clearly depressed in 2011–2012, it is hard to believe that future reform was playing a definite role in the falling amount of loans. But when demand picked up in 2013, the banks did not follow. As Basel III/CRD was about to be implemented, the banks lowered their RWA to meet the regulatory capital standard, and it is likely that they did this by cutting first the most capital intensive assets, such as corporate loans. The lowering of the interest rate down to zero by the relaxed monetary policy beginning in late 2011 was not enough. In 2014 and 2015, demand for loans from NFC grew stronger without the effective loans outstanding to rise. It seems that forward guidance and extreme monetary policy, although they were theoretically justified to deliver a boost to corporate borrowing, could not work as the banks were frightened by projected implementation of further capital buffers to be decided by unpredictable authorities: while the financial macroeconomists were theorizing lowering risk aversion through clever monetary policy, banks were experiencing rising uncertainty aversion in front of a regulatory future they could no longer see through or influence.

The remaining questions are whether this state of affairs is going to last, and what can be done to ease up the recovery.

15.4 From Prevision to Recommendations

A recent initiative by the European Commission gives us some insights into what is going to happen in the next few months (Sect. 15.4.1). Then we offer some recommendations to lead the next steps of banking regulation and business-driven growth (Sect. 15.4.2).

15.4.1   Plausible Next Months

Loans to NFC are not likely to restart strongly as there is a backlog of troubled assets (non performing loans in Italian banks, for instance), plus uncertain future steps of regulation. Even straightforward incentives such as the SME supporting factor, which amounted to reducing by almost 30 % the capital charges for loans to SME, were not met with any success in 2015 (EBA 2016b). This might be considered as a sign of extreme uncertainty aversion by the banks.

Fortunately, as EBA (2016b), the SME supporting factor will continue to incentivize lending to SME in the near future, and it will be subjected to further close monitoring. That will enable to track as early as possible either the furthering of uncertainty aversion or the shift to a lesser risk-averse bank asset choice policy. It is not unlikely that further regulatory evolution will be necessary to trigger this latter move.

15.4.2   Tuning Regulation to Trigger Growth

If we have been correct in diagnosing that the binding factor of corporate lending was anticipated regulation by banks, then it seems crucial to address that particular source of bank uncertainty aversion. We have identified competition among authorities as a possible source of uncertainty aversion, this concept being effective both at the legal and supervisory level. In order to ease up this concern, it might be fruitful to move toward a more consistent design and implementation of the regulatory package. A pause for assessment of the existing reforms, as asked for by the European Parliament, seems reasonable.

As we have shown, regulatory capital is a example of potential competition among authorities; it was decided by up to three different authorities at three different levels without any consistency checks. Moving away from the coordination issues implied by competition among authorities would imply aligning the role of stakeholders: this could be achieved only via a consistent regulatory framework. One could think that the supervisor should basically check the compliance of capital requirements and internal models with regulations; while a banking authority could design the models to measure the risks experienced by the banks. Eventually, the acceptable level of risk with every institution (i.e. microprudential) must be decided by the law, while the systemic risk policy might be taken care of by a higher level authority, either purposive or political, which would set up dedicated capital pockets to address designated risks, the breakdown among banking institutions would be made according to risk measures provided by models designed by the banking authority.

In this "pyramidal" model (supreme macroprudential authority deciding "risk budgets," banking authority designing risk measurement models, supervisor verifying that they are correctly implemented into banks) there seems to be no conflict among authority… but possible agency conflicts: these might be addressed through classical incentives. At least, the signal to banks would be clear and reliable, excluding uncertainty aversion. Macron (2016) made a very clear point about such risk budgets. Rodarie (2015) has shown that if implemented correctly, they would require the political leaders to take full responsibility for their choices. While this would mean a deep change of the principles of overall regulatory architecture, with a long time to go, it is possible to advance in the meantime.

In the meantime, the broken piping of corporate financing might be fixed by using different vehicles. For instance, securitization might help either direct funding of middle-market companies through Collateralized loan obligations (CLO) or indirect funding of SMEs by securitizing other credits (RMBS for instance) thus freeing up regulatory capital to grant new SME loans. A more precise review of the options offered by securitization appears in Daphné Héant et al., Chap. 16, this volume. It is up to the member states to develop their financial ecosystem, as has been the case in the last few months: Renzi has developed private equity (Politi 2016) in Italy, while in France, the projected law Sapin 2 in its art. 33 is allowing life insurance companies to shift investments to purposely set up pension funds in order to switch from the Solvency 2 to Solvency 1 regulatory regime. The implied regulatory capital relaxation would make it easier to invest in stocks or other corporate liabilities, which are too heavily charged under S2. Schackmann-Fallis and Weiss (2014) are advocating that banks are providing the businesses with stable and reliable funding, which should not be substituted by tempting new gadgets; it is clear that with overly regulated banks, any opportunity might be overexploited by the shadow banking system. Hence the need for consistency among stakeholders.

15.5   Conclusion

The EU, which was not the origin of the financial crisis, has almost lost a growth cycle to the USA. Our analysis has shown that the negative effect of the Basel III package expected by the pre-QE studies are almost annihilated today. The recession must then have other causes: falling corporate lending volumes resulted from falling demand in the aftermath of the financial crisis, but this is longer the case. The EU is trying to incentivize corporate lending via forward guidance as well as the "supporting factor" of cutting down the Basel capital requirements. The macroeconomic theorists are trying to account for the future success of monetary policy around a zero nominal interest rate via the risk-taking channel. All these clever initiatives have failed to deliver. As a consequence, we might infer that banks are simply not taking any risks: rather than appealing to risk aversion, we would like to argue that the banks seem especially embarrassed by future regulatory developments, which appear remote and uncertain. The binding constraint for corporate lending and growth in the EU is therefore plausibly a combination of banks' expectations of future regulation and strong uncertainty aversion. While we offer some mitigation prospects (Sect. 15.4.2), we hope that the theoretical developments of the recent years will quickly yield both theoretical advances and practical results.

References

Antipa, P., & Matheron, J. (2014). Interactions between monetary and macroprudential policies. *Financial Stability Review, 18,* 225–239.

BCBS. (2014). *Basel III: The net stable funding ratio.* Available on: http://www.bis.org/bcbs/publ/d295.pdf

BCBS. (2015, December). *Second consultative document standards revisions to the standardised approach for credit risk.* Available on: http://www.bis.org/bcbs/publ/d347.pdf

Brundsen, J. (2015, October 1). European Commission changes tone over financial regulation. *Financial Times.*

EBA. (2014). *Second report on impact assessment for liquidity measures under Article 509(1) of the CRR.* Available on: https://www.eba.europa.eu/regulation-and-policy/liquidity-risk

EBA. (2015). *EBA report on net stable funding requirements under Article 510 of the CRR.* EBA/Op/2015/22.

EBA. (2016a). *Opinion of the European Banking Authority on the implementation of the regulatory review of the IRB approach.* EBA/Op/2016/01.

EBA. (2016b). *EBA report on SMEs and SME supporting factor.* EBA/OP/2016/04. Available from: https://www.eba.europa.eu/-/eba-publishes-the-report-on-smes-and-the-sme-supporting-factor

EC. (2013). *Capital requirements—CRD IV/CRR—Frequently asked questions.* EC MEMO 13/690. http://europa.eu/rapid/press-release_MEMO-13-690_fr.htm

ECB. (2015). The transmission of the ECB's recent non-standard monetary policy measures. *ECB Economic Bulletin, 2015*(7), 32–51.

EP. (2016). European parliament resolution of 19 January 2016 on stocktaking and challenges of the EU financial services regulation: Impact and the way forward towards a more efficient and effective EU framework for financial regulation and a Capital Markets Union, P8_TA(2016)0006.

Hale, T. (2016, April 11). Italian banks extend gains on rescue fund hopes. *Financial Times*.

Institute of International Finance. (2010). *Interim report on the cumulative impact on the global economy of proposed changes in the banking regulatory framework*. Online.

Institute of International Finance. (2011). *The cumulative impact on the global economy of changes in the financial regulatory framework*. Online.

JC. (2016). *Joint Committee report on risks and vulnerabilities in the EU financial system*. JC 2016 17.

Macron, E. (2016). Interview. *Risques, 105*, 11.

Pigou, A. C. (1943). The classical stationary state. *Economic Journal, 53*, 343–351. doi:10.2307/2226394.

Politi, J. (2016, June 12). Private equity fights Italy tax changes. *Financial Times*.

Sanderson, R. (2016, March 16). Corporate Italy risks 'asphyxia', warns business chief. *Financial Times*.

Schackmann-Fallis, K.-P., & Weiss, M. (2014). Régulation des marchés financiers et financement des entreprises. *Revue d'économie financière, 2*, 209–232.

Wise, P. (2016, April 29). Court blocks Novo Banco bond move. *Financial Times*.

16

Higher Quality Securitization

Daphné Héant, Sophie Vermeille, and Yann Coatanlem

16.1 Introduction

Caught red-handed at the epicentre of the 2008 subprime crisis, securitization has a bad reputation. It is at the heart of the ominously named "shadow banking" system, an intricate web of loosely regulated financial intermediaries. In the aftermath of one of the worst economic crises in decades, many lawsuits have pitted banks, investors and regulators against each other in high-profile cases centred on securitization. Owing to the understandable loss of investor confidence post-crisis and European regulation introduced

Daphné Héant, structured credit investor, member of Club Praxis.
Sophie Vermeille, president of the think tank Droit et Croissance, lawyer at DLA Piper, researcher at Laboratoire d'économie du droit at Paris II Panthéon—Assas and lecturer at Paris II.
Yann Coatanlem, president of Club Praxis and director of research at Citigroup.
Special thanks to Pierre-Charles Pradier for his careful review and insightful comments.

D. Héant (✉)
Club Praxis, New York, NY, USA

S. Vermeille
Droit et Croissance and DLA Piper and Laboratoire d'économie du droit at Paris II Panthéon, Paris, France

Y. Coatanlem
Club Praxis and Citigroup, New York, NY, USA

R. Douady et al. (eds.), *Financial Regulation in the EU*,
DOI 10.1007/978-3-319-44287-7_16

in 2011, securitization volumes in Europe plummeted from €594 billion in 2007 to €216 billion in 2014.[1]

On the other hand, the Federal Reserve and the European Central Bank (ECB) have partly focused their economic recovery programmes on the over $10 trillion global securitization market through "quantitative easing" measures.[2] More recently the ECB, the European commission, the Basel Committee and the European Banking Authority (EBA) have approached securitization under a new angle. Lord Hill, former European Commissioner for financial stability, declared in February 2015: "We should look again at whether the 'skin in the game' rules work effectively for high-quality securitisations."[3] In September 2015 the European Commission concluded: "Securitisation is an important element of well-functioning financial markets. Soundly structured securitisation is an important channel for diversifying funding sources and allocating risk more efficiently within the Union financial system. It allows for a broader distribution of financial sector risk and can help to free up originator's balance sheets to allow for further lending to the economy. Overall, it can improve efficiencies in the financial system and provide additional investment opportunities. Securitisation can create a bridge between credit institutions and capital markets with an indirect benefit for businesses and citizens (through, for example, less expensive loans and business financing, credits for immovable property and credit cards)."[4] Aiming to rekindle this market, the European Commission published a proposal for new regulation "laying down common rules on securitisation and creating a European framework for simple, transparent and standardised securitisation and amending" previous relevant directives.

What is securitization? What is its role in the economy? Why have regulators been ambivalent about restricting its use and promoting its growth? This chapter will go over the basics of securitization, discuss the merits and flaws of current regulation and outline future challenges on the path to the European Capital Markets Union.[5]

---

[1] http://www.wsj.com/articles/eu-proposes-new-capital-rules-to-boost-securitization-1443610493

[2] http://www.urban.org/sites/default/files/alfresco/publication-pdfs/2000375-The-Rebirth-of-Securitization.pdf

[3] Financial Times, 17 February 2015

[4] *Regulation of the European Parliament and of the Council laying down common rules on securitisation and creating a European framework for simple, transparent and standardised securitisation and amending Directives 2009/65/EC, 2009/138/EC, 2011/61/EU and Regulations (EC) No 1060/2009 and (EU) No 648/2012*, 30 September 2015

[5] The authors for this analysis contributed to a Club Praxis report in April 2015. Section 4 by Sophie Vermeille was integrally copied and translated from French by Pierre-Charles Pradier: http://www.club-praxis.com/?p=1658.

16.2 Securitization

Securitization is a financial process by which loans are consolidated and sold to investors under the form of securities named "tranches." The proceeds from the sale of the tranches finance the purchase of the "underlying loans." Priority of payment and loss absorption on these tranches is contractually predetermined. A tranche's yield increases with its risk and it is generally rated by rating agencies. A tranche can be bought or sold independently from the underlying loans. More specifically, while an initial investor may lose faith in the financial prospects of a tranche, the sale of his security will not result in the underlying loans being sold in the market.

Securitization is in its essence a transfer of risk from the institutions which lend to finance individuals and companies' projects (e.g. banks) to investment institutions which benefit from longer term funding (e.g. insurance companies, pension funds, asset managers).

Securitization and the product it creates can be complex. Simplistically, however, the content of books neatly ordered in a library or in a messy pile remains the same. Similarly, taken as a whole, securitization does not transform bad loans into good securities or good loans into bad securities. Securitization is but the mere container of credit; it allocates losses to some tranches and insulates others, but the aggregate amount of loss is unchanged. Asset quality is paramount to performance, and the European Commission highlighted that "AAA-rated U.S. securitisation instruments backed by residential mortgages (RMBS) reached default rates of 16% (subprime) and 3% (prime). By contrast, default rates of EU RMBS never rose above 0.1%" (Fig. 16.1).

Securitization applies to numerous types of financing: mortgages (RMBS), commercial loans (CMBS), student loans, credit cards, auto loans, aircraft leases (ABS), and loans to high yield companies (CLO: Collateralized Loan Obligation) on which we will focus in more depth in Sect. 16.4.

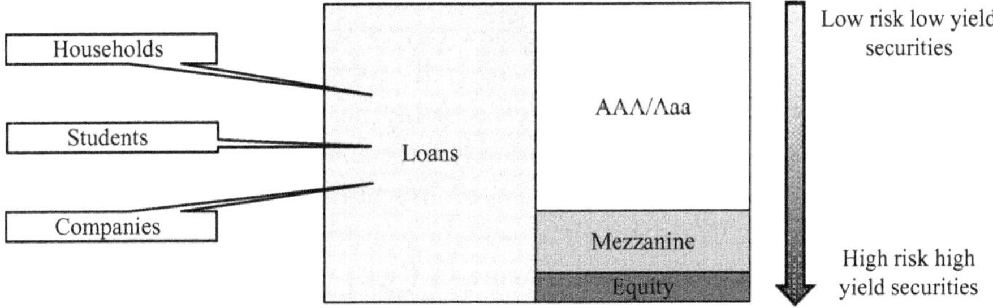

Fig. 16.1   Securitized product (SPV)

Financing	Short Term		Long Term		
Lendee	Companies	Individuals	Individuals	Companies	
Securitized Product	ABCP	ABCP	RMBS, ABS (Student Loans, Credit Cards)	CMBS, Balance Sheet CLOs	*Balance Sheet originated & Passively managed*
				Open Market CLO	*Open Market sourced & Actively managed*
Number of loans per pool		thousands to tens of thousands		tens to hundreds	

Fig. 16.2 Securitization categories

Securitization can be either short term (Asset Backed Commercial Paper) or long term (sometimes over a decade). Each type of securitized product has slightly different structural features generally dictated by its underlying assets or by investor needs. Most structured products are "static" or "passively managed." A static deal's underlying pool of loans amortizes through early repayment ("prepayment") or default. No additions or exchanges are made to the original loan pool. Passively managed deals' prepaid loans may be automatically reinvested in very similar assets (e.g. for credit card deals). A CLO's loans can be either originated on a bank's balance sheet (static or passively managed deal) or sourced in the open market and "actively managed" by a CLO manager. The CLO manager makes changes to the original portfolio, buying and selling loans on a discretionary basis. The matrix below offers a simplified overview of these features (Fig. 16.2).

The flow chart categorizes securitization participants: in white the companies or individuals who need to finance their projects and the investors who provide that financing because they wish to invest their money productively. The "white cell" participants have a need which is serviced by the "black cell" participants. These "black cell" participants are often banks (but not always). The originators create loans, the structurers package them together in a special purpose vehicle (SPV) and the syndicators sell them to investors. The structurers need the advice of lawyers to structure the SPV on solid legal footing and the validation of rating agencies to standardize and opine on the creditworthiness of tranches (both "grey cell" participants). This assessment of creditworthiness came under much scrutiny post-crisis as rating agencies had failed to determine risk appropriately, especially in the securitization of tranches of securitized products (so called "resecuritizations"). In Sect. 16.3, we will examine how regulators have sought to mitigate this issue. Finally, in actively managed securitizations, a manager ("grey cell" participant) oversees the SPV after it is created and ensures that dozens of tests focused on portfolio

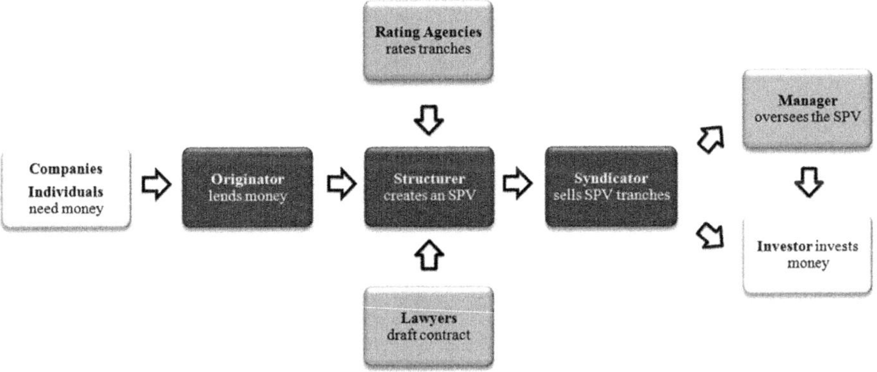

Fig. 16.3 Securitization participants

quality and tranche safety remain in compliance while buying and selling the underlying credits of the SPV for the benefit of the investor (Fig. 16.3).

Investors are mostly institutional: banks, insurance companies, pension funds or asset managers. In Europe, since the 2008 crisis, securitization has widely been used as collateral by banks to access liquidity from central banks. Unfortunately, as the Basel Committee commented, "issuance placed with third-party investors is still very low, with the exception of auto loan ABS and UK and Dutch RMBS, most of which are placed with the market" (Fig. 16.4).[6]

16.3 European Commission Proposal 2015/0226 (COD)

The European Commission (February 2015), the Basel Committee on Banking Supervision, (December 2014), the European Banking Authority and the Bank of England together with the ECB (March 2015) all insisted on the development of a "simple, transparent and standard" (STS) securitization framework. The European Commission published a regulation proposal (hereafter named SR). It states the framework's objectives, the regulatory requirements for all securitized products and the more stringent constraints to qualify for an STS label (which should benefit from lower capital charges).

---

[6] Basel Committee on Banking Supervision, *Criteria for identifying simple, transparent and comparable securitisations*, December 2014.

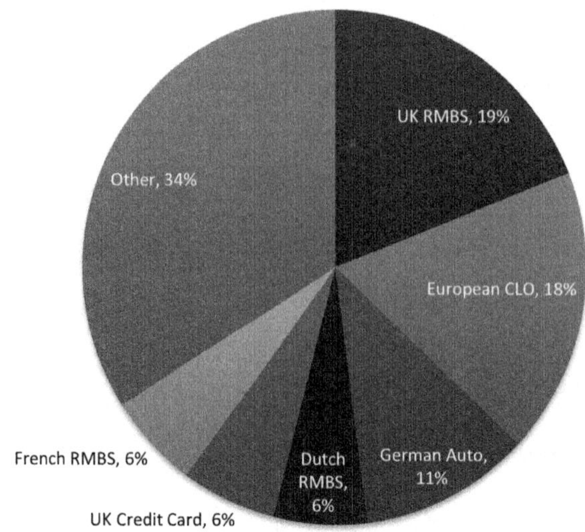

Fig. 16.4 Issuance placed with investors, 2nd Quarter 2015 (*Source*: DATA from AFME, SIFMA)

SR is 76 pages long, and this section will only highlight a few main features of the regulation, which should come into force in 2018.[7]

16.3.1 Rationale, Concerns and Incentives

The European Commission's objective is to foster the "development of a simple, transparent and standardised securitisation market" which "constitutes a building block of the Capital Markets Union (CMU)." The framework should "promote integration of EU financial markets, help diversify funding sources and unlock capital, making it easier for credit institutions and lenders to lend to households and businesses." The European Commission estimates that "if the securitisation market would return to pre-crisis average issuance levels and new issuance would be used by credit institutions to provide new credit, these would be able to provide an additional amount of credit to the private sector ranging between €100-150bn. This would represent a 1.6% increase in credit to EU firms and households."

As much as the European Commission sees potential in promoting securitization it is also wary of the pitfalls of the last crisis. "It is essential to prevent

---

[7] http://www.lexology.com/library/detail.aspx?g=3bbb3de9-6c6f-4b08-8910-7d18ea7e070d

the recurrence of purely 'originate to distribute' models. In those situations lenders grant credits applying poor and weak underwriting policies as they know in advance that related risks are eventually sold to third parties. Thus, the exposures to be securitised should be originated in the ordinary course of the originator's or original lender's business pursuant to underwriting standards that should not be less stringent than those the originator or original lender applies to origination of similar exposures which are not securitised." This concern is completely warranted; the "alignment of interest" between creators of securitization (originators, sponsors,[8] issuers) and investors is at the heart of securitization regulation.

Investment in tranches of securitized products is very capital intensive in Europe.[9] The proposed regulation on securitization (2015/226 COD) comes with a companion text (2015/225 COD) amending the Capital Requirements Regulation (575/2013/EU), hereafter named CRR. Implementation measures of "lower" level, such as capital requirements for insurance companies (DR 2015/35/EU) or liquidity requirements for banks (DR 2015/61/EU) will be fine tuned by delegated regulations of the Commission once the regulation proposals have been approved. Non-STS securitized investments will still be allowed but with heavier capital charges. This design is clairvoyant, as it doesn't ban innovation; it simply makes it less appealing economically until it has been vetted.

16.3.2 General Rules for all Securitizations

Compliance with SR regulation is assessed on three dimensions: investor due diligence, originator/sponsor risk retention and deal transparency.

Firstly the European Commission reminded investors that no label should release them from appropriate analysis. The due diligence criteria (sound analysis and verification of risk retention compliance) and transparency criteria (quarterly reports and deal documentation) are sensible and should already be part of any responsible investor's analysis. It may appear obvious but most of the blame for the subprime meltdown was placed on originators/sponsors and rating agencies while investors were troubled little for their lack of homework. The "new EU framework does not replace the need for investors

---

[8] "'sponsor' means a credit institution or investment firm as defined in Article 4(1) points (1) and (2) of Regulation (EU) No 2013/575 other than an originator that establishes and manages an asset-backed commercial paper programme or other securitisation transaction or scheme that purchases exposures from third-party entities."

[9] http://www.solvencyiinews.com/europe/anything-is-possible-in-sii-securitisation-charges-revamp.

to conduct thorough due diligence. It also does not control for credit risk in the securitised loans—investors have the full range of investment possibilities to suit their risk-reward preferences available to them. The concept of 'simple, transparent and standardised' (STS) refers to the process by which the securitisation is structured and not the underlying credit quality of the assets involved. It therefore does not mean that some non STS securitisations, for instance implying less simple structures, could not be formed of underlying exposures with appropriate credit quality features." This approach contrasts with the USA's "qualified" securitizations (such as qualified mortgages), which are exempted from risk retention. The focus on "simple structures" rather than "quality assets" has benefits (the regulator doesn't need to continuously assess the appropriate level of risk of each asset class) and drawbacks (regardless of the historical performance of the loans considered, all securitizations require the same risk retention level).

Secondly the risk retention criteria (the hardest to comply with) are those already defined in the CRR published in January 2011. Nomura summarizes: "The rules require that the originator, sponsor or original lender retain, throughout the life of the deal, an unhedged 'material net economic interest' of at least 5 % in the transaction, in one of five ways:

- 5 % of each tranche in the securitization [vertical slice]
- 5% seller interest, in revolving deals or deals with revolving exposures (e.g., credit cards)
- Retention of 5% of randomly selected exposures which would have otherwise been securitised, as long as the number retained is at least 100
- 5% first-loss tranche(s) [horizontal slice]
- 5% first-loss retention in each of the underlying loans in the securitisation.

[…] An originator cannot be the risk-retainer if it is an entity 'established or operated for the sole purpose of securitising exposures'. This provision was added at the recommendation of the EBA to close a perceived loophole in the current legislation by which risk retainers could circumvent the spirit of the requirement. This has caused concern particularly in the European CLO market, where some funds act as originator risk retainers."[10]

How costly is risk retention in terms of reduced volumes of securitization? The impact is hard to evaluate because post crisis credit markets haven't regained their 2007 vigor. Is lack of issuance in Europe due to economic

---

[10] *A Guide to the New Securitisation Regulation in Europe*, Nomura, October 2015.

weakness or overly punitive regulation? Risk retention in the USA will be implemented in December 2016 so issuance in 2017 should provide better insight.

The European Commission has decided that the burden of proof of risk retention be on the originator/sponsor rather than the investor for European securitizations. For foreign securitizations, a European investor will bear the burden of proof however. This is a sensible decision as the investor cannot always verify that the originator/sponsor is holding his risk retention piece. In prior legislation the issue of cross-border investment hadn't sufficiently been addressed. In the new version European investors may invest in non-EU securitized products as long as they comply with the general securitization rules defined by the European Commission. Additionally, non-EU securitized products can apply for STS status.

The European Commission divides the securitized products landscape into "long- term" and "short-term" securitizations, "cash" underlying assets and "synthetics," simple securitizations and "resecuritizations." However, the parceling could have been even more granular, acknowledging the differences between *balance sheet* transactions and *open market* ones (cf. matrix chart, Sect. 16.2). Indeed, there is a better alignment of interest in open market actively managed transactions (where a manager buys loans originated by others and is paid when they perform) than in balance sheet transactions. In the latter case the bank has originated the loans itself and securitizes them to free its balance sheet. The bank benefits from asymmetric information on the quality of the assets securitized. The bank can hardly be impartial when it directly benefits from choosing to securitize its weaker credits or creating structures with more lenient terms.

Interestingly Guillaume Eliet, managing director of regulation policy at the French agency, the AMF, said "There should be a regulated entity to manage the vehicle in the interests of investors at every step and to make sure there is no conflict of interest."[11] The comment was intended to mean that a regulated entity should determine whether a deal is STS or not (as opposed to the European Commission's proposal that it be determined by the originator/sponsor of the deal). However, Managers of CLOs (deemed non STS by SR) ironically fit the description. They are regulated and "manage the vehicle in the interests of investors at every step" thanks to proper incentives (see Sect. 16.4).

Across all securitized products, the volume of balance sheet transactions is far larger than that of open market deals. This may explain why both US and

---

[11] "France warns that EU securitisation push lacks ambition," *Financial Times*, October 2015.

European regulation have disregarded this critical difference. However open market deals have the potential to grow significantly if they aren't too highly penalized by regulation. In the USA, open market CLOs were among the first securitizations to reemerge post crisis. Sect. 16.4 will advocate for a differentiated treatment.

Proposal 1 Create a separate category for "open market" securitizations and give some credit to the transparency and alignment of interest they provide when considering risk retention levels.

16.3.3 Additional Rules Specific to STS Securitizations

Why did the European Commission insist on making securitization "simple, transparent and standardized"? Securitization is complex because hundreds to thousands of credits are pooled together. The assessment of risk no longer relies on the knowledge of a specific borrower but becomes statistical, focusing on aggregated metrics. Securitization is opaque because tranche investors did not grant individual loans themselves. They relied on an originator to create the loans, a syndicator to create the securitization and sometimes a manager to oversee it after creation. The interests of these parties are not always well aligned with the investor. Securitization is not standardized because each time an issuer wishes to sell credits to a more or less diversified investor base, it draws structurers, lawyers and rating agencies into the negotiation of a unique contract. This contract is often hundreds of pages long and reflects the tug of war between all of the participants and especially between senior and junior investors of a securitization.

The European Commission made 29 proposals to mitigate those issues and grant the STS label (see Annex). We will highlight a few with the asset classes which fail a requirement in parenthesis. A "simple" securitization cannot be actively managed on a discretionary basis (CLO) nor can it be a resecuritization (CDO^2). It cannot contain "transferable securities", in particular, bonds (CLO, CBO) or loans to credit impaired borrowers (Non Performing Loan RMBS). To be considered "transparent" the repayment of a securitization's tranches cannot rely on asset sales (CMBS) and there must be at least five years of historical data available on the underlying assets. To be considered "standard" a securitization's originator/sponsor must satisfy "risk retention" and the payments on its tranches must be sequential at least as soon as credit metrics fail predefined tests.

Interestingly, the Volcker Rule in the Dodd–Frank Act (US regulation) also prohibits banks from owning CLO tranches with underlying bonds. This caused CLOs issued prior to the regulation and not grandfathered in to sell their high yield bonds and amend their legal documentation (which required the approval of a majority of all the investors in each tranche, investors who are not always aligned in their interests). Though the process was very tedious and less than half of former CLOs became compliant (thus forcing banks to sell their positions), US CLOs did not have a very large portion of their assets invested in bonds so the economic impact of the transition was muted. In Europe however, CLOs have a larger allocation to bonds due to a smaller leveraged loan market. Above and beyond a regulation's restrictiveness, the decision to make it apply retroactively to previously issued deals, which deals to grandfather in and how long non-compliance is tolerated, are particularly sensitive. When poorly handled, synchronized expeditious sales of non-compliant deals can cause large losses to financial institutions.

16.3.4   Issues Arising from the Regulation

While the European Commission rightly requires originators to report certain metrics on a regular basis it does not specify the underlying loan data to be made available (even though they require that same data of investors for due diligence) nor does it insist on metric quality. Companies are audited so the risk of fraudulent metrics is greatly reduced but individuals are not held accountable to the same degree. Many issues in US subprime securitizations came from originators allowing individuals to declare their income themselves ("stated income" versus "verified income").

Proposal 2 Consumer-based (student loans, mortgages, etc.) securitization originators must require proof of certain metrics, in particular income.

SR states that "Originators, sponsors and SSPE's should make freely available the information to investors, [...] on a website [...] such as the 'European Datawarehouse'." Centralization and easy access to information is indeed paramount. The European Commission could go a step further and extend France's recent Macron Law, Article 169 to the EU.[12] The law allows the French central bank to share the FIBEN database (which includes pro-

---

[12] Macron law, Article 169 modifying section L. 144-1 of the Monetary and Financial Code.

prietary ratings on companies) with banks, central banks, insurance companies and asset managers as was recommended by the French Council of Economic Analysis. The Bank of England and the ECB also support the effort towards "the availability of key performance metrics" on Small and Medium Enterprises (SMEs).[13] The framework could be further extended to individuals (Americans have FICO scores). However, great caution must be exercised in the choice of metrics utilized and the protection of sensitive personal information.

Proposal 3 Allow central banks across the EU to share with financial firms the data they have on companies' creditworthiness (extension of the Macron Law, Article 169). Similarly a credit rating score for individuals could be developed.

Again in the spirit of transparency, the European Commission has required that originator/sponsors provide a model of each securitization's cashflow payments. Given the bias of a seller to make a securitization appear at its best by tweaking one of the dozens of parameters of the model, it would be even better to require that an independent modeler also be in charge of that process. Today Intex has established itself in a number of asset classes and provides helpful modeling over the life of a deal. However, they do not model a securitization until after it is sold to investors and there are often significant differences between a bank's cashflows and those on Intex immediately post-sale. Furthermore, while most US RMBS and open market CLOs are already well modeled on Intex this is not the case for all student loan deals or balance sheet securitizations. Moody's Analytics and Bloomberg are both ramping up their cashflow modeling capabilities, which should provide diversity of opinion and enhanced asset coverage for investors.

Proposal 4 An independent securitization modeling company should model each securitization prior to sale to investors. That company's main source of income should be investor access fees not fees from the originator/sponsor.

The Commission mentions the possibility to securitize loans to SMEs. "First of all, [the policy options] should help SME financing through two specific channels: SME lending, through SME ABS, and short-term lending, through simple and transparent ABCP conduits. Secondly, the initiative

---

[13] Bank of England, European Central Bank, March 2015.

should provide banks with a tool for transferring risk off their balance sheets." Not all loans are well suited for securitization. In the USA "middle market" CLOs have emerged (see issuance chart, Sect. 14.4.2) but middle market loans (MML) are to companies with an EBITDA (earnings before interest, taxes, depreciation and amortization) between $10 million and $60 million. For very small companies, proximity with a banker and exchange of information on an ongoing basis have advantages that securitization cannot provide. Furthermore, middle market loans are quasi-illiquid, meaning that they can rarely be sold on a secondary market. In that sense they are very similar to a mortgage but the balance of the loan is larger.

Proposal 5 Regulators should tread with caution in securitizations involving SME loans. A higher level of risk retention could be warranted.

Regardless of whether SME CLOs emerge in Europe, banks will get relief from other types of securitization and those funds could benefit SMEs through a trickledown effect. Alternatively, a securitization used as collateral for the central bank but where no tranches are sold to third party investors could be a favourable intermediate solution. In France, five large banks (BNP Paribas, BPCE, Crédit Agricole, HSBC France and Société Générale) issued €2.65 billion of ESNI (Euro Secured Notes Issuer) securities on their corporate loans in April 2014.[14]

Alongside the publication of SR, the European Commission also proposed a regulation amending CRR. Capital treatment for securitization is still very punitive but the new regulation provides some relief. Capital charges on the senior tranche of a securitization are capped to the level of capital required on its underlying loans. This cap makes sense as a senior tranche on a pool of loans carries less risk than that pool of loans!

However, rules have become so complex that banks are having a hard time calculating the capital required for Basel III and for the Federal Reserve's "Comprehensive Capital Analysis and Review" (CCAR). Convergence of regional regulation on capital quality, leverage ratios, liquidity leverage ratio and net stable funding ratio is critical.

Proposal 6 Regulators should assist banks in their Basel III capital calculation (Risk-Weighted-Assets computed from "Supervisory Formula

---

[14] AGEFI: http://www.agefi.fr/articles/la-bce-adoube-le-vehicule-de-titrisation-de-la-place-de-paris-1367847.html.

Approach" (SFA) and "Simplified Supervisory Approach" (SSFA) methods,[15] in particular by providing a centralized database.

The positive impact of the capital relief in the CRR amendment may be completely muted by other regulations. In particular an interim impact analysis for the Fundamental Review of the Trading Book (FRTB) was released in November 2015 by the Basel Committee on Banking Supervision.[16] J.P. Morgan's research assessed the capital charge on some junior debt tranches of CLOs for example to be between two to three times the market value of the position.[17] This was particularly troubling as a bank can only lose its capital once on any tranche purchased. The level of capital required on CLO AA tranches was over 40 times the level required under Basel 2.5 rules. J.P. Morgan said: "We reiterate that the FRTB rules as currently proposed would result in bank capital charges for fixed income trading books becoming extremely onerous and could lead to drastic changes in the pricing of inventory (to cover higher capital costs), downsizing of operations, or an exit of some broker dealers. There could be unintended collateral damage to the real economy given CLOs' provision of liquidity and financing to corporates." The rationale for these levels of capital charges was unclear. Several associations representing financial markets' participants wrote an open letter to the Federal Reserve and other regulators to reach a more viable agreement.[18]

The final FRTB rules (see Table 16.1) are to be implemented in 2019, though most banks are already adapting to them in anticipation. Though far more onerous than Basel 2.5's charges, they are still more reasonable than the November 2015 proposal. For example, a generic AA rated CLO tranche will require a bank to keep 20 % of its market value on its balance sheet which is 9.6 times the ~2 % currently required under Basel 2.5 but far less than the 95 % initially suggested. This illustrates the iterative nature of regulations in striking a balance between stability and growth (Table 16.1).

J.P. Morgan's assessment is only at the tranche level. Above and beyond CLOs, rules on correlation inter- and intra-asset classes may decrease the additional capital needed for the bank to comply with FRTB on their aggregated balance sheet.

Informal discussions with banks' trading desks suggest that the rules make structured products less attractive to the point where banks may chose to exit

---

[15] Cf. (Basel Committee on Banking Supervision, December 2012).

[16] http://www.bis.org/bcbs/publ/d346.htm.

[17] J.P. Morgan, 5 November 2015.

[18] http://www.sifma.org/issues/item.aspx?id=8589957660.

Table 16.1 Estimated Capital Requirement for CLOs under FRTB

		Current SSFA		Proposed FRTB		Final FRTB		
Rating	Credit Quality	Risk weight (in %)	Capital as % of MV (in %)	Risk weight (in %)	Capital as % of MV (in %)	Risk weight (in %)	Capital as % of MV (in %)	Capital ratio to current SSFA
AAA	Senior IG	20	2	328	34	86	9	4.3
AA	non-Senior IG	40	2	908	95	192	20	9.6
A	non-Senior IG	43	4	1137	119	357	37	8.3
BBB	non-Senior IG	187	20	1389	146	608	64	3.2
BB	HY/NR	602	63	2673	281	1043	109	1.7
B	HY/NR	1190	125	3035	319	1404	147	1.2
Equity	HY/NR	1250	131	2319	243	1359	143	1.1

Data Reproduced with the kind permission of J.P. Morgan

some asset classes entirely. The warning is credible as many banks have already curtailed or exited some of their fixed income trading businesses over the last couple of years, partly due to regulation.[19] This will be detrimental to investment liquidity: the ability for an investor to buy or sell an asset quickly and in large size without affecting its price or incurring large transaction costs.

Quantifying the impact of specific regulation on asset liquidity is beyond the scope of this chapter, but it is a central concern of institutional investors as well as some regulators such as the US treasury which stated that "regulations have created multiple constraints likely to curtail liquidity when it is really needed."[20] The process of writing wise new regulation is made more complex by its interaction with existing and forecasted regulations.

Proposal 7 Regulatory institutions must cooperate with each other and ask for market representatives' comments to achieve best results. A review of regulation should be conducted after it is enacted to track whether its impact on investment liquidity, market competition, business consolidations and exits isn't so severe as to outweigh its benefits.

The European Commission exempts "public authority"-backed securitization from certain constraints. "In accordance with existing EU law, certain exceptions should be made for cases when securitised exposures are fully, unconditionally and irrevocably guaranteed by in particular public authorities." More detail should be provided on what the European Commission has in mind. Is this sentence a placeholder for legislation on future guaranteed

---

[19] http://www.businessfinancenews.com/26659-morgan-stanley-to-dismiss-400-employees/.

[20] https://www.treasury.gov/resource-center/data-chart-center/quarterly-refunding/Documents/Charge_2.pdf.

securitized products? What type of institution would qualify for these exemptions? Not all European "public authorities" have the same creditworthiness, and guarantees on securitized tranches should not be given lightly. A review of the Fannie Mae and Freddie Mac bailout during the 2008 crisis could be useful in assessing the negative consequences of a public authority backing securitizations.

Proposal 8 Provide more clarity and limits to exemptions from regulation by "public authorities."

16.4 Case Study: CLO: High Yield Corporate Financing

16.4.1 CLO Characteristics

Open market CLOs differ from other securitizations in two important ways.

Firstly, their underlying corporate loans are quoted daily on secondary markets with reasonable liquidity. While only the originator has detailed knowledge of the credit quality of a student loan or a mortgage, corporate loans are initially underwritten by multiple credit firms and the loan is continually traded. The price at which the corporate loan is exchanged carries a lot of information on the credit quality of the company it references. This reduces the information asymmetry between the originator and end investor and potential moral hazard. While a student loan is in the tens of thousands of dollars and an average mortgage is in the hundreds of thousands of dollars, a corporate leveraged loan is in the hundreds of millions of dollars. The larger size entices more credit analysts to study that loan's value, providing a transparency which is unique in the securitized sector. Additionally, companies' financial statements are audited, which further reduces the risk of fraudulent information being conveyed to investors.

Secondly, an open market CLO is actively managed. The "manager" is in charge of swapping corporate loans which might be undergoing credit stress with others which offer better loss adjusted prospects. These trades are regulated by dozens of rules in a contract agreed to by all investors and the manager at investment inception. The manager receives a subordinate management fee and incentive fee dependent on the performance of the CLO, aligning his interests with those of tranche investors. While there is more uncertainty through time on the loans held in an actively managed CLOs than in a static

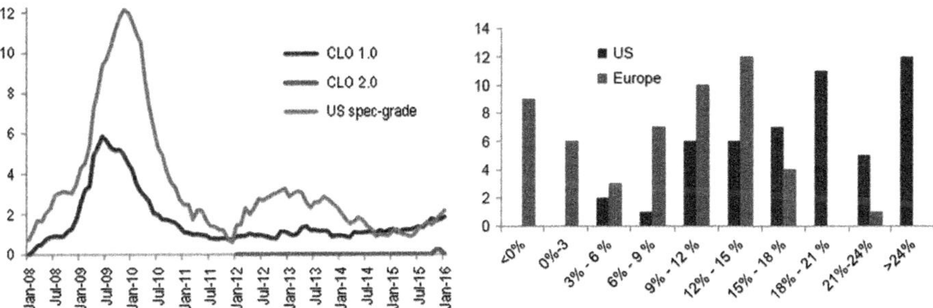

Fig. 16.5 Loan defaults (%) in CLO vs. the market and CLO Equity return distribution through the crisis (for deals issued 2005-2007). (*Source: Charts published courtesy of Citigroup*)

RMBS (which is probably why the European Commission excluded CLOs from being STS), there is also closer monitoring and possible avoidance of credit deterioration. Detailed monthly reports on CLO positions have further mitigated the negatives of this tradeoff. A manager's ability to reinvest the proceeds of loan sales and prepayment through a crisis can materially enhance investors' returns while a static structure would be handcuffed. Static structures in a crisis are generally better for senior tranches while actively managed structures can be better for junior tranches. Figure 16.5, provided by Citigroup,[21] shows how CLO managers are able to reduce their clients' exposure to defaults, and achieve good performance even during times of financial stress (Fig. 16.5).

The structural and credit features described shape investors returns. While US RMBS performance through the 2008 crisis was abysmal, US open market CLOs issued in 2006-2007 have on average compensated investors well (see Fig. 16.5, RHS for distribution of returns on the most subordinate tranche). Using Moody's historical data, Citigroup provides some insight into default rates on debt tranches of corporates, RMBS, CMBS and CLO (see Table 16.2). The data is provided for five- and ten-year averages over the last 20 years. CLOs both in the USA and Europe compare favourably with other asset classes even though they include pre 2003 issuance when CLOs were mainly composed of corporate bonds rather than loans and experienced high defaults during the 2001 crisis (Table 16.2, Figs. 16.6 and 16.7).

Taking a step back, corporate securitization is not a replacement for standard corporate credit funds or banks' balance sheets. In fact, these different types of investors coexist beneficially. When standard funds must liquidate loans in times of duress, CLOs are a natural buyer. Symmetrically, CLOs

---

[21] *Loan retention vehicle (and CLO) investment primer*, Citigroup, September 2015.

Table 16.2 Global CLO Cumulative Loss Rate (1993–2014)

	Cohort Size	5 Yrs (in %)	10 Yrs (in %)
US CLO Aaa	1916	0.0	0.0
US CLO Aa	906	0.0	0.0
US CLO A	912	0.0	0.0
US CLO Baa	1055	0.3	2.6
US CLO Ba	731	1.4	12.7
US CLO B	104	15.9	
EUR CLO Aaa	468	0.0	0.0
EUR CLO Aa	290	0.0	0.0
EUR CLO A	280	0.0	0.0
EUR CLO Baa	357	0.2	0.2
EUR CLO Ba	225	2.7	4.0
EUR CLO B	42	5.0	7.8
US Investment Grade	n. d.	0.7	
US Speculative Grade	n. d.	13.3	
US ABS (IG)	17941	1.7	3.8
US ABS (SG)	347	24.4	41
US subprime RMBS (IG)	22842	43.5	57.2
US subprime RMBS (SG)	1108	91.8	95.9
US CMBS (IG)	11970	9.8	15.6
US CMBS (SG)	2762	35.0	60.9

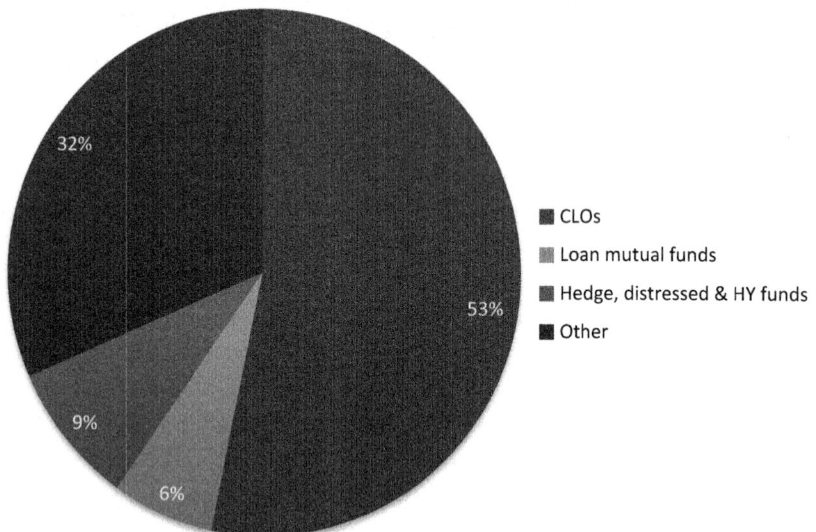

Fig. 16.6 2013 Investors

cannot function properly without the availability of a liquid secondary credit market fostered by standard funds. In the USA both CLOs and standard credit funds are well developed (see Fig. 16.7 on leveraged loans funding sources)

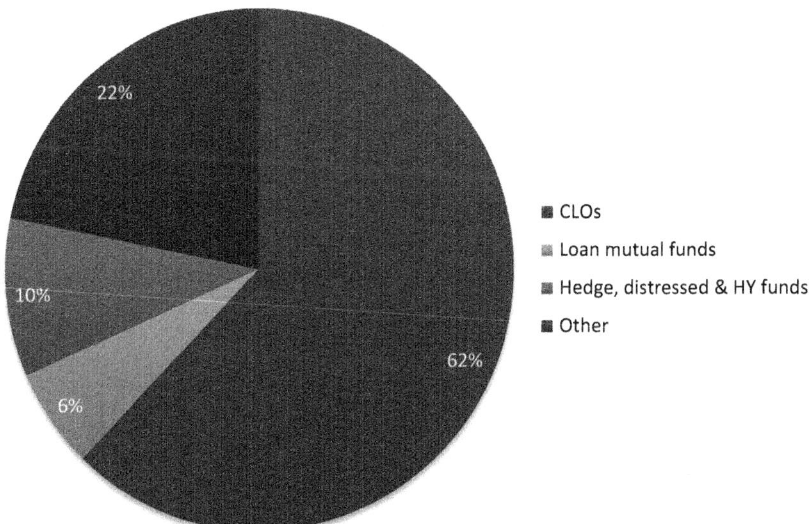

Fig. 16.7 2014 Investors

while in Europe both are in nascent stages. The last section of this chapter will focus on measures to encourage the development of better corporate credit markets through insolvency legislation reform.

16.4.2 Level of Risk Retention Capital

Before the 2008 crisis investors required that managers invest a significant amount of their own capital (a few million dollars) in the riskiest tranche of the CLO (equity) alongside their investors. The profit on this investment was added to subordinate management fees paid after debt received its interest payment and the incentive fee which managers receive after the equity tranche had achieved a 12 % return on investment.[22] The equity commitment was large enough to ensure alignment of interest but reasonable enough so small managers could be economically viable.

After the subprime crisis, regulators understandably wished to correct the misalignment of interest between originators and investors across all securitizations. Europe got a head start at "risk retention" or "skin in the game" regulation in January 2011 with Article 122a of the Capital Requirements

---

[22] The incentive fee return hurdle is generally 12 % but it varies in each CLO, in practice between 10 % and 15 %.

Directive,[23] and CRD4 (May 2013),[24] followed in the USA by section 941 du Dodd–Frank Act (October 2014).[25] The European version of risk retention was covered in Sect. 16.3.3 and requires that the originator/sponsor of a securitization keep an economic interest of 5 % in each CLO.

While the 5 % risk retention regulation makes perfect sense for an "originate to distribute" business model or balance sheet securitizations, it is unclear that it is useful for open market CLOs which already had subordinate management fees, incentive fees and often 1 % of capital invested in the riskiest tranche. However, more risk retention will always appear safer so the costs of that marginal increase in safety must be evaluated.

There are CLO managers harboured by large investment banks (e.g. CSAM), insurance companies (e.g. AXA) or asset managers (e.g. Blackrock), but there are also some standalone firms managing a few CLOs which are known only in their field. The latter "boutiques" have a few dozen employees and issue around two CLOs a year. Risk retention will be around $25 million per CLO ($500 million * 5 %) while ordinary average yearly revenue from each CLO is $2.5 million (0.5 % * $500 million).[26] These "boutiques" are insufficiently capitalized for that business model even assuming it makes economic sense. To comply with regulations they will either need a large injection of capital or to be acquired by the larger managers who have long-term capital to spare. While there was worldwide debate post-crisis concerning the moral hazard of "too big to fail", risk retention regulation has ironically resulted in "too small to survive" regulation in the CLO market.

If most CLO managers were large the regulator might consider boutique manager disappearance a small price to pay for increased market stability, but in fact a majority of managers are small. Citi research estimates that only CLO managers with $5 billion in post-crisis CLOs (CLO 2.0) would be able to invest 5 % in their future CLOs without any outside financing or coinvestment. "Just one third of US CLO managers will (barely) be able to issue and retain 5% risk without additional help, which will raise investor concern about manager concentration."[27] Assuming some of the smaller managers can access reasonably priced financing on 80 % of their vertical strip, Citigroup research estimated that up to 80 % of managers could survive the regulation, but that now seems optimistic. Even some of the largest CLO managers are

---

[23] Committee of European Banking Supervisors, December 2010.

[24] Cf. http://ec.europa.eu/finance/bank/regcapital/legislation-in-force/index_en.htm#maincontentSec1.

[25] https://www.fdic.gov/regulations/reform/dfa_selections.html#941.

[26] CLO incentive fees are only distributed after the CLO Equity achieves an IRR around 12 %, which is generally after the deal is liquidated (four to ten years after issuance).

[27] *Vertical Slice Financing: A Sensible CLO Solution*, Citigroup, August 2015.

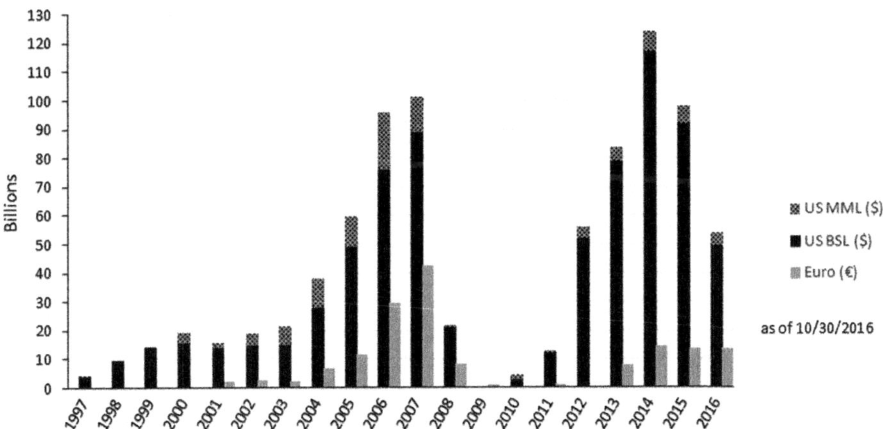

Fig. 16.8 US and Euro CLO Annual Issuance (*Source*: Intex, S&P, Moody's, Wells Fargo Securities. *Published with the kind permission of Wells Fargo Securities*)

trying to sell their firms to large insurance companies or private equity firms which can commit the capital required.[28] The volume of US CLOs issued in 2016 as of October 30th is down around 36 % relative to what it was at the same time in 2015. The US market could follow the post-crisis European path. While corporate financing backed by CLO issuance in Europe in 2014 was 34 % of 2007 levels, in the USA Broadly Syndicated Loan (BSL) CLOs achieved ~130 % (risk retention will apply in December 2016) (Fig. 16.8).

In better news, some CLO managers have anticipated the December 2016 deadline by issuing compliant deals. They are signaling to skeptical investors that they can survive the regulation, which gives them a marketing advantage. They are also focusing on US/Europe dual compliance (which we discuss in Sect. 16.4.3). Recently the law firm Maples and Calder conducted a survey of CLO managers,[29] which supports the hope that at least a third and potentially half of 2015 managers would be able to comply with regulation (Figs. 16.9 and 16.10).

As discussed in Sect. 16.3.2 guessing how much of EU CLOs' demise is due to economic reasons and how much is due to regulation is tricky. After risk retention regulation is implemented in December 2016, US issuance volumes could plummet as they have in Europe but there could also be height-

---

[28] http://www.bloomberg.com/news/articles/2015-11-05/conning-to-buy-octagon-in-junk-bet-add-12-8-billion-of-assets.

[29] http://www.maplesandcalder.com/fileadmin/uploads/maples/Documents/PDFs/Risk_Retention_Survey_of_US_CLO_Managers_-_Feb2016.pdf.

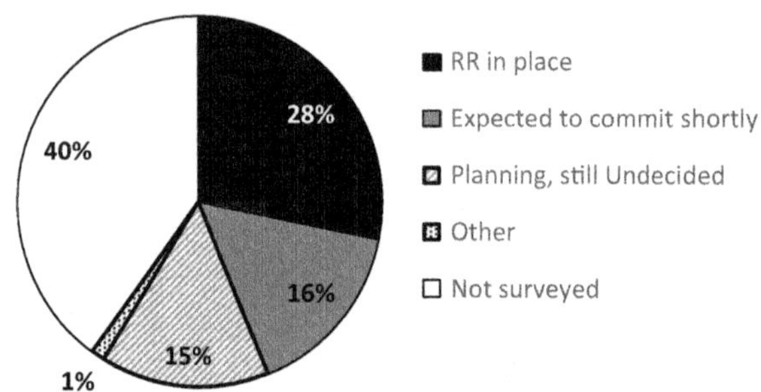

Fig. 16.9   Risk Retention Survey of CLO Managers Active in 2015 (*Source*: Maples and Calder. Reproduced with the kind permission of Maples and Calder)

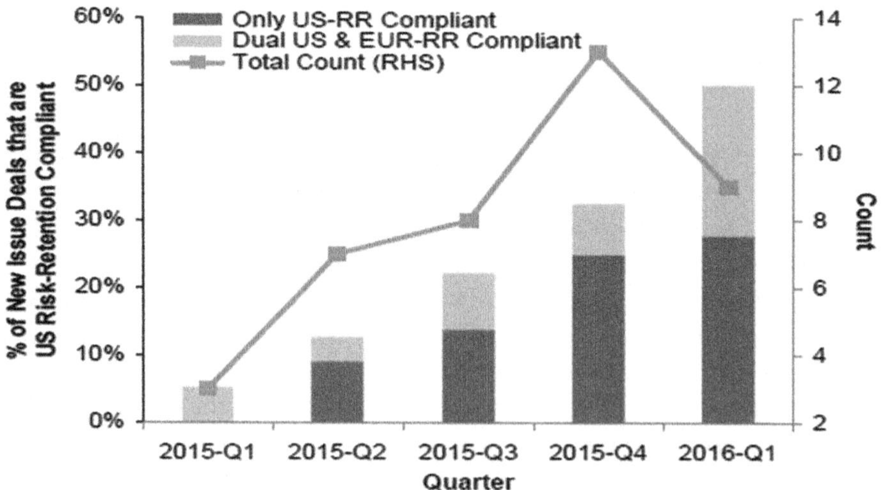

Fig. 16.10   % of US Risk-Retention Compliant New Issue Deals Increasing (*Source*: Morgan Stanley Research, S&P LCD. Reproduced with the kind permission of Morgan Stanley)

ened merger activity, with very large managers issuing at a faster pace to make up for some of the lost volume.

In anticipation of the deadline for this paradigm shifting regulation, managers have been searching for legal solutions to dilute the amount of capital they must ultimately commit to risk retention. Many managers will choose to comply with the "vertical strip" option (see Sect. 16.3.2). As they do not have enough capital to put to work they will find banks or insurance companies to provide financing (up to around 80 %) on that strip. This financing must be long-term locked up capital as boutique managers cannot risk margin calls on assets they cannot sell per the law. Unfortunately, banks are unlikely to be able to provide such financing as the capital treatment of such investments is quite unfavourable in Basel III.

Above and beyond financing, managers in the USA may seek partners to shoulder the risk retention piece in Manager Owned Affiliated funds (MOA) or Capitalized Manager Vehicles (CMV). US GAAP (generally accepted accounting principles) would allow a manager to "control" an MOA with only 10–20 % of economic ownership which will result in the retention capital being 0.5 % to 1 % (10–20 % economic interest * 5 % risk retention). This solution requires less capital than investors were asking of managers pre-crisis and it will result in lower to no liquidity on the commitment made by the partnering investors. It may also subject these investors to cross collateralization risk (investors would no longer be exposed to only one CLO at a time) and manager counterparty risk. Before this regulation the bankruptcy of a small manager had no economic impact on a CLO investor, as the manager merely provided a credit analysis service and did not "own" the assets. These solutions to the regulation increase systemic risk, decrease investor flexibility and safety and in my view do not even satisfy the spirit of the law, as the "skin in the game" must be diluted. Some of these schemes are bound to backfire. Michael Hanin, a legal specialist, mentioned: "The fact that regulators know the industry was disappointed, at least in part, by those final rules, is a recipe for increased regulatory focus".[30] A simpler rule could have been proposed which would have been subject to less interpretation.

Proposal 9 Open market CLO managers should only be required to retain 1 % of the sum of the initial liabilities. That capital should be invested solely in the equity tranche of the securitization. It should be provided by the manager, not through an affiliate fund, that is, that 1 % should not be diluted. The "Qualified CLO" proposal by the LSTA should be given due consideration as a best effort suggestion by the industry to satisfy the spirit of regulation.[31]

This 1% rule would apply to open market CLOs only; in the case of balance sheet CLOs just as in all balance sheet securitizations, the 5 % regulation is appropriate and does not apply disproportionate pressure as the issuing entities are generally large institutions which can and already usually retain

---

[30] Creditflux, October 2015.

[31] http://webcache.googleusercontent.com/search?q=cache:7fBTLRnQBGsJ:www.lsta.org/document/default/download/file/f08638f5-9a98-11e5-af38-0050568e41f7+&cd=1&hl=en&ct=clnk&gl=us.

that capital. Each securitization sector must be thoroughly investigated to determine the appropriate level of risk retention.

Unfortunately, regulation is often quite political. In the USA the mortgage sector at the heart of the subprime crisis was exempted from risk retention in the case of "qualified mortgages." Similar exemptions prevail in auto loans because of the powerful automobile lobby. Senator Barney Frank "said one of the shortfalls of the Dodd-Frank Act was the exclusion of auto dealers from regulation by the Consumer Financial Protection Bureau. Frank said auto dealers lobbied their way out of the Act. Global banks 'don't even come close' to the political power that auto dealers have."[32]

CLOs are not the only way to finance medium sized corporations' projects, but they are an efficient one which should not be disregarded especially when so much financing relies on banks in Europe with weak risk appetite in the post-crisis environment. A simple rule, not easily circumvented through legal loopholes, but with a risk retention level which enables boutiques to survive should be preferred.

Proposal 10 Regulators could observe market evolution and increase or decrease risk retention level within the existing framework to speed up or slow down securitization in the same way that central banks use the interest rate to manage the economy.

16.4.3 International Convergence

We will now examine how various regional regulators introduce legal complexity even when the spirit of their rules coincides.

Investors benefit from regional diversification and the ability to invest everywhere increases the allocation of capital to where it is most productive. It is beneficial to investors, to companies and to the global economy. When regulation is complex but also regionally determined it becomes very difficult, onerous and sometimes impossible for institutions to comply with regulations everywhere. In the case of CLO risk retention both the European and American regulators require 5 % retention but the format of ownership is different. In particular:

1) The notional on which the 5 % is applied is the sum of the face value of all
   liabilities at inception in the USA and the sum of the face value of all assets

---

[32] http://www.globalcapital.com/article/q77tcy6bg69s/risk-retention-exemption-riles-barney-frank.

Sponsor

- Most of the European 2.0 CLOs issued in this regulatory environment have been met by CLO Manager's meeting the role of "Sponsor" to the transaction.

- This requires meeting certain MiFID registration and can often prove restrictive from a capital and regulatory standpoint, as, for example, the CLO Manager can no longer qualify as an AIFM (Alternative Investment Fund Manager)

Originator

- An entity can meet the role of "Originator" it if has been deemed to Originate a significant proportion of asset throughout the transaction.

- This has been interpreted as meaning that at any point in time greater than 50% of the CLO assets must have come from the Originator vehicle

- The Originator must have had meaningful risk exposure in the assets it originates

---

Fig. 16.11 Sponsor and Originator (*Source*: Citi Research. *Reproduced with the kind permission of Citi Research*)

at all times in Europe. The American rule is preferable because compliance need be calculated only at inception. If a manager buys a loan at a price of 95 with a face value of 100 then he might have increased his investors' profits but the risk retention capital he retains in the structure will need to be increased as the face value of his assets has increased. Thus European CLO managers must invest more than 5 % in their CLOs in case they manage the structure profitably! The uncertainty around capital needed in time and the misalignment of incentives (what is good for investors is bad for the manager) is unfortunate.

2) A European "sponsor" must be MIFID compliant,[33] but US managers cannot obtain that accreditation without having a European affiliate. There is no valid ground for that protectionism.

In summary, a European a manager can comply through the Sponsor route or the Originator route. In the USA a manager can comply through the Manager Owned Affiliate route or Capitalized Manager route (Figs. 16.11 and 16.12).

As US Managers can rarely be MIFID compliant, if they wish to have European investors they must be a European "originator." Citigroup's illustration below depicts a solution lawyers are currently contemplating for dual compliance (US MOA and EU Originator) (Fig. 16.13).

European regulators wish to promote "simple" securitizations but regional divergence in regulation results in anything but simplicity!

---

[33] *Markets in Financial Instruments Directive.*

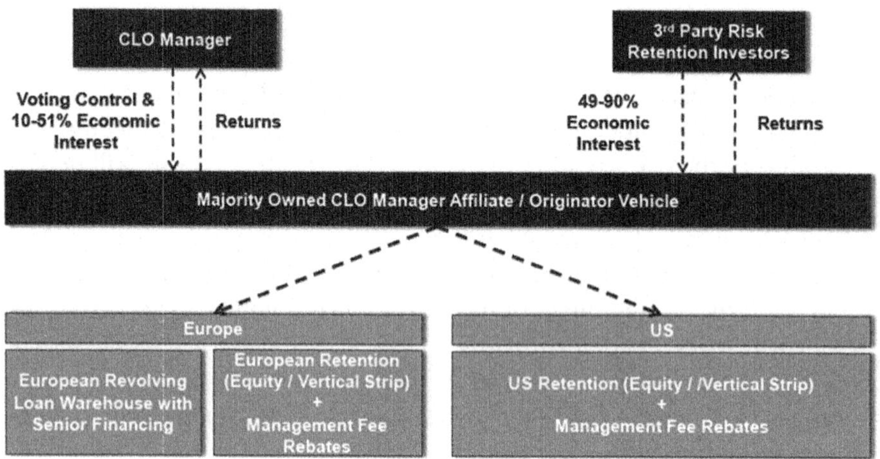

Fig. 16.12 Majority Owned Affiliate and Capitalized Manager Vehicle (*Source*: Citi Research. *Reproduced with the kind permission of Citi Research*)

Fig. 16.13 Potential solution for dual compliance (US MOA & EU Originator). (*Source*: Citi Research. *Reproduced with the kind permission of Citi Research*)

Proposal 10 Ensure harmonization of risk retention rules between the European Union (EU) and the USA.

16.5 Insolvency Law Reform in Europe

As mentioned in Sect. 16.4.1, CLOs benefit from a healthy competitive corporate loan market with a large diversified pool of investors. In Europe, unfortunately, investors must hire both sector experts (industrials, healthcare, telecoms, etc) as well as regional legal experts (France, the UK, Spain, etc.).

This is costly to financial institutions so they restrict their footprint in some countries. As a result, financial markets are shallower in Europe than in the USA. Greater convergence of insolvency law across Europe would go a long way to reduce investors' burden in assessing the outcome of a failed investment. It would also achieve an important step towards the European Capital Markets Union on regulators' agenda.

Proposal 11 European countries' insolvency laws should converge towards a framework similar to the American Chapter 11.

What follows is much inspired by the French case, but many European countries experience similar issues. Convergence of European countries' insolvency law would:

1) Unify conditions governing the calculation of loss given default in underlying corporations in order to achieve uniform EU-wide rules and level the playing field.
2) Grant investors a certain degree of predictability of the level of loss given default. The US rule provides investors with the certainty that their level of loss will depend almost entirely on the borrower's distress level and their seniority ranking. In France, and more generally in Europe, investors face risks related to inefficient law and insufficiently trained courts.
3) Restore the balance between the rights of creditors and shareholders. French insolvency law sometimes gives all the power to shareholders, even though they bear none of the negative consequences of their decisions, as they have already lost all of their investment in the debtor company. Such situations, which economists call moral hazard, make firms and their creditors, including their employees, worse off. No wonder capital investors as well as lenders are reluctant to invest when French firms, while remaining viable, experience financial distress. This is why the market for funding distressed firms is underdeveloped in France compared to its major trade partners. As a result, the cost of credit for distressed firms is overly expensive. Interest rates in the 15–30 % range and overcollateralization where the value of assets pledged to lenders is four to five times the amount lent, are not unusual.
4) More specifically, overhaul French insolvency law to give viable businesses the best chance of recovery and success, and cause the least possible harm to stakeholders of failed businesses, that is, customers, employees, suppliers, lenders, shareholders, and even the wider community, including public finances.

16.5.1 Firms of Significant Size (Debt Could be Securitized)

It is necessary to prevent the shareholders of viable distressed firms who refuse to take responsibility from delaying settlement. Similarly, unsecured creditors and junior creditors should be prevented from blocking any transfer, balance sheet restructuring or debt reduction that would allow the firm to survive.

Providing strong incentives to shareholders and creditors to negotiate a contractual agreement consistent with their respective rights and interests as quickly as possible should be preferred. Therefore, the rules of collective proceedings must respect existing agreements between the various categories of investors as much as possible. These rules should carefully avoid any breach of equality caused by undue wealth transfers as a result of a substantial change in the order of priority of payments and loss absorption.

If negotiations fail, transfer of control must be to the benefit of so-called pivotal creditors. These stakeholders should be identified once the company's value has been assessed and creditors' claims have been ranked according to their priority rights.

Creditors shall be classified into three broad categories. Senior creditors can expect to recover their entire claim while junior creditors' claim shall be written off. In the middle, the so-called pivotal creditors will recover only a portion of their debt and make a tradeoff while assessing the viability of the company.

Only they should be entitled to choose the best outcome for they are the only ones to suffer the economic consequences of their decisions. The financial outcome of the other categories of creditors having already been established contractually, they are not required to take additional risk. Pivotal creditors should thus have the opportunity to convert their claims into shares and replace the initial shareholder who disappears.

In this framework, the judge enters the battlefield only once the war is over. He either validates and enforces the agreement between stakeholders or supplements it if negotiations have failed. The judge's decision to evict stakeholders must be so certain it constitutes a sword of Damocles for shareholders reluctant to deal with creditors. Avoiding to call upon a judge offers multiple benefits: the stakeholders reduce their cost of litigation; the company decreases the value destroyed by long and uncertain insolvency proceedings; the community does not bear the cost of the procedure. This virtuous sword of Damocles ensures the pertinence of negotiated solutions, while the uncertainty that currently weighs on creditors (particularly pivotal creditors) has the opposite perverse effect.

This type of procedure is at the heart of the American Chapter 11, a framework which deserves to be broadcast throughout Europe. In the USA, it has allowed companies to quickly find new resources and rebound on a healthier basis.

16.5.2   Small and Medium Businesses

For these businesses (with a balance sheet size too small to absorb the costs involved in insolvency proceedings), there should be a simpler and faster procedure. Transfer of control should be in favour of secured creditors according to a procedure designed to minimize transaction costs. Banks play a central role in this type of procedure; British and Swedish experience is conclusive.[34]

16.6   Conclusion

Regulation is a powerful medium to shape financial markets, promote stability and orient innovation. In developed economies it has become a prominent tool of governments and central bankers. Today dozens of institutions, hundreds of employees and thousands of pages of legislation govern what is legal, what is encouraged and what is not. Some rules are crafted with foresight, others display very confusing features and language. The complexity of regulation rivals the complexity of markets, its understanding and implementation comes at large cost to financial firms and ultimately the economy. It is critical that each new piece of legislation weigh that burden and benefit with great wisdom. The balance between overly broad legislation that wrongly crushes a small subsector, and overly minute rules which hinder innovation and could be circumvented, is a hard one to strike. As the French revolutionaries duly noted, "great responsibility follows inseparably from great power."[35]

---

[34] For further reference see a Praxis report on business support (Club Praxis, November 2013), a report by the think tank Law & Growth with the support of Labex Louis Bachelier (Droit & Croissance, November 2014) and the proposals from the Council of Economic Analysis (Plantin, Thesmar & Tirole, 2013).

[35] Convention Nationale, May 1793.

16.7 Annex

Appendix A.1 Summary of Simple, Transparent and Standardised (STS) Securitisation Criteria (*Source*: European Commission and Nomura)

Requirement type	Component	Requirement
Simplicity	Transfer of Assets	Asset transer must be true-sale, with no severe claw back provisions.
	Encumbrance	Seller must provide representations and warranties that the loans are not encumbered or otherwise in a condition adversly affecting its enforceability.
	Pool Management	**Active portfolio management on a discretionary is not allowed**
	Asset Inclusion Criteria	The loans must meet predetermined and clearly defined eligibility criteria
	Homogeneity	The loans must be homogenous by asset type
	Full Recourse	**The loans must be contractually binding and enforceable with full recourse to debtors**
	Re-securitisation	The underlying exposures should not include other securitisations or transferable securities
	Periodic Payments	The loans must have defined periodic payments streams relating to rental, principal, interest payment or rights to receive income from assets
	Ordinary Course Underwriting	The loans must be originated in the ordinary course of originator's or original lender's business, and underwriting should not be less stringent than for loans kept on balance sheet
	Seller Expertise	Originator or original lender must have expertise in the underlying loans' asset type
	Self-Certification	For residential loans, the loan should not be marketed or underwritten on the premise that the information provided by the borrower might not be verified by the lender. The borrowers' credit worthiness must be assessed in accordance with the relevant regulation.
	Credit Impairment	There should be no loans in default or loans to credit-impaired borrowers, at the time of transfer to the securitisation
	Seasoning	Borrowers must have made at least one payment prior to transfer, except in case of revolving deals of certain loan types (credit cards, trade receivables, etc).

Appendix A.1 (continued)

Requirement type	Component	Requirement
Transparency	Principal Redemption	Repayment of bonds must not be "substantially" reliant on sale of assets
	Historical Data	Investors must have access to historical performance information of similar assets, for at least 5 years for retail exposures, and 7 years for non-retail exposures
	Verification	Independent verification for a sample of exposures (95% confidence level) is required
	Liability Model	Originator or sponsor must provide a deal cashflow model prior to and after securitisation
	Transparency	Originator/sponsor must meet transparency requirements of the Securitisation Regulation (Article 5) and provide the necessary documents and information before pricing
Standardisation	Risk Retention	Originator, sponsor or the original lender must satisfy the risk retention requirement of the Securitisation Regulation (Article 4)
	Rate/FX Risk	Rate and currency risks must be mitigated, and derivatives, if any, must be for hedging purposes only, underwritten and documented according to international standards
	Interest Rates	Referenced rates on assets and liabilities must be generally used market rates
	Waterfall (non-revolving deals)	If event of enforcement/acceleration, the waterfall must be sequential with no substantial cash trapping. The structure must have performance triggers which result in sequential payments. There should be no provisions for a reverse waterfall and no forced liquidation of collateral
	Triggers (revolving deals)	The structure should have early amortisation events or triggers for termination of revolving period (if any), based on performance of loans, insolvency of originator / servicer etc.
	Waterfall & Trigger Clarity	Payment priorities and triggers must be clearly specified, and changes reported in a timely manner
	Servicer Expertise	The servicer must have expertise in servicing the underlying loans
	Servicing Process	The transaction documentation must have clear definitions and actions relating to borrowers in arrears and default
	Counterparty Roles	Responsibilities and obligations of servicer, trustee and other ancillary service providers must be clearly specified
	Counterparty Continuity	There must be provisions to ensure continuity of servicer, swap providers, liquidity providers and other counterparties in the event of a counterparty default
	Resolution Process	The transaction documentation must contain provisions and voting rights and how investor conflicts are to be resolved

17

Essay on the State of Research and Innovation in France and the European Union

Antoine Kornprobst and Raphael Douady

17.1 Introduction

Innovation in the economy is an important engine of growth, and no economy, whatever its complexity and degree of advancement, whether it is based on industry, agriculture, high tech or the providing of services, can be truly healthy without innovating actors within it. The aim of this chapter written by an expert in applied mathematics working in finance, not by an economist or a lawyer, is not to provide an exhaustive view of all the mechanisms in France and in Europe that seek to foster innovation in the economy and to offer solutions for removing all the roadblocks that still hinder innovation; indeed such a study

This work was achieved through the Laboratory of Excellence on Financial Regulation (Labex ReFi) supported by PRES heSam under the reference ANR10LABX0095. It benefited from French government support managed by the National Research Agency (ANR) within the project Investissements d'Avenir Paris Nouveaux Mondes (Investments for the Future Paris New Worlds) under the reference ANR11IDEX000602.

The author gratefully acknowledges the help of **Maximilien Nayaradou** (Finance Innovation), **Henry Marty-Gauquié** (Banque Européenne d'Investissement), **Philippe Roy** (Cap Digital) and **Emmanuel Kornprobst** (Rouen University of Law) whose guidance while exploring this subject was very much appreciated.

A. Kornprobst (✉) • R. Douady
LabEx RéFi and CES, Université Paris 1 Panthéon-Sorbonne, Paris, France

R. Douady et al. (eds.), *Financial Regulation in the EU*,
DOI 10.1007/978-3-319-44287-7_17

would go far beyond the scope of this chapter. What is modestly attempted here is firstly to show what currently works well and what needs to perfected as far as innovation is concerned in France and Europe, then secondly to offer some solutions and personal thoughts about how to boost innovation.

Those solutions will mostly be articulated through the development of business and research clusters such as Finance Innovation or Cap Digital that provide a favourable setting in which start-up companies in a particular sector of activity can be born and prosper, as well as through some European institutions such as the European Investment Bank (EIB) that, among its other missions, helps young companies, especially innovating ones, to obtain all the funding they need to secure their future, and to ensure not only their continued existence but a strong expansion of the number of jobs they offer. Innovation, whatever the field of activity, is not the exclusive domain of start-ups and Small and Medium-sized Enterprises (SMEs), of course, indeed it could be argued on the contrary that a majority of the economic innovation is made by either large multinational companies or the state behind large public companies or universities. Still, it is often in reality through partnerships between large institutional agents and small young companies, or the sale of a start-up to a large company, or the funding by a large company of a researcher's project, that real innovation takes place, and our study will aim to demonstrate that fact.

In France, as in all countries, the state of innovation is best described by a National System of Innovation (NSI) that takes into account the actors of innovation (fundamental and applied researchers, innovating entrepreneurs, business and research clusters), the structures of innovation (SMEs, multinationals, universities, the state, European institutions, etc.) and the results of innovation (economic growth, lower unemployment).

Innovation is always based on research in all its forms (fundamental, experimental, applied) that leads to the creation of intellectual property. That intellectual property can, for example, take the form of patents that are submitted in France to the Institut National de la Propriété Industrielle (INPI) and which are protected by the law for 20 years, in the form of patented inventions (that do not have the same legal status as patents but enjoy equivalent protections) or the form of know-how protected by the laws governing trade secrets. Innovation in the economy could be defined as exploiting this intellectual property originating from research to produce goods and services. Actual production is ensured by public, private or hybrid public/private companies that can either be the original proprietor of the intellectual property, having funded the research, or having rented the intellectual property through licensing, or having acquired the intellectual property and associated technology by purchasing a small start-up company. For instance, Google bought YouTube and Facebook bought What's App.

An NSI constitutes six components: Human Resources, Public Research, Private Research, Relationship between Industry and Science, Innovating Entrepreneurs and General State Policy. Each of those components has to be evaluated individually and in relation to one another in order to obtain an overview of the state of innovation in a country. Globally, although France possesses excellent research and a remarkable dynamism among its actors of innovation, its NSI is quite poor according to a 2011 report by the European Commission (OECD 2014): it ranked eleventh among the European Union's 27 members at the time (Croatia joined in 2013), and it was classified as an "innovation follower" rather than an "innovation leader." France possesses excellent NSI components which unfortunately tend to fail at interacting with each other; this results in a lot of red tape that stifles innovation.

17.2 The Tools of Innovation and Economic Growth

17.2.1 The Legal Framework of Innovation

17.2.1.1 Public Research and Innovation Structures

The first important characteristic of research in France that differs from almost all of the other OECD (Organisation for Economic Co-operation and Development) member states is the key part of the state in its financing. Indeed, the French state provides around 50 % of all research and development expenses in France, compared with around only 30 % in Germany and the UK, according to a 2014 report by the OECD (2014). Moreover, these research expenses are not limited to traditional domains such as national defence or nuclear energy but extend to civilian research and development. The second exclusive characteristic of French research is the relatively minor role played in public research by the universities themselves: instead, this role is taken by the major public research administrations, which are recognized to be among the best in the world in their respective fields of expertise. These public research administrations include the CNRS (Centre National de la Recherche Scientifique/National Centre for Scientific Research), the CEA (Centre d'Études Atomiques/Centre for Nuclear Research), the CNES (Centre National d'Études Spatiales/National Centre for Space Research), the

INRIA (Institut National de Recherche en Informatique et en Automatique/ National Institute for Computer Science), the INSERM (Institut National de la Santé et de la Recherche Médicale/National Institute for Health and Medical Research), the CNET (Centre National d'Études des Télécommunications/ National Centre for Information Technology), and many others, so that each major field of public research has its own public administration.

The CNRS, for example, has over 33,000 people on its payroll and administrates over 1,100 research laboratories (including 40 located abroad). Its annual budget reaches €3.3 billion, including almost €700 million of its own resources, which means money that comes from contracts with private sector counterparties, public institutions such as the ANR (Agence Nationale de la Recherche/National Agency for Research) or European institutions. Between 2007 and 2011, an average of 43,000 peer-reviewed publications were produced each year under the CNRS brand and the CNRS also filled between 600 and 800 patents each year. Those patents are often licensed to the private industrial sector, which can translate excellence in scientific research into real economic growth. Indeed, the CNRS has a long tradition of establishing joint ventures (3,000 per year on average) with large French industrial actors, public universities, other public research administrations or other private research institutions. The CNRS is also very active as a real economy actor of its own, applying its research and producing economic growth through the creation, under the CNRS brand, of many start-up companies by members of its staff (more than 1,100 since 1999).

This importance of the state in French research and innovation has traditionally created a "vertical" structure where public research administrations were often associated with on the one hand large companies, sometimes partly state owned, of the aeronautics, space, nuclear, transportation, public utilities or telecommunications sector, or on the other with start-up companies born of a patent filled by a public research administration. Medium-sized companies in the middle were typically excluded from these arrangements, leaving them with only a marginal role to play in research and innovation in the French economy. Moreover, this vertical structure created a tendency to concentrate the top decision and policymaking at ministerial level (Defence Ministry, Transport Ministry, Education Ministry, etc.), which fostered short-term political interference to the detriment of a sound business strategy. Indeed, this vertical structure of research and innovation in the French economy was not immune to criticism, as the 2012 *Rapport de la Mission d'Évaluation Relative au Soutien à l'Économie Numérique et à l'Innovation* (Report of the Committee for the Development of the Economy and Innovation in the Digital Age)

(Ministère des Finances 2012), published by the Finance Ministry, underlined. Some of its main conclusions were:

1. There is a vertical compartmentalization of research that, to this day, negatively impacts the training, either initial or during their whole career, of engineers and researchers, thus limiting the potential for interdisciplinary collaborative work, which is essential for true innovation to take place.
2. Since there is a partial disconnection between the world of research, dominated as we have seen by public money and thus geared toward reaching the goals of research and innovation of the public sector, and the world of business and industrial development, the question of the profitability of the main orientations, decided at the top political level, of French research and innovation policies needs to be raised more often. Only a research and innovation policy that aims at being profitable in the medium to long term has a chance to foster real economic growth in the country.
3. There is to this day too much opacity and too much rigidity in the way research projects are financed and not enough freedom allowed for researchers, especially those who are intent on creating start-up companies, to make their project evolve. As a matter of fact, financing is very often tied to a series of rules and criteria established by the state that do not always take into account the evolution of the economy, consumer habits, social structure or the environment.

These structural flaws of the traditional research and innovation structure in France are compounded by the worsening flaws in the French education and higher learning systems, and the public universities are often in competition with the Grandes Écoles (public or private) which have much more selective entry exams. Public universities, owing to a lack of material means and questionable policy decisions over the last few decades, tend to have difficulties in providing a good level of education to the students, especially at bachelor level (i.e. an education that will enable students to find a job). While the French education system is good at producing world-class researchers, engineers and business people, it lags behind in offering young people proper technical training in the IUT (Institut Universitaire de Technologie/Technical Training Universities) and through the deliverance of diplomas such as the BTS (Brevet de Technicien Supérieur/Qualified Technician Certificate), which are essential for innovation to work in the real economy. As a matter of fact, that cutting edge start-up company created by a CNRS researcher will need qualified IT technicians, marketing and communication people, and so on, to function and develop, and that is very often difficult to find in France, despite persistent high unemployment.

Despite all these structural flaws in its research and innovation system, France has been trying since the late 1990s to correct its past mistakes and bring its NSI closer in terms of efficiency to those of its OECD peer countries. Many legislative and administrative decisions were taken to boost the efficiency of French research and innovation, and that tendency has been accelerating since the advent of the euro and ever closer European integration. Among the top measures taken, we can underline:

1. Incentives to increase technological transfers between the public and private sectors through a series of legislative measures since 1994.
2. Creation since 2004 of business and research clusters on the American "Silicon Valley" model.
3. Creation of a very attractive special tax status for researchers and employees who come and establish themselves in France at the invitation of a French company (Code Général des Impôts (CGI)/Tax Code, art.81.B).
4. Creation in 2006 of the ANR and of the AERES (Agence d'Évaluation de le Recherche et de l'Enseignement Supérieur/National Agency for the Evaluation of Research and Higher Learning Education) that has since been renamed the Haut Conseil de l'Évaluation de le Recherche et de l'Enseignement Supérieur/High Council for the Evaluation of Research and Higher Learning Education.
5. Establishment since 2010 of successive PIAs (Programmes d'Investissement d'Avenir/Programs for Future Investments).
6. Introduction in 2008 of a new legal status for French public universities that grants them a higher degree of autonomy. In particular, universities are opening up to the public sector with the goal of developing applied research inside new UMRs (Unité Mixtes de Recherche/Hybrid Research Units), which are often administrated by the CNRS and designed to meet the needs of businesses.

17.2.1.2   Private Research and Innovation Structures

In recent years France has developed its legal structures to support risk capital, as in the UK. However, unlike in Germany, in France there are only a limited number of public–private partnership funds that specialize in supporting SMEs that foster innovating technologies: according to the *Rapport de la Mission d'Évaluation Relative au Soutien à l'Économie Numérique et à l'Innovation* (Ministère des Finances 2012), only three such funds existed in 2012, but more are being created.

On the other hand, all the European Union (EU) states have created structures, whether through tax policy or legislative initiatives, to support research and development; such as Oséo in France, the Technology Strategy Board, Regional Growth Fund and Research Councils in the UK, the ZIM (Zentrales Innovationsprogramm Mittelstand/Central Innovation Programme) since 2008 in Germany and the Vinnova programme in Sweden.

In France, a large selection of private research structures can be found, most having been created with the goal of unleashing the potential of public research and gearing it towards innovation in the real-world economy and the private sector. Among those structures, we can give the following examples:

1. Private research centres that have been approved by the Higher Learning Education and Research Ministry and can therefore receive public money.
2. Centres de Coordination de Recherche et de Développement (CCRDs/ Centres for the Coordination of Research and Economic Development) that have been created inside large multinational companies with the task of coordinating all research policies, planning re-search programmes, administrating laboratories and of course maximizing all possible tax advantages for the company by optimizing all research that it pays for with respect to existing government tax relief programmes and research subsidies.
3. The status of Jeune Entreprise Innovante (JEI/Young Innovating Enterprise) that can be awarded by the Finance Ministry to new SMEs (even a one-person company in the case of a start-up). Such a tax status confers many advantages to young companies on the condition that they be eligible for the CIR (Crédit Impôt Recherche/Tax Relief for Research), about which we will talk more later and which is basically a tax deduction computed from the amount of money a company spends on its research activities, for at least 15 % of its functioning costs. Moreover, at least 50 % of their capital must be held by private individuals, SCRs (Sociétes de Capital Risque/ Risk Capital Firms), FCPs (Fonds Communs de Placement/Mutual Investment Funds), SFIs (Sociétés Financières d'Innovation/Financial Firms for Innovation), public research establishments or other JEIs. If those conditions are met, the JEI enjoys a complete exemption from corporate tax and social security contributions as well as a partial exoneration of capital gains tax for investors who will, at a given time, sell their shares in the company.

4. The status of Jeune Entreprise Universitaire (JEU/Young Enterprise with
   Academic Roots) was created on the model of the JEI with the same tax
   relief advantages, but is specific to companies created by researchers working for a public research and higher learning institution. The JEU status
   has been designed to encourage professors, researchers or even college
   students to become entrepreneurs and to monetize their research in order
   to derive extra income from it and create jobs in the real economy. A JEU
   has to be created by someone working in a higher learning institution, has
   to have an economic activity based primarily on its creator's research and
   needs to be based on a convention signed between the higher learning
   institution and the new entrepreneur.

Despite all this, research expenses toward economic innovation in France
remains limited in comparison with some other EU states such as Germany
and the Scandinavian countries. This situation may not be the consequence of
a lack of dynamism in French research and development, however, but merely
an expression of the fact that the most innovating economic sectors in France
(luxury goods, agribusiness and food processing, tourism, high value added
services, etc.) are traditionally not as much in need of scientific and technological research as the dominant economic sectors in countries such as Germany.

17.2.1.3 Business and Research Clusters ("*Pôles de Compétitivité*")

The business and research clusters, which are still too few in France compared
to their numbers in the UK and, especially, the USA are a key factor in cooperation between the public and the private sector. These *pôles de compétitivité*
consist of "areas," which can be physical or not, where private companies,
higher learning establishments and research institutions, both public and private, converge and pool resources to create a high degree of synergy for innovation, technological advancement and economic growth. In their respective
fields of activity, those business and research clusters provide all the means of
research as well as sources of financing so that new innovating companies can
be born and existing businesses can thrive. In France, examples of such *pôles
de compétitivité* can be found in Cap Digital for the IT sector and Finance
Innovation for the financial sector. Their action is determinant in fostering
innovation and economic growth in the country.

In France, business and research clusters have been created since 2004
by the Comité Interministériel d'Aménagement et de Compétitivité des

Territoires (CIACT/Interministerial Committee for the Development and Competitiveness of the Regions) to support research programmes approved by the state. Tax incentives toward the creation of such structures have been somewhat lowered since 2010 because their profits are no longer exempt from taxation, but they remain exempt from all local taxes such as the *contribution économique territoriale* (regional tax to finance economic subsidies). Today, in most economic sectors from nanotechnology to finance, there are around 71 research and business clusters in France and six of them have a truly global perspective. These encouraging results remain modest when compared with the business and research clusters, technological innovation centres and business incubators that can be found in the USA or, to a lesser extent, in the UK. As a matter of fact, those countries possess world-class giants, such as Silicon Valley in California (6,000 companies concentrated on 1.5 square kilometres and supported by Stanford University with its 15,000 students, including nearly 9,000 post-graduates) or the East London Tech City (informally known as "Silicon Roundabout," it groups together 800 high-tech companies).

17.2.2 A Flawed System: Comparison with Other Developed Countries

Despite all these public and private structures and the high efficiency of some of them, which confers on France a worldwide reputation of excellence in some fields of research and innovation, and despite a clear amelioration of competitiveness in the past few decades when it comes to research and innovation in France, the system remains deeply flawed. Research and innovation in France remains burdened by many legal and administrative constraints and the *Tableau de Bord de l'Union de l'Innovation* (Benchmark of Innovation in the Union) (European Commission 2015) which is published every year by the European Commission ranks France as 11th among the member countries, on par with the Netherlands, Belgium and the UK as an "innovation follower" rather than an "innovation leader" like Sweden (1st), Denmark (2nd), Finland (3rd) and Germany (4th). This disappointing position for France in the field of innovation, according to the European Commission, is somewhat mitigated, however, by its better results regarding the quality of its researchers and the number of its peer reviewed publications (7th and 8th, respectively, according to the same study). France has admittedly increased the performance of its research and innovation system between 2007 and 2014 but tends to evolve slower than its European partners because, according to the same study by the European Commission, it was 8 % above the EU average in 2012 but only 6 % above the EU average in 2014.

This disappointing situation is confirmed by France's position of 14th among EU countries in the ranking of national economies by public-private partnerships. The insufficient amount of private sector investment in French SMEs as well as the amount of risk capital available in the economy as a whole is also worrisome, but this is an EU-wide problem because, while the global amount of innovation in the European economy has been stable over the past decades, the number of innovating private sector companies, especially SMEs, is decreasing. The stable level of innovation at an EU-wide level hides deep inequalities in the situation of individual countries. Indeed, the recent progress of some states, such as Latvia, Bulgaria, Ireland or the UK, compensates for the difficulties of others, and therefore the EU as a whole remains behind the countries that lead the world for innovation, such as the USA, Japan or South Korea.

It has to be noted, however, that all these comparative studies are only taking into account the overall quantity of innovation in the economy and do not permit us to draw any conclusions on the quality of the research and innovation structures of a country. Moreover, the profitability of the research and development investments in France are not properly measured by these studies, and to do so we would need to use the theory of options and cash flows that the investments are capable of creating, as detailed in the work of Professor Raimbourg, published as part of the encyclopedic *Ingénierie Financière* (Financial Engineering) book of reference published by Dalloz Action (Raimbourg 2015a).

Another notorious flaw of the French research and innovation system is rooted in the French, and to some extent European, business culture. Indeed there is not enough of a "risk culture" in Europe: the business projects that get started must come to term otherwise they are regarded as a serious, even borderline shameful, failure. The bankruptcy and liquidation laws in France and Europe in general tend to be very punitive toward investors who do not succeed, and therefore any entrepreneur who starts a company that doesn't get off the ground is often considered to be a "loser" in European business culture. That situation tends to diminish the dynamism of potential entrepreneurs who want to minimize the risks above everything else, even at the cost of missing business opportunities. This is totally different in the USA where it is much easier to rebound after a business failure. Excessive and overly complicated rules and regulations, as well as redundancy and sometimes even incoherence between individual member countries' national regulations, produce a lot of red tape that also, compounded with a very high cost of capital, tends to smother innovating businesses in Europe.

17.3 The Financing of Innovation in Enterprises

The financing of innovation in French and European enterprises is of three kinds: public financing by the state, private financing and European financing.

17.3.1 Public Financing

Public financing of innovation is essentially geared toward research. First of all, this public financing takes the form of tax reductions or exemptions. The Organismes Publics de Recherche (OPR/Public Research Institutions) are entitled since the Loi de Programme pour la Recherche (Research Planning Bill) of 18 April 2006 to a complete exemption from all taxation on any profits generated by their research activity within the constraints of their public interest mission. These provisions for the OPR concern primarily:

1. The public research administrations such as the CNRS and the public higher learning institutions such as the public universities (e.g. Paris I Panthéon Sorbonne University).
2. The legal entities created with the goal of administrating a research project or with the goal of coordinating the research activities of a network of other research institutions, including other OPRs. This is the case for example of the Laboratoires d'Excellence (LabEx/Laboratory of Excellence) that operate under the aegis of the ANR.
3. The research foundations that are recognized by the government as Fondation Reconnue d'Utilité Publique (Foundation Carrying out a Public Interest Mission), such as for example the Pasteur Institute, which is a world leader for medical research.

Moreover, enterprises from the private sector are entitled to deduct the donations they make to the OPRs from their taxable profits, up to a limit of 0.5 % of their total revenue figure.

Besides these tax advantages, the traditional "vertical" structure of the French research and innovation system makes it so that the public financing of research and innovation often takes the form of direct government subsidies or loans, subsidized or not, delivered to public, private or hybrid entities by a number of government agencies. Among the most important programmes and institutions involved in financing innovation in France, we can cite the following for their important role:

1. Direct subsidies provided, within the constraints of European law which tends to limit such practices at the member state level, by the central French government through various ministries or by local governments at various levels (Municipal, Départemental, Régional)
2. Subsidies and loans to innovating companies as well as research grants offered by the large state-owned (or hybrid with a majority of the capital held by the state) companies such as Electricité de France (EDF/French Electric Power Company) or Société Nationale des Chemins de Fer Français (SNCF/French National Railway Company).
3. The Agence de l'Environnement et de la Maîtrise de l'Énergie (ADEME/ Agency for the Supervision of Energy and Environmental Policy) provides subsidies and loans to SMEs and start-up companies that are innovating in the field of energy production and storage. Its main goal is to foster in France the development of green and renewable energy in the context of the energy transition that is currently taking place in all advanced economies worldwide and to make that transition profitable, so that cleaner energy doesn't only make sense from an environmental point of view but from a business point of view as well.
4. State subsidies provided to firms that participate in the Conventions Industrielles de Formation par la Recherche (CIFRE/Higher Education Through Industrial Research) programme which consists of a company, from the large multinational group to the start-up, providing a grant and one of his or her two research codirectors (the other research director has to be a university professor) to a doctoral student whose research is centred on the company's activity.
5. Oséo, which is legally a private bank specialized in providing loans to innovating SME's, but with a *délégation de service public* (public service mission). It was merged in June 2013 with the Fond Stratégique d'Investissement (FSA/Investment Planning Fund) and other state financial institutions such as the enterprise division of the Caisse des Dépôts et Consignations (CDC) to create the Banque Publique d'Investissement (BPI France/ French Public Investment Bank). Oséo and the BPI are providing funding to innovating enterprises, especially young SMEs through loans, loan guarantees and direct investments.

All these state-controlled mechanisms to fund research and innovation in the private sector must not hide the fact that it is the universities, public research administrations such as the CNRS and other OPRs which are the key players in research and innovation in France. A similar situation exists in the USA, albeit with the major difference that most large universities, while often receiving some public funding, are essentially private institutions. In the USA, the law goes much further than in France and most EU countries in recognizing the key role of universities in research and innovation with the Bayh–Dole Act of 1980, which confers to universities the exclusive property of their research results. While French universities and OPRs do not usually enjoy such a level of independence from the state, they are still the keystone in the research networks that link the private sector, the public sector and risk capital firms in order to convert scientific and technological advancement, obtained through research, into real economic growth and job creation.

Since the creation of the Programmes d'Investissement d'Avenir (PIA/Programs for Future Investments) by legislative action on 9 March 2010, global state policy about innovation and research funding in France has been articulated around six major axes with the aim of creating a coherent research and innovation funding programme that covers all aspects of scientific and technological progress, including fundamental research, industrial development, as well as education and of course job creation and economic growth. Those six major axes are the following:

1. Support higher learning and education with the goal of creating world-class research centres.
2. Foster the valorization of fundamental research through its applications in the economy with the goal of increasing and accelerating the transfers of ideas and people between private and public research and the creation of start-up companies by the researchers.
3. Provide financial incentives to the industrial sector so it can help support the development of innovating start-ups and SMEs through training, know-how transfers and financial assistance.
4. Support the energy transition and the advent of clean and renewable energy production in France.
5. Support the digital economy and the development of a world-class telecommunication infrastructure in France.
6. Support medical research and the biotechnology sector.

The drafting and management of the PIAs is entrusted to the Commissariat Général à l'Investissement (CGI/National Investment Commission) that coordinates all government programmes in support of research and innovation in France and makes sure that all the concerned institutions (ANR, BPI, CDC, etc.) are acting in an efficient fashion to maximize the benefit to the economy and the public in general. The PIAs also play a key role in coordinating large-scale scientific endeavours that require the pooling of the resources of many business and industry agents, research institutions as well as the support, both material and financial, of the state. These large-scale projects typically revolve around cloud computing, big data mining, a smart electrical grid and renewable energy, for example.

The advent of the PIAs has had a very strong positive influence on the French NSI, and these programmes help make up for other flaws in the French research and innovation system and help France overcome many of the deficiencies of its traditional (and archaic) "vertical" system of research and innovation. The PIAs allow for an optimum management of private investment subsidized by public money and a better prioritization of the innovating business projects so that the state can better allocate its limited resources to the projects that have the best chances to translate research results into economic growth, the production of innovating products or services and the creation of jobs. The PIAs also permit a better coordination between academic and business agents and facilitates exchanges between those two worlds.

The clear beneficial effects of the PIAs on the French NSI since the programme was initiated are tending to fade nowadays according to the Cour des Comptes (State Audit Office). Indeed, according to its 2 December 2015 report (Cour des Comptes 2015), the first PIA (PIA1) which started in 2010 was faithful to the initial mission and did produce tangible results, but the second PIA (PIA2) was launched in 2014 before the results of PIA1 could fully have come to fruition and before a proper macroeconomic and statistical study of the effects of PIA1 could have been conducted. Moreover, PIA2 has sometimes been used to finance projects that may not have been relevant as innovating projects capable of producing economic growth. According to the Cour des Comptes, up to 20 % of the investment spending under PIA2 may have been mismanaged. The current objective is to correct this course deviation by the advent of a third PIA (PIA3), which would have a better managed budget and tighter fiscal policy and which would be placed under the direct authority of the Prime Minister.

Besides considerations about the efficiency of the successive PIAs, their actual size in terms of investment by the state is also smaller than it seems, and this tends to blur the budget evaluation of those programmes. As a matter of fact the amounts of money really available to fund innovation in the economy (€24 billion for PIA1 and €10 billion for PIA2) are smaller than those announced (€35 billion for PIA1 and €12 billion for PIA2), because a sizable portion of the PIAs (around €9 billion) take the form of non-expendable endowments, meaning that the public money is invested elsewhere and only the revenues generated by those investments are available to fund research and innovation. Taking all these facts into consideration, the adjusted global level of investment that the French government is providing to boost research and innovation in France has been stable at best since 2010, and it doesn't seem that the successive PIAs have measurably increased that amount. Moreover, despite the clear beneficial effect of the PIAs, according to a 2014 report by the OECD (2014), France still lags behind other OECD countries in terms of public expenses for education, including higher education, expressed as a percentage of GDP (gross domestic product; France ranks 18th among OECD member countries) and in terms of public expenses for research and development (France ranks 19th among OECD member countries).

17.3.2 Private Financing

The form that private sector financing of innovation and research will take inside a given company and the means available to that company of obtaining funding will depend essentially on its size. A difference has to be made between the funding of research and development by a company using its own funds or through investments coming from other private companies, and the risk capital companies or risk capital funds. With regard to the private funding of innovation, the French system includes most of the other mechanisms found in other advanced economies but their level of development and availability, especially regarding the availability of cheap capital for start-ups, often lacks behind what can be found in the NSI of world leaders of innovation such as the USA. In the following section, we will explore the major means of private financing of research and innovation available to businesses in France, starting from the large listed companies whose shares are publicly traded on a stock exchange down to the start-up.

17.3.2.1 Companies That Have Access to the Stock Market

Companies that are listed on a stock market are usually large corporate entities, which can also be conglomerates regrouping multiple large companies for tax reasons. They often have subsidiaries purely dedicated to research and development in their field of activity. Some of those subsidiaries may be based in France, especially those that specialize in fundamental research, but they are also often located abroad, again with the goal of lowering their taxes, in countries which have a more favourable patent and intellectual property regime than the French system. Those patents filled abroad may afterwards be sold or licensed internally to their parent company or to other companies operating in France. This raises the question of the transfer prices regarding the localization of profits generated by the selling or licensing of patents, which was studied by H. Hamaekers in a report for the Inter-American Center of Tax Administration (Hamaekers 1999). For its part, France established a new committee, which is tasked with checking the fairness and lawfulness of those transfer prices. It is called the Mission d'Expertise Juridique et Économique Internationale (MEJEI/Committee of Experts on International Legal and Economic Matters), and it was established by decree of the Finance Ministry on 13 March 2013.

These large companies are the source of most of the research and development expenditures in the public sector. Indeed, according to a report by BPI France (2015), only 96 large companies represent around 34 % of the research and development investment financed by the private sector in France. For those large companies, research and innovation is usually self-financed using their own cash flows. Even though these large listed companies usually have extensive financial means at their disposal, the very high rate of corporate tax $(33\frac{1}{3}\%)$ in France tends to discourage investment in research and innovation, which is often not regarded as absolutely essential to the business model of the company or the moving of those activities abroad where the rate of taxation may be lower. Indeed, as far as large listed companies are concerned, since they are funding their own research, considerations about the various regimes of taxation in France determine their research and innovation strategy. In that regard, the most important points to consider are the following:

1. **Tax regime for research towards patents**. Research and development costs incurred towards the creation of a patent or patented invention can be deducted from the taxable profit of a company, without any ceiling. This covers all the phases of production of the patent or patented invention, including fundamental research, technological development and product tests. This constitutes a very important financial advantage in terms of liquidity for a company as long as it conducts research with the goal of producing patents and new patented products.
2. **Tax regime for patents**. In France the tax regime for patents is relatively attractive when compared with other European countries such as the UK with its Patent Box system. The most important tax advantages in France regarding patents are the following:

   a) For patents that have been filled or acquired, it is permissible to deduct from the taxable profit (corporate tax or personal income tax depending on the legal structure of the company) an amortization equal to one-fifth of the value of the patent each year during five years, even though patents are protected by the Institut National de la Propriété Industrielle (INPI/French Patent Office) for 20 years. This disposition is designed to increase the cash flow of businesses.

b) When a patent or patented invention is sold or licensed, a reduced taxation rate of 15 % is applied on the capital gain of the transaction instead of the usual 33 $\frac{1}{3}$ % rate, except if the transaction is taking place between two companies which are related, for example a transaction between a subsidiary and its parent company. In case the sale price is lower than the actual value of the patent or patented invention, then the entirety of the loss can be deducted from the corporate tax or the income tax, depending on the legal structure of the business.

c) When a patent is added to the assets of a company in exchange for shares of its capital, then the company does not have to pay a registration fee even if the patent has already been exploited.

d) For private individuals, the value of patents is not added to the total wealth in the computation of the Impôt de Solidarité sur la Fortune (ISF/Solidarity Tax on Wealth).

Despite this attractive tax regime for patents, the relatively heavy taxation of businesses in France (corporate tax, social security costs, etc.) has a clear negative impact on innovation. In fact, a common tax optimization scheme for a French company consists of conducting research in France in order to benefit from all the financial programmes designed to lower its costs, after which the patent produced by that research is filled abroad in ad hoc legal structures based in a tax haven country or territory, and finally that same patent is sold to the original French company, which benefits from the tax deduction associated with the sale of a patent.

3. **The Crédit Impôt Recherche** (CIR/Research Tax Credit). The CIR in France is one of the most generous tax deduction programmes geared toward fostering research and innovation among all the OCDE countries according to Daniel Boucher (2011). It is available for all companies and businesses in France, regardless of their size or legal form, as long as they have research and development expenses (fundamental research, applied research, experimental development and prototypes, etc.), whatever their field of activity. Since it is, as we have already seen, the large listed companies which account for most of the research and development expenses of the private sector in France, it is naturally those same listed companies that benefit the most from the CIR. The CIR is equivalent to the Research and

Experimentation Tax Credit in the USA and the R&D Tax Credit in the UK, but it doesn't have any real equivalent in Germany, which relies exclusively on other programmes, such as the ZIM, which we mentioned earlier and is a very efficient tool for funding research and innovation in businesses, especially for SMEs.

The CIR consists of a tax credit that concerns the taxable profit (corporate tax or personal income tax depending on the legal structure of the company). It represents each year one of the three largest losses of tax revenue for the state. If the tax credit is larger than the amount of the tax that is due, then the balance is reimbursed by state after at most three years or even sometimes immediately as, for example, in the case of a JEI. The CIR is equal to 30 % of the research expenses up to €100 million and 5 % above. Every year, the research expenses of a company are computed by summing the following items:

a) The amortization of patents.
b) The salaries of researchers and the corresponding social security contributions.
c) A lump sum equal to 75 % of the amortization of patents plus 50 % of salaries of researchers and the corresponding social security contributions. This lump sum is designed to take into account all the other expenses related to the research activity in the company (rents, transports, computers, equipment, etc.).
d) The expenses corresponding to subcontracting research to another company or to a public institution, with a ceiling of €10 million.
e) Various other costs associated with research, such as INPI fees and technology watch.

On top of all these, there is another tax credit called CIR Innovation (Research Tax Credit for Innovation) that is reserved for SMEs. It is a tax credit corresponding to 20 % of the expenses incurred towards ameliorating the efficiency of existing products without the intervention of researchers or the filling of new patents. The ceiling of the CIR Innovation is €400,000 per year.

The CIR programme is very expensive for the state. It costs around €5 billion per year in the form of lost tax income, and this cost is expected to grow to €7 billion in lost tax income in coming years, when the programme reaches cruising speed. According to the OECD (2014), this represents an amount four to six times larger than the combined government subsidies given to foster research and innovation in the private sector and one-third of the costs incurred toward research and development in the public sector (which from a legal point of view do not include the CIR). Given its very large cost, the CIR programme has naturally come under review, and the question of its efficiency in supporting research and innovation in the French economy has naturally been posed many times in the political debate. While the CIR is undeniably an important programme with a lot of potential to foster innovation in the French economy, and there have been some impressive results over the years, as demonstrated by the work of the Observatoire du CIR (http://observatoire-du-cir.fr), it remains somewhat controversial. Indeed, the Cour des Comptes published a report in September 2013 (Cour des Comptes 2013) that underlines flaws in the CIR system, and calls its efficiency into question, especially given its high cost to the state. While also proposing many reforms to improve the efficiency of the CIR, some of the main conclusions of that report were:

a) The efficiency of the CIR regarding its main objective, which is to increase the research and development investments of the private sector, is difficult to precisely quantify. Moreover, the increase in those research and development investments doesn't seem to reflect the tax advantage offered by the state.
b) Managing the CIR is difficult, both for the companies that benefit from it and for the French tax administration. Much of the red tape could be removed by allowing online filling of CIR documents.
c) The tax administration is unable to properly target its controls and tax audits in order to uncover companies which are abusing the CIR. A large part of the problem lies in the opacity and the complexity of the rules governing the CIR.
d) The Ministry of Education and Higher Learning doesn't have the resources needed to assure its mission of supervision of the research activities of the companies that benefit from the CIR.

17.3.2.2   Companies That Aren't Listed on the Stock Market

For these companies, which are typically of intermediate size, self-funding of research and innovation is usually not an option because they do not possess enough own funds and the necessary cash flows generated by a high turnover. They aren't listed on a stock market, which means that they cannot raise capital through the sale of shares on the stock market, which remains the most efficient method of equity financing. They will encounter difficulties obtaining loans and guarantees to finance research and innovation from the banking sector as well because, especially in the current financial crisis climate, innovating SMEs represent a very high risk for the banks. Because of the stringent banking regulations, at the French, European and international level with the Basel III recommendations, banks will find themselves in no position to offer loans to risky SMEs. This fact is one of the main conclusions of a 2013 report by the European Commission (Eurostat, European Commission, Ipsos MORI 2013). These financial and banking rules and regulations clearly serve an important purpose in defending the global financial and banking system against systemic events similar to those created by the Lehman Brothers collapse of 2008, which was precipitated by the subprime crisis taking root in the US real-estate sector, where banks and other financial institutions had the unfortunate habit of offering a very large number of bad and extremely risky loans to struggling people who had little chance of ever repaying them. However, effectively forbidding banks to offer risky loans stifles innovation in the economy as well. Leverage ratios and own funds requirements of Basel III in particular tend to have the pernicious effect of starving innovating SMEs of the much-needed capital they need to develop their activity and/or of rendering access to capital too expensive for them, because the cost for the banks of providing that capital has become too high. A middle ground has to be found in future between security and avoiding smothering innovation in the economy, because while all those new banking regulations might help prevent another Lehman Brothers, they might also unfortunately kill the next Google or Facebook before it is born.

To remedy this situation, France has created many legal and financial structures designed to provide much-needed capital to innovating companies of intermediate size so that they can develop their activity. Those many private equity initiatives and venture capital trusts are sometimes more efficient than stock markets in providing capital to innovating SMEs created by dynamic entrepreneurs, according to Harris et al. (2014). Among those structures, the most notable are:

1. The **Fonds Communs de Placement pour l'Innovation** (FCPI/Mutual Investment Funds for Innovation). Those structures are collective investment funds that are neither companies nor trusts from a legal point of view. They are basically just an "account" that is being managed by a bank or another financial institution and they are a particular kind of FCP. The structure of an FCP and the steps toward its creation are always the same, be it designed for innovation in the economy or not:

a) First, a banking establishment creates an account (the FCP) which is designed to receive deposits from both private investors and businesses. The legal form of the FCP specifies the ways the bank will have to manage it. For example, the bank will have to invest the deposits into a given sector of activity (innovating companies for the FCPI), or into the economy of a given country or territory, or into a given kind of business.
b) Investors then place their money in the FCP and receive in exchange shares of the FCP, which are expected to increase in value with time and which may be sold later on, generating a capital gain.

At least 70 % of the assets of an FCPI must be invested in the capital of unlisted companies of less than 500 employees and which are considered as being "innovative" according to the following criteria:

a) They must have research expenses eligible for the CIR representing at least one-third of their total revenue.
b) They have to be able to provide evidence for the creation of innovating products, techniques or services.
c) At least 70 % of their capital must be held by private individuals, or a public research establishment, or other innovating companies of the same kind, according to the criteria that we have just detailed.

In order to support the development of the FCPIs, a special tax reduction system has been put in place for private individuals who invest in them by purchasing shares. The main provisions of this tax reduction programme are the following:

a) There is first of all a tax credit (informally called "*réduction Madelin*" in the name of a former French finance minister of the mid-1990s, Code Général des Impôts (CGI)/Tax Code, art.199 terdecies-0A), that is of the same nature as the British Enterprise Investment Scheme (EIS), and which is equal to 18 % of the yearly investment into FCPI shares, with a ceiling of €50,000 per year for a single person and €100,000 per year for a married couple, under the condition that the shares be kept for at least five years.
b) Then there is a tax advantage known as "*non-imposition immédiate*" (delayed taxation) which consists of adding the revenues and capital gains generated by the FCPI shares to the value of those shares (which

may be sold at a later date) without immediate taxation by way of the personal income tax.

c) Finally, if the shares are kept for at least five years, there is a complete exemption of the personal income tax corresponding to capital gain generated by the sale or acquisition of those shares.

Moreover, these FCPI structures allow investors to benefit from the experience of professionals specialized in funding research and innovation in the economy and in handling innovating companies as well as the inherent risks associated with them. F. Moulin and D. Schmidt detail in their book "*Les Fonds de Capital Investissement, Principes Juridiques et Fiscaux*" (2015) how investing in FCPIs permits benefiting from people with knowledge of the innovating SME's business ecosystem, to achieve economies of scale and to pool the risks.

Despite the many tax advantages, the FCPI structure seems to be losing its attractiveness among investors. Indeed, there were around 97,000 owners of FCPI shares in France in 2014, down from 145,000 in 2008, and the total amount invested in FCPI's has dropped by 32 % during the same period according to A. Vion in *Les Echos* newspaper of 16 April 2015 (Vion 2015).

2. **Other private equity structures**. Besides the FCPIs, many other structures, which may differ from one another with regard to their size, scope and target companies, exist in France to finance the research and innovation of the SMEs. They all revolve around private equity and can take various legal forms. All these legal structures benefit from a tax exemption on their profits (exemption of the corporate tax or of the personal income tax depending on their legal form).

a) The **Fonds Communs de Placement à Risque** (FCPR/Mutual Fund for Risky Investment) Those funds have essentially the same legal form as FCPIs but they are specialized in "risky investments," which in particular can be investments in innovating companies.

b) The **Sociétés de Capital Risque** (SCR/Risk Capital Firm) Those firms are financial companies specialized in asset and portfolio management. Their mission is to help the launch of new companies which are active in research and innovation by investing at least 50 % of their assets in the capital of unlisted innovating SMEs or in the capital of innovating companies with a small capitalization and limited access to the stock market.

c) The **Sociétés Unipersonnel les d'Investissement à Risque** (SUIR/ One Person Company Dealing with Risky Investment) Those financial firms are similar in structure to the SCRs, but they consist of only one shareholder who has to be a private individual.

d) The **Sociétés Financières d'Innovation** (SFI/Financial Firm for Innovation) Those firms, which have to be registered with the Finance Ministry and are subjected to government oversight, support research, innovation and technological advancement in the economy by funding the development of SMEs involved in the elaboration of new products and services. They must invest at least one-third of their assets in innovating projects. Their investment can take the form of a direct acquisition of shares of the capital of innovating SMEs or they can provide to them intellectual property assets such as patents relevant to their innovation.

Moreover, besides the *"réduction Madelin"* that we mentioned earlier, there is also for private individuals a reduction of the ISF equal to 50 % (CGI, art. 885-0 bis) of the investment in shares of the capital of SMEs from an EU country (not only innovating SMEs) that operate in the industrial, commercial, arts and crafts, agribusiness or service sectors, but not in the financial sector. The ceiling for the ISF reduction is of €45,000 per year, and this tax deduction cannot be cumulated with the *"réduction Madelin"* on the personal income tax.

Despite all these programmes and structures designed to boost private investment into innovating SMEs, the French system is still far behind the American system in terms of efficiency and dynamism. Indeed, France doesn't have in its legal system something as versatile as the status of Small Business Investment Company (SBIC). SBICs are basically private businesses specialized in investing in SMEs which can use their own funds as well as loans that have been guaranteed by the federal SBA (Small Business Administration). In the American business landscape, one can also find the New Market Venture Capital Companies (NMVCC), which specialize in investing in the capital of SMEs located in economically underprivileged regions of the USA, and which also support research and innovation. In the UK, there used to be the Capital for Enterprise Limited (CfEL) until it was merged in October 2013 with the Department for Business, Innovation and Skills (BIS) to become part of the British Business Bank programme. It continues under this new form its mission of providing financial assistance to British SMEs and start-up companies, and the programme is considered to be close to being as successful as its American counterparts. In France, progress still needs to be made, and the Finance Ministry underlined in its Report of the Committee for the Development of the Economy and Innovation in the Digital Age (Ministère des Finances 2012) that:

1. When it comes to funding research and innovation in the economy, there is still in France an insufficient role played by the "business angels" and venture capital (France is even below the average of the EU for the availability of venture capital expressed as a percentage of GDP) and that situation persists despite the creation of the Fond National d'Amorçage (FNA/ National Fund for Start-up Companies) which represents only around €100 million of investment per year. This may have to do with legal restrictions (for example the obligation in some cases to sell the start-up to a European company) that may apply when the entrepreneur attempts to sell a successful start-up that benefited in one way or another from public funding. Indeed, it is often the business strategy of start-up company creators to intend from the beginning to sell the company later on to an industry leader (to give two very famous examples mentioned earlier: Facebook bought What's App and Google bought YouTube), and this sale is often the only real compensation the original entrepreneurs get for their work, because in the growth phase they often get no salary from the fledgling company they created.
2. The availability of risk capital is still insufficient in the "middle stage" of the life-cycle of a typical start-up company. That is the investment that is supposed to take over the funding of the start-up after an initial phase of funding led by the original investors themselves and their families.
3. Technical and legal hurdles need to be overcome to permit successful start-up companies at a later development stage to access the stock market more easily, thus raising the prospect of raising more capital or being acquired by a larger firm in France.

17.3.2.3   The Case of the Start-Up Companies

Start-up companies are usually very small companies (Très Petites Entreprises (TPE)) which are born around "key-persons" (sometimes a single entrepreneur) who usually plan to exploit the economic potential of their own research, patents or patented inventions. The typical economic and financial strategy behind the set-up of a start-up company based on original scientific research is the following:

1. Researchers or inventors provide their patents, patented inventions or know-how to the newly created company that starts to develop around those "key persons". There is something like a bet in a project like this: if the company succeeds and grows, then the key persons will get rich by selling their shares of the capital later on, but if the company fails the loss will be theirs and they will get nothing.

2. The compensation of the key persons usually doesn't take the form of a salary which is much too expensive from the point of view of a small company because of all the taxes and social security contributions associated, and not attractive enough from the point of view of the entrepreneur. This compensation will, hopefully, take the form of the capital gain generated from the sale by the key persons of their participation in the company (their shares of the capital). Once the key persons have severed their link with the company they created, they sometimes start over and create another company and attempt to be, in the jargon of the start-up creators' community, "serial winners."

In order to facilitate start-up creation, which is associated with innovation and dynamism in the economy, France created a series of legal protections, financial structures and instruments as well as a special legal status for start-up creators, much like the USA with the Employee Stock Ownership Plans (ESOP). The key points of the French system regarding start-up creation are the following:

1. Upon entry of the inventor/entrepreneur into the new start-up (or into an existing start-up that wishes to develop a new product using his or her research), he or she brings a patent, patented invention or know-how and may receive in exchange several kinds of financial instruments, such as:

   a) The Obligations Convertibles en Actions (OCA/bonds convertible into shares) or the Obligations Échangeables en Actions (OAE/bonds exchangeable for shares). The precise workings of these financial instruments are explained in details in the work of Jean-Claude Augros (1987) and of Philippe Raimbourg (2015b), but the basic idea is for the inventor to enter the company as a mere lender and to exit as a shareholder.

   b) The Bons de Souscription de Parts de Créateur d'Entreprise (BSPCE/share warrants for entrepreneurs), which enable the future creation of new shares earmarked for the key persons of the start-up company.

c) The Attributions Gratuites d'Actions (AGA/attribution of free shares) that are reserved for the key persons upon creation of the start-up company. Their precise workings are detailed in the work of P. de Fréminet (2010).

d) The stock options (SO) that are designed to provide compensation for the key persons by giving them the right, upon creation of the start-up, to buy shares of the company in the future at a given strike price (call option). Assuming the value of the shares will increase over the years, the SO allows the key persons to realize a future capital gain. Obviously, the risk lies in a depreciation or stagnation of the value of the shares.

All these dispositions therefore permit to compensate an inventor/entrepreneur, not with a salary but with a future capital gain on the sale of shares, when he or she eventually leaves the start-up. This capital gain corresponds to the added value the inventor/entrepreneur provided to the start-up through his or her research, innovation and management skills. It has to be noted that this compensation arrangement has been for a few years less and less profitable because it is based on the difference between the taxation levels of capital gains and salaries. Indeed, salaries tend to be more expensive from a tax optimization point of view and they also include social security contributions. However, this difference between the levels of taxation of capital gains and salaries are currently being called into question, and many of the tax advantages of the usual compensation system of start-up creators are in the process of being adjusted downwards, as the levels of taxation of capital gain and salaries converge in many cases. This analysis is detailed in the work of A. Guillemonat, and O. Ramond, who published an in-depth review of current management packages in the tenth issue of the *Revue de Droit Fiscal* in 2015 (Guillemonat and Ramond 2015).

2. Upon exit of the inventor/entrepreneur from the start-up company, the sale of his or her shares generates a capital gain. This capital gain is admittedly subject to taxation under the same terms as dividends from equity (progressive rate of 0 %–45 %, plus social security contributions), except for BSPCE which are taxed at a flat rate of 19 % plus social security contributions; however, a tax deduction is offered depending on the duration the shares were kept by the inventor/entrepreneur. This tax reduction can climb up to 85 % for shares of an SME which have been acquired within ten years of the creation of the company. Moreover, upon exiting the start-up and selling his or her shares, the inventor/entrepreneur may claim further tax reductions under French law by invoking the taxation regime

that is reserved to the *"revenus exceptionnels"* (exceptional revenue). Today, in order to benefit from those dispositions, the key persons aren't required to have top management responsibilities inside the start-up or to be officially heading the company, as was mandatory in the past.

Many other structures, which may be public, private or hybrid, support the creation of start-up companies in France, in every field of activity, and the innovation and dynamism they bring into the economy. To cite only a few, we can mention:

1. The important role played by the *pôles de compétitivité* and the *pôles d'innovation* (business and research clusters), as we have already seen when discussing the tools of innovation and economic growth. Those business and research clusters provide funding to the fledgling companies but their action isn't limited to that and they also offer legal advice, practical and technical advice and support for the entrepreneurs or would-be entrepreneurs who have the project of exploiting their innovating ideas by creating a start-up. In France, Cap Digital fulfils this mission in the information technology sector and Finance Innovation fulfils this mission for start-up companies in the financial sector, especially supporting the newly born companies through its programme of *"projets labélisés"* (approved projects), which gives financial start-ups the recognition and visibility they need to thrive in a very competitive business landscape.
2. The emerging role played by "crowdfunding" companies and online platforms. As a matter of fact, despite the many funding opportunities that we have seen, sometimes an entrepreneur cannot have access to private equity, government subsidies or loans and can only count on his own funds to start a company. This is where the crowdfunding solutions available in France may play a determinant role. These solutions (Anaxago, Wiseed, Finance Utile, etc.) serve as intermediaries between "microinvestors" and the would-be founder of a TPE. They are the middle ground between a proper investment fund and family investment. They also have the advantage of relying on professionals with knowledge of the TPE ecosystem, such as the Conseillers en Investissement Participatif (crowdfunding advisors), which is a label recognized by the Finance Ministry, who can vet the projects and provide valuable advice to both the investors and the entrepreneurs.

17.3.3 European Financing

17.3.3.1 European Programmes

The funding of European research and innovation policy has been since 1984 articulated around the Programmes Cadres de Recherche et Développement Technologique (PCRDT/Framework Programme of Research and Technological Development), but European research policy only reached its true potential with the creation in January 2000 of the Espace Européen de la Recherche (EER/European Research Area) by the European Commission under the initiative of Philippe Busquin, who was then European Commissioner for research and authored several reports underlining the deep flaws in the European research system and its inability to transform scientific research into economic growth. Over the years, the greater role taken by the EIB in funding research and innovation also accounts for the much more efficient nature of the research and innovation system in the European economy today.

The eighth PCRDT named *"Programme Cadre pour la Recherche et l'Innovation"* (Framework Programme for Research and Innovation) is part of the *Europe 2020* programme, which is a ten-year strategy proposed by the European Commission on 3 March 2010 and covering the period 2014–2020. According to an official report authored by José Manuel Barroso for the European Commission (2010), the goals of the programme are to maximize research and innovation funded by the EU, to foster economic growth that is sustainable, inclusive and employment-generating, and to face the great challenges in European society and economy. Toward those goals, the programme must create a coherent series of structures and institutions spanning the entire research and innovation ecosystem from fundamental research to the introduction on the market of new innovating products and services.

The objectives and the budget of each PCRDT are set by the Conseil Européen de la Recherche (ERC/European Research Council) under the direct supervision of the European Commission, which calls upon independent experts for the selection phase and the evaluation of projects, which are chosen after a public invitation to tender and are published afterwards in the *Official Journal of the European Union*. The seventh PCRDT lasted seven years had a budget of €50.5 billion, to which should be added €2.7 for the legally separate, but structurally integrated, Euratom project on nuclear research between 2007 and 2012. The eighth PCRDT is envisioned to have a budget of €80 billion until 2020, including estimations of €25 billion for cutting edge scientific projects, €18 billion for industrial innovation which includes nanotechnology, nanoelectronics and so on, and €32 billion for major challenges in European society, which includes public health, agriculture, clean energy and the energy transition, and marine research.

17.3.3.2   The European Investment Bank (EIB)

The EIB was established in 1958 under the Treaty of Rome. It is a non-profit international financial institution whose shareholders are the EU member states. It functions as a long term lending institution and its primary mission is to financially support economically sound projects that are important for European integration and the future of the EU. The EIB is the main shareholder of the European Investment Fund (EIF), possessing 62 % of its capital. The EIB is taking a very active role in support of European Commission policies, especially the current European Commission Investment Plan for Europe (ECIPE), known informally as "Juncker's plan," and in that framework it created the European Fund for Strategic Investment (EFSI).

The role of the EIB and its satellite organizations (EIF, EFSI, etc.) in the funding of innovation in Europe is crucial and represents a large part of the bank's activity even though it has other important missions, outside the scope of this study, such as financing infrastructure projects in Europe (bridges, hospitals, etc.) and facilitating European integration and economic stability in Europe. The role of the EIB in fostering innovation in Europe became even more important in the context of the current global financial crisis. Indeed, the funding of innovation has suffered a lot since the 2008 financial crisis, which started in the summer of 2007 as the subprime crisis in the USA. In the first semester of 2009, for example, there was almost no credit offered by the banks, which brought the real economy and innovation in particular to a standstill. The EU member states intervened to prevent the banks going under by establishing programmes similar those of the American Federal Government (quantitative easing, etc.), which were deeply unpopular because they were seen by the general public as a gift made to the banks. In reality they weren't: they were loans offered to the banks from the states, and the banks did pay them back in full in the years that followed, which even generated a profit for the states. In fact, since those loans were a lot more expensive than interbank lending, had it been available at the time, banks were in a hurry to reimburse the states and move on. Even though those rescue packages for the banks were successful in preventing a total banking and financial collapse, the availability of credit has never fully recovered to this day in France and in Europe, and innovation suffers a lot because of this.

In this context of a credit crunch, it is the SMEs that suffer the most because they are the ones that are quickly asphyxiated in the absence of funding. One of the principal missions of the EIB is to help SMEs find funding; not by directly giving them loans as it doesn't have the infrastructure and local branches needed to interact with individual clients directly, but by providing traditional commercial banks with incentives to lend to those SMEs, especially innovating SMEs. The EIB can provide credit to banks on the condition that they use those guarantees exclusively to lend to SMEs. These SMEs need of course to have a sound business plan and they have to be able to reimburse their loan, since the EIB, while it is a not for profit organization, is also not an institution that hands out economic and financial aid. These EIB guarantees make lending to innovating SMEs and start-ups an activity that is more attractive, less risky and more profitable for banks. The guarantees induce several beneficial effects for banks and they also generate leverage, which is typically quite high, in the order of a factor of 8 to 15; but it remains safe because it is powered not by mere speculation but by the status of the EIB as a trustworthy European institution, on the same level of standing and trust as the European Central Bank (ECB).

Specifically, the advantages that banks get from EIB guarantees in exchange for offering loans to SMEs, especially innovating ones, can be listed as follows:

1. A **rate advantage**: because lending to young unproven companies, especially those that are producing innovating products, which may or may not succeed commercially, is riskier for a bank, it may refuse to do so in general, therefore young innovating companies do not get the credit they desperately need to grow and succeed. The EIB guarantee (usually 40 %–50 % of the value of the loan) allows the bank to be compensated for the risk it is taking and to finance that risk. Because of that guarantee of the EIB, the bank can lower its lending rate or take more risk at a given rate, which is currently still quite low and fixed by the ECB.

2. An **equity advantage**: offering credit to subprime agents has become considerably more expensive for banks since Basel III regulations started to come into effect, accompanied by a great increase in the complexity of rules and regulations for the banking sector, which are becoming more and numerous every year. There were, for example, 47 separate new rules in France in 2009 for the banking sector alone. Because these prudential reg-

ulations force banks to have ever-increasing levels of equity to back up their loans, which is crippling and expensive, banks will greatly prefer to lend to SMEs that have a low risk of failing (a baker's shop, for example) rather than innovating ones, created by an entrepreneur who believes he or she has a revolutionary product based on new research. Even if the entrepreneur who believes he or she has a revolutionary product could in theory be the founder of the new Google or Facebook, banks just cannot take the risk of lending money to that person: in the current regulatory atmosphere it just wouldn't make business sense. The guarantee from the EIB allows banks to lower their risk to the level where it makes good business sense to use their precious equity, demanded by the regulator, to back up a loan to an innovating company, thus fostering research and innovation in the economy.

3. A **balance of payment advantage**: this is directly linked to the regulatory requirement for the banks to have equity to back up the loans. Indeed, the loans that are guaranteed by the EIB and which are, in the bank's view, potentially toxic because they are offered to small unproven, often innovating companies, can through legal mechanisms be, at least partially, removed from the bank's balance of payment, thus eliminating the need for the bank to commit more equity and own funds to back them up. In the context of the current financial crisis, large banks usually do not have liquidity problems; it is the regulatory high level of equity needed to back up loans which is the limiting factor to providing credit for the real economy, and especially to the innovating agents of that economy. Therefore the banks need the guarantees offered by the EIB much more than they would need extra liquidity, provided by the EIB or the ECB.

The EIB can also help to foster innovation in Europe through its participation in the EIF. Unlike the EIB, which specializes in very large, multi-billion euro operations with commercial banks and does not deal with SMEs directly, the EIF has a more local approach and specializes in smaller operations focused on individual business projects which go through a rigorous vetting process. In most cases, the EIF will act as a fund of funds, participating in specialized risk capital funds that in turn provide financing for very innovating, cutting edge start-up companies. In that respect, the EIF is acting a lot like a business angel or venture capitalist, except that its primary motivation as a European institution is to make those companies succeed for the greater good of the economy, rather than short- or medium-term profit; and in that regard, the EIF also forfeits most of the rights that a traditional investor would demand, such as the right to have a say in the business decisions and general strategy of the companies it invests into. The specialized funds that the EIF is working with have the know-how and the experience to properly evaluate the chances of success and the soundness of the business plan of those start-up companies in their field of expertise. Vetting these projects, which may be very cutting edge and based on a newly filled patent, is a very hands-on, very local business. These specialized risk capital funds (around 45 of them in France and 460 in the EU) provide much-needed capital investment to innovating start-ups (maybe the next Google), which are too small to have access to the stock market and which are also too risky to have access to bank loans.

Finally, the EIB finances innovation in Europe in the framework of Juncker's plan through the EFSI, which is designed to work in concert with European Commission economic policies. For example, the EIB has intensified its action, especially toward SMEs and innovating SMEs with the framework of Juncker's plan. As a matter of fact, in 2008 it issued €57 billion of guaranteed loans to banks among which 30 % were earmarked for the SMEs, and in 2014 that commitment had increased to €77 billion of guaranteed loans to banks, of which 30 % again was earmarked for the SMEs. The EIB and EIF also launched the InnovFin initiative in the framework of the European Commission's Horizon 2020 programme, which is an EU-wide research and innovation programme with nearly €80 billion in funding between 2014 and 2020, as we have already seen. InnovFin consists of financing tools as well as advisory services designed to boost research and innovation by attracting investors, and thus help all companies, from the start-up to the multinational, that wish to participate in the programme, to be more innovating. The EIB also helps supervise and finance many Public Private Partnership (PPP) projects, which are an important vector of innovation in the European economy.

17.4 Conclusion

As a conclusion, we can say first of all that, when it comes to research and innovation that foster sustainable economic growth and the creation of jobs in the economy, both France and the EU have progressed a lot in recent years. While some worrisome flaws remain in the French NSI, structural reforms in the framework of European integration, and often on the American model, keep on improving the situation. While France may not be ranked by the European Commission as one of the top innovating countries in Europe at the moment, as we have seen, it does remain a key player with world-class research institutions and dynamic entrepreneurs. To come back to the six modules that constitute an NSI, we could say that France has excellent individual parts but that the interactions between those parts sometimes needs to be perfected. Regarding *human resources*, France still lags behind other European countries when it comes to offering young people an education that will enable them to be competitive in an innovating economy and to give them the opportunity to be innovators themselves. Of course, the French higher education system produces world-class researchers and engineers, in all fields of science, and the French business schools are ranked among the best in the EU and the world; but this excellence "at the top" is not enough. A healthy innovating economy also needs qualified technicians, accountants, marketing and communication people, whose work is essential for research and innovation to be translated into successful companies, from the start-up to the multinational, and economic growth. They are the kind of people that the French education system, despite recent reforms in a good direction, seems incapable to produce, despite high unemployment in the country.

Regarding *public research*, France with its many large and world-renowned public research administrations, such as the CNRS, is at the cutting edge of science and technology in many fields, but there is still, despite recent progress in the right direction, an insufficient mobility, both of ideas and of people, between the world of public research and the world of private research, business and innovation in the economy. *Private research* is in good shape as well, as an NSI module of its own, and it benefits from a lot of help from the French state and the EU as well. However, the very favourable tax regimes and various financial structures designed to foster research and innovation in France and in Europe cannot fully compensate for the very heavy taxation and social security contributions that are burdening businesses, stunting investment and stifling innovation in the economy at French and European level. Of course it is not that simple but, taking a few shortcuts, we very often see a situation like this: scientific research is conducted in France while corresponding economic innovation is taking place in countries with lower taxes. Steps are being taken, both at French and European level, to counter situations like this, but more needs to be done. Moreover, as we have seen, the majority of private research and innovation is still being done by a handful of large companies, which are precisely those with the means to fully exploit every French tax reduction programme such as the CIR, while at the same time they have the means to move production abroad where taxes are lower and/or labour legislation is laxer than in France. Innovating SMEs and start-up companies are having a more and more important role in private research, supported by business and research clusters such as Finance Innovation or Cap Digital, French institutions such as BPI France and European institutions such as the EIB, but despite remarkable progress, especially given the current global financial crisis, a lot still needs to be done to help innovating SMEs and start-up companies thrive.

When it comes to the ***relationship between industry and science***, the French system still retains to this day many characteristics of its traditional, and obsolete, "vertical" structure. That traditional system was based on research and scientific policy being decided at the top political level and articulated around traditionally state-controlled industries such as national defence, nuclear power, aeronautics and space. Today, the relationship between industry and science is becoming more "horizontal" in France, and research is becoming better adapted to the needs of the economy, in every field of economic activity, especially as industrial research and development partnerships are created involving companies, large and small, from other countries inside the EU.

Innovating entrepreneurs are many in France, and their dynamism is world-renowned and an important engine of economic growth. As we have seen, many highly efficient structures and programmes exist in France and at the European level that help the creation and continued funding of start-up companies as well as SMEs. There are attractive tax reduction systems for start-up creators, many private equity structures that also benefit from tax advantages, and business and research clusters, which offer not only financial help but legal and material help also, and of course the actions of the EIB, which enables commercial banks to offer loans to risky SMEs and start-ups in a very difficult global financial situation. Despite all this, a lot still needs to be done in France to facilitate the work of innovating entrepreneurs and to render the French system as attractive as the American or British system regarding the creation of start-up companies: in France, there are still a lot of legal and administrative roadblocks that innovating entrepreneurs have to negotiate, unfortunately.

Finally, ***general state policy***, the last NSI module, is supposed to be the cement that binds together all the other parts into a coherent whole. Many countries have had a highly efficient global state strategy for research and economic innovation for decades. This is the case in the USA, with the Office of Science and Technology Policy, which advises the President and helps define general federal policy regarding research and innovation. This is also the case in Germany kond the UK. France used to lag far behind in that regard and for decades, general state policy for research and innovation remained either essentially absent or tainted with short-term political manoeuvring that completely lacked vision and a long-term sustainable plan to boost research and innovation in the French economy. This situation has been greatly improving recently, however, especially with the advent of the PIAs, in concert with the process of European integration. At the European level, France is naturally part of the Europe 2020 programme, started in 2010, that fixed precise objectives, for individual member countries and the EU as a whole, regarding research and innovation in the economy. There is, for example, the goal of reaching a figure of 3 % of GDP for research and development investments, while it stands at 2.5 % in France today. There is also the goal of having at least 40 % of new generations graduating from a higher learning institution and obtaining a diploma. This "union of the innovation" is under the supervision of the European Commission, which may propose objectives and make yearly recommendations to member states regarding research and innovation. It is inside this European framework and through partnerships with other EU countries that French state policy has the best chance of finally becoming the cement binding together all the remarkable assets that France possesses in its NSI. Indeed, it is as a part of Europe that France will eventually achieve its true potential as a world leader in scientific research and economic innovation.

References

Augros, J.-C. (1987). *Finance, options et obligations convertibles* (2 ed.). Paris: Economica.

Barroso, J. M. (2010). *Europe 2020, Une Stratégie pour une Croissance Intelligente, Durable et Inclusive* (p. 12). Bruxelles: Commission Européenne. www.ec.europa.eu/eu2020/pdf/COMPLET%20FR%20BARROSO%20-%20Europe%202020%20-%20FR%20version.pdf

Boucher, D. (2011). *Le Crédit Impôt Recherche*. Paris: LexisNexis.

BPI France. (2015, February). *Rapport sur l'Évolution des PME*. Paris: La Documentation Française. http://www.ladocumentationfrancaise.fr/rapports-publics/154000148/

Cour des Comptes. (2013 September). *L'évolution et les Conditions de Maîtrise du Crédit d'Impôt en Faveur de la Recherche.* http://www.ccomptes.fr/Actualites/Archives/L-evolution-et-les-conditions-de-maitrise-du-credit-d-impot-en-faveur-de-la-recherche

Cour des Comptes. (2015, December 2). Le Programme d'Investissement d'Avenir. http://www.ccomptes.fr/Accueil/Publications/Publications/Le-programme-d-investissements-d-avenir

de Fréminet, P. (2010). Revue Historique du Régime des Options de Souscriptions ou d'Achat d'Actions et des Attributions Gratuites d'Actions, Droit Fiscal 2010, n°16, comm. 281.

European Commission. (2015). *Tableau de Bord de l'Union de l'Innovation*. http:// www.horizon2020.gouv.fr/cid88734/tableau-de-bord-de-l-union-de-l-innovation.html

Eurostat, European Commission, & Ipsos MORI. (2013). *SME's access to finance survey, analytical report*. Brussels: European Commission.

Guillemonat, A., & Ramond, O. (2015). Management Packages: Comment Différencier le Bon Grain de l'Ivraie en Matière Fiscale, Droit Fiscal, n°10, comm.181.

Hamaekers, H. (1999, September). *Taxation vis-à-vis international relations and the use of new technologies; Transfer pricing at the beginning of the XXI century*. Inter-American Center of Tax Administration.

Harris, R. S., Jenkinson, T., & Kaplan, S. N. (2014, October). Private equity performance: What do we know? *The Journal of Finance, 69*(5), 1851–1852.

Ministère des Finances. (2012, January). Rapport de la Mission d'Évaluation Relative au Soutien à l'Economie Numérique et à l'Innovation. http://www.igf.finances. gouv.fr/webdav/site/igf/shared/Nos_Rapports/documents/2012/2011-M-060-02.pdf

Moulin, F., & Schmidt, D. (2015). *Les Fonds de Capital Investissement, Principes Juridiques et Fis-caux* (3 ed.p. 40). Paris: Gualino.

OECD. (2014). *Examens des Politiques d'Innovation en France—Rapports de l'OCDE*. http://www.oecd.org/fr/sti/inno/innovation-france-ocde.pdf

Raimbourg, P. (2015a). *Ingénierie Financière. Évaluation des Laboratoires de Recherche, des Brevets et des Activités de Recherche et Développement* (3e édition, n°111.83). Dalloz Action.

Raimbourg, P. (2015b). *Ingénierie Financière* (3e édition, n°132). Dalloz Action.

Vion, A. (2015, 16 April). Capital-Investissement: Plateformes de Crowdfunding Equity ou FCPI-FIP ? *Les Echos*.

Name Index

Note: Page numbers followed by "n" denote notes.

Subject Index

Note: Page numbers followed by 'n' refer to foot notes.

Printed by Printforce, the Netherlands